Politics in the European Union

Politics in the European Union

Stephen George

Ian Bache

OXFORD
UNIVERSITY PRESS

OXFORD

UNIVERSITY PRESS

Great Clarendon Street, Oxford OX2 6DP

Oxford University Press is a department of the University of Oxford.
It furthers the University's objective of excellence in research, scholarship,
and education by publishing worldwide in

Oxford New York

Athens Auckland Bangkok Bogotá Buenos Aires Cape Town
Chennai Dar es Salaam Delhi Florence Hong Kong Istanbul Karachi
Kolkata Kuala Lumpur Madrid Melbourne Mexico City Mumbai Nairobi
Paris São Paulo Shanghai Singapore Taipei Tokyo Toronto Warsaw

with associated companies in Berlin Ibadan

Oxford is a registered trade mark of Oxford University Press
in the UK and in certain other countries

Published in the United States
by Oxford University Press Inc., New York

British Library Cataloguing in Publication Data
Data available

Library of Congress Cataloging in Publication Data
Data available
ISBN 0–19–878225–X

10 9 8 7 6 5 4 3 2 1

Typeset in ITC Stone
by RefineCatch Limited, Bungay, Suffolk
Printed in Great Britain by
The Bath Press, Bath

Preface

When we began work on this book some three years ago, we thought it would be a major task. We were right. Over that period we have managed, just about, to stay good friends. Our collaboration has been frank and forthright and we hope the book is better for this.

As is usual for a project of this duration, we have accumulated a number of debts. Stephen George would like to thank Neill Nugent and his publishers Palgrave for permission to use material that was originally researched and drafted as part of a collaborative project; some of this material was also used in Neill Nugent's book *The European Commission* (Palgrave, 2000), which explains any similarity there may be in the wording and argument of small parts of the two books. We would both like to thank Tim Barton, Angela Griffin, and Miranda Vernon at Oxford University Press, and various anonymous readers for their helpful comments at different stages of the writing process. Above all, though, we would like to thank Linda and Pamela for their continued support.

Stephen George
Ian Bache
November 2000

Contents

Part Four Institutions

Part Five Policies

Table of Contents

Part Three **The Member States**

Part Four Institutions

Part Five   Policies

List of Figures

List of Tables

List of Boxes

Abbreviations and Acronyms

AASM	Associated African States and Madagascar
ACP	African, Caribbean, and Pacific
APEC	Asia Pacific Economic Cooperation
BBC	British Broadcasting Corporation
BDI	Bundesverband der deutschen Industrie
Benelux	Belgium, The Netherlands, and Luxembourg
BKartA	Bundeskartellamt (German Cartel Office)
BSE	bovine spongiform encephalopathy
CAP	Common Agricultural Policy
CBI	Confederation of British Industry
CCC	Coalfield Communities Campaign
CdP	Commissariat du Plan (French Economic Planning Commission)
CDU	Christian Democratic Union
CEEC	Committee for European Economic Cooperation
CEN	European Committee for Standardization
CENLEC	European Committee for Standardization of Electrical Products
CEPS	Centre for European Policy Studies
CET	Common External Tariff
CFSP	Common Foreign and Security Policy
CGT	Confédération Générale du Travail
CI	Community Initiative
CJD	Creutzfeldt-Jakob Disease
COPA	Committee of Professional Agricultural Organizations of the European Community
CoR	Committee of the Regions and Local Authorities
COREPER	Committee of Permanent Representatives
COSAC	Conference of European Affairs Committees of the Parliaments of the European Union
CSCE	Conference on Security and Cooperation in Europe
CP	Comparative Politics
CSU	Christian Socialist Union (Germany)
DDR	Deutsche Demokratische Republic (East Germany)
DG	Directorate General
DTI	Department of Trade and Industry (Britain)

EAGGF	European Agricultural and Guidance Fund
EBRD	European Bank for Reconstruction and Development
EC	European Community
ECB	European Central Bank
ECHO	European Community Humanitarian Aid Office
ECHR	European Court of Human Rights
ECO	European Cartel Office
ECOFIN	Council of Economic and Finance Ministers
ECSC	European Coal and Steel Community
ECJ	European Court of Justice
ECU	European Currency Unit
EDC	European Defence Community
EdF	Electricité de France
ESCB	European System of Central Banks
EDF	European Development Fund
EEA	European Economic Area
EEC	European Economic Community
EES	European Economic Space
EFTA	European Free Trade Association
EIB	European Investment Bank
EMCF	European Monetary Co-operation Fund
EMF	European Monetary Fund
EMI	European Monetary Institute
EMS	European Monetary System
EMU	Economic and Monetary Union
EP	European Parliament
EPA	European Parliamentary Assembly
EPC	(1) European Political Community (till 1952); (2) European Political Co-operation
ERDF	European Regional Development Fund (see also RDF)
ERM	Exchange Rate Mechanism
ERP	European Recovery Programme ('Marshall Plan')
ERT	European Round Table of Industrialists
ESC	Economic and Social Committee
ESF	European Social Fund
ESPRIT	European Strategic Programme for Research and Development in Information Technology
ETUC	European Trade Union Confederation

EU	European Union
EUA	European Unit of Account
EUF	European Union of Federalists
EURACOM	European Action for Mining Communities
Euratom	European Atomic Energy Community
EUREKA	European Research Co-ordination Agency
FO	Foreign Office (Britain)
FDP	Free Democrat Party (Germany)
FN	Front National (National Front, France)
FYROM	Former Yugoslav Republic of Macedonia
GATT	General Agreement on Tariffs and Trade
GDP	Gross Domestic Product
GNP	Gross National Product
HMSO	Her Majesty's Stationery Office
IAR	International Authority for the Ruhr
IBM	International Business Machines
IBRD	International Bank for Reconstruction and Development
ICSID	International Centre for Settlement of Investment Disputes
IDA	International Development Association
IFC	International Finance Corporation
IGC	Intergovernmental Conference
IMF	International Monetary Fund
IMPs	Integrated Mediterranean Programmes
INTUG	Information Technology User Group
IPE	International Political Economy
IR	International Relations
ISPA	Pre-accession structural instrument
ITO	International Trade Organization
JHA	Justice and Home Affairs
MAFF	Ministry of Agriculture, Fisheries and Food (Britain)
MCAs	Monetary Compensation Amounts
MEP	Member of the European Parliament
MIGA	Multilateral Investment Guarantee Agency
MRP	Mouvement Républicain Populaire (France)
NAFTA	North American Free Trade Association
NATO	North Atlantic Treaty Organization
NFU	National Farmers' Union (UK)

NUM	National Union of Mineworkers (Britain)
NPD	National Democratic Party (Germany)
NTB	Non-Tariff Barrier
OECD	Organization for Economic Cooperation and Development
OEEC	Organization for European Economic Co-operation
ONP	Open Network Provision
OPEC	Organization of Petroleum Exporting Countries
OSCE	Organization for Security and Cooperation in Europe
PASOK	Panhellenic Socialist Party (Greece)
PCP	Portuguese Communist Party
PHARE	Poland–Hungary: Actions for Economic Reconstruction
PR	Proportional Representation
PS	Parti Socialiste (Socialist Party, France)
PSP	Portuguese Socialist Party
PTT	Post, Telegraph, and Telephone Companies
QMV	Qualified Majority Voting
RDF	Regional Development Fund
Rechar	Community Initiative programme for the conversion of coal mining areas
RPF	Rassemblement du Peuple Français (Gaullist Party, France)
RPR	Rassemblement pour la République
SDP	Social Democratic Party (Britain)
SEA	Single European Act
SPD	Sozialdemokratische Partei Deutschlands (Social Democratic Party, Germany)
Stabex	System for the Stabilization for Export Earnings
TABD	Transatlantic Business Dialogue
TACIS	Technical Assistance for the Commonwealth of Independent States
TEC	Treaty for establishing the European Community
TENS	Trans-European Networks
TEU	Treaty on European Union
UDF	Union pour la Démocratie Française
UNICE	Union of Industrial and Employers' Confederations of Europe
UN	United Nations
US	United States
USSR	Union of Soviet Socialist Republics
VAT	Value Added Tax
WEU	Western European Union
WTO	World Trade Organization

Introduction

IN 1951, six European states signed the Treaty of Paris to form the European Coal and Steel Community. This agreement began a process of European integration which now, some fifty years later, involves fifteen European states in a broad and complex set of political and economic arrangements that is the European Union (EU). The purpose of this book is to chart the main developments in this process of integration and to disentangle some of the complexities of current arrangements.

While we would argue that there is no easy separation between economics and politics, this book is explicitly concerned with politics in the European Union. Thus, we address some of the standard issues of the discipline: is the EU developing into a super-state of some sort? If so, of what sort? Have national governments voluntarily surrendered sovereignty to European institutions, or are there forces at work dragging member states towards ever closer union against the will of the governments?

To root the questions firmly in a theoretical structure, **Part One** of the book reviews the main academic debates about the process of European integration and the nature of the EU. Because this is a book about the politics of the EU, views from the political studies literature are particularly central to this review. While we recognize that many important insights into EU politics would be gained from placing this review alongside literature on the EU from other disciplines such as economics, law, and sociology, we are bound by limits of time, space, and competence. Moreover, as the reader will observe, the political studies community itself speaks with many voices on this issue and providing a path through these debates is no small challenge. For those who wish to place our review alongside theor-

ies of European integration from other disciplinary perspectives, Michelmann and Soldatos (1994) provide a good starting point.

A review of theories is in itself important to prepare students for further reading on the subject, which will inevitably be informed by some theory or other. In addition, the review of theories here is also important in drawing out the themes that run throughout the book. In the Conclusions to the theory chapters we identify four main themes and several subsidiary themes. The main themes are: whether the EU is an intergovernmental or a supranational organization; the importance of legitimacy to the EU; the role of vested interests and of ideas in the development and functioning of the EU; and the importance of the wider global environment within which the EU is situated to understanding its development. In the Conclusion to each chapter we have situated the material in the context of the relevant themes.

Part Two traces the history of European integration from the end of the Second World War in 1945 through to 1999. Here we have concentrated on presenting the broad picture of developments, leaving the details on specific institutions and specific policies for later chapters. There is no clear separation that can be made between narrative and interpretation, and we have brought out differences in interpretation of EU history wherever they seem appropriate, and also wherever they illustrate the themes and debates that underlie the book.

Part Three deals in detail with the relationship of each of the three largest member states with the European Union and provides introductory material on the other member states. To give equal consideration to every member state was not a practical proposition, so we have settled for the unsatisfactory compromise of including thumbnail sketches of all the other twelve states in a single chapter.

Part Four looks at the EU's institutional arrangements and also the role of organized interests in the decision-making process. Of all the institutions that were set up by the treaties, four are undoubtedly important. They are the Commission, the Council, the European Parliament (EP), and the European Court of Justice (ECJ). Each of these has a separate chapter in Part Four, as does the subject of organized interests. The other institutions appear in the first chapter in Part Four, which is devoted to explaining the institutional architecture of the EU. The rest of Part Four is mainly concerned with the academic debates that have developed around the role of the main institutions. Again, the conclusions to the chapters try to relate these specific debates to the wider themes of the book.

Part Five discusses five of the main policy areas for which the EU has competence. There are more policies than are covered here. Here, we attempt to provide background and analysis for five policies with sufficient depth to stimulate further investigation. If we succeed in conveying something of the approach that we favour, we should supply students with an intellectual toolkit of questions with which they can analyse other policies for themselves.

We encourage the reader to be critical in reading this book. No book, and no argument, is complete. We have sought to explain our selection of material more fully in the separate introductions to the different parts of the book. Yet there are inevitably important omissions. As the process of European integration has accelerated, the academic literature on the subject has grown exponentially. In part, we address this problem by pointing the reader in the direction of other literature at the end of each chapter. In part, though, we just have to accept that the European Union is a dynamic entity, a 'moving target'. However much we capture the essence of the beast here, we are aware that our contribution, as with all others, is locked in time and space and should be understood as such by the reader.

Part One

Theory

This part of the book consists of three chapters. These three chapters trace the development of theoretical approaches to understanding the EU and outline contemporary theories.

WHY THEORY?

Our understanding of the world is guided by our particular conceptual lenses or theoretical models, whether this is explicit or implicit. There has been no shortage of models applied to understanding the European Union. While no book can provide comprehensive coverage of all models and approaches, we provide an overview of what to us appear to be the most important. Necessarily, our own conceptual lenses influence the content of this overview. However, there is a consensus among scholars that the study of the European Union has been characterized by two distinct theoretical phases. The first phase was dominated by approaches from *international relations*; the second phase saw these approaches accompanied and amended by insights from *public policy* and *comparative politics*. In broad terms, the first two chapters of this part of the book correspond to these two phases.

The most straightforward way of understanding this theoretical shift is to see it as a move away from treating the EU as an international organization similar to others (e.g. NATO) to seeing it as something unique among international bodies. The uniqueness here relates both to the nature and to the extent of its development. This means that in at least some areas of activity the EU displays properties more akin to national political systems than to those of international organizations.

In many ways, the inclusion of a third chapter in this section of the book is most revealing of our 'take' on the study of the EU. Our position is that while the traditional international relations theories set out in **Chapter 1 Theories of European Integration**, and the newer theoretical developments set out in **Chapter 2 Theories of EU Governance**, all contribute to the understanding of the EU, we feel that they share a similar weakness. This weakness is a particular neglect of placing developments in the EU in the context of developments beyond its boundaries. Put briefly, **Chapter 3 Beyond EU Studies,** argues that the insights from the study of *international political economy* are an essential complement to other theories which seek to understand the European Union.

Theories of European integration

'international theory' has been too readily written off by contemporary writers seeking to offer theoretical treatments of the EU

(Rosamond 1999: 19)

SUMMARY

The dominant approaches to understanding the early phase of European integration came from international relations (IR). In particular, the study of integration was dominated by the competing approaches of neofunctionalism and intergovernmentalism. Although neofunctionalist theory neatly fitted events in the 1950s and early 1960s, subsequent events led to its demise and the rise of intergovernmentalist explanations. While theorizing European integration has moved on significantly from these early approaches, much of what followed was either framed by this debate or developed as a rejection of it. The debate about whether the EU is an intergovernmental or a supranational institution still dominates much of the academic work on the subject.

Introduction

The signing of the Treaty of Rome in 1957 by the governments of France, Germany, Italy, and the Benelux states (Belgium, the Netherlands, and Luxembourg) began the process commonly referred to as European integration (see Box 1.2, p. 10). This process has meant that the economies of participating states, and subsequently other policy areas, have been increasingly managed in common. Decisions previously taken by national governments alone are now taken together with other governments, and specially created European institutions. Governments have relinquished the sole right to make legislation over a range of matters (national sovereignty), in favour of joint decision-making with other governments (pooled sovereignty). Other tasks have been delegated to European institutions.

It was something of a surprise to academic theorists of IR when governments in western Europe began to surrender their national sovereignty in some policy areas. For the first half of the twentieth century the nation-state seemed assured of its place as the most important unit of political life in the western world, especially in Europe. As such, the process of European integration constituted a major challenge to existing theories and generated an academic debate about the role of the state in the process. The two competing theories that emerged from IR to dominate the debate over early developments in European integration were neofunctionalism (E.B. Haas 1958; Lindberg 1963) and intergovernmentalism (Hoffmann 1964; 1966).

Before discussing these two main positions in the debate, it is necessary to consider the intellectual context from which the idea of European integration emerged. Below we look first at the functionalist ideas of David Mitrany on how to avoid war between nations, then at the ideas of the European federalists, and finally at the 'federal-functionalism' of Jean Monnet. We then turn to look at first neofunctionalism and then intergovernmentalism.

The intellectual background

To understand the ideas that fed into the first attempts to theorize European integration, it is useful to start with one of the approaches that was influential after the Second World War about how to avoid another war. This 'functionalist' idea, which was particularly associated with the writings of David Mitrany, informed the United Nations movement. It was a theory of how to achieve world peace, rather than a theory of regional integration, and it took a very different approach to the question from the European federalists, who wanted to subordinate national governments to an overarching federal authority. The ideas of both the functionalists and the federalists were brought together in the 'functional-federalism' of Jean Monnet, which in turn provided one important source of intellectual inspiration for the neofunctionalist theory of European integration.

Mitrany and functionalism

David Mitrany (1888–1974) was born in Romania, but spent most of his adult life in Britain and the United States. He was not a theorist of European integration. His concern was with building a *Working Peace System*, the title of his Fabian pamphlet (Mitrany, 1966; first published 1943). For Mitrany, the root cause of war was nationalism. The failure of the League of Nations to prevent aggression prompted debate even before the outbreak of the Second World War about a new type of international system. For those who blamed the failure of the League on its limited powers, the response was the development of an international federation. In other words, the League had not gone far enough and the same mistake should not be repeated:

henceforth, nations should be tied more closely together.

Mitrany did not agree with the idea of federation as the means of tying states together. He opposed the idea of a single world government because he believed that it would pose a threat to individual freedom. He also opposed the creation of regional federations, believing this would simply reproduce national rivalries on a larger scale. Any political reorganization into separate units must sooner or later produce the same effects; any international system that is to usher in a new world must produce the opposite effect of subduing political division.

Instead of either of these possibilities—a world federation or regional federations—Mitrany proposed the creation of a whole series of separate international functional agencies, each having authority over one specific area of human life. His scheme was to take individual technical tasks out of the control of governments and to hand them over to these functional agencies. He believed that governments would be prepared to surrender control because they would not feel threatened by the loss of sovereignty over, say, health care or the co-ordination of railway timetables, and they would be able to appreciate the advantages of such tasks being performed at the regional or world level. As more and more areas of control were surrendered, states would become less capable of independent action. One day the national governments would discover that they were enmeshed in a 'spreading web of international activities and agencies' (Mitrany, 1966: 35)

These international agencies would operate at different levels depending on the function that they were performing. Mitrany gave the example of systems of communication. Railways would be organized on a continental basis; shipping would be organized on an intercontinental basis; aviation would be organized on a universal basis. Not only would the dependence of states on these agencies for their day-to-day functioning make it difficult for governments to break with them, the experience of the operation of the agencies would also socialize politicians, civil servants, and the general public into adopting less nationalistic attitudes and outlook.

Spinelli and federalism

A completely different approach to guaranteeing peace was devised during the war in the ranks of the various Resistance movements. It was a specifically European movement, and whereas Mitrany aimed explicitly to depoliticize the process of the transfer of power away from national governments, federalists sought a clear transfer of political authority.

The European Union of Federalists (EUF) was formed in December 1946 from the wartime Resistance movements. It was particularly strong in Italy, where the leading figure was Altiero Spinelli. Federalism appealed to the Resistance groups because it proposed superseding nationalism. It is important to bear in mind that whereas in Britain (and Russia) the Second World War was a nationalist war (in the former Soviet Union it was 'the great patriotic war'), in countries such as France and Italy it was an ideological war. Resistance fighters drawn from Communist, Socialist, and Christian democratic groups were in many cases fighting their own countrymen—Vichy supporters in unoccupied France, Italian Fascists in Italy.

While being held as political prisoners of the Fascists on the island of Ventotene, Spinelli and Ernesto Rossi (1897–1967) produced the Ventotene Manifesto (1941), calling for a 'European Federation'. It argued that, left alone, the classes 'most privileged under old national systems' would seek to reconstruct the order of nation states at the end of the war. While these states might appear democratic, it would only be a matter of time before power returned to the hands of the privileged classes. This would prompt the return of national jealousies and ultimately, to renewed war between nation states. To prevent this development, the Manifesto called for the abolition of the division of Europe into national, sovereign states. It urged propaganda and action to bring together the separate national Resistance movements across Europe to push for the creation of a federal European state.

The EUF adopted the Ventotene Manifesto, and began agitating for an international conference to be called which would draw up a federal constitution for Europe. This ambitious proposal was designed to build on what Milward called, 'the wave of hope for a better world and a changed future for the human race which had swept across Europe' and which included an 'extraordinary wave of enthusiasm for European federation' (Milward, 1984: 55).

The strategy of the EUF was to exploit the disruption caused by the war to existing political structures in order to make a new start on a radically different basis from the Europe of national states. They aimed to achieve a complete break from the old order of nation-states, and to create a federal constitution for Europe. Their Congress took time to organize, though. It eventually took place in The Hague in May 1948 (see Ch. 4, p. 48). By that time the national political systems had been re-established, and what emerged from the Congress was an inter-governmental organization, the Council of Europe, not the new federal constitutional order that the federalists had hoped for. Many federalists then turned to the gradualist approach that was successfully embodied in the European Coal and Steel Community (ECSC).

Monnet and functional-federalism

The plan for the ECSC was known as the Schuman Plan because it was made public by the French Foreign Minister Robert Schuman, but it is generally accepted that it was drawn up within the French Economic Planning Commission (*Commissariat du Plan*), which was headed by the technocrat Jean Monnet. It was the task of the Planning Commission to guide the post-war reconstruction and modernization of the French economy, and it was through his experiences in this task that Monnet came to appreciate the economic inadequacy of the European nation-state in the modern world. He saw the need to create a 'large and dynamic common market', 'a huge continental market on the European scale' (Monnet, 1962: 205). He aimed, though, to create more than just a common market.

Monnet was a planner: he showed no great confidence in the free-market system, which had served France rather badly in the past. He placed his faith in the development of supranational institutions (see Box 1.1, p. 8) as the basis for building a genuine economic community which would adopt common economic policies and rational planning procedures. Coal and steel were only intended as starting points.

Box 1.1 **Supranational institutions**

'Supranational' literally means 'above the national'. A supranational institution is one that has power or influence going beyond that permitted to it by national governments. An international institution, in contrast, is one that results from the co-operation of national governments, and has no power beyond that permitted to it by those governments.

The aim was to extend integration to all aspects of the west European economy; but such a scheme would have been too ambitious to gain acceptance all at once. There had been a clear indication of this in the failure of previous efforts to integrate the economies of France, Italy, The Netherlands, Belgium, and Luxembourg.

There was also a new factor in the equation, the key factor prompting Monnet's plan: the emergence in 1949 of a sovereign West German state. For Monnet the existence of the Federal Republic of Germany posed two problems in addition to that of how to create an integrated western European economy. The first problem was how to organize Franco-German relations in such a way that another war between the two states would become impossible. To a French mind this meant how to control Germany. The pooling of coal and steel production would provide the basis for economic development as a first step towards a 'federation of Europe', and by stimulating the expansion of those industries for peaceful purposes would provide an economic alternative to producing war materials for those regions of Europe that had been largely dependent on providing military material. The second problem facing Monnet was the very practical one of how to ensure adequate supplies of coking coal from the Ruhr for the French steel industry. The idea of pooling Franco-German supplies of coal and steel would tie the two states into a mutual economic dependency, in addition to taking out of the immediate control of the national governments the most basic raw materials for waging another war

Mitrany (1966) described Monnet's strategy as 'federal-functionalism'. It is not clear, though, how far Monnet was a federalist at all. He might be seen as a supreme pragmatist who proposed the ECSC as a solution to the very practical problems described above. To solve these problems Monnet adopted a solution similar to that of Mitrany: remove control of the strategically crucial industries—coal and steel—from the governments and put it in the hands of a free-standing agency. This was the High Author- ity of the ECSC, and in Monnet's original plan it was the only institution proposed. The development of other supranational institutions came from other pressures (see Ch. 5, pp. 62–3). The High Authority was the prototype for the later Commission of the EEC, which became central to the neofunctionalist theory of European integration.

International relations theories of European integration

Realism was the dominant approach in IR in the 1950s. It assumed that sovereign states formed the fundamental units of analysis for understanding international relations. The appearance of the EC therefore provided fertile ground for those who wished to develop a critique of this dominant approach. Neofunctionalism was the name given to the first theoretical attempt to understand European integration. Its implied critique of realism led to a counter-theory from within a broadly state-centred perspective, which became known as intergovern-mentalism. The debate between these two broad positions has evolved over time, but the central issues of dispute remain much the same today as they were in the 1950s.

Neofunctionalism

Starting with the analysis of the ECSC by Ernst Haas (1958), a body of theorizing about European integra-tion known as neofunctionalism was built up in the writings of a group of US academics (see Box 1.2, p. 10). These theorists drew on the work of Mitrany and Monnet in particular. In addition to Haas, the main figures in this school of analysis were Leon Lindberg (1963, 1966), and Philippe Schmitter (1970).

Neofunctionalism was a pluralist theory of inter-national politics. In contrast to the more traditional realist theories, it did not assume that a state was a single unified actor; nor did it assume that states were the only actors on the international stage. In the concepts that it used it anticipated later writings on global interdependence (Keohane and Nye, 1977).

In the first period of European integration, neo-functionalism appeared to be winning the theor-etical debate. Neofunctionalism sought to explain 'how and why they (states) voluntarily mingle, merge and mix with their neighbours so as to lose the factual attributes of sovereignty while acquiring new techniques for resolving conflict between them-selves' (Haas 1970: 610). There were four key parts to the neofunctionalist argument:

1. The concept of the 'state' is more complex than realists suggested.

2. The activities of interest groups and bureaucratic actors are not confined to the domestic political arena.

3. Non-state actors are important in international politics.

4. European integration is advanced through 'spill-over' pressures.

In contrast to realists, neofunctionalists argued that the international activities of states were the outcome of a pluralistic political process in which government decisions were influenced by pressures from various interest groups and bureaucratic actors. In common with the general tenor of US political science at the time, it was often assumed that these pressures constituted the complete explanation for government decisions. So, if the analyst could

Box 1.2 European integration

European integration has a number of aspects, but the main focus of Chapter 1 is on *political* integration. E. B. Haas (1968: 16) provided a definition of European political integration as a *process*, whereby:

political actors in several distinct national settings are persuaded to shift their loyalties, expectations and political activities toward a new center, whose institutions possess or demand jurisdiction over the preexisting national states. The end result of a process of political integration is a new political community, superimposed over the preexisting ones.

Implicit in Haas's definition was the development of a European federal state. More cautiously, Lindberg, provided a definition of political integration as a process, but without reference to an end point:

political integration is (1) the process whereby nations forego the desire and ability to conduct foreign and key domestic policies independently of each other, seeking instead to make *joint decisions* or to *delegate* the decision-making process to new central organs; and (2) the process whereby political actors in several distinct national settings are persuaded to shift their expectations and political activities to a new center.   (1963: 149)

The first part of this definition refers to two 'intimately related' modes of decision-making: sharing and delegating. The second part of the definition refers to 'the patterns of behaviour shown by high policy makers, civil servants, parliamentarians, interest group leaders and other elites' (Lindberg 1963: 149), who respond to the new reality of a shift in political authority to the centre by reorientating their political activities to the European level.

identify the strength and direction of the various pressures accurately, it would be possible to make predictions about government behaviour in international relations.

Using the concepts that were later called 'transnationalism' and 'transgovernmentalism' (Keohane and Nye, 1977: 129–30), neofunctionalists expected nationally-based interest groups to make contact with similar groups in other countries (transnationalism), and departments of state to forge links with their counterparts in other states, unregulated by their respective foreign offices (transgovernmentalism).

Neofunctionalists pointed to the activities of multinational corporations to illustrate their argument that non-state actors are important in international politics. However, for neofunctionalists, the European Commission was the most important non-state international actor. The Commission was believed to be in a unique position to manipulate both domestic and international pressures on national governments to advance the process of European integration, even where governments might be reluctant. This contrasted with realist explanations of international relations that focused exclusively on the international role of states.

Neofunctionalists used the concept of spillover to explain how once national governments took the initial steps towards integration, the process took on a life of its own, and swept governments along further than they anticipated going. As Lindberg (1963: 10) put it:

In its most general formulation, 'spillover' refers to a situation in which a given action, related to a specific goal, creates a situation in which the original goal can be assured only by taking further actions, which in turn create a further condition and a need for more action, and so forth.

Two types of spillover were important to early neofunctionalist writers: functional and political. A third type, cultivated spillover, was added by later theorists to explain the part played by the Commission in fostering integration.

Functional spillover argued that modern industrial economies were made up of interconnected parts. As such, it was not possible to isolate one sector from others. Following this understanding, neofunctionalists argued that if member states integrated one functional sector of their economies, the interconnectedness between this sector and others would lead to a 'spillover' into other sectors. Technical pressures would prompt integration in those related sectors, and the integration of one sector would only work if other functionally-related sectors were also integrated. For example, if a joint attempt were made to increase coal production across member states, it would prove necessary to bring other forms of energy into the scheme. Otherwise, a switch by one member state away from coal towards a reliance on oil or nuclear fuels would throw out all of the calculations for coal production. In addition, any effective planning of the total energy supply would involve gathering data about future total demand, implying the development of overall plans for industrial output across member states. (For other examples see Box 1.3, p. 11.)

To this technical logic of functional spillover, the neofunctionalists added the idea of political spillover, and set perhaps more store by this than by functional spillover in explaining the process of integration. Political spillover involved the build-up of political pressures in favour of further integration within the states involved. Once one sector of the economy was integrated, the interest groups operating in that sector would have to exert pressure at the supranational level, on the organization charged with running their sector. So the creation of ECSC would lead to the representatives of the coal and steel industries in all the member states switching at least a part of their political lobbying from national governments to the new supranational agency the High Authority. Relevant trade unions and consumer groups would follow suit.

It was argued that once these interest groups had switched the focus of their activity to the European level, they would rapidly come to appreciate the

---

Box 1.3 Three illustrations of functional spillover

1. From removing tariff barriers to a common monetary policy

If tariff barriers (i.e. import taxes) were removed on trade between member states, this would not in itself create a common market. So long as the rates of exchange between national currencies were allowed to fluctuate, prices would be unpredictable and no genuinely unified market would develop. At the same time, national governments would find it much more difficult to control their economies' performance once they could no longer turn to tariffs to regulate imports. They would be forced to use their individual powers over monetary policy to change the exchange rate more often, thereby increasing monetary instability and making a genuine common market even less likely. The removal of tariffs would therefore increase the pressure for governments to surrender control over their national exchange rates as well: it would prove necessary to move towards a common monetary policy in order to make a reality of the common market.

2. From a common monetary policy, to a common economic policy, to a common regional policy

A common monetary policy would make it almost impossible for governments to control their domestic economies, because it would deprive them of their last instrument for regulating imports and exports. Thus monetary union would imply full economic union, with economic policy being regulated centrally for the whole area of the common market. Without the adoption of a common economic policy, it would be doubtful whether the monetary union would hold anyway, because economic policy is one of the key determinants of currency stability. If some governments adopted more inflationary policies than others did, the value of the currency used in countries that were trying to avoid inflation would be undermined. So macro-economic policy would have to be centrally controlled; but this would prevent governments from helping the weaker regions of their own national economies, and this responsibility would also have to be assumed at the centre, implying a common regional policy.

3. From a common agricultural policy to a common monetary policy

A different line of progress to the same conclusion as example 2 could be traced by starting from an attempt to construct a common agricultural policy, aimed at the equalization of food prices throughout six states. This policy would run into severe difficulties if national currencies were allowed to fluctuate relative to one another. What would start out as a common level of prices, expressed in a neutral accounting unit, would become several price levels if all the exchange rates were to change. So pressure would build up for agricultural policy to be complemented by the tying together of exchange rates, thus restricting fluctuations. From this point the logic of functional spillover proceeds just the same way as in example 2, from monetary union to economic union to a common regional policy.

benefits available to them as a result of the integration of their sector. Further, they would also come to understand the barriers that prevented these benefits from being fully realized. As the main barrier would be that integration in one sector could not be effective without the integration of other sectors, these interest groups would become advocates of further integration and would lobby their governments to this end. At the same time they would form a barrier themselves against governments retreating from the level of integration that had already been achieved. This was important, because such a retreat would be the one alternative way in which pressures caused by functional spillover could be resolved. In addition, governments would come under pressure from other interest groups which would see the advantages accruing to their counterparts in the integrated sector and realize that they could profit similarly if their sectors of the economy were also integrated.

For Haas, the driving force of political integration was the calculated self-interest of political elites:

The 'good Europeans' are not the main creators of the regional community that is growing up; the process of community formation is dominated by nationally constituted groups with specific interests and aims, willing and able to adjust their aspirations by turning to supranational means when this course appears profitable   (Haas, 1966: p. xxxiv).

Neofunctionalists looked for spillover pressures to be encouraged and manipulated by the Commission. It was expected both to foster the emergence of EC-wide pressure groups and to cultivate contacts behind the scenes with national interest groups and with bureaucrats in the civil services of the member states, who were another group of potential allies against national governments (Tranholm-Mikkelsen 1991). This was the third type of spillover, which was known as cultivated spillover because it involved the Commission cultivating the contacts and the pressure on governments.

In the 1950s, neofunctionalist theory neatly fitted events, particularly in explaining the transition from the ECSC to the European Community (EC). Events in the 1960s were less supportive. The beginning of the end for neofunctionalist theory in its original manifestation came in the early 1960s and in particular the use of the veto by de Gaulle, leading to the 'empty chair' crisis of 1965–6 (see Ch. 8, pp. 92–3).

National governments had power and were clearly prepared to use it to determine the nature and pace of integration:

By 1967 Haas was already attempting to cope with the possibility that De Gaulle had 'killed the Common Market' by revising his theory to account for the prospect of 'disintegration', and by 1975 he was announcing the 'obsolescence of regional integration theory' (Caporaso and Keeler 1995: 36–7).

Intergovernmentalism

In response to the neofunctionalist analysis of European integration, a counter-argument was put forward by Stanley Hoffmann (1964; 1966). This argument drew heavily on realist assumptions about the role of states, or more properly, the governments of states in international relations. Essentially there were three parts to Hoffmann's criticism of neofunctionalism.

1. European integration had to be viewed in a global context. Regional integration was only one aspect of the development of the global international system. The neofunctionalists predicted an inexorable progress to further integration; but this was all predicated on an internal dynamic, and implicitly assumed that the international background conditions would remain fixed. This criticism became particularly relevant in the light of events in the global situation in the early 1970s.

2. National governments were uniquely powerful actors in the process of European integration: they controlled the nature and pace of integration guided by their concern to protect and promote the 'national interest'.

3. Although, where 'national interests' coincided governments might accept closer integration in the technical functional sectors, the integration process would not spread to areas of 'high politics' such as national security and defence.

Hoffmann rejected the neofunctionalist view that governments would ultimately be overwhelmed by pressures from elite interest groups to integrate. However, his argument departed from classical realism, in which states were treated as unified rational actors, with little importance attached to domestic politics. Hoffmann's intergovernmentalist position was more sophisticated than that of realists in this respect, and his political awareness was also greater than that of the neofunctionalist writers who tended to adopt a rather simplified pluralist view of political processes.

Hoffmann claimed the neofunctionalist argument was based on 'false arithmetic' which assumed that the power of each elite group (including national governments) was approximately equal, so that if the governments were outnumbered they would lose. In addition, he argued that government decisions could not be understood simply as a response to pressure from organized interests, but that often political calculations led governments to take positions to which powerful groups were hostile (Hoffmann, 1964: 93). These political calculations were driven by domestic concerns. In particular, the impact of integrative decisions on the national economy and on the electoral prospects of the party in government were also determined by political calculations.

Hoffmann acknowledged that actors other than national governments played a role in the process of integration. He recognized that in the 'low-politics' sectors (e.g. social and regional policy) interest groups did influence the actions of governments: but as he pointed out, they were not the only influence. Other influences included government officials (particularly on economic matters) and also the electoral considerations of the party or parties in office (Hoffmann, 1964: 89). However, he considered national governments to be the ultimate arbiters of key decisions. The governments of states were said to be uniquely powerful for two reasons. First, because they possessed legal sovereignty; and second because they had political legitimacy as the only democratically-elected actors in the integration process. In this view, where the power of supranational institutions increased it did so because governments believed it to be in their national interest.

In Hoffmann's picture of the process of European integration, governments had much more autonomy than in the neofunctionalist view. The integration process remained therefore essentially intergovernmental: it would only go as far as the governments were prepared to allow it to go.

However, Hoffmann also pointed to the fact that European integration was only one aspect of the development of international politics. That insight led to a more restrictive view of government autonomy. In this respect Hoffmann, like the realists, stressed the external limitations on autonomy: states were seen as independent actors, but their governments were constrained by the position of the state in the world system.

Liberal intergovernmentalism

Andrew Moravcsik (1993) provided a later and more rigorous version of the intergovernmental explanation of the EC. Like Hoffmann, Moravcsik started from a critique of neofunctionalism. He restated the argument that neofunctionalism failed to explain developments in the EC itself, but he put more weight on a theoretical critique. In particular, he argued that the self-criticisms of the neofunctionalists themselves had to be taken seriously. He identified (Moravcsik, 1993: 478–80) three such self-criticisms:

1. theories of European integration had to be supplemented (or even be supplanted) by more general theories of national responses to international interdependence;

2. the development of common policy responses needed to be looked at as much as did institutional transfers of competence; the emphasis on formal transfers of authority to the EC often concealed a failure to effect a real surrender of sovereignty;

3. unicausal theories were inadequate to deal with the phenomenon under consideration; more than one theory was needed to grasp the complexity of EC policy-making

Instead of reviving neofunctionalism, Moravcsik argued that these criticisms should be taken seriously, and a theory constructed that took account of them. He believed that all of the points could be accounted for if the analysis of the EC was rolled into what he called 'current theories of international political economy' (Moravcsik 1993: 480).

Moravcsik's approach, like that of Hoffmann, assumed that states were rational actors, but departed from traditional realism in not treating states as black boxes or billiard balls. Instead it was assumed that the governments of states were playing what Putnam called 'two-level games' (Putnam 1988). A domestic political process determined their definition of the national interest. This constituted the first part of the analysis and determined the position that governments took with them into the international negotiation.

This approach built on the undeveloped argument of Hoffmann about the role of domestic politics, but in some ways it was less sophisticated in its account of domestic politics than was that suggested by Hoffmann. Moravcsik's view of domestic politics, which he called a liberal view, was essentially the same as that of the neofunctionalists, which we have called above a pluralist view. The primary determinant of the preferences of a government was the balance between economic interests within the state. He was frequently criticized for this rather restricted view of the domestic political process (Wincott, 1995: 601; Forster, 1998: 357–9; Caporaso, 1999: 162; Wallace, 1999: 156–7)

The second part of the analysis was to see how conflicting national interests were reconciled in the negotiating forum of the Council of Ministers. This process was divided into two logically sequential stages. The first stage was to reach agreement on the common policy response to the problem that governments were trying to solve. The second stage was to reach agreement on the appropriate institutional arrangements. Moravcsik (1999: 21–2) gave the example of monetary union: it would be impractical to try to understand the negotiations over the constitution of a European Central Bank without first understanding the objectives which the bank was being set up to achieve.

The analytical framework of liberal intergovernmentalism was applied in Moravcsik (1999) to five key episodes in the construction of the EU:

- the negotiation of the Treaties of Rome (1955–8)

- the consolidation of the common market and the Common Agricultural Policy (CAP) (1958–83)

- the setting up of the first experiment in monetary co-operation and of the European Monetary System (EMS) (1969–83)

- the negotiation of the Single European Act (SEA) (1984–8)

- and the negotiation of the Treaty on European Union (TEU) (1988–1991).

On the basis of these case studies Moravcsik came to the following conclusions:

1. The major choices in favour of Europe were a reflection of the preferences of national governments, not of the preferences of supranational organizations.

2. These national preferences reflected the balance of economic interests, rather than the political biases of politicians or national strategic security concerns.

3. The outcomes of negotiations reflected the relative bargaining power of the states; the delegation of decision-making authority to supranational institutions reflected the wish of governments to ensure that the commitments of all parties to the agreement would be carried through rather than federalist ideology or a belief in the inherent efficiency of international organizations.

However, he was criticized for his choice of case studies. As Scharpf (1999: 165) put it:

Since only intergovernmental negotiations are being considered, why shouldn't the preferences of national governments have shaped the outcomes? Since all case studies have issues of economic integration as their focus, why shouldn't economic concerns have shaped the negotiating positions of governments? And since only decisions requiring unanimous agreement are being analysed, why shouldn't the outcomes be affected by the relative bargaining powers of the governments involved?

The alternative would have been to look at the smaller-scale day-to-day decisions that constitute the bulk of the decisions made within the EU. Here the picture might be very different. Supranational actors might have more influence, and national preferences might be less clearly defined and less vigorously defended. We look at some of these arguments later in the book (Chs. 19 to 21, pp. 233–73).

Conclusion

Essentially the same academic debate about the process of European integration has been going on for over four decades. Central to this debate is the nature and role of the state. In intergovernmental perspectives, European integration is a process whereby the governments of states voluntarily enter into agreements to work together to solve common problems. Some constraints operate on the autonomy of national governments, but they remain in control of the process. The alternative perspective suggests that although governments started the process, it soon took on a life of its own which went beyond the control of the governments. This 'intergovernmental–supranational debate' forms the first of the themes that recur throughout this book.

These questions are of more than just academic interest. The nature of the EU, and where the process is going, are fundamental issues of political debate in the member states of the EU today. However, there is some irony in how explanations of the process of integration have been used. In the 1950s and 1960s, neofunctionalist ideas were eagerly embraced by members of the Commission as a blueprint for constructing a united Europe. Today, opponents of further integration implicitly invoke the neofunctionalist idea that the process is no longer under control and threatens national identity. Conversely, intergovernmentalist arguments are more likely to be voiced by the advocates of further steps, who echo Hoffmann and Moravcsik in reassuring hesitant European public opinion that the governments of states remain in charge: that sovereignty is only 'pooled', not lost.

Underlying the political arguments about the nature of the EU are assumptions about the legitimacy of transferring sovereignty away from the nation-state which form the second recurring theme of this book. This is sometimes presented as a problem of the 'democratic deficit' that exists at the level of the EU (Box 22.7, p. 284), with the implication that it can be solved by increasing the powers of the European Parliament (EP). However, Eurosceptics often argue that democratic accountability cannot be established at the European level because there is

no such thing as a European people. Democracy can only operate within the context of national cultures. If an attempt is made to force the diverse peoples of Europe into an artificial union, nationalism will be stirred up rather than abolished. The peoples of Europe are too different from one another, their histories, cultures and values too diverse for them to be brought together in one state. In this view the problem is not simply a democratic deficit, but a legitimacy deficit (Box 1.4, p. 15). Some defenders of further integration would agree that there is a legitimacy deficit, but would also argue that legitimacy

---

Box 1.4 Legitimacy

Legitimate government is accepted by the people to whom it applies as being more than an externally imposed system of rules. They believe that it is justified in some way. Beetham and Lord (1998) identified three different dimensions of legitimacy. They argued that political authority was legitimate to the extent that:

- established rules are followed in acquiring or exercising the authority;

- socially accepted beliefs about the rightful source of authority and the proper ends and standards of government are adhered to;

- the authority is recognized by other legitimate authorities and by the appropriate subordinates.

Generally, international institutions have secured legitimacy through the approval of the legitimate governments of member states. This is an indirect rather than direct form of legitimacy. However, for many, the extent of European integration demands more direct political legitimacy than for other international institutions. Indeed, if it is accepted that the EU institutions are supranational, rather than merely international (see Box 1.1, p. 8), then they clearly do require direct legitimation. The problem for the EU is the distance between its institutions and the citizens, and the absence of a common European identity.

can be built at the European level through building a sense of European identity.

Finally, the emphasis of both the neofunctionalists and Andrew Moravcsik on the role of vested interests, or pressure groups, raises a third theme. This is also a central topic in theories of EU governance that are discussed in the next chapter, and we will come back to it in the conclusion to that chapter.

KEY POINTS

The intellectual background

- David Mitrany was not a theorist of European integration, but his ideas were influential on those who later advocated integration.

- His main concern was to prevent war between states, and he proposed to do this by taking routine functional tasks out of the hands of national governments and giving them over to international agencies.

- He was opposed to world government because it would be inimical to freedom, and to regional federations because they would just reproduce the conditions that had produced wars between states at a bigger level.

- European federalism attracted strong support among the Resistance groups in war-time Europe.

- The leading intellectual figure was Altiero Spinelli. He advocated a 'constitutional break' at the end of the war, with a move directly to supersede the system of sovereign states with a federal constitution for Europe.

- The Resistance movements did not manage to organize the Congress that was intended to adopt this new constitution until 1948, by which time national political elites were already installed in the European states.

- The outcome of the Hague Congress was the Council of Europe, an intergovernmental body that fell far short of the aspirations of the federalists.

- The Schuman plan for the ECSC was devised by Jean Monnet, the head of the French economic planning commission.

- Monnet had realized the inadequacy of the European nation-state as an economic unit in the modern world, and believed it was necessary to create a European-scale economy.

- He was also concerned with two other problems: how to control Germany, and how to ensure adequate supplies of coking coal for the French steel industry.

- The idea of a coal and steel pool solved all of these problems by taking the first, limited step towards a European-scale economic zone, taking strategic industries out of the hands of the German government, and giving France access to Ruhr coal.

International relations theories of European integration

- IR theory in the 1950s was dominated by realism. This theory treated nation states as the fundamental units of international relations. It did not lead to any expectation that the governments of states would voluntarily surrender their sovereign control over policy.

- Because realism was ill equipped to explain the emergence of European integration, the first theorists of the process posed a direct challenge to the realist assumption in IR.

- Neofunctionalism suggested that European integration was a process that once started would undermine the sovereignty of states to a greater extent than envisaged by the governments when they took that first step.

- The challenge to realism produced a response that stressed the intergovernmental nature of the process.

- Neofunctionalism argued that states are not unified actors, but that the definition of the national interest is the result of a pluralistic political process in which the government of the state negotiates with interest groups.

- Interest groups were seen also to be important international actors, their activities crossing state boundaries.

- The concept of spillover was central to the neofunctionalist theory. Functional spillover, political spillover, and cultivated spillover would lead the process of European integration to run out of the control of national governments.

- Hoffmann argued that neofunctionalists had made three mistakes: regional integration was not a self-contained process, but was influenced by a wider international context; states were uniquely powerful actors because they possessed formal sovereignty and democratic legitimacy; and integration in low politics sectors would not necessarily spillover into high politics sectors.

- Moravcsik's liberal intergovernmentalism incorporated the neofunctionalist insight that national interests are defined as part of a domestic pluralist political process; but he denied the importance of supranational actors and insisted that governments remained in control of the process of European integration.

- Moravcsik proposed a two-level analysis of EU bargaining, in which governments' preferences were determined at the domestic level, and then used as the basis for intergovernmental negotiations at the European level.

- For Moravcsik, the primary determinant of a government's preferences was balance between economic interests within the state.

- Moravcsik divided intergovernmental negotiations into the reaching of agreement on a common policy response to a problem, and the reaching of agreement on the appropriate institutional arrangements.

QUESTIONS

1 What relevance have Mitrany, Spinelli, and Monnet for the theory of neofunctionalism?

2 Why did neofunctionalists believe that once the first steps had been taken in the process of European integration, other steps would inevitably follow?

3 What are the main arguments of intergovernmentalism?

4 How might global international factors affect European integration?

5 How might domestic political factors affect European integration?

FURTHER READING

An excellent recent discussion of integration theories is to be found in: B. Rosamond, *Theories of European Integration* (Basingstoke and London: Macmillan, 2000).

Other accounts can be found in: L. Cram, 'Integration Theory and the Study of the European Policy Process', in J. Richardson (ed.), *European Union: Power and Policy-Making* (London: Routledge, 1996), pp. 40–58; and in S. George, 'The European Union: approaches from international relations', in H. Kassim and A. Menon, *The European Union and Industrial Policy* (London and New York: Routledge, 1996), pp. 11–25.

Neofunctionalism is elaborated, expanded, and defended in: J. Tranholm-Mikkelsen, 'Neo-functionalism: Obstinate or Obsolete? A Reappraisal in the Light of the New Dynamism of the European Community', *Millennium* 20 (1991), 1–22.

The earliest statement of liberal intergovernmentalism is in A. Moravcsik, 'Preferences and Power in the European Community: A Liberal Intergovernmentalist Approach', *Journal of Common Market Studies* 31 (1993), 473–524; a later statement of the theory, which differs subtly, is given by him in *The Choice for Europe: Social Purpose and State Power from Messina to Maastricht* (London: UCL Press, 1998).

2 Theories of EU governance

a newer generation of scholars, uninspired by debates between intergovernmentalism and neofunctionalism . . . struck out on their own

(Caporaso, 1998: 341).

SUMMARY

As European integration progressed, the academic focus began to shift from explaining the integration process to examining the EU as a political system. As such, EU scholars increasingly drew on approaches from comparative politics and public policy. While some attempts to escape the supranational–intergovernmental dichotomy have proved more successful than others, the study of the EU has nonetheless broadened considerably beyond the traditional IR debate.

Introduction

The academic debate about European integration is still dominated by the theoretical stand-off between intergovernmental and supranational interpretations. Other voices have begun to emerge, though, which reject that dichotomy. Approaches to understanding the EU have been advocated that do not derive from international relations, but draw instead on comparative politics and public policy analysis, while other analysts have tried to find a median between the entrenched intergovernmental and supranational positions. All of these approaches turn away from the focus of IR theories on the process of European integration, and instead treat the EU as a political system that is already in existence, and try to explore 'the nature of the beast'.

This chapter looks first at attempts to study the EU using concepts and theories drawn from comparative politics, particularly 'new institutionalism', then at attempts deriving from the analysis of public policy. It then turns to two theories of governance in the EU that have come to prominence in recent years, one of which characterizes the EU as a system of multilevel governance and one which discusses it as a system of supranational governance.

The study of the EU as comparative politics

In a seminal article, Simon Hix (1994) issued a call to scholars within the discipline of comparative politics to wake up to the existence of the EU as a suitable subject for study using their established concepts. He heeded his own call a few years later, producing a textbook on the EU that took a radically different approach to the subject.

Instead of asking questions such as how far the EU was dominated by the member states and how far it operated as an autonomous entity, Hix (1999: 1) asked questions that derived from the study of comparative politics:

How is governmental power exercised? Under what conditions can the Parliament influence legislation? Is the Court of Justice beyond political control? Why do some citizens support the central institutions while others oppose them? How important are political parties and elections in shaping political choices? Why are some social groups able to influence the political agenda more than others?

The approach succeeded in shifting the focus away from the study of European integration as a process to *'how the EU works today'* (Hix, 1999: 1; emphasis in original). The main perspective from comparative politics that has been applied to the EU is 'new institutionalism'.

New institutionalism

One adaptation of an approach that was originally applied to the study of domestic politics that Hix drew upon was new institutionalism (March and Olsen, 1984, 1989, 1996). It would be more accurate to refer to two sets of approaches—rational choice institutionalism and historical institutionalism.

New institutionalism was a reaction to the behavioural approaches that had come to dominate political science in the 1970s. Behaviouralism itself had been a reaction against formal institutional analyses of government and politics which had lost sight of the real political processes that lay behind the formal structures of government.

New institutionalism argued that the reaction against the old, formal institutional analyses had gone too far; that the importance of institutions in structuring political action had been lost. In the words of Bulmer (1998: 368) '[t]he core assumption of this approach is that *institutions matter*'.

One thing that was new about this variety of institutionalism was that institutions were not just defined as the formal organizations that the old institutionalism had recognized—such as parliaments, executives, and judicial courts—but extended to include informal patterns of structured inter-action, such as policy networks (see below). At the same time, new institutionalism recognized that formal institutions were more important than behaviouralists had suggested. Behaviouralism focused on groups in society, and tried to under-stand the influence that these 'societal actors' had on political decisions. The formal institutions were treated as neutral arenas within which the struggle for influence between the different societal actors was carried out. New institutionalists disagreed with this perspective in two ways. First, they argued that formal institutions were not neutral arenas, since formal institutional structures and rules biased access to the political process in favour of some soci-etal groups over others. Second, they argued that institutions could be autonomous political actors in their own right.

Rational choice institutionalism focused particu-larly on the constraints that institutional structures imposed on actors. In trying to understand the behaviour of political actors it was important to identify the parameters that were set by the fact that they were acting within a specific framework of rules. So, the activities of interest groups would reflect the procedures that prevailed for the passage of the legis-lation that affected them, the access points that were available to them in that process, and the previous relationships that they had established with key decision-makers.

In the case of the EU, whether interest groups chose to try to influence legislation through national governments or through the Commission and the European Parliament (EP) would reflect:

- the relative openness to those groups of the national government actors compared with the supranational actors
- the extent to which the process was intergovernmental (e.g. what decision-rules applied within the Council of Ministers)
- what role the EP had in the final decision.

If national decision-making was dominated by other interest groups, then 'outsider' groups trying to influence EU policy might turn to the supranational institutions because they would be more likely to get their voices heard there. In competition policy

decisions, for example, national monopoly sup-pliers, which had a close working relationship with national government officials, would tend to work through national channels. In contrast, potential competitors, who wanted to see the dismantling of the advantages that the national monopoly sup-pliers enjoyed at the national level, would be more likely to turn to the Commission because it was dif-ficult for them to obtain access to the national decision-makers and easier for them to obtain access to the supranational institutions.

Where unanimity applied in the Council of Minis-ters, it would be more important to lobby at the national level because one vote against a proposal could block it; but where Qualified Majority Voting (QMV) applied the potential influence of the Com-mission would be greater, making it a more attractive target for lobbying. In areas where the powers of the EP were extended under the SEA, the TEU, and the Treaty of Amsterdam (see Ch. 18, pp. 223–6), inter-est groups began to lobby the EP more extensively than they had previously, and to do so more than did interest groups in policy sectors where the powers of the EP remained restricted to the consult-ation procedure.

Rational choice institutionalists also made a sig-nificant contribution to understanding the ways in which supranational actors could obtain a degree of autonomy from national governments, allowing them to make their own input to the policy process (Pollack, 1997). Applying what is known as principal–agent theory, rational choice institutional-ists pointed to the difficulties of principals (the national governments) in keeping a check on the activities of their agents (the central institutions).

- As the range of delegated tasks increased, so the difficulties of monitoring what the agents were doing would increase.

- As the number of principals increased with successive enlargements of membership, so the agents could play off the preferences of different coalitions of principals against the attempts of other principals to restrain them.

- As QMV expanded, so the constraints on the Commission in constructing a winning coalition in support of its proposals were reduced.

Historical institutionalists placed emphasis on the

argument that political relationships have to be viewed over time. Their approach argued that decisions were not made according to an abstract rationality, but according to perceptions and within constraints that were structured by pre-existing institutional relationships. Institutions incorporated values and norms which affected the way in which actors perceived the choices open to them. They also argued that once a decision was made, it was subject to unanticipated consequences over time.

Central to historical institutionalism was the concept of 'path dependence'. Once one decision was made it tended to block off some potential avenues for development of policy and made it more likely the policy would continue to develop in the same direction. In extreme cases, path dependence could turn into 'lock-in' (Pierson, 1996) where other avenues of policy were entirely closed off by the bias towards the existing route that was built into the system. This could explain why policies such as the CAP proved so resistant to reform even after their negative effects had become obvious.

Applying historical institutionalism to the EU led to a further critique of intergovernmental analyses, and revealed further reasons for thinking that national governments might not be entirely in control of the process of integration. Intergovernmental analyses tended to focus on the historic decisions, represented mainly by revisions to the treaties. What happened between these historic decisions was treated by intergovernmentalists as simply the working through of the decisions. Historical institutionalists argued that after the decision had been taken it would be likely to produce unanticipated and unintended outcomes. This might be because of a simple failure to think through the implications; but it might be for one or both of two other reasons (Pierson, 1998: 41). First, the preferences of governments might change over time. For example, the preference for a common agricultural policy based on price support might have been a rational response to conditions in the 1960s in Europe, when security of food supplies was a paramount concern, but no longer appropriate in the changed circumstances of

the 1990s when technological advances had removed this concern. Second, national governments might change. For example, the EC directives on social policy to which a British Labour government had agreed were not to the liking of the Conservative governments between 1979 and 1997.

Even where preferences changed, governments would find it extremely difficult to change the decision. One reason for this was the institutionalization of the policy sector. Initial policy choices tended to structure subsequent patterns of behaviour, thus creating path dependence. Once the CAP was in place, structured relationships developed between European farmers' representatives, the relevant Commission officials, and national agricultural policy officials which crystallized into a European-level policy community (see pp. 23–4 below, and Ch. 24, pp. 305–23) which was very resistant to change.

A second reason why governments found it difficult to change a decision was because the voting rules in the Council of Ministers made it very difficult to get agreement to move back from a policy once it was agreed. Where, as with agriculture, the rule was unanimity, it was impossible to retreat so long as one member state benefited from the status quo and refused to move from it. This was sometimes referred to as 'the ratchet effect'. Even where QMV applied, in order to effect change it was necessary to construct a coalition representing more than a simple majority of states (the exact number depending on the weighting of the votes of the members of the coalition, and therefore on the identity of the states involved). It was impossible where the changed preference involved only a few states or, as in the case of social policy quoted above, only one state.

The insights of new institutionalism fed into a number of studies of specific EU polices, such as the single market programme (Armstrong and Bulmer, 1998). They also informed more elaborated frameworks of analysis such as the multilevel governance approach, and analysis of the EU as a system of supranational governance, both of which are dealt with later in this chapter.

The study of the EU as public policy analysis

Richardson (1996a) took up Hix's call to approach the EU from different disciplinary directions, but instead of organizing the study around the concepts of comparative politics, he advocated organizing it around the concepts that he and others had been using for some time to study the policy-making process within member states. He argued in particular for the application of two concepts: policy networks and epistemic communities. The first of these concepts was originally developed in studies of public policy-making in the United States and later became prominent in Britain, particularly through the work of Rhodes (1988). Ironically, the second concept originally arose from the study of international relations and then fed back into domestic policy analysis.

Policy networks

The policy network concept as applied at the national level refers to relationships between interest groups and governments. Marsh and Rhodes (1992b) defined a policy network as 'a set of resource-dependent organisations'. By this they meant that each of the groups that made up the policy network needed something that the others had in order to fulfil its own objectives. The types of resources that actors could bring to a policy network included constitutional-legal, organizational, financial, political, and informational.

Although the terms have been used in slightly different ways by different writers, Richardson (1996a) appeared to accept the Marsh and Rhodes idea that 'policy network' is a generic term, and that types of policy networks range on a spectrum from closely-knit policy communities to loose issue networks. The characteristics of these different types of policy network are listed in Box 2.1, p. 23.

The applicability of the policy networks framework to the analysis of the EU was questioned by Kassim (1994). He argued that EU processes were not settled enough to allow policy networks to emerge. Interest groups used different channels to influence decisions; sometimes national, sometimes EU-level.

> ### Box 2.1 Policy communities and issue networks
>
> A policy community is marked by:
>
> - limited membership;
> - stable membership over long periods of time;
> - a high level of interaction between the members;
> - shared values between members;
> - some degree of equality in the distribution of resources;
> - a relative balance of power and influence between members.
>
> An issue network, in contrast, is marked by:
>
> - large and diffuse membership;
> - frequent shifts in the membership;
> - fluctuating frequency of contact between members;
> - lack of shared values;
> - marked inequality in the distribution of resources;
> - marked inequality in power and influence within the network.

The multinational character and institutional complexity of the EU made it difficult to delimit policy networks, and particularly to identify the relevant public sector actor. Sometimes national agencies would be key, sometimes the Commission, sometimes other EU-level institutions. The institutions themselves often acted as lobbyists in the EU in pursuit of their own objectives.

One of the scholars who had advocated the use of policy networks replied to Kassim (Peterson, 1995a). He questioned Kassim's insistence on the fluidity of EU policy-making procedures, arguing that while some sectors remained fluid, others were settling into more stable patterns. Indeed, he argued that the Commission was so under-resourced that it had to try to enter into stable relationships with partners whom it could trust, who had information that it could use. While he accepted Kassim's points about the complexity of the role of institutions in the EU in comparison with national institutional arrangements, he argued that the policy networks approach was perfectly compatible with new institutionalist analyses of the EU, which allowed theorization of the working of institutional relations. While he accepted that the delineation of policy networks at the EU level was a difficult task, Peterson insisted that this did not make it a less important one.

Peterson's most interesting observation, though, was the need to be clear about the level of the policy-making process that was being analysed. He argued that the policy networks model was best able to explain what he called 'the policy-shaping decisions', when proposals were being formulated and before a political decision was taken which 'set' the policy (Peterson, 1995a: 400). In a subsequent article, the same author expanded on this argument (Peterson, 1995b). He here identified three 'levels' of analysis in EU decision-making. The highest level he termed the 'super-systemic' or 'history-making' decisions. These were mainly decisions taken by national governments in the European Council or at IGCs, and were most fruitfully analysed using inter-governmental ideas. The second level he termed the 'systemic' or 'policy-setting' stage. At this level a combination of intergovernmental and inter-institutional analysis was needed to understand outcomes. The third level he called the 'sub-systemic' or 'policy shaping' stage. At this level policy networks

were a useful concept for understanding how policy options were formulated in bargaining between the Commission Directorates-General, national civil servants, and private actors (see Box 2.2, p. 24).

Epistemic communities

Whereas policy networks are held together by resource interdependence, epistemic communities are knowledge-based groups. An epistemic community was defined by Haas (1992: p. 3) as:

a network of professionals with recognised expertise and competence in a particular domain and an authoritative claim to policy-relevant knowledge within that domain or issue-area.

The members of an epistemic community shared both normative beliefs and causal beliefs, i.e. they held a common set of values about what was right and desirable, and a common set of assumptions about how to achieve those goals. They also agreed on notions of validity, so they had a common basis for settling differences of opinion between themselves, and they shared a common policy enterprise, so that they were all involved in efforts to solve the same problems.

Epistemic communities were likely to exercise particular influence over policy when policy-makers faced conditions of uncertainty about the likely consequences of policy choice. Such uncertainty was particularly high where international co-ordination

Box 2.2 Levels of analysis in EU decision-making

Level	Type of decision	Dominant actors	Rationality
super-systemic	history-making	European Council, National governments in IGCs European Court of Justice	political, legalistic
systemic	policy-setting	Council of Ministers, Committee of Permanent Representatives (COREPER)	political, technocratic administrative
sub-systemic/meso-level	policy-shaping	Commission, committees, Council groups	technocratic consensual, administrative

Reproduced from *Journal of European Public Policy* 2/1 1995: 71.

of policy was concerned. Success in such situations was heavily dependent on the actions of other states. There was also a high degree of uncertainty about the possible unforeseen consequences. In these circumstances state actors were highly likely to turn to epistemic communities because they were not sure how to define the national interest.

Members of transnational epistemic communities can influence state interests either by directly identifying them for decision makers or by illuminating the salient dimensions of an issue from which the decision makers may then deduce their interests. The decision makers in one state may, in turn, influence the interests and behavior of other states, thereby increasing the likelihood of convergent state behavior and international policy coordination, informed by the causal beliefs and policy preferences of the epistemic community   (Haas, 1992: 4).

Haas's perspective suggested that epistemic communities were useful as a means of helping the governments of states to think their way through situations of uncertainty, and to provide a common framework of analysis which could act as a guarantee that states that tried to co-ordinate policy would all work along the same lines. However, going beyond Haas's arguments, epistemic communities might also be used by supranational actors such as the European Commission as a means of furthering the Europeanization of policy. The expert analysis that they provided, and the policy prescriptions that they advocated, if they pointed in the desired direction, could form a powerful lever for supranational actors to move states in the direction of common European solutions to problems that confronted them.

Multilevel governance

Multilevel governance has strong antecedents in neofunctionalism, but is less a theory about the process of European integration and more a theory about the nature of the EU that has emerged from that process. In that respect it is entirely in line with the approach advocated by Hix (1999).

Multilevel governance was first developed from a study of EU structural policy and was later extended into a fuller theory. An early definition by Gary Marks (1993: 392) spoke of:

the emergence of *multi-level governance*, a system of continuous negotiation among nested governments at several territorial tiers—supranational, national, regional and local.

In this context, Marks was referring particularly to the way in which EU structural funds were administered: to the implementation stage of policy (see Ch. 27, pp. 374–6). However, in conjunction with other writers, he subsequently extended the concept to cover the policy-making phase as well (Marks, Hooghe, and Blank, 1996). While accepting that integration involved intergovernmental bargains, multilevel governance theorists reasserted the neofunctionalist critique of realism, that individual governments were not in control of the process.

Marks, Hooghe, and Blank made three key points against the intergovernmental view, some of which echoed the arguments of new institutionalists:

1. Collective decision-making involves loss of control for the governments of individual states.

2. Decision-making competencies in the EU are shared by actors at different levels, not monopolized by the governments of states.

3. The political systems of member states are not separate from each other, as Moravcsik assumed, but are connected in various ways.

While Marks, Hooghe, and Blank accepted the central role of the Council of Ministers in EU decision-making, they pointed to a number of constraints on the ability of individual governments to control the outcomes of such collective decision-making. The use of qualified majority voting in the Council was an obvious constraint: any individual government might be outvoted. The Luxembourg Compromise (see Ch. 8, pp. 92–3) did allow a government to exercise a veto if it felt that its vital national interests were threatened, but the prevailing culture in the Council worked against frequent use of this option, making it a rather blunt instrument for maintaining national sovereignty. So, while it was true that governments might be able to attain desired objectives by pooling their sovereignty, that was not the same as arguing that their control of the process remained intact.

Supranational institutions might be created by member governments to assist them, as Moravcsik argued, but these did not remain under close national government control. For intergovernmentalists, national governments could ultimately choose to rein in the power of these institutions. For multilevel governance theorists this was difficult in practice because changes to the role of supranational institutions required unanimous agreement, which was difficult to secure with so many member states.

Another reason why Marks, Hooghe, and Blank believed governments had difficulty in controlling supranational institutions was because the state itself was not a unified actor. Moravcsik accepted this in his liberal intergovernmentalist position so far as defining the national interest was concerned. He saw a domestic pluralistic process taking place. Marks, Hooghe, and Blank went further by arguing that the determining of the national interest was not purely a domestic matter. Sections of the government, and non-state actors, would form alliances with their counterparts in other member states, which might influence national governments' negotiating positions on EU matters. These alliances would not be under the control of the core institutions of the national government, such as the Foreign Office or the Prime Minister's Office. The Commission in particular would be able to exploit the existence of these 'transgovernmental' and 'transnational' networks of actors to promote their policy preferences within the 'domestic' politics of member states.

Rather than a coherent theory, multilevel governance was an eclectic collection of points that were primarily directed at what its advocates saw as the misrepresentation of the nature of the EU by the intergovernmental theorists. It did contain some elements of an explanation for the development of the EU: but it was primarily concerned with the static analysis of the nature of the EU. This meant that it lost the basis for the analysis of political dynamics that was present in neofunctionalism. This dynamic element was recovered in a later theorization of the EU as a system of supranational governance.

Supranational governance

Starting from the intergovernmentalism versus supranationalism debate, a team of scholars led by Wayne Sandholtz and Alec Stone Sweet (1998) claimed to offer an alternative that cut through the dichotomy. It was an approach that drew on the transactionalism of Karl Deutsch (1953, 1957) and on new institutionalism as applied to the EU, although the authors themselves located the origins of their approach in neofunctionalism.

Fundamental to the approach was the argument that if the EU was to be analysed as an international regime, as Moravcsik insisted it could be, then it had to be seen not as a single regime but as a series of regimes for different policy sectors. The authors therefore sought to explain the different levels of supranationalism that existed in different policy sectors. The three key elements in their approach were the development of transnational society, the role of supranational organizations with meaningful autonomous capacity to pursue integrative agendas, and a focus on European rule-making to resolve what they called 'international policy externalities'. By this last phrase the authors meant the unintended effects on one country of policies being followed in another country, such as the pollution of the air in one country by smoke from factories in a neighbouring country.

Following Deutsch, Stone Sweet and Sandholtz (1997) argued that transactions across national boundaries were increasing. As they increased, so a supranational society of relevant actors would emerge. These actors would favour the construction of rules to govern their interactions at the supra-national level because nationally-based rules would be a hindrance to them. If companies that operated across national boundaries had to comply with different rules in every member state, this would impose additional costs on their activity. A good example here is merger control (Box 2.3, p. 27). Another example of what the authors call the emergence of supranational society is provided by the case of the emergence of a supranational telecommunications regime (Box 2.4, p. 27).

The construction of rules at the supranational level would result in the 'Europeanization' of a sector: that is the regulation of the sector would be at the EU level. Once the initial step is taken in the Europeanization of a policy sector, Stone Sweet and Sandholtz argued that the consolidation of the supranational regime would proceed through the emergence of European rules. Actors working within the new framework of European rules would start to test the limits of those rules. They would seek clarification from the adjudicators—administrators and courts. These clarifications would not only establish the precise meaning of rules, but would also and at the same time modify them. The actors would then face a different set of constraints, which would be tighter than the previous constraints, because more

precise, and the actors would adjust their behaviour accordingly. As rules became more precise, so they would tend to develop away from the original intentions of the member states, and would simultaneously become more difficult to modify in any different direction. This pointed to the same process as in the historical institutionalist concept of path dependence.

Branch and Øhrgaard (1999) argued that Stone Sweet and Sandholtz had not succeeded in escaping the intergovernmental–supranational dichotomy, but had instead offered a mirror-image of Moravcsik's liberal intergovernmentalism. In particular they argued that both theories privileged certain types of actors, and therefore certain types of decisions; and that both theories classified actors as either intergovernmental or supranational in a way that ensured that they would oversimplify the complexity of the

---

Box 2.3 The emergence of supranational society—merger control

Two companies in the same sector operating across national borders might decide to merge so as to rationalize their operations and reduce their costs. To do so they might have to get the approval not just of national monopoly and merger authorities in their two states of origin, but also in all those states where either company or both combined had a significant proportion of the relevant market. To avoid this situation of 'multiple jeopardy' we would expect to see considerable support from large companies for the transfer of merger approval to the supranational level, giving them a one-stop approval procedure to negotiate, and this is what has actually happened.

(Cini and McGowan, 1998)

Box 2.4 The emergence of supranational society—telecommunications

In the 1980s the sector was dominated by national monopoly suppliers, the nationalized Postal, Telegraph, and Telephone companies (PTTs). These national suppliers formed parts of policy communities consisting of the PTTs, the officials in the relevant national ministries, and the suppliers of switching equipment, who were also nationally-based and who had a guaranteed market from the PTTs. Sandholtz (1998) showed how the domination of the sector by these national policy communities came to be challenged by a coalition of users of telecommunications who demanded cheaper and more technically advanced services than were provided by the PTTs. These users formed a supranational coalition for change, allying with the Commission and with the British government, which had liberalized its own telecommunications market and wished to extend liberalization to the other national EC markets. Gradually the pressure from this coalition eroded the hold of the PTTs on the policy preferences of national governments and opened a window of opportunity for the Commission to get proposals through the Council of Ministers for opening up national markets to competition.

nature of the EU. According to Branch and Øhrgaard, Moravcsik gave a privileged role in his theoretical framework to national actors and intergovernmental bargains. He therefore concentrated on episodes, the grand bargains, which were highly likely to demonstrate the value of these concepts. On the other side of the mirror, Stone Sweet and Sandholtz gave a privileged role to transnational business actors and supranational actors, and to the operation of supranational rules of governance. They therefore concentrated on routine decision-making in policy sectors that were concerned with economics and trade, which were highly likely to demonstrate the value of these concepts.

Branch and Øhrgaard also argued that both Moravcsik and Stone Sweet and Sandholtz equally made the mistake of treating evidence of influence on policy decisions by supranational actors as necessary and sufficient evidence of supranational integration, and evidence of decisions remaining in the hands of national governments as necessary and sufficient evidence of intergovernmentalism. In contrast, Branch and Øhrgaard argued that not all European integration was driven forward by transnational and supranational actors. In fields such as social policy, the process had been driven by national governments anxious to correct for the effects of the economic integration that *had* been driven by transnational and supranational actors. They further argued that European integration could not simply be equated with the influence of supranational actors. In the field of the Common Foreign and Security Policy (CFSP) (see Ch. 28, pp. 395–401),

although the mechanisms remained intergovernmental and the formal power of the supranational institutions remained limited, academic experts agreed that the process involved much more than just diplomatic consultation. CFSP was a form of European integration that did not involve supranational governance.

A further criticism of Stone Sweet and Sandholtz's approach is that the framework of analysis ignored the wider context within which the process of Europeanization takes place. This criticism points to an omission that is curious given the association of one of the authors, Sandholtz, with a seminal analysis of the emergence of the single market (Sandholtz and Zysman, 1989) which put particular stress on the wider context of global capitalism in explaining the emergence of the policy. This study is examined in Chapter 25 (see pp. 330–1). In the empirical studies contained in the book that they edited (Sandholtz and Stone Sweet, 1998), the influence of the wider capitalist system did not emerge very clearly. For example, Sandholtz (1998) explained the emergence of the supranational European society in the telecommunications sector without referring to the deregulation of US telecommunications, which both put European-based companies who were consumers of telecommunications at a disadvantage in comparison with their US competitors, and led to intense pressure from the US government for the European market to be opened to entry by US telecommunication providers (Dang-Nguyen *et al.*, 1993; Fuchs, 1994). This inadequacy in the analysis reflected the inadequacy in the theory.

Conclusion

Attempts to get away from the deadlock in the debate between intergovernmentalists and supranationalists over the nature of the EU have involved scholars from disciplines other than international relations, particularly comparative politics and policy analysis, applying the concepts that are their stock-in-trade to the EU. Such approaches yield a number of insights, especially concerning the more routine decisions of the EU. Such decisions may not be as monumental as the 'history making decisions', but, as Richardson (1996a: 29) said, they constitute 'the nine-tenths of the 'policy iceberg' that is below the water line', and 'some means has to be found of analysing it'.

The analysis of public policy in particular raises again the theme that was mentioned at the end of

Chapter 1: that of the role of interest groups. Ideas of policy networks put the emphasis squarely on the links between interest groups and policy-makers. The motive force of policy-making is conceived to be vested interest. This reproduces at the micro-level the insight of neofunctionalists that European integration would be driven forward more by interests responding in a rational, self-serving manner to the changed circumstances produced by the existence of the EC than by any idealistic commitment such as that shown by the federalists. Liberal intergovernmentalism also emphasizes interests rather than ideas as the key to analysing the EU. However, the concept of an epistemic community modifies this emphasis on interest, and brings ideas back into the analysis. The experts who make up the epistemic communities are not driven by self-interest, but by a commitment to a set of ideas or theories.

Historical institutionalism also brings ideas back in. The other type of new institutionalists, rational choice institutionalists, analyse the logical responses of actors to the institutional rules that they face, and so are working on the same lines as neofunctionalists and liberal intergovernmentalists. Historical institutionalists put a great deal of emphasis on the values and norms that actors develop within institutionalized relationships over time. These values and norms can be interpreted as ideas that actors hold, perhaps not fully consciously, which affect and at least partially explain their behaviour. While rational choice theorists, neofunctionalists, and liberal intergovernmentalists would all tend to argue that the existence of the EU structures the responses of actors because it provides a new set of rules within which they pursue their interests, historical institutionalists would tend to argue that the existence of the EU affects the way in which the actors perceive their interests, their aims, and objectives. The theme of the role of interests in the EU is therefore also about the role of ideas.

Finally, the problem with the application of concepts that were originally derived from the study of domestic political systems is that they may lose the sensitivity to the influences of the wider international system that is the strength of approaches derived from international relations. The absence of such a dimension was one of the most telling criticisms made by Hoffmann of neofunctionalism. This in itself indicates that the problem does not necessarily lie in the disciplinary origins of the theories. After all, neofunctionalism is generally perceived to have derived from a liberal pluralist tradition in the study of international relations. The other side of this argument is that the study of politics and public policy within states ought not to be innocent of wider international influences either. Globalization is a phenomenon that erodes the distinction between domestic and international studies (see Ch. 3, pp. 38–41).

Despite these qualifications, approaches derived from the study of domestic systems do tend to neglect the wider international context. This is particularly evident in the frameworks devised by Marks *et al.* and by Stone Sweet and Sandholtz which were devised to go beyond the intergovernmental versus supranational dichotomy. The impact of that wider context is the subject of the next chapter.

KEY POINTS

The study of the EU as comparative politics

- Hix (1994 and 1998) advocated a 'new' approach to studying the EU. His concern was not with the IR debate over the process of integration, but with the question of how the EU operated as a political system.

- *New institutionalism* argued that analysts had lost sight of the importance of institutions in structuring political action. New institutionalist approaches can be divided between *rational choice institutionalism* and *historical institutionalism.*

- Rational choice institutionalism emphasized the argument that the behaviour of political actors was shaped by the specific framework of rules within which they operated.

- Historical institutionalism emphasized the argument that political relationships have to be viewed over time and that decisions are shaped by the nature of pre-existing institutional relationships.

The study of the EU as public policy analysis

- Richardson (1996*a*) took up Hix's call to approach the EU from different disciplinary directions by advocating the application of two concepts: policy networks and epistemic communities.

- A *policy network* is a set of resource-dependent organizations. Policy networks range from tightly-knit policy communities to loosely-bound issue networks.

- Kassim (1994) argued that EU processes were not settled enough for policy networks to emerge. Peterson (1995*a*) argued that while some EU policy sectors remained fluid, others indeed had developed into policy networks.

- *Epistemic communities* are knowledge-based groups that are most likely to be influential when policy-makers face uncertainty over policy choices.

Multilevel governance

- Multilevel governance has strong antecedents in neofunctionalism, but is a theory of the nature of the EU rather than a theory of the process of European integration.

- While accepting that integration involved intergovernmental bargains, multilevel governance theorists argued that individual governments were not in control of the process. Actors at supranational and subnational levels played a key role also.

- While initially established by national governments, supranational EU institutions develop a degree of autonomy from the control of governments.

- Transnational and transgovernmental alliances mean that states are open to external influences. The Commission is able to exploit this situation to promote its own agenda.

Supranational governance

- The approach of supranational governance was located in neofunctionalism, but also drew on transactionalism and new institutionalism.

- Stone Sweet and Sandholtz argued that the EU should be studied not as one international regime, but as a series of regimes for different policy sectors.

- In this view, the increase in transactions across national boundaries would lead to a supranational society that would favour the construction of supranational rules to regulate its activities

- Branch and Øhrgaard argued that Stone Sweet and Sandholtz had not escaped the intergovernmental–supranational dichotomy. Rather, they had privileged certain types of actors and also classified actors as either intergovernmental or supranational in a way that oversimplified the complexity of the EU.

- The approach of Stone Sweet and Sandholtz can be further criticized for failing to place the analysis in the wider context of developments in global capitalism.

QUESTIONS

1 Why are approaches from international relations less dominant in the study of the EU than previously?

2 Assess the utility of the various new institutionalist approaches to the study of the EU

3 What are the advantages of applying the policy networks approach to EU decision-making?

4 How far is the EU system characterized by multi-level governance?

5 To what extent have Stone Sweet and Sandholtz moved beyond the supranational–intergovernmental dichotomy?

FURTHER READING

The clearest statement of dissatisfaction with approaches to the EU based on theories of international relations is S. Hix, 'The Study of the European Community: The Challenge to Comparative Politics', *West European Politics* 17 (1994), 1–30. The clearest statements of the new institutionalist approach as applied to the EU are to be found in P. Pierson, 'The Path to European Integration: A Historical and Institutionalist Analysis', *Comparative Political Studies* 29 (1996), 123–63, and S. Bulmer, 'New Institutionalism and the Governance of the Single European Market', *Journal of European Public Policy* 5 (1998), 365–86. Epistemic communities are explained in P. Haas, 'Introduction: Epistemic Communities and International Policy Coordination', *International Organization* 49 (1992), 1–35. The application of policy networks and policy communities is debated in H. Kassim, 'Policy Networks, Networks and European Policy-Making: A Sceptical View', *West European Politics* 17 (1994), 15–27, and J. Peterson, 'Policy Networks and European Policy Making: A Reply to Kassim', *West European Politics* 18 (1995), 389–407. The classic statement of multilevel governance is G, Marks, L. Hooghe, and K. Blank, 'European Integration from the 1980s: State-Centric v Multi-Level Governance', *Journal of Common Market Studies* 34 (1996) 341–78. Supranational governance is outlined in A. Stone Sweet and W. Sandholtz, 'European Integration and Supranational Governance', *Journal of European Public Policy* 4 (1997), 297–317, developed in W. Sandholtz and A. Stone Sweet (eds.), *European Integration and Supranational Governance* (Oxford: Oxford University Press, 1998) and contested in A. P. Branch and J. C. Øhrgaard, 'Trapped in the Supranational–Intergovernmental Dichotomy: A Response to Stone Sweet and Sandholtz', *Journal of European Public Policy* 6 (1999), 123–43.

3 Beyond EU studies

SUMMARY

European integration takes place in a global context. In the immediate post-war years this context was provided by the cold war and US hegemony within the capitalist world. The United States used its hegemonic position to create the conditions for the global development of capitalism. This undermined its own economic dominance within the global system, and fostered the emergence of a new phase of capitalism, marked by globalization. This global system is believed to reduce the opportunities for individual states to follow autonomous economic policies. The pressure is for all states to adopt policies that resemble those previously characterized by European academics as 'the Anglo-Saxon model'. While the EU might be viewed as an attempt by European states to counter the influence of globalization through collective action, the policies that have been agreed at EU level resemble the Anglo-Saxon model more than they do the policies that had previously characterized the member states.

Introduction

European integration does not take place in isolation from the wider world of which Europe is only one part. One of the criticisms that Stanley Hoffmann made of neofunctionalist theory was that it paid insufficient attention to the global context. Hoffmann was specifically referring to the Atlantic relationship, and to security issues. The same argument can be applied to the global economic context within which the EC/EU operates. However, it is not just neofunctionalism that can be criticized in this way. While intergovernmentalists regularly acknowledged the importance of external factors in relation to European integration, the relationship between the two remained underdeveloped within this paradigm also. Approaches from comparative politics focused on the nature of EU governance, but to the extent that these approaches considered the effects of global factors on internal EU developments at all, such factors were taken as given and not explored.

In short, theorizing the EU to date has been characterized by a paucity of attempts to link the process of European integration and the nature of EU governance with developments in the wider world. This chapter explores the relationship between the EU and the broader international context. To explore this relationship further we need to look beyond the mainstream approaches and theories applied to understanding the EU.

The chapter focuses on two theoretical concepts which help us to understand the relationship between the EU and the wider global system. The first of these is the concept of hegemony; the second the concept of globalization. Illustrations are given of the way in which these concepts can be applied to the history of the post-war capitalist world. This goes beyond theory to its application, but it is necessary to do so because these concepts only make sense in a concrete historical context. So, hegemony is first outlined and discussed in the post-war context; then globalization is similarly outlined and discussed.

Hegemony

Thousands of pages have been written contesting the definition of capitalism, much of it with a political inspiration. Does capitalism necessarily involve private ownership of the means of production, as Marx argued? Left-wing Socialists who wanted to define the former USSR as a system of 'state capitalism' were forced to argue that it did not. They preferred to define it as simply 'production for sale in the market', as opposed to what they considered to be production for 'socially useful' purposes. It is not necessary to get into these disputes. The capitalist system in the post-war world was predominantly marked by private ownership of the means of production; but there were state-owned enterprises producing for sale in the market which could hardly be considered as other than part of the system.

If capitalism is a system predominantly marked by private ownership, unless ownership degenerates into monopoly, it is a decentralized system. The many producers of goods and services are in competition with each other; but they also have a common interest in the maintenance of the whole system. Capitalism can only operate in a context of political stability, with a legal structure to enforce contracts, clear and enforced rules on the ownership of property, a stable means of exchange (money), and protection of the market mechanism itself against distortions by the actions of powerful individuals, corporations, and governments. The system also has to be secured against external threat.

So long as capitalism operates mainly at the national level, the state performs these functions for the national system as a whole. Political stability is maintained through the maintenance of social stability, backed by the threat or use of force should it break down. In other words, the state has a responsibility to try to make sure that the grievances of citizens do not lead to the breakdown of order, and the responsibility to restore order through policing actions if it does break down. One important part of the law-and-order function of the state is the protection of property. Another aspect of the state's role in maintaining property rights is the maintenance of a system of civil law to settle ownership disputes. Civil law is also important to ensure that contractual disputes can be arbitrated; and the criminal law can be invoked in cases of dishonest disregard for contractual obligations. National currencies provide the stable means of exchange under nationally-based capitalism. The protection of the market against distortion by powerful individuals and corporations is the responsibility of government agencies such as that known in Britain as the Office of Fair Trading; and monopoly and merger commissions try to prevent any one company becoming so powerful that it can distort the market in its favour. Protection against distortion of the market by the state itself is perhaps the most difficult aspect, although national constitutions are constructed in part to provide some safeguards. Finally the state provides the armed forces to protect the system from external threat.

Once capitalism breaks the bounds of the nation-state and starts to operate internationally, there are difficulties about who will perform these functions for the system as a whole, because the system reaches beyond the geographical limits of any single state. There are two possible solutions to the problem: either states can co-operate to provide the conditions in which capitalism can operate internationally; or one state can perform the functions for the system as a whole. The difficulty with either solution is that the governments of states tend to be far from impartial when it comes to capitalist enterprises. Governments will tend to support the efforts of their own national capitalist enterprises over those of other states. This is simple self-interest. National firms create jobs and prosperity in their country, and the politicians benefit from the public popularity that accompanies jobs and prosperity. Such national competition puts barriers in the way of co-operation to manage the international system. It also causes problems for the other solution: that one state performs these functions for the whole system.

When this second solution operates, the dominant state is known as the 'hegemon', or 'hegemonic state'. This comes from the Greek word for a leader, and at its weakest the term simply refers to the leading state within the international system or regional sub-system. In modern usage, though, the term has taken on stronger connotations of a state that exercises dominance over other states. In the realist tradition this refers primarily to military dominance, but the concept has been developed in the work of Robert Keohane (1984) and in the critical theory of Robert Cox (1996), in a direction that embraces the ideas of political economy.

US hegemony

At the end of the Second World War, the United States was unquestionably the strongest economic and military power in the world. The other industrial states, including the USSR, had been severely weakened by the war. The United States did not enter the war until 1941; its economy had already benefited from non-participation, and it was geographically insulated from the physical destruction that affected other combatants. As a result, the US administration was able to construct a post-war economic system that embodied its belief in multilateral free trade and the free movement of capital. The structure was to be given stability by a system of fixed exchange rates between currencies. It was defended from the external threat posed by the USSR through NATO, the military alliance that the USA dominated.

The institutional underpinnings of the economic system were agreed at a conference at Bretton Woods in New Hampshire in 1944. They were the International Monetary Fund (IMF) (Box 3.1, p. 35) and the International Bank for Reconstruction and Development ('the World Bank') (Box 3.2, p. 35). The General Agreement on Tariffs and Trade (GATT) (Box 3.3, p. 36) was added later. But the system only worked because the United States was prepared to play a leading and directive role.

Box 3.1 **The International Monetary Fund (IMF)**

The IMF was set up in 1944:

- to promote international monetary co-operation;
- to facilitate the expansion and balanced growth of international trade;
- to promote stability in exchange rates;
- to assist in the establishment of a multilateral system of payments in respect of trade between member states;
- to contribute to the elimination of foreign exchange restrictions;
- to provide short-term and medium-term loans to states experiencing temporary balance of payments difficulties.

(*Source:* IMF Web Site *http://www.imf.org/external/about.htm*)

The US dollar was placed at the centre of the new monetary order. It was to be fully convertible into gold at a rate of $35 per ounce, so that it could be considered as good as gold. This was feasible because most of the world's stocks of gold were in the United States at the end of the war, a reflection of the strength of its economy. The values of other currencies were then fixed in terms of dollars. The dollar itself became an international reserve currency, which central banks were prepared to accept as payment in external dealings rather than insisting on payment in their own national currencies. In this way it was hoped that the dollar would be able to finance an increase in world trade that might otherwise be constrained by a lack of international liquidity. But this could not work unless other members of the system were able to accumulate dollars. To allow that to happen, the United States was prepared to accept discrimination against its exports in the form of limitations on the convertibility of national currencies into dollars, while at the same time sending large quantities of dollars to western Europe in the form of Marshall Aid and private transfers of capital. Of course, the private transfers of capital benefited US business interests by allowing them to buy major shares in West European industry, and to set up subsidiaries of their own companies in western Europe. But the ending of the dollar shortage was beneficial to the whole of the capitalist world.

Box 3.2 **The World Bank**

The International Bank for Reconstruction and Development (IBRD) was founded in 1944 to give loans to states to aid their economic recovery. It is now one of five organizations closely associated institutions that together constitute the World Bank Group:

- the IBRD, which provides loans and development assistance to middle-income countries and creditworthy poorer countries;
- the International Development Association (IDA), which is focused on the poorest countries, providing them with interest-free loans and other services;
- the International Finance Corporation (IFC), which promotes growth in the developing world by financing

private sector investments and providing technical assistance and advice to governments and businesses;

- the Multilateral Investment Guarantee Agency (MIGA), which helps encourage foreign investment in developing countries by providing guarantees to foreign investors against loss caused by non-commercial risks;
- the International Centre for Settlement of Investment Disputes (ICSID), which provides conciliation and arbitration facilities for the settlement of investment disputes between foreign investors and their host countries.

(*Source:* World Bank Group Web Site *http://www.worldbank.org/html/extdr/about/wbgis.htm*)

Box 3.3 The General Agreement on Tariffs and Trade (GATT)

The GATT was negotiated in 1947 and started operation on 1 January 1948. It consisted of a standing conference for the negotiation of tariff cuts, and an agreement that all such cuts would be multilateral, not bilateral. This was embodied in the principle of 'most favoured nation treatment' for all signatories of the agreement: any trade concession extended by one member to another had to be extended to all other members.

It was originally intended that the GATT would be one part of an overarching International Trade Organization (ITO), but this proposal ran into resistance in the US Congress, and never received ratification.

The GATT held eight rounds of multilateral trade negotiations, culminating in the Uruguay Round which opened in Punte del Este, Uruguay in 1986 and was not completed until 1994. It was this Round that focused attention on the trade-distorting effects of the EU's common agricultural policy. One of the agreements in the Uruguay Round was the creation of a new World Trade Organization (WTO), which began operation on 1 January 1995. Its functions are:

- to administer WTO trade agreements;

- to act as a forum for trade negotiations;

- to handle trade disputes;

- to monitor national trade policies;

- to provide technical assistance and training for developing countries;

- to co-operate with other international organizations.

(*Source:* WTO Web Site *http://www.wto.org/*)

From 1947 to 1958 the United States voluntarily and deliberately ran a deficit on its balance of payments. It covered this deficit by printing more dollars, which were accepted by other states as payment for their exports because the dollar was still backed by massive gold reserves. The dollars that the United States printed were also used for direct investments in western Europe and elsewhere. At the same time the United States took the lead in pushing through a series of tariff cuts under GATT auspices, which took tariffs between the signatories down to very low levels. The result was an unprecedented expansion in world trade, which grew between 1955 and 1969 by 8.4 per cent per annum. At the time, the United States was unable to take full advantage of the tariff cuts, but it hoped to be able to do so in the future.

By 1958 this programme had been so successful that all the western European states had been able to return their currencies to full convertibility with the dollar. However, the United States was unable to restore its balance of payments to surplus (Box 3.4, p. 36). Initially it had difficulty in taking advantage of the new trading possibilities open to it; that was corrected to some extent when the Kennedy Administration came to office and adopted a programme of economic and trade stimulation that soon produced massive surpluses on the current account of the balance of payments. These were

---

Box 3.4 Balance of payments

The balance of payments of a country is the record of its foreign trade in goods and services plus its foreign capital transactions over any specific period of time. It is normally divided into the current account, the trade in goods and services, and the capital account, foreign capital transactions. If the total amount of exports of goods and services, plus the total amount of capital investment in the country by nationals of other states exceed the total amount of imports of goods and services plus the total amount of overseas capital investment by nationals of the state, the balance of payments will be in surplus. It imports and outward investment exceed exports plus inward investment, the balance of payments will be in deficit.

---

more than offset, though, by the deficit on the capital account because of the continuing outflow of dollars for overseas investment and for defence purposes.

Defence against the threat to the system posed by the USSR was one of the essential functions of the hegemonic power. The United States had to turn part of its economic wealth into military capability to perform this function. At the same time, the threat to the capitalist world helped to ensure that the leadership of the United States was largely unquestioned.

During the period of greatest tension, from the end of the World War to the death of Stalin in 1953, the West displayed great unity behind US leadership. There was a strong perception of a common threat from Communism, both ideologically and militarily; and this perception made a considerable contribution to bringing about Franco-German reconciliation (see Chs. 4 and 5, pp. 49–66).

The prosperity that western Europe enjoyed during the 1950s and 1960s was essential to the early success of the EC. It resulted from the success of an international economic system that was dominated and directed by the United States, and was centred on the industrialized capitalist states of the northern hemisphere. The end of the era of prosperity and rapid economic growth was associated with the demise of that system.

By the end of the 1960s, the economic dominance of the United States was already seriously eroded by the success of the western European and Japanese economies. During the 1970s, the collective centrality within the system of these states was diminished by challenges from the Third World and by the partial integration of the Soviet bloc states into the system. These changes put a strain on the rules and institutions that had ordered the system, and though there was no collapse into anarchy, the international economic context within which the EC functioned in the 1970s was marked by a much higher degree of turbulence than had been the case in the previous two decades. Perhaps the most obvious example of this turbulence was the 1973 decision of the Organization of Petroleum Exporting Countries (OPEC) (Box 3.5, p. 37) to force a quadrupling in the price of oil. This finally pushed a capitalist economic system that was already teetering on the brink, over the edge into recession.

During the 1970s the United States found it increasingly difficult to maintain stability within the capitalist world, and looked to the EC to play a part. This led some commentators to argue that the era of US hegemony had ended. However, that judgement, considered by some at the time to be premature, looked unsound following the second oil crisis, which was sparked off by the overthrow of the Shah of Iran in January 1979. While western Europe struggled to overcome the recession that the rise in the price of oil provoked, both Japan and the United

---

Box 3.5 Organization of Petroleum Exporting Countries (OPEC)

OPEC was created at a conference of petroleum exporting states in Baghdad in 1960. The founder members were Iran, Iraq, Kuwait, Saudi Arabia, and Venezuela. They were later joined by eight other Members: Qatar (1961); Indonesia (1962); Libya (1962); the United Arab Emirates (1967); Algeria (1969); Nigeria (1971); Ecuador (1973–92) and Gabon (1975–94). OPEC's objective is to co-ordinate and unify petroleum policies among Member Countries, in order to secure fair and stable prices for petroleum producers; an efficient, economic and regular supply of petroleum to consuming nations; and a fair return on capital to those investing in the industry.

(*Source*: OPEC Web Site *http://www.opec.org/ 193.81.181.14/xxx1/history.htm*)

States made rapid recoveries based on the adoption of new technologies.

The 1980s were a decade of intense economic and technological competition between the United States, Japan, and western Europe. A whole new generation of advanced technologies revolutionized the capital goods industries, and threatened to relocate the centre of the capitalist world in whichever of these states could establish itself as the technological leader. Partly as a result of the impossibility of competing in this new technological race, the USSR finally gave up its attempt to create a separate economic system centred on itself, and moved under Mikhail Gorbachev belatedly to join the capitalist world system.

The end of the cold war had profound implications for the nature of the international system. First, it left the United States as the only military superpower. Second, though, it changed the nature of the security threat. Instead of needing defence from an external threat, the system now required internal policing efforts. It was by no means clear that the United States was equipped to play this role. Its military superiority was based on weapons that would not necessarily be suitable for the type of action that would be needed under the new conditions. Also, once the cold war had finished, the legitimacy of the

United States as a policing agent was open to question as never before. During the confrontation with the USSR, the United States had frequently justified its military interventions in other countries as necessary to protect the system against Communism, which was assimilated to Soviet aggression. With no big external enemy, the threat from Communism was less of a justification for intervention. This applied also to the justification given by US governments to the US public to justify these military adventures. Domestic resistance to US involvement in military action overseas, which had already been provoked by the Vietnam war, increased after the end of the cold war.

Economically the picture was also less clear-cut by the end of the century. The success of the United States in creating the conditions for the global development of capitalism had fostered the emergence of what some argued was a new phase of the system, characterized by the term 'globalization'.

Globalization

Globalization is variously defined. On some definitions, it is no more than a contemporary term to describe a set of processes that have a long history; but more commonly globalization is taken to refer to a new phenomenon of linkages transcending existing territorial boundaries. Although it has cultural and social aspects, it is generally perceived to be driven by economic imperatives.

Most definitions of globalization imply that we are seeing the emergence of an economic system that goes beyond being merely international. An international economic system is marked by trade between companies that are situated in different states. A global system implies the emergence of multinational companies which operate in a number of states, and which own especial loyalty to no one state. Most definitions also mention the emergence of global flows of capital, which have increased dramatically in the last part of the twentieth century. These flows are both of investment capital and liquid capital (Box 3.6, p. 38). The implication of increased flows of investment capital are that states are in competition with each other to provide the most attractive conditions for investment. If they try to impose higher taxes or more restrictive rules than their competitor states, they will lose investment to those other states. The implication of the high levels of liquid capital flows is that states are unable to manage the value of their currency, and, at least in the short-term, the value of a currency may bear little relationship to the underlying strength of the real economy.

> ## Box 3.6 Investment capital and liquid capital
>
> - *Investment capital* refers to assets that are invested in a country in the form of factories, businesses, etc.
>
> - *Liquid capital* refers to assets that are placed into bank deposits or similar sources from which they may quickly be withdrawn and transferred elsewhere.

The question of the degree of control that states have over this process is the subject of academic dispute. The term 'globalization' is often used as though it was a process beyond the control of governments, which constrains them in the policies that they can follow. However, there are those who argue that globalization is a myth (Hirst and Thompson, 1996). On this view, globalization is only a continuation of the internationalization of capitalist activity that has been happening for a long time, and in fact the present 'global' economy is less open than was the international economy between 1870 and 1914. Most so-called multinational corporations are actually large national companies that trade internationally. The myth of globalization is used as an argument to prevent national governments from trying to control the forces of capitalism; but if governments co-ordinated their efforts they could regulate global markets. A third view (Amoore *et al.*,

1997; Payne, 2000) is that globalization has two aspects. On the one hand, there is a sense in which developments that are largely independent of governments, such as technological advances, have changed the scale of operation of capitalist enterprises and made it more difficult for governments to regulate their activities. On the other hand, the responses of states to these developments have themselves fed the process. Technology makes it possible to move funds across international exchanges at speeds never envisaged in earlier periods, and this poses problems for governments in regulating the process. They could respond by investigating new, perhaps collaborative ways of regulating the exchanges; but they have mostly responded by capitulating to 'the inevitable' and lifting capital controls. This response makes a reality of the globalization of capital markets; but it could have been otherwise.

It is important in this context to see that globalization is a process, not a fixed condition. It is not the case that globalization started on a particular date; it is a name given to changes in the capitalist system that have developed in the post-war period. At each stage in this development the responses of the governments of states have been important in determining whether the process is given another twist. It may appear to states that they are responding to forces beyond their control, and for any one individual state this may be true; but the collective result of the responses of individual states has been to keep the process going. It also follows that it is false to discuss globalization in terms simply of state responses to an exogenous variable. Not only is the process itself fed by the actions of states; it also affects the outlooks of governments, and even the institutional arrangements for governing states. This is particularly true of the EU.

The EU and globalization

At first sight, the emergence of the EU as a regional grouping seems to be in contradiction with the direction and thrust of globalization. It is true that to some extent the project of European integration, which started as a response to the problems of post-war reconstruction, became a process of responding to the evolution of the international system. However, the European project has always been one of open regionalism.

Open regionalism means that policy is directed towards the elimination of obstacles to trade within a region, while at the same time doing nothing to raise external tariff barriers to the rest of the world   (Gamble and Payne, 1996: 251).

There has been no voice in the debate about the nature of the EU that has advocated closing western Europe off from the global system. The central debate has been between the British position and the French position. Until very recently the German government was prepared to subordinate its view to that of the French in the interests of maintaining the Franco-German alliance. The British position has

favoured global free trade and free movement of capital. It has seen the freeing of trade within the EU as a stepping stone to this end. The French position has seen the EU as a means of organizing European capitalism to compete more effectively on world markets. It has been a 'strategic trade' view rather than a 'free trade' view. But it has never advocated the EU being a closed trading bloc. Instead it has argued the case for the liberalization of national markets to be accompanied by the introduction of European-level industrial and technology policies to build up and promote European champions, companies that could compete effectively with US and Japanese companies on world markets.

These debates reflect differences in national approaches to the management of capitalism. French governments have generally been less willing than British to accept that the free market should determine the shape of the national economy, and have favoured a larger role for the state (George, 1989). However, the belief that there has been a quantitative and qualitative change in the extent and nature of global economic transactions has affected the policies of individual states, and the nature of the process of European integration. Rhodes and van Apeldoorn (1997: 171) argued that, while there was still considerable diversity among the national 'capitalisms' in western Europe in the late 1990s, both globalization and European integration were 'eroding national particularities'. Distinctive national systems were being replaced by systems that embodied the ideas of liberalization, balanced budgets, and primary emphasis on anti-inflationary monetary policies.

The acceptance of these policies implied the dismantling of the different national systems that were set up after the war. These varied in the emphasis that they put on different elements in the mix, hence the diversity noted above; but they typically involved some or all of the following: extensive welfare provision, paid for out of taxation; a steering role for the state in the economy; significant state ownership in some sectors of industry; a role for the representatives of organized labour in economic policy-making; an implicit guarantee that wages would increase to allow workers to share in the benefits of economic growth; some degree of job security for the workforce. These variations on a European model of capitalism can be contrasted with the 'American' model that prevailed in the United States, which gave a much smaller role to state regulation of the economy, and a much bigger role to market forces than did the European models.

Globalization has placed the distinctive features of the European models under strain. High taxes to support a high level of welfare provision provide a disincentive to investment, which under conditions of globalization is more likely to be redirected to states with lower tax burdens. State interference in the working of the market economy is another incentive for potential investment to go elsewhere, to find bases for production that are regulated with a lighter touch, leaving management more flexibility to respond to changing market conditions. State ownership of industry acts as a barrier to penetration of national markets from outside, and so has come under sustained attack from multinational producers; while selling off state shares in industry ('privatization') has proved to be a useful source of revenue

for governments trying to keep their budget deficits within acceptable margins. The reaction of organized labour to privatization and to attempts to reduce welfare commitments has been obstructive, encouraging governments to minimize the involvement of the representatives of organized labour in policy-making. Maintaining wage increases, especially in the public sector, is dependent on maintaining rates of economic growth, and at certain periods has proved difficult without increasing budget deficits. Job security translates into inflexibility in labour markets, and has been identified as the biggest problem preventing Europe from benefiting from the advent of new, potentially labour-saving technologies to the same extent as the United States.

Within the EU, leading states have embraced policies of liberalization with varying degrees of enthusiasm. Since 1979, when Margaret Thatcher was first elected, Britain has moved to a position close to that of the United States. It has promoted liberal policies of removing capital controls, privatizing publicly-owned enterprises, and deregulating labour markets. Essentially the same policies have been continued under the New Labour government of Tony Blair, which has also tried to convert the rest of the EU to support them. Rhodes and van Apeldoorn (1997: 171) argued that, beyond the changes occurring in national 'capitalisms', there was also a question of what kind of socio-economic order, or 'model of capitalism' was emerging within the supranational regime of the EU. Debate over the future economic, social, and political structure of the EU in the light of the impact of globalization became central to the history of European integration during the period when Jacques Delors was President of the Commission (see Chs. 11 and 12, pp. 114–28), and has remained so since.

Some of the voices that resisted market-oriented policies in this debate may have been genuinely rejecting the alleged logic of globalization for economic and social policies. However, the extent to which the market-oriented policies have prevailed suggests another explanation. Governments faced with the prospect of having to dismantle their postwar national systems because of the impact of globalization, might protest in public so that they can avoid having to accept responsibility for unpopular measures at home. As Mitchell Smith (1997) explained, the claim that 'the Commission made me do it' can provide governments with a strategic advantage in domestic politics, allowing them to achieve their real objectives while allowing the Commission to take the blame. At the same time this can have a negative effect on the image of the Commission, and of the EU as a whole, in the state concerned. It can contribute to the EU being seen as a negative, even malign influence, and so undermine its popularity and legitimacy.

Conclusion

One of the themes that underlies the analysis of the EU in this book is that the regional process of European integration cannot be fully understood except by taking into account the effect on western Europe of the wider global international system within which it is embedded. Two aspects have been particularly emphasized in this chapter: the post-war hegemony of the United States, and the process of globalization.

There is little dissent from the view that the United States was the hegemonic power in the immediate post-war era, but there is considerable disagreement about when or even whether US hegemony came to an end. It is clear that the United States has remained a significant player on the international scene, and that the attitude of successive US administrations to the development of the EU has been important. The role of the United States will be a consistent theme of the analysis in this book. The impact of globalization on the member states of the EU is another theme of the book, which is particularly examined in Part Three. The related question of what kind of system the EU itself will turn out to be will recur throughout the discussion of the policies of the EU in Part Five.

There is one other aspect of this discussion based on the impact of globalization that is significant. The move away from national capitalisms to a more uniform system based on market disciplines has contributed to the undermining of the legitimacy of governments in Europe. In some cases governments have tried to displace the blame onto the EU, and this has contributed to an undermining of the legitimacy of the EU itself. Legitimacy is a theme that was identified in the conclusion to Chapter 1, and recurs at various points in the analysis that follows.

KEY POINTS

Hegemony

- To operate successfully, capitalism requires that certain key functions be performed by a public agent.

- These functions are performed by the state so long as capitalism remains a national phenomenon.

- Once capitalist enterprises start to operate across state boundaries, there is a need for the same functions to be performed internationally.

- In the post-war world the United States, as the strongest state, performed these functions for the system as a whole. It laid the role of the 'leader' or 'hegemon'.

- The system came under strain as the economic dominance of the United States was eroded in the 1960s.

- To some extent the United States re-established its economic dominance (except over Japan) in the 1980s by rapid adoption of new technologies to production.

- The end of the cold war left the United States as the only military superpower in the world, but also made it more difficult for it to justify its domination of other states.

Globalization

- Globalization refers to the emergence of an economic system in which capitalist enterprises operate on a genuinely global scale, and no longer own especial loyalty to one state.

- It is a system in which capital flows freely from state to state, so governments have to compete with each other to provide the most attractive conditions for investment.

- The EU as a regional grouping can be seen as a response by the governments of the member states to the problems posed for them by globalization.

- The EU has always been an example of 'open regionalism'.

- Responses to globalization have led to the dismantling of post-war national systems for managing capitalism and their replacement by more liberal, market-oriented policies. Different member states of the EU have embraced these developments with different degrees of enthusiasm.

- A debate has ensued over the 'model of capitalism' that should apply to the EU as a whole.

- Some governments have put the responsibility for unpopular measures that have been necessitated by the effects of globalization onto the EU, and so undermined its legitimacy.

QUESTIONS

1 To what extent has the US hegemony influenced the process of European integration?

2 In what ways is an understanding of globalization important for understanding the process of European integration?

3 How does the models of capitalism debate add to our understanding of EU politics and policy?

FURTHER READING

An excellent starting point for further reading on the issues discussed in this chapter is a special issue of the journal *Current Politics and Economics of Europe* on 'Theorising the EU at the Turn of the Century', vol. 9, no. 2. Other clear and informative discussions are provided by Rosamond (1999, 2000).

The linkage between regionalism as a general (rather than just a European) phenomenon and world order is explored through the essays in: A. Gamble and A. Payne (eds.), *Regionalism and World Order* (Basingstoke and London: Macmillan, 1996).

The definition of a new agenda for the study of IPE in: A. Payne, 'Globalization and Modes of Regionalist Governance', in J. Pierre (ed.), *Debating Governance* (Oxford: Oxford University Press, 2000) is an important contribution to the emerging debate which has influenced the analysis in this book.

Part Two

History

Deciding where to begin a history is often difficult, but not really in this case. While there were attempts to integrate Europe before the twentieth century, the end of the Second World War in 1945 provided the catalyst for the phase of European integration with which we are familiar today. There is little dispute among historians that 1945 is the most appropriate starting point for discussing the events leading to the creation of what is today the European Union. Thus, while we reflect briefly on previous attempts to integrate Europe, our point of departure here is the end of the Second World War.

The history we present is largely a familiar account of developments in European integration in the second half of the twentieth century. It is a story often dominated by personalities, which is decontextualized by its authors to exclude the significance of broader social, economic, and political forces in shaping events. Our purpose in presenting this account is partly because it is the function of a textbook to cover the most recognized contributions in the field of study. However, it is also because we feel there is some intrinsic value in the selections we have made. Our own distinctive contribution is developed primarily in the conclusions to the chapters, where we seek to add to the familiar story a broader understanding of events, drawing on the themes of the book that are explored in the conclusions to the chapters in Part One: the tension between supranational and intergovernmental explanations; the role of interest groups; the issue of legitimacy; the models of capitalism; and the broader international political and economic context. In other words, we argue that *individuals matter*, but that their actions can only be understood in relation to the structures which both influence and give meaning to their actions.

Finally, as with all histories, we have had to make choices about how our history is organized. Here, we follow a conventional path. In our opening chapters we focus on the history of 'important' decisions, in particular those leading to the Treaties establishing the European Communities. Later in the section we identify phases in the process of European integration that are distinguished by the pace of events: for example, the 'dark ages' of European integration. Towards the end we return again to a focus on events leading to key decisions.

As time passes, it is likely that events and developments in post-war integration that seem important to observers now may seem less important to future generations. Conversely, matters less obvious at the beginning of the twenty-first century will grow in importance. Similarly, the distinct eras in the process of integration that we identify will demand redefinition at some future date. In this sense, all histories are inevitably transient and imperfect. Thus, the basis on which we organize our history is nothing more than an informed choice in the light of current understanding.

4 Europe after the war

If Europe were once united in the sharing of its common inheritance, there would be no limit to the happiness, to the prosperity and the glory which its three or four hundred million people would enjoy.

(Winston Churchill, Zurich 1946)

SUMMARY

Attempts at European integration have a long history; but most have taken the form of conquest. While the outbreak of the Second World War illustrated the force of nationalism in Europe, its aftermath provided conditions for moves towards a consensual approach to European unity. In particular, the ideology of a European federation had attracted support within resistance movements during the war. The Hague Congress in May 1948 was a direct attempt by the federalists to introduce a new system of governance for post-war Europe that would have bound states together in a federation. The Council of Europe, which was set up as a result of the Congress, fell well short of that ambition.

The development that actually led to the first concrete steps of European economic integration was the breakdown of co-operation between the USSR and the western Allies, and the emergence of the cold war. Economic conditions in western Europe in 1945–6 provided fertile conditions for Communist ideas, and in response to this threat the United

States offered Marshall Aid to facilitate the reconstruction of the west European economies. That aid came with the condition attached that the plans for spending the money should be developed by the European states jointly, not separately. However, attempts by the United States to insist that the funds should be administered in a genuinely supranational manner were blocked.

Introduction

Our starting point for this discussion of European integration is the end of the Second World War: but the idea of European integration is not unique to this era. Politicians and intellectuals alike aspired to European unity over two centuries. Plans for achieving perpetual peace in Europe by overcoming the division into nation states can be traced back at least to the early eighteenth century, and the *Project for Perpetual Peace* of the Abbé de Saint Pierre (Forsyth *et al.*, 1970: 128). At a practical level, though, moves for European unity took the form of attempts by one nation or another to dominate Europe through conquest. Both France under Napoleon and Germany under Hitler could be accused of trying to forge European unity in this way.

Whereas attempts at enforced European *political* integration foundered, the potential benefits of *economic* integration proved attractive to European political elites. Yet nineteenth-century free-trade experiments across nation-states were short-lived, while early customs unions were specific to regions within nation states (Box 4.1, p. 46). Ultimately these experiments in economic integration suffered the same fate as attempts at political unity.

Movements in favour of peaceful integration emerged in Europe after the First World War, but the political settlement after the war was based on the peaceful co-existence of nation-states rather than integration. The failure of the League of Nations (Box 4.2, p. 47) to sustain peace was rapid and complete, with the resurgence of nationalism in the 1920s and 1930s. The pro-integration groups emerging in Europe after 1918 were unable to offer any practical solutions to this. The outbreak of the Second World War destroyed hopes of European unity.

Box 4.1 Free trade areas, customs unions, common markets, and economic areas

Free trade area: Member states remove all tariff and quota barriers to trade between themselves, but retain independent trade policies with the outside world.

Customs union: A free trade area, but with a single set of rules on trade with the outside world.

Common market: A customs union, but with the addition of free movement of factors of production, including capital and labour.

Economic union: A common market with the addition of unified economic and monetary policies.

Source: Swann (1995: 12–13)

The aftermath of the war, though, provided the origins for the modern movement for European integration.

Emerging from the war physically devastated, Europe began a process of both economic and political reconstruction. The idea of European unity was present in this process from the outset, as the ideology of federalism had attracted a great deal of support during the war. However, the story cannot be told simply in terms of ideals. Although influential figures showed some degree of attachment to the concept of federalism, the steps that were taken were informed by hard-headed realism about what was necessary for reconstruction to succeed. They were also taken in the context of an emerging cold war that divided the continent on ideological lines.

Box 4.2 The League of Nations

- The League of Nations was inspired by the vision of US President Woodrow Wilson. Its Covenant was drawn up at the Paris Peace Conference in 1919, but the US Congress refused to ratify the Treaty so the United States never became a member of the League.

- The League Covenant committed the states that signed to respect the sovereignty and territorial integrity of other states, and not to resort to force to resolve disputes, but to submit them to arbitration by the League.

- The League's institutional structure consisted of a General Assembly, in which all member states were represented, and a Council. The Council had four, then later six permanent members—Britain, France, Italy, Japan; then Germany from 1926, and the USSR from 1934.

- Between 1931 and 1939 the League failed to deal effectively with aggression by Japan, Italy, Germany, and the USSR. In 1935 Japan and Germany withdrew from membership.

- Although it failed to prevent war, the League did successfully establish a number of special agencies working at a functional level to deal with matters such as health and the protection of labour. The success of these bodies may have influenced the thinking of David Mitrany (see Ch. 1, pp. 6–7).

The end of the war, federalism, and the Hague Congress

The war in Europe had extensively destroyed physical infrastructure, disrupted economic production, and caused severe social dislocation. Roads, railways, and bridges had been destroyed by allied bombing or by the retreating German army in its attempt to slow the advance of the allied forces. According to Laqueur (1972: 17–18) coal production at the end of the war was only 42 per cent of its pre-war level; pig iron output in 1946 was less than one-third of that in 1938; and crude steel output was about one-third of what it had been before the war. There were millions of refugees wandering around Europe trying to return to their homes, or without any homes to return to.

Accompanying the economic and social dislocation, there was political dislocation as governments that had collaborated with the Nazis were displaced. Germany and Austria remained occupied and divided between the occupation zones of the allies. Elsewhere, there was a mood in favour of change; a feeling that there should be no return to the pre-war elites and the pre-war ways.

This mood particularly benefited parties of the left. In Britain a Labour government was elected in 1945 with a massive majority, despite the Conservatives being led by the wartime hero Winston Churchill. In France, the provisional government that was set up in 1945 was presided over by General de Gaulle, the conservative leader of the Free French forces which had fought on outside of the occupied country; but the first elections favoured the parties of the internal Resistance, particularly the Communists but also the Socialists and the centre-left Christian party, the *Mouvement Républicain Populaire* (MRP). In Italy, although the Catholic south ensured the emergence of a large conservative Christian Democratic Party, the Communists dominated in the industrial north.

The mood for change also fed a strong popular sentiment in the countries that had suffered from Fascism, in favour of a decisive move away from nationalism in the post-war reconstruction. Ideas favouring European federalism gained support, particularly in Italy, but also in France, Germany, and elsewhere in continental Europe, although not in Britain or the Scandinavian countries.

The European Union of Federalists (EUF) was formed in 1946 from the wartime Resistance movements. It attempted to exploit the disruption caused to existing political structures by the war to make a new start on a basis radically different from the Europe of nation-states, and to create a federal constitution for Europe, as part of a more distant plan for global unity. However, it took until 1947 to organize the conference that was supposed to pave the way to the new constitution, by which time national governments had already been restored to office everywhere. The conference, the European Congress, eventually took place in The Hague in May 1948.

The Congress attracted considerable attention at the time. It was attended by representatives of most of the political parties of the non-communist states of Europe, and its Honorary President was Winston Churchill, who had used a speech in Zurich in 1946 to call for a united Europe. Churchill had implied in the Zurich speech that Britain, with its Commonwealth of Nations, would remain separate from the 'United States of Europe' to which he referred. Britain, along with the United States and possibly the USSR, would be 'friends and sponsors of the new Europe'. The vital development in this project would be a 'partnership' between France and Germany. Beyond this, and the 'first step' of forming a Council of Europe (Box 4.3, p. 48), Churchill did not detail how the process toward European unity should proceed.

The Hague Congress was an occasion for fine speeches, but it gradually became apparent that the British were not interested in being part of a supranational organization that would compromise their national sovereignty. While the Congress did lead to the creation of the Council of Europe, this was so dominated by national governments that there was little realistic prospect of it developing in the federal direction that the EUF hoped.

The Council of Europe still exists today, and it has many solid achievements to its credit. In particular, it was responsible for adopting the European Convention on Human Rights in 1950, and it maintains both a Commission on Human Rights and a Court of Human Rights; the former to investigate alleged breaches of such rights by governments, and the latter to rule definitively on whether a violation of rights has occurred. It also serves useful functions as

---

Box 4.3 **The Council of Europe**

Founded in 1949 as a result of the 1948 Congress of Europe in The Hague, the Council of Europe is not connected to the EU and should not be confused with the European Council, which is the name of the institutionalized summit meetings of the EU Heads of State and Government.

The Council of Europe is an intergovernmental organization based in the French city of Strasbourg. It originally had ten members, and now has forty one.

Its main institutions are:

- the Committee of (Foreign) Ministers

- the Parliamentary Assembly, consisting of 245 members of national parliaments, with 245 substitutes

- the Congress of Local and Regional Authorities of Europe

- the Secretariat;

- the European Commission of Human Rights

- the European Court of Human Rights.

Its main role is to strengthen democracy, human rights and the rule of law throughout its member states. It is active in enhancing Europe's cultural heritage, and it acts as forum for examining a whole range of social problems, such as social exclusion, intolerance, the integration of migrants, the threat to private life posed by new technology, bio-ethical issues, terrorism, drug trafficking, and other criminal activities.

Since 1989, the Council of Europe has become the main political focus for co-operation with the countries of central and eastern Europe, as and when these have opted for a democratic form of government. The Council of Europe has laid down a series of common principles governing the protection of national minorities, actively supported the democratic transition process, and strengthened its machinery for monitoring its members' respect for their undertakings.

(*Source:* Council of Europe World Wide Web site: http://www.coe.fr/eng/present/about.htm)

a meeting place for parliamentarians from the diverse member states, and a forum for the co-ordination of measures such as environmental protection. This all falls far short of the hopes of the EUF.

European integration was not to be achieved in one great act of political will, because the will was not there. Some blamed the failure of the Council of Europe to develop in a federal direction on the atti-tude of the British; but the truth is that no national government, once installed, was willing to surrender much of its power. In 1947 the attention of governments was still focused on national economic reconstruction, not on superseding the nation state. Yet there were soon more insistent pressures on the governments to move away from national sovereignty than those that the federalists could muster.

The Cold War

To understand the origins of the EU it is essential to see them in the context of the emerging cold war between the capitalist West and the Communist Soviet Union. Before the Second World War, advocates of a European union had assumed it would stretch to the borders of the USSR. But as relations between the former allies deteriorated throughout 1946 and into 1947, it became clear this would be a project confined to the western part of the continent.

Agreement was reached at an Allied summit meeting in Yalta in 1945 to divide Europe at the end of the war into 'spheres of influence'. This was intended by the western Allies to be only a temporary arrangement, but the Soviet Union soon started to make it permanent. Regimes friendly to the USSR were installed in those countries of central and eastern Europe which at Yalta had been assigned to the Soviet sphere. This led Churchill to make a speech in Fulton, Missouri in March 1946 in which he talked about an 'iron curtain' descending across Europe. The speech did not receive a sympathetic hearing in Washington, where the prevailing mood was still in favour of co-operation with the USSR; but this mood changed in the course of 1946.

In September 1946 Communist insurgents restarted a civil war in Greece. This was a decision that could not have been taken without the agreement of the Soviet Union. In 1945 Stalin had ordered the Greek Communists, who controlled large areas of the country, not to continue with an armed insurrection against the government that the British had installed in Athens. Greece was in the British sphere of influence according to the Yalta agreement, and it seemed that whatever unwelcome moves Stalin might be making in the Soviet sphere, he was at least intent on respecting the limits set at Yalta. The recommencement of hostilities in Greece threw that interpretation into doubt. During 1946, too, the Soviet Union refused to withdraw its troops from Persia, which was also outside its sphere, and made territorial demands on Turkey.

The weather in the European winter of 1946–7 was particularly severe, and put considerable strain on the economic recovery that was underway (Box 4.4, p. 49). This had direct consequences for the emergence of the cold war. In February 1947, London

---

Box 4.4 1947: Economic crisis?

Marshall presented the American people with a vision of Europe in crisis in 1947. People were starving. The economy had broken down. Milward (1984: 3–4) contested this orthodox view. He denied there was a crisis, although he accepted that there was a serious problem about the ability of the west European states to build and sustain international trade because of a lack of convertible currencies to finance it. In his view the Marshall Plan was entirely political in its conception and objectives, although its means were entirely economic. The misleading representation of the economic position in Europe was designed to get the agreement of the US Congress to the reconstruction programme.

informed Washington that it could not afford to continue economic and military aid to Greece and Turkey. In response, President Truman asked Congress in March 1947 for $400 million of economic and military aid for Greece and Turkey. To dramatize the situation, he spoke of the duty of the United States to assist 'free peoples who are resisting attempted subjugation by armed minorities or by outside pressures'. This became known as the Truman doctrine, and it marked a clear statement of intent by the US Administration to remain involved in the affairs of Europe and the wider world, and not to allow isolationist sentiments within the country and within Congress to force a withdrawal from an international role.

Perhaps even more significant in converting the US Administration to Churchill's view, was the collapse of the Four-Power Council of Foreign Ministers, a standing conference to discuss the administration and future of Germany. Soviet intransigence in that forum, and the eventual walk-out of the Soviet representative in April 1947, convinced those who were trying to negotiate on behalf of Washington that it was not possible to work with the USSR. From that point on the emergence of separate West and East German states became gradually inevitable.

A second direct consequence of the bad winter and economic setback of early 1947 was that waves of strikes spread across France and Italy. In both cases the strikes were supported by Communists, who engaged in revolutionary anti-capitalist rhetoric. In the light of events in Greece, this was interpreted as further evidence of the Soviet Union attempting to undermine stability outside its sphere of influence, although in both cases it may have been an incorrect interpretation. Certainly in France, where the Communist Party was part of the coalition government, the strikes appeared to take them by surprise. However, it was very difficult for the French Communists not to support their core electorate, and indeed not to interpret the strikes as evidence of the imminent collapse of capitalism. The other parties in the French coalition responded by expelling the Communists from the government: the Truman Administration responded with the Marshall Plan.

The Marshall Plan and the OEEC

On 5 June 1947 George Marshall, the US Secretary of State, announced that the United States Administration proposed to offer financial and food aid to Europe to assist in its economic recovery (Box 4.5, p. 50). Suspicious of US motives, the USSR and its allies rejected the offer. There were some grounds for this suspicion: the American gesture went far beyond simple altruism to a concern with economic self-interest.

Marshall Aid offered an injection of dollars into the European economy, which would finance trade between the European states and the United States, and trade between the European states themselves. This was a policy much favoured by those sections of US industry that were involved in exporting. It was less favoured by those sections of US industry that were oriented towards the domestic market, and that suspected that they would pay the bill for European reconstruction without gaining the benefits. This section of domestic opinion was strongly represented within Congress, and so it was by no means a foregone conclusion that the Administration would get its plans through Congress. Following the Soviet Union's rejection of aid, Truman and Marshall were able to justify the Plan as part of the same response to the threat of Communism as was the Truman Doctrine. Marshall argued that economic conditions

---

Box 4.5 The Marshall Plan

- The European Recovery Programme (ERP) was announced by US Secretary of State George C. Marshall in a speech at Harvard University on 5 June 1947.

- It involved the United States giving a total of $13bn. in financial aid to the states of western Europe. The assistance was offered to the states of eastern Europe, but they declined under pressure from the Soviet Union.

- The European states that accepted held a conference in July 1947 in Paris, and set up the Organization for European Economic Co-operation (OEEC) to facilitate the unified response that the United States required.

in western Europe in 1947 were so serious that they provided a breeding ground for Communism. The struggle had to be waged by economic as well as military means.

Whether it was motivated by genuine concern for the condition of western Europe, or by economic considerations that had more to do with lobbying by the larger US corporations, Marshall Aid came with strings attached. The US Administration was committed to the idea of free trade. It was concerned to see what it described as 'European integration', meaning that national economic barriers to trade should be broken down. Both of the motives discussed above would support this position. Given that the Administration genuinely believed that free trade would strengthen the west European economies, integration was compatible with the stated aim of strengthening western Europe against Communist expansion. However, it was also compatible with the aim of creating a large and exploitable market for US exports and for investments by US multinational corporations.

The United States insisted that decisions on the distribution and use of Marshall Aid be taken by the European states jointly. To effect this, a body known as the Committee for European Economic Co-operation (CEEC) was set up. Despite the professed aim of allowing the Europeans to make their own decisions on the use of the aid, the United States was represented on this committee, and because it was contributing all the funds, it clearly had some economic and political leverage. The CEEC was transformed in April 1948 into a more permanent body, the Organization for European Economic Co-operation (OEEC).

For Marshall and other members of the US Administration, OEEC was to be the basis for the future supranational economic management of Europe. Nobody was quite clear what 'supranational' meant in this context, but it certainly meant breaking down national sovereignty in economic affairs. In particular, the US view was that western Europe should become a free-trade area as the first step towards global free trade.

This was not a vision that particularly appealed to the governments of the European states involved. The British did not particularly want to be tied into any arrangement with the Continental states. The French had already embarked on their own recovery programme which was based on a much more restrictive view of the role of free trade and the free market. Other governments shared some of the French concern to keep as much control as possible over their own economies, giving away sovereignty neither to a supranational organization nor to the workings of the international free market.

Crucial to the economic and political stance of the European states was the position of Germany. Whether the German economy and state would be reconstituted was still an open question when CEEC began operations. The US wanted the decisions to be made by the OEEC. Germany's neighbours were simply not prepared to see that happen. In particular, they were nervous about the extent of political leverage the United States was able to exercise within OEEC because of its economic influence as the sole contributor to the reconstruction funds. However, despite its economic leverage, the United States simply did not have sufficient political weight to overcome the combined opposition of Britain, France, and the smaller European states to allowing OEEC to develop as a powerful supranational organization (Milward 1984: 168–211).

The body within OEEC controlling policy and administration was the Council of Ministers, which consisted of one representative from each member state. Decisions taken by the Council were binding on members but each member state retained the right of veto. While effective within its limited remit, the OEEC promised little in terms of further integration.

Despite its limitations, the OEEC continued its work for twelve years and, according to Urwin (1995:22) 'played a major role in driving home the realization that European economies were mutually dependent, and that they prospered or failed together'. In 1960, the OEEC was superseded by the Organization for Economic Co-operation and Development (OECD), which had a broader remit, concerned with issues of economic development both in Europe and globally (Box 4.6, p. 52).

Box 4.6 **The OEEC and OECD**

Founded in 1948 to oversee the implementation of the Marshall Plan, the OEEC originally had fifteen members. In 1949 the newly-independent Federal Republic of Germany became a member. In 1950 the United States and Canada became associate members.

In 1961 the OEEC was transformed into the Organization for Economic Co-operation and Development (OECD), with the USA and Canada as full members.

The OECD aims

- to promote economic co-operation between industrialized countries

- to co-ordinate development assistance to the third world

- to provide a forum for the resolution of problems of world trade and economic growth.

Box 4.7 **Benelux**

- The term Benelux is an acronym made up of the first parts of the names of the member states: *Be*lgium, the *Ne*therlands, and *Lux*embourg.

- The governments of these three states adopted a customs union while in exile in London in 1944, and extended this to an economic union on 1 January 1948.

- The aim of the Benelux economic union is to achieve common employment and social security policies, close co-ordination of macro-economic and budgetary policies.

- Benelux forms a passport-free area.

- The institutions of Benelux are:

  — Committee of Ministers

  — Interparliamentary Council

  — Economic and Social Council

  — Court of Justice

  — Secretariat.

Germany

The German problem came increasingly to dominate the debate about the future of Europe. For the United States and Britain the future of Germany was inevitably linked to the emerging cold war. For France and Germany's smaller neighbours it was still a question of how to prevent the re-emergence of a threat to their sovereign independence from Germany itself.

Initially Germany's neighbours tried to protect themselves through a traditional military alliance, in which British participation was seen as crucial. This approach produced the Treaty of Dunkirk between Britain and France in March 1947, and the Treaty of Brussels between Britain, France, and the Benelux states (Box 4.7, p. 52) in March 1948. Both alliances were aimed more at forestalling German aggression than they were against the Soviet Union.

The French also tried to prevent the emergence of any German state. Ideally the French Foreign Office would have liked to have kept Germany under permanent allied occupation. Failing that, it wanted the former German state to be divided into a large number of small separate states. By 1949 it had become apparent that this was not going to happen. Again the crucial dynamic was the rapidly emerging cold war. In 1948 the Soviet Union walked out of Allied talks on the future of Germany. The United States and Britain responded by starting to prepare the Anglo-American zones for independence. The French were left in no doubt that they were expected to merge their occupation zone into the new West German state, which would be created under the plans for independence. Once the Federal Republic of Germany came into existence in 1949, the French policy had to be rethought.

Conclusion

Several of the themes that run throughout the book are already apparent in this chapter: the problems of legitimacy and national identity; the conflict between managed capitalism and free market capitalism; and the necessity of understanding what was happening in Europe in a more global context.

The governments that took office in post-war western Europe faced a series of challenges. They faced a demand from their electorates both for security from the economic problems that had afflicted pre-war Europe, and from further war. They faced a lack of popular confidence in the ability of the sovereign national state to meet these demands. They faced a challenge from federalism, which offered an alternative way of organizing Europe politically, but one that would have removed the levers of power from the hands of national governments. They faced an even more serious challenge from Communism, an ideology that promised to deliver the economic security that people doubted capitalism could deliver. They faced demands from the United States that they reconstruct their economies in a way that would open them to foreign competition, which if met would have reduced the ability of national governments to control the impact of the market on their electorates.

The success of Socialist governments in many west European states in the first post-war elections indicated the extent of the desire among the people of western Europe for a fairer and more managed economic system. It was in response to this demand that the first steps were soon taken in the construction of the welfare state systems, and an active role for the state in economic management began to be mapped out. The distinctive European model of capitalism began to emerge. Before these systems could work, though, there had to be economic recovery from the war. This proved elusive in the early years.

The United States showed itself to be willing to finance recovery through the Marshall Plan, in return for reconstruction being on the basis of liberal market economies that were open to competition. To ensure this openness, the United States insisted that recovery plans be constructed on a European basis, not a national basis. West European governments had to cope with a demand that they surrender some of their ability to control their national economies as the price for US financial assistance.

So the first tentative steps towards some form of west European economic integration were taken in response to a combination of internal and external pressures on governments. The decisions were undoubtedly intergovernmental: there were no supranational institutions to push the process forward at this stage. They were taken by governments whose legitimacy had to be established. Recourse to nationalism was not an option for gaining legitimacy because of the popular lack of confidence in the nation-state following the war. On the other hand, embracing federalism implied a surrender of authority and control that most national governments were unwilling to undertake. The most efficacious way of gaining legitimacy was to provide economic growth, but this required the support of the dominant economic power in the post-war world, the United States. Support was offered on condition that the economic recovery plan go beyond the nation-state. This was not a demand for a surrender of political sovereignty, and was therefore easier for the west European states to accept than a full-blown move to a federal constitution. At the same time the governments were able to adopt federalist rhetoric. They could appear to be moving in a popular direction while not losing control of the process.

At the same time, the insistence by the United States that the reconstruction be based on open market systems did threaten the post-war models of managed capitalism. The implications of opening national economies to external competition was that jobs would be lost in some sectors. The European models of capitalism could only be reconciled with open markets if there were high rates of economic growth, so that any jobs lost to competition were replaced by new jobs generated by this growth. This was a gamble, but it was a gamble that the national governments had no choice but to make. Unless the post-war economic recovery could be got underway, there would be no jobs to be lost. In the end the influence of the United States, exercised through the conditions attached to the Marshall Plan, was decisive.

KEY POINTS

The end of the war, federalism, and the Hague Congress

- The Second World War caused great economic and social dislocation and created a mood for political change. In general, this mood favoured the left, and federalist ideas also gained support in much of continental Europe. This led to the formation of the European Union of Federalists (EUF) in 1946.

- The Hague Congress of 1948 promised much in terms of integration, but in the end delivered little beyond the Council of Europe and this was dominated by national governments.

The Cold War

- The post-war process of European integration has to be understood in the context of emerging tension between the capitalist West and the communist Soviet Union.

- As the Soviet Union began to install friendly regimes in the countries of central and eastern Europe, Churchill spoke of an 'iron curtain' descending across Europe.

- As economic and political tensions in Europe grew, the 'Truman doctrine' of 1947 declared the United States' intention to maintain an active role in world affairs.

- Following the principles of the Truman doctrine, the 1947 Marshall Plan provided US aid to assist the recovery of European economies.

- The Committee for European Economic Co-operation (CEEC) was set up to administer Marshall aid, and included US representation. This temporary body was replaced by the permanent Organization for European Economic Co-operation (OEEC) in 1948. The OEEC was ultimately superseded by the Organization for Economic Co-operation and Development (OECD) in 1960, which had a remit beyond European recovery.

- The issue of how to deal with Germany came to dominate the European agenda. In particular, its neighbours were keen to prevent any resurgence of German aggression.

- When the Soviet Union walked out of talks on the future of Germany in 1948, Britain and the US advanced plans for an independent West German state.

QUESTIONS

1 In the aftermath of the Second World War, was some form of European integration inevitable?

2 Consider the argument that the post-war process of European integration was driven primarily by economic concerns.

3 How important was the United States in the process of European integration immediately after the Second World War?

FURTHER READING

The early post-war period is not particularly well written-up, except as part of wider histories. For the whole history of European integration D. W. Urwin, *The Community of Europe: A History of European Integration since 1945* (London and New York: Longman, 2nd edn. 1995) and Urwin, *Western Europe since 1945: A Short Political History* (London and New York: Longman, 4th edn., 1985) should be treated as standard reference sources.

A particularly controversial account of the early post-war origins of European integration is given by: A. S. Milward, *The Reconstruction of Western Europe, 1945–51* (London: Routledge, 1984).

For more information on European federalism, see: M. Burgess (ed.), *Federalism and federation in Western Europe* (London: Croom Helm, 1986), and *Federalism in the European Union: Political Ideas, Influences and Strategies* (London and New York: Routledge, 1989).

5 The Schuman Plan for coal and steel

By pooling basic production and by instituting a new High Authority, whose decisions will bind France, Germany and other member countries, this proposal will lead to the realization of the first concrete foundation of a European federation indispensable to the preservation of peace.

(Schuman Declaration)

SUMMARY

In May 1950 the French Foreign Minister, Robert Schuman, proposed a scheme for pooling the coal and steel supplies of France and Germany, and invited other European states who wished to participate to express an interest. The idea involved a surrender of sovereignty over the coal and steel industries. It was devised by Jean Monnet, a French civil servant, and addressed practical problems for France that arose from the establishment of the Federal Republic of Germany. The first problem was how to avert the threat of future conflict between France and Germany; the second was how to ensure continuing supplies of coal for the French steel industry once the Ruhr region reverted to German sovereign control.

The plan was welcomed by the German Chancellor, Adenauer, and the Benelux states and Italy indicated that they would wish to participate. The British government declined an invitation to take part. The negotiations between the six states that did wish to participate were marked by hard bargaining in defence of national interests, but eventually agreement was reached on what became the European Coal and Steel Community.

Introduction

On 9 May 1950 the French Foreign Minister, Robert Schuman, announced a plan for France and Germany to pool coal and steel production under a High Authority, and invited other European nations to join them. Four other states (Belgium, Luxembourg, The Netherlands, and Italy) did agree to join what became the European Coal and Steel Community (ECSC). Britain declined an offer to become a member. The Six signed the Treaty of Paris in April 1952, and the ECSC came into operation in July 1952 (Box 5.1, p. 57).

It is clear that the ECSC project involved a considerable surrender of sovereign control over the coal and steel industries, which raises the question of why the governments of the participating states were prepared to agree to this. This chapter examines the reasons for the participation of the six states, and for the non-participation of Britain. It also looks at the negotiations that led from the Schuman Plan to the ECSC.

Box 5.1 The Schuman Plan

- Robert Schuman presented his plan as a contribution to safeguarding world peace.

- It was based on the premise that the key to peace was European unity, and in particular overcoming the old hostility between France and Germany.

- This would not be achieved all at once, but unity could be built through concrete achievements that would build solidarity.

- To this end the French government proposed a limited plan to place Franco-German production of coal and steel under a High Authority in an organization that would be open to other European countries to join.

- This would be a decisive first step in the federation of Europe. It would make war between France and Germany not only unthinkable, but also materially impossible. It would lay the foundation for the economic unification of the participating states.

National positions and the origins of the ECSC

In the following analysis the positions of the six founder states are examined, and then that of Britain. The analysis starts with France, the country that proposed the scheme, then looks at Germany, without whose participation the scheme would never have got off the ground. The Benelux states are considered together because their reasons for participation were extremely similar. Italy's reasons for joining the negotiations require a little more explanation. Britain's reasons for not joining are important for the future relationship between Britain and the EC.

France

The plan for the ECSC was known as the Schuman Plan because it was made public by the French Foreign Minister, Robert Schuman. He was born in Luxembourg, lived in Lorraine when it was part of the German empire, was conscripted into the German army in the First World War, and only became a French citizen after the war when Alsace and Lorraine reverted to French sovereignty. Thus he had a particular reason for wanting to reconcile the historic conflict between the two countries.

Milward (1984: 395–6) argued that the Foreign Ministry must have played a role in devising the plan, but the more generally accepted view is that it was drawn up within the French Economic Planning Commission (Commissariat du Plan—CdP), which was headed by Jean Monnet (Box 5.2, p. 58). It was the task of the CdP to guide the post-war reconstruction and modernization of the French economy, and it was through his experiences in this task that Monnet came to appreciate the economic inadequacy of the European nation state in the modern world. As he himself put it:

For five years the whole French nation had been making efforts to recreate the bases of production, but it became evident that to go beyond recovery towards steady expansion and higher standards of life for all, the resources of a single nation were not sufficient. It was necessary to transcend the national framework. (Monnet, 1962: 205)

The wider framework that Monnet had in mind was an economically united western Europe. He saw the need to create a 'large and dynamic common market', 'a huge continental market on the European scale' (Monnet, 1962: 205). But he aimed to create more than just a common market. Monnet was a planner: he showed no great confidence in the free-market system, which had served France badly in the past. He placed his faith in the development of supranational institutions as the basis for building a genuine economic community which would adopt common economic policies and rational planning procedures.

Coal and steel were only intended as starting points. The aim was to extend integration to all aspects of the west European economy; but such a scheme would have been too ambitious to gain acceptance all at once.

Europe will not be made all at once, or according to a single plan. It will be built through concrete achievements which first create a *de facto* solidarity (Schuman Declaration 1950).

There had been a clear indication of this need for incrementalism in the failure of various post-war efforts to integrate the economies of France, Italy, The Netherlands, Belgium, and Luxembourg. Although negotiations for an organization to be known as 'Finebel' had proceeded for some time, they were on the verge of collapse in 1950. Besides, the new factor in the equation, and the key factor

---

Box 5.2 Jean Monnet

Jean Monnet (1888–1979) was born into a small brandy-producing family in Cognac. He left school at 16, and after a period gaining experience of financial affairs in London, he worked for the family business, travelling widely.

In 1915 he was declared unfit for military service, and spent the war instead in the civil service. He rose rapidly to the position of representative of the French government in London.

After the war he was appointed deputy secretary-general of the League of Nations, but he returned to private life when the family firm got into difficulties in 1922. He subsequently became an investment banker and financier.

In the Second World War he worked first for the British government in Washington, then for de Gaulle in Algiers. He was instrumental in preventing the British and Americans from replacing de Gaulle, who in 1946 appointed him as head of the CdP.

He devised both the Schuman Plan and the Pleven Plan for a European Defence Community (EDC).

He was the first President of the High Authority of the ECSC between 1952 and 1955. Following the defeat of the proposed EDC in the French National Assembly, he resigned from the High Authority to be free to promote further schemes for European integration, setting up the Action Committee for the United States of Europe.

prompting Monnet's plan, was the emergence in April 1949 of a sovereign West German state.

For Monnet the existence of the Federal Republic of Germany posed two problems in addition to that of how to create an integrated west European economy. The first was how to organize Franco-German relations in such a way that another war between the two states would become impossible. To a French mind this meant how to control Germany. The pooling of coal and steel production would provide the basis for economic development as a first step towards a 'federation of Europe', and would change the future of those regions devoted to producing munitions, which had also been 'the most constant victims' of war.

The solidarity in production thus established will make it plain that any war between France and Germany becomes not merely unthinkable, but materially impossible (Schuman Declaration).

The problem of how to control Germany remained at the heart of the process of European integration throughout the early post-war period.

The second problem facing Monnet was the very practical one of how to ensure continuing adequate supplies of coking coal from the Ruhr for the French steel industry. The idea of pooling Franco-German supplies of coal and steel was not new: similar schemes had been proposed on many occasions previously (Gillingham, 1991*b*: 135; Duchêne, 1994: 202). In fact the idea of pooling coal and steel supplies had featured in two recent publications, one from the Assembly of the Council of Europe and the other from the UN Economic Commission for Europe (Urwin, 1995: 44). These reports were concerned with the very practical problems affecting the coal and steel industries of Europe. There was excess capacity in steel, and a shortage of coal. This combination was of particular concern to Monnet, whose recovery plan for France involved expanding steel-producing capacity. The French steel industry was heavily dependent on supplies of coking coal from the Ruhr.

At the end of the war, the Ruhr region of Germany had been placed under joint Allied control. Its supplies of coal had been allocated between the various competing users by the International Authority for the Ruhr (IAR), which had been established in April

1945. It seemed unlikely that this arrangement could be long continued once the Federal Republic was constituted, which raised the question of how France could ensure that it continued to get access to the supply of scarce Ruhr coal which its steel industry needed. The coal and steel pool had the potential to achieve this.

In summary, Monnet's reasons for proposing the plan to pool Franco-German supplies of coal and steel were a combination of taking a first step on the road to complete integration of the west European economy, finding a way to organize Franco-German relations which would eliminate the prospect of a further war between the two states, and solving the problem of how to ensure continued access for the French steel industry to supplies of coking coal from the Ruhr. That Schuman essentially accepted this thinking, informs the standard explanation for France's participation in the Schuman Plan.

Germany

Konrad Adenauer, the Chancellor of the Federal Republic, accepted the Schuman Plan with alacrity. Yet if the proposal had been made to serve French interests, why was the German Chancellor so keen on it?

As with Schuman, one of the factors was a commitment on the part of Adenauer to the ideal of European integration. Like Schuman, Adenauer came from a border region, in his case the Rhineland. Like Schuman, he was a Roman Catholic and a Christian Democrat. In accepting the Schuman Plan, Adenauer committed himself to Franco-German reconciliation and to European integration. This does not mean, though, that he acted only for idealistic reasons. There were also very practical reasons for Adenauer's acceptance of the Schuman Plan. The Federal Republic needed to gain international acceptance; Adenauer wanted to make a strong commitment to the capitalist West; and the new German government was looking for a way of getting rid of the IAR.

The legacy of the Nazi era and of the war had left Germany a pariah nation. It had also left it divided into two separate states, the Federal Republic in the west and the Democratic Republic in the east.

Adenauer wanted to establish the Federal Republic as the legitimate successor to the pre-war German state, but also as a peace-loving state that would be accepted as a full participant in European and international affairs. Adenauer also wanted to establish the western and capitalist orientation of the Federal Republic beyond question or reversal. This was important to Adenauer because the Social Democratic Party (*Sozialdemokratische Partei Deutschlands*—SPD) was arguing for the Federal Republic to declare itself neutral in the emerging cold war, in the hope that this would facilitate re-unification of the country. As well as being strongly anti-communist, Adenauer believed that the Democratic Republic was dominated by the Soviet Union, and he feared the cultural influence of Russia would be damaging to the vitality of German culture and to the process of moral renewal in the aftermath of Nazism, which, as a devout Catholic, he believed to be essential. (Milward, 1992: 329–30).

The importance for Adenauer of getting rid of the IAR was both political and economic. Politically it was important to him that the region be integrated into the Federal Republic. Economically, the Ruhr had always been one of the powerhouses of the German industrial economy, so it was important to the prospects of economic recovery that it be unchained from the restrictions that the IAR placed on its industrialists. There was a risk that in accepting the Schuman Plan, Adenauer would commit his country to a relationship from which French industry would gain at the expense of German industry. However, Adenauer was confident that German industrialists could stand up for their interests within a coal and steel pool (Gillingham, 1991*a*: 233).

The Benelux States

The reason why the Benelux states agreed to enter the negotiations for the ECSC was the same in each case: they could not afford to stay out of any agreement between France and Germany on coal and steel. These commodities were essential to the economies of the three states, and there was a high degree of interdependence between the industries in the border regions of France and Germany, and those in

Belgium and Luxembourg particularly. There was also support in all three states for any moves that promised to reduce the risk of war between their two larger neighbours.

Italy

Italian reasons for joining in the negotiations require a little more explanation than the reasons for Benelux participation. Italy is not geographically part of the same industrial region as the other participants, so there was not the same inevitability about its involvement. In many ways the reasons for Italian participation in the negotiations resembled those of Germany more closely than those of the Benelux states.

Like Germany, Italy was governed by Christian Democrats; and as in the case of Adenauer (and of Schuman) the individual who dominated the government was a Roman Catholic and someone who originated in a border region. Alcide di Gasperi came from the Alto Adige region of Italy, which had been part of the Austro-Hungarian empire before the First World War. Like Germany, Italy had to rebuild its international reputation after the war. Mussolini had been Hitler's ally and had ended up as his puppet. Like Germany, Italy was on the front line in the emerging cold war. Geographically, it had a land frontier with the Communist state of Yugoslavia, and only the Adriatic Sea separated it from Albania. At the end of the war there had been a serious risk that the Italian Communist Party would take over the country in democratic elections, and it remained the largest single party in terms of support. Di Gasperi therefore had a similar need to that of Adenauer in Germany to enmesh his country in a complex of institutional interdependencies with the capitalist west, to establish its western and capitalist identity politically, economically, and in the minds of its own people.

Britain

The other state that was invited to participate in the conference that followed the Schuman Plan was Britain. The negative attitude of the British government has been extensively analysed (Dell, 1995; George, 1998: 19–22; J. W. Young, 1993: 28–35; H. Young, 1998).

All accounts accept that there were certain peculiarities of the British position that made it highly unlikely that its government would welcome the proposal. Whereas in continental Europe, nationalism had been discredited through its association with Fascism, in Britain Fascism had never succeeded, and the war had been fought as a national war. Unlike the other states, Britain had neither been defeated nor occupied in the war. There was not the same sense in Britain of discontinuity with the past. The attitude of the British governing elite was that Britain was not just another European state. It was a world power with global responsibilities. Although this attitude has been described as a 'delusion of grandeur' (Porter, 1987) it had some basis in reality. Britain still had a considerable empire; British companies had interests in all parts of the world; and British armed forces were globally deployed in keeping the peace, or acting as a bulwark against communist encroachment.

The perception at the time was that Britain was economically far stronger than the other western European states, and that tying the future of the British economy to that of the German and French economies was dangerous. Britain had adequate indigenous supplies of coal, and the Labour government had just completed the nationalization of the coal and steel industries. Having campaigned over many years for nationalization, the Labour Party was unlikely to surrender control once it had been achieved. Also, European integration was at this time particularly associated with the leader of the Conservative Party, Winston Churchill. Although there were some Labour Party members who participated in the Hague Congress and remained supporters of a united Europe, the idea was associated with the opposition, not the government.

To add to these general factors, Ernest Bevin, the Foreign Secretary, was personally upset that he had no forewarning of Schuman's announcement. Dean Acheson, the US Secretary of State, was told about the Plan in advance by the French Prime Minister, Georges Bidault; and Acheson subsequently met Bevin, but did not mention the Plan. As Acheson had been given the information in confidence, this was reasonable enough; but it led Bevin to see a Franco-American plot to seize the initiative away from Britain in the formulation of plans for western Europe (Young, 1998: 52). Bevin's annoyance was increased when the French government insisted that all those who wished to participate in the scheme must accept the principle of supranationalism. This condition was pressed by Monnet, who was concerned that otherwise the outcome would be another intergovernmental organization. He must have known that it would be an impossible condition for the British government to accept, given the strong attachment of the Labour Party to national sovereignty, and perhaps he did not really want British participation at the outset. It was, after all, the British who had been primarily responsible for the watering down of the commitment to supranational institutions in the Council of Europe.

The British government did not immediately reject the demand for a commitment to supranationalism. Instead, the French were asked to specify exactly what they meant by the phrase, to spell out the full extent of the surrender of sovereignty that was envisaged and its effects. After some three weeks of inconclusive discussions of the implications of supranationalism, Schuman announced on 1 June 1950 that the principle was non-negotiable, and that any state that wanted to be involved in the negotiations must accept it by 8.00 p.m. on 2 June. The British Cabinet immediately rejected this condition.

From the Schuman Plan to the Treaty of Paris

Negotiations between the six began on 20 June, with all delegations supposedly committed to the principle of supranationalism. However, both the Belgians and the Dutch had reservations, as became apparent once the opening session was completed and the substantive negotiations began on 22 June (Duchêne, 1994: 209).

Monnet insisted that the French delegation should be hand-picked by himself, and he rigorously excluded representatives of the French coal and steel industries from influence in the process. This was not the case with the other delegations, which consisted of diplomats and officials from the national energy ministries, who were open to influence from the affected industries.

There followed months of hard bargaining during which various departures were made from the original principles set out in Monnet's working document (Box 5.3, p. 62). These concessions were

necessary to make a success of the negotiations. That they had to be made reinforces the view that most participants were concerned to use the ECSC to further their own national interests. The biggest concessions were made by the Germans, for whom the main potential advantage of the Schuman Plan was the opportunity it offered to get the removal of the constraints imposed by the IAR.

At the end of the war, the Allies had forced the deconcentration of the coal and steel industries in Germany, and the break-up of the cartels that had restricted competition. From the German point of view this only served to give an artificial advantage to their French competitors. The IAR acted to prevent reconcentration and re-emergence of cartels, so the German industrialists wanted to get rid of it. But they did not want the High Authority of the ECSC to take over those functions from the IAR, whereas Monnet was determined that the High Authority would do exactly that.

From the French point of view, concentration was dangerous because it gave too much political influence to the large industrial concerns. The support of the Ruhr industrialists for Hitler had contributed to the Nazis coming to power. Cartelization was a device which, in Monnet's eyes, acted as a restraint on competition. In this view he was strongly supported by the United States.

The role of the US Administration in the negotiations was vital. Not officially represented at the talks, the United States nevertheless exerted a tremendous influence behind the scenes. A special committee was set up in the US Embassy in Paris to monitor progress, and it acted as a sort of additional secretariat for Monnet. For the United States the cartel arrangements were an outrageous interference with the operation of market forces, and could not be tolerated. There was initially less concern about the concentration issue because the size of the units involved would still be much smaller than those in the United States. However, after the outbreak of the Korean War in June 1950, the US Administration came to the reluctant conclusion that Germany would have to be rearmed. In this context, the issue of not

---

Box 5.3 Bargaining concessions in the ECSC negotiations

- At the insistence of the Dutch, supported by the Germans, a Council of Ministers, consisting of representatives of national governments, was added to the institutional structure to curtail the supranationalism of the High Authority.

- At the insistence of the Belgians, a special 'equalization tax' on efficient coal producers was agreed, which would be used to subsidize the modernization of inefficient mines. In practice this amounted to a subsidy from Germany to Belgium.

- At the insistence of the Italians, the Italian steel industry was allowed to maintain tariffs against the rest of the participants for five years, and to continue to import cheap coking coal and scrap metal from outside the ECSC. As with the Belgian coal mines, there was to be an equalization fund to finance the modernization of inefficient Italian steel plant, although this was much smaller than the coal equalization tax.

allowing the emergence of the industrial conglomerates that had supported the previous militaristic German regime became more significant in US minds.

After months of hard negotiation, the United States cut through the arguments and forced a settlement. On 3 March 1951 Adenauer was summoned to see John J. McCloy, the US High Commissioner in Bonn, who told him that the delays caused by the Germans were unacceptable, and that 'France and the United States had no choice but to impose their own decartelization scheme' (Gillingham, 1991*a*: 280). Despite vigorous protests from the Ruhr producers, Adenauer accepted the ultimatum because for him the political gains of the ECSC were paramount, and he could not afford to allow the process to collapse.

It appeared, then, that although Monnet's concept had been severely modified, the essential purpose had been achieved of creating a supranational body which could exercise some control over the coal and steel producers in the interests of promoting efficiency and competition.

The High Authority was funded through a direct levy on Europe's coal and steel firms and had a wide brief on taxes, production, and restrictive practices. Alongside it were established a Council of Ministers consisting of national government representatives, and a Common Assembly. In addition, a Consultative Committee to the High Authority was established to represent producers, employers and consumers. More significantly in terms of future integration, a Court of Justice was set up with judges drawn from the national judiciaries to rule on the legality of the High Authority's actions.

Conclusion

The first steps in the process of European integration were taken not primarily because of any commitment to the ideas of the federalists, but in response to practical problems. Schuman, Adenauer, and de Gasperi may have had personal reasons for wanting to see a move away from nationalism, but the architect of the ECSC, Jean Monnet, was concerned with solving immediate and longer-term problems. The two immediate problems were, first the reconstruction of the two industries that were central to the European economies of the day, coal and steel, and second how to accommodate West Germany within the system of capitalist European states without reviving the risk of war, and without serious damage to the French steel industry. In the longer term, he was looking at how to ensure that Europe would be competitive in comparison with the United States. The way in which solutions to practical problems became the basis for advances in European integration recurs throughout the story of the founding and evolution of the European communities.

Another consistent theme of the story of European integration is the tension between free-market capitalism and planned capitalism. The system of planned capitalism, or managed markets, is sometimes known by the French word *dirigisme*. Monnet saw very clearly the economic necessity for western Europe to move away from the fragmentation of national markets to form a single large market. He did not consider that the way to achieve this was through the immediate creation of a free market. He wanted the process to be controlled by planners, such as himself, and to proceed economic sector by economic sector. The end result, though, would be a managed European market rather than managed national markets. This theme is returned to in the conclusion to Chapter 7 (p. 84).

The importance of the background of the cold war was again evident in the launch of the ECSC. The breakdown of co-operation between the Soviet Union and the western Allies led to the creation of a West German state, posing the problems of how to handle Germany and how to ensure adequate coking coal for French steel manufacturers. It coloured the reaction of the governments to the Schuman Plan, particularly in Germany and Italy where the theme of the search for a new national identity was particularly prominent. In both states the governments wanted to find a way of consolidating their position in the western capitalist camp. ECSC offered a way of embedding their states into the capitalist west, and they could appeal to the idea of European federalism as a way of convincing their electorates that the move was a good one.

This did not mean that the governments of any of the states that agreed to take part in ECSC were prepared to sell short their national interests as they perceived them. A consistent theme of the history of European integration is that advances are made only after hard bargaining between governments. This bargaining tends to produce package deals that give something to everyone. E. B. Haas (1968: 155) said of the Treaty of Paris that set up the ECSC (see Box 5.4, p. 64):

The very ambiguity of the Treaty . . . made this pattern of convergence possible. Something seemed to be 'in it' for everybody and a large enough body of otherwise quarrelling politicians was persuaded to launch the first experiment in deliberate integration.

In this process of bargaining, the United States was a central actor. Although not having a formal seat at the negotiating table, the US Administration exerted influence on the negotiations and imposed its position on the maintenance of the cartels. Many episodes in the process of European integration can only be fully understood with reference to the position of the United States, which was often either directly involved, or was a factor in the reckoning of the participants.

Finally, the analysis that has been presented here focuses on the interests of states as interpreted by their governments, not on the activities of interest groups. In Chapter 1 (p. 9) a distinction was drawn between realist and pluralist theories of international relations. For realists, states are the only significant actors in the international arena. For pluralists, other actors such as interest groups are also significant. In the case of neofunctionalism, a key role was allocated to organized interests. However, even Haas, the founding father of neofunctionalism, could not tell the story of the foundation of the ECSC in terms of interest group pressures. He examined the positions of all the key interest groups in the various states, and was able to show that they affected the detail of the positions taken up by national governments; but in the end the agreement to the ECSC was based on an independent interpretation of the national interests of the participating states taken by the governments of those states. However, this should not be so surprising, because neofunctionalism was essentially a theory about how the interests would react to the first steps in the process of European integration. ECSC *was* the first step. The time for neofunctionalist analysis had not yet arrived.

Box 5.4 Extract from the Treaty of Paris

Preamble to the Treaty of Paris establishing the European Coal and Steel Community

The President of the Federal Republic of Germany, His Royal Highness the Prince Royal of Belgium, the President of the French Republic, the President of the Italian Republic, Her Royal Highness the Grand Duchess of Luxembourg, Her Majesty the Queen of the Netherlands,

Considering that world peace can be safeguarded only by creative efforts commensurate with the dangers that threaten it,

Convinced that the contribution which an organized and vital Europe can make to civilization is indispensable to the maintenance of peaceful relations;

Recognizing that Europe can be built only through practical achievements which first of all create real solidarity, and through the establishment of common bases for economic development;

Anxious to help, by expanding their basic production, to raise the standard of living and further the works of peace;

Resolved to substitute for age-old rivalries the merging of their essential interests; to create, by establishing an economic community, the basis for a broader and deeper community among peoples long divided by bloody conflicts; and to lay the foundations for institutions which will give direction to a destiny henceforward shared.

Have decided to create a European Coal and Steel Community . . .

KEY POINTS

National positions and the origins of the ECSC

- The reactions to the proposal for coal and steel known as the Schuman Plan, and the reasons for accepting it, varied from state to state.

- The French government saw the coal and steel pool as a way to solve its problem with the emergence of a West German state, and as a way to guarantee supplies of coal from the Ruhr.

- The German government saw participation in the scheme as a route back to international respectability, and Adenauer saw in it a means of consolidating West Germany's capitalist identity.

- For the governments of the Benelux states there was no choice but to participate in a coal and steel pool that involved France and Germany, so interdependent were their economies.

- The Italian government saw the scheme as a potential protection against a Communist takeover.

- The British Labour government was unsympathetic to involvement in any economic union with other European states, and coal and steel had just been nationalized, so the sectors could not have been less well chosen to encourage British participation.

From the Schuman Plan to the Treaty of Paris

- Negotiations over the Schuman Plan led to significant changes to reflect national interests.

- Ultimately, however, the US played an important 'behind the scenes' role in shaping an agreement which angered German steel producers but which Adenauer accepted because for him the political gains from the ECSC were paramount.

- While Monnet's initial concept was modified, the agreement still created a supranational body, the High Authority, with some control over domestic coal and steel producers.

- Established alongside the High Authority was a Council of Ministers, a Common Assembly and a Court of Justice to rule on the legality of the High Authority's actions.

QUESTIONS

1 What persuaded five states to sign up to the ECSC?

2 Why was Britain not initially involved in the ECSC?

3 Assess the importance of the US on the agreement to establish the ECSC

4 To what extent was the creation of the ECSC a victory for Monnet's ideas?

FURTHER READING

There is a considerable literature on the Schuman Plan. The outline of the negotiations is ably recounted by D. W. Urwin, *The Community of Europe: A History of European Integration since 1945* (London and New York: Longman, 2nd edn. 1995), but for a detailed insight into the process the account given by F. Duchêne, *Jean Monnet: The First Statesman of Interdependence* (New York and London: W. W. Norton and Co., 1994) is indispensable. Most of J. Gillingham, *Coal, Steel, and the Rebirth of Europe, 1945–1955* (Cambridge: Cambridge University Press, 1991) is devoted to the build-up to the negotiations and the negotiations themselves, and E. B. Haas, *The Uniting of Europe: Political, Social and Economic Forces, 1950–1957* (Stanford, Calif.: Stanford University Press, 1968) contains information on the positions of all the main actors, scattered through a book that is organized thematically rather than chronologically.

For the revisionist view that the ECSC was not a move away from state autonomy but a means of protecting it, the reader should turn to A. Milward, *The European Rescue of the Nation State* (London: Routledge, 1992).

The British failure to take seriously the Schuman Plan is recounted in E. Dell, *The Schuman Plan and the British Abdication of Leadership in Europe* (Oxford: Clarendon Press, 1995).

6 The European Defence Community, the European Political Community, and the road to the Rome Treaties

In the Autumn of 1952, there were not one but three prospective Communities, two pillars and the roof of a potential European union. Covering coal, steel, defence, arms production and perhaps elements of foreign policy—that is, economic and political functions close to the core of the state—they provided the outline of a federation in the classic style. To achieve so much would be extraordinary three or four years from a standing start and less than a decade after the war. On the other hand, there were disturbing signs that all this might be a house of cards resting on the fate of the European Army

(Duchêne 1994: 234–5)

SUMMARY

While the development of the ECSC (Ch. 5, pp. 56–66) set much of the tone and framework for future developments in European integration, it was largely overshadowed at the time by negotiations to establish a European Defence Community (EDC). Connected with the EDC were plans to create a European Political Community (EPC) to provide democratic European structures for co-ordinating foreign policies. This radical plan collapsed in 1954 with failure to secure agreement on proposals for EDC. Despite this, and perhaps because of it, the integration project was relaunched in 1955. This relaunching ultimately led to the Treaties of Rome in 1957, which established the European Economic Community (EEC) and the European Atomic Energy Community (Euratom).

Introduction

Although we now know that the ECSC was the first step on the road to the EU, it was overshadowed in the minds of contemporaries by the negotiations on another plan devised by Monnet, the Pleven Plan for a European Defence Community (EDC). The failure of this proposal was perhaps as much responsible as the successes and failures of the ECSC in explaining the initiatives that led to the Treaties of Rome.

The EDC initiative was accompanied by a proposal for a European Political Community (EPC). This provided federalists with another opportunity to pursue their strategy of 'the constitutional break', moving directly from a Europe of nation-states to a federal constitution for Europe. The feasibility of doing this was no greater in 1953 than it had been in 1948, and for the same reason: the governments of the states were not prepared to surrender their sovereignty. The positive reception given to the Schuman Plan had shown that this was not true in strictly limited areas that were not central to the identity and survival of the state; but the proposal for a general surrender of sovereignty had been too much for the governments of the states participating in the Con-

gress of Europe, and it would almost certainly have been too much for the governments that were involved in the EPC proposal. There was a logic behind arguing that the EDC could not function properly without centralized political direction. Had the EDC been accepted, then EPC might have had to follow. In the event, the EDC collapsed. Although it was like the ECSC in proposing a surrender of sovereignty in a specific sector, it was unlike ECSC in that the sector, defence, was absolutely central to the issues of identity.

With the collapse of the EDC and EPC, the radical federalist strategy of a direct attack on the system of nation-states disappeared from this story. It was not attempted again. Instead, federalists rallied to the gradualist approach that had been suggested by the Schuman Plan. The failure of EDC/EPC, and the success of ECSC, led to proposals for further 'functional' steps towards closer integration between the six states that made up the ECSC. This chapter examines first the record of the Pleven Plan, then the circumstances that produced this so-called 'relaunching' of European integration.

The Pleven Plan

Following the collapse of the four-power administration of Germany, the cold war developed rapidly. In April 1949 a mutual defence pact, the North Atlantic Treaty, was signed in Washington between the United States, Canada, and ten west European states (Britain, France, the Benelux states, Iceland, Italy, Norway, and Portugal). This set up the North Atlantic Treaty Organization (NATO). In the same month the Federal Republic of Germany came into existence. In June 1950 Communist North Korea invaded capitalist South Korea. The ensuing civil war involved the United States, acting under the auspices of the United Nations, on the side of the South, and the Soviet Union and Communist China on the side of the North. It had a profound impact on western thinking about security.

Like Korea, Germany was divided into capitalist and Communist states. While Korea was at that time geographically peripheral to the main global balance of power, Germany was not. The fear in the West was that the Korean invasion was a precursor to an invasion of West Germany from East Germany. In this context, and because the United States was committing troops to the Korean conflict, the US administration decided that the Europeans had to make a bigger contribution to their own defence. In particular, they reluctantly decided that there was no alternative to reconstituting a German army.

This idea alarmed the French. For them it was unthinkable that a German army should come back into existence. Monnet tried to solve the problem with a proposal based on the same principles as his plan for ECSC. Under his scheme for a European Defence Community, instead of having a German army, he proposed to pool the military resources of France and Germany into a European army. There would be German soldiers, but they would not wear German uniforms, and they would not be under German command. The corollary, of course, was that the French army would at least partially disappear into the same European force. Monnet's proposal did however allow France and the other participants, except Germany, to have their own national armies alongside the European army (Box 6.1, p. 69).

As with the pooling of coal and steel, a European army was not a new idea. A similar proposal had been made by the French representatives in the Consultative Assembly of the Council of Europe in August 1950, and had received the support of the Assembly, but had been blocked in the Council of Ministers. Monnet now formalized the idea, making an explicit link to the ECSC. The plan was publicly launched by the French Prime Minister, René Pleven, an old collaborator of Monnet, on 24 October 1950.

Despite the election in Britain in October 1951 of a

Box 6.1 The European Defence Community

Proposed by the French Prime Minister René Pleven, on 24 October 1950, but devised by Jean Monnet, the 'Pleven Plan' was a response to the demand from the United States for the rearmament of Germany in the light of the outbreak of the Korean War.

A Treaty was signed by the six ECSC member states on 27 May 1952. It proposed the creation of a European army consisting of 14 French divisions, 12 German, 11 Italian, and 3 from the Benelux states. The command of the army would be integrated, but there would be no divisions of mixed nationality.

The EDC would have had a similar institutional structure to the ECSC:

- a Council representing the member states, with votes weighted according to each state's contribution to the European army;

- a Commission;

- an Assembly.

Article 38 of the Treaty made provision for a common external policy. The ECSC Parliamentary Assembly was to provide a plan for this, which became the draft Treaty for a European Political Community (EPC).

The EDC was rejected by the French National Assembly on 30 August 1954.

Conservative government under Churchill, who professed to be a supporter of European integration, the British were unwilling to become involved in plans for the EDC. The US administration was initially cautious, but Monnet talked round the new NATO Supreme Allied Commander in Europe, Dwight D. Eisenhower, and his support swung the administration behind the scheme (Duchêne, 1994: 231). Adenauer welcomed the idea, seeing in it a way of finally ending the Allied occupation of West Germany. The other four states that had joined in the Schuman Plan signed up to talks for essentially the same reasons as they had joined ECSC: the Benelux states did not feel that they could stand aside from such an initiative between their two larger neighbours, and Italy continued to seek acceptance into the European states system.

At Monnet's prompting, Pleven made it a condition of progress on the EDC that the ECSC Treaty be signed first. This was particularly resented in Germany, because Monnet had accompanied preparation of the Pleven plan with a hardening of his attitude towards the position of the German steel cartels in the talks on the Schuman Plan. This had stalled the talks: Adenauer and the German negotiator, Hallstein, felt that they were being railroaded into accepting an unfavourable agreement on the ECSC in order to secure negotiations on the EDC. They were not mistaken. Gillingham (1991*b*: 146) was clear that these two developments were linked in Monnet's mind. Indeed, the same author (1991*a*: 264) went so far as to suggest that the Pleven Plan 'saved the Schuman Plan'. This sort of cross-bargaining worked both ways, however. Duchêne (1994: 250) believed that one explanation for Monnet's failure to press home the Treaty provisions against the Ruhr cartels when he became President of the ECSC High Authority was that Adenauer warned him that any premature action on this front would jeopardize the ratification of the EDC Treaty in the German parliament.

A problem with the proposed EDC was the plan for a common European army without a common foreign policy. The proposed institutions of the EDC would not be able to provide this. At the insistence of Italy, a clause was inserted into the draft treaty linking the EDC with the creation of a European Political Community to provide a democratic dimension to

---

Box 6.2 The European Political Community

The Treaty for the European Defence Community made provision in Article 38 for the Parliamentary Assembly of the ECSC to draw up plans for a common external policy for the six states.

The opportunity was seized on by federalists within the Assembly to draft a Treaty for a European Political Community.

In the course of its work the ECSC Assembly was supplemented by members of the Parliamentary Assembly of the Council of Europe.

The draft Treaty was adopted by this *ad hoc* Assembly on 10 March 1953. It proposed:

- a two-chamber European Parliament consisting of a People's Chamber that would be directly elected every five years, and a Senate of indirectly elected members from national parliaments

- a European Executive Council that would have to be approved by both chambers of the parliament, but once in office would have the power to dissolve the People's Chamber and call new elections

- a Council of National Ministers

- a Court of Justice.

The EPC collapsed with the failure of the French National Assembly to ratify the EDC in August 1954.

---

the project. Plans were to be drawn up by the Common Assembly of the EDC, but as delays in ratifying the treaty stretched out the process, Paul-Henri Spaak, the Belgian Premier, suggested that the Common Assembly of the ECSC, enlarged in membership so as to resemble the proposed EDC Assembly, should prepare the EPC proposal (see Box 6.2, p. 70). The EPC would not be just a third community, 'but nothing less than the beginning of a comprehensive federation to which the ECSC and EDC would be subordinated' (Urwin 1995: 64).

The fate of the EPC was inevitably linked to the fate of the EDC. The EDC treaty had been signed in May 1952, but it had not been ratified by any of the signatories when the EPC proposals emerged. In fact, the EDC treaty was 'rotting before the ink was dry' (Duchêne 1994: 233). Its prospects were crucially dependent on French support, but the French government only signed it on the 'tacit condition that no immediate attempt should be made to ratify it' (Duchêne 1994: 233). German rearmament, even as part of a European army, was unpopular in France. Pleven only managed to get approval for his proposal from the National Assembly by 343 votes to 220. By the time that the intergovernmental negotiations were completed, there had been elections in France and the parliamentary arithmetic did not indicate a clear majority for ratification. In consequence, successive prime ministers refused to bring the treaty to the Assembly for ratification, fearing that its failure would bring down their government. This prevarication, which went on for almost two years, caused exasperation in the United States, and led Secretary of State John Foster Dulles in December 1953 to threaten an 'agonizing reappraisal' of policy. Eventually the Treaty was submitted to the National Assembly by the government of Pierre Mendès-France at the end of August 1954, but the government gave it no support, and indicated that it would not resign if the Assembly voted against ratification. The EDC treaty was not ratified and the demise of the EDC was accompanied by the collapse of the EPC.

The issue of European defence was eventually solved according to a formula proposed by the British government. The Brussels Treaty of 1948 was extended to Germany and Italy; a loose organization called Western European Union (WEU) was set up to co-ordinate the alliance; an organic link was made with NATO, to which Germany and Italy were admitted. Adenauer achieved his aim of securing an Allied withdrawal from the whole of West Germany (although not Berlin), and a German army was formed, although it was hedged around with legal restrictions on operating beyond the borders of the Federal Republic. The WEU appeared to contemporary observers to be an organization of no particular

---

Box 6.3 **The Western European Union**

Following the collapse of the EDC, the British government proposed an alternative security structure for western Europe. This involved Italy and Germany becoming signatories to the Brussels Treaty of 1948, by which Britain, France, and the Benelux states had committed themselves to treat any act of aggression against one as an act of aggression against all.

The Western European Union (WEU) which resulted began work on 6 May 1955. Its headquarters were in London. Its institutions consisted of:

- a Council of Foreign and Defence Ministers;

- a Secretariat, headed by a Secretary-General;

- an Assembly (based in Paris), made up of the member states' representatives in the Parliamentary Assembly of the Council of Europe.

From the outset WEU was overshadowed by NATO. It was only in the 1980s that it began to assume any significance beyond its original purpose as a means of giving a British security guarantee to Germany's neighbours so that they would agree to German rearmament.

In the 1980s the WEU took on a new role as a bridge between the EC and NATO in the context of efforts to forge a European security and defence identity.

The Treaty on European Union (signed February 1992) contained as an annex a Declaration on WEU which said: 'WEU will be developed as the defence component of the European Union and as a means to strengthen the European pillar of the Atlantic Alliance.'

In June 1992 the WEU Council endorsed future WEU involvement in conflict prevention and peacekeeping operations. These are known as the 'Petersberg tasks'.

Today the WEU brings together twenty-eight states divided into Members, Associate Members, Observers, and Associate Partners to discuss issues of common concern related to security and defence in the new Europe.

Member States: Belgium, France, Germany, Greece (joined 1995), Italy, Luxembourg, the Netherlands, Portugal, Spain, the United Kingdom.

Associate Members: the Czech Republic, Hungary, Iceland, Norway, Poland, Turkey.

Observers: Austria, Denmark, Finland, Ireland, Sweden.

Associate Partners: Bulgaria, Estonia, Latvia, Lithuania, Romania, Slovakia, Slovenia.

importance because it was overshadowed by NATO. However, like other organizations that were set up in the post-war period, it was later to acquire functions that had not been envisaged at the time when it was formed (Box 6.3, p. 71).

The other practical significance of the EDC episode, or rather of the related EPC initiative, was that it kept the federalist idea alive. As Gillingham (1991a: 349) put it, it 'kept the cadres in being, dialogue moving, and served as a learning experience'. The importance of this became clear with the 'relaunching of Europe' which followed the collapse of EDC.

Defence was not an obvious next step after coal and steel in the process of 'building mutual trust through concrete achievements'. It was not an issue with a low political profile, but a sensitive issue that struck to the heart of national sovereignty. Had it not been for the international crisis of the Korean War, it would surely not have surfaced at this stage. Monnet himself may have been of this view. Duchêne (1994: 229) reports that several people who were working close to Monnet at the time had the impression that he regarded the EDC scheme as premature. After winning over Eisenhower, Monnet took no further part in the negotiations on the plan, and this unusual degree of detachment led one sympathetic American official in Paris to criticize Monnet for his lack of commitment to the project (Duchêne 1994: 233).

Messina

In November 1954, Monnet announced that when his first term as President of the High Authority of the ECSC ended in February 1955, he would not seek a second term. Citing the collapse of the EDC, he said that he wanted to free his hands to work for European unity. He then formed an organization called the Action Committee for the United States of Europe, consisting of leading political and trade union figures from the member states of the ECSC, but also from Britain and other states.

The main proposal to come from the Action Committee was for a European Atomic Energy Community (Euratom). It was accompanied by a plan to extend the sectoral responsibilities of the ECSC to cover all forms of energy, and transport. Nothing came of these latter proposals, although transport was given a special place in the Treaty of Rome (EEC). The member governments were simply not interested in extending the remit of the ECSC.

Also accompanying the proposals from the Action Committee was a proposal from Beyen, the Dutch Foreign Minister, for a general common market. Richard Mayne (1991: 115) maintained that this scheme also originated with Monnet, but he offered no evidence for this, and it is a view that is flatly rejected by other writers. Duchêne (1994: 269–72) provided evidence that Monnet actually rejected the idea of a general common market, believing that it was too ambitious, and might produce another EDC débâcle.

There was no great enthusiasm for further sectoral integration. In so far as business interests expressed support for further integration, it was for an extension of the market aspect of the ECSC, not for the centralized regulatory functions of the High Authority. The lesson that was learned from ECSC was that sectoral integration would not work. As The Economist (11 Aug. 1956) reported:

In the last four years the Coal and Steel Community has proved that the common market is not only feasible but, on balance, advantageous for all concerned. But it has also shown that 'integration by sector' raises its own problems of distortion and discrimination. The Six have therefore chosen to create a common market for all products rather than continuing to experiment with the sector approach.

On 4 April 1955, Spaak circulated a memorandum to the governments of the six states of the ECSC proposing that negotiations begin on the extension of sectoral integration to other forms of energy than coal, particularly nuclear energy, and to transport. The proposal met with a cool response; only the French government supported it. Beyen then pressed the case for a relaunch based on the idea of a general common market.

The Federal German government reacted very positively to Beyen's proposal, but in France the idea of a general common market was strongly rejected by industry, which argued that it would not be able to compete with German industry. French politicians had generally accepted this argument, but there was a growing belief that the excuse could not be used forever, and that French industry would never be competitive until it had to compete. At this stage, though, the mood in France was not conducive to taking such a step, which may explain why Monnet was reluctant to advocate it.

Spaak subsequently met with the Dutch Prime Minister, Joseph Bech, and as a result of that meeting, a formal Benelux initiative was launched combining Monnet's ideas for further sectoral integration with Beyen's idea of a general common market. This proposal was circulated in late April 1955, and was discussed at the beginning of June in Messina in Italy at a meeting of the heads of government of the six, which had originally been called to decide on a successor to Monnet as President of the High Authority of the ECSC.

Agreement was reached at Messina to set up a committee under the chairmanship of Spaak to study the ideas in the Benelux memorandum. The French government was not enthusiastic, and appeared not to expect anything to come of the talks, but it was difficult for France to block them so soon after its rejection of the EDC. Because the agreement to hold talks was reached in Messina, the negotiations took that name. In fact most of the meetings were held in Brussels. Their success was unexpected, except perhaps by optimistic partisans of integration like Spaak. In fact, the success of the Spaak Committee, which met in Brussels between July 1955 and March 1956, owed a great deal to his energetic and skilful chairing of the proceedings. Also very important, though, were the changed circumstances between the original Messina meeting and the actual negotiations.

One very important change was in the government of France: Guy Mollet, the leader of the Socialist Party, became Prime Minister in 1956. Having originally been sceptical about European integration, Mollet had become convinced that French

industry needed to be opened up to competition if it was ever to achieve the sort of productivity gains that lay behind the remarkable German economic recovery. He had also become a member of Monnet's Action Committee, and Duchêne (1994: 287) maintained that a relationship developed between Monnet and Mollet similar to the earlier relationship between Monnet and Schuman.

Mollet was brought to office by the deteriorating situation in Algeria, where French settlers were under attack by the nationalist Front for the Liberation of Algeria. The war that developed there was traumatic for the French, and dominated the nation's attention so that the negotiations in Brussels were able to proceed without attracting much notice from critics. But Algeria was only one of the international events of 1956 that had an effect on the outcome of the Messina negotiations. In October the Soviet Union invaded Hungary to suppress an anti-communist national movement which had the sympathy of the Hungarian army. Hungary brought home to western Europeans once again the reality of the cold war that divided their continent. More directly, the Suez Canal crisis also blew up in October.

The nationalization of the Suez canal by Egyptian President Gamal Abdel Nasser not only caused outrage in France, as it did in Britain; it also offered the French a possible excuse to topple Nasser, whose pan-Arab rhetoric inflamed the situation in Algeria, and whose regime was suspected of sheltering and arming the Algerian rebels. However, once the nationalization had been effected, Nasser gave no further cause for outside intervention. The canal was kept open to international shipping; it was business as usual under new ownership. To foment an excuse to invade, the French government colluded with the Israeli government and hatched a scheme that was subsequently sold to the British government of Anthony Eden. Israel would invade the canal zone; the French and British governments would demand an immediate withdrawal from the canal by the armed forces of both sides. Egypt would certainly refuse, and the combined Franco-British force would then move in to occupy the canal zone and reclaim the canal. The fall of Nasser was confidently expected to follow.

However, the invasion failed because in the face of opposition from the Soviet Union and, more significantly, from the United States, the British government decided to pull out. France could not carry through the operation alone. The episode was perceived in France as a national humiliation at the hands of the Americans, but also as a betrayal by the British who were believed to be too subservient to US wishes. It fed support for the nationalist position of Charles de Gaulle, who subsequently came to office as first president of the new Fifth Republic in May 1958. It also fed into the Messina negotiations, helping them to reach a speedy and successful conclusion.

Directly, Suez underlined much more than events in Hungary the impotence of France in the post-war world of superpowers. It gave support to the concept of France acting together with other European states. Indirectly, the clear signs that this episode marked the beginning of the end for the government of Mollet, and the strong indications that he would be succeeded by de Gaulle, who had always opposed European integration, accelerated the efforts to reach agreement. A 'rush to Rome' began in an effort to get the Treaties signed before de Gaulle came to office and aborted the whole experiment.

The road to the Rome Treaties

The agreements reached in the Spaak Committee were a series of compromises between different national positions, particularly those of France and Germany. Central to the agreement detailed in the Spaak Report of March 1956 was the creation of the general common market favoured by the German government. Although Mollet believed that this step would be good for France as well as for Germany, he had to negotiate concessions that would allow him to get the Treaty ratified in the French National Assembly. There were three main areas where the French government extracted concessions: Euratom, agriculture, and relations with France's overseas territories and dependencies.

Euratom was attractive for many French politicians because they saw it as a means of obtaining a subsidy from Germany for the expensive process of developing nuclear energy, which in turn was linked to the development of nuclear weapons. Although Mollet personally believed that France should confine itself to the peaceful use of nuclear energy, the sentiment in the National Assembly in the aftermath of Hungary and Suez was very much in favour of an independent French nuclear deterrent. Euratom offered the opportunity to devote more national resources to the weapons programme, while depriving Germany of a national nuclear capability, and guaranteeing French access to uranium from the Belgian Congo.

Agriculture was given a separate chapter in the EEC Treaty. Its inclusion, not as part of the general common market, but as in effect a further extension of sectoral integration was another factor that was important in ensuring French ratification of the Treaty. For the French governments of the Fourth Republic, agriculture was both politically and economically important. Politically, small farmers had a disproportionate electoral importance under the voting system that was used in the Fourth Republic. The small farmers were inefficient producers, but were determined to retain their independence, which in effect meant that they had to be subsidized by the state through a national system of price-support. By transferring this cost to the common EEC budget, the French state again obtained a subsidy from the more prosperous Germans. Economically, France also had an efficient agricultural sector, and actually produced a considerable surplus of food, so the guarantee of a protected market for French agricultural exports was another concession that helped to sell the EEC Treaty within France.

In the context of decolonization and the war in Algeria, it was very important for all French governments to ensure that the special links with the former colonies were maintained. There were considerable French economic interests that were dependent on trade with these overseas dependencies and territories, and there was a general sentiment in France in

Box 6.4 **Extract from the Treaty of Rome (Euratom)**

The Preamble to the TREATY OF ROME establishing a EUROPEAN ATOMIC ENERGY COMMUNITY
(Signed 1957, brought into effect January 1958)

RECOGNIZING that nuclear energy represents an essential resource for the development and invigoration of industry and will permit the advancement of the cause of peace,

CONVINCED that only a joint effort undertaken without delay can offer the prospect of achievements commensurate with the creative capacities of their countries,

RESOLVED to create the conditions necessary for the development of a powerful nuclear industry which will provide extensive energy resources, lead to the modernization of technical processes and contribute, through its many other applications, to the prosperity of their peoples,

ANXIOUS to create the conditions of safety necessary to eliminate hazards to the life and health of the public,

DESIRING to associate other countries with their work and to cooperate with international organizations concerned with the peaceful development of atomic energy,

HAVE DECIDED to create a European Atomic Energy Community

colonies, was the third important factor to allow the Treaty to obtain ratification in France.

On each of these points the German government made considerable concessions. There was no sympathy for Euratom in German industrial or government circles; the Germans would have preferred to leave agriculture to national management, and to continue to allow food to be imported as cheaply as possible from the rest of the world; and there was no enthusiasm for supporting the last vestiges of French colonialism. However, in order to obtain the considerable prize of the common market in industrial goods, the German government was prepared to make these concessions to France.

The other major bargaining concession was made to Italy in the form of the inclusion in the Treaty of a commitment to reducing the differences between prosperous and poor regions. This was the Italian government's attempt to claim a subsidy from Germany, given that the problems of the south of Italy represented the main regional disparity within the original six member states.

The Spaak Report was agreed by the governments of the six member states in May 1956. The Spaak Committee was transformed into a conference with responsibility for drafting the necessary treaties. In March 1957, two treaties emerged: one for the EEC; the other for Euratom. The treaties were signed by national governments in Rome in the same month, prior to being passed on for domestic ratification. If the failure of the EDC had meant several steps backwards in the process of integration, the Treaties of Rome promised a major leap forward (Boxes 6.4, p. 75, and 6.5, p. 76).

favour of the link. The continuation of this special relationship, by guaranteeing preferential access to the common market for the products of the former

Conclusion

Several of the persistent themes of this story emerge once more in this chapter. The influence of the cold war on the whole EDC episode is clear, as is the role of the United States in the affairs of western Europe during this period of its hegemony of the capitalist world. However, the fate of the EDC is vindication of

the functionalist analysis, that a head-on attack on sovereignty would be resisted, whereas gradual steps to tie states together might succeed.

It is contestable whether the opening of negotiations on the EEC is vindication of the neofunctionalist argument that spillover would operate to

---

Box 6.5 **Extract from the Treaty of Rome (EEC)**

Preamble to the TREATY OF ROME establishing the EUROPEAN ECONOMIC COMMUNITY)
(Signed 1957, brought into effect January 1958)

DETERMINED to lay the foundations for an ever closer union among the peoples of Europe,

RESOLVED to ensure the economic and social progress of their countries by common action to eliminate the barriers which divide Europe,

AFFIRMING as the essential objective of their efforts the constant improvement of the living and working conditions of their peoples,

RECOGNIZING that the removal of existing obstacles calls for concerted action in order to guarantee steady expansion, balanced trade and fair competition,

ANXIOUS to strengthen the unity of their economies and to ensure their harmonious development by reducing the differences existing between the various regions and the backwardness of the less favoured regions,

DESIRING to contribute, by means of a common commercial policy, to the progressive abolition of restrictions on international trade,

INTENDING to confirm the solidarity which binds Europe and the overseas countries and desiring to ensure the development of their prosperity, in accordance with the principles of the Charter of the United Nations,

RESOLVED by thus pooling their resources to preserve and strengthen peace and liberty, and calling upon the other peoples of Europe who share their ideal to join in their efforts,

HAVE DECIDED to create a European Economic Community

---

move integration forward once the first steps had been taken. The line of spillover from ECSC to Euratom is clearer, and was the line of progression favoured by Monnet. However, the proposal for Euratom was countered, rather than complemented, by the proposal from the Benelux states for a general common market. In this can be seen the tension between *dirigisme* and free-market approaches to integration. The general common market was designed to open national markets by removing tariffs, at that time the main barrier to free trade. It stood in marked distinction to the Euratom proposal to extend the system of planning of the 'commanding heights' of the economy from coal and steel to what was expected to be the new main source of energy.

Monnet's scheme also reflected the need to gain the acceptance of the French political elite. France was developing nuclear energy as a priority project, so it could be expected to support Euratom, which offered France the prospect of a subsidy from the other member states for its research and development costs. A free market in industrial goods was less likely to find favour in a country where there was less industrial efficiency than in West Germany. However, things were changing in France. There was a growing awareness among the political elite that if France were to keep up with its German neighbour it had to modernize its economy. Euratom, and concessions on agriculture and overseas territories, were necessary sweeteners to sell the package to the French National Assembly; but the assertion, often made, that the EEC was a deal between German industry and French agriculture hides the truth, that for certain sections of the French political elite the common market was a useful tool to sweep away the protectionism that was stifling French economic growth. Another theme that reappears later in the story emerges here: the use of the EEC as an excuse for governments to carry through unpopular measures that they believe to be necessary but wish to blame somebody else for.

There is no strong evidence that a commitment to maintaining the momentum of integration was a motive for the acceptance of the EEC by the political elite in any of the member states. Events in Algeria, Suez, and Hungary did, though, bring home to them the weakness of European states in an era of superpowers, and made clinging together more attractive. These dramatic incidents also impacted on public opinion, and reinforced a general sentiment in favour of federalist ideas. Suez and Algeria in particular caused a crisis of identity among the French public that allowed their government to push through the Treaties of Rome behind a rhetoric of maintaining the momentum of integration. At the same time, the account given here shows that the Messina negotiations were no exception to the rule that national interests will be strongly defended in all moves in the direction of integration.

KEY POINTS

The Pleven Plan

- While the ECSC is often seen as the first step on the road to the EU, negotiations over the Pleven Plan for a European Defence Community were considered more important at the time.

- The outbreak of the Korean war led to US demands for German rearmament.

- To head off the creation of a West German army, Monnet devised what became known as the Pleven Plan for a European Defence Community in which German troops would be under European command.

- Adenauer reacted positively because it offered a means of ending the Allied occupation of West Germany.

- The EDC became linked with a proposal for a European Political Community.

- Both projects collapsed when the French National Assembly refused to ratify the EDC Treaty.

Messina

- Following the collapse of EDC/EPC, Monnet launched initiatives for the revival of European integration based on extending the ECSC model to other forms of energy, especially atomic energy, and to transport.

- The Benelux states supported a general common market for industrial goods.

- The two sets of proposals were discussed together in the Messina negotiations.

- The negotiations were given impetus by international events in 1956: the war in Algeria; the invasion of Hungary by the USSR; and the Suez crisis.

The road to the Rome Treaties

- The Treaties of Rome involved compromises between France and Germany.

- The French price for accepting the general common market in industrial goods was German agreement on Euratom, the common agricultural policy, and a preferential relationship with the EEC for the former French colonies.

- Italy was allowed to have a commitment in the EEC Treaty to create a regional policy.

QUESTIONS

1 Why did proposals for a European Defence Community fail in the 1950s?

2 Consider the extent to which the Pleven Plan saved the Schuman Plan

3 Explain the significance of the Messina negotiations

4 What were the key intergovernmental bargains on the road to the Rome treaties?

FURTHER READING

The Pleven Plan and the abortive attempt to create a European Defence Community is less written about than the Schuman Plan, but it is the subject of E. Fursdon, *The European Defence Community: A History* (London: Macmillan, 1980).

As with the Schuman Plan, F. Duchêne, *Jean Monnet: The First Statesman of Interdependence* (New York and London: W. W. Norton and Co., 1994), 229–32, provides an insider account.

7 The ECSC and Euratom

In itself, this was a technical step, but its new procedures, under common institutions, created a silent revolution in men's minds

(Jean Monnet 1962: 208).

SUMMARY

The ECSC survived the EDC débâcle and began operation in July 1952 under the presidency of Jean Monnet. Although it had considerable powers at its disposal, it proceeded cautiously in using them, but still found itself in conflict with national governments who were reluctant to relinquish actual control over the two key industries. These conflicts increased after 1958 when de Gaulle became President of France. Euratom only began operations in 1958, and immediately ran into the same problems that were afflicting the ECSC by this time.

Introduction

This chapter examines the independent existence of both the ECSC and Euratom up to the merger of the High Authority and Euratom Commission with the EEC Commission in July 1967. The 1967 merger was effectively a takeover of both Euratom and the ECSC by the EEC. In the interim both the High Authority and the Euratom Commission ran into conflicts with the governments of the member states, particularly with the French government after de Gaulle became President of France in 1958. Their difficulties had

several parallels, and could lead to the conclusion that they were failed experiments. However, Monnet himself claimed that the ECSC at least contributed to changing perceptions of what was necessary to make European integration work. This chapter asks what lessons can be learned from the experience of these two 'failed' attempts at supranational regulation, and identifies issues that can be later applied to the EEC.

The European Coal and Steel Community

In the original plan for the ECSC there was only one central institution, the High Authority. During the negotiations a Council of Ministers and a European Parliamentary Assembly (EPA) were added to the institutional structure. This reflected concern about the power and possible *dirigiste* nature of the High Authority, but did not allay that concern.

While coal producers were ambiguous about supranational *dirigisme*, most of them hoping for some degree of support for their troubled industry, steel producers were generally hostile to this aspect of the Schuman Plan. German industrialists in particular opposed the *dirigiste* element to the Plan, and the Federal German government supported them. The governments of the Benelux countries also had severe doubts about the role of the High Authority. It was at the insistence of these governments that a Council of Ministers was included in the institutional structure of the ECSC, alongside the High Authority.

Although its independence was reduced from Monnet's original proposal, the High Authority was still given considerable formal powers. Diebold (1959: 78–9) considered that:

It was truly to be an imperium in imperio, wielding powers previously held by national governments and having some functions not previously exercised by governments.

Despite these powers, in practice the High Authority proceeded very cautiously. It was in a constant state of tension with the governments of the member states, which did not take easily to having their sovereignty circumscribed by a supranational body. The Council regularly rejected proposals of the High Authority that conflicted with national interests. For this reason the High Authority needed a strong president who could impose his authority. In their comprehensive history of the ECSC. Spierenburg and Poidevin (1994: 649) argued that the first two presidents, Monnet and René Mayer, fitted this description, as did the last president, Del Bo, although by the time he took office in 1963 the High Authority was already in its twilight years. The two intervening presidents, Finet and Malvestiti, did not carry the same weight (Box 7.1, p. 81).

Even taking account of this difficult relationship with the Council, E. B. Haas (1968: 459) considered that, 'in all matters relating to the routine regulation of the Common Market, the High Authority is independent of member governments'. Because of this independence, those governments that were concerned about the possible *dirigisme* of the High Authority took care to nominate as their members people who were not themselves committed to this outlook. For Milward (1992: 105) the most notable

---

Box 7.1 The High Authority

The High Authority of the ECSC had nine members, two each from France and Germany and one from each of the other member states, the ninth member to be co-opted by the other eight; its seat was in Luxembourg. It had five Presidents:

- Jean Monnet (1952–5)

- Rene Mayer (1955–7)

- Paul Finet (1958–9)

- Piero Malvestiti (1959–63)

- Rinaldo Del Bo (1963–7).

It had the power under the Treaty of Paris to obtain from firms in the coal and steel sectors the information that it required to oversee the industries, and to fine firms that would not provide the information or evaded their obligations (Article 47).

It could impose levies on production, and contract loans to raise finance to back investment projects of which it approved (Articles 49–51), and it could guarantee loans to coal and steel concerns from independent sources of finance (Article 54). It could also require undertakings to inform it in advance of investment programmes, and if it disapproved of the plans could prevent the concern from using resources other than its own funds to carry out the programme (Article 54).

---

feature of the members of the High Authority was that they never liberated themselves from their national governments. Monnet became the first president of the High Authority, but found himself at the head of a group of people who were not in sympathy with his own view on its role. E. B. Haas (1968: 459) argued that in 'the ideology of the High Authority, the free enterprise and anti-*dirigiste* viewpoint . . . definitely carried the day'.

This way of presenting the issue is perhaps a little misleading. It suggests that Monnet was in favour of intrusive public-sector intervention and was opposed by other members who favoured free competition. In fact, one of the things that Monnet wanted the High Authority to do was prevent the reformation of the coal and steel cartels, organizations of producers to regulate the industries by collaboration on prices and output. Monnet wanted such regulation as there was to be carried out by the High Authority; but he was also committed to preserving competition between producers. The other members of the High Authority were committed to preventing it from interfering with self-regulation of the markets, not to competition. Perhaps this is what Haas meant by a 'free-enterprise' viewpoint, but the terminology tends to suggest that less regulated markets were the objective. In any case, Monnet was frustrated in his policy objectives for the High Authority.

He was also frustrated in his organizational object-

ives. Mazey (1992: 40–1) argued that Monnet wanted a small, supranational, non-hierarchical, and informal organization; but that internal divisions, bureaucratization, and pressures from corporatist and national interests foiled him in this. Internal divisions between members of the High Authority itself were reproduced within the administration, and when combined with the non-hierarchical structure that Monnet adopted, this led to increasing problems of administrative co-ordination, delays, and duplication of effort because of overlapping competencies.

However, as the demands for administering the common market for coal and steel grew, so did the bureaucratic nature of the High Authority. Problems of co-ordination increased as the different Directorates of the ECSC developed different links with interests and producers in the member states. The consequence was that in the first three years of its operation, 'the administrative services of the High Authority were . . . transformed from an informal grouping of sympathetic individuals into a professional bureaucracy which, in terms of its structure and 'technocratic' character, resembled the French administration' (Mazey, 1992: 43).

When the ECSC was proposed, coal was in short supply; but by 1959 the increasing use of oil had led to over-capacity in the industry. This became a crisis in 1958 when a mild winter and an economic downturn produced a serious fall in demand. Although economic growth picked up in the second quarter of 1959, stocks of coal at the pit-head continued to accumulate because of a second mild winter, low transatlantic freight costs which allowed cheap imports of US coal, and an acceleration of the switch from coal to oil. The High Authority diagnosed a manifest crisis, and in March 1959 asked the Council of Ministers for emergency powers under Article 58 of the Treaty. However, this request failed to achieve the qualified majority necessary, primarily because neither France nor Germany was prepared to grant the extra powers to the High Authority that it requested.

This was one of a series of crises in the history of the European Communities that shook the collective morale of the central bureaucratic actors. The immediate effect was to make it very difficult for the High Authority to respond to the crisis. It had to resort to palliative measures such as social assistance, and a restructuring plan for the Belgian industry, which was hardest hit by the crisis. More fundamentally:

The High Authority's powerlessness revealed the inadequacy of sectoral integration for which it was responsible and which did not cover competing energy sources—oil and nuclear energy (Spierenburg and Poidevin, 1994: 652).

The realization that the attempt to integrate in one sector could not be successful unless integration were extended to other sectors might have led to an increase in the competencies of the High Authority. The Council of Ministers did ask the High Authority to undertake the co-ordination of energy supplies and to draw up plans for a common energy policy; but by this time the Treaties of Rome had come into effect, creating the two new communities, the EEC and Euratom, each with its own Commission.

The decision to make a new start with new institutions, rather than extending the competencies of the High Authority, inevitably produced a conflict between the established bureaucratic actor and the newcomers. Although the High Authority helped the two Commissions to get started by seconding many of its experienced staff, 'there were undeniable jealousies that precluded closer union between the three executive bodies' (Spierenburg and Poidevin, 1994: 652).

Finet complained about the 'poaching' of High Authority staff by the Commissions of Euratom and the EEC (Spierenburg and Poidevin, 1994: 381) and there were tensions both over issues of responsibility and budgetary matters. The Commissions, one headed by a Frenchman and the other by a German, had the support of the French and German Governments on these matters. More generally, governments were content to see responsibilities of the High Authority transferred to the less supranational new Commissions.

Yet the ECSC could claim partial success for its activities, for example in limiting restrictive practices in the coal and steel sectors. More importantly, for Monnet, the creation of the ECSC laid vital foundations for further European integration:

It proved decisive in persuading businessmen, civil servants, politicians and trade unionists that such an approach could work and that the economic and political advantages of unity over division were immense. Once they were convinced, they were ready to take further steps forward (Monnet 1962: 208).

While the supranational instincts of the High Authority were kept under control by national governments, it was significant for future developments in European integration that both the Assembly and the Court of Justice were supportive of its supranational efforts. The Court in particular 'stamped its imprint on the ECSC, and in doing so built up a body of case law, an authority, and legitimacy that could serve as foundations for the future' (Urwin 1995: 56).

Six years after signing the Treaty of Paris establishing the ECSC, the six parliaments ratified the Treaty of Rome establishing the Economic Community, taking the major step towards the creation of a Common Market for all goods and services. Monnet (1962: 211) spoke of a 'new method of action' in Europe, replacing the efforts at domination by the nation-states 'by a constant process of collective adaptation to new conditions, a chain reaction, a ferment where one change induces another'.

Euratom

The Euratom Commission had similar powers and responsibilities to those of its sister institution, the EEC Commission (Box 7.2, p. 83). While the EEC Commission made skilful use of these powers during its first decade to push forward the process of integration, the Euratom Commission failed to make any significant progress. Illness forced the resignation of its first president, Louis Armand, in the first year. Armand was replaced in February 1959 by Etienne Hirsch, a former colleague of Monnet's at the CdP. Delays over recruitment and establishing priorities meant that by the time the Euratom Commission really began work in 1960, the context in which it had been created had changed. In particular, the easing of the coal shortage and reduced concern about dependence on oil from the Middle East in the post-Suez period removed some of the urgency on the development of nuclear energy.

Box 7.2 **The Euratom Commission**

The Euratom Commission consisted of five members, one from each member state except Luxembourg, which had no national nuclear-power programme. During its time it had three presidents:

- Louis Armand (1958–9),

- Etienne Hirsch (1959–62),

- Michel Chatenet (1963–7).

It was charged to ensure that the member states fulfilled the terms of the Treaty:

- it had the sole right to propose measures to this end to the Council of Ministers;

- it had a duty to oversee the implementation of agreements;

- it represented the Community in the negotiation of agreements with the outside world;

- it was answerable to the European Parliamentary Assembly (EPA) for the proceedings of the Community

---

The delay in the start of Euratom operations also allowed national rivalries to become embedded. France, with the largest nuclear research programme had expected the bulk of the subsidies available, but Italy and West Germany rapidly developed their programmes following agreement on Euratom. After 1959, France, which was then under the leadership of de Gaulle, was less enthusiastic about Euratom than it had been. The Hirsch Euratom Commission clashed with the French government over both the right of the Commission to inspect French plutonium facilities and the Commission's decision to divert funds to a joint programme of reactor development with the United States. On the first, Hirsch found no support in the Council of Ministers. On the second, however, the Commission won a majority vote in the Council. Yet even this victory was hollow, as the French government subsequently insisted that budgetary decisions be taken on the basis of unanimity. Thus in both instances of conflict with the French government, the Commission's position was ultimately weakened. Further, de Gaulle refused to renominate Hirsch as president and his successor, Michel Chatenet, was less assertive in his leadership of the Commission.

From 1962 onwards Euratom drifted into deeper crisis. In 1964 there was deadlock over the size of the budget, which was eventually resolved only at the cost of the Commission having to make massive cutbacks in the already modest remaining research programme. A second crisis in 1966 meant that Euratom went into the merger year of 1967 having to survive on the system of 'provisional twelfths' which allowed no more than one-twelfth of the previous year's budget to be spent each month until agreement was reached on the new budget.

A number of explanations have been offered for the failure of Euratom (Scheinman, 1967). First, because it dealt with a single functional sector, the Commission was unable to offer national governments trade-offs in other policy areas to secure deals on nuclear power. Second, the external environment that favoured the creation of Euratom had changed by the time it became operative. Moreover, internal rivalry between member states increased and was consolidated with the election of de Gaulle. France was particularly important here because the matter of nuclear power development was a key issue for the French government that was closely linked to the high politics issue of nuclear weapons. Perhaps the key weakness of the Euratom Commission was that it failed to develop a transnational network of interests around the nuclear energy issue which could create a momentum that would overcome national rivalries. In sum, while the Euratom Commission faced inevitable constraints, it also failed to deploy tactics that were important to the relative success of the EEC commission.

Conclusion

In the history of the ECSC and Euratom we can see the struggle between *dirigisme* and free-market economics; the fragmentation of the supranational executives that was later to afflict the EC Commission; and the assertion of national control over supranational institutions, but also the first stirrings of independence among the supranational institutions.

The story of *dirigisme* versus free-market economics that is told here offers a warning against a simple assumption that the first is about unwarranted interference in the beneficent workings of the market, while the second is about competition from which the consumer will benefit. In fact it was Monnet, the champion of a *dirigiste* approach, who wanted to create genuine competition in the market for steel by breaking up the German cartels, which were clearly organizations in restraint of trade. The advocates of free-market economics were in reality defenders of monopolistic practices. Capitalism is a system that tends to monopoly and monopolistic practices, and to avert that, constant regulation and monitoring is necessary. This is one of the functions that the state can perform for national economies. Among business elites, advocates of market economics are often motivated more by a desire to avoid state regulation so as to leave them free to adopt monopolistic practices than they are by an abstract commitment to the public good. In the EC/EU competition policy has proved to be an important supranational power.

The bureaucratization of the High Authority prefigured the bureaucratization of the EC Commission, which was to prove one of its weaknesses in the 1970s (see Ch. 10, p. 107). Bureaucratization involved among other things the fragmentation of the High Authority into directorates that operated in relative isolation from each other and formed tightly integrated 'policy communities' with key interest groups. This phenomenon is central to understanding the later history of the EC, and especially the operation of the Common Agricultural Policy (see Ch. 24, pp. 305–23).

Finally, the assertion of national control over the supranationalism of the High Authority and the Euratom Commission is clear. If we were to focus only on these forerunners of the EC Commission, the lesson to be drawn would have to be that the member states were suspicious of supranational tendencies in the institutions they had created, and were capable of restraining them. But the first stirrings of the supranational ECJ offered a different lesson for the future. The body of case law that the ECJ began to build up was not particularly controversial, and was not widely noted at the time: it was, however, laying the basis for an independent supranational institution of the future (see Ch. 22).

KEY POINTS

The European Coal and Steel Community

- The High Authority was not as powerful as originally planned, but still had considerable formal independence. It needed strong leadership to be successful, but this was only available during part of its existence.

- There was considerable suspicion of Monnet's *dirigiste* tendencies among national governments who consequently nominated members to the High Authority who were mostly not sympathetic to Monnet's aims.

- Monnet tried to run the High Authority on informal lines, but it became internally divided and increasingly bureaucratized.

- The hostility of de Gaulle to supranationalism exacerbated matters after 1958; Adenauer preferred the Commission of the EEC, which was headed by his associate Hallstein.

- Excess supply of coal led to a crisis in 1959. The Council of Ministers refused the High Authority emergency powers to deal with the crisis. This precipitated a collapse of morale in the High Authority.

- Rivalry emerged between the High Authority and the two new Commissions, of the EEC and Euratom.

- Despite its shortcomings, Monnet believed that the ECSC pioneered the development of a community method of working.

Euratom

- By the time that Euratom began operation the energy crisis that existed when it was negotiated had disappeared. Instead of a shortage of coal there was a glut.

- Whereas France had the only developed programme of research on nuclear energy in the mid-1950s, by the end of the decade Germany and Italy also had independent programmes in competition with that of France.

- The French government refused to co-operate with the Euratom Commission and the Commission never managed to build a supportive network of industry groups or technical experts to help it counter French obstructionism.

QUESTIONS

1 How important was leadership to the development of the ECSC?

2 What were the intergovernmental constraints on the operation of the ECSC?

3 How important was leadership to the development of Euratom?

4 What were the intergovernmental constraints on the operation of Euratom?

5 What lessons could be learned from the history of the ECSC and Euratom for advocates of European integration?

FURTHER READING

Several books are devoted to, or contain extensive sections on the experience of the early communities: W. Diebold Jr., *The Schuman Plan: A Study in Economic Cooperation: 1950–1959* (New York: Praeger, 1962); J. Gillingham, *Coal, Steel, and the Rebirth of Europe, 1945–1955* (Cambridge: Cambridge University Press, 1991); E. B. Haas, *The Uniting of Europe: Political, Social and Economic Forces, 1950–1957* (Stanford, Calif.: Stanford University Press, 1968).

There is one indispensable work on the ECSC: D. Spierenburg and R. Poidevin, *The History of the High Authority of the European Coal and Steel Community: Supranationality in Action* (London: Weidenfeld, 1994).

On the Euratom there is less. The most revealing piece is a short monograph, L. Scheinmann, 'Euratom: Nuclear Integration in Europe', *International Conciliation* no. 563 (1967). There is also a discussion of the adoption of Euratom in A. Milward, *The European Rescue of the Nation State* (London: Routledge, 1992), 200–11.

8 The EEC: 1958–67

. . . to lay the foundations for an ever closer union among the peoples of Europe

(Preamble to the Treaty of Rome establishing the European Economic Community)

SUMMARY

From its creation, the EEC was the most important of the three Communities. Driven by the vigorous leadership of Commission President Walter Hallstein, the EEC made a successful start, illustrated by agreement to accelerate the timetable for creating a customs union between the six. The first real setback came when de Gaulle unilaterally rejected the British application for membership in 1963. A second and more serious crisis in 1965 prompted de Gaulle to withdraw his ministers from Council meetings. The eventual compromise on this damaged the morale of the Commission and undermined the prospects for further integration. The destiny of the project remained firmly in the hands of individual governments and not with supranational institutions, which was what de Gaulle had wanted.

Box 8.1 The institutional arrangements of the EEC

The Commission consisted of nine Commissioners appointed by national governments: two each from France, Germany, and Italy, one each for Belgium, Luxembourg, and the Netherlands. While national appointees, Commissioners were not supposed to advocate national interests but to protect the European ideal. The Commission's primary tasks were to make proposals to the Council of Ministers and to implement the Treaty of Rome. (On the Commission see Ch. 19, pp. 233–45.)

The Council of Ministers consisted of one representative from each member state. Provision was made for it to vote on proposals from the Commission by qualified majority vote (QMV). For these purposes, seventeen votes were allocated among the six member states: four each to France, Germany and Italy; two each for Belgium and the Netherlands; and one vote for Luxembourg; a qualified majority required twelve votes, ensuring that a decision required the support of at least four states. However, in the first stage, prior to the completion of the common market, it was agreed that all decisions would be taken by unanimity. (On the Council see Ch. 20, pp. 246–58.)

The European Parliamentary Assembly (EPA) of 142 members was a purely consultative body. Although provision was made in the Treaty for direct election, initially the members were nominated by national parliaments from among their own members.) (On the European Parliament see Ch. 21, pp. 259–73.)

The ECJ was made up of seven judges: one from each member state, plus one appointed by the Council. (On the ECJ see Ch. 22, pp. 274–87.)

Introduction

It was not obvious in 1957 which of the two new communities, the EEC or Euratom, would become the more important. Within a few years, though, Euratom had lost all momentum. The merger of the three communities in 1967 was effectively a takeover of Euratom and the ECSC by the EEC.

This development reflected the remarkable success of the EEC in achieving its objectives over most of the first decade of its existence. If attempts to create a European Political Community had been ambitious, the development of EEC was no less so, although the political implications were less obvious. The explicit task was to create a common market within fifteen years. Nonetheless, the Treaty of Rome establishing the EEC implied political integration.

The institutional arrangements of the EEC followed those of the ECSC, with a supranational Commission as the equivalent of the High Authority, a Council of Ministers and a Parliamentary Assembly. In addition, an Economic and Social Committee played an advisory role. Finally, the European Court of Justice (ECJ) was established to interpret the provisions of the Treaty of Rome and to act as arbiter in disputes on Community decisions (Box 8.1, p. 88).

The early years: 1958–1963

For the whole of its separate existence, the Commission of the EEC had only one President. Walter Hallstein had been the State Secretary in the Foreign Office of the Federal Republic of Germany, and had been in charge of the German team during the negotiation of the EEC. Hallstein's appointment was accepted unanimously, a remarkable development only twelve years after the war.

The very lack of a sense of drama in the choice of a German for the most important of the new posts was not only a tribute to Hallstein's achievements and reputation but proof of giant progress since the Schuman plan (Duchêne, 1994: 309).

Close to Chancellor Adenauer in his views on west European integration, Hallstein was in no doubt about the political nature of the Commission. In a book published in 1962 he made clear that in his view the logic of economic integration not only leads on toward political unity it involves political action itself.

We are not integrating economics, we are integrating policies . . . 'Political integration' is not too bold and too grandiose a term to describe this process. (Hallstein, 1962: 66–7)

Hallstein was backed in this view of the role of the Commission by the energetic Dutch Vice-President and Commissioner for Agriculture, Sicco Mansholt. Between them Hallstein and Mansholt gave vigorous leadership to the Commission, which according to one observer constituted 'a relatively united, committed partisan organisation' (Coombes, 1970: 259).

The morale of the Commission was increased by its success in getting the Council of Ministers to agree to an acceleration of the timetable for the achievement of a customs union in 1962. It went on to broker agreement on the level of the common external tariff (CET), and at the same time to negotiate acceptance of a Common Agricultural Policy (CAP).

The EEC Treaty (Article 14; now removed) specified a precise timetable for the progressive reduction of internal tariffs. On the original schedule it would have taken at least eight years to get rid of all such tariffs. This rather leisurely rate of progress reflected the concerns of specific industrial groups about the problems of adjustment involved in the ending of national protection. However, once the treaty was signed and it became obvious that the common market was to become a reality, those same industrial interests responded to the changed situation facing them. Even before the treaty came into operation on 1 January 1958, companies had begun to conclude cross-border agreements on co-operation, or to acquire franchised retail outlets for their products in other member states. Just as the neofunctionalists had predicted, changing circumstances led to changed behaviour.

So rapid was the adjustment of corporate behaviour to the prospect of the common market that impatience to see the benefits of the deals that were being concluded and of the new investments that were being made soon led to pressure on national governments to accelerate the timetable. Remarkably, the strongest pressure came from French industrial interests, which had opposed the original scheme for a common market.

On 12 May 1960 the Council of Ministers agreed to a proposal from the Commission to accelerate progress on the removal of internal barriers to trade and the erection of a common external tariff, and on the creation of the CAP. Pressure had come only for the first of these to be accelerated. Progress was slow on agriculture, the negotiations having been dogged by disagreements over the level of support that ought to be given to farmers for different commodities. But the issues were clearly linked: progress on the CAP to accompany progress on the industrial common market had been part of the original deal embodied in the EEC treaty.

It seemed that in keeping the linkage between the two issues in the forefront of all their proposals to the Council of Ministers, the Commission had played a manipulative role that coincided with the view of neofunctionalism about the importance of central leadership. Indeed, it is possibly from the performance of the Commission in this period that the importance of leadership from the centre was first theorized and added to the emerging corpus of neofunctionalist concepts. This interpretation, though, was later contested by Moravcsik (1998: 233) (Box 8.2, p. 90).

As described by Lindberg (1963: 167–205), the progress of the EC between 1958 and 1965 involved the Commission utilizing a favourable situation to promote integration. Governments found themselves trapped between the growing demand from national interest groups that they carry through as rapidly as possible their commitment to create a common market, and the insistence of the Commission that this could only happen if the governments were prepared to reach agreement on the setting of common minimum prices for agricultural products.

These agreements were engineered by the skilful use of the 'package deal': linking the two issues together, and not allowing progress on one without

---

Box 8.2 Neofunctionalist and intergovernmentalist views of the Acceleration Agreement

Lindberg (1963) took the role of the Commission in the success of the EEC in the 1960s as clear evidence of its centrality to the process.

However, this interpretation was strongly contested by Moravcsik (1998: 231–3). According to this intergovernmentalist interpretation 'the Commission was ineffective and repeatedly sidelined' (Moravcsik, 1998: 233). Its

proposals were often ignored, and were only successful when they paralleled proposals made by key member states. Although the Commission made the final proposal on which agreement was reached (as it had to under the rules of the EEC), this was often the opposite of what the Commission had originally proposed.

---

commensurate progress on the other. In that way, each member state would agree to things in which it was less interested in order to get those things in which it was more interested. It was just such a package deal that the French president Charles de Gaulle was to reject in spectacular fashion in 1965, plunging the EEC into crisis. However, before that, in 1963, there was a warning of the problems that lay ahead.

The 1963 crisis

As Urwin (1995: 103) noted,

To some extent, the Commission could be so active because the national governments, through the Council of Ministers had been content to allow it to be so. Even President de Gaulle had on the whole been quite circumspect about the Commission.

However, Commission influence and the apparent smooth progress of the EEC received a setback in January 1963 when President de Gaulle unilaterally vetoed the application for membership from the British government. The most comprehensive history of this episode is Ludlow (1997), on which the following account is largely based.

Having declined the invitation to be present at the creation, Harold Macmillan announced in the House of Commons in July 1961 that the British government had decided to apply for membership of the EEC. The development was not welcomed by Walter Hallstein, who saw it as potentially disruptive to the smooth progress of integration among the six. It was also unwelcome to de Gaulle, who had ambitions to use the EEC as a platform for the reassertion of French greatness in international affairs.

To this end de Gaulle tried to get agreement between the Six on co-operation in foreign policy, which he believed that France would be able to dominate. From 1960 it was agreed that the foreign ministers of the member states would meet four times yearly. De Gaulle also developed a special relationship with the German Chancellor, Konrad Adenauer. This relationship was important in securing support for de Gaulle's plans to extend political co-operation between the six. The matter was subsequently considered by a committee chaired by the French official, Christian Fouchet (Box 8.3, p. 91). The Fouchet negotiations on political co-operation were taking place in 1961 when the British application was lodged, but they had already run into some difficulties over proposals for foreign and defence policy.

British entry did not fit de Gaulle's plans: it would have provided an alternative leadership for the four other member states, whose governments were suspicious of him and wished to resist French domination. Technically, de Gaulle could have vetoed the application, but politically he was in no position to do so. In addition to Fouchet, there were negotiations proceeding in 1961 on two issues that were of

Box 8.3 The Fouchet Plan

In 1961 President de Gaulle proposed to the other members of the Communities that they consider forming what he called a Union of States. This would be an intergovernmental organization in which the institutions of the existing three Communities would play no role. It would involve the member states in pursuing closer co-operation on cultural, scientific, and educational matters, and, most significantly, in the co-ordination of their foreign and defence policies.

At summit meetings in 1961 it was agreed to set up a committee under the chairmanship of the French Ambassador to Denmark, Christian Fouchet, and subsequently to ask the committee to prepare a detailed plan for such co-operation.

This 'Fouchet Plan' proposed a confederation of states with a Council of Ministers, a Consultative Assembly of seconded national parliamentarians, and a Commission. However, unlike the Commissions of the EEC and Euratom, this Commission would not be a supranational body with independent powers, but would consist of officials from national Foreign Ministries.

Box 8.4 The *acquis communautaire*

- The term *acquis communautaire*, often abbreviated to simply *acquis*, is one of those French phrases for which it is difficult to find a precise English translation. A French–English dictionary would define *acquis* as something like 'acquired knowledge' or 'accumulated experience'; but the connotation in this phrase is much more like 'heritage'. The *acquis* is the body of laws, policies, and practices that have accumulated over the lifetime of the European Communities, and now the European Union. Any new member state joining the EU has to accept the *acquis* as part of its terms of entry.

- The adjective '*communautaire*', when applied to the *acquis* or to other nouns, means more than just 'of the (European) community'. It has connotations of something that is in sympathy with the co-operative spirit that informed the original EC.

- The term '*communitaire*', which can be found all too frequently in texts on the EU, is simply an incorrect and horrible piece of 'Franglais'.

crucial importance to France: the common agricultural policy, and new association terms for Africa. Also, de Gaulle did not want to make it more difficult for the pro-French position of his ally Adenauer to prevail in Bonn.

The approach that de Gaulle chose to adopt was to allow negotiations on enlargement to open, but to instruct the French delegation to set the price high in the hope that the terms would prove unacceptable to the British government. The French position was presented as defending the Treaty of Rome and the community *acquis* (see Box 8.4, p. 91). Both had been so strongly influenced by French demands that their defence was almost the same as the defence of the French national interest. Because the French demands were couched in *communautaire* language, it was very difficult for the other member states to resist them. They were torn between support for British membership and a desire not to dilute the achievements of the EEC to date.

The negotiations did not collapse, but they went on so long that de Gaulle was eventually presented with the excuse that he needed to issue his unilateral veto: the deal on nuclear weapons that was reached between Macmillan and US President John Kennedy at Nassau in December 1962. Macmillan persuaded Kennedy to sell Britain Polaris missiles to carry Britain's independent nuclear weapons. This was presented by de Gaulle as clear evidence that the British were not yet ready to accept a European vocation, and used as justification for bringing to an end negotiations that had stalled in late 1962 anyway.

The other member states reacted angrily to the veto. Given that the negotiations had run into difficulties, the anger was directed less at their enforced ending than at the way in which de Gaulle had undermined the system of collaborative working which had begun to emerge in the Six, and within which the others had operated throughout the negotiations.

The 1965 crisis

A more fundamental and considerably more serious crisis began in July 1965, when de Gaulle withdrew France from participation in the work of the Council of Ministers in protest at a proposal from the Commission concerning the financing of the Community's budget.

Once agreement had been reached on the details of the CAP, the question arose of how the policy would be funded. For the first time the EEC would have a budget that went beyond the salaries and administrative costs of the central institutions. The Commission proposed that instead of the cumbersome method of annual contributions negotiated between the member states, the Community should have its 'own resources'. These would be the revenue from the common external tariff (CET) on industrial goods and the levies on agricultural goods entering the Community from outside, which would be collected by national customs officials at their point of entry into the EEC, and then handed over to Brussels, after the deduction of 10 per cent as a service charge. The justification was that the goods might be intended for consumption in any part of the Community, and it was therefore unreasonable that the revenue should accrue to the state through which the goods happened to enter the common market.

What was questioned by the French President, however, was another aspect of the proposal. Using the method of the package deal, the Commission linked the idea of having its own resources with a proposal for an increase in the powers of the EPA, giving it the right to approve the budget. The argument for this was that if the revenues passed directly to the EEC without having to be approved by national parliaments, there would be a lack of democratic scrutiny, which could only be corrected by giving that right to the EPA.

President de Gaulle, however, objected to this increase in the powers of a supranational institution, and when discussion became deadlocked he showed how important he held the issue to be by imposing a French boycott of all Council of Ministers meetings from June 1965. This action was subsequently termed the 'empty chair crisis'. In essence, the dispute was about the very nature of the Europe that the Six were hoping to build. For de Gaulle, primacy had to be given to the interests of national governments.

After six months an agreement was reached between France and the other five member states in Luxembourg. The so-called 'Luxembourg Compromise' of January 1966 represented a considerable blow to the process of European integration. First, there was agreement not to proceed with the Commission's proposals: funding of the budget would continue to be by national contributions. Second, France demanded that there be no transition to majority voting in the Council of Ministers. This move had been envisaged in the original treaties once the customs union was complete and completion was on schedule for January 1966. Under the terms of the Luxembourg Compromise, governments would retain their right to veto proposals where they deemed a vital national interest to be at stake. This agreement was a serious blow to the hope of the Commission that brokering agreement on further integrative moves would be easier in the future.

Third, France made four other demands: that the President of the Commission should no longer receive the credentials of ambassadors to the EEC; that the information services be taken out of the hands of the Commission; that members of the Commission should be debarred from making political attacks on the attitudes of member states; that the Commission should not reveal its proposals to the EPA before they were presented to the Council of Ministers, as it had with the controversial package on the budget.

The terms of the deal precipitated a collapse of morale in the Commission. In particular, the authority of Hallstein and Mansholt was undermined by the episode. Some Commissioners had warned against a confrontation with de Gaulle on supranationality, but Hallstein and Mansholt had overruled them (Camps, 1967: 47). Neither was to regain the air of invincibility that he had acquired in the past. Hallstein withdrew his name from the list of nominations for the presidency of the new combined Commission of the ECSC, EEC, and Euratom that was due to take office on 1 July 1967, and simply served out the remainder of his term. Mansholt stayed on as a Commissioner, but did not put his name forward for the presidency.

Conclusion

The struggle between supranationalism and inter-governmentalism is the clear theme of this chapter. The neofunctionalist interpretation of the history of European integration seems to get both its strongest support and its greatest challenge from the period under consideration. The support comes from the story of the acceleration agreement as told by Leon Lindberg. The setback came from the actions of de Gaulle in vetoing British entry in 1963 and in boycotting the Council of Ministers in 1965.

The acceleration agreement resulted from pressure from business interests for an acceleration of the original timetable for the creation of the common market. This vindicates the neofunctionalist argument that changed circumstances change attitudes and behaviour. The exploitation of this demand by the Commission to lever the member states into accepting a general acceleration of their timetable, for the agricultural negotiations as well as for the reduction of industrial tariffs, vindicates the argument that the central supranational actor can act in conjunction with interest groups to push governments into taking further integrative steps. However, it should be noted that this interpretation has been strongly contradicted by Andrew Moravcsik (1999: 159–237). It is also incontestable that the pressure came not from transnational interest groups, as neofunctionalist theory predicted that it would, but from national groups, especially French business interests. The linkage to agriculture was hardly a surprise given that the two issues had been linked in the original package, and the French government itself could not simply bow to the wishes of French business and ignore the wishes of French farmers. Moravcsik's historical research indicates that the deals were not cut by the Commission but by the governments of other member states.

The 1965 dispute over the funding of the budget certainly illustrates the continued ability of national governments, even of a single national government, to stop the process of European integration in its tracks. It also prefigures, though, another theme that becomes more prominent later in the story. The Dutch government insisted that, if the budget was to be funded from the EC's own resources, the EP must be given some control over the budget. The Dutch argument was that national parliaments would lose their ability to exercise democratic scrutiny and control of the budget once the own-resources system of financing was introduced, so to ensure that there was some democratic oversight the EPA would have to be given some control. There is an aspect of spillover here. If the success of a policy is defined not just as the instrumental 'does it work', but also in terms of the extent to which it can be seen as an example of democratic decision-making, there is spillover from the removal of decisions from national parliamentary control to the increase in the powers of the EP. When this did not take place, there emerged a democratic deficit within the EC. Governments did not worry too much about the democratic deficit until it began to undermine the legitimacy of the EC in the eyes of their electorates. This was an early example of the Dutch parliament pointing to the potential for such a democratic deficit to open up.

KEY POINTS

The early years: 1958–63

- The EEC Commission under the presidency of Walter Hallstein was very proactive in promoting integration.
- Its apparent successes included getting agreement from the member states to accelerate progress on creating the common market and the CAP.

The 1963 crisis

- In 1961 President de Gaulle proposed that the member states of the Communities try to agree on intergovernmental political co-operation. Negotiations on the 'Fouchet Plan' were going on when the British government applied for entry to the Communities.
- De Gaulle did not want to see Britain become a member, but rather than risk collapsing the Fouchet negotiations he allowed negotiations on membership to begin.
- French demands in the entry negotiations seemed to be designed to raise the price of entry to an unacceptable level.
- When the Fouchet negotiations came near to collapse, and the entry negotiations did not, de Gaulle unilaterally vetoed British entry.

The 1965 crisis

- In 1965 the Commission proposed a system of financing the CAP that would have given the EEC its own financial resources. This was linked to a proposal to increase the budgetary powers of the EPA.
- De Gaulle rejected the increase in the powers of the EPA, and when agreement could not be reached he withdrew France from participation in the work of the Council of Ministers.
- In January 1966 France was persuaded to resume its place in the Council, but it insisted as the price of doing so that the planned move to QMV be abandoned. This was accepted in the so-called 'Luxembourg Compromise'.
- The crisis precipitated a crisis of confidence in the Commission.

QUESTIONS

1 Why was the Hallstein Commission able to flourish while the High Authority of the ECSC and the Commission of Euratom were perceived as threats to the national sovereignty of governments?

2 Why was the British application for membership in 1963 rejected?

3 What lessons can be drawn for integration theory (see Ch. 1, pp. 5–18) from the experience of the EEC between 1958 and 1967?

FURTHER READING

When we get to the establishment of the EEC the range of reading extends considerably. A. Milward, *The European Rescue of the Nation State* (London: Routledge, 1992) is still relevant, and a similar but subtly different perspective is taken by A. Moravcsik, *The Choice for Europe: Social Purpose and State Power from Messina to Maastricht* (London: UCL Press, 1998), 86–158.

The standard account of the early years of the EEC is L. Lindberg, *The Political Dynamics of European Economic Integration* (Stanford, Calif.: Stanford University Press; London: Oxford University Press, 1963); but this is rejected by Moravcsik (1998: 158–237).

On the British application in 1961, see P. Ludlow, *Dealing with Britain: The Six and the First UK Application to the EEC* (Cambridge: Cambridge University Press, 1997).

9

After Luxembourg: the 'Dark Ages' of European integration?

The period from the early 1970s to the early 1980s has often been characterized as the doldrums era or the 'Dark Ages' for the Community

(Caporaso and Keeler, 1995: 37)

SUMMARY

If the period up to the 'empty chair' crisis was characterized by relative harmony between member states and steady progress on integration, the decade following the 'Luxembourg Compromise' began with limited expectations. Signs of a revival began with the Hague Conference in 1969, but the revival was limited by a downturn in economic circumstances. In addition, the accession of three new member states, two of which were opposed to supranationalism, made the prospects for further integration bleak. Although there were some achievements, scholars generally saw this period as the low point of European integration.

Introduction

Whereas the 1960s had been an era of high rates of economic growth within a reasonably stable (if militarily threatening) international environment, the 1970s were times of turbulence and flux in the international economic system. Three factors were particularly important: the collapse of the international monetary system (1971); the OPEC oil crisis (1973); the onset of 'stagflation' (Box 9.1, p. 97) producing economic divergence in the EC.

The economic recession that started in 1971, and that really began to bite after the December 1973 rise in the price of oil, made governments more defensive and less inclined to agree to integrative measures that would weaken their ability to preserve domestic markets for domestic producers. As the economic context changed, the pace of European economic integration slowed and there was no advance towards political union. Uncertainty within member states restricted the scope for Commission activism. The Hallstein Commission was initially given tremendous credit for promoting integration in the period following the signing of the Treaties of Rome. However, subsequent reassessments suggested that in fact it had done little beyond fill out the details of

---

Box 9.1 **Stagflation**

- Governments follow several economic policy objectives simultaneously. One consistent objective is economic growth. Another is monetary stability.

- Without growth the economy will stagnate, or worse, sink further and further into recession, with the loss of investment and jobs. Without monetary stability there will be inflation: prices will increase.

- Economists used to believe that there was a trade-off between economic growth and inflation. Policies could either promote economic growth, at the price of higher inflation; or they could focus on restraining inflation at the cost of lower rates of economic growth.

- This belief was based on the writings of John Maynard Keynes, who argued that stagnation and recession in an economy were usually caused by a lack of effective demand. Consumers did not have the money in their pockets to buy goods, and so factories had to reduce production to the level of output that could be sold. That meant laying off workers, which meant that there were even fewer consumers with the money in their pockets to buy goods. There was a vicious downward spiral of insufficient demand leading to production cuts, leading to lower demand.

- To counteract such a tendency, most post-war European governments followed policies of running budget deficits to maintain levels of demand. They spent more than they received in tax revenues. This pumped purchasing power into the economy. If too much purchasing power was injected, demand would run ahead of increased output, and prices would rise. Hence the believed trade-off between economic growth and inflation. On the other hand, if governments refused to increase purchasing power, there was a risk of stagnation and recession. The trick was to get the balance right.

- In post-war Europe different governments made different national choices about where to strike the balance. West German governments were very much at the cautious end of the spectrum, risking lower growth in return for low inflation. French governments were at the other end of the spectrum, tolerating high rates of inflation in order to promote high rates of growth (see Ch. 26, pp. 343–4).

- Following the OPEC decision to raise the price of oil at the end of 1973, the western economies entered a period when the trade-off did not appear to work. They all experienced increased rates of inflation as the price rises for oil fed through into higher industrial production costs and produced rises in the prices of other goods. Their attempts to control inflation by tightening budgetary policy damaged rates of economic growth. They experienced the worst of all worlds: stagnation with inflation, or 'stagflation' as it was known.

agreements that had been made between the member states in the Treaty of Rome.

If this view is correct, then for the Commission to play an active role required a new mandate from the member states. During this period the Commission had four presidents (Box 9.2, p. 98). Neither Jean Rey nor Franco Malfatti had that mandate, and besides they were both preoccupied with the difficult issues involved in combining the three executive bodies of the ECSC, EEC, and Euratom into a single Commission.

When a new mandate was given, at a summit meeting in The Hague in December 1969, it involved completion of the financing arrangements for the EC budget, enlargement to take in Britain and the other applicant states, progress to economic and monetary union, and trying to develop a common foreign policy. The first of these was easily accomplished. The second was successfully carried through for three of the four applicants, but at considerable cost in terms of time and resources for the Commission. Economic and monetary union might have been the mandate that the Commission needed to produce a new impetus to integration, but as Tsoukalis (1977) argued, this decision was more akin to the decision to negotiate on the EEC than it was to the Treaty of Rome itself. As we shall see, this proved to be an intractable issue. Progress on co-ordination of foreign policy was made in a purely intergovernmental framework.

Not only were these issues more difficult in themselves: the overall context of the period was unfavourable to further integration. The Luxem-

---

> ## Box 9.2 **Presidents of the Commission, 1967–1977**
>
> 1967–70   Jean Rey (Belgium)
> 1970–72   Franco Maria Malfatti (Italy)
> 1972   Sicco Mansholt (the Netherlands)
> 1973–77   François-Xavier Ortoli (France)

bourg agreement that ended the French boycott in January 1966 effectively meant that the national veto was retained on all matters that came before the Council of Ministers. Although the Commission had operated with a veto system in the 1960s, the further integration progressed, the more likely it was that particular vested interests would come under challenge, and that individual states would try to block measures. The problem was exacerbated by enlargement, which brought into membership two more states, Britain and Denmark, that were opposed to supranationalism. The cumulative effect of these developments was to ensure that the second decade of the EEC was not marked by the rapid progress on integration that had marked the first decade.

This chapter examines in more detail the Hague summit and its attempt to relaunch the European project; it assesses the degree of success achieved in each of the four main objectives. It also looks briefly at the origins of one of the major institutional innovations of the period, the formalization of the periodic summit meetings of heads of government as the European Council.

The Hague Summit

The resignation of President de Gaulle in April 1969 appeared to free the way to further integration. De Gaulle was succeeded by his former Prime Minister, Georges Pompidou, who soon let it be known that he did not object in principle to British membership.

Also in 1969 there was a change of government in Germany. The SPD, which had been the junior coali-

tion partner to the Christian Democrats for the previous three years, became the larger partner in a coalition with the Free Democrat Party (FDP). Willy Brandt, the new Chancellor, intended to pursue an active policy of improving relations with the Communist bloc, but was anxious to demonstrate that this *Ostpolitik* did not imply any weakening of German commitment to the EC (see Ch. 14, p. 155).

As a result of these two changes, a summit meeting of heads of government was convened in The Hague in December 1969 with the explicit aim of relaunching European integration. This Hague Summit declared the objectives of completion, widening, and deepening. Completion meant tidying up the outstanding business from the 1965 crisis: moving the EC budget from dependence on national contributions to a system of financing from its own resources. Widening meant opening accession negotiations with Britain and other likely applicants. Deepening meant taking the next steps in the process of European integration, specifically in the direction of economic and monetary union and closer political co-operation. The objectives of completion and widening were successfully met; less so the objective of deepening.

Completion

Completion was achieved relatively easily. A system was agreed for the EC to have as its own resources the levies on agricultural products entering the EC under the CAP, and the revenues from the common customs tariff on imports of non-agricultural products from outside of the EC.

There were the usual compromises, but France did accept some budgetary role for the EPA, giving it the right to propose amendments to those parts of the budget that were not classified as 'compulsory expenditure' under the treaties, and to propose modifications to the items of 'compulsory' expenditure. The Council of Ministers, acting by qualified majority, could amend the amendments, and could refuse to agree to the modifications, so in effect it retained the final say on the budget. The distinction between compulsory and non-compulsory expenditure defined expenditure under the CAP as compulsory, so making the bulk of the budget difficult for the EP to amend. Nevertheless, there was an acknowledgement that the EP should have some role in scrutinizing the budget, and there was the prospect that deepening would lead to a larger budget in which agriculture was not so dominant, so there would be more areas of non-compulsory expenditure.

Widening

Negotiations with four applicant states—Britain, Ireland, Denmark, and Norway—opened in June 1970, and were successfully completed by January 1972. Referendums were then held on membership in Ireland, Denmark and Norway. The first two produced clear majorities in favour of entry, but in September 1972 the Norwegian people, not for the last time, rejected membership. In Britain, the Conservative Government of Edward Heath refused to hold a referendum, arguing that it was not a British constitutional instrument; but parliamentary ratification was successfully completed. So on 1 January 1973 the six became nine.

While enlargement achieved the objective of widening the membership of the EC, it was to cause problems as well. The new member states entered at a time when the economic growth of the 1960s had already started to slow, and was about to receive a further setback when the Organization of Petroleum Exporting Countries (OPEC) quadrupled the price of oil in December 1973. Not having experienced the positive benefits of membership, neither the governments nor the peoples of these new member states had the same degree of psychological commitment to the idea of European integration as had those of the original six members. In addition, in Britain in particular there was considerable scepticism about the merits of the EC. Edward Heath was personally strongly committed to membership, but he never managed entirely to convince his own Conservative Party; and Heath was soon displaced as Prime Minister when he lost the general election early in 1974, and Harold Wilson once again formed a Labour government.

While in opposition, the Labour Party had been riven with dissension, and membership of the EC had been a central issue. Several of Wilson's cabinet ministers from 1964–70 were committed to British membership. Wilson himself was also convinced of the necessity of membership. But a majority in the party was still opposed, and the pressure from this majority meant that Wilson could not give unqualified approval to entry when Heath negotiated it. On the other hand his own certainty that membership was necessary, and the importance of the pro-membership minority within the leadership of the party, made it impossible for him to oppose entry. The result was an ingenious compromise of opposition to entry on the terms negotiated by the Conservative government. Labour went into the 1974 election committed to a full renegotiation of the terms of entry with a threat (or promise) of withdrawal if 'satisfactory' terms could not be agreed.

The renegotiation involved serious disruption to other business in the EC, at a time when there were several important issues on the agenda. It also involved a great deal of posturing and nationalist rhetoric from the British government. What it did not involve was any fundamental change in the terms of entry. Nevertheless, the renegotiated terms were put to the British people in a referendum in June 1975, with a recommendation from the government that they be accepted, which they were.

The two-to-one vote in the referendum in favour of Community membership was a passing moment of public favour. Soon the opinion polls were again showing majorities against membership. Britain had joined at a bad time, and the continuing economic difficulties of the country could conveniently be blamed on the EC. Although the Labour opponents of membership had to accept, for the time being, the verdict of the referendum, they lost no opportunity to attack the EC, and Wilson was prepared to accept this if it diverted attention away from his failure to solve the economic difficulties of Britain. He himself continued to take a strongly nationalistic line in EC negotiations, as did his Foreign Secretary, James Callaghan, who succeeded him as Prime Minister in March 1976.

By succeeding in widening its membership, the EC placed another barrier in the way of further integration. Yet it is a mistake to blame Britain alone for blocking further integration. Certainly Britain became an awkward partner; but as Buller (1995: 36) argued: 'everybody consciously attempts to be obstructive every now and again in European negotiations. It is all part and parcel of politics in this kind of environment.' The degree of awkwardness of all member states increased during this period of economic problems.

Deepening

Attempts at deepening co-operation between member states met with limited success. The two main objectives agreed at The Hague were 'economic and monetary union by 1980' and the creation of a common foreign policy.

Economic and Monetary Union (EMU)

This was the logical next step in the building of the EC. Economic union meant that the member states would, at most, cease to follow independent economic policies, and at least would follow co-ordinated policies. This would remove distortions to free competition and would help to make a reality of the common market. Monetary union meant, at most, the adoption of a single Community currency, at least the maintenance of fixed exchange rates between the currencies of the member states.

In 1969 there were the first major realignments of member states' currencies since the EC had started, and the prospect of monetary instability threatened to hinder trade within the common market by introducing an element of uncertainty into import and export deals. In this context, monetary union was seen as a means of making the common market effective.

Following the Hague summit, a Committee was set up under the chairmanship of Pierre Werner, the Prime Minister of Luxembourg, to produce concrete proposals on EMU. It reported within a few months, and in February 1971 the Council of Ministers adopted a programme for the achievement of EMU in stages between 1971 and 1980. The institutional centrepiece of the scheme was the 'snake-in-the-tunnel', an arrangement for approximating the exchange rates of member currencies one to another while holding their value jointly in relation to the US dollar. It was to be accompanied by more determined efforts to bring national economic policies into line, with Finance Ministers meeting at least three times per year to try to co-ordinate policies. Thus there would be progress on both monetary and economic union, the two running in parallel.

The 'snake' did not last long in its original form. It was destroyed by the international monetary crisis that followed the ending of the convertibility of the dollar in August 1971. Only after the Smithsonian agreements of late 1971 had restored some semblance of order to the world monetary system was it possible to attempt once again a joint Community currency arrangement, this time with the participation of the four states that had just completed the negotiation of their entry to the EC. That was in April 1972: but it took under two months for this second snake to break apart. In June the British government had to remove sterling from the system and float it on the international monetary markets. Italy was forced to leave in February 1973. France followed in January 1974, rejoined in July 1975, but was forced to leave again in the spring of 1976. In every case the currency had come under so much speculative pressure that it had proved impossible to maintain its value against the other currencies in the system.

By 1977 the snake had become a very different creature from that which had been envisaged. Of the nine members of the EC, only West Germany, the Benelux states, and Denmark were still members (Ireland had left with Britain, the Irish punt being tied to the pound sterling at that time). In addition, two non-member states, Norway and Sweden, had joined. Yet during 1977 even this snake was under strain, and Sweden was forced to withdraw the krona.

European political co-operation (EPC)

This was the more successful attempt at deepening, ironically since it was only included in the Hague objectives as a concession to France. President Pompidou was dependent for his majority in the French National Assembly on the votes of the Gaullist party of which he was himself a member. De Gaulle had opposed giving budgetary powers to the EP, and Pompidou agreed to this at The Hague. De Gaulle had also opposed British entry to the EC. He had made it clear when a second British application was tabled in May 1967 that there was no point in entering into negotiations, because he would veto British membership. Pompidou had made it equally clear that he was prepared to enter into negotiations, and perhaps even to accept British membership if satisfactory terms could be agreed. Both of these departures from Gaullist orthodoxy were controversial in his own party, and he needed concessions at The

Hague in order to be able to sell the package to this domestic constituency.

One of de Gaulle's pet projects had been to set up a system of intergovernmental political co-operation between the member states of the EC. This was the basis of the Fouchet Plan, which had been under discussion at the same time as the first British application, and had finally collapsed as a result of the French veto on British entry (Ch. 8, p. 91). It was therefore unsurprising that Pompidou should look for a commitment to revive this project as part of the price for his co-operation on completion and widening. It was agreed at The Hague to set up a committee under the chairmanship of Viscount Etienne Davignon, a senior official in the Belgian Foreign Ministry, to devise machinery for co-operation between the member states on foreign policy issues. This committee reported in October 1970, and the system that it recommended became the basis for some successful diplomatic initiatives. Indeed, European Political Co-operation came to be seen as one of the few bright spots in the bleak years of the 1970s.

One of the successes was the formulation of a common position on the Middle East, which allowed the EC to pursue its clear interest in improving trade with the Arab OPEC states in the 1970s, through the Euro-Arab dialogue. In 1980 this common policy culminated in the Venice Declaration, which went further than the United States was prepared to go in recognizing the right of the Palestinians to a homeland. The nine member states were also extremely successful in formulating a common position at the Conference on Security and Co-operation in Europe (CSCE) in Helsinki in 1975, and at the follow-up conferences in Belgrade in 1977, and Madrid in 1982–3. Again the common position adopted by the EC ran somewhat contrary to the position of the United States, which regarded the Helsinki process with some suspicion as running the risk of legitimating Communist rule in eastern Europe. Third, the Community states achieved a high degree of unity in the United Nations, voting together on a majority of resolutions in the General Assembly, and developing a reputation for being the most cohesive group there at a time when group-diplomacy was becoming much more common.

Admittedly there were also failures for the policy of European political co-operation. On balance, though, there were more substantive successes than there were failures. However, all of this remained officially intergovernmental, rather than being rolled up into the more supranational procedures of the EC, so there was a question mark over whether it could be considered to be an advance for the process of European integration. On the other hand, the actual working of the system was less strictly intergovernmental than the formal procedures, a point that is explored further in Chapter 28 (see pp. 395–8).

The European Council

Mid-way through this period, there were again coinciding changes of government in both France and Germany, which strengthened the Franco-German relationship. Georges Pompidou died in office in 1974, and was succeeded by Valéry Giscard d'Estaing, who was not a Gaullist, although he was dependent on the Gaullist party for a majority in the National Assembly. In Germany, Brandt resigned following the discovery that an East German spy had been part of his personal staff, and was succeeded by his former Finance Minister, Helmut Schmidt.

These changes brought to office two strong national leaders who had an excellent *rapport*, and who dominated the EC for the next six years. They were not, though, particularly committed to reviving the process of supranational integration. Their approach was pragmatic rather than ideological, and they were prepared to use any instruments that presented themselves to deal with the problems that their countries faced.

In 1974 Giscard called a summit meeting to discuss his proposal that the EC should institutionalize summit meetings. The smaller member states were suspicious of this proposal, which sounded very Gaullist, but Giscard got strong backing from Schmidt, and it was agreed to hold meetings of the heads of state and government three times every year under the title the 'European Council'. At the same time, as a concession to the fears of those governments who saw in this a weakening of the supranational element of the EC, agreement was reached to hold direct elections to the EP in 1978. The British government was reconciled to this by concessions on the renegotiation of its terms of entry that was taking place at the same time.

Direct elections were not actually held until 1979 because the British government was unable to pass the necessary domestic legislation in time to hold the election in 1978. In the long run the decision to hold direct elections was far from insignificant. In the short to medium term, though, the creation of the European Council was much the more significant outcome of Paris, 1974.

The European Council was from the outset an intergovernmental body. It had no basis in the Treaties until the Single European Act came into force in July 1967. It became the overarching institution of the EU in the Treaty on European Union. Yet to this day it is not directly answerable to the EP, nor subject to judicial review by the ECJ (Ch. 20, pp. 248–50). In the 1970s it was symbolic of a profoundly intergovernmental era in the history of the EU.

Conclusion

In this period, when US hegemony began to falter, the EC had to deal with an increasingly turbulent international environment. The theme of the impact of the wider system on developments within the EC is clearly illustrated here. The retreat into covert national protectionism, to preserve jobs for nationals, was a direct consequence of the shadow that recession cast over the process of European integration. The sceptical attitudes of the British and Danish people to the advantages of European integration were not produced by the recession, but the failure of membership of the EC to produce tangible economic benefits reinforced their prejudices.

Domestic politics were the other side of the faltering of economic growth. In the original six member states, the compromise on the principle of an ever closer union of the peoples of Europe reflected both the shallowness of that commitment among the political elites, and the fact that to retain office they needed to win votes among their own electorate. One of the consistent paradoxes of European integration has been an increasing divorce between politics and policy in the EC. Politics has remained firmly national, while policy has become increasingly Europeanized. This tension existed even in the early stages of the process, and the adverse economic conditions of the 1970s exposed it graphically.

Domestic politics can also be seen at work in the attitude of the British Labour government to the renegotiation of Britain's terms of entry to the EC. The objectives of the renegotiation could have been achieved, perhaps could have more easily been achieved, through the normal process of intergovernmental negotiations within the context of the EC. That the demands were made into a high-profile renegotiation was primarily due to the need of the Prime Minister, Harold Wilson, to satisfy the critics of EC membership within his own party, and to convince the British people that he had won a series of 'victories' on their behalf in the negotiations. The disruption that this approach caused to the functioning of the EC was a high price to pay, but the tension between domestic politics and European integration is again very apparent, as in this case is the primacy of domestic politics.

In this period intergovernmentalism seemed to hold sway. The main innovations of the period were the creation of the European Council, which to a large extent was an attempt to reclaim leadership of the EC for national heads of government, and the beginning of the European Political Co-operation (EPC), an intergovernmental process of co-ordinating foreign policy. The main integrative initiative, the 'snake in the tunnel' system designed to move the EC towards monetary union, collapsed in the face of the global turbulence in currency markets. There was little in the period onto which the neofunctionalists could cling as evidence of their theory being vindicated.

KEY POINTS

The Hague Summit

- Changes of leadership in France and Germany in 1969 appeared to free the way for further European integration. The result was The Hague summit, which declared the objectives of completion, deepening and widening.

- The objectives of completion and widening were successfully met; less so the objective of deepening.

- *Completion* was achieved through allowing the EC to have its own resources for the first time. The EP was also given some budgetary powers.

- *Widening* was achieved through the entry of Britain, Denmark and Ireland into the EC in 1975.

- Deepening of co-operation on foreign policy through European Political Co-operation had some success; less so co-operation on monetary union.

The European Council

- In 1974, the new president of France Giscard d'Estaing called for the institutionalization of summit meetings of EC Heads of State and Government. He received support for this from the new West German president Helmut Schmidt.

- It was agreed that these meetings be institutionalized under the auspices of the European Council and would be held three times each year.

- The creation of the European Council symbolized a profoundly intergovernmental period in the history of European integration.

QUESTIONS

1 To what extent is it accurate to describe the two decades after the Luxembourg Compromise as the 'dark ages' of European integration?

2 What were the difficulties in achieving the objectives of completion, widening, and deepening that were agreed at the Hague Summit in 1969?

3 What lessons could future leaders learn from the early attempts to co-operate on issues of (*a*) monetary union; (*b*) foreign policy?

FURTHER READING

This whole period is dealt with extensively by D. W. Urwin, *The Community of Europe: A History of European Integration since 1945* (London and New York: Longman, 2nd edn. 1995), 146–79. K. Middlemass, *Orchestrating Europe: The Informal Politics of European Union, 1973–1995* (London: Fontana, 1995), 73–110, calls the years between 1973 and 1983 'The Stagnant Decade'. A. Moravcsik, *The Choice for Europe: Social Purpose and State Power from Messina to Maastricht* (London: UCL Press, 1998), 238–313, focuses on monetary co-operation and the European Monetary System. British entry is ably dealt with in C. Lord, *British Entry to the European Community under the Heath Government of 1970–4* (Aldershot: Dartmouth, 1993).

10 The European Community into the 1980s

European integration was considered dead in the water in the 1970s and barely ten years later the European Community was being hailed as the new superpower for the twenty first century.

(Mutimer, 1994: 42)

SUMMARY

The early 1970s marked a low point in European integration, but signs emerged in the late 1970s of the EC turning a corner. Roy Jenkins, a prominent British politician, became President of the Commission in the late 1970s, and managed to enhance the prestige of the institution in ways that carried over to the next decade and his successor. A policy success was recorded with the successful launch of the European Monetary System (EMS). The external reputation of the EC was indicated by further applications for membership from Greece, Portugal, and Spain, although negotiating their terms of entry did rather dominate the attention of the Commission for a long period, and so their application was a problem as well as a sign of revival. A more serious problem was the British government's claim for a rebate on its contributions to the EC budget. Only when this issue had been resolved would it prove possible to build on these signs that the EC had turned the corner and move forward to new initiatives and new developments.

Introduction

During the early 1970s European integration appeared to have stalled. The first signs of a revival appeared in the late 1970s during the Commission presidency of Roy Jenkins. In this period there were three significant signs of revival: the agreement to involve the Commission in the summitry that had come to mark the Franco-German approach to solving common problems; the agreement to open negotiations with Greece on membership; the agreement to set up the European Monetary System (EMS).

Despite these signs of progress, the 1980s began with the EC facing a number of problems that demanded a response. Problems of diminishing European competitiveness in relation to the United States, and increasingly in comparison to Japan, were becoming a major concern to governments. In addition to the ongoing problem of eliminating internal trade barriers, the CAP continued to draw heavily on Community resources and the British government was intent on obtaining a rebate for its contribution to the budget. Finally, there was a third enlargement to incorporate Portugal and Spain, which although a sign of the continued attraction of the EC to non-members, nevertheless took up a large proportion of the time of the Commission.

The Jenkins Commission

The authority of the Commission was strengthened by the presidency of Roy Jenkins between 1977 and 1981. Jenkins was an established political figure with considerable experience in government. He had held all the major posts in the British cabinet other than Prime Minister. As such, his appointment raised great expectations amongst those who regretted the decline in the authority of the Commission. Perhaps not all of those expectations were fulfilled. However, Jenkins did enhance the position of the president, and therefore of the Commission, by securing agreement from the Heads of State and Government that he should be present at meetings of the international economic summits, which had previously been restricted to the leaders of the major industrial nations. This development was strongly resisted by Giscard d'Estaing, but was strongly supported by the smaller member states, who felt excluded from an important economic decision-making forum, and who therefore wished to see the President of the Commission present to act as a spokesperson for the EC as a whole (Jenkins, 1989: 20–2).

Jenkins also undertook a fundamental reform of the internal structure of the Commission, attempting, against considerable opposition from vested interests, to remove some of the causes of the bureaucratization that had been identified as one of the reasons for its decline in influence (Jenkins, 1989: 310, 376). Although he was not completely successful, he did have some impact, and the strong leadership he demonstrated in tackling this problem was probably responsible for earning him the nickname that was a gallicization of his name, but also suggestive of an autocratic manner: 'Roi Jean Quinze'.

The European Monetary System

In the policy field there was one very significant development in the late 1970s. The decision taken at the Brussels European Council in December 1978 to create the European Monetary System (EMS) did not exactly constitute a revival of EMU, but it did provide a basis for a future step in that direction.

As explained in the previous chapter, the snake had by 1977 become a system which embraced only five member states of the EC, together with two non-members. During 1977 even this truncated snake was under pressure from international speculation, and Sweden was forced to withdraw. In this far from promising context, Jenkins launched an initiative that met with a certain amount of initial scepticism about its feasibility even from colleagues within the Commission. In a lecture at the European University Institute in Florence, in October 1977, he called for a new attempt to start the EMU experiment (Jenkins, 1977).

The following year Helmut Schmidt and Giscard d'Estaing came up with a joint proposal for what became the EMS. In July 1978, the European Council meeting in Bremen agreed to pursue the idea, and in December 1978, meeting in Brussels, agreed to create what looked remarkably like another snake. It would be more flexible than its predecessor, allowing wider margins of fluctuation for individual currencies, and it would be accompanied by the creation of a new European currency unit (ecu). The ecu would take its value from a basket of the national currencies of the member states, and it would be used in transactions within the EMS. A stock of ecus would be created by each member state depositing 20 per cent of its gold and 20 per cent of its foreign currency reserves with a European Monetary Fund (EMF). If a government was having difficulty in holding the value of its currency in relation to the other currencies in the system, it could apply to the EMF for short-term loans, and later if necessary for medium-term loans, up to a predetermined limit, from the central reserve. The loans would be denominated in ecus. It was hoped that ecus would gradually become the normal means of settlement of international debts between EMS members, thus forming the basis of a common Community currency.

In addition to France and West Germany, the Benelux states and Denmark supported the EMS. After initial hesitation, Italy and Ireland agreed to become full participants. But Britain declined to put sterling into the joint float against the dollar, although it was included in the basket from which the value of the ecu was calculated. Despite the scepticism that had greeted Jenkins's initiative, the EMS did get off the ground, and this time the snake did hold together, so that the scheme must be judged a relative success in the context of the overall history of attempts to move towards EMU (see also Ch. 26, pp. 344–7).

The Mediterranean enlargements

In 1974 two significant events took place in the Mediterranean. Turkey invaded Cyprus, and a revolution in Portugal overthrew the right-wing Caetano government. Each led to an application for membership of the EC. Subsequently, political developments in Spain led to a Spanish application.

Greece had concluded an Association Agreement with the EC in 1964. This had envisaged eventual membership, but in 1967 Greece entered a period of military dictatorship which precluded an application. The inability of the Greek military to prevent the Turkish occupation of Cyprus precipitated the collapse of the dictatorship, and in June 1975 the new democratic Greek government sought membership of the EC as a means of consolidating democracy. In January 1976 the Commission issued a very cautious Opinion on the ability of Greece to adapt to membership, but political and strategic considerations led the Council of Ministers to accept the application and order the opening of negotiations. Democracy had to be shored up; but also Greece had to be prevented from swinging to the far left and reorienting itself towards the Communist bloc. The negotiation of terms of entry for Greece was not easy, and it took up a great deal of the time of the Commission between July 1976 and May 1979, when the Accession Treaty was signed. Nevertheless, the launching of the negotiations gave a new role to the Commission and put it back at the centre of the EC.

An application from Portugal followed the Greek application in March 1977. Again there were political and strategic reasons for accepting it. The Portuguese revolution threatened to run out of the control of the pro-capitalist forces, and to fall into the hands of extreme left-wing groups that would have emphasized relations with the Third World. The Socialist International, with the German SPD taking a lead, provided support to the Portuguese Socialist Party (PSP), and so when the PSP was elected to government in 1976 there was not much doubt that it would apply for EC membership, nor that the application would be accepted.

Similar political and strategic considerations applied in July 1977 to the acceptance of an application from Spain following the death of the dictator Franco and the restoration of democracy there. In the Spanish case, membership of the EC was held out as a bonus if it decided also to join the NATO alliance. Given Spain's strategic position in the Mediterranean, this was a vital interest of the western alliance.

Whereas the first of these applications stimulated a revival of the role of the Commission, handling three sets of difficult negotiations became a problem, and the Portuguese and Spanish Accession Treaties were not signed until 1985.

The British budget rebate

Another issue that caused problems for the EC in the 1980s was the British budgetary rebate. Although budget contributions had been central to the renegotiation, already by 1976, while transitional arrangements still limited the extent of its contributions, Britain was the third biggest net contributor to the EC budget, behind Germany and Belgium. In 1977, still under transitional arrangements, the British net contribution was the second highest to that of Germany. By mid-1978 it was becoming apparent that once the transitional period of membership ended in 1980, Britain would become the largest net contributor to the budget.

This situation arose because:

1. Britain imported more goods, especially foodstuffs, from outside the EC than did other member states, and therefore paid more in import levies.

2. Low direct taxes meant that British consumers spent more in proportion to the relative wealth of the country, and Britain therefore contributed more to the budget in VAT receipts;

3. Payments out of the budget were dominated by the CAP, and Britain had a small and efficient farming sector which meant that it received less than states with larger agricultural economies.

The developing position was unacceptable to the Labour government. The Foreign Secretary, David Owen, told the House of Commons that the situation whereby 'the United Kingdom has the third lowest per capita gross domestic product in the Community' yet was already the second highest net contributor to the budget, 'cannot be good for the Community any more than it is for the United Kingdom', and promised that the government would 'be working to achieve a better balance, especially in relation to agricultural expenditure, to curb the excessive United Kingdom contribution' (*Hansard*, 14 Nov. 1978, col. 214).

In fact the Labour government never had the opportunity to work for a better balance because it lost office in the June 1979 election to the Conservatives under Margaret Thatcher. The new government soon took up the same theme concerning the budget. Shortly after coming into office, Sir Geoffrey Howe, the Chancellor of the Exchequer, announced that the size of the problem was far greater than the Conservatives had realized while in opposition, and something would have to be done about it urgently.

Margaret Thatcher raised the issue at her first European Council in Strasbourg in June 1979, soon after her election victory. Her presentation there was moderate and reasonable, and the complaint was offset by an announcement on the first day of the meeting that Britain would deposit its share of gold and foreign currency reserves with the European Monetary Co-operation Fund that had been set up to administer the EMS. The move was widely interpreted as a sign that sterling would soon join the exchange rate mechanism of the EMS. Discussion of the budgetary issue at Strasbourg was brief and limited to agreeing a procedure for analysing the problem. The Commission was asked to prepare a report by September; this would be discussed by Finance Ministers, then revised in time for the next European Council in Dublin in late November.

At that November 1979 Dublin European Council Thatcher adopted an entirely different tone. She insisted that the Commission proposal of a rebate of £350 million was unacceptable, and that she would not accept less than £1 billion. The French said that they would not agree to more than £350 million, which the British would have to accept as full and final settlement of their claim. This provoked an argument that lasted ten hours, in the course of which Thatcher upset her partners by her uncompromising demands for what she insensitively described as Britain's 'own money back'.

This was the tone that Thatcher persistently adopted in negotiations for the next four-and-a-half years. During that time several temporary abatements of the British contributions were agreed, but a permanent settlement eluded all efforts to bridge the gap between what the British Prime Minister demanded and what the other member states were prepared to pay. British tactics became increasingly obstructionist on other issues, and relations with the other states became increasingly strained. Relations reached their nadir in May 1982. Britain was blocking agreement on agricultural price increases for 1982–3, linking agreement to a permanent settlement of the budgetary dispute. Finally, the Belgian presidency called a majority vote on the agricultural prices. Britain protested that this breached the Luxembourg Compromise, but the vote went ahead and was passed. Several of the other states, though, appeared shocked at their own behaviour. It seemed apparent that a settlement of the British dispute was necessary before progress could be made in other areas.

Leadership changes

The confluence of challenges facing the EC at the beginning of the 1980s coincided with the appointment of Gaston Thorn to the Commission presidency in 1981. Member States generally welcomed Thorn's appointment. Although he took over at a difficult time, there was a feeling that he was uniquely well qualified for the job, as few people had a wider experience of the EC. Early in his presidency there were two significant changes among the national leaderships with which Thorn would have to work.

In May 1981 François Mitterrand defeated Giscard d'Estaing in the French presidential election. This result was consolidated a month later by a victory for Mitterrand's Socialist party in elections to the National Assembly. The change broke apart the Franco-German axis because Helmut Schmidt had less in common with the Socialist president than he had with the conservative Giscard. In particular, the Socialist government came into office committed to tackling unemployment rather than emphasizing low inflation as its predecessor government had done. However, a U-turn in economic policy in 1983 brought France more into line with the neo-liberal and deregulationist tendencies already evident in West Germany and Britain.

The second change in political leadership came in West Germany itself. Although the SPD/FDP won the 1980 Federal election, dissension within the coalition was increasing in the face of the economic problems the country was facing. Within the SPD, the left-wing and the trade unionist membership were demanding some measures of reflation to relieve unemployment, which in 1981 stood at 1¼ million. But at the same time, the FDP was returning to its basic principles of economic liberalism, represented most strikingly by the Economics Minister, Otto von Lamsdorff. The clash between the two parties over economic affairs led to the eventual breakdown of the coalition. The FDP changed partners and allowed the CDU/CSU into office, with Helmut Kohl, the CDU leader, as chancellor.

Kohl emphasized continuity in his foreign policy, but it was expected that he would develop a warmer relationship with Thatcher than Schmidt had. This was partly because the milder personality of Kohl was less likely to clash with the forthright manner of the British Prime Minister, and partly because of a mutual interest in attacking socialism.

Moves to revive the EC

By the start of the 1980s there was an acceptance within both national governments and the Commission that the response to challenges facing the EC required, in part at least, institutional reform to facilitate easier and more effective decision-making.

The first response came in September 1981 from the foreign ministers of Germany and Italy, and was known as the Genscher–Colombo Plan. This plan called for a new European charter which would supersede the Treaties of Paris and Rome as the basic constitutional document of the Communities, and would bring European political co-operation,

together with the EC, under the joint direction of the European Council. This would only be a formalization of the existing situation, although Genscher and Colombo also wished to improve the decision-making ability of the Council of Ministers by increasing the use of majority voting, to expand the functions of the European Parliament, and to intensify foreign policy co-operation in security matters.

The plan received a cool response in the Council, as had an earlier proposal led by Altiero Spinelli— now a senior figure in the European Parliament—

which sought to diminish the institutional position of the Council in favour of the Parliament and Commission. Yet while these two sets of proposals made no immediate impact on integration, they contributed to the European Council beginning a new round of negotiations on the question of political union and possible revision of the treaties.

On the economic front, attempts by Thorn and his Vice-President and Commissioner for the Internal Market, Karl-Heinz Narjes, to highlight the problems faced by industrialists in trading across national borders within the EC met with little response from national governments. Governments were determined to reserve jobs for their own nationals (read 'voters') by tolerating, or even themselves erecting, non-tariff barriers to trade, and by giving public contracts exclusively to national companies. Yet Thorn, Narjes, and particularly Vice-President Etienne Davignon, the Commissioner for Industrial Policy, laid the groundwork for the agreement that was concluded under the following Delors presidency to free the internal market of all these obstacles by the end of 1992.

Thorn and Narjes maintained a constant propaganda campaign against barriers to a genuine internal market. This campaign had an effect in raising awareness of the issue, especially when it was taken up by a group of Members of the European Parliament (MEPs) who called themselves the Kangaroo Group because they wanted to facilitate trade that would 'hop over' national boundaries. The work of Davignon was less public, but possibly more influential in persuading governments to accept change. He called into existence a network of leading industrialists involved in the European electrical and electronics industries to discuss their common problems in the face of US and Japanese competition. Out of these discussions came the Esprit programme of collaborative research in advanced technologies; but more significantly there also arose the European Round Table of Industrialists, which was to become an influential pressure group pushing governments into taking measures to liberalize the internal market of the EC.

Fontainebleau

The European Council meeting at Fontainebleau in June 1984 marked a turning point in European integration. First of all, the summit resolved the British budgetary question, in the context of an agreement at Fontainebleau to cut back on CAP expenditure and to increase the Community's own resources through an increase in VAT contributions by member states. The agreement settled five years of dispute and opened the door for reform of the CAP.

The meeting also agreed to set up an *ad hoc* committee on institutional affairs, which came to be known by the name of its Chair, James Dooge of Ireland. The report of this committee became the basis for the institutional changes that were later to be made, alongside the fundamental policy commitment to completion of the internal market.

Conclusion

The first signs of the revival of the EC were ambiguous. The initiative to launch the EMS did not mark a new commitment to further European integration. Whatever Jenkins's motives for proposing a revival of monetary union, the EMS fell well short of being that. It was actually a response by West Germany to the threat posed to German exports by the US policy of benign neglect of the external value of the dollar. The themes that are relevant here are the impact of the global system on developments in the EC, and the defence of national interest by the larger member states. Later the EMS was to form the basis on which a new attempt at monetary union could be built, but this illustrates another consistent theme of the story: that steps taken in pursuit of national interest can often have unintended consequences that favour further European integration.

The continued decline of US hegemony drew the

EC into playing a larger international role, and this was the main motive behind the Mediterranean enlargements of the EC in this period. The development of the EC was still being played out against the background of the cold war, and it was a fear that political instability might open the way for Communist influence which inspired the leading states of the EC to push for the membership of Greece, Portugal, and Spain despite the obvious economic weaknesses of these states. Again, the unintended consequences of these decisions were arguably to advance European integration, because the new member states became a powerful lobby for the extension of the structural funds of the EC, which eventually accounted for one-third of the EC budget, second only to the CAP.

The influence of domestic politics came through again in the British dispute over the budget rebate. Margaret Thatcher used the technique that Harold Wilson had adopted very successfully in the renegotiation of British terms of entry. She adopted a confrontational and nationalistic tone, which played well to a domestic audience, but caused disruption to the smooth operation of the EC.

At the same time there were the first stirrings of a more active role for the Commission in this period. The agreement to allow the President of the Commission to attend meetings of the economic summits reflected the concerns of smaller member states that the era of summitry might become the era of large states dominating smaller states. Again, a step that was negotiated from a viewpoint of defending national interest had positive implications for the strength of supranationalism.

On the other hand, the internal reforms by Jenkins indicated the problem of bureaucratization of the Commission, a problem that Jenkins did not manage to solve. Nevertheless, the increasing activism of the Thorn Commission, which is often unfairly treated as ineffective, showed the extent to which the presidency of Jenkins had marked a turning point in the self-confidence of the Commission, and paved the way for Delors.

KEY POINTS

The Jenkins Commission

- As Commission President, Roy Jenkins managed to secure a place at international economic summits for the Commission for the first time.

The European Monetary System

- Following a call from Jenkins to renew attempts at monetary union, the European Council passed a proposal by Schmidt and Giscard for a European Monetary System (EMS) in 1978.

- The new EMS would be more flexible than its predecessor, but Britain declined to put sterling in a joint float against the US dollar.

The Mediterranean enlargements

- Following a difficult period of negotiations, the accession of Greece to the Community was agreed in 1979. Portugal and Spain, who applied later, were eventually accepted into the EC in 1985.

The British budget rebate

- Britain was set to be the largest net contributor to the Community budget by 1980. The tactics of the Thatcher government over the issue jeopardized progress in other areas until a satisfactory solution was found.

Leadership changes

- The appointment of Gaston Thorn to the Commission presidency in 1981 coincided with important leadership changes in France and Germany.

Moves to revive the EC

- The challenges facing the EC in the early 1980s demanded a response. The Genscher–Colombo plan proposed institutional reforms that received a cool response from the Council. However, Commission plans for freeing the internal market began to win over national governments.

- The resolution of the British budgetary question at Fontainebleau allowed for progress on both the internal market and institutional reform.

QUESTIONS

1 Assess the significance of the Jenkins Commission to the subsequent revival of European integration in the 1980s.

2 Assess the significance of the EMS in the process of Economic and Monetary Union.

3 What were the difficulties involved in expanding the EC to include Greece, Portugal and Spain?

4 In the early 1980s, why were proposals on institutional reform less acceptable to national governments than proposals to free the internal market?

5 What was the significance for European integration of the leadership changes that occurred in 1981?

6 To what extent was the Thatcher government justified in disrupting progress in other policy areas to secure a budgetary refund?

FURTHER READING

For an insider account of the early part of this period see R. Jenkins, *European Diary, 1977–1981* (London: Collins, 1989). The British budget rebate issue is explained more fully in S. George, *An Awkward Partner: Britain in the European Community* (Oxford: Oxford University Press, 1998), 137–65. D. W. Urwin, *The Community of Europe: A History of European Integration since 1945* (London and New York: Longman, 2nd edn. 1995), 195–228 puts particular emphasis on the problems of enlargement and the initiatives for political integration such as the Genscher-Colombo plan.

11 The Single European Act

[T]he SEA . . . had potential for revolution, suggesting a shift in the existing balance of power away from the member states towards the Community institutions.

(Urwin, 1995: 231)

SUMMARY

After the relative stagnation of European integration in the 1970s and into the start of the 1980s, the mid-1980s marked a turning point. When a new Commission assumed office in 1985 under the presidency of Jacques Delors it offered a visible symbol of a new start under dynamic leadership. Delors championed the scheme for a new integrative push through the means of freeing the single market. This initiative was named the '1992 programme'. This economic project was linked to a programme of institutional reform that would have far-reaching implications for the way in which the EC made decisions, although those implications were not all immediately apparent.

The Single European Act marked a key moment in the history of European integration. It was the collective response of European Community states to the global economic challenges of the late twentieth century and marked a new phase in European integration. By the end of the decade the EC had cast off the image of Eurosclerosis and was demonstrating a dynamism that had hardly seemed possible five years earlier.

Introduction

In the last chapter the first signs were identified of the EC making a new start after the stagnation of integration in the 1970s. The June 1984 Fontaine-bleau agreement on British budget contributions was a very significant development, clearing out of the way an issue that had dominated attention for the previous five years and opening the way to new initiatives. These new initiatives began at Fontaine-bleau itself, with the creation of the Dooge Committee on institutional reform. A more dramatic initiative was made early in 1985 by the new president of the European Commission, Jacques Delors (see Box 11.1, p. 115). He proposed that the EC should set itself the target of removing a whole series of barriers to free trade and free movement of capital and labour that had grown up during the 1970s. This project would be pursued with a target date for completion of the end of 1992.

The single market programme was economic in focus, but it was intended to have far-reaching political consequences. From the outset it was linked to certain institutional reforms, particularly the introduction of qualified majority voting (QMV) into the proceedings of the Council of Ministers, thus overcoming the blockage to progress imposed by the veto system. It was also intended to revive the momentum of integration, because Delors believed that the freeing of the internal market would lead to spillover into other policy sectors. In particular he believed that it would not be feasible to have the single market without strengthening the degree of social protection available to workers at the EC level; and that the single market would set up a momentum towards monetary union.

Despite British reluctance to see these further developments, the Thatcher government wanted to

---

Box 11.1 Jacques Delors

Jacques Delors was born in Paris in 1925. His father was a middle-ranking employee of the Bank of France, and the son went to work for the Bank straight from school. The young Delors was active in Catholic social movements, and became a devotee of the doctrine of 'personalism', a form of Christian socialism associated with the philosopher Emmanual Mounier. Delors was also an active trade unionist. In the 1960s he moved from the Bank to a senior position in the French Planning Commission, which had been created by Jean Monnet. Although he was an adviser to the Gaullist Prime Minister Jacques Chaban-Delmas at the end of the 1960s and in the early 1970s, he subsequently joined the reformed Socialist party of François Mitterrand, and was elected to the European Parliament in 1979 as a Socialist. When Mitterrand became President of France in 1981, Delors became Finance Minister in the Socialist government. He was instrumental in moving the government away from policies of economic expansion that were not working and were undermining the value of the currency. He played a crucial role in the negotiation of the 1983 realignment of currencies within the exchange rate mechanism of the European Monetary System, and won the respect of the German government in the process. In 1985, with strong support from Chancellor Kohl of Germany as well as from Mitterrand, he became President of the European Commission, a post that he retained for ten years.

---

see the single market programme itself put into place. Subsequently the British Prime Minister tried to block the further developments, but in the meantime the success of Delors's initiative revived the self-confidence of the Commission, which had already begun to recover under Jenkins and Thorn. It also led to a revival of theoretical interpretations of the EC that emphasized the role of the Commission and other supranational actors, thus rekindling the supranational–intergovernmental debate about the nature of the EC, which had lain dormant during the 'doldrums years' of the 1970s and early 1980s.

This chapter examines the initiative taken by Delors, and the SEA itself. It looks at the provisions of the SEA, particularly the institutional reforms that it introduced, and then briefly at two issues that are discussed in more detail in Chapter 25 (see pp. 324–40), the debate over the role of the Commission in getting it accepted and problems of implementing what had been agreed.

1985: a watershed year

Delors had been Finance Minister in the 1981–3 French Socialist governments, which had tried to tackle the problem of unemployment in France by reflating the economy. The result had been a serious balance of payments crisis as the reflation did little to restore full employment, but did suck in imports. There had been two views on how to respond to this. One had been to withdraw from the European Monetary System, and to impose import controls, in contravention of France's EC obligations. The other, of which Delors had been the strongest advocate, had been to revert to national policies of balancing the budget by cutting public expenditure, and to develop a European solution to the problem of unemployment (Ch. 15, pp. 173–4). That view had prevailed, and Delors's advocacy of it made him acceptable to both Germany and Britain as a nominee for the Commission presidency. It had been tacitly accepted that the presidency of the Commission would be given to a German candidate if the Federal Government wished to take it up; but Kohl chose to throw his weight behind Delors.

The Brussels European Council of February 1985 instructed the Commission to draw up a timetable for the completion of the single market. Within a few months of taking office, the British Commissioner for Trade and Industry, Lord Cockfield, produced a White Paper listing the barriers that needed to be removed for there to be a genuine single market inside the EC. This listed some 300 separate

measures, later reduced to 279, covering the harmonization of technical standards, opening up public procurement to intra-EC competition, freeing capital movements, removing barriers to free trade in services, harmonizing rates of indirect taxation and excise duties, and removing physical frontier controls between member states. The list was accompanied by a timetable for completion, with a final target date of the end of 1992.

At the Milan European Council in June 1985 the objectives of the White Paper and the timetable for its completion by the end of 1992 were agreed by the Heads of Government. A massive publicity campaign would be organized to promote the project. It was also agreed, against the protests of the British Prime Minister, to set up an Intergovernmental Conference (IGC) to consider what changes were necessary to the original treaties in order to achieve the single market, and to consider other changes to the institutional structure that had been recommended by an *ad hoc* committee under James Dooge which had been set up at the Fontainebleau European Council a year earlier. This IGC drew up what became the Single European Act (SEA), which was agreed by the heads of government at the Luxembourg European Council in December 1985, and eventually ratified by national parliaments to come into effect in July 1987. Thus was born the 1992 programme, which did more than any initiative since the Treaties of Rome to revitalize the process of European integration.

The Single European Act

Although modest in the changes that it introduced in comparison with the hopes of federalists in the European Parliament and within some member states (particularly Italy), the SEA rejuvenated the process of European integration. The intention of the SEA appeared relatively modest, seeking to complete the objective of a common market set out in the Treaty of Rome. By the early 1980s, the need for member states to compete in world markets, especially against the United States and Japan, was an overriding concern. A single European market would increase the specialization of production at company level and allow greater economies of scale, leading to more competitive firms. The issue of monetary union as an accompaniment to the single market was not addressed at this stage of developments.

While ostensibly an economic project, in its proposals for institutional change, the SEA:

had potential for revolution, suggesting a shift in the existing balance of power away from the member states towards the Community institutions. The radical political implications of the economic target of a common market—the single internal market—were there for all to read in the document ... while the issues of political and economic integration are closely interlinked, the parallel debates tended to muddy the waters of each   (Urwin, 1995: 231).

In retrospect at least, the political implications of the SEA are clear (Box 11.2, p. 117). At the time, though, the SEA was largely seen as a mechanism for implementing the commitment made at Milan to achieve the single market. This goal was not contested by member states. Moreover, the Commission was concerned with emphasizing the practical rather than the political implications of aspects of the reform. Only in the final section of the White Paper did the Commission refer to the wider implications of the internal market project, acknowledging that 'Just as the Customs Union had to precede Economic Integration, so Economic Integration has to precede European Unity' (European Commission, 1985: 55). Despite the political implications of the single market being deliberately understated by the Commission, the proposed institutional reforms proved the most controversial aspect of the project.

Institutional reforms

While ostensibly a project to complete the single market, the SEA contained important institutional reforms which were to be of lasting significance for European integration (Box 11.2, p. 117). In particular, the SEA introduced qualified majority voting (QMV) in the Council of Ministers. QMV was designed to speed-up decision-making by reducing substantially the number of areas in which individual states could reject progress by use of their veto. QMV would apply to measures related to the freeing of the internal market, although certain measures, including the harmonization of indirect taxes and the removal of physical controls at borders, were excluded at British insistence. Without the extension of QMV, the internal market project was likely to be delayed and possibly lost through inter-governmental disputes.

The codification of the commitment to QMV as a formal amendment of the founding treaties, and as part of a potentially wider reform of the institutional procedures for making decisions, was resisted strongly by Prime Minister Thatcher. The whole issue of institutional reform was one of several where the

---

Box 11: 2 **The political provisions of the SEA**

- It introduced qualified majority voting (QMV) for single-market measures.

- It increased the legislative powers of the European Parliament in areas where QMV applied.

- It incorporated European political co-operation (EPC) into a treaty text for the first time.

- It incorporated in the Preamble a reiteration of the objective of an economic and monetary union.

- It incorporated in the Preamble a commitment by the member states to 'transform relations as a whole among their States into a European Union'.

British government differed from most of its continental European partners. Mrs Thatcher insisted at Milan that no institutional reform, and so no IGC, was necessary. However, it seems that she was persuaded by her Foreign Secretary, Sir Geoffrey Howe, and her adviser on European affairs, David Williamson, that unless a legally binding commitment were made to an element of majority voting in the Council of Ministers the measures necessary to implement the Cockfield White Paper would never be agreed.

The freeing of the internal market was supported by all the member states, and it coincided with the belief of the British Prime Minister in universal free trade. On the other hand, it was also an excellent issue for the new Commission to make into the centrepiece of its programme. As Helen Wallace (1986: 590) explained:

The internal market is important not only for its own sake, but because it is the first core Community issue for over a decade . . . which has caught the imagination of British policy-makers and which is echoed by their counterparts elsewhere . . . The pursuit of a thoroughly liberalized domestic European market has several great advantages: it fits Community philosophy, it suits the doctrinal preferences of the current British Conservative government, and it would draw in its train a mass of interconnections with other fields of action.

Whereas doctrinal preferences may be sufficient explanation for British support of the internal market project, the support of other member states perhaps needs a little further explanation.

One important factor was the support given to the freeing of the market by European business leaders, some of whom formed the European Round Table of Industrialists in 1983 to press for the removal of the barriers to trade that had developed. This pressure occurred in the context of a generalized concern amongst governments about the sluggish recovery of the European economies from the post-1979 recession in comparison with the vigorous growth of the US and Japanese economies. In particular, the turning of the tide of direct foreign investment, so that by the mid-1980s there was a net flow of investment funds from western Europe to the United States, augured badly both for the employment situation in Europe in the future, and for the ability of European industry to keep abreast of the technological developments that were revolutionising production processes.

It was in response to the worry that Europe would become permanently technologically dependent on the United States and Japan that President Mitterrand proposed his EUREKA initiative for promoting pan-European research and development in the advanced technology industries. This concern also lay behind the promotion by the new Commission of framework programmes for research and development in such fields as information technology, bio-technology, and telecommunications (Sharp and Shearman, 1987). But when European industrialists were asked what would be most likely to encourage them to invest in Europe they replied that the most important factor for them would be the creation of a genuine continental market such as they experienced in the United States.

It was therefore in an attempt to revive investment and economic growth that governments other than Britain embraced the free-market programme. The pressure to break out of the short-termism that had prevented the EC from making progress in the 1970s and early 1980s came partly from interest groups, but also from the economic situation that faced governments. The EC, as only one part of the global capitalist economy, was seeing investment flow away from it to other parts of the global economy, and was already being left behind in rates of economic growth and in technological advance by rival core-areas within the system. It was a calculation of the common national interests of the member states that led them to agree a new contract, in the form of a White Paper and the Single European Act.

The role of the Delors Commission

The emphasis that Delors put on the single market was part of a carefully considered strategy. During the autumn of 1984 he considered a variety of candidates for the role of the 'Big Idea' that would relaunch European integration (Grant, 1994: 66). Initially attracted to completion of EMU, following the relative success of the EMS, Delors ultimately decided that the idea of completing the internal market was the best starting point. This project was firmly within the boundaries of integration established by the Treaty of Rome. Even more important, perhaps, with policies of market liberalization adopted by key member states, the single market project stood the best chance of winning the support of even the most Euro-sceptic governments, Britain's in particular. Moreover, successful completion of the 1992 project had implications for a wide range of Community policies. Most notably, the project would inevitably prompt reconsideration of the advantages of monetary union as a complement to the single market and would also lead to demands for strengthening EC social and regional policies from the member states most likely to be adversely affected by the internal market.

Few dispute that the Delors Commission played a pivotal role in developing and pushing forward the single market programme as a means to the end of ever closer union. The emergence of the programme and eventually the drive towards full monetary union and the adoption of a social charter, all bore the hallmarks of a plan devised in Paris in the light of the failures of the 1981–4 French economic experiment. Delors and the British Commissioner Cockfield worked together closely on developing and promoting the project. Cockfield faced accusations from the British Prime Minister that he had 'gone native' in his support for wide-ranging European integration, and it was no great surprise when Thatcher chose not to renominate him to the Commission in 1988.

Under Delors the Commission regained the high profile it had under Hallstein, and, irrespective of whether the Hallstein Commission had been the genuine motor of integration, the Delors Commission certainly appeared to play that role by the 1980s. But it was only able to play that role because of the support Delors received from Mitterrand, and because of the diplomatic skill of Mitterrand himself in ensuring that other member states, Germany above all, were carried along with the plan.

Implementing the SEA

While national governments were initially slow to implement the measures detailed in the SEA, businesses began to take advantage of the emerging opportunities offered by the 1992 project. Company mergers accelerated to take advantage of EC-wide economies of scale. The business publication *The Economist* (1988) noted that in 1987 there were 300 major mergers compared with only sixty-eight in the previous year. In comparison, by November 1987 the Council of Ministers had adopted only sixty-four of the measures set out in the White Paper (Dinan, 1994: 150).

The core problem of implementation related to accompanying measures to the SEA, in particular, the demands of southern member states for adequate compensatory mechanisms to balance the adverse effects of market liberalization. While a number of member states were reluctant to commit greater resources to Community regional aid, ultimately these demands had to be satisfied to protect the 1992 programme. Subsequently, at the Brussels European Council of February 1988, Heads of Government agreed to a doubling in the allocations to the structural funds to promote greater cohesion as a complement to the internal market.

Conclusion

This was the period in which the EC was revitalized, and with it the theory of neofunctionalism. The debates surrounding the origins of the single market programme are considered further in Chapter 25 below (see pp. 330–3). Interpretations of the relevant importance of different factors certainly vary, but there is a considerable body of analysis that attributes a central role to the European Commission under Jacques Delors, and to the European Round Table of Industrialists. Two of the actors whom neofunctionalists had predicted would be influential appeared to be influential in this landmark decision:

the Commission and transnational business interests. Neofunctionalism also received support from another development: the speed with which businesses responded to the announcement of the 1992 programme to conclude mergers and announce new investment plans vindicated the argument that changed circumstances would lead to changed attitudes and behaviour.

However, the interpretations that emphasized the role of supranational actors did not go along with neofunctionalism in seeing spillover as the dynamic force that produced the 1992 programme. There is general agreement that global economic developments were the catalyst for the acceptance of the single market. The remarkable economic recovery of the United States and Japan from the second oil crisis contrasted starkly with the sluggishness of the west European economies. Not only was there a marked conjunctural difference in performance: the success

of the United States and Japan was based on the adoption of new technologies into their production processes that threatened to leave western Europe with an obsolete industrial base unless investment could be revived.

In exploiting the problems that the changed global economic environment posed for national governments, Delors acted as a 'policy entrepreneur', a concept that is explored further in Chapter 25 below (see pp. 328–31 and 335). However, he did not mobilize the Commission to support this role by carrying through the reforms that had eluded Jenkins. It remained a bureaucratized and fragmented body. Rather than reform its procedures, Delors chose to short-circuit them, using an informal network centred on his personal *cabinet* as the agents for pushing through the necessary initiatives. This was to store up problems for the future that would lead directly to a substantial crisis in the late 1990s.

KEY POINTS

1985: a watershed year

- In February 1985, the European Council instructed the Delors Commission to draw up a timetable for the completion of the single market. In June 1985, the Council agreed to the Commission's proposals and the 1992 timetable for completion.

- An IGC on institutional reform, drew up what became the Single European Act.

The Single European Act

- The SEA rejuvenated the process of European integration.

- In retrospect, the broad political significance of the institutional reforms of the SEA became clear. At the time, most actors and observers saw the SEA in the context of the completion of the single market

- While the British government was instinctively averse to QMV, this was accepted as necessary to achieve the completion of the single market by 1992

- On the whole, governments were persuaded of the need of the SEA by the desire to revive investment and economic growth in the context of greater competition from and technological dependence on Japan and the US.

- For Delors the single market programme was the 'Big Idea' that would relaunch European integration

- While the Commission regained its high profile through the single market project and played a key role in its development, the support of key member governments was essential to its ultimate success.

- Companies were quick to take advantage of the opportunities provided by the single market project, but implementation of SEA measures varied across member states. However, the doubling of the structural funds to compensate poorer member states for market liberalization was a major breakthrough on this.

QUESTIONS

1 Why was completion of the internal market the most appropriate issue for relaunching European integration in the 1980s?

2 Explain the significance of the Delors Commission in the relaunch of European integration in the 1980s

3 What were the problems involved in implementing the provisions of the SEA?

4 To what extent were national governments unaware of the political provisions of the SEA?

FURTHER READING

C. Grant, *Delors: Inside the House that Jacques Built* (London: Nicolas Bealey Publishing) and G. Ross, *Jacques Delors and European Integration* (Cambridge: Polity Press) both give accounts of what went on within the Delors Commission.

For the analysis of the Single European Act, begin with D. R. Cameron, 'The 1992 Initiative: Causes and Consequences', in A. Sbragia (ed.), *Euro-Politics: Institutions and Policymaking in the 'New' European Community* (Washington, DC: Brookings Institution, 1992), 23–74, and continue with W. Sandholtz and J. Zysman, '1992: Recasting the European Bargain', *World Politics* 95–128. A. Moravcsik, *The Choice for Europe: Social Purpose and State power from Messina to Maastricht* (London: UCL Press, 1998), 314–78, or his chapter 'Negotiating the Single European Act', in R. O. Keohane and S. Hoffmann (eds.), *The New European Community: Decisionmaking and Institutional Change* (Boulder, San Francisco, and Oxford: Westview Press), 41–84.

12 Maastricht and beyond

More than the SEA, the Maastricht treaty helps to clarify the rules of the game and the international competénces *of the emergent Euro-polity.*

(Schmitter, 1996: 1)

SUMMARY

The success of the 1992 project revived European integration. However, the difficult issue of monetary union had yet to be addressed. Following the collapse of Communism in eastern Europe and the reunification of Germany, the future of European integration was once again brought into focus. The result was the Treaty on European Union, signed in Maastricht in December 1991, which brought agreement on moves towards a single currency and further institutional reforms. The subsequent problems over ratifying the Treaty within member states highlighted the gap that had emerged between elite and mass attitudes to integration generally and the single currency specifically.

Introduction

The 1992 project was a tremendous success. It led to a revival of investment in Europe, which had been stagnating. Companies anticipated the arrival of the single market by engaging in cross-border mergers and joint production arrangements. The EC experienced a wave of business euphoria, which ensured that the work of public officials in actually agreeing the necessary measures did not waver. By the target date of the end of 1992, 260 out of the consolidated list of 279 measures that had been identified in the White Paper had been agreed in the Council of Ministers, a staggering 95 per cent success rate (Pelkmans, 1994: 103).

However, the freeing of the market was not the end of the project so far as Delors was concerned. He saw it as a first step that implied further extensions of integration. In particular he argued for a social dimension to the project, and for its completion by agreement on monetary union. On both of these issues he had the support of a majority of the governments of the other member states, but was implacably opposed by the British Prime Minister, Margaret Thatcher.

The British government rejected the proposed Social Charter, which Mrs Thatcher described as 'Marxist' (Urwin 1995: 231). The proposal for worker representatives on company boards was a particular problem for the Thatcher government. Despite subsequent revisions to the proposed Social Charter, the UK government refused to sign, leaving the remaining eleven governments to sign an agreement on social policy outside of the treaty.

To add to the complexity of the situation, in the course of 1989 and 1990 the world changed beyond all recognition. The collapse of Communism throughout central and eastern Europe left western governments facing a situation that was unexpected and complex. In particular the rapid movement to German unity inserted a new element into the calculations of the leaders of other west European states.

This chapter examines the moves towards monetary union, the impact of the collapse of Communism on the EC, the terms of the Treaty on European Union (TEU), and the aftermath of its signing, when public opinion began to turn away from support for European integration.

Towards Maastricht

Monetary policy had been largely absent from the SEA, but the logic of the internal market suggested at least some harmonization of taxation policies. Following the SEA there had been growing support for a single currency controlled by a European central bank, but the British government rejected this concept. Despite British opposition, the heads of government agreed in Hanover in June 1988 to set up a committee of central bankers and technical experts, under the chairmanship of Delors, to prepare a report on the steps that needed to be taken to strengthen monetary co-operation. The subsequent 'Delors Report' proposed a three-stage progress to monetary union leading to a single currency by

1999. The report was presented to the June 1989 meeting of the European Council in Madrid, which on a majority vote of eleven to one (Thatcher voting against) agreed to convene an IGC to prepare proposals for changes to the treaties to allow movement to a monetary union.

These events were accompanied by the dramatic collapse of Communism in the Soviet Union and other central and eastern European countries. This forced a serious reconsideration of the political aspects of the EC. The immediate impact was the destabilization of the geographical area immediately to the east of the EC and, more positively for the EC, the opening up of potential new markets and new sites for investment for west European capital. In addition, the collapse of Communism raised the prospect of German reunification.

This 'acceleration of history' as Delors called it impacted on the EC and on Delors's plans for its development. In particular, the prospect of a reunified Germany caused alarm in the neighbouring states, particularly over a possible resurgence of German nationalism. A more immediate concern was that the new Germany would turn its attention more to the east and become less concerned with its obligations to western Europe.

Chancellor Kohl of Germany shared these concerns. Kohl had not hitherto been noted for providing strong or dynamic leadership, but he seized the opportunity to go down in the history books as the person who reunified his country. At the same time, however, he did not want to be remembered as the Frankenstein who created a new monster in the centre of Europe. Such concerns led directly to the convening of a second IGC on political union to run alongside the one that had already been called on monetary union. Although Delors supported the move, it was not part of his plan. The political union IGC together with that on monetary union meant that the Maastricht Treaty became a very high profile issue: 'a treaty too far' as Lady Thatcher later described it.

The two IGCs met throughout 1991, and their proposals were incorporated into the TEU which was signed in Maastricht in December of that year, and which created the European Union (EU). Britain, under the new premiership of John Major, agreed to the TEU only when a chapter on social policy had been removed from the main text, and only when it was agreed that Britain could opt out of the final stage of monetary union if its Parliament so decided.

The Treaty on European Union

Intergovernmental negotiations leading up the Maastricht Summit of December 1991 were tough and much of what was agreed reflected the lowest-common-denominator bargaining position of governments. Nonetheless, Maastricht marked a further big step on the road to European integration. Heads of governments agreed a three-pillar structure for the EU. This consisted of the EC Pillar (economic and social affairs) and the intergovernmental pillars of Common Foreign and Security Policy (CFSP) and Justice and Home Affairs (JHA) (Fig. 18.1, p. 214).

In addition to agreement on monetary union, the powers of the EP were strengthened at Maastricht through the extension of the co-decision procedure, which gave Parliament greater legislative power in a range of policy areas (Ch. 18, pp. 225–6). More generally, EC competencies were extended in a number of areas including education and training, environment, health and industry. Built on compromise, the TEU included something positive for the EC institutions and each of the member states involved.

After Maastricht

Although agreed by the heads of governments, the decision to move to a single currency raised concerns within member states. Notably, this decision caused a collapse of support for the EU in Germany itself, where the Deutschmark was held in high regard as the factor that had facilitated post-war prosperity. Problems were made worse when the German currency union took effect, following the decision to convert East German Ostmarks at an artificially high rate into Deutschmarks. This led to inflationary tendencies in the unified Germany, which were suppressed by the Bundesbank (the German central bank) raising interest rates. This in turn solidified resistance within Germany to European monetary union, and therefore to Maastricht. It also pushed the buoyant European economies into recession, which made it more difficult to sell Maastricht to European citizens, who were already rather alarmed by the pace of change that was being proposed.

It was against this background that the Danish referendum in June 1992 rejected the Treaty (Ch. 17, p. 202). It was only when concessions were made on monetary union—giving Denmark similar opt-out rights to those of Britain—and on some other issues of concern, that it was narrowly accepted in a second referendum in May 1993. Perhaps even more significantly, the treaty was only accepted by the French public by the narrowest of margins (50.3 to 49.7 per cent) in September 1992.

In Germany there was no referendum, but the strength of public concern about monetary union was such that the Bundestag demanded the right to vote on the issue again before any automatic abandonment of the Deutschmark in favour of a common European currency. This move, in effect, unilaterally claimed for Germany the opt-out that Britain and Denmark had negotiated. There was clear evidence of serious public discontent with the Treaty in other member states, not least in Britain.

The Commission became caught in this wave of popular discontent about the pace of integration. Delors was personally associated with the proposals on monetary union, which caused the greatest concern in Britain and Germany. He had also adopted a very high profile in the run-up to the ratification débâcles. In particular, his ill-timed statement shortly before the Danish referendum to the effect that small states might have to surrender their right to hold the presidency of the Council of Ministers in a future enlarged EC was seen as a contributory factor to the negative vote in Denmark.

Delors's comments about small states were actually made in the context of an entirely different debate about enlargement of the EC. The success of the 1992 programme had led to concern among the members of the European Free Trade Association (EFTA) that they were not sharing in the investment boom that 1992 precipitated. Led by Sweden, these states began to broach the question of membership of the EC. Delors was against this because he believed that further enlargement would dilute the degree of unity that could be achieved, and he proposed instead a way in which the EFTA states could become part of the single market without becoming full members of the EC. Membership of the European Economic Area (EEA) would involve the EFTA states adopting all the relevant commercial legislation of the EC, without having any say in its formulation. It was never likely to be a satisfactory agreement for the governments of those states, who would thereby be surrendering sovereignty over large areas of their economies; more significantly, it did not convince the businesses that were diverting their investments from EFTA to inside the EC. All the EFTA states decided to press ahead with membership applications, but Switzerland withdrew its application after the Swiss people rejected the EEA in a referendum in December 1992; and the Norwegians again rejected membership in a referendum in November 1994.

Sweden, Finland, and Austria became members of the EU on 1 January 1995. The EU that they joined was not the self-confident one that they had applied to join. As well as disagreement about the future direction, and signs of public disaffection with the whole exercise, the EMS had effectively collapsed during the ratification problems. Britain had withdrawn and floated sterling, and other states had only been able to remain inside because the bands of permitted fluctuation had been widened from 2.25 per cent to 15 per cent either side of parity.

Delors had started his long period as President of the Commission with a considerable triumph in the single market programme. He ended it with that achievement somewhat overshadowed by the hostile reaction of public opinion in much of Europe to the Maastricht Treaty. Yet whether it was reasonable to blame the Commission for this débâcle is very doubtful. Delors had been upset at the extent to which the Commission had been ignored during the IGCs that prepared the TEU, and had opposed several of the provisions of the Treaty. However, he had adopted such a high profile during his period as President, and had been so closely associated personally with the most unpopular provision of the Treaty, for monetary union, that it was easy for the governments of the member states to pass the blame onto him personally and the institution of which he had been president for ten years.

Conclusion

Delors approached the single market programme as the first step in a wider programme of integration. There is no doubt that he was familiar with the central concepts of neofunctionalist theory himself, as evidenced in his inaugural address to the sixth annual conference of the Centre for European Policy Studies (CEPS) in 1989 (CEPS, 1990: 9–18). Delors expected and intended that the economic liberalization programme would be followed by both monetary union and an extension and deepening of social policy. Here the theme of the tension between types of capitalism re-enters the story, because the British Prime Minister, Margaret Thatcher, objected strongly to the idea that either of these things was entailed by the 1992 programme. While her objection to monetary union can be interpreted as a reflection of her commitment to an intergovernmental view of the EC, her objection to the social dimension of the single market programme was clearly a reflection of her adherence to a different concept of how capitalism should be organized in the late twentieth century. That particular debate was to continue after the political demise of Thatcher.

While personal convictions cannot be written out of the explanation for Margaret Thatcher's opposition to both monetary union and an EC social policy, the question of the personal position of her successor, John Major, is less important. The fact is that Major had little choice but to negotiate opt-outs for Britain on both issues at Maastricht because of the domestic political constraints that he faced, which were in turn the legacy of the Thatcher years. The primacy of domestic politics, a consistent theme of these chapters, re-emerges here, as does the theme of the conflict between different ways of organizing capitalism.

The collapse of the exchange rate mechanism of EMS gives strong support to the argument that the evolution of the EC can only be understood against the background of an understanding of global economic forces. The globalization of monetary markets, and the increase in the quantity of liquid capital traded across the international exchanges, made it impossible for the system to be maintained in the form that had functioned for years to stabilize European exchange rates, and gave added force to the argument that only a single currency would provide the stability that was necessary to ensure the smooth and complete functioning of the single market, even though the British government chose to interpret the episode as evidence that the infrastructure was not yet in place for a single currency.

Neofunctionalism received some additional support from the applications for membership by the EFTA states. The idea of spillover was extended to cover the idea of geographical spillover, and this appeared to cover the case of the EFTAns. Once the single market was a reality, the attitude and behaviour not just of businesses based inside the EC, but also of businesses based in the rest of western Europe, changed. The result was an inflow of investment to the single market zone, and an imperative for those states that remained outside to join. When the half-way-house of the EEA failed to convince businesses that it would constitute full membership of the single market, the EFTA states were forced to reconsider their position on full membership. Again the relative impotence of individual state governments in the face of the forces of contemporary capitalism was illustrated.

It was in this period that the cold war finally came to an end, although the impact of the uncertainty that this change in the background conditions of the EC produced was only fully felt in the next period, after Maastricht. The collapse of Communism may have given additional momentum to a process that was already under way, in the same way that Algeria, Hungary, and Suez gave additional momentum to the Messina negotiations in the late 1950s; but the 'acceleration of history' did not dramatically change the agenda of the IGCs that were already scheduled.

Finally, the developments after Maastricht illustrate a theme that had been largely neglected by governments and analysts until then: the importance of legitimacy for the process of European integration. In a majority of member states, the EC had an independent legitimacy of its own because it represented the 'good' of European integration (see Ch.

14–17, pp. 147–210). The aftermath of Maastricht raised questions about whether this was still the case. At the same time, governments did not hesitate to undermine further the legitimacy of the EC/EU by blaming it for unpopular measures that they felt needed to be taken, but for which they were reluctant to accept the responsibility themselves, for fear of weakening their electoral position.

KEY POINTS

Towards Maastricht

- In June 1989, the European Council agreed to Delors's three-stage plan for monetary union by 1999, despite British opposition

- The collapse of Communism in Central and Eastern Europe and the prospect of a reunified Germany focused minds on the political aspects of European integration.

- In 1991, IGCs were held on both monetary union and political union. The proposals of these IGCs were incorporated into Treaty on European Union, signed at Maastricht in December 1991.

- The Treaty on European Union marked a major step on the road to European integration. It extended EC competencies in a range of areas and strengthened the powers of the European Parliament.

After Maastricht

- The decision to move to a single currency caused concern within member states, not least Germany, which had a strong attachment to the Deutschmark

- The TEU was rejected by the Danish following a referendum in 1992 and was only accepted in 1993 following major concessions. A referendum in France (1992) was only narrowly in favour.

- By the time Austria, Finland, and Sweden became members of in 1995, the EU was not the confident one they had applied to join.

- The Commission became caught up in the wave of unpopularity affecting the EU. Delors's high profile presidency ensured that he was the focal point of much criticism.

QUESTIONS

1 Why was the British government so opposed to monetary union and a social dimension to European integration?

2 What was the significance of the collapse of Communism in central and eastern Europe for developments in the EU in the early 1990s?

3 Assess the significance of the Treaty on European Union in the history of European integration

4 What explains the problems experienced in ratifying the TEU?

FURTHER READING

The negotiation of the Treaty is analysed by J. Baun, 'The Maastricht Treaty as High Politics: Germany, France and European Integration', *Political Science Quarterly* 110 (1996), 605–24. A. Moravcsik, *The Choice for Europe: Social Purpose and State Power from Messina to Maastricht* (London: UCL Press, 1998), 379–471

The aftermath of the signing of the Treaty is analysed in: B. Criddle, 'The French Referendum on the Maastricht Treaty, September 1992', *Parliamentary Affairs* 46 (1993), 228–38; D. Baker, A. Gamble, and S. Ludlam, '1846–1906–1996? Conservative Splits and European Integration', *Political Quarterly* 64 (1993), 420–34, and 'The Parliamentary Siege of Maastricht 1993: Conservative Divisions and British Ratification of the Treaty of European Union', *Parliamentary Affairs* 47 (1994), 37–60; H. Rattinger, 'Public Attitudes towards European Integration in Germany and Maastricht: Inventory and Typology', *Journal of Common Market Studies* 32 (1994), 525–40.

13 The EU after 1995

. . . flexibility, according to its proponents, promised a new principle and a new tool for responding to differences in the enthusiasms and capabilities of the member states of the EU to take on new tasks of policy integration. In the period following Maastricht, it had become evident that subsidiarity was both a contested concept and a muddled guide for practice.

(Wallace, 2000: 175)

SUMMARY

The period after the signing of the Maastricht Treaty was dominated by the issue of monetary union. With a majority of states keen to move to a single currency by 1999, other issues remained secondary. By 1994, the prospect of flexible European integration was clearly on the agenda, which suggested that a hard-core of member states that wished to go ahead with closer integration should do so. Increasingly prominent in the post-Maastricht era was the proposed enlargement of the EU to include states of central and eastern Europe. This enlargement would require substantive changes to both EC institutional arrangements and policies. Ultimately, the 1997 Treaty of Amsterdam which attempted the necessary adjustments, was more modest than advocates of further integration and enlargement would have liked.

Introduction

On 1 January 1995 the membership of the EU expanded to fifteen with the accession of Austria, Finland, and Sweden. On the same date, Jacques Santer became president of the European Commission for a five-year term. He inherited an agenda that included further enlargement, an IGC to review the TEU, and monetary union. He also inherited the legacy of the concerns and suspicions that had arisen over the TEU, and the role of the Commission in promoting integration. This led him to adopt as an unofficial mission-statement a formula that had already been advocated by the British Foreign Secretary Douglas Hurd: do less but do it better. However, not everyone in the EU wanted to do less. Despite the unfavourable move in public opinion, voices in both France and Germany were raised in favour of an arrangement that would allow those states that wished to do so to forge ahead with closer integration, not being held back by those which were more hesitant.

This chapter examines first the debates over monetary union, particularly the form that it would take. The framework decision to move to a single currency left the detail of the rules that would govern the new system to be negotiated, and this process revealed differences in outlook between the French and German governments in particular. The chapter then reviews significant changes in governments in the leading member states, before looking at the debate over flexible integration. Finally it turns to the issue that dominated the horizon of the EU at the end of the millennium: the prospective enlargement to central and eastern Europe.

Monetary union

The agreement that had been reached at Maastricht represented a compromise between the positions of states with very different perspectives on the issue. Those compromises had to be sorted out in order for the programme for monetary union to go ahead. During 1995, the decisions on the detail of the monetary union began to be settled, generally in favour of the German view. These included agreement that the location of the European Central Bank (ECB) would be in Frankfurt, and that the new currency would be called the Euro, not the ecu as the French wished, because that name was not liked by the German public. More significantly, during 1996 it was agreed that the convergence criteria set out in the TEU (Box 26.2, p. 349) would have to be met precisely, with no fudging of the issue, and that there would continue to be a stability pact after the single currency came into existence. French hopes for more political control over the monetary policy of the ECB were also dashed (Ch. 26, pp. 350–1).

The efforts of the member states that wished to participate in the single currency to meet the convergence criteria were hindered by the continuation of recession in Europe. During 1995, it was decided to abandon the earlier of the two possible starting dates for the single currency, 1997, because it was obvious that not enough states, if any, would fully meet the convergence criteria by then. There was also doubt about how many would achieve the targets by 1999, the second of the two possible starting dates. In France and Belgium the efforts of the governments to reduce the level of their budget deficits to the 3 per cent target led to strikes and disruption. The imposition of lower public spending on economies that already had high levels of unemployment was a sure recipe for political problems.

However, in the course of 1996 and 1997 a surprising number of states did manage either to achieve or to approach the targets. This caused concern in Germany, because the idea that Italy in particular could possibly observe the conditions of the stability pact in perpetuity was not considered credible. There was a fear that the German public might reject a Euro of which Italy was a part. As the trend in the Italian economy moved in the direction of the targets, so the insistence of the Germans that the targets be treated as absolutes grew. On the budget deficit, which was treated as the most important criterion, the German Finance Minister, Theo Waigel, and the President of the Bundesbank, Hans Tietmeyer, insisted that 3 per cent meant exactly 3 per cent or less, not 3.1 per cent even. This was clearly an attempt to set the target at a level that Italy would

not be able to reach. The irony was that Germany missed the 3 per cent deficit target in 1996, and looked like missing it again in 1997. A single currency without German participation was inconceivable, yet the continuing problems posed for the German economy by the absorption of East Germany threatened to disqualify it from membership on its own criteria.

All of this caused some glee within the British Conservative government, which found the whole project of monetary union extremely difficult. For domestic political reasons the government could not join the single currency, even if it met the convergence criteria; but if the project went ahead without it there was a risk that British economic interests would be damaged, and that British political influence within the EU would be permanently diminished. So it was with a certain air of wishing rather than predicting that the Prime Minister John Major had said in an article in 1993 that 'economic and monetary union is not realisable in present circumstances' (*Economist*, 25 Sept. 1993). While there might have been some justification for this view in 1993, by the end of 1997 it was apparent that the single currency would start on schedule in 1999, and although it was not clear which member states would be members, it began to look as though all those that wished to join, except Greece, would be in a position to do so.

Changes of government

There were several significant changes of governments during this period. In Germany the government of Chancellor Kohl continued uninterrupted, but the authority of the Chancellor was called into question by a number of difficulties on policy and a number of electoral setbacks. In Britain the Conservative government of John Major experienced a series of defeats in parliamentary by-elections, which reduced its majority. This, combined with the increasingly militant anti-EU position of a significant number of its own MPs, left the government with little room for manoeuvre, and its discourse on the EU became increasingly negative.

In France there were two changes of government. In May 1995 the Gaullist Jacques Chirac was elected President in succession to the Socialist François Mitterrand. There was already a conservative majority in the National Assembly, from which Chirac nominated Alain Juppé as his Prime Minister. However, when parliamentary elections were held in April 1997, the Socialist Party won the largest share of seats, and formed a coalition with the Communists.

Chirac's initial actions as president were viewed with some concern in Germany. His decision to permit the testing of nuclear weapons in the Pacific met with protests throughout the EU, including in

Germany. Only the British government supported Chirac on this. Together with the common experience of working together in Bosnia, this incident led to a measure of agreement between France and Britain. Chirac at one stage suggested that France might learn something from the British approach to the EU. However, he gradually came back into line with the position of his predecessor.

Flexible integration

During 1994 the German CDU/CSU parliamentary group produced a paper, jointly authored by Karl Lamers and Wolfgang Schauble, which suggested that a hard core of member states that wished to go ahead with closer integration should do so. A similar approach, envisaging a Europe of concentric circles with France and Germany at its centre, had been outlined by the French Prime Minister, Edouard Balladur in an interview published two days before the German paper.

These ideas were prompted primarily by the increasingly obstructionist stand taken by the British Prime Minister, John Major on all suggestions for further integration. Shackled by a small parliamentary majority and with a significant number of his own backbench MPs hostile to further integration of Britain with the rest of the EU, Major had become an increasingly uncooperative partner. Faced with the apparent determination of the French and German governments to push ahead with monetary union, and with other measures that would be unacceptable to the parliamentary Conservative Party, Major himself had begun to contemplate the possibility of extending the arrangements that had been agreed at Maastricht for Britain to opt-out of monetary union and an integrated social policy.

In September 1994 Major gave the William and Mary Lecture at the University of Leiden. He used it as an opportunity to expound the idea of flexible integration. On the basis that trying to force all the member states into the same mould would crack that mould, he called for an agreement that if some states wanted to integrate more closely, or more rapidly than others, they should be allowed to do so. On the other hand, it was important that no state should be excluded from participation in closer integration in a policy sector if it was willing and able to participate. This principle led Major to reject the idea of a 'hard core' Europe, although he did advocate a hard core of basic policies from which no state could opt-out. These were international trade obligations, the single market, and environmental protection. Looking ahead, Major argued that bringing prosperity and stability to the states of central and eastern Europe was an historic task that required the enlargement of the EU. That enlargement would produce such a variety of member states in size, shape, economic and industrial profile, philosophy, history, and culture that it would require the introduction of the flexibility that he was advocating.

In January 1995, the former French President Valéry Giscard d'Estaing published two articles in the daily *Le Figaro* in which he went further and argued for a new Treaty with an explicit federal aim. Since British membership, the existing EU had lost sight of that ultimate objective. Giscard believed that it would be impossible to get back on course for a federal Europe so long as the British government was able to block every step. The new treaty would be separate from the EU Treaties, and would exclude Britain and other countries that were reluctant to embrace the federal vocation of European integration. In common with the previous contributors to this debate, Giscard also mentioned the impending further enlargement of the EU to the east. This he considered inevitable; but in common with John Major, he believed that it would be impossible to proceed down a federal road with so many and so diverse a range of members. So as well as British obstructionism, the proposed enlargement figured prominently in this debate about the need for flexibility.

Enlargement

All member states paid lip-service to the principle of enlargement of the EU to the east, but some states were keener than others. For Germany the enlargement was an absolute priority; it was also strongly supported by Britain and the Scandinavian countries. However, France, Italy, and Spain had reservations. When the shift was made from the general issue of supporting enlargement to the discussion of the detailed steps that were needed to make a reality of the aspiration, even the strongest supporters were not necessarily prepared to accept the full implications.

Germany's commitment to enlargement was based largely on security considerations. Following reunification, Germany was once again a central European state, having borders with Poland and the Czech Republic. Instability in the region would be right on Germany's doorstep, and admitting its nearest neighbours to the EU was seen as a way of guaranteeing their stability. There were also economic considerations. Before the war German companies and banks had been the leading foreign investors in central Europe, and soon after the collapse of Communism German investment began to flow into the area. Guaranteeing the security of those investments was another reason for the German government's support of membership for the central European states.

British motives for welcoming enlargement were less immediately obvious, but reflected a combination of security, economic, and political considerations. In terms of security, British governments since the war had continued to support the principle of global stabilization even where British investments were not immediately involved. This was a habit of statecraft that dated back to the period before the First World War when Britain was the hegemonic power in the world and shouldered responsibility for policing the international capitalist system. That responsibility had largely passed to the United States in the period since the Second World War, but British governments had consistently supported such efforts at global stabilization. In the situation after the end of the cold war, the United States administrations of both Bush and

Clinton made it clear that they expected the EU states to play a leading role in stabilizing central and eastern Europe, and membership of the EU was specifically pressed by the Clinton administration as a means of achieving this.

In economic terms, British support for further enlargement reflected the hope that British business would be able to profit from access to a larger market. Politically, however, this enlargement would also imply a looser EU less likely to move in a federal direction. Thus in both economic and political terms, eastern enlargement suited the Conservative government of John Major.

While the governments of France and the Mediterranean states could see the arguments for enlargement to the east, and even accepted them, they were apprehensive about the effect that such an enlargement would have on the EU.

- First, they were concerned that an eastern enlargement would shift the balance of power in the EU decisively to the north, especially coming immediately after the accession of Austria, Finland, and Sweden.

- Second, and related to the first point, they were concerned that the problems of the Mediterranean, which affected them more than instability in the east, would be relegated to a secondary issue. Instability in North Africa, particularly civil war in Algeria, were already having an impact on them in the form of refugees, and threats to their companies' investments in the region.

- Third, they feared that EU funds that came to them through the CAP and the structural funds would be diverted to support for the central and east European economies.

Their concern that attention would be diverted from the problems of the Mediterranean was recognized by the German government when it held the presidency of the EU in the second half of 1994. Agreement was reached at the Essen meeting of the European Council in December 1994 to launch an initiative on North Africa and the Middle East. This assumed more tangible form during 1995 under the successive French and Spanish presidencies, culminating in a major conference in Barcelona from 23 to 29 November 1995 involving the EU member states, the Maghreb states (Algeria, Morocco, and Tunisia), Israel, Jordan, Lebanon, Syria, Turkey, Cyprus, and Malta. The central and eastern European states were also represented. The conference agreed on a stability pact for the Middle East on the model of the Conference on Security and Co-operation in Europe (CSCE) and the EU agreed to contribute $6bn. in aid and $6bn. in European Investment Bank (EIB) loans to the economic development of the region.

The problem of accepting the implications of a commitment to enlargement to the east were apparent in November 1995 when the Commission proposed that agricultural imports from six central and east European states (Bulgaria, the Czech Republic, Hungary, Poland, Romania, and Slovakia) be increased by 10 per cent a year. Britain, Denmark, The Netherlands, and Sweden supported the proposal. France and the Mediterranean states opposed it, indicating that they would only be prepared to accept an increase of 5 per cent a year. Germany, which was ostensibly the strongest supporter of enlargement, joined the Mediterranean states in opposing the Commission's proposal. This indicated the strength of the farming lobby in Germany, and the fragmented nature of decision-making in the country which allowed the Agriculture Ministry to adopt a line so clearly incompatible with the official policy as enunciated by the Chancellor's office.

Box 13.1 Applicant countries

Country	Year	
Turkey	1987	
Cyprus	1990	
Poland	1990	
Switzerland	1992	(application withdrawn same year)
Hungary	1994	
Slovak Republic	1995	
Romania	1995	
Latvia	1995	
Estonia	1995	
Bulgaria	1995	
Lithuania	1995	
Czech Republic	1996	
Slovenia	1996	
Malta	1998	(application reactivated)

The same contradiction in policy emerged after July 1997 when the Commission published its *Agenda 2000* report on the future direction of the EU in the likely context of enlargement. The German Farm Minister, Ignaz Kiechle, publicly stated that the proposed reforms of the CAP were unnecessary. He received no reprimand for this from Chancellor Kohl. In addition to the reform of key policies, the eastern enlargement had implications for the decision-making procedures of the EU. This came to be one of the key issues in the IGC which led up to the Treaty of Amsterdam. (On enlargement, see also Ch. 29, pp. 407–24.)

The 1996 IGC

Originally the 1996 IGC was intended to review the working of the TEU. Provision for such a review was written into the agreements that were reached at Maastricht in December 1991. However, nobody expected the ratification of the TEU to take as long as it did, with the result that the review started after only two and a half years of experience of the new arrangements. The difficulties in ratifying the TEU also meant that there was little appetite for further fundamental change. Increasingly the IGC came to be seen as primarily about preparing the ground for the eastern enlargement. There were several institutional issues that needed to be addressed if the EU were to enlarge to over twenty members: the size of the Commission and the EP; the rotation of the presidency of the Council; the extent of QMV; and the weighting of votes under QMV.

The Commission already had twenty members in 1995, and that was already too many for the number of portfolios available, as Jacques Santer found out when he tried to allocate responsibilities without upsetting either national sensibilities or the *amour propre* of his colleagues in the College of Commissioners. Enlargement threatened to produce an unwieldy organization. The British government offered to relinquish its second Commissioner if the other large states would agree to do so, but this was not an easy concession for the others. For Italy and Spain in particular, having two Commissioners was a matter of national pride, singling out their countries as larger member states on a par with Germany, France, and Britain. Even if there had been unanimous agreement to dispense with the second Commissioners, the problem of too many Commissioners would have remained.

The EP would also become unwieldy if the same rough formula that had been used up to the 1995 enlargement were applied to further member states. Clearly there had to be some limit put on the numbers; but that had implications for the existing distribution of seats.

With twelve members, and the presidency of the Council changing every six months, there were six years between presidencies for any one state (see Ch. 20, pp. 254–5). This meant that all the expertise that had been acquired for one presidency was lost by the time the next one came round. There was also concern that the next enlargement would involve mostly small states, as had the 1995 enlargement. Small states often had problems with servicing the presidency. The problems had been eased since the Troika system had come into operation, whereby the present, previous, and immediate future presidents co-operated (see Ch. 20, p. 255). However, the situation was rapidly approaching where there might not be a large state in the Troika much of the time.

On QMV, the German and French governments wanted to see an extension to cover areas under the JHA pillar of the TEU, but the British Conservative government was adamantly opposed to any extension of QMV. The British government was also, along with Spain, one of the strongest advocates of a re-

weighting of the votes under QMV. Because the number of votes allocated to a state was not directly proportional to its population, the increase in the number of small member states had produced a situation in which measures could be passed under QMV with the support of the representatives of a decreasing proportion of the total population of the EU. In the original EC of six states, votes representing 70 per cent of the population were needed to pass a measure; by 1995 this had been reduced to 58.3 per cent; and on the basis of reasonable assumptions about the identity of the members, and therefore about the numbers of votes to which they would be entitled on the existing formula, with twenty-six member states the proportion required could be as low as 50.3 per cent. The French government supported the idea of a re-weighting of votes, but the German Chancellor was hesitant because of the concern expressed by the smaller member states that this would be yet another step towards downgrading their role.

Beyond these specific institutional issues, each member state went to the IGC with particular issues that it wished to push. Sweden, Denmark, and the Netherlands were concerned to increase the accountability and transparency of Council business, and proposed that a freedom of information clause be written into the Treaty. Sweden was also a leading mover in pressing for a chapter on employment policy to be added to the Treaty. In March 1996 the Swedish government called a meeting in Oslo to build support for this proposal: France, Germany, Britain, and Italy were not invited. Britain wanted reform to the working of the ECJ, having suffered several adverse judgments at its hands. Britain and France both pressed for an enhanced role for national parliaments in the policy-making process. France and Germany pressed the flexibility issue hard; they also co-operated in putting forward proposals to move towards incorporating the WEU into the EU, something which was strongly opposed by the neutral member states (Austria, Ireland, and Sweden) and by Britain.

The IGC was preceded by a 'Reflection Group' which met in the second half of 1995 under the Spanish presidency. This consisted of representatives of the Foreign Ministers and two members of the EP. It had a remit to seek the views of other institutions on progress towards European union, and possible amendments to the TEU, and to prepare a report on the issues that should form the agenda of the IGC. When he reported on the work of the Group in December 1995, the Spanish Foreign Minister Carlos Westendorp said that there was agreement that the IGC should not aim at fundamental reform, but be about necessary changes; in particular it should be seen as one part of the process of eastern enlargement. Werner Hoyer, the German representative on the Reflection Group, indicated publicly that the work of the Group had soon deteriorated into an exchange of national positions, and warned that there was a risk of the IGC turning into a confrontation between integrationists and intergovernmentalists.

The IGC itself opened officially in Turin on 29 March 1996. The special European Council that was called to inaugurate it was dominated, though, by the ban on exports of British beef which had been imposed in the aftermath of the announcement that bovine spongiform encephalopathy (BSE) in cattle, with which British herds were particularly infected, could be the cause of Creutzfeldt–Jakob disease (CJD) in humans. As British efforts to get the ban lifted made little progress over the coming weeks, John Major threatened to block progress in the IGC, and to refuse to sign any Treaty that emerged from it until the ban was lifted. His government did in fact veto just about every item of EU business over which it could exercise a veto until an agreement was reached on a phased lifting of the ban.

This incident marked the final breach between the British Conservative government and the rest of the EU. Patience was already exhausted before Major threatened to block agreement on a new Treaty unless two changes were made to the existing one. First, he demanded agreement to allow the reversal of a decision of the ECJ that a directive on a 48-hour maximum working week must apply to Britain, despite the British government's opt-out from the social protocol, because it was a health-and-safety issue and so covered by the SEA. Secondly, he demanded that changes were made to the common fisheries policy, to prevent fishing boats from other member states buying quotas from British fishermen.

There were some indications that the IGC was deliberately prolonged into 1997 in the hope that the British general election would produce a change of government, which it did. The Labour government under Tony Blair indicated immediately that while its priorities would remain those of its predecessor, it would not block a Treaty over any issue other than that Britain must be allowed to retain its border controls. The way was thus cleared for agreement on the text of a new Treaty at a European Council in Amsterdam in June 1997.

The Treaty of Amsterdam

Agreement was reached at Amsterdam on a rather modest Treaty. In particular, no agreement could be reached on the institutional reforms that were believed to be essential to pave the way for enlargement. Also, there was little extension of QMV because Chancellor Kohl retreated from his earlier advocacy of the principle, and actually blocked its extension to cover:

- industrial policy
- social policy
- certain aspects of the free movement of labour.

As a result of what may have been an oversight, the failure to extend QMV to them did not lead to withdrawal of the linked proposal to increase the powers of the EP in these three areas, so the EP was given the right to amend or reject proposed legislation in two-dozen areas which were brought under co-decision for the first time.

Dutch plans to extend majority voting into eleven policy areas, ranging from cultural activities to industrial policy, ran into German resistance. Kohl insisted that these extensions would undermine the position of the German Länder. The only two extensions of QMV that were agreed were for research programmes and compensatory aid for imports of raw materials. In addition, new areas were agreed in which QMV would apply from the start:

- countering fraud
- encouraging customs co-operation
- collating statistics
- laying down rules for the free movement of personal data.

On the number of Commissioners, a compromise was reached that if more than two and fewer than six new members joined, the Commission would continue to have one representative from each member state, although Spain insisted that it would only surrender its second Commissioner in return for changes in the weighting of votes in the Council, which could not be agreed.

Rules on allowing flexible integration were agreed:

- in the first pillar, it would be triggered by QMV, although with the veto retained if a member state insisted that the development would jeopardize its vital national interests
- in the second pillar (CFSP) the system would be 'constructive abstention'

- in the third pillar, special opt-outs for Britain, Ireland, and Denmark would allow the others to proceed without them.

It was agreed that a zone of freedom, security, and justice for EU citizens would come into force within five years of ratification. Member states that violated fundamental freedoms faced loss of voting rights in the Council of Ministers. Complete freedom of movement was pledged for all individuals within the EU, but the UK and Ireland were allowed to retain border controls. Decisions on immigration, visas, and asylum were to be subject to unanimity for at least five years, and then reviewed, but with a veto on change.

On CFSP, it was agreed that the Council Secretary-General would represent the EU to the outside world. QMV would be used on implementing foreign policy measures, but any state which believed its vital national interests were at stake could exercise a veto. The WEU might be incorporated into the EU in the future, but Nato was reaffirmed as central to Europe's defence.

Conclusion

In the latest period the EU has entered a context of tremendous uncertainty in both its global context and its internal functioning. Enlargement to eastern Europe was the biggest item on the post-Maastricht agenda, and threatened or promised to transform the EU itself beyond all recognition. A definite tension developed between the will of all member states to consolidate democracy and capitalism in eastern and central Europe and the willingness of any member state to accept economic sacrifices to allow that enlargement to happen. Willing the end did not appear to mean necessarily willing the means. Domestic politics assumed priority too often when it came to trying to agree the details of reforms to the common policies and to the central institutions that everyone agreed were necessary to facilitate the enlargement.

As with the EC and the Mediterranean enlargements in the 1970s, eastern enlargement in the forthcoming twenty-first century was part of the enhanced security role for the EU in the world after the decline of US hegemony. So was the need to progress the CFSP, which was incorporated into the TEU. Here immediate national economic interests were less directly involved, so there was the prospect of progress; but national cultural differences emerged, as did differing national security interests. The CFSP forum also provided Britain with an opportunity to be more centrally involved with the EU, alongside France as the two states with the most efficient professional armies. Germany remained hampered by a suspicion throughout central Europe of Germans in uniforms, and a reluctance among the German people themselves to see German forces committed to military operations in other countries.

The concern within Germany was partly about a re-emergence of German militarism, but it was also about the impact on the legitimacy of the EU if German lives should be lost in pursuit of objectives set through the CFSP. The attitudes of the publics of France and Britain were different, being accustomed to their national forces forming part of UN peace-keeping operations. The legitimacy of the EU in Germany was severely shaken by the decision to adopt the single currency, and by what appeared to be the centralization of functions that had previously been the responsibility of the Länder. It was this last concern that caused Helmut Kohl to back-track at Amsterdam from his previous insistence that there should be more qualified majority voting.

Concern to prevent further slippage of powers from the national or sub-national level to the supra-national level was apparent throughout the EU by the time of Amsterdam. With the changes in government in France, Germany, and Britain the future of policy looked uncertain. The first indications were that a new form of co-operation was emerging which cast the Commission in a different role as an impartial arbiter and referee of agreements for co-ordinated national action rather than as enforcer of legally binding commitments. The role of the ECJ was also affected by this development. The EU perhaps stood on the threshold of a new era in its development, but it was too early to get any real perspective on this as the twentieth century drew towards its close.

KEY POINTS

Monetary union

- In 1995, details of monetary union began to emerge. The ECB would be located in Frankfurt and the single currency would be called the 'Euro'.

- Although recession hindered attempts by some states to meet the convergence criteria, the single currency stayed on course for a 1999 launch.

Flexible integration

- In 1994 the idea of flexible integration became widespread. This was the notion that some member states should integrate further and faster than others.

Enlargement

- While member states were generally supportive of further enlargement to include countries of central and eastern Europe, there were a number of concerns over the impact this would have on key policies, such as agriculture, and also on decision-making procedures.

The 1996 IGC

- The 1996 IGC focused on the institutional changes necessary to prepare for further enlargement. This IGC was also marked by conflict over the British 'beef' crisis, which resulted in the Major government blocking agreement on a range of issues.

The Treaty of Amsterdam

- Resulting from the 1996 IGC, this Treaty was relatively modest in scope. In particular, it did not contain the decision-making reforms deemed necessary for enlargement.

QUESTIONS

1 What is meant by 'flexible integration' and why did this idea flourish in the mid-1990s?

2 What concerns did existing member states have over further enlargement of the EU to include countries of central and eastern Europe?

3 Why did the 1996 IGC fail to achieve the institutional reforms necessary for further enlargement?

FURTHER READING

Useful guides to the Treaty of Amsterdam are European Commission, *The Amsterdam Treaty: A Comprehensive Guide* (1999) and A. Duff, *The Treaty of Amsterdam: Text and Commentary* (London: Federal Trust/Sweet & Maxwell, 1997).

On the politics that led up to the Treaty, see G. Edwards and A. Pijpers, *The Politics of European Treaty Reform: The 1996 Intergovernmental Conference and Beyond* (London, and Washington, DC: Pinter, 1997).

A reaction to Amsterdam from an intergovernmentalist perspective is A. Moravcsik and K. Nikolaïdes, 'Explaining the Treaty of Amsterdam: Interests, Influences, Institutions', *Journal of Common Market Studies* 37 (1999), 59–85. Other analyses are offered by E. Philippart and G. Edwards, 'The Provisions on Closer Co-operation in the Treaty of Amsterdam', *Journal of Common Market Studies* 37 (1999), 87–108 and Y. Devuyst, 'The Community-Method after Amsterdam', *Journal of Common Market Studies* 37 (1999), 109–20.

Chronology

1945

February	Yalta Summit
May	End of World War II

1946

September	Civil war breaks out in Greece
September	Winston Churchill's 'United States of Europe' speech in Zurich
December	European Union of Federalists (EUF) formed

1947

February	British government tells US administration that it cannot continue aid to Greece and Turkey
March	Truman Doctrine announced in US Congress
March	Treaty of Dunkirk signed by Britain and France
April	Soviet walkout of Four Power Council of Foreign Ministers
June	Marshall Plan announced
July	Committee for European Economic Co-operation (CEEC) set up

1948

January	Benelux states commence economic union
March	Treaty of Brussels signed by Britain, France, and Benelux states
April	Organization for European Economic Co-operation (OEEC) replaces CEEC

May	European Congress, The Hague

1949

April	Federal Republic of Germany established
April	North Atlantic Treaty signed in Washington, DC, setting up NATO
April	International Authority for the Ruhr (IAR) established
May	Council of Europe formed

1950

May	Schuman Plan for coal and steel announced (Schuman Declaration)
June	Korean War begins
October	Pleven Plan for a European Defence Community (EDC) launched
November	Council of Europe adopts European Convention on Human Rights

1951

March	US give ultimatum to Adenauer on acceptance of anti-cartel powers for High Authority of ECSC
April	Treaty of Paris signed, establishing the European Coal and Steel Community (ECSC)

1952

May	European Defence Community (EDC) Treaty signed in Paris
July	ECSC begins operation

1953

March	Draft Treaty for a European Political Community (EPC) adopted
September	European Convention on Human Rights comes into force

1954

August	EDC Treaty rejected by French National Assembly (collapse of EPC)
October	Treaty creating Western European Union (WEU) signed
November	Monnet announces that he will not stand for a second term as President of the High Authority of the ECSC

1955

April	Spaak memorandum to ECSC states proposing an extension of sectoral integration
April	Beyen memorandum on behalf of the Benelux states proposing a general common market
June	Messina conference agrees to set up Spaak Committee to consider future of integration
October	Monnet sets up Action Committee for the United States of Europe

1956

March	Spaak Report published
May	Governments agree Spaak Report
June	Start of 'Messina negotiations' based on the Spaak Report
October	USSR invades Hungary to put down anti-communist uprising
October	Suez crisis

1957

March	Completion of 'Messina negotiations'
April	Treaties of Rome (establishing the EEC and Euratom) signed

1958

January	EEC and Euratom begin operations: Walter Hallstein is the first President of the EEC Commission, Louis Armand the first President of the Euratom Commission

1959

January	Customs duties within the EEC cut by 10 per cent

1960

May	Acceleration agreement on the common market and agricultural policy between six EC states
December	Organization for Economic Co-operation and Development (OECD) supersedes OEEC

1961

February	Paris summit agrees to set up committee under Christian Fouchet to review co-operation
March	Fouchet negotiations begin
July	Association Agreement signed with Greece
August	Britain, Denmark, and Ireland apply for membership of the EC

1962

April	Norway applies to join the EEC
December	Nassau agreement between Macmillan and Kennedy

1963

January	De Gaulle announces his veto of British membership

1965

April	Merger Treaty signed
July	Start of French boycott of the Council of Ministers

1966

January	Luxembourg compromise

1967

May	Britain, Denmark, and Ireland make a second application for membership of the EC
July	Norway makes a second application for membership of the EC

July	Sweden applies for EEC membership
July	Merger Treaty takes effect: Jean Rey is first Commission President for all three communities (ECSC, EEC, Euratom)
December	France blocks agreement on opening negotiations with the applicant states

1968

July	Merger Treaty comes into effect
July	Customs Union completed and common external tariff established

1969

December	Hague summit: the 'relaunching of Europe'

1970

June	Membership negotiations begin with Britain, Ireland, Denmark, and Norway
July	Franco Malfatti becomes President of the European Commission
October	Davignon Report on European political co-operation

1971

February	Werner Report on economic and monetary union
August	Ending of the convertibility of the US dollar into gold marks the collapse of the Bretton Woods international monetary system
December	Smithsonian agreements on international monetary regime to replace Bretton Woods

1972

January	Completion of membership negotiations with Britain, Ireland, Denmark, and Norway; accession treaties signed
March	Sicco Mansholt becomes President of the European Commission
March	Start of the 'snake in the tunnel' system of EC monetary co-ordination
May	Irish referendum in favour of EC membership

September	Norwegian referendum rejecting EC membership
October	Danish referendum in favour of EC membership
October	Paris summit

1973

January	François-Xavier Ortoli becomes Commission President
January	First enlargement of EC from six to nine member states
February	Italy forced to leave the 'snake'
December	OPEC oil crisis

1974

January	France forced to leave the 'snake'
July	Turkish invasion of Cyprus
December	Paris summit: agrees to direct elections to the EP and creation of the European Council

1975

March	First European Council meeting in Dublin
June	British referendum agrees continued membership of EC
June	Greek application for membership of EC
July	France rejoins the 'snake'
August	Signing of the 'Final Act' at the Conference on Security and Co-operation in Europe (CSCE) in Helsinki

1976

January	Commission Opinion on Greek application: not very favourable
April	France leaves the 'snake' for the second time
July	Opening of Greek accession negotiations

1977

January	Roy Jenkins becomes President of the European Commission
March	Portuguese application for membership of the EC
July	Spanish application for membership of the EC

October	Jenkins lecture at the European University Institute, Florence: calls for a new attempt at monetary union

1978

July	Bremen European Council agrees to pursue proposal from Schmidt and Giscard for a 'zone of monetary stability in Europe'
October	Opening of accession negotiations with Portugal
December	Brussels European Council agrees to create the European Monetary System (EMS)

1979

February	Opening of accession negotiations with Spain
March	EMS begins
May	Greek Accession Treaty signed
June	First direct elections to the European Parliament
November	Dublin European Council: Thatcher demands a British budgetary rebate

1980

June	Venice Declaration of the EC member states on the situation in the Middle East

1981

January	Gaston Thorn becomes President of the European Commission
January	Greece becomes a member of the EC
November	Genscher-Colombo Plan

1983

January	Stuttgart European Council signs Solemn Declaration on European Union

1984

February	European Parliament approves draft treaty on European Union
June	Fontainebleau European Council: British budgetary dispute settled; Dooge Committee on institutional reform set up

1985

January	Jacques Delors becomes President of the European Commission
February	Brussels European Council: mandates Commission to produce a plan for the single European market
June	Cockfield White Paper on the freeing of the internal market
June	Portuguese and Spanish accession treaties signed
June	Milan European Council: 1992 programme agreed
December	Single European Act (SEA) agreed in principle by heads of government at Luxembourg European Council

1986

January	Portugal and Spain join the EC
February	SEA signed by Foreign Ministers in Luxembourg (nine states) and subsequently the Hague (the remaining three states).

1987

April	Turkey applies for EC membership
July	SEA comes into effect

1988

February	Brussels European Council: agrees to a doubling of the structural funds
June	Hanover European Council: sets up the Delors Committee on monetary union
September	Margaret Thatcher's Bruges speech

1989

June	Delors Report on monetary union
July	German monetary union
July	Austria applies for EC membership
September	Start of collapse of Communism in eastern Europe
October	Delors lecture to the College of Europe in Bruges

1990

July	Stage 1 of Economic and Monetary Union begins
July	Cyprus applies for EC membership

July	Malta applies for EC membership
October	Re-unification of Germany; five new Länder become part of the EC

1991

July	Sweden applies for EC membership
December	Maastricht European Council: agrees principles of Treaty on European Union (TEU)

1992

February	Maastricht Treaty on European Union signed
March	Finland applies for EC membership
May	Switzerland applies for EC membership
June	Danish referendum rejects TEU
September	French referendum accepts TEU
September	British forced to withdraw from exchange rate mechanism of EMS
November	Norway applies for EC membership
December	Swiss referendum rejects membership of the European Economic Area in a referendum: Swiss government withdraws application for membership of EC

1993

May	Second Danish referendum accepts TEU
November	Treaty on European Union comes into effect

1994

January	Stage 2 of Economic and Monetary Union begins
April	Hungary applies for EU membership
April	Poland applies for EU membership
June	Austrian referendum in favour of EU membership
October	Finnish referendum in favour of EU membership
November	Swedish referendum in favour of EU membership
November	Norwegian referendum rejects EU membership

1995

January	Austria, Finland, and Sweden become members of the EU
January	Jacques Santer becomes President of the European Commission
June	Romania applies for EU membership
June	Slovak Republic applies for EU membership
October	Latvia applies for EU membership
November	Estonia applies for EU membership
December	Lithuania applies for EU membership
December	Bulgaria applies for EU membership
December	Madrid European Council decides on 'Euro' as the name for the single currency

1996

January	Czech Republic applies for EU membership
June	Slovenia applies for EU membership
March	Intergovernmental Conference to review TEU officially opens in Turin

1997

June	Amsterdam European Council: agreement on terms of Treaty of Amsterdam
July	Publication of Commission's *Agenda 2000* on eastern enlargement and the reform of the CAP and structural funds
October	Treaty of Amsterdam signed

1998

March	Opening of accession negotiations with Cyprus, Czech Republic, Estonia, Hungary, Poland, and Slovenia

1999

January	The Euro comes into operation, although national notes and coins alone remain in circulation until 2002
March	Resignation of the Santer Commission
March	Berlin European Council: agrees on a financial perspective for 2000–6, reform of CAP and structural funds, and to nominate Romano Prodi as the next President of the Commission.
May	Treaty of Amsterdam enters into force
May	Prodi becomes President of the Commission.

Part Three

The member states

Of all the sections to this book, the selection of content for this part is perhaps most controversial. This section has four chapters: each of the first three deals separately with one member state (Germany, France, and Britain), while the fourth is merely a sketch of the remaining twelve.

CHOICE OF STATES

Ideally, we would have given substantial coverage to each of the fifteen current member states and also discussed prospective members. However, constraints of time and space forced us into making choices for case study states. Here we have retreated to conventional practice somewhat by focusing on the 'Big Three' states of the European Union. These are not only big states in terms of population, but in many explanations of European integration, the actions of the governments of these states have been seen as pivotal. A notable example is Moravcsik (1991, 1993, and 1998—see Ch. 1 pp. 13–14) who explains key developments in European integration in terms of the convergence of preferences of these three governments.

Few observers would doubt the significance of the role played by the Big Three in the process of European integration. Most agree that the Franco-German axis following the Second World War was the essential relationship driving forward a united Europe. For many, this relationship remains pivotal. However, in our selection of case study states here, we are aware that there is a danger of simply reinforcing perceptions of the importance of the Big Three. We would warn the reader against adopting this perception easily: logic suggests that as the EU has expanded, and continues to expand, their importance is diluted. In this context, our section on the 'other' member states serves merely as an introduction to their relationship with the EU.

# 14 Germany

SUMMARY

In the early post-war years, West Germany developed an identity that was anti-communist, pro-western, and favourable to European integration. Throughout most of the lifetime of the EC/EU, German politicians have been able to take decisions that supported further

European integration against a background of a permissive consensus in public opinion. Following the reunification of Germany in 1990, the five new Länder were readily incorporated into the EC. After the TEU, Germany's leaders had to be more sensitive to domestic public opinion on the EU. Public attachment to the Deutschmark caused resentment at the proposal for a single European currency. Despite this, at the end of the decade, Germany remained at the heart of the European integration process.

Introduction

Germany has been at the centre of developments in European integration since the Second World War. Along with France, Germany has been seen as the driving force in shaping the integration process. Yet while broadly supportive of the integration process, domestic political changes have altered German priorities over time. Moreover, German reunification in 1990 created a new set of domestic challenges that demanded a response within the European context.

This chapter traces the development of Germany from the Second World War and its involvement in the process of European integration. The chapter takes in turn a number of factors impacting on Germany's relationship with its European neighbours:

- cultural
- constitutional and institutional
- public opinion
- the economic structure
- political developments.

Germany and European integration

Until October 1990 Germany was divided by the cold war into two states: the Federal Republic (West Germany) and the Democratic Republic (East Germany). West Germany was one of the founder members of the EC, and the most prosperous. Following reunification, the new German state was the largest member of the EU both in size of population and in economic strength, although the absorption of the former East Germany proved to be a prolonged and difficult process which weakened the German economy as a whole.

Germany has consistently supported European integration, despite being the biggest net contributor to the budget. This reflects the sense of national identity that was constructed after the war under the leadership of Konrad Adenauer. On the detail of EU policy, German attitudes reflect:

- cultural attitudes that predate the Second World War
- a decentralized constitution
- coalition politics
- an economic structure that is oriented to manufacturing and to exporting.

Cultural factors

At the end of the Second World War the German people were disoriented. Defeat, and guilt for the excesses of Nazism, were added to by the division of the country into two states. In this situation the people of West Germany were offered two alternative visions of their future. The Social Democratic Party (SPD) advocated the reunification of Germany, and was quite prepared to accept that this would involve neutrality in the emerging cold war. The Christian Democratic Union (CDU) and its allies, under the leadership of Konrad Adenauer, repudiated such an approach and followed a line of faithful adherence to the western camp in the cold war.

The result of the first federal election in 1949 was therefore very important for the future self-identity of West Germany. The identity that Adenauer fostered for the West German state was that it was:

- the inheritor of all that was best in German history
- an integral part of the western system of states
- a loyal and trusted ally of the United States.

When the French launched their initiatives for European integration, the response of Adenauer reflected the compatibility between this idea and the orientation that he had sought for the new West German state.

This identity was accepted by a large part of the West German electorate, which partly explains the dominance of electoral politics by the CDU in the 1950s. It had created a state identity in its own image. In order to make any impact in this state, the SPD had to adapt and accept most of its tenets. Once it was in office, the SPD also had to be careful to balance any moves that it made to improve relations with the East by moves to reassert its commitment to the West, so that it could not be accused of a return to neutralist tendencies.

CDU electoral success in the 1950s and 1960s was also due to the economic progress over which the CDU-led governments presided. Between 1950 and 1960 the average annual increase in the GNP of the Federal Republic was 7.9 per cent, compared with an average of 5.5 per cent for the OECD. The Economics Minister, Ludwig Erhard, attributed the success to his economic policy of a firm commitment to free-trade and free-market principles. Erhard set the pattern of economic thinking in the Federal Republic into a shape that it retains today.

At the same time, this free-market orientation had to adapt to older cultural attitudes that persisted from before the Second World War. The commitment of the German people to social solidarity and community meant that German capitalism took on a distinctive pattern. This 'Rhine capitalism' emphasized:

- co-operation between management and workers
- high levels of job security and social security
- protection of economic activities that were crucial to the survival of local communities.

It is often contrasted with the Anglo-Saxon form of capitalism that was practised in the United States, and increasingly Britain, where the level of social protection and co-operation is less important, and free-market economics is emphasized more consistently.

In one respect, though, German cultural attitudes were in line with the most orthodox form of market economics. Because of the traumatic experience of hyper-inflation in the inter-war Weimar Republic, the German people emerged from the war committed to a belief in the virtues of 'sound money'. While other European states were prepared to risk inflation in order to maintain high levels of economic activity, the Germans never embraced Keynesian economics. Protection against any erosion of the value of the currency was a fundamental of West German economic policy.

Constitutional and institutional factors

Bulmer and Paterson (1987: 240) described policy-making in the Federal Republic as based on 'sectorization, incrementalism and consensual relationships within discrete policy communities'. This situation arose partly out of the cultural commitment to social solidarity. Decisions were not taken without consulting all affected interests. It also arose out of constitutional and institutional arrangements that were imposed on Germany at the end of the war.

The most important factor limiting decisive decision-making in post-war Germany was the Federal constitution. This was in keeping with German tradition, but also reflected the aim of the allies to prevent a strong centralized state emerging which might again be subject to takeover by extremists, as had happened with the Nazis. The German Federal system gives significant powers to the regional authorities or 'Länder' (see Box 14.1, p. 150).

The federal structure therefore complements the cultural orientation to consensus politics. The same applies to the electoral system of proportional representation, overlaid on a constituency system (see Box 14.2, p. 151). The proportional system makes it unlikely that any one party will gain an overall majority. Coalition government is the norm. Every government since 1949 has been a coalition. In all but two of these, the small liberal Free Democrat Party (FDP) has been the junior coalition partner—first to the CDU/CSU, then to the SPD. This has given an added element of continuity to government policy across changes of major coalition party.

A third feature of the German institutional system that contributes to weak central control is the existence of constitutionally guaranteed independence for certain key agencies. Of these the most important is the central bank, or Bundesbank. The cultural prejudice in favour of sound money means that the Bundesbank is constitutionally required to follow monetary policies that keep inflation in check. It has done this rigorously, by raising interest rates when it saw any sign of inflation increasing, even when it proved politically embarrassing for the federal government.

Under the European Monetary System (EMS), the

Box 14.1 **The German federal system**

After the Second World War, the Federal Republic of Germany was divided into eleven Länder, or states (ten in West Germany, plus West Berlin). Following reunification in 1990 a further five eastern Länder were added. The Länder have considerable autonomy under the constitution. They have directly elected assemblies that can levy taxes, and have considerable independent powers in the fields of education, policing, internal security, the administration of justice, and the control of the communications media.

The governments of the Länder are represented at federal level in the upper house of the federal parliament, the Bundesrat. The lower house, the Bundestag, has to get the approval of the Bundesrat for any legislation that affects the Länder. In effect, this means almost all domestic legislation because the Länder are responsible for implementing even those policies that are the constitutional prerogative of the Federal government. The

political composition of the Bundesrat is therefore very important to the effectiveness of the Federal government. Elections take place in the Länder at different times, and there is rarely a year when there are no Land elections. The Federal government has to be in a constant condition of electoral alert both to protect the position of the coalition parties in the Land elections, and also to try to maintain a majority in the Bundesrat.

Issues between the Federal government and the Länder governments are not only debated on the level of inter-party politics. They are also subject to intra-party politics. The parties themselves are decentralized organizations, and even a party-political majority in the Bundesrat does not guarantee that the Federal government will be able to get agreement to its proposals. All the Land governments jealously protect the independence of the Länder against encroachment either from the Federal government, or from the EC/EU.

Box 14.2 **The German electoral system**

In Germany, every voter casts two votes: one for the constituency member, and one for a party. The constituency contest is decided on a simple majority basis: the winner is the candidate with the highest number of votes. This elects half the members of the lower house, the Bundestag. The party votes are then counted, and the other half of the seats are distributed to people on the party lists in such a way as to give as nearly as possible a parliament that reflects in its overall party balance—constituency members plus members from the party lists—the proportions of votes cast for the parties in the non-constituency part of the ballot. There is a 5 per cent threshold which any party has to surmount in order to be awarded any seats at all. This is to reduce the chances of extremist parties entering the Bundestag.

level of interest rates in Germany determined the level in the rest of the EMS member states. However, the Bundesbank continued to set rates purely with an eye on the inflationary prospects in Germany, and without reference to the effects on the other EMS states. This was one factor that inclined the other states to favour moving to a single currency.

Successive Presidents of the Bundesbank have never hesitated to criticize government policy, and such is the prestige and popular support for the bank in Germany that governments ignore such criticisms at their peril. Policy has to be co-ordinated with this important independent actor. The only example of the Bundesbank being overridden was when Helmut Kohl decided in 1990 that the currency union with the former German Democratic Republic would proceed on the basis of a rate of exchange between the Deutschmark and the Ostmark of which the Bundesbank did not approve. Kohl got his way, but the bank then imposed increases in interest rates to soak up the inflationary pressure that the currency union generated, and contributed to an economic downturn that may eventually have cost Kohl the 1998 election.

Public opinion

In line with the sense of identity that Adenauer fostered, German public opinion on European integration was consistently supportive throughout the post-war period. This meant that German governments could make concessions in negotiations in the EC which might run against public sentiment, but be able to get acceptance of their decisions by arguing that they were necessary to further European integration. Public support was maintained until the TEU, but then it plummeted (see Ch. 12, pp. 124–5).

The key factor in the change was the decision to abandon the Deutschmark and adopt the single European currency. The Deutschmark had become the symbol of Germany's rehabilitation after the war, and of its economic success. As well as the commitment to the symbolic aspect, there was a widespread fear that the single currency would be less stable than the Deutschmark. The German people did not believe that other European peoples had the same commitment as they had to a stable currency.

Other factors contributed to a cooling of public support for the EU. Once the single market was fully operative, the Germans found that some of their most treasured national institutions were under attack from Brussels. A series of competition cases brought against Germany proved very sensitive. An Austro-German agreement on book pricing, which the Commission held was in restraint of competition, was believed by the Germans themselves to be a necessary protection for small booksellers and a guarantee that German-language books would continue to be profitable for publishers to produce. An investigation into whether the locally-based Landesbanks were receiving an unfair advantage in competition with other banks, because they were underwritten by the Länder, also provoked public resentment.

Economic structure

The economic structure of a country affects the policies of its government in two ways. First, governments have to follow policies that they believe will benefit their own state's economy. Second, the economic structure affects the pattern of interest group pressures that the government faces.

The economic structure of West Germany was laid down in the 1950s, which is also when the economy experienced its fastest rates of growth. Factors contributing to the high growth rates of this decade were:

- availability of large quantities of skilled labour

- low wages

- high investment rates

- the role of the 'big three' banks (the Deutscher, the Dresdner, and the Kommerz).

In all west European economies after the war there was high demand for labour from industry. In every case this was satisfied in large part by the movement of population from rural areas. Agricultural productivity increased, agricultural employment fell, and industrial employment rose. In West Germany, though, there was another source of labour. While there was a decline in the rural population, there was also a steady influx of East German refugees from the Communist regime. The largest influx was at the end of the war. When the Federal Republic was established, 10 million people, a quarter of the total population, were refugees or expellees from the East. Between 1949 and 1961 another 2.5 million refugees entered West Germany from East Germany, comprising eventually 10 per cent of the workforce, and almost equalling the number entering industry from agriculture. These workers were generally more skilled and better educated than the rural population, which enabled West Germany to specialize in more advanced technological sectors of production than other states.

One effect of the steady influx of refugees was to keep wages low, even for skilled workers. Low wages meant higher profits, which allowed West Germany to maintain the highest level of investment as a proportion of GNP in western Europe. The government also gave generous tax incentives for investment.

The big three commercial banks, which had been split up by the allies as part of the process of deconcentration, soon reconstituted themselves. They were actively involved in financing industrial expansion, and performed a planning and co-ordination role that in other economies was performed by the state (Shonfield, 1969: 246–55).

After the building of the Berlin Wall in 1961 the supply of East German labour stopped. By that time, though, the pattern of West German strength in the technologically advanced industries, and particularly in the capital goods industries, was solidly established. The underlying strength of the West German economy was shown during the recession of the 1970s. It recorded the lowest levels of inflation and unemployment in the EC, despite high dependence on imported oil which quadrupled in price in the early 1970s.

The features of the economic structure that was established are identified in Box 14.3, p. 153.

Box 14.3 Features of German economic structure

Economic features	*Political implications*
Agricultural sector remained relatively large This was the consequence of the supply of labour from East Germany.	Small farmers continued to be an influential pressure group.
High degree of concentration in industry Between 1954 and 1967 the share of the fifty largest concerns in West Germany in total industrial turnover increased from 25 per cent to 42 per cent; a higher level of concentration than in any other west European economy. (Hardach, 1976: 222)	The government faced a dominant force of large-scale national enterprises.
Small-scale enterprises flourished However, because of the co-ordinating role of the banks, which were the main suppliers of capital to small enterprises, they were guided into areas where they complemented and were dependent on the larger concerns.	There was no strong independent pressure on government from small concerns.
Multinational investment (mainly of US origin) Attracted by the strength of the economy, political stability, the skilled workforce, and the initially low level of wages, this investment continued even after 1961, when wages began to rise. Between 1961 and 1974 West Germany received the bulk of all foreign direct investment in developed capitalist states. (Schlupp, 1980: 187)	This sector of German industry shared the commitment of the native enterprises to an open economy.
A general acceptance by large and small enterprises of an 'export mystique' (Kreile, 1977: 777) The government encouraged this export orientation by maintaining the Deutschmark at an artificially low exchange rate throughout most of the 1950s and 1960s. Only when the inflow of speculative funds to the Deutschmark threatened to undermine domestic anti-inflation policies did the government bow to pressure from its partners in the OECD. It revalued the Deutschmark upwards by 5 per cent in 1961 and then by a more realistic 9.3 per cent in 1969.	There was no conflict on such questions as the desirability of free trade.
The economy was strong in the technologically advanced industrial sectors (particularly capital goods) Demand throughout western Europe for capital goods during the post-war reconstruction was one of the reasons for the rapid expansion of the West German economy in the 1950s. In the 1960s, the slower pace of demand for this type of good led to a slowing of West German growth. This key sector of the economy led to pressure on government to open up new markets for capital goods.	The conversion of the ideologically anti-communist West German industrial class to improved relations with the East in the 1970s owed a great deal to their hope of finding new outlets for an industry which had a heavy dependence on exports.
From 1959, the government encouraged the export of capital This was to offset the embarrassingly large trade surpluses that were sustained by the undervalued currency. There was a steady increase in West German investments abroad. Large national corporations became multinational. By 1975, West German external investment had reached the same level as foreign investment in West Germany. (Kreile, 1977: 778)	This led to pressure on the government to follow more active international policies in order to protect those investments.

Political developments

To the surprise of many observers, the conservative Christian Democratic Union (CDU) won the largest number of seats in the first elections to the federal parliament, or Bundestag, which took place in 1949. It had been widely expected that the Social Democratic Party (SPD) would be the largest party. However, this belief was based on an extrapolation of pre-war patterns of voting, and ignored a number of important factors, especially the hostility of the Roman Catholic Church to the SPD. The division of the country reduced the Protestant population in West Germany and left it with a small Catholic majority. These voters were influenced by clerical support for the Christian Democrats. More generally, the SPD's appeal was not helped by it continuing to profess a commitment to Marxism, which was purely theoretical, but which made it look too much like the East German Socialist Unity Party for the comfort of many West German voters.

The other important factor in the success of the CDU was the personal popularity of its leader, Konrad Adenauer. A man untainted by participation in the politics of the failed Weimar Republic, or by any suggestion of collaboration with the Nazis, Adenauer was able to present himself as a symbol of German respectability. He was also known as the party leader who had the closest working relationship with the Allies. In many ways, the 1949 result was a personal triumph for him, which he used as the basis for dominating the CDU through to the early 1960s.

The CDU also managed to absorb most of the other small parties of the right and centre during this period of dominance, with two exceptions. The Christian Social Union (CSU) continued as a separate entity in Bavaria. Although often referred to as the Bavarian wing of the CDU, it was consistently to the right of the CDU in its social policies, and its leader had a national profile. The Free Democrat Party (FDP) managed to survive as an independent party by skilfully exploiting the one weakness in the CDU's electoral appeal: its association with the Roman Catholic Church. Although the CDU went out of its way to stress its non-confessional nature,

the strong support given to it in its early years by the Catholic Church, and the domination of the party by the Catholic Adenauer, meant that it was still unacceptable to some Protestant middle-class voters. It was to these people that the FDP appealed. In other respects the profile of its electorate was very similar to that of the CDU, but it was geographically strongest in the Protestant north of the country, and at its weakest in the Catholic south. It attracted a smaller share of the rural vote than the CDU (including here the Bavarian CSU) because the pattern of farming meant that there were more rural votes available in the Catholic south. However, farm-votes were an important ingredient in its overall support. It attracted fewer working-class votes than the CDU, which were more likely to go to the SPD in Protestant areas, but which did go to the CDU/CSU in significant numbers where religion interfered with a class-based pattern of voting. The FDP also attracted a high proportion of votes from immigrants from East Germany, who were as virulently anti-communist as Adenauer, but were also likely to be strongly Protestant.

Although the electoral niche occupied by the FDP gave it only a small percentage of the vote, coalition politics allowed it to exercise influence out of proportion to its size. With the exception of 1957, when the CDU/CSU won an absolute majority of seats for the only time, the FDP was an essential coalition partner. It used this position to unseat Adenauer from the Chancellorship in 1963, by which time his authority in the government had been seriously eroded. The FDP also brought about the fall of his successor, Erhard, by withdrawing from the coalition in 1966.

This move was taken in the face of a growing economic crisis, with which the FDP did not wish to be associated; but it temporarily backfired. The CDU responded by inviting the SPD to join it in a 'Grand Coalition', and the FDP was left out in the cold as the only opposition party in the Bundestag.

The rise of the SPD

For the SPD, the Grand Coalition was the opportunity it had been awaiting. It too had been forced to adjust to the new national identity. In 1959, at its Bad Godesburg Conference, it had adopted a new constitution that left out all mention of Marxism, and propounded the distinctly CDU-sounding economic line of 'as much competition as possible, as much planning as necessary'. It also accepted the foreign-policy orientation that Adenauer had given to the state. In 1961, it fought the election with a new Chancellor candidate, the popular young mayor of West Berlin, Willy Brandt, and made up ground on the CDU. All that it lacked was governmental experience, to prove that its leaders were capable of managing the CDU-state. That was what the Grand Coalition offered the SPD. At the cost of defections by traditional Socialists and the formation of an extra-parliamentary opposition by the student movement, the opportunity was taken.

SPD ministers made an impression on the public during the next three years. Economics Minister Karl Schiller introduced computer forecasting into the making of governmental economic policy, and appeared thereby to cure the economic crisis within a year. Vice-Chancellor Willy Brandt opened negotiations on the normalization of relations with the German Democratic Republic, and with other members of the Communist bloc, and received public recognition for it at a time when there was a general relaxation in East-West tensions and a feeling in West Germany that it was all right to follow this route if the United States was prepared to approve it.

In the 1969 election the SPD fought against its coalition partners, and only just failed to beat them. The CDU/CSU remained the largest single party in the Bundestag, but it was unable to form a government because the FDP agreed to form a coalition with the SPD. This represented a considerable gamble for the FDP, because it stood to lose votes among its traditional conservative supporters as a consequence. The issue that brought the two parties together was the development of a new *Ostpolitik* (Eastern policy), which sought to normalize relations with eastern Europe.

The demand for an improvement in relations with eastern Europe had grown amongst the electorate as a new generation of voters came of age, and as the cold war eased. It had received considerable strengthening when important sections of West German industry rallied to the idea, with an eye on the trading possibilities. The CDU was torn by internal dissension on the issue, with a strong element of traditional anti-communism preventing decisive action. When the CDU did come round to tolerating cautious moves, those moves were taken by the Grand Coalition, and the credit went to Brandt. As a former mayor of West Berlin, Brandt had long been associated with a call for improving relations with East Germany.

However, the new coalition had to accommodate itself to the West German sense of identity. It was important for the SPD that it should not be open to accusations of returning to its former demands for the unity of the two Germanies in a neutral state. Therefore, the new Chancellor, Brandt, was careful to balance his *Ostpolitik* with a reaffirmation of West German commitment to the EC. He was as instrumental as the new French President Pompidou was in making the 1969 summit a relaunching of the EC; and he was also careful to try to establish US approval for all his steps in Eastern Europe. Overall, his policy was a diplomatic and electoral success. He won a new majority for the SPD/FDP coalition in the 1972 election, before handing over to Helmut Schmidt in 1974.

Germany under Schmidt

With Schmidt the Federal Republic emerged as the leader of the EC, and a major world power in its own right. Brandt's success with his *Ostpolitik* had added a new element to the West German national image: as a state that played an independent role in world politics. Imbued with a new feeling of self-confidence, the West German people were ready to see their country build upon its economic success with more diplomatic forcefulness. Schmidt was just the man for the part; and his close personal relationship with Giscard d'Estaing, who became President of France in the same year as Schmidt became Chancellor of Germany, soon led to talk of a Franco-German condominium in Europe.

Notionally, Giscard was a conservative-liberal politician, while Schmidt was a Socialist; in practice the two were not politically far apart. Although leader of the SPD, Schmidt was more often found on the side of the conservative-liberal FDP in internal disputes within the coalition government. He was able to win election victories for the coalition in 1976 and 1980, at a time when the general climate of opinion in the Federal Republic was tending steadily more to the right, simply because he was widely regarded as the best conservative Chancellor on offer.

However, following the 1980 election a growing rift emerged between the coalition partners about how to tackle the economic problems caused by a large increase in the price of oil in 1979. The FDP Economics Minister, Otto Graf Lambsdorff, stressed the need to deal with a budget deficit that resulted from lower tax revenues and higher unemployment payments. For its part, the SPD wanted to spend more public money on a job-creation programme for the unemployed.

The FDP itself was internally split on the question, and the uncertainties and dissension within the party contributed to a rapid drop in its popularity. In the 1980 Bundestag election it had secured 10 per cent of the vote; its second-best result ever. However, by 1982 the FDP had fallen to the point where, in Land elections in Hamburg and Hesse, it failed to clear the 5 per cent hurdle below which a party receives no seats at all.

Hamburg, always an SPD stronghold, provided a shock to Schmidt's party too, when the CDU emerged from the election there in June 1982 as the largest single party. So by the end of the summer both coalition partners were unsettled. Tension within the government was brought to a head in September by the publication of a 34-page memorandum from Lambsdorff to Schmidt. In this, the Economics Minister called for tax cuts to encourage investment and enterprise, to be accompanied by cuts in social expenditure to close the budgetary deficit. The SPD leadership collectively attacked Lambsdorff's ideas as a danger to the social consensus.

On 17 September, the four FDP ministers resigned from the government. On 1 October, the FDP joined with the CDU and CSU in passing a constructive vote of no confidence in the Chancellor, which resulted in Helmut Kohl becoming Chancellor. Schmidt, who had heart-trouble, announced shortly afterwards that he would not stand again as Chancellor, for health reasons. Thus ended a period during which the Federal Republic had experienced the strongest leadership since Adenauer, and during which it had emerged as a leading diplomatic actor both within the EC and on the wider world stage.

The Kohl chancellorship

Kohl was not initially seen as a strong leader in the style of Schmidt, and he took over a coalition government that was probably more rent by division than the SPD/FDP coalition that it replaced. The FDP moved to the right because of the change of coalition partners, largely because of the defection from it of many of those members who had opposed the switch. Nevertheless, there remained a considerable gulf between the FDP on the one side of the coalition and the CSU on the other side, especially over foreign policy.

Hans Dietrich Genscher, the FDP leader, remained Foreign Minister, and continued to advocate a balanced approach to the West and East within the context of a clear commitment to NATO. This had been the line of the SPD/FDP coalitions. Although as Schmidt had become increasingly disillusioned with the United States, Genscher had often appeared in the latter years of that government to be the advocate of *Westpolitik* against the SPD's enthusiasm for cultivating closer relations to the East, in defiance of US policy under President Reagan. In the new coalition, Genscher, performing the same balancing act, appeared as the champion of continuing *Ostpolitik* against the strident demands of the CSU for a clearer alignment of the Federal Republic behind the confrontationist policies of the United States towards the Soviet Union and its allies.

Despite differences within the coalition, the new government was confirmed in office by the electorate in March 1983. Elections were deferred until then at the behest of the FDP, to give it time to recover from the disruption caused by the decision to change partners. In the gap between the fall of Schmidt and the holding of the elections signs emerged that the economy was reviving. Unfair though it may have been for the new government to get credit for this, it probably helped to produce an increase in the CDU's vote to bring it neck-and-neck with the SPD, even without the CSU vote added on. More important, though, was probably the disappearance of Schmidt as the SPD Chancellor candidate, and the instability that loss of office produced within that party, which experienced an apparent swing to the left.

The other factor that may have contributed to the decline in the vote for the SPD was the success of the Greens. The Greens took 5.6 per cent of the national vote and became the first new party since 1957 to gain seats in the Bundestag. Environmentalism cut across the traditional left-right divisions of German politics, but the support for the Greens ate significantly more into the electorate of the SPD and the FDP than into that of the CDU/CSU. The success of the Greens indicated the high level of concern over environmental issues, fuelled by the death of the German forests because of acid rain; no Federal government could afford to overlook this concern in the future. The Greens also opposed both the construction of nuclear power stations and the stationing of nuclear weapons on German soil.

Despite the CDU and CSU between them gaining 49 per cent of the seats in the 1983 election, the presence of 27 Green Party representatives deprived them of an absolute majority. This necessitated the continuation in the coalition of the FDP, which had just managed to clear the 5 per cent hurdle with 6.9 per cent of the vote. This outcome meant a continuation of internal coalition bickering. Yet despite all the signs of disagreement within the coalition and weakness in the Chancellor, the government parties were able to win another election victory in January 1987. This was largely the consequence of the remarkable turn around in the country's economic fortunes. The FDP did better in the election than either of its coalition partners, increasing its support from 6.9 per cent to 9.1 per cent, while both the other parties lost ground to a somewhat revived SPD.

In the last months of 1989 the government's attention was dominated by the need to move rapidly towards economic, and possibly political unification with the German Democratic Republic. This move was deemed necessary to prevent a flood of refugees entering the Federal Republic and putting an intolerable strain on the social fabric there. In rising to this challenge, Chancellor Kohl began at last to look the part of a leader of international stature. He moved rapidly and decisively when faced with the historic opportunity to reunite his country.

Reunification

Economic and monetary union between the two German states took place in July 1990, and on terms that were extremely favourable to East Germans (see Box 14.4, p. 158). In August 1990 the two Germanies signed the unification treaty. In September, this was followed by the so-called 'Two Plus Four' Treaty between the two German states and the states that had defeated and occupied Germany at the end of the war (Britain, France, the United States, and the Soviet Union). Unification took place in October, and the in December the first post-war all-German elections were held. The governing coalition won the elections with 54.8 per cent of the vote.

It was not long, however, before discontent began to grow in both East and West. In April 1991 there were demonstrations in East Germany against rising unemployment. The Treuhand, the state agency charged with the reconstruction of the formerly Communist East German economy, had no choice but to close many loss-making plants as a prelude to the sale of the assets to West German companies. Jobs that had been guaranteed under Communism disappeared under capitalism. The East German people, who had no experience of the effects of a market economy, reacted strongly to this loss of their livelihoods. At the same time, the higher taxes that were levied to pay for the absorption of East Germany caused discontent in the West. Opinion polls showed the popularity of the government in steady decline throughout 1991, especially in the East.

Although unification had been rushed through in an attempt to stem the flood of refugees from East to West, it did not achieve this objective because of the poor condition of the East German economy. West Germany also became the target of economic refugees from throughout the former Communist bloc. The influx of asylum-seekers caused an increase in anti-foreigner sentiment amongst the West German population. Physical attacks against foreigners increased, and support for extreme right-wing parties increased in Land and local elections during 1992.

The newly unified Germany also found itself under international pressure to contribute to the various UN operations that were proliferating during this period. This sparked off a considerable political debate. There was genuine concern amongst many Germans that their armed forces should not be deployed abroad. For some this was based on a fear of history repeating itself; although for many it was based on less altruistic feelings of concern for the safety of German youth in places such as Somalia and Bosnia. Eventually, in the course of 1993, it was agreed to allow German forces to enforce the no-fly zone in Bosnia, and to send 1,600 troops to Somalia to assist the relief operation there. In July 1994 the Constitutional Court ruled that, contrary to what most Germans believed, the Basic Law did not prevent German forces from taking part in collective defence or security operations outside the NATO area. The new Germany took another step towards developing its status as a world power.

The Maastricht Treaty

At the same time as the debate over German involvement in UN operations was taking place, the German parliament was debating the ratification of the Maastricht Treaty, which proved to be another factor adding to the problems of the government. It became apparent from opinion polls that a majority of the German population was hostile to the provisions of the Treaty on monetary union. There was a

---

Box 14.4 Reunification Terms

Against the advice of the Bundesbank, Kohl insisted that individuals' savings in the East German Ostmark be exchanged one for one for Deutschmarks up to a limit of:

- 2,000 marks for children under 15 years old,

- 4,000 marks for adults,

- 6,000 marks for those over 60.

The conversion for all other purposes would be at 2 to 1. Even the latter figure was clearly unjustified by the relative strength of the two currencies, but it did go some way to protect the value of the savings of individuals and small businesses.

widespread reluctance to give up the Deutschmark, which had been an anchor of stability throughout the post-war period. The experience of the monetary union with East Germany further undermined support for a similar experiment in unifying with other currencies: the result of all-German monetary union had been higher taxes and higher interest rates. Such was the reaction against European monetary union that the Bundestag was only prepared to ratify the Treaty if it was guaranteed that the government would respect a parliamentary vote on whether to proceed to the final stage of adopting a European single currency. When consulted on the issue, the Constitutional Court ruled that not only did the Bundestag have a right to make such a demand, it had a duty to do so; it also ruled that German participation in a monetary union would have to receive the assent of the Court.

In October 1994 the governing coalition won yet another electoral victory, against an unfavourable economic context but also against a weak opposition. The CDU/CSU took 41.5 per cent of the vote nationally, against the SPD's 36.4 per cent. Together with the FDP's 6.9 per cent, the coalition was returned to office, but with only a ten-seat majority in the Bundestag. However, the steady loss of control of Land governments meant that the Bundesrat was in the hands of the opposition parties. Despite an image of stability in the midst of what was a turbulent political scene throughout Europe, the position of the German government was not strong following the election. It subsequently weakened further as the FDP vote started to collapse in Land elections.

After the election, Kohl continued to defend the single currency project despite its unpopularity. Paradoxically, the extent of the domestic opposition that he encountered strengthened his hand in EU-level negotiations, so that Germany seemed to get its own way on almost every issue concerning the details of EMU (see Ch. 26, pp. 349–52). Kohl also managed to get most of what he wanted on eastern enlargement (see Ch. 13, pp. 133–4). These successes gave the impression of Kohl as the strong man of Europe. Especially after the replacement of Margaret Thatcher by the less forceful John Major as British Prime Minister, and of François Mitterrand by Jacques Chirac as French President, Kohl's position appeared secure.

The external image of the iron Chancellor belied the internal position. Kohl remained a weak leader, unable to control the pluralism of the German political system. The slowness with which Germany implemented the single market became an embarrassment, but reflected the unwillingness of the government to confront domestic vested interests. In November 1995 Germany opposed a proposal from the Commission for more rapid opening of the EU market to agricultural exports from the states of central Europe. This was in conflict with the Chancellor's strong advocacy of rapid progress to granting the same states full membership of the EU, but reflected capitulation to the German farm lobby.

Kohl's biggest domestic problems were over the economy and the single currency. Germany had insisted on rigorous application of the 'Maastricht criteria' for membership of the single currency (see Box 26.2, p. 349). This was to ensure that the German economy would not be harnessed to weaker economies that would drag it down. Unfortunately, the persistence of high unemployment in Germany made it increasingly likely that it would not itself meet the convergence criteria. Plans to reduce the ratio of public debt to GDP were not implemented in the face of strong opposition; and the suggestion that there would have to be further cuts in public expenditure even to meet the short-term requirement that the budget deficit should not exceed 3 per cent of GDP led to calls for a delay to the start of EMU until after the recession had ended.

The Länder were the most vocal critics of Kohl's commitment to the single currency. In June 1998 there were reports that the Chancellor had done a deal with the Land governments: they would stop criticizing the single currency and in return he would oppose further transfers of competencies to Brussels that affected the Länder. At Amsterdam, Kohl turned from having been previously a strong advocate of the extension of QMV and the absorption of second pillar (Justice and Home Affairs) issues into the EC pillar, to being the main blockage on such changes.

While Kohl could try to neutralize opponents by making deals with them, the persistent poor performance of the economy was something that he could not address by making deals. In September 1998 his coalition lost office to the SPD under Gerhard Schröder, in coalition with the Greens.

The Schröder government

The new coalition had a rough first few months. Schröder had to assert his authority over the Green environment minister, Jürgen Trittin, on the issue of the decommissioning of nuclear power stations, and over his SPD colleague, the Finance Minister Oskar Lafontaine. Lafontaine formed a close alliance with the French Socialist government, and particularly with the French Minister of Finance, Dominique Strauss-Kahn. Together they caused problems between Germany and Britain by insisting on pursuing an EU policy of tax harmonization; and they put pressure on the new ECB to lower interest rates as a response to continued sluggish economic growth. This did not coincide with the image that Schröder wanted to give his government. He was personally closer to the new social democracy of British Labour Prime Minister Tony Blair than to the rather more traditional socialism of the French government.

In March 1999, Lafontaine resigned following a confrontation with Schröder. Soon after, in June 1999, Blair and Schröder jointly launched an agenda for economic reform entitled 'Europe: The Third Way, Die Neue Mitte' which rejected 'measures leading to a higher tax burden and jeopardizing competitiveness and jobs in the EU'. It called for the reduction of taxes on hard work and enterprise, and said that public expenditure as a proportion of national income had reached the limits of acceptability. These were all tenets of the 'New Labour' approach of Blair, and were far from the positions of the French Socialists.

The document did not go down well with the rank-and-file of the SPD, and when the party suffered a series of embarrassing defeats in Land elections, Lafontaine publicly blamed the adoption of the new approach. For a time it looked as though Schröder might retreat from his programme of modernization in the face of these setbacks and this criticism. When the giant Holzmann construction company found itself in serious financial trouble in November 1999, Schröder declared that it would be amazing if the Deutsche bank, the company's main creditor, allowed it to go bankrupt. Schröder met with representatives of the company and the bank to press the need to find a rescue package. At about the same time, the Chancellor criticized the hostile takeover bid launched by the British mobile communications firm Vodafone AirTouch for the German telecommunications giant Mannesmann.

However, the Holzmann case produced another response from the government that pointed in a different direction. Shortly after the Chancellor's meeting with the interested parties, the new Finance Minister, Hans Eichel, announced that he would be introducing legislation to allow German banks and corporations to divest themselves of their cross-holdings in other German companies without incurring capital gains tax. This apparently technical measure signalled that the government had listened not only to the Holzmann side of the case, but also to the Deutsche bank. All German commercial banks had actually been trying to reduce their exposure to business failures among the big traditional German companies by divesting themselves of their substantial shareholdings for some time. This was in line

---

Box 14.5 German governments since 1949

(Prior to reunification the references are to governments of the Federal Republic of Germany only)

Dates	Chancellor	Coalition parties
1949–63	Konrad Adenauer	CDU + CSU + FDP*
1963–6	Ludwig Erhard	CDU + CSU + FDP
1966–9	Kurt-Georg Kiesinger	CDU + CSU + SPD
1969–74	Willy Brandt	SPD + FDP
1974–82	Helmut Schmidt	SPD + FDP
1982–98	Helmut Kohl	CDU + CSU + FDP
1998–present	Gerhard Schröder	SPD + Greens

* In the first Bundestag there were also minor conservative parties in the coalition, but these were soon absorbed into the CDU.

with the need to respond to the challenge of regional and global competition in the banking sector. The accumulated share holdings from the past threatened the German banks with just such a situation as had arisen in the Holzmann case. Covering themselves against such eventualities tied up reserves that they might otherwise use to expand and to support new ventures in sectors such as information technology.

Schröder's comment on the Vodafone AirTouch bid for Mannesmann also proved to be less than the reversion to old attitudes that some analysts in the financial markets had painted it. After the initial expression of concern, the government stood back and allowed the bid to run its course. This resulted in a former German industrial champion falling into foreign ownership. Although the government responded by saying that it would conduct an inquiry into the country's takeover laws, there was no real expectation that this would produce any changes.

Towards the end of 1999, a scandal over CDU funding during the Kohl era made it considerably easier for Schröder to take this line. This scandal effectively eliminated the CDU in the short term as a credible electoral force. This development provided a window of opportunity for the government to push forward with its modernization programme to bring Germany more into line with the requirements of the modern globalized capitalist economy.

Conclusion

Germany, like all the member states of the EU, has had to adapt itself to the reality of existence in a rapidly changing world. Post-war West Germany constructed a particularly successful form of capitalism that went under the title of the social market economy. Although this featured a strong commitment to the idea of market economics, it was to a modified form into which the state would intervene vigorously where necessary to maintain social stability. What post-war German citizens wanted above all was prosperity combined with security. The social market economy provided both.

The persistent economic problems of the early 1980s were the first sign that the West German model might be getting left behind by the rapid changes in other parts of the world, particularly the United States and Asia. The commitment of the Kohl governments to the single market programme represented a response to the problem posed by the globalization of capitalism. In providing a regionalist response to globalization, though, it increased the effects of regionalization. As the strongest economy within the EC, Germany might have been expected to benefit; but the creation of the single market made it feasible for German companies to produce in other parts of the EC where labour costs were lower than in Germany. The single market did not produce the boost to German investment that the government might have hoped for.

Problems were exacerbated by the reunification of West and East Germany. This was a historic opportunity that the government could hardly spurn, but it brought with it the need for higher taxes in the west to provide the funds to develop the crumbling infrastructure of the east. At the same time, the opening up of investment opportunities in the rest of the former Communist bloc gave a further boost to the tendency of German companies to become multinational and to produce outside their high-cost homeland.

The efforts of the SPD/Green coalition under Gerhard Schröder to address the issues that were threatening to undermine German competitiveness involved unpopular measures that went against the commitment of the German people to the social market economy. To head off political discontent, the government was not averse to blaming the EU on issues such as the removal of the privileged status of the Landesbanks. However, this did nothing to enhance the legitimacy of the EU in Germany, which had plummeted after the conclusion of the TEU.

KEY POINTS

Cultural factors

- The victory for the CDU in the first election in the Federal Republic allowed Adenauer to foster a sense of identity for the West German state that was anti-communist, pro-western, and favourable to European integration.

- Adenauer's Economics Minister, Ludwig Erhard attributed the economic miracle of the 1950s, to his free-market, free-trade principles. These became part of the self-identity of the Federal Republic.

- The commitment to free-market, free-trade principles was overlaid by older cultural values of commitment to social solidarity and community to produce the distinctive model that is known as 'Rhine capitalism'.

- On monetary policy, German cultural attitudes strongly favoured a policy that gave primacy to combating inflation.

Constitutional and institutional factors

- The Federal German constitution gives considerable autonomy to the constituent states, the Länder. They also control the upper house of parliament, the Bundesrat.

- The electoral system institutionalizes coalition governments, which further constrains the freedom of manoeuvre of the Federal government.

- Key state agencies are constitutionally independent of the government. The most important is the Bundesbank.

Public opinion

- Throughout most of the lifetime of the EC/EU, German politicians could take decisions that supported further European integration against a background of a permissive consensus in public opinion. After the TEU it became more difficult to do so.

- The main issue that caused resentment was the proposal for a single European currency. The German people did not want to abandon the Deutschmark.

- Competition cases brought by Brussels were seen as illegitimate interference with the institutions of the German way of life.

Economic structure

- West Germany established a strong position in technologically advanced industries, and particularly the capital goods industries, after the war. This was based on skilled labour fleeing East Germany, low wages, high investment rates, and co-ordination of industrial activity by the big banks.

- This alternative supply of labour allowed the agricultural sector to escape rationalization: small farmers remained an influential interest group.

- A number of factors placed pressure on governments to maintain an outward-looking economic policy. These included: industrial concentration; the synergy between large and small enterprises; inward investment by foreign multinationals; the general acceptance of an export orientation; and the heavy dependence of the capital goods industries on exports.

- From the early 1960s investment by German companies abroad increased. This led to pressure on the government to become more politically active in foreign affairs to protect those investments.

Political developments

- 1949–66 West Germany was dominated by the CDU, under the leadership of Adenauer until 1963, then briefly under Erhard. During this period, the main features of the state were established.

- 1966–9 'Grand Coalition' of the CDU/CSU with the SPD. During this period, the SPD established its credentials as a credible party of government.

- 1969–82 the SPD led coalition governments with the FDP, and held the Chancellorship, first under Brandt then, from 1974, under Schmidt. Brandt's Chancellorship was marked by the normalization of relations with eastern Europe (the *Ostpolitik*), Schmidt's by West Germany's emergence as an international political actor of influence.

- 1982–9 the CDU/CSU/FDP formed a coalition under Helmut Kohl that was marked by internal dissension and weak leadership.

- 1989–90 Kohl emerged as a leader of stature when he seized the opportunity offered by the collapse of Communism to reunify Germany.

- 1990–8 Kohl played a dominant role in European politics, but faced increasing pressures domestically, especially because of the poor performance of the economy.

- September 1998 the CDU/CSU/FDP coalition lost office to an SPD/Green coalition under Gerhard Schröder.

QUESTIONS

1 How important have domestic political changes been to Germany's attitude to European integration?

2 Why has opposition to monetary union been particularly strong in Germany?

3 What was the impact of re-unification on Germany's approach to the EU?

FURTHER READING

The starting point for further reading on German Politics is: G. Smith, W. E. Paterson, and S. Padgett (eds.) *Developments in German politics 2* (Basingstoke: Macmillan, 1996).

Specifically on Germany and Europe: B. Heurlin (ed.) *Germany in Europe in the Nineties* (Basingstoke: Macmillan, 1996); P. J. Katzenstein, *Tamed power: Germany in Europe* (Ithaca, NY, and London: Cornell University Press, 1997); D. Marsh, *Germany and Europe: The Crisis of Unity* (London: Mandarin, 1995).

Although it is now tremendously dated, having been written before the reunification of Germany, there has been little to improve on the analysis offered of the domestic bases of Germany's policy in the EC in: S. Bulmer, and W. Paterson, *The Federal Republic of Germany and the European Community* (London: Allen & Unwin, 1988). The same authors have more recently written an article on the same subject: 'Germany in the European Union: Gentle Giant or Emergent Leader?', *International Affairs* 72/1 (1996), 9–32.

15 France

SUMMARY

In post-war France, Charles de Gaulle played an important role in fostering a French identity which was pro-Europe and distinctly anti-American. French public opinion on European integration fluctuated throughout the post-war period, but remained generally positive enough to allow French politicians to maintain a central role in the process. However, the referendum on the TEU produced only a very narrow majority in favour of ratification. This was in the context of heightened concerns about the economic and social effects of membership of the EU. Following the referendum, the EU remained a controversial issue. Politicians could no longer take it for granted that public opinion would back them in supporting further integration.

Introduction

Perhaps more than any other state, France has been central to the process of European integration. As the state most vulnerable to a resurgent Germany after the war, France had the greatest motivation for securing European co-operation. Despite major domestic political and economic changes, France has remained generally supportive of the integration project at both the elite and mass levels throughout the post-war period.

This chapter traces the development of France from the Second World War and its involvement in the process of European integration. The chapter takes in turn a number of factors impacting on France's relationship with its European neighbours:

- cultural;
- constitutional and institutional;
- public opinion;
- the economic structure;
- political developments.

France and European integration

The Second World War did not destroy the French national identity in the same way as it did the German. Nevertheless, it was a difficult experience for the French. Defeat and occupation were severe blows to national pride. The internal conflict between collaborators and the Resistance left a deep impression on post-war attitudes and politics. The need to avoid war in the future was universally accepted, although how to achieve that was less clear.

For the first thirteen years of the post-war period, French politics returned to something like their pre-war pattern of ideological divisions and extreme fragmentation, except that overt nationalism was muted. During this period politicians had less influ-ence on policy than did officials, or technocrats as they were known. Then in 1958 the Fourth Republic gave way to the Fifth, and to the strong government of Charles de Gaulle.

Politically, de Gaulle made a similar impression on France to that which Adenauer made on Germany: he fostered an identity within which his successors had to work. Economically the Fifth Republic continued a process of modernization that had begun under the Fourth. This gradually transformed the pattern of economic interests which governments had to take into account when defining the national interest.

Cultural factors

The first cultural factor that has been of consistent relevance to understanding French attitudes to European integration is nationalism. France was one of the first modern states, and one of the first modern nations. Nationalism has an appeal both to the conservative right and to the republican left in France.

At the end of the war the traditional French right was discredited by its collaboration with the Nazis. The political forces that were in the ascendant were almost all on the left and centre-left of the political spectrum. The parties that emerged from the internal resistance were the Socialists, the Communists, and the Social Christians who formed the Mouvement Républicain Populaire (MRP). These parties did not promote nationalism as a value because of its association with Nazism.

The one conservative figure of stature was General Charles de Gaulle, who had led the Free French forces from outside France. De Gaulle became Prime Minister of the first post-war provisional government, but soon realized that he would not be able to govern in conjunction with the left-wing parties and resigned to construct his own political support. His success in building up the Rassemblement du Peuple Français (RPF) as a force based on traditional nationalism indicated that the pattern of political parties in the Fourth Republic did not accurately represent the balance of political opinion in the country.

The discrediting of the French right at the elite level was not an accurate reflection of opinion at the mass level. The Vichy regime (see Box 15.1, p. 167), which was condemned by the politicians who were on the winning side, had not been unpopular with a large part of the French people. Nor did left-wing voters necessarily see the war as an ideological war against Nazism, which was the interpretation of those who had been active in the Resistance. For many ordinary people on the left it had been a national war against the Germans.

A gap therefore opened up between the range of political options on offer under the Fourth Republic, and the preferences of the electorate. This gap was filled by the Gaullist RPF, which used nationalism to appeal to voters across the political spectrum. When the Fourth Republic collapsed under the pressure of a colonial war in Algeria, de Gaulle was able to return to office on his own terms, creating a strong presidential system of government with himself as president.

Just as Adenauer set the tone of West German politics by giving the state and the electorate a new national identity, so de Gaulle, after he became president, set the tone of French politics by reviving an old sense of national identity. French nationalism is historically linked with an anti-Anglo-Saxon attitude that originally was directed against Britain, but was easily transferred to the United States when that country became the standard bearer of what to the French is Anglo-Saxon imperialism. Nationalism created a sense of national pride which remained to act as a limitation on those who followed de Gaulle.

At the same time as he appealed to traditional French nationalism, de Gaulle presided over an economic transformation of France which completed the movement that was already underway from a rural to an urban society. Yet this process was masked by a political discourse that idealized the rural France that de Gaulle's policies were destroying. The Gaullist rhetoric fed off and helped to sustain another aspect of French national culture: an attachment to the countryside and to the peasant way of life that gave farmers a disproportionate influence over French policy. Even in the 1990s, by which time France had become a post-industrial nation with a heavy dependence on services, it was difficult for French governments to accept an agreement in the GATT Uruguay Round that would have freed trade in services (see Ch. 28, pp. 392–3). This was because French farmers objected to the provisions on agriculture and had the sympathy of a significant part of the urban population.

At the end of the war, the need for economic modernization to keep France in touch with Germany was clearly perceived at the elite level, but was not accompanied by an unambiguous commitment to free trade. Economic liberalism had not served France well in the past, and the technocrats who took control of the post-war reconstruction were wedded to a belief in the virtues of *dirigisme*, a system of managed capitalism or 'indicative planning' in which the state not only retained a considerable

---

Box 15.1 **The Vichy regime**

Following the German invasion, in 1940 France was split internally into a *zone annexée*, joined to Germany, a *zone occupée*, controlled by the German authorities, and a *zone libre*, within which a government was reconstituted at Vichy, in central France. This government was led by Marshal Pétain, a military hero of the First World War. However, the Vichy government was increasingly subject to the demands of the German forces and became identified as a collaborationist regime.

(*Source*: Stevens 1996: 19)

holding in industry itself, but also co-ordinated the investment decisions of private firms. This was the spirit that informed Monnet's plan for the ECSC, and it was the aspect of ECSC that caused the biggest problems between France and Germany.

The whole process of restructuring the French economy involved active government participation. Although the attitude towards indicative planning varied between different presidents, there was never the free-market orientation that marked West German economic policy. Even after 1976, when Raymond Barre became Prime Minister and announced that France in future must respond to market discipline, this did not mean a withdrawal of government from an active role in the economy. In fact, more was achieved in this direction by the subsequent Socialist governments under the presidency of Mitterrand; but they continued to use a discourse of state intervention, so reducing the impact on cultural attitudes among the public.

There was also a very different attitude in France from that in Germany on what was believed to be the trade-off between inflation and economic growth. Whereas the German culture was deeply attached to the principle of sound money, even at the expense of lower rates of growth, the French elite was determined above all that France should not fall far behind Germany in economic growth. The risk of inflation was worth taking to achieve this. Their attitude encouraged the belief among the French people that if growth slackened and unemployment threatened to increase, the state would intervene to stimulate the economy and prevent them from having to make sacrifices.

The attitude of the elite to inflation changed in the 1970s in response to the recession that began in 1974. However, it was more difficult to change the public culture in respect to the short-term sacrifices that were necessary in order to restrain inflation.

Constitutional and institutional factors

The French administrative system has traditionally been highly centralized. Although some reform in a decentralizing direction took place under in the early 1980s under a Socialist government (the Defferre reforms of 1982), French regions and localities have nothing like the autonomy that the German Länder have from the Federal German Government.

At the level of central government, there is a traditional hierarchy within the state apparatus that leads to a greater coherence of policy than is achieved in less centralized systems. Wright (1990) argued that the effectiveness of this hierarchy had been undermined by the increasing sectorization of policy, with autonomous policy communities developing in different policy sectors. However, at the EU level the French administration still has the reputation of being very coherent in its positions across negotiations on different issues.

Under the Fourth Republic, the strength of the administrative system contrasted with the fragmentation of the political system (see Box 15.2, p. 168).

Box 15.2 The Fourth Republic

The constitution of the Fourth Republic was modelled on those of previous republics. It was a system that centred on the legislature, the National Assembly. Elections were by proportional representation, which produced a multi-party system in which all governments had to be coalitions between several parties. These coalitions often fell apart over specific issues, and governments were frequently replaced between elections.

The result was weak political control over the administration, and a disproportionate influence of technocrats over policy.

De Gaulle tried to remedy this in the constitution of the Fifth Republic. So urgent was the crisis in France that was caused by the Algerian war (see Ch. 6, p. 73), and so indispensable was de Gaulle to

Box 15.3 The French electoral system

The system of a directly elected president and a directly elected parliament produces the potential for incoherence in policy. This is especially so because the president is elected for a seven-year period and the parliament for five years. However, the president has the power to dissolve the parliament and call new elections. Successive presidents have used this power to hold parliamentary elections immediately after their own election if the existing parliament did not contain a majority of their supporters. In most cases, the electorate has responded by providing the majority that the president needs to ensure presidential control over policy.

Box 15.4 Cohabitation

Cohabitation first happened in 1986, when a change to proportional representation for National Assembly elections allowed the right to form a coalition under Jacques Chirac as Prime Minister, while the Socialist François Mitterrand remained President. In the 1988 presidential elections, Mitterrand was returned to office and immediately dissolved the National Assembly. His Socialist party won a majority in the consequent election, so restoring the relationship between president and government that was intended by the framers of the constitution.

In 1993, for the second time during Mitterrand's presidency, the right won a majority in parliamentary elections. This time Mitterrand appointed not Chirac, but Edouard Balladur to be Prime Minister. Although Chirac formally nominated Balladur, Mitterrand made it clear that he had made the choice of which individual to appoint (Stevens, 1996: 63). This time the cohabitation ended with the presidential victory of Chirac.

The third example of cohabitation began in 1997, when Jacques Chirac was President. He made a mistake in calling early elections to the National Assembly at a time when the conservative government was not popular, and the Socialists were returned at the head of a left-wing coalition with the Communists and Ecologists.

resolving the crisis, that he was able to dictate the terms on which he would return to office. He asked for and got a new constitution in which the centre of authority was not the National Assembly but the President. After de Gaulle's first term as President, from 1965 onwards, the President was given added legitimacy by being directly elected. Nevertheless, most observers believed that the new constitution, by weakening parliamentary powers, further strengthened the influence of the administration in policy-making (see Box 15.3, p. 169).

Although the system normally produces a president who has a majority in the National Assembly, there have been three periods of what is known as *cohabitation*. This is when the president has been of one political family and the government has been from the other side of the political divide (see Box 15.4, p. 169).

During these periods of *cohabitation* it is not clear where the balance of political power lies, and there may sometimes be contradictions in French policy. Under what were once considered 'normal' circumstances for the Fifth Republic, it was clear that the President was the dominant figure. This was certainly the case with de Gaulle, Pompidou, and Giscard d'Estaing. Even during the first two periods of cohabitation there was not much doubt that Mitterrand was in control. The position was less obvious during the second cohabitation of Chirac and Jospin. On the first two occasions of cohabitation there was a sense that this was an abnormal period, which would return to normality following the presidential elections (Stevens, 1996: 63). However, this third period was potentially five years long, and 'demonstrated the desire of many French voters to swap the concentration of political power in the President's hands for a more balanced distribution of power within the French executive' (Cole and Drake, 2000: 32).

Public opinion on European integration

During the Fourth Republic, public opinion on European integration was generally positive. The fear of war, and acceptance of the need for reconciliation with Germany were important factors. The policy was, nevertheless, controversial. The Communists in particular opposed the ECSC and EC as capitalist plots, and the high level of support that they enjoyed in France contributed to a higher level of negative responses. On the other hand, the Socialists and Christian democrats supported the policy, and their electorates followed their lead.

Over most of the history of the EC/EU, levels of support for European integration in France, though lower than in Germany, remained positive. They fluctuated according to circumstances and leadership, reaching lower levels during de Gaulle's disputes with the EC in the mid-1960s, higher levels during the period in the mid-1970s when Giscard took a leading role in EC affairs. However, just as the TEU precipitated a crisis in German public opinion on the EU, so it did in France. Guyomarch, Machin, and Ritchie (1998: 97–8) identified six factors that helped produce only a very narrow Yes vote (51 per cent to 49 per cent) in the 1992 French referendum on the ratification of the Treaty (see Box 15.5, p. 170).

The same authors pointed to the fact that the controversy generated by the referendum led to an increase in interest in the EU. This meant that in the 1994 elections to the EP the turnout in France increased against the EU-wide trend, from 50.4 per cent in 1989 to 55 per cent (Guyomarch *et al.*, 1998: 101).

> ## Box 15.5 **Factors in the 1992 French referendum**
>
> - High unemployment and the argument of the No campaign that under the TEU the government would no longer be able to take effective action to create jobs.
>
> - Concern that further integration would lead to a weakening of the level of social security.
>
> - hostility to the MacSharry reforms of the CAP (see Ch. 24, pp. 316–17).
>
> - Concern at the effects on previously protected sectors of the economy of the opening of the domestic market.
>
> - Concern at the what was seen as interference by Brussels with aspects of the traditional French way of life, including the right to produce and eat unpasteurized cheese, and to shoot migrating birds.
>
> - Splits in all the main parties on their attitude to the TEU, which deprived the electorate of clear leadership.
>
> (*Source*: Guyomarch, Machin, and Ritchie, 1998: 97–8)

As in Germany, politicians could no longer rely on a permissive consensus of public opinion. Following the referendum the number of issues where France was in conflict with the EU increased, increasing the need for governments to take up principled positions in defence of French national interests.

Economic structure

Where West Germany experienced its economic miracle in the 1950s, with a slowing of growth rates in the 1960s, the French economy did not really take off until the arrival of the Fifth Republic. A respectable annual average of 4.6 per cent growth in the 1950s was followed by a more than respectable annual 5.8 per cent in the 1960s (Fohlen, 1976: pp. vi and 100). The Fourth Republic laid the basis for

> ## Box 15.6 French trade within the franc zone
>
> In the early 1950s trade with the franc zone (mainly colonies and ex-colonies) accounted for 40 per cent of all French trade: by 1970, this proportion had dropped to 5 per cent. The EC took 52.5 per cent of total French exports in the period 1968–70, as against only 12 per cent that were sold to the countries of the franc zone (Sautter, 1982: 453).
>
> In 1954, France sold more goods in Algeria than it exported to West Germany: by 1970 West Germany was France's largest trading partner (Fohlen, 1976: 103).

this acceleration, though, by the efforts of the Planning Commission to promote the modernization of the economy.

Between 1949 and 1962, 1.8 million workers left agriculture, almost one-third of the total agricultural labour-force (Sautter, 1982: 453). Within the industrial sector the share of total output from the traditional industries, such as textiles and clothing, declined, while the share of more modern industries such as engineering and chemicals and metal manufacture increased. In these leading sectors, the state planners fostered a new spirit of enterprise, so that growth was seen as a positive factor for which it was worth taking risks. An older attitude, which favoured caution and protection, prevailed in other industrial sectors, but the previous domination of a small-business mentality even in large businesses was effectively ended. This was perhaps the major contribution made by the planners of the Fourth Republic to the success experienced in the Fifth Republic.

De Gaulle contributed political stability. He also ended the Algerian war, which released much-needed labour for the industrial expansion, and ended the last of the colonial links that had diverted French trade into unprofitable channels (see Box 15.6, p. 171).

These trends were encouraged by highly interventionist Gaullist governments, which also fostered the continuation of other changes that had begun under the Fourth Republic. Between 1960 and 1970 another 1.3 million workers left agriculture (Ald-

croft, 1978: 178). In industry, the government promoted concentration of ownership, so that the pattern of economic interests came increasingly to be dominated by large national corporations. At the same time, despite considerable Gaullist rhetoric about the promotion of national firms and the need to keep the French economy in French hands, foreign investment accelerated. Multinational corporations, mainly US in origin, gained control over important sections of French productive capacity (see Box 15.7, p. 171).

The result of these changes in the nature of industrial control was that French governments increasingly faced a pattern of interest-group pressure which paralleled that facing West German governments: a combination of large national enterprises and multinational corporations, with a common export orientation. There remained important differences, though. The small-business sector, which in West Germany was structurally integrated with the large national and multinational concerns, in France was concentrated in the declining industrial sectors, and did not share the orientation towards growth and export of the larger companies. Because of the conservative nature of the political support for de Gaulle, the small businesses were not entirely without influence.

Then there were regional problems in France that led to political pressure on the government. While economic development in West Germany was geographically spread over most of the country, this was not so in France. Here, the south and east, together with Brittany, did less well than central regions from

> ## Box 15.7 Multinational corporations in France
>
> In 1960, 8 per cent of industrial turnover in France was under foreign control; by 1980 this had risen to around 25 per cent. However, in the most advanced sectors of the economy the proportions were much higher. In the capital goods and chemical industries foreign control was around 40 per cent by 1980, and in computers and agricultural machinery it was over 50 per cent
>
> (Cox, 1982: 15, table 1.3; 16, table 1.6)

the expansion of industry, and remained predominantly rural and relatively poor. At the same time, the north suffered particularly from the decline of the old nineteenth-century industries that were concentrated there.

Finally, but very importantly, the reduction of the numbers working in agriculture did not mean a decline in its economic importance. In 1974, agricultural exports still made up nearly a fifth of total French exports, and agricultural output amounted to 5.9 per cent of Gross Domestic Product (GDP). In comparison, West Germany was a net food importer throughout the post-war period, and in 1974 agriculture only accounted for 3 per cent of its GDP.

From the start of the presidency of Giscard d'Estaing efforts were made to restructure the economy towards high-technology goods and capital goods. These efforts continued under the Socialist governments after 1981. Their failure is clear in figures for the end of the 1980s quoted by Hall (1990: 184). France's share of world exports of high-technology products was only 6 per cent, compared to 22 per cent for Japan, 18 per cent for the United States, 12

per cent for the Federal Republic, and 8 per cent for Britain. The strength that France had long held in agriculture, armaments, vehicles, and luxury goods was balanced against a weakness in capital goods, household appliances, and mass-produced consumer goods. The pattern was little different from that which had existed before the extensive efforts at restructuring.

This pattern had changed little by the end of the 1990s. France did, however, emerge as a major exporter of services, a factor that had to influence government policy. In 1995, services accounted for 46.6 per cent of GDP and France was the second largest exporter of services in the world after the United States.

By 1995, the pattern of French trade was very strongly oriented towards the rest of the Europe. The EU accounted for 64 per cent of both imports and exports, with Germany alone accounting for 18 per cent of both imports and exports. This degree of interdependence acted as a powerful constraint on government economic policy.

Political developments

The parties of the Fourth Republic were divided on economic modernization and on European integration. The political forces that favoured modernization were themselves divided by the old cleavage of religion. Both the Socialists and the MRP were in favour of economic modernization and European integration, but were unable to collaborate in government because the MRP was a Catholic party, and Socialist supporters were anti-clerical.

De Gaulle managed to avoid the religious division by appealing to nationalism, and using this as the cover for modernizing the economy. However, his nationalism was not easy to reconcile with the abandonment of national sovereignty to the EC. While he understood the need for France to take part in the economic aspects of the EC, he opposed the political implications of closer integration. (For presidents of

Box 15.8 Presidents of the French Fifth Republic

1959–1969	Charles de Gaulle
1969–1974	Georges Pompidou
1974–1981	Valéry Giscard d'Estaing
1981–1995	François Mitterrand
1995–	Jacques Chirac

the Fifth Republic see Box 15.8, p. 172; for prime ministers see Box 15.9, p. 173.)

De Gaulle resigned in 1969. His successor, Georges Pompidou, needed to attract the support of the successors of the MRP while placating the hardline nationalists in the Gaullist party. The result

Box 15.9 **Prime Ministers of the French Fifth Republic**

Jan 1959–April 1962	Michel Debré
April 1962–July 1968	Georges Pompidou
July 1968–June 1969	Maurice Couve de Murville
June 1969–July 1972	Jacques Chaban-Delmas
July 1972–May 1974	Pierre Messmer
May 1974–August 1976	Jacques Chirac
August 1976–May 1981	Raymond Barre
May 1981–July 1984	Pierre Mauroy
July 1984–March 1986	Laurent Fabius
March 1986–May 1988	Jacques Chirac
May 1988–May 1991	Michel Rocard
May 1991–April 1992	Edith Cresson
April 1992–April 1993	Pierre Bérégovoy
April 1993–May 1995	Edouard Balladur
May 1995–May 1997	Alain Juppé
May 1997–	Lionel Jospin

was a contradictory pattern of pro- and anti-EC moves.

Pompidou died in office in 1974. His successor, Valéry Giscard d'Estaing, was not a Gaullist. He had his own political party, the Independent Republicans (later named the Republican Party). This had formed part of the *majorité* under de Gaulle and Pompidou, but had retained its separate identity as a modernizing force close to the centre. Even more than Pompidou, Giscard needed the votes of the centre to win a majority. François Mitterrand had forged the left into a cohesive alliance, and in the 1974 presidential election Giscard only beat Mitterrand by less than 1 per cent of the vote.

Giscard's first government contained a high proportion of politicians from the pro-EC centre parties, but he had a Gaullist Prime Minister, Jacques Chirac. The ambiguity on policy towards the EC that had marked Pompidou's presidency continued, but Giscard was more influenced by the pro-EC centre, and in 1976 Chirac resigned over Giscard's support for direct elections to the EP. However, he dared not withdraw Gaullist support for the *majorité* because of the strength of the challenge from the left. Giscard was therefore free to follow a more pro-EC policy, although he also had to respect the popularity across the political spectrum of de Gaulle's brand of nationalism.

Giscard was able to pursue a close alliance with West Germany within the context of these constraints. De Gaulle had sanctioned such a policy by his close relationship with Adenauer. In addition, West Germany under Schmidt was becoming increasingly critical of the United States. An alliance with West Germany allowed Giscard to take up positions that were independent of the United States, while satisfying the centre that he was pro-European.

At the same time, Giscard was no more content than his predecessors (or his successor) to allow France to be economically the weaker partner in this relationship. His economic policy was designed to close the gap between France and Germany. Particularly under Prime Minister Raymond Barre, whom Giscard appointed in 1976, it involved a considerable effort to restructure the economy. This involved a move away from traditional industries such as steel to free capital for investment in new sectors. However, this process was inevitably socially disruptive. When combined with the deleterious economic effects that followed the Iranian revolution and the second oil-price shock of 1979, this process contributed to Giscard's defeat in the 1981 presidential election.

Mitterrand's victory in May was consolidated the following month by a victory for his Socialist Party in elections to the National Assembly. They won 285 out of 491 seats, and together with their Communist allies had a majority of 167 seats. As in the presidential election, Gaullist voters appeared to have stayed away from the polls in large numbers. Commentators at the time suggested they were respecting the tradition inherited from de Gaulle of allowing the President to govern by allowing him his parliamentary majority.

The new government, which included Communist ministers, embarked on an expansionary economic policy, in contrast to the austerity policies of the Barre government. Reducing unemployment was identified as the primary target. In taking this line, the French government was breaking with a consensus that had emerged amongst the advanced capitalist states: that reflation would not work, and would only fuel inflation.

The failure of the policy illustrated the degree of

interdependence of the French economy. By expanding the economy at a time when the other EC economies were still in recession, the government succeeded only in sucking imports into the country. The balance of trade went dramatically into deficit, and the French franc came under severe downward pressure, threatening its position within the ERM.

Although voices on the left urged Mitterrand to suspend France's membership of the ERM, the President backed his Finance Minister, Jacques Delors, and negotiated realignments of parities within the ERM. The West Germans were persuaded to shoulder some of the burden of adjustment by revaluing the Deutschmark. This move assisted French exports to the Federal Republic. However, the price that the Germans insisted on was a complete reversion of French economic policy to bring it back into line with the consensus that inflation was the primary threat to future prosperity. Because of this, the freeze on wages and prices that the Socialist government felt obliged to introduce in June 1982 was just the start of a two-year period of austerity.

The failure of the 1981–4 economic experiment illustrated most graphically the effects of interdependence on the ability of any government to manage the French economy as it wished. Yet the same effect had been obvious much earlier, and the adoption by the Barre government of a rhetoric of bowing to the market marked a degree of acceptance of this fact of contemporary life. It was impossible to follow economic and monetary policies that were radically out of line with those of other EC members. Moreover, the increased internationalization of financial markets had removed from the French state one of its main levers for getting private companies to comply with its plans; its virtual monopoly in the first two post-war decades over sources of finance for industrial expansion.

After 1984 Mitterrand accepted the limitations that interdependence placed on autonomous government action and adopted the EC as the vehicle for the realization of his policy objectives. This change of direction came too late to prevent the electorate punishing the Socialists in the 1986 parliamentary elections for earlier policy failures. A change in the electoral system, introducing proportional representation in place of the two-ballot constituency system, minimized the damage to the Socialists, who managed to retain 206 seats. The change also allowed the extreme right-wing National Front to gain 35 seats that would otherwise have gone to the parties of the more moderate right. The Communists also won just 35 seats. The Gaullist Rassemblement Pour La République (RPR) and the Union Pour La Démocratie Française (UDF) got 148 and 129 seats respectively. This was not enough for an absolute majority, but enough for Chirac, as the nominated candidate for Prime Minister of both the main conservative parties, to win a vote of confidence. This was achieved with the support of the National Front and other small right-wing groups.

There now began an experiment in power-sharing, or *cohabitation*. Jacques Chirac became Prime Minister, but Mitterrand made it quite clear that he intended to see out his full seven-year term as President. From 1986 to the presidential election in 1988 France had a two-headed executive, each head pointing in a different political direction.

Chirac's image as Prime Minister was of a man who tried to do too much too quickly, and had little patience with constitutional niceties. He also failed to end the periodic outbreaks of violence over industrial restructuring in the country that had marred the latter months of the Socialist government, a problem that he had promised to solve. In the April 1988 presidential election Mitterrand beat Chirac comfortably, and appointed the Socialist Michel Rocard as Prime Minister.

Problems began to mount for Mitterrand, though, following the reunification of Germany in 1990. The difficulties in the German economy sparked off a recession in France that led to rising unemployment, which translated into increasing discontent with the Rocard government. In an attempt to boost the government's flagging popularity, Mitterrand replaced Rocard in May 1991 with Edith Cresson, at the time France's most popular Socialist politician. However, Cresson's popularity immediately began to dip, as did Mitterrand's own ratings once the temporary boost of the Gulf War disappeared. Following poor results for the Parti Socialiste (PS) in regional and cantonal elections early in 1992, Mitterrand dismissed Cresson and replaced her with Pierre Bérégovoy, but the change did nothing to revive the flagging fortunes of the PS.

In September 1992 it was revealed that Mitterrand

was suffering from a serious illness, which called into question his ability to see out the remainder of his presidential term. In March 1993 the PS, weakened by a series of corruption scandals as well as by continuing high levels of unemployment, was heavily defeated in elections to the National Assembly. The RPR and UDF between them took 75 per cent of the seats, and Edouard Balladur was appointed Prime Minister, ushering in another period of *cohabitation*.

France was now taking on the aspect of a nation under siege. To the economic problems were added concern about the effects of the GATT agreement that had been reached in the last months of the Socialist government, and which threatened in particular French agriculture. There was also growing anti-immigrant feeling, which was exploited by the extreme right-wing Front National (FN) of Jean-Marie Le Pen. The FN took 12.4 per cent of the vote in the first ballot of the 1993 elections, playing on the reaction to the Maastricht Treaty, to the GATT deal, and to unemployment.

However, Balladur insisted on honouring the GATT agreement, and continued to follow the policy of tying the value of the French franc to that of the Deutschmark, the policy known as the *'franc fort'*. He introduced a programme of privatization of state companies, but had to delay the sale of Air France following protest strikes by air crew. He also had to drop plans to lower the national minimum wage for young people, which was an attempt to create more jobs, after protests by students.

After Jacques Delors, bloodied by the Maastricht ratification *débâcle*, announced that he would not be a presidential candidate for the PS, it became likely that a conservative would win the 1995 election to succeed the ailing Mitterrand. Balladur stood, but his association with economic policies that continued to cause pain counted against him. Jacques Chirac emerged from a clutch of candidates to take the presidency in a run-off ballot against the PS candidate Lionel Jospin. The margin of victory was surprisingly narrow, at just over 5 per cent (52.6 to 47.4 per cent). The low turnout did not augur well for the stability of the new government under Alain Juppé, that was appointed by Chirac.

Within the year Juppé, was facing widespread strikes against the plans of his government to cut social welfare, change the rules on public sector pensions, and streamline the state railway system ahead of possible privatization. In November 1995 the country was brought almost to a halt by striking public sector workers, and during December protests began to turn unpleasant, with attacks on property and police. Eventually Juppé, was obliged to abandon his plans for reform of pensions and privatization of the railways. However, he insisted that other cut-backs in expenditure were still needed if France were to meet the Maastricht criteria for entry to the single currency.

This issue was uppermost in Chirac's mind when he decided in April 1997 to hold parliamentary elections a year ahead of schedule. It seemed clear that a further round of public expenditure cuts would be necessary in the coming year for France to meet the Maastricht criteria. These would be unpopular, and probably hand the election to the Socialists. Chirac hoped, therefore, to win a majority before implementing the cutbacks. Unfortunately, the electorate had not forgotten the winter of 1995-6, and the Socialists won the election, ushering in a further period of *cohabitation*.

Conclusion

Adapting to the demands of globalization is difficult for any state. For France it has been particularly difficult. The post-war socio-economic system that was established in France emphasized exactly those elements that seem to be most a handicap to competing in the globalized economy. Mobile capital is attracted to locations that have low taxes and limited state intervention. France has established social stability based on a system of state support that requires high taxes; and state intervention in the operations of large corporations has been the norm. Attempts to move away from the system of extensive social welfare have been met by direct action that has disrupted normal commercial life. In addition, the resistance of public-sector trade unions to privatizations has reinforced the reluctance of state planners to surrender their dominant position.

Added to these problems of transition has been the difficulty of finding a political discourse that will legitimate the dismantling of the post-war structures. De Gaulle set the tone for all subsequent French political discourse. His legacy included rejection of Anglo-Saxon hegemony. Any attempt by governments of either the left or right to effect structural transformation in the French system have to be presented as a way of strengthening France in the world. Change cannot be justified by reference to ideas of Anglo-American provenance such as Clinton and Blair's 'New Democrat/New Labour' project. Nor would the phrase beloved by Margaret Thatcher work in France, 'There is no alternative'. The French philosophical outlook rejects the idea that human societies should allow their fate to be determined by impersonal economic forces.

For successive French governments the EC/EU has been seen as a regionalist response to the loss of autonomy by the nation-state in the face of the globalization of capitalism. If states cannot control the forces of capitalism alone, they must pool their sovereignty to exercise control collectively. However, this view of the aims and objectives of the project of European integration has not been shared by all France's partners, and particularly not by the British. The German position has lain somewhere between the French and British, but the arguments have increasingly gone against the French view, leading to tension between France and the EC/EU.

It is difficult to tell whether the Jospin government accepts the necessity of economic restructuring and the social restructuring that goes with it, or whether it is being swept along with a tidal wave of change that is generated by the global system, magnified by the economic regionalization of the single market programme, and to which French corporations are being obliged to respond. France at the end of the twentieth century was changing. The state was reducing its direct holdings in commercial concerns. Industry and services were becoming more multinational. The size of the state budget deficit was being brought under control. At the same time, the Socialist government was protesting to its domestic constituency that it was compelled to meet the requirements of membership of the single currency. Alongside this, the government demanded that its partners in the EU make control of unemployment a priority. Yet the plan for combating unemployment that the EU accepted was marked not by the higher public spending that the French government had implied it was asking for. Instead, the EU provided measures to train the unemployed and to encourage small-business start-ups that were perfectly compatible with the Middle Way/Neue Mitte paper that the British Labour Party and the German SPD produced.

It is clear that France will never easily subscribe to ideas that have been accepted elsewhere within the capitalist system. Just as French engineers have persisted in solving problems in a peculiarly French way, as illustrated by the construction of nuclear power stations (see Ch. 7, pp. 83–4), so French intellectuals and politicians will continue to search for distinctively French ways of solving the problems of existence in a globalizing capitalist system. However, these ideas have to be compatible with France's obligations as a member of the EU. France's economic welfare is too closely tied up with the success of the EU for it to be otherwise. If a distinctively European way forward can be found, for which the French government can claim a large part of the credit, then it will be easier for France and the EU to effect the adaptation to the new realities that face all member states in the twenty-first century.

KEY POINTS

Cultural factors

- Conservative attitudes among the French people survived the war, but traditional nationalism was not on offer from the mainstream political parties in the Fourth Republic. The demand was supplied by the RPF of Charles de Gaulle, who seized power as a candidate of national unity when the Fourth Republic collapsed in 1958.

- De Gaulle revived nationalism and gave it a distinct anti-American, and to a certain extent, anti-British flavour.

- Under both the Fourth and Fifth Republics the French economy was transformed, but de Gaulle concealed the extent of the social revolution over which he presided by adopting a discourse that emphasized the virtues of rural France. This played on a sense of identity with the peasant farmer among the French people, and reinforced it.

- The economic culture of the French elite placed emphasis on maintaining high rates of economic growth rather than on maintaining monetary stability.

- The French people came to believe that if they were faced with economic hardship, the state would intervene.

- A change in elite attitudes to inflation and growth in the 1970s was not shared by the public, particularly so far as it implied tolerating high levels of unemployment.

Constitutional and institutional factors

- France is a centralized system of government with some autonomy given to the regions and localities, but it is far from a federal system.

- The system of administration is hierarchical and therefore has a high degree of coherence. It is also highly efficient.

- Under the Fourth Republic, the political system produced fragmentation and weak government at the political level. This allowed the technocrats of the administration to exercise considerable influence over policy.

- In the constitution of the Fifth Republic, de Gaulle created a strong presidential system that allowed the reassertion of political control. The administration still played a large role in policy-making.

- Normally the direction of French government is clear because of presidential domination. However, when the majority in the National Assembly is from a different political grouping to the President this can introduce ambiguity into French policy.

Public opinion

- French public opinion on European integration fluctuated throughout the post-war period, but remained generally positive.

- The referendum on the TEU produced a very narrow majority in favour of ratification. This was in the context of heightened concerns about the economic and social effects of membership of the EU.

- Following the referendum, the EU remained a controversial issue. Politicians could no longer take it for granted that public opinion would back them in supporting further integration.

Economic structure

- The economic planning by technocrats in the Fourth Republic paid off with high growth rates in France in the early years of the Fifth Republic.

- There was a considerable movement of labour off the land throughout the 1950s and 1960s, but agriculture continued to be an important export industry.

- The restructuring of the economy involved a decline in older industries and the promotion of newer industries such as engineering and chemicals. Different business philosophies prevailed in the declining and expanding sectors.

- Under de Gaulle the pattern of French trade reoriented away from the former colonies to the EC.

- Gaullist promotion of concentration meant that large national firms came to dominate; but there was also considerable inward investment by multinationals, especially in the more advanced technological sectors.

- Small businesses were concentrated in the declining industrial sectors, but were politically significant during the Gaullist years because of their electoral influence.

- Efforts by both conservative and Socialist governments after 1974 to strengthen the high-technology sectors of industry were not particularly successful; but the services sector did grow considerably in importance.

Political developments

- De Gaulle overcame the religious divisions that prevented the political forces in favour of modernization from co-operating in the Fourth Republic. He modernized the economy behind a smokescreen of nationalist ideology.

- His successor, Pompidou, had to try to please both nationalist supporters of de Gaulle and centrist supporters of European integration.

- Giscard d'Estaing faced a similar dilemma, but it was eased after the Gaullists under Chirac left his government in 1976. Giscard pursued a close alliance with West Germany.

- Giscard's attempts to restructure the economy led to the victory of the left under Mitterrand in 1981.

- At first the Socialist governments tried unilaterally to reflate the French economy. After 1982 they started to retreat from this policy, and in 1984 Mitterrand adopted European integration as the centrepiece of his policy.

- The Socialists lost the 1986 parliamentary elections, and there followed two years of *cohabitation* between Mitterrand as President and Chirac as Prime Minister. Mitterrand handled this relationship better, and won a second term of office in 1988. Parliamentary elections gave the left a majority, and a series of Socialist governments followed.

- In 1993, the Socialists were again defeated in parliamentary elections. This produced a brief period of *cohabitation* until the 1995 presidential election, which Chirac won.

- In 1997, Chirac called early elections to the National Assembly, which returned a majority for the left. There followed a period of *cohabitation* between Chirac and the Socialist Prime Minister, Lionel Jospin.

QUESTIONS

1 How important have domestic political changes been to France's attitude to European integration?

2 What explains the generally supportive view of European integration within the French public?

3 How important was de Gaulle in shaping the general tenor of France's relationship with the rest of Europe after the war?

FURTHER READING

Of the many general texts on the government and politics of France, two that can be strongly recommended are: A. Cole *French Politics and Society* (Hemel Hempstead: Prentice Hall, 1998); A. Stevens *The Government and Politics of France* (Basingstoke and London: Macmillan. 1996).

The essential starting point for further reading specifically on France and the EU is: A. Guyomarch, H. Machin, and E. Ritchie, *France in the European Union* (Basingstoke and London: Macmillan, 1998).

Recommended shorter pieces that cover the most recent developments are: H. Drake and S. Milner, 'Change and resistance to change: management of Europeanisation in France', *Modern & Contemporary France* 7/2 (1999) 165–78; A. Cole and H. Drake, 'The Europeanization of the French polity: Continuity, Change and Adaptation', *Journal of European Public Policy* 7/1 (2000) 26–43.

16 Britain

SUMMARY

The Second World War did not alter the fact that the British people felt more affinity with the Commonwealth and the United States than with the rest of Europe. This fact, along with a strong cultural attachment to the ideas of national and parliamentary sovereignty, meant that public opinion in Britain was less positive about European integration than in Germany or France. For the most part, British leaders have done little to change this inherent public Euroscepticism. Thus, Britain was a late applicant to the EC and, as a member, has been something of an 'awkward partner' in the eyes of other member states.

Introduction

Often portrayed as an 'awkward partner' in relation to European affairs, Britain is nevertheless a major player in the process of integration. A combination of factors both internal and external to Britain delayed entry into the European Community until 1973. Since that time it has been regarded as one of the 'big three' players in European politics. Despite this, domestic cultural and economic circumstances have set Britain apart from the more pro-integrationist tendencies of France and Germany.

This chapter traces the development of Britain from the Second World War and its involvement in the process of European integration. The chapter takes in turn a number of factors impacting on Britain's relationship with its European neighbours:

- cultural
- constitutional and institutional
- public opinion
- the economic structure
- political developments.

Britain and European integration

The problem of economic decline, and the attempts of successive governments to halt that decline and to modernize the economy dominated politics in post-war Britain. Membership of the EC was conceived as part of the process of modernization. European integration was not adopted as a valuable end in itself, but primarily as a means to an economic end. There was no sense that nationalism and the nation-state were outdated concepts to be superseded by a European identity.

Nationalism in Britain, as in France, was not discredited in the war. On the contrary, in Britain successful resistance to invasion and ultimate victory strengthened it. There was an important difference, though, between the sense of self-identity implied by French nationalism and that implied by British nationalism.

Although imperialism had played a part in the development of French nationalism, there was never any doubt about France's European identity. For the British, Europe began on the far side of the English Channel, and there was a tradition of Britain remaining aloof from European affairs as far as possible. For the average British citizen there was a greater identification with the white settler populations of Australia, Canada, New Zealand, and South Africa than with the peoples of France, Germany, the Low Countries, and Italy.

This difference in national identity reflected an economic orientation that also was not directed towards Europe. Trade with the Commonwealth and with the world beyond Europe generally was extremely significant for the British economy. Other, non-trading links became increasingly important in the post-war world, especially through the investments of British companies abroad, and this continued to give British policy-makers a different perspective on the EC even after membership.

Cultural factors

In 1945, the British people saw themselves as victors in a nationalist war. Neither among the elite nor among the people at large was there any sense that nationalism was discredited, nor that British national identity needed to be rethought. It was assumed that Britain would go on dominating economically and politically in the post-war world. This perception changed only slowly.

Through a long period of imperialism and hegemony, the British people had developed a sense of their uniqueness that bordered on condescension towards other peoples. This was particularly pronounced in the attitudes to France and Germany. Several factors in British culture made the country ill-suited for participation in the first experiments in European integration, and to some extent continue to form a cultural barrier between Britain and the rest of Europe (see Box 16.1, p. 182).

Successive post-war governments did nothing to counteract these popular prejudices, and indeed most British ministers probably shared them. Legitimacy continued to be based on the defence of national sovereignty. It was very difficult for any government to confess that it was about to surrender any element of sovereignty. This cultural commitment finds an echo only in France among the other EU member states.

On economic and social issues, British culture was divided. Greenleaf (1983: 14–28) argued that the British political tradition had two poles, libertarianism and collectivism. There was no simple correspondence between these ideal types and political parties. Elements of both appeared in the programmes of all the political parties. During the 1950s and 1960s the collectivist elements in the cultural mix grew strong, encouraged by full employment, the welfare state, and the unwillingness of even Conservative governments to challenge the industrial power of the trade unions. This trend contributed to the so-called 'British disease' of industrial relations blighted by strikes. It culminated in the winter of 1978–9, when strikes paralysed the country, and destroyed the Labour government (see below under 'Political Developments').

Under Margaret Thatcher the power of the trade unions was broken, by brute force in the case of the coal miners, but more generally by high levels of unemployment that accompanied a rapid restructuring of the economy. At the same time, the government lost no opportunity to extol the virtues of individualism and enterprise. The cultural effect was to reduce the collectivism that had marked post-war Britain; but collectivism never disappeared from the national cultural mix, and acted as a constraint on the reforms of the Thatcher governments.

It could be argued that Thatcher made a similar mark on the British sense of self-identity to that made by Adenauer on Germany and by de Gaulle on France. After Thatcher there could be no easy return to the degree of collectivism of the period between 1945 and 1979. The economic culture in particular was shifted significantly in the direction of enterprise. The weakness of the trade unions and the acceptance by the British people of the validity of market reforms put British political leaders in a much stronger position to pursue the policies that were necessitated by globalization than were their counterparts in Germany or France. This showed in the adoption by the Labour government that was elected in 1997 of many of the Conservatives' policy positions.

Where Germany and France subscribed to versions

Box 16.1 British Euroscepticism

Noel Currid (1998) examined the discourse used by those who described themselves as 'Eurosceptics' during several of the key parliamentary debates on the relationship with the EC/EU. He showed that the following themes recurred:

- prejudices against France and Germany;

- prejudices in favour of the Commonwealth;

- an attachment to the 'special relationship' with the United States of America;

- an attachment to national parliamentary sovereignty.

of 'Rhine capitalism', Thatcher's reforms made Britain a leading proponent of the virtues of the US model of capitalism based on flexible labour markets and an open economy with little direct state involvement. This division came to be significant in the triangular relationship between the three largest member states of the EU, which determined the nature of the EU itself.

Constitutional and institutional factors

Britain remains a highly centralized political system. Before 1997 it was even more centralized. Local government had no constitutional autonomy, and what it had been granted by custom and practice was clawed back by the Thatcher governments. Local government finances were controlled by central government, and its functions were reduced by reforms that created a variety of new quasi-autonomous agencies such as Training and Enterprise Councils. Other functions, such as water supply, were privatized.

While Scotland and Wales (to a lesser extent) had traditionally retained a degree of administrative devolution, it was 1997 before a political devolution accompanied this. Here again, devolved authority was greater in Scotland. While the Labour government established Regional Development Agencies in England after 1997, there was no sign that the government was prepared to devolve further responsibilities to the English regions during its first term in office. Labour's devolution policies were born of political commitments that Tony Blair had made in order to win the leadership. Whether, as Prime Minister, he welcomed the weakening of central control that they implied was open to question.

In short, during the whole of the period covered by this book, pressures from sub-central tiers of government did not seriously deflect the policy-making authority of British central government.

Central government

While the British political system is itself centralized, there is a further centralization of power within the Cabinet and especially within the office of the Prime Minister. The extent to which British government had become 'presidential' was a favourite question of writers of textbooks. Most writers agreed that the answer depended in large part on the individual involved. Margaret Thatcher was certainly a strong Prime Minister; John Major was not; Tony Blair appeared to be more in the Thatcher mould.

The 'first past the post' electoral system contributes to the potential strength of British Prime Ministers (Box 16.2, p. 183). This system maximizes the chance that one political party will gain an overall majority of seats in the parliament. Minor parties tend not to be elected, and the constituency system exaggerates national swings in votes to produce a larger than proportional swing in the numbers of seats won or lost. Therefore, British Prime Ministers generally do not have to form coalition governments, as their Continental counterparts normally do (see Box 16.3, p. 184). This gives them a very different perspective to their EU partners on the necessity for making compromises and deals.

Box 16.2 The British electoral system

- The British system is known as 'first-past-the-post in single-member constituencies'.

- The country is divided into 659 geographical constituencies, each of which has one seat in the House of Commons.

- The electors cast a single vote for their preferred candidate.

- The votes in each constituency are counted, and the candidate with the highest number of votes is declared elected.

Box 16.3 British Governments since 1945

Date	Party	Prime Minister
1945–51	Labour	Clement Attlee
1951–5	Conservative	Winston Churchill
1955–7	Conservative	Anthony Eden
1957–63	Conservative	Harold Macmillan
1963–4	Conservative	Sir Alec Douglas Home
1964–70	Labour	Harold Wilson
1970–4	Conservative	Edward Heath
1974–6	Labour	Harold Wilson
1976–9	Labour	James Callaghan
1979–90	Conservative	Margaret Thatcher
1990–7	Conservative	John Major
1997–	Labour	Tony Blair

The civil service has a reputation for professionalism and impartiality both in advising governments and in implementing legislation. Indeed, there have been complaints from British businesses at the efficiency with which the civil service has implemented and enforced EC legislation. Business complains that in other member states the rules are not so rigorously enforced, which gives an unfair advantage to competitors in those countries. In 1996, the Minister for Public Services in the Major government, John Freeman, issued a guide to civil servants entitled *Implementing European Law* which aimed to avoid 'over implementation' of EU legislation.

EU policy-making

EU policy-making is formally co-ordinated through the Cabinet Office. As Edwards (1992: 77) explained:

The system that has evolved since 1973 is one that places emphasis on the Cabinet Office and particularly its European Secretariat. To that extent, 'Europe' has been a factor reinforcing the trend noted by a succession of commentators in the 1970s towards the assumption of powers by Cabinet or groups of Cabinet ministers within the Cabinet Office.

The importance given to the European Secretariat of the Cabinet Office perhaps indicated the determination of the Prime Minister to maintain control of EU policy. Margaret Thatcher was believed to be of the view that the Foreign Office (FO) had become too 'pro-European' and could not be trusted to direct policy. However, the fact that the FO remained the formal link between Whitehall and the UK Permanent Representation in Brussels inevitably gave it a strong hand.

Other departments of state with a degree of independence in the role they played from an early point in Britain's membership of the EC were the Ministry of Agriculture, Fisheries, and Food (MAFF); the Department of Trade and Industry (DTI); and the Treasury. By the 1990s, though, very few policy sectors did not have a European dimension.

The appearance of unity may hide a pluralist process in which each department pursues its own agenda, driven to some extent by its relationship with its own domestic policy network. Nevertheless, the co-ordination clearly works, and 'the instructions given to those negotiating on the part of the UK are reportedly among the tightest and most strictly adhered to of all the member states—even more so than the French with their equally centralized system' (Edwards, 1992: 74).

Public opinion on European integration

Given the deep-rooted historical prejudices outlined under the heading 'Cultural Factors' above, the first surprise in studying British public opinion on the EU is that 'opinion on European integration has not been as negative as is commonly supposed' (Nugent, 1992: 176). There has usually been a majority (albeit small) in favour of closer integration. On the other hand, 'British opinion has been significantly out of line with the average Community opinion' (Nugent, 1992: 179). The proportion of the population supporting integration has been some 10 to 15 per cent lower than the Community average, and the proportion opposing it some 5 to 10 per cent higher.

The second point to make about public opinion is that there is a generational difference. 'Every survey of British views on Europe finds that younger people are the most positive' (Grant, 1998: 150). Put the other way round, the age cohort over 55 is generally much more negative than the younger cohorts.

A third point is that negative attitudes are not strongly held. European integration is not at the forefront of most people's concerns about the world. This in turn suggests that public opinion responds to a lead from the political elites rather than the other way around.

However, the British Social Attitudes survey for 1997 found a 'perverse' trend in British public opinion on the EU. In the 1980s, when Margaret Thatcher was Prime Minister and was openly Euro-sceptical, attitudes became increasingly sympathetic to a stronger relationship with the EU. In 1997, with a more sympathetic government, public opposition

---

Box 16.4 British public opinion and the EU

- In 1983, 53 per cent of the population favoured continued membership of the EU, and 42 per cent favoured withdrawal.

- In 1991, 77 per cent wanted continued membership, and the proportion advocating withdrawal had declined to 16 per cent.

- In 1997, 55 per cent favoured continued membership, while the number advocating withdrawal had risen to 28 per cent. The 'don't knows' had risen to 17 per cent from a steady 5–6 per cent over many previous years. Only 17 per cent were content to lose the pound, exactly the same percentage as were prepared to see the Euro phased in alongside the pound.

---

was on the rise (see Box 16.4, p. 185). The report concluded that, 'Even with the presumed weight of government support behind the proposition, a referendum victory on Britain's adoption of the Euro will be hard to achieve.' (Jowell *et al.*, 1998: 176.)

Economic structure

From the early 1950s, the performance of the British economy persistently failed to match that of its main competitors. Between 1950 and 1969 Britain achieved a steady 3 per cent average annual increase in industrial output. This was high by historical standards, but it was approximately half the rate of increase of the six member states of the EC. Also, the rate of inflation in Britain was higher than in any of the six except France; and Britain's export performance was poor, with imports increasing more quickly than exports, whereas the two increased in parallel in the six.

There was some improvement in the 1960s over the 1950s. British industrial production increased by 3.5 per cent per annum in this decade, compared to around 5 per cent in the EC six. However, British rates of inflation remained higher. And while in its first year of Community membership Britain managed to match West Germany's 5 per cent growth, the onset of the world recession at the end of that year exposed the continuing underlying weakness of the British economy.

From 1974 to 1979 British GDP increased by an annual average of less than 1.3 per cent, compared to West Germany's 2.5 per cent and France's 3 per cent. In the same period, the average rate of inflation in Britain was 15.5 per cent, compared to 5 per cent for West Germany and 11 per cent for France.

Explaining Britain's relative economic decline

Much discussion has taken place of the reasons for Britain's relatively poor economic performance in this period. Three factors frequently cited are:

- labour problems
- management failings
- government economic policy.

Together, these factors combined to prevent adequate modernization to meet the challenges of an increasingly international market place.

Labour problems

Problems with labour concerned both labour-supply and adaptability. Labour-supply was a problem in Britain in the 1950s, before it became a problem elsewhere in western Europe, because Britain had no surplus agricultural population to feed industrial expansion. The consequent tightness of the labour market allowed British workers to achieve bigger wage increases in the 1950s than their counterparts elsewhere in western Europe.

Britain also had a long tradition of trade-union organization which was unbroken by defeat by Fascism; nor was the self-confidence of British workers destroyed by national defeat in war. This contributed to the high wage increases. More importantly though, it enabled British workers to resist changes in the shape of the economy, and in work routines in new industries, which hindered adaptation of the nineteenth-century industrial structure to the post-war world.

Management Failings

Although trade-union militancy became a favourite explanation of Britain's economic failings by the late 1960s, blame has also been attributed to the conservatism of the other side of industry. Realization of the need for change came slowly. Production of textiles, clothing, steel, and ships continued to dominate the thinking of large industrial concerns through to the mid-1950s, without any apparent realization of the need to diversify. The labour shortages that hampered the expansion of the newer engineering and chemical industries were exacerbated by the actions of employers in the traditional areas. These employers refused to accept that the lower demand for their products was permanent. Consequently, they hoarded underemployed labour rather than risk releasing workers and then having difficulty in recruiting when the expansion of demand came, as they were sure that it would.

Government economic policy

Unlike the position in France, there was no attempt by any section of the administrative or political elite in Britain to change these attitudes in industry. Government economic policy, guided by the permanent civil servants in the Treasury, was directed throughout the 1950s to preserving the external value of the pound sterling. This was done mainly by attempting to dampen down domestic demand, which was outstripping industrial production and so pulling in imports.

Concern about the external value of the currency in part reflected the strength of the financial sector in the British economy. Britain was unique among European states in having a financial sector that was largely independent of national industrial interests. The City of London's role as the supplier of banking and insurance services to the whole world derived from the days of British hegemony, when sterling was the major international currency. Although Britain's place as the leading capitalist power was taken over by the United States after the Second World War, with the dollar becoming the dominant international reserve currency, the financial expertise of the City allowed it to play a key role. However, until the development of the Eurodollar market, that role could only be maintained if the strength of sterling was maintained, otherwise funds would not be held in sterling in London, but would be transferred to New York or elsewhere. Thus, the maintenance of the external value of the pound, and the absence of any controls on the flow of capital in and out of London were two of the primary objectives of the City.

That they were also primary policy objectives of British governments throughout the 1950s was the result not so much of overt pressure by the City as of the acceptance by politicians and by the Treasury of the economic assumptions that most favoured the City; what Marxist writers described as the hegemony of the financial sector within the British capitalist class. That hegemony extended also to industrial capitalists, who continued to accept the economic doctrine of *laissez-faire* even when it no longer served their interests.

Modernization strategies

The economic policies of the 1950s failed to consolidate international confidence in the pound, and this led to a change of direction in 1960. Under direct pressure from the Federation of British Industry, the Conservative government accepted that the only way of permanently ensuring the stability of sterling was to promote economic growth and encourage an increase in exports to strengthen the balance of payments. After 1960, governments began to pursue interventionist policies to encourage industrial modernization. However, this did not mean the end of the policy of support for the pound. This was demonstrated in 1966–7, when Harold Wilson was prepared to brake back heavily on the domestic economy rather than devalue the currency. The modernization strategy had its limits, and those limits were reached when the value of the pound came under threat.

Other constraints on the modernization strategies of both Conservative and Labour governments before 1979 were the trade unions, and the weight of certain sections of industry.

The unions
In West Germany the trade unions generally accepted the definition of national interest propounded by the government and industrialists, because they benefited from it. In France, membership of trade unions was low, so union leaders could simply be ignored by the planners in the Fourth and Fifth Republics. In Britain the trade unions were strong enough to make their voice heard even when there was a Conservative government, and that voice was often, although not invariably, independent of that of the industrialists.

It is not easy, though, to identify a coherent pressure on British governments from the trade unions. At times their voice was strongly in favour of modernization of the economy, but then it would protest equally strongly about the implementation of the measures necessary to meet that demand. This is explained partly by the different perceptions of the leadership and of the rank and file. The leaders often accepted the arguments for modernization, but they had to respond to their members' protests about job losses in declining industries, about changes in their working conditions, and about pay restraint.

Industry
On the other side of industry there was also ambiguity in attitudes to economic modernization, despite a certain homogeneity about the scale of British industry. A process of concentration of industrial ownership between the wars was complemented by a wave of mergers and take-overs which began late in the 1950s. This meant that by the end of the 1960s, 'the concern of authentically corporate character (as distinct from that of essentially individualist character) had become not merely a common, nor even just a predominant, but virtually the exclusive type throughout manufacturing industry' (Murphy, 1973: 805–6). Britain had fewer small firms than either Germany or France. The dominance of large corporations was strengthened by the existence of nationalized concerns which between them employed 8.5 per cent of total employees (Murphy, 1973: 804, table 11.49). In the new industries such as automobiles and chemicals there was also considerable multinationalism, both by British firms with extensive interests abroad and by US firms with production units in Britain.

These sections of industry had different interests to press on government. The large national concerns, which were mainly concentrated in the declining industries of textiles, shipbuilding, and steel, were intermittently protectionist in their demands. These firms also sought incomes policies to help them resist the wage demands of their employees, who were highly unionized. The multinationals, on the other hand, favoured open markets and world free trade; and they were more inclined to buy industrial peace by granting high wage rises; especially if these could be linked to increases in productivity.

The rise of the multinationals
After 1979 the Thatcher governments cut through this tangle of contradictory pressures by siding

unequivocally with the City of London and the multinational corporations, and opening the British economy to international competition. This led to a painful restructuring of the economy that destroyed much of the old industrial base. Prosperity returned primarily to the south-east of the country, partly as a spin-off from the tremendous success of the City of London. The City was quick to take advantage of the deregulation of capital movements to confirm its position as one of the three leading financial centres of the world, alongside New York and Tokyo.

Microelectronics companies, mainly Japanese or American, moved into the Thames valley and parts of the Scottish highlands to take advantage of labour that was cheap by European standards. Investment by Japanese manufacturers of cars and electrical goods increased in the face of hostility from the EC

to the volume of Japanese exports: production in Britain allowed them to circumvent export quotas throughout the Community, and for a variety of reasons, including lower wages, Britain was favoured over other member states.

Largely as a result of the arrival of multinationals that used Britain as a production base for sales to the EC market, in the period between 1972 and 1995 British trade with the EC grew from around one-third of total exports and imports to over half. In 1995, 57 per cent of all British exports went to the rest of the EC and 54 per cent of British imports came from the rest of the EC. In comparison, exports to and imports from North America were both 14 per cent of the totals, little changed from 1972 when North America accounted for 16 per cent of exports and 17 per cent of imports (OECD, 1987, 1996).

Political developments

The post-war Labour government: 1945–1951

Between the end of the war and the start of the 1970s the Labour and Conservative Parties alternated in office. To the surprise of many people, who expected that Winston Churchill's wartime leadership would produce a Conservative victory, Labour won the first general election in 1945 with a substantial majority. The Labour government proceeded to put through a programme of economic and social reforms that included the nationalization of important sectors of industry and the creation of a National Health Service. The popularity of this programme is indicated by the extent to which it was accepted by the Conservatives, and became the basis of a broad consensus on domestic policy that lasted through to the 1970s.

The Labour government also necessarily presided over a period of economic restraint, an inevitable consequence of the dislocation caused by the war. The weariness this produced in a people who had suffered for too many years contributed to such a

drastically reduced majority for Labour in February 1950 that another election had to be held in September 1951. This time, as a result of Britain's electoral system, the Conservatives won despite polling fewer votes than Labour, and so were in office in time to claim credit for the effects of the world economic boom that was just beginning. On this basis they held office for the next thirteen years, under four Prime Ministers: Churchill until 1955, Anthony Eden from 1955 to 1957, Harold Macmillan from 1957 to 1963, and Alec Douglas-Home briefly from Macmillan's resignation to the general election in 1964.

Conservative control: 1951–1964

During these thirteen years of Conservative government, there was first a recovery in national self-confidence, then a steady decline. The Suez crisis of 1956 is often seen as a turning-point in Britain's post-war history: it emphasized the relative weakness of Britain in world affairs, and sparked a bout of national self-examination which extended beyond matters concerned with foreign and defence policy to a questioning of the performance of the economy.

British economic growth in the 1950s was extremely high by historical standards, but the sense of well-being that this generated was gradually undermined by the realization that other European states were performing better. Balance of payments crises became a recurrent problem, as imports expanded faster than exports, and inflation rose more rapidly than in the economies of Britain's competitors. Governments found themselves trapped into a 'stop-go' cycle, expanding the economy through the stimulation of demand, only for the balance of payments to plunge into deficit so that demand had to be reined back to avert a sterling crisis.

By 1960, concern was such that the government, under pressure from the Federation of British Industry, decided to embark on a programme of modernization of the economic structure. This implicit confession that all had not been as well as it had been portrayed during the previous decade played into the hands of the Labour Party. Labour presented itself as a more dynamic modernizing force, and, helped by scandals that undermined the moral authority of the government, won the 1964 general election with a very narrow majority.

The Wilson governments: 1964–1970

Labour, under the leadership of Harold Wilson, consolidated its victory and increased its majority substantially in 1966. Elected on a programme that stressed the need for Britain to undergo a technological revolution, it soon found itself grappling with intractable obstacles. One was the balance of payments, which because of the weak export performance of the British economy continued in chronic deficit. Eventually the pound sterling had to be devalued in 1967. Another problem was the resistance of the trade unions to the modernization programme. The failure of the Wilson government to deal with industrial militancy undermined its authority and led to a narrow Conservative victory in 1970.

The Heath years: 1970–1974

In opposition to the 1964–70 Labour governments, the Conservative Party adopted a new leader, Edward Heath, and a new economic programme, based on a radical rejection of state intervention in the economy and a commitment to the free market. Yet during its first two and a half years in office the new government abandoned or reversed almost all of its policies. Its determination not to use public money to support inefficient firms ('lame ducks') was abandoned to save Rolls-Royce from bankruptcy. Aid that had been withdrawn from the Upper Clyde Shipbuilders was restored. Public expenditure rose to record heights. In 1972, a phased prices and incomes policy was introduced to combat inflation.

This reversal of the free-market policies on which the government had been elected was partly a response to the realities of economic management in a rapidly changing world, and partly a retreat from the politically unacceptable consequences of the original policies.

The policy to which Heath was most strongly committed (other than membership of the EC) was reform of the trade unions. Here, Heath saw a fundamental role for the state, and he picked out of the wastepaper basket the plans that Wilson had scrapped for bringing industrial relations under legal regulation. His Industrial Relations Act ran into determined and predictable opposition from the trade unions, but Heath pressed ahead with it because he saw it as a fundamental part of any programme for solving Britain's economic problems. However, his confrontational approach led to industrial turmoil, helped to undermine the popularity of his government, and strengthened the position of the left within the Labour Party.

The failure of Heath reinforced the position within the Conservative Party of the ideological proponents of the free market, who were able to claim that it was his abandonment of the original economic programme which was responsible for the failure.

The return of Labour: 1974–1979

When Wilson returned to office in 1974 he had to deal with political problems at three levels.

1. Within his own party he faced pressure from the left, led by Tony Benn, who argued that the 1964–70 Labour governments had failed because they had not implemented Socialist policies.

2. At the parliamentary level, he had to contend with not having a majority between February and October 1974, which meant that he had to ensure that he could win support from the minor parties.

3. He had to deal with a country that was deeply divided.

The trade unions had mobilized against Heath's government, and the National Union of Mineworkers had contributed to the downfall of the government. In reaction, elements of other social classes were restive. Soaring inflation hit particularly those socio-economic groups that were unable to insulate themselves from its effects by demanding high increases in wages, as the larger trade unions were able to. Hostility to the trade unions was rife and was stirred up by the popular press. Trade unionists in response had become defensive and uncooperative.

In these circumstances, the primary task of the new government was to restore some sort of social harmony; but this was not easy in the face of a serious economic crisis provoked by the 1973 rise in oil prices. In an attempt to control high inflation, the government introduced a system of price controls combined with voluntary wage restraint through the medium of a 'social contract' with the trade unions. The other side of this contract was a programme of social reforms that the country could ill afford in its straitened circumstances.

Wilson resigned as Prime Minister in March 1976, and James Callaghan took over. Within weeks he faced a sterling crisis that eventually forced Britain to apply to the IMF for a loan; this was only given with conditions attached. The IMF conditions meant a final retreat from the extensive programme of social welfare measures that had formed the basis of the Labour Manifesto in 1974. This led some backbenchers on the left of the party to feel that the leadership had forfeited any claim on their loyalty, which made it very difficult for the Whips to ensure solid support for the government. By March 1977, after defections and by-election defeats, the government did not even have an overall majority.

In the circumstances the government formed a pact with the Liberal Party, which also had no wish to see a general election at a time when opinion polls indicated a possible landslide Conservative victory. David Steel, the new Liberal leader, agreed to support the government in return for a regular input into discussions of future business. In addition, Steel wanted commitments from Callaghan to introduce legislation to facilitate direct elections to the European Parliament and to try to make progress on the devolution of powers to a Scottish Assembly. Unfortunately, Labour backbenchers opposed both of these demands. So Callaghan found himself facing a situation that is common in Continental European politics, where coalition government is normal, but rare in British politics, of having to reconcile the conflicting demands of maintaining intra-party and inter-party support.

The 'Lib-Lab pact' allowed the government to survive into the 1977–8 parliamentary session, by which time the economic indicators had improved again. There was considerable speculation that the Prime Minister would call an autumn election, but he decided to wait until after the winter. This was a mistake. Attempts by the government to hold the line against inflationary pay increases broke down when they failed to stop the Ford motor company from awarding its workers a 15 per cent rise. That opened the floodgates for massive claims from several groups of workers, including petrol-tanker drivers and road haulage workers, whose strikes in support of their claims caused shortages of heating fuel and of food in the shops. They were followed by strikes in the public sector that produced the closure of hospitals, the appearance of piles of rubbish in the streets, and the contamination of water supplies. These bitter industrial battles caused the defeat of the Callaghan government in March 1979. The Conservatives were elected on a platform that included a commitment to abandon pay policy and to weaken the power of trade unions.

The Thatcher governments: 1979–1990

Following the defeat of the discredited Heath government in 1974, Margaret Thatcher was elected leader of the Conservative Party in the following year. The main lines of Thatcher's economic programme were based on:

- rejection of incomes policies
- the aim of reducing of trade union power
- the desire to combat inflation through tight control of the money supply
- lower income tax
- an end to subsidies for inefficient nationalized industries.

For the first three years of its term of office, the new government faced a world recession sparked off by the 1979 rise in the price of oil. Despite this, the government introduced a number of deflationary measures in 1979, including a budget that fulfilled its manifesto pledge to reduce income tax, but almost doubled VAT from 8 to 15 per cent. To combat inflation, interest rates were increased from 12 to 14 per cent in June, and to 17 per cent in November. These measures, the recession in the rest of the world, and the persistently high value of sterling that was a result of its status as the currency of an oil-producing state, combined to produce a serious downturn in economic activity in Britain in 1980. Bankruptcies and unemployment both soared to unprecedented heights, and the government's popularity fell to correspondingly low levels in opinion polls.

In this context, Thatcher's declared aim of reducing public expenditure proved difficult to achieve. The higher levels of unemployment increased social security payments, and efforts to make nationalized industries more efficient imposed short-term costs. In an attempt to prevent public expenditure from actually rising, the government began to look for savings in every possible direction. Prescription charges were increased, regional aid was cut, the fees of overseas students were increased by several hundred per cent, and the price of school meals and council house rents were raised.

The turning-point for Thatcher came in 1982. Its most dramatic manifestation was the war with Argentina over the Falkland Islands. The invasion by Argentina of this small remnant of the British Empire provided Thatcher with an opportunity to demonstrate her resolve and patriotism, which she was quick to seize. She dispatched a naval task-force to the islands amidst a revival of popular jingoism,

and refused to allow mediation efforts to stand between her and a complete military victory. The professional British forces, against the conscript and less well-equipped Argentinians, predictably achieved the military victory.

One effect of the Falklands conflict was to transform the popularity of Thatcher, whom opinion polls had at one stage shown to be the most unpopular Prime Minister of the post-war period. It dispelled attempts to portray her as less concerned about the national interest than her opponents in the opposition parties and within her own party. This claim had been given credence by policies such as ending controls on the movement of capital out of the country. The military victory combined with signs of an economic upturn to secure a second term of office for the Conservatives in 1983.

By 1983 unemployment, although still high, was no longer increasing; inflation had been brought back down from the record high levels that it attained in the first two years of the government; and industrial output had begun a slow recovery. In the context of serious division within the opposition Labour Party, enough people were convinced that the Conservatives provided the best prospects for economic security to assure the government of re-election.

The Labour Party had split in the autumn of 1980, with several of its more prominent members leaving to form the Social Democratic Party (SDP). An alliance between the SDP and the Liberals proved a popular home in by-elections for voters who disliked Thatcherism, but also were not attracted by the leftward drift of the Labour Party in opposition. Although the Alliance attracted 25.4 per cent of the votes cast in 1983, the effect of the electoral system was that it only won 23 seats in Parliament (Liberals 17, SDP 6). The main result of the Alliance challenge was to allow the Conservatives to win a large majority of seats, 397 of the 650, on just 42.4 per cent of the vote.

The election cleared the way for the next phase of the Thatcher government's radical restructuring of British society and the British economy. Following the election, the struggle to reduce the power and influence of the trade unions became a priority. The government prepared for and then provoked conflict with the National Union of Mineworkers (NUM), a union that had long been in the vanguard of working-class militancy and had played a major role in bringing down the Heath government, in which Margaret Thatcher had been a minister. In addition, the government introduced new legislation on strikes and picketing. The success of the government's strategy for defeating the NUM was a decisive moment in undermining the authority of organized labour in Britain. Alongside this strategy, the government also accelerated its programme of denationalizing public-sector concerns, a process that it called 'privatization'.

Although the government's passage was not entirely smooth, the economy remained the most important factor influencing voting intentions, and Britain's success in this respect continued. Despite a significant drop in the price of oil, which reduced revenues from the North Sea, economic activity continued at a high level, with only a minor setback in the second half of 1985. The decline in the price of oil contributed to a depreciation in the value of sterling from mid-1985, which in turn contributed to a sharp revival of exports. Unemployment started to come down from the middle of 1986, and wage increases continued to run well ahead of inflation. By early in 1987 more people in Britain were feeling better off than at any previous time since 1979. The government was therefore able to call a general election in the spring of 1987 with every prospect of a comfortable victory. This is precisely what it achieved, although not before receiving something of a scare from the opinion polls during the campaign itself.

The new leader of the Labour Party, Neil Kinnock, ran a much better campaign than had his predecessor Michael Foot in 1983, and, in the view of many people, a better campaign than the Conservatives. Nevertheless, the result was very similar to that of 1983, with the alliance of the Liberal and Social Democratic parties splitting the anti-Thatcher vote with Labour. This allowed a Conservative victory by an even larger percentage of seats than in the previous election.

Thatcher's personal position both domestically and internationally was already strong before the election: it was even stronger after it. Domestically, the scope for criticism within the Conservative Party was reduced by her very success, although the gov-

ernment was to run into some opposition from its own backbenchers over some of its domestic legislative programme. Internationally, Thatcher's position as the longest-serving European head of government appeared to give her an opportunity to play a leading role in the EC and on the wider world stage. Yet before the end of 1990 Thatcher had been replaced as Prime Minister by John Major.

The main cause of Thatcher's downfall was Europe, although there were other contributory factors, in particular the replacement of the domestic rates, a local tax based on property values, by the Community Charge, a poll tax. This regressive tax was extremely unpopular even among Conservative voters. Conservative MPs became increasingly restive as the government's ratings in the opinion polls fell well below those of Labour, and the Prime Minister's personal rating fell even further. However, with time before the next election, this factor alone would probably not have precipitated the fall of Thatcher.

Her downfall was caused by her increasingly negative statements on European integration, and particularly on monetary union. In reply to questions in the Commons on the Rome meeting of the European Council in October 1990, Thatcher asserted that she would not 'hand over sterling and the powers of this House to Europe' (*Hansard*, 30 Oct. 1990, col. 873). This statement was so far out of line with the more pragmatic position of the government as to prompt the resignation of her Deputy Prime Minister, Sir Geoffrey Howe. In his resignation speech Howe made a strong attack on Thatcher's positions over Europe which was all the more damaging because of his reputation for mildness in political debate (*Hansard*, 13 Nov. 1990, cols. 461–5).

The day following the speech, Michael Heseltine, a former cabinet Minister who remained very popular within the Party, announced that he would stand against Thatcher in the annual leadership election that was about to take place. Enough Conservative backbench MPs were disillusioned with Thatcher's leadership for her to fail to get the number of votes needed on the first ballot to defeat Heseltine. Her colleagues persuaded her that there was a serious risk that if she stood in the second ballot she might be defeated. Given her dislike for Heseltine, she decided to step aside to clear the way for other members of the cabinet to stand against him. Her own chosen successor was her Chancellor of the Exchequer, John Major, and this support certainly helped him to win the leadership.

The Major years: 1990–1997

Despite demands from the Opposition that he call an immediate election, Major decided to hang on in the hope that the economic indicators would improve. The recession that had started in the latter half of 1990 tightened its grip in the first half of 1991. Interest rates were high, inflation was high, unemployment was rising, and output was falling. This was no context in which to choose to hold an election. However, things did not get much better; so, running out of time, and with no sign of an economic recovery on the horizon, Major went to the country in April 1992.

He faced one of the toughest electoral tasks of the post-war period: to try to win an election when the economy was apparently mired in recession. Yet, after a hard-fought campaign, he did it, helped by some serious misjudgements by the Labour Party. It was a narrow victory, though, and left him with a precarious majority in Parliament.

As time went by, the voices of the 'Euro-sceptics' in the Conservative Party became more insistent, and the concessions made by the government became more frequent. The image of an internally divided party under a weak leader contributed to the defeat of Major in the 1997 election.

There was also a strong sense in the country that after seventeen years of Conservative rule it was time for a change. Labour under Kinnock had reformed itself into a credible party of government. Kinnock resigned after Labour's election defeat in 1992, and was succeeded briefly by John Smith, who unfortunately died within months of taking over. His successor, Tony Blair, moved the Labour Party even further into the new, post-Thatcher centre ground of British politics. 'New Labour' adopted many of the policies of its Conservative opponents, thereby reassuring the middle-class English voters who were vital to its chances of winning. So successful was it in this that it won the election with a massive majority of 177 over all other parties.

The Blair government 1997–

In some policy areas, the Blair government retained the principles of Conservatism. This was most evident in its declared intention to restrict public spending for the first two years to the targets set by the previous government. Arguably its most radical commitment was to constitutional reform. Within six months of taking office the government signalled its commitment to constitutional reform by holding successful referendums on devolution in both Scotland and Wales. In England, limited decentralzsation was provided through creation of Regional Development Agencies.

On Europe, the new government promised a more co-operative and conciliatory approach than that of previous Conservative governments. In its eighteen years of opposition the consensus of the Labour party, and of the British labour movement more generally, had moved from a position of open hostility to the process of European integration to one in favour. An important factor in this was the experience of eighteen years of Conservative government. During this period, key constituencies of the Labour movement had received support and sympathy from Brussels when little was available from the British government. Labour local authorities, deprived of finance under Conservative regional policy, placed greater emphasis on securing European assistance. British trade unions, on the receiving end of domestic legislation, sought protection from the EC/EU. Through networking on such issues, Labour figures developed good relations with the Commission officials and other EU actors. In other words, there is some evidence that Labour's 'turn to Europe' was partly the responsibility of Conservative policies.

Shortly after taking office, Labour signalled its new approach to Europe by signing the Social Chapter which had been rejected by the Major government at Maastricht. The government also struck a more conciliatory tone than its predecessor over institutional changes proposed at Amsterdam (Sowemimo, 1999: 349). Yet while the Labour government was keen to co-operate, it could ill afford to be seen by its electorate as too compliant. As such, it was keen to emphasize its desire for a 'leadership' role within Europe, which could be sold to its domestic constituency in patriotic terms.

Yet while in some respects the Blair government began to return Britain to Europe's mainstream, the issue of the single currency provided a major obstacle to it adopting a central role. Despite apparent support for joining the Euro within the government, public opinion remained opposed to such a move. The consequence was that Labour's policy on this issue was for its first two years of office officially neutral: Britain would only join the single currency if and when it looked certain to benefit the economy. This position later altered subtly, however, to the presumption that Britain would join 'when the economic circumstances were right'.

Squaring this circle would be the major challenge of the Blair government in relation to Europe. On the one hand, there were signs that the government believed it to be in the country's long-term economic interest to be part of the Euro and also necessary for Britain to play a lead role in European affairs. On the other hand, British political elites had done little to challenge the Euroscepticism of the public which was now proving to be a burden to the government. This public hostility to the Euro, encouraged by important sections of the national press, ensured that no decision would be taken on British entry until after the next general election.

Conclusion

A constant process of leapfrogging takes place between industrial and post-industrial economies. The leaders at one stage will find themselves being overtaken by national economies that lagged behind them, but which consequently had to restructure, giving them a lead at the next stage. Because it was less successful in the post-war world than either Germany or France, the British economy had to be restructured. Several attempts failed. Eventually the Thatcher governments succeeded.

Restructuring is always a painful business and the suffering is always felt unevenly; inevitably, therefore, the social groups most likely to suffer resist restructuring. Thus the political project of restructuring a national economy is always problematical. A successful project, in a democratic state, has to legitimate itself through an ideology. In the case of both Germany and France the ideology of Europeanism provide some of that legitimation. In Britain the failure of the political class to sell the idea of Europe to a population that remained wedded to the nineteenth-century doctrine of nationalism did not allow that vehicle to be used. Instead, Margaret Thatcher rode the nationalist vehicle, which involved engaging in fierce public disputes with the rest of the EC.

The nature of the restructuring itself left Britain open to the full force of globalization. Initially this involved a rapid depletion of the old industrial base, with severe social costs. This was followed by the emergence of a flexible and open economy that was remarkably successful in attracting foreign direct investment. It was also an economy that relied heavily on services. The price of this shift was the replacement of secure well-paid jobs in traditional industries with often insecure and relatively low-paid jobs in services. By the end of the millennium, the service sector accounted for over 40 per cent of GDP and employment in Britain. Industrial production, although it still accounted for 65 per cent of exports, only accounted for around 20 per cent of output and employment. The national interest would inevitably be determined more by the interests of the financial service industries than the engineering industries.

It was not clear at the end of the millennium where the interests of the financial services lay in terms of closer British involvement in the EU, and particularly in terms of British membership of the single currency. It was clear, though, that manufacturing industry had a heavy reliance on the European market. Moreover, the exchange rate risk of being outside of the single currency weighed heavily on the minds of those multinational firms that had located in Britain precisely in order to access the EU market.

At the same time, the continued strength of nationalism in British political culture made it very difficult for the government to opt for membership of the single currency, and indeed for it to convince the British people that closer European integration was desirable. The decision of the Conservative Party in opposition to transform itself into an openly Eurosceptic party which was opposed to membership of the single currency made it all the more politically risky for the Labour government to commit itself to such a step. The economic transformation of Britain had not been accompanied by a sufficient change in political culture to allow the Labour government to place Britain at the heart of Europe any more convincingly than its predecessor had been able to.

KEY POINTS

Cultural factors

- British nationalism was conditioned by the history of imperialism, and marked by a sense of the superiority of Britain over other European nations. The war did not undermine nationalism in Britain.

- The British people felt more affinity with the Commonwealth and the United States than with the rest of Europe.

- There was a strong cultural attachment to the ideas of national and parliamentary sovereignty.

- Social and economic attitudes were marked by an ambiguity between beliefs in libertarianism and collectivism. Both elements were present throughout the post-war period, but collectivism predominated until 1979.

- The Thatcher governments of 1979–90 actively worked to swing the balance back towards individualism. Thatcher's Conservative successor, John Major, took up this legacy, as did the Labour government of Tony Blair that followed.

Constitutional and institutional factors

- Until the devolution reforms of the Blair government, sub-central government in Britain was weak and had little influence on central government policy. Even after devolution, local government had little autonomy.

- Power within the government tended to be concentrated in the cabinet and particularly with the Prime Minister.

- The electoral system produces majorities for the winning party, which means that British governments are generally not coalitions, unlike most continental European governments.

- The civil service is highly efficient and respected. There is rivalry between departments of state, but these are resolved before British officials negotiate in Brussels.

Public opinion

- Public opinion in Britain has been less positive about European integration than has public opinion in Germany or France, but there has generally been a small majority in favour.

- Younger people tend to be more positive about the EU than those over the age of 55.

- The salience of the EU as an issue is not high.

- Public opinion has not consistently followed the lead of politicians either for or against developments in the EC/EU

Economic structure

- The post-war performance of the British economy was poor compared to that of other west European states.

- Labour shortages, trade union resistance, and the influence of the older industrial interests hindered attempts to tackle the problems. Management was locked into outmoded thinking and was slow to respond to the changing economic environment.

- Government policy was obsessed with maintaining the value of the pound sterling. This reflected the strength of the financial sector in the City of London.

- The Thatcher governments cut through the domestic resistance to reform by allowing the older sectors of industry to go bankrupt in the recession that followed the 1979 rise in oil prices. This also contributed to undermining the strength of the trade unions.

- The resources that were freed by the bankruptcies were taken up by inward investment by US and Japanese multinationals which wanted to use Britain as a low-cost business-friendly manufacturing base for entry to the EC market.

- These developments contributed to a reorientation of British trade, so that by 1995 over half of all British exports and imports were exchanged with the rest of the EC.

Political developments

- The post-war Labour government introduced popular reforms which laid the basis of the welfare state and nationalized key industries. The acceptance of these reforms by the Conservative Party laid the basis for a post-war consensus that lasted until the 1970s.

- From 1951 until 1964 there were thirteen years of Conservative government. During this period concern grew about national economic performance, and the first attempts were made to modernize the economy.

- The 1964–70 Labour governments also tried to carry through a programme of economic reform, but failed in the face of external constraints and opposition from the trade unions.

- The 1970–4 Conservative government retreated from its commitment to free-market solutions to Britain's economic problems. It also came into conflict with the trade unions over the reform of industrial relations. Its credibility was destroyed by a prolonged miners' strike.

- The Labour governments between 1974 and 1979 tried to buy the co-operation of the trade unions with reform in return for high levels of public expenditure. Eventually it too collapsed in the face of trade union intransigence, and the strikes of the winter of 1978–9 brought Britain to the edge of anarchy.

- The Conservative governments of Margaret Thatcher carried through the free-market approach to economic restructuring that Heath had tried and abandoned. The result was high levels of bankruptcy and unemployment. The government was saved from defeat by division within the opposition and the takeover of the Labour Party by its left wing.

- Thatcher eventually left office after provoking splits within her own party over the EC.

- John Major was unable to govern effectively because of these splits in the Conservative Party, combined with a small majority in parliament.

- During the period from 1983 to 1987 the Labour Party was reformed under the leadership of Neil Kinnock.

- In 1997, 'New Labour' won a convincing victory under Tony Blair. While generally more co-operative on European matters than its predecessor, the Labour government faced public Euroscepticism which restricted its scope for assuming a central role.

QUESTIONS

1 What explains Britain's late entry into the European Community?

2 Why has Britain been regarded as an 'awkward partner' in its relations with other member states?

3 How important have domestic political changes been to Britain's attitude to European integration?

FURTHER READING

Of the many general introductions to British politics, perhaps the most accessible is: B. Jones (ed.), *Politics UK* (3rd edn., London: Prentice Hall, 1998).

On British policy in the European Community the basic text is: S. George *An Awkward Partner: Britain in the European Community* (3rd edn., Oxford: Oxford University Press, 1998)

This analysis is complemented (as the title suggests) by: Royal Institute of International Affairs, *An Equal Partner: Britain's Role in a Changing Europe: Final Report of the Commission on Britain and Europe* (London: RIIA, 1997).

A more journalistic account can be found in: H. Young, *This Blessed Plot: Britain and Europe from Churchill to Blair* (Basingstoke and London: Macmillan, 1998).

Reviews of recent developments include: S. George, 'Britain: Anatomy of a Eurosceptic State', *Journal of European Integration*, 21/1 (1999) 1–19; J. M. O. Sharp, 'Will Britain lead Europe?', *World Today*, 53/12 (1997) 316–19; M. Sowemimo, 'Evaluating the Success of the Labour Government's European Policy', *Journal of European Integration*, 21/4 (1999) 343–68.

Other member states

SUMMARY

For the original member states, pro-EU sentiment was strong. However, each state had its own reasons for joining and each had its own national interests to pursue. This was true of subsequent members also. So Ireland, for example, felt compelled to join along with Britain because of their close trade relationship. At the same time, however, Irish politicians saw membership as an opportunity to reduce its dependence on Britain. Greece, Portugal, and Spain hoped membership would support domestic political stability as well as provide economic benefits. Each new member has brought with it issues that demand an EU response. For some, the experience of membership has consolidated or improved public perceptions of European integration. For others, the experience has heightened public Euroscepticism, particularly in the 1990s.

Introduction

According to Andrew Moravcsik's (1993; 1998) analysis, the development of European integration can be understood fully by reference to the preferences and bargaining strategies of the larger member states of the EC/EU. Yet even Moravcsik occasionally has to bring the positions of other member states into the analysis in order to explain particular outcomes. While the positions of France, Germany, and Britain may be particularly influential, the EU consists of fifteen members. In most cases the pattern of support for a measure from other member states can be extremely influential. First, the Germans in particular are very sensitive to the feelings of the smaller states. Second, just in voting terms it is possible for a

measure that is supported by two of France, Germany, and Britain to be blocked if sufficient of the other states can be persuaded to vote against it. For these reasons it is important to understand the general orientation of the other member states.

This chapter gives a sketch of the position of each of the members. Here, we indicate the main reasons for joining the EC/EU, the state of domestic public opinion on European integration, the economic stake of the country in EU membership, and the particular issues on which individual member state governments feels it necessary to take a distinctive stance. We proceed in the chronological order in which countries became EC/EU members.

The original member states

France and Germany were discussed in Chapters 14 and 15 respectively (pp. 147–79). This section focuses on the other original member states: Belgium, Luxembourg, The Netherlands, and Italy.

Belgium

When France and Germany agreed to pool their supplies of coal and steel in an attempt to avoid future conflict, there was no doubt that Belgium would join them. The Belgian economy in the post-war period was heavily dependent on the coal and steel indus-

tries, and on French and German markets. There was also general approval for steps that would reduce the likelihood of war between Belgium's two large neighbours. Whether measured by public opinion or by the actions of its government, Belgium has remained consistently the most pro-EU of the member states. There are two reasons for this, one political, the other economic.

The political reason concerns the weakness of the Belgian state, which has practically ceased to exist. The country has since its origins been divided between Dutch-speaking Flemish Belgians and French-speaking Walloon Belgians. Inter-communal conflict became endemic in the 1960s. This was a result of economic changes that led to a decline of the industrial base of the Walloon part of the country, which had previously dominated Belgium, and the rise to prosperity of the previously agricultural Flemish part, based on its exploitation of the EC to attract outside investment in chemicals, rubber, and automobile manufacture.

In the early 1970s, in an attempt to end the conflict, the country was divided into three largely autonomous territories: Flanders, Wallonia, and Brussels. Such was the extent of the devolution of powers to these units that they even operated separate economic policies. Such a fragmented state had very little will to defend its sovereignty, and incorporation within a federal Europe seemed to Belgians on all sides of the language divide to be the best solution to their problems.

This pro-European sentiment was strongly reinforced by the economic benefits that flowed to Belgium from EC membership. Not only did it become a leading recipient of foreign direct investment, which was targeted on the EC market as a whole; it also benefited from Brussels becoming the effective capital of the new Europe.

On most issues, the Belgians have stuck close to the positions of the Franco-German alliance. Again, this makes both political and economic sense. Politically, the Walloons have always looked to France as their natural defenders, while the Flemish population has looked to Germany. Economically, the Belgian economy has become little more than an adjunct to the French and German economies, so there are unlikely to be issues of national interest which do not coincide with the positions of Belgium's two large neighbours.

Luxembourg

This small country of only 450,000 inhabitants has provided two Presidents of the European Commission (Gaston Thorn and Jacques Santer), and until 1999 it was the only member state to have done so. As the smallest state of the EU by a considerable margin, the idea of autonomy is relatively meaningless for Luxembourg. The country is economically entirely dependent on the EC market for its considerable prosperity. It has therefore embraced

European integration wholeheartedly and almost unquestioningly, and consistently comes at or near to the top of the list in terms of percentage support for integration in the *Eurobarometer* polls.

Because of the importance to Luxembourg of making the EU work, its government often plays the role of mediator in disputes between its larger neighbours. This does not mean, though, that it has no independent interests to pursue. Following the decline of the steel industry, Luxembourg has developed as a leading 'offshore' financial centre. Because of this, it is sometimes the ally of the British government in opposing EC rules that might provoke the flight of financial business to other centres, such as Switzerland.

Luxembourg also benefits from the single market in a peculiar way. Because it has a small and wealthy population it needs to raise less revenue from taxation than other states. Consequently, it has the lowest rates of VAT in the EU. This makes it the major destination for cross-border shoppers, who can make considerable savings on consumer goods, and off-set the cost of travelling to Luxembourg by filling their fuel tanks with the cheapest petrol or diesel in the EU. This means Luxembourg has been less than enthusiastic about attempts to introduce harmonized bands for VAT at EU level.

The Netherlands

As with the other two Benelux states, there was little option for the Netherlands but to join the ECSC and EEC, given the high level of economic dependence on its their neighbours. There was also a strong sentiment among the Dutch people in favour of international organization as a means of avoiding future wars. Public opinion has remained positive towards European integration.

The Dutch have remained much more independent of the Franco-German alliance than their Belgian neighbours have. The Netherlands is a larger country than Belgium (around 15 million population, compared to 10 million), with a more diverse economic base. Its foreign policy has been marked by an attempt to carve out an independent sphere of action for a medium-sized country by joining international regimes such as the EC. It has always resisted proposals that might lead to the EC being dominated by the big powers.

For that reason, the Dutch were consistent champions of British entry, seeing this as the best counterweight to the attempts of France under de Gaulle to claim the leadership of the organization. In recent years, the Dutch government has found itself at loggerheads with the Germans, especially during Helmut Kohl's period as Chancellor. This again has made the Dutch sometimes allies of the British.

As a former global power in its own right, and a maritime mercantile nation in the twentieth century, the Netherlands has always been more global in its perspective than some other members of the EC. It has been a strong supporter of United States hegemony, and therefore also of the NATO alliance. This has made the Dutch suspicious of attempts to establish a separate security and defence dimension to the EC.

Italy

Italy was the odd one out of the six founder member states. It had a much lower degree of trade dependence with the rest of the original EC than any of the other members. The motivation of the Italian political elite for joining was political. Italy was close to the front line of the cold war, and had a strong Communist Party. The anti-communist coalition governments, led by the Christian Democrats, wanted to create an identity for Italy that was capitalist and west European. Anti-communism meant that the Italian Christian Democrats were strong supporters of NATO, and the commitment to supporting the United States was stronger in the 1950s and 1960s than the commitment to the EC. Nevertheless, the choice for Europe was another important part of that anti-communist strategy.

The decision to join the ECSC, and later the EEC, was a choice of future. In making this historic choice, Italian governments were helped by public support for the principle of European integration. Italy was one of the strongholds of federalist thinking during the war, and the most prominent post-war European

federalist, Altiero Spinelli, was an Italian (see Ch. 4, pp. 47–8).

Membership of the EC benefited the economy of the north of Italy tremendously, and tied its industrialists into dependence on the markets of France and Germany. The south of Italy remained underdeveloped, but after 1975 it became the largest beneficiary of the new European Regional Development Fund (ERDF) (see Ch. 27, pp. 361–84). This consolidated the popularity of the EC in that part of the country.

In terms of population, Italy is one of the larger member states, at 57 million about the same as France and the UK. In terms of GDP it has been rapidly catching up with France, and on some calculations has overtaken Britain. However, its diplomatic weight has never been as great as either. Partly this has been because of the chaotic state of Italian domestic politics. Government coalitions changed with remarkable frequency during the 1960s and 1970s. In the late1980s, following the end of the cold war, the system was thrown into further disarray by the need for a fundamental restructuring.

Italian political leaders have been irritated by the way that the Franco-German alliance within the EC has often ignored them. At times, this has led them to work with the British; especially on issues related to security and defence, where their mutual strong attachment to the Atlantic alliance has helped the two see eye-to-eye. Following the 1973 enlargement, the Italian government also worked for a time together with the British government to get agreement on the setting up of the ERDF, from which they were both likely to benefit. On the other hand, the strength of Italian commitment to the principle of integration has also led to conflicts with the British. These reached their nadir in 1985 when the Italian presidency pushed to a vote the question of whether to set up an IGC in the face of opposition from the then British Prime Minister, Margaret Thatcher.

Since the enlargements of the 1980s, the Italians have often worked together with the other Mediterranean member states to ensure that their interests, especially in the structural funds, have not been overlooked by the northern member states.

The 1973 entrants

Britain was discussed in Chapter 16 (pp. 180–97). Here we focus on the other 1973 entrants, Denmark and Ireland.

Denmark

Danish membership of the EC was prompted by the British application. The importance of agricultural exports to Britain persuaded the Danish government of the day that it could not afford to remain outside of the EC if Britain was going in. However, according to Petersen (1993), Denmark's attitude to the EC/EU has always been support for the economic aspects of integration, but opposition to any development of political integration. It was on the understanding that they were entering an economic common market that the Danish people voted for membership in a referendum in 1972, by 63 per cent to 37 per cent. It was support for the economic project of the single market that produced a 56 per cent to 44 per cent vote in favour of the SEA in 1986. Concern about the political integration envisaged by the TEU contributed to its rejection in the 1992 referendum by 50.7 per cent to 49.3 per cent.

This is not the whole of the story of the Maastricht referendum, however. Unlike Norway, where opposition to membership of the EC was always strongest in the rural areas of the north, in Denmark farmers and fishermen had usually been strong supporters of the EC. Danish opposition to membership had been concentrated in Copenhagen and the other urban areas. In 1992, concern about the reforms of the CAP and the Common Fisheries Policy reduced the 'yes' vote in rural areas, and may have been sufficient to make the difference between a narrow 'yes' and a narrow 'no'.

Subsequently, the concessions that the Danish government negotiated at the Edinburgh European Council in December 1992 allowed it to achieve a narrow majority in favour of ratification of the Treaty in a second referendum. Nevertheless, public suspicion of the possible political implications of monetary union kept Denmark outside of the single currency.

On other issues the Danes have found natural allies in the other Nordic member states, Sweden and Finland, over questions such as environmental protection, social protection, and transparency in the governance of the EU.

Ireland

Like Denmark, Ireland felt that it had little choice but to join the EC when Britain did. Over 60 per cent of Irish exports went to the United Kingdom. Irish citizens resident in the UK had voting rights, as did British citizens resident in the Republic; and the links between the Republic of Ireland and Northern Ireland went beyond economics in ways that made the drawing of a boundary between them unthinkable. At the same time, though, Irish politicians welcomed the opportunity that EC membership offered them to diversify economically and politically away from domination by Britain.

The economic effects of membership were dramatic. First, Ireland benefited considerably from the EC structural funds. At one time these amounted to as much as 3 per cent of Irish GDP. Second, Ireland has been a major beneficiary of the CAP. Combined with the effect of the structural funds, CAP receipts have transformed the traditionally impoverished Irish countryside.

In the 1970s Ireland became a major recipient of inward direct investment, both from other parts of the EC to take advantage of lower labour costs, but also from the United States. The large Irish-American business community in the United States welcomed the opportunity to invest in 'the old country' once it gave access to the EC market. A young population meant a flexible workforce, and the Irish government offered considerable incentives for investors. These advantages kept the investment flowing throughout the 1980s and 1990s.

The aim of diversification away from dependence on the British market was achieved. By 1995, only 26 per cent of Irish exports were going to the UK. At the same time, Irish governments were able to operate with a degree of autonomy of the British government inside the EC that it had been difficult for them to achieve outside.

Under these circumstances, it is hardly surprising that Ireland has become one of the leading pro-EU member states. The main difficulty has been about neutrality. Moves to give a security and defence dimension to the EU have caused the same problems for Ireland as they have for some of the 1985 entrants (see below).

The 1980s entrants

Greece

Greece joined the European Community in 1981. From the origins of the EC in the 1950s, Greek governments showed a desire to develop strong links for essentially political reasons. First, as a country in the Balkans, Greece had Communist neighbours, and there were voices within the country that advocated an identity for Greece that was oriented towards regional co-operation with these Balkan neighbours. These voices were also pro-communist. As for Italy, orienting towards the EC was a decision taken in the context of the cold war and the choice of a destiny. Second, the Greeks wanted 'to countervail what [was] seen as the tilt in favour of Turkey, both of NATO and in particular of the United States' (Tsakaloyannis, 1981: 138).

In 1962, Greece concluded an Association Agreement with the EC that envisaged eventual membership. In 1967, a military dictatorship was installed in response to a leftward swing of Greek democratic politics. In response, the Association Agreement was suspended. It was reactivated after the collapse of the dictatorship in 1974. The new Greek government applied for full membership of the EC in June 1975.

In January 1976, the Commission gave a rather negative official opinion on the Greek application, but it was overridden by the Council of Ministers. Here political considerations prevailed over economic. Popular feeling in Greece was running against NATO because the United States had failed to act against the Turkish occupation of the north of Cyprus in the summer of 1973. Greek forces were withdrawn from the NATO command structure, and there was a threat of a complete withdrawal from the alliance. In this context, it became more important to shore up the southern flank of NATO than to worry about the cost of accepting a poor new member state.

Greece has been a substantial beneficiary from the EC structural funds and the Cohesion Fund, and part of the alliance in favour of maintaining and extending such funding. In other respects, though, it has been a difficult partner. The Greek left never accepted membership of the EC, so when the Panhellenic Socialist Party (PASOK) has been in office it has tended to ally with Britain and Denmark in opposing moves to closer integration. On foreign policy issues, Greek governments of both right and left have found it difficult to align themselves with the majority of member states. This reflects both geo-strategic and cultural differences.

As a Balkan state, Greece has a direct interest in developments in the sub-region. This led it, for example, to oppose the recognition of the independence of the Former Yugoslav Republic of Macedonia against the unanimous decision of all the other member states. It has been obstructionist about allowing the EU to develop any links with Turkey, which caused difficulties when Turkey was originally not included among the prospective new member states for the post-2000 enlargement. For cultural as well as geo-strategic reasons, Greece was more sympathetic to the position of the Serbs in Yugoslavia than were other EU members.

Spain

Spain joined the European Community in 1986. Until December 1978, when it adopted a new constitution, Spain was unable to join the EC because it was not a parliamentary democracy. A Spanish application for associate membership of the EC in 1962 was rejected on these grounds. Prior to full membership, only a preferential trade agreement between the EC and Spain existed, signed in 1970.

Following the death of the dictator Franco in 1975 the country effected a transition to democracy and market capitalism. Part of this process was membership of the EC. Membership was seen both as a guarantee of democratic stability and as a means of gaining access to the core market of the EC for Spanish goods. At the same time as wanting to access the EC market for its own goods, Spain sought a degree of temporary protection for its own market.

Throughout the accession negotiations Spain maintained a broad consensus in favour of EC membership. Despite this, the Spanish government was able to use the newness and fragility of the democratic framework as a bargaining ploy in the negotiations. It demanded an extended transition period, and substantial subsidies from the richer members of the EC for its economic development. The subsidies were negotiated in the form of the structural and cohesion funds, where Spain emerged as the leader of a coalition of the Mediterranean states and Ireland (see Ch. 27, pp. 368–81). The other big interest of Spain is in the Common Fisheries Policy. Spain has the biggest fishing fleet in the EU.

While central government maintains a pivotal role in relation to the EU, the post-Franco era has been marked by differing degrees of decentralization of power to the Spanish regions: a process of *asymmetric federalism*. EU membership has opened up new opportunities for the stronger regions to deal directly with Brussels. More generally, central government has been obliged to acknowledge the demands of influential regions in formulating its EU policies. EU structural policy was identified as one area where the scope for subnational influence had grown, particularly in the 1990s (Bache and Jones, 2000).

Portugal

Portugal joined the European Community in 1986. Spain's smaller neighbour on the Iberian Peninsula also lived under dictatorships until 1974. When the dictatorships collapsed following unsuccessful colonial wars in Angola and Mozambique, the Portuguese revolution threatened to run out of the control of the pro-capitalist democratic forces. For nearly two years there was political turmoil, with strong support for the Portuguese Communist Party (PCP) and for other left-wing political forces that had little sympathy for the PCP, but were equally anticapitalist.

To head off the possibility of Portugal being lost to the capitalist economic system and from the NATO alliance, European political forces took a number of initiatives. These were channelled not through governments, but through the political parties. The most prominent initiative came in the form of support from the Socialist International for the Portuguese Socialist Party (PSP) of Mario Soares. This initiative was headlined by the German SPD, which provided the PSP with funds, aid in establishing electoral and research centres, and public support in the form of visits by leading social democrats, most notably Willy Brandt. In 1976, a PSP government under Soares was elected in Portugal, and when it applied for membership of the EC it was guaranteed the support of West Germany whatever the budgetary implications.

Public opinion on the EU in Portugal has generally been positive, and like the other Mediterranean states, Portugal has been a strong defender of the structural funds, from which it has benefited considerably.

The 1995 entrants

Austria

At the end of the war, Austria, like Germany, was an occupied and divided state. In 1955, the western Allies and the USSR reached agreement on a mutual withdrawal of their armies of occupation in return for a guarantee of Austrian neutrality. Neutral status was therefore imposed on Austria, but it soon became the basis of national self-identity. The end of the cold war opened up the prospect of ending the neutral status, but public opinion remained attached to it.

Membership of the EC became tied up with the whole question of neutrality and national identity. It was pursued, though, for primarily economic reasons. In the light of the single market, Austria, like the other EFTA states, was concerned at the risk to its exports. At the time, exports to the EC comprised two-thirds of all Austrian exports. At the same time, the political elite saw membership as a means of pushing through a programme of economic reform, while minimizing the political risks by putting the responsibility on the EC (Kaiser, 1995: 412).

In terms of the type of capitalism that operates in different states, Austria had a very corporatist and statist system. Corporatism expressed itself in institutionalized links into the decision-making process for the peak interest groups representing capital and labour. Statism expressed itself in a large nationalized sector to the economy and an extensive welfare state. During the 1980s, business interests became increasingly concerned at the disadvantages they suffered in comparison with competitors in other European states. Cumbersome decision-making processes and the high cost of maintaining both the inefficient state sector and the welfare state provisions were seen as causes of this. Politicians were already looking for ways of dismantling the old system when first the EC's single market programme, then the collapse of Communism in central and eastern Europe brought the issue to crisis.

The debate on EC membership centred on concerns about both economic and military security. The economic security concerns were that jobs would be lost both to the EC, because of discrimination against Austrian exports, and to the post-communist central European states because of their lower wage rates. Military security became a dominant concern with the outbreak of war in the former Yugoslavia, right on the borders of Austria.

The referendum in June 1994 produced a surprisingly large vote in favour of membership, by 66.6 per cent to 33.4 per cent. This perhaps reflected the high level of cross-party support by leading politicians, and all but one of the national newspapers. Opposition came only from the right-wing populist and nationalist Freedom Party and the environmental Greens.

Although the referendum was comfortably won, public opinion soon began to turn against the EC. This reflected the unpopularity of the reforms to dismantle the corporatist and statist system. These reforms were blamed on membership. Also the determination of the government not to be left behind in a second tier of membership by moves to develop the CFSP, ran counter to the continued attachment of a majority of the Austrian population to the doctrine of neutrality. Another factor may have been the government's decision to accept large numbers of refugees from the fighting in former Yugoslavia, although this was not itself a direct consequence of EC membership. Austrians have a traditionally conservative culture, and the influx of large numbers of outsiders who would dilute the traditional culture was one of the fears that was stirred up by the Freedom Party during the referendum campaign. By the end of the 1990s, the EC was less popular in Austria than in any other member state except Sweden, and the Freedom Party made significant gains in the 1999 federal election.

Within the EU, Austria has a particular concern for agricultural issues, reflecting the importance of agriculture not only to the economy but also to the national culture. The appointment of Franz Fischler as Agriculture Commissioner in the Santer Commission, and the renewal of his tenure in the same post in the Prodi Commission, reflected the priorities of the Austrian government and the need to reassure the Austrian agricultural lobby. Other issues of concern to Austria are the environment, eastern enlargement, and the development of the CFSP.

On the environment, Austria has joined the coalition of states in favour of high levels of environmental protection. The issue of nuclear power also hangs in the air as a possible issue of controversy. The Austrians have voted not to generate electricity from nuclear power stations. However, the liberalization of the EU energy market may provoke a backlash against the requirement that electricity generated by nuclear power stations in other member states has to be available for sale in Austria.

Eastern enlargement is a fraught and difficult issue for the Austrians. On the one hand, they want to see early enlargement to take in their close neighbours in Slovenia and Croatia. They are also anxious that the central European states should be obliged to conform to EU standards on environmental protection and health and safety. The first of these is partly to protect their own environment; both are because of the fear of unfair competition for investment. Enlargement is also seen as the best means of ensuring the stability of the region on which Austria borders.

Comment has already been made above on the dilemma that Austrian governments face on CFSP. On the one hand, they do not want Austria to become a second-class member of the EU, and this implies being fully involved with moves towards a CFSP. An effective EU security policy is also an important safeguard for Austrian national security given Austria's position close to the less stable regions of central Europe. On the other hand, the Austrian sense of national identity has come to be closely associated with neutrality, and moves towards a CFSP add to the unpopularity of EU membership with the people.

Sweden

In the 1970s Sweden had two serious political problems about joining the EC: its neutrality in the context of the cold war, and its high standards of welfare, which the Swedish people feared would be undermined by EC membership. In 1972, having concluded a favourable free trade agreement with the EC, it seemed that Sweden had managed to achieve all the economic benefits of membership without the political drawbacks of actually joining (Jerneck, 1993: 24). This view was not revised until the 1980s and the declaration of the 1992 programme to free the internal market.

The effect of the single market programme on the investment plans of large Swedish companies such as Volvo, Aga, and SKF was that they began to look for manufacturing bases within the single market. In response, the Swedish government began negotiations for membership of the European Economic Area (EEA). This was a scheme devised by Jacques Delors to allow those countries that had a high degree of trade dependence on the EC to have access to the market without having full membership. Had such an arrangement proved possible and acceptable, it would have constituted in effect an upgrading of the favourable trade agreement that Sweden had held with the EC since 1972. However, the agreement proved unsatisfactory for two reasons. First, Sweden and the other EEA applicants were expected to adopt the whole of the single market legislation of the EC without having any effective say in its formulation. Second, the companies that the EEA was designed to reassure about their access to the EC market remained unconvinced that there would never be discrimination against Swedish exports. As such, they continued to plan to switch production from Sweden to inside the EC.

In October 1990, as part of a package of measures to rebuild confidence in the context of sustained speculative pressure against the krona, the Swedish government announced publicly its intention to apply for membership of the EU. Jerneck (1993) gives six reasons for this change of policy:

- increasing concern that the internal market would lead to discrimination against Swedish goods;
- concern that the world was dividing into trading blocs, and that Sweden would be left out in the cold;
- dissatisfaction with the terms of the EEA;
- a narrowing of the gap in welfare provision between Sweden and the EU member states as a result of the need to control government expenditure in Sweden and the beginning of the social dimension of the single market programme;

- a change in the position of the powerful Swedish trade unions in the light of the above narrowing of welfare differences, and their concern at the power of multinational corporations to divert investment away from individual states with higher welfare costs;

- the changing security climate as the cold war came to an end, which weakened the neutrality constraint on membership.

The referendum on membership in November 1994 produced a narrow 'yes' vote by 52.2 per cent to 47.8 per cent (almost exactly the same percentages by which Norway rejected membership a short time later). Yet, within a short time after membership, public opinion had turned decidedly negative.

Finland

During the cold war, Finland occupied a unique position. Its geographical location next to the USSR meant that is was in an extremely precarious position. Although Finnish governments consistently referred to Finland as a neutral state, geo-strategic realities obliged it to sign a Treaty of Friendship, Co-operation, and Mutual Assistance with its Communist neighbour in 1948. Although Finland developed as a prosperous capitalist economy, the USSR remained its main trading partner; and this trade was in effect based on barter. Finland received imports of oil and gas from the USSR and paid for them with exports of various manufactured goods (Arter, 1995: 362–5).

Even before the collapse of Communism in the USSR, and the subsequent collapse of the Russian economy, Finland suffered from the changes that Gorbachev introduced as part of his policy of *perestroika*. Attempts by the USSR to attract foreign currency into the country led to a reorientation of energy exports away from Finland towards the rest of western Europe (Arter, 1995: 367). The economic difficulties that followed the end of the Gorbachev era only deepened a recession that had already started in Finland by 1990.

The economic imperative to diversify its own trade left Finland with little option but to look to the EC. Initially it was content to take part in the negotiations for the EEA. This arrangement suited Finland because it appeared to allow access to the single market without the government having to address the vexed issues of neutrality and agriculture. However, when Sweden decided to explore full membership of the EC in November 1991, Finland felt that it could not risk being left out and launched its own application (Arter, 1995: 367–8).

Public opinion was volatile during the negotiations. The level of support among farmers was very low, and there was general public concern about the implications of EC moves towards a CFSP. There was strong support for membership, though, from big business. This sector was concerned about the inadequacy of the EEA arrangements to prevent discrimination against Finnish exports. It was also anxious to reap the benefits of the increased economic stability that full membership promised (Arter, 1995: 377–8). In the pro-membership campaign, these economic arguments were combined with invocation of the threat from Russia. This invocation was given added force during the referendum campaign by the emergence to prominence of the Russian nationalist politician Vladimir Zhirinovsky. Zhirinovsky openly advocated reconstructing the Russian empire of which Finland had once been a part (Arter, 1995: 370).

The result of the referendum, which was held on 16 October 1994, was 57 per cent for and 43 per cent against membership. Analysis of the results indicated that the strongest support came from the 18–25 age-group (68 per cent pro). Arter (1995) suggested that the positive vote of this younger group was a vote for a new national identity as west Europeans. The lowest vote by age-cohort was in the next generation up, the 26–35 age-group (55 per cent pro), for whom neutrality was part of their sense of identity. The generation over 65 remembered a time before 'Finlandization' and the 1939–40 and 1941–4 wars against the USSR. This was a factor in explaining their 64 per cent in favour of membership.

Whereas in some other member states a narrow vote in favour of membership was followed by a decline in the popularity of the EU, in Finland the opposite happened. The population accepted the decision once made, and embraced the new sense of identity. *Eurobarometer* polls showed Finland to have above-average levels of support for the EU and for further European integration.

Conclusion

The position of each member state on any specific issue will reflect the impact of that issue on what is perceived by the government to be the national interest of that state. At the same time, what is perceived to be in the national interest is coloured by general attitudes to European integration. These underlying perceptions reflect the reasons why the states joined the EC in the first place.

Economic factors are obviously relevant to determining a state's position on a particular issue. However, in terms of the general attitudes to European integration, the more fundamental factor in most cases is linked to the slightly vague concept of national identity. Where membership of the EC was seen at the time as a positive step to choose a national identity that was west European, democratic, and capitalist there is generally a lasting legacy of goodwill towards the EU which takes consistent disappointments over a long period of time to destroy. Of the states covered in this chapter, this sort of choice for Europe was made at different times by Belgium, the Netherlands, Luxembourg, Italy, Ireland, Greece, Spain, Portugal, and Finland. In all of these states public sentiment in favour of the EU remains strong, and this in turn influences government policies.

On the other hand, where membership was chosen for essentially pragmatic reasons, as it was for Denmark, Austria, and Sweden, the commitment to European integration has not been internalized. Setbacks to the flow of economic benefits soon erode public support, and this in turn affects the positions taken up by the governments of these states.

This is not much different from the conclusions drawn for the three most prominent member states which were considered in the earlier chapters in this section of the book. Germans remained committed to European integration for a long time despite having to make considerable contributions to the common budget, because the EC was central to the western, democratic capitalist identity chosen in the Adenauer era. French commitment was shallower: so long as Europe was constructed in the French interest there was support, but when things began to go against the French support waned quickly. In the case of Britain, the choice was based on a purely pragmatic economic calculation, and when the benefits were not obvious the support was withdrawn.

KEY POINTS

The original member states

- Pro-EU sentiment is strong in the original member states. Nevertheless, each state has its own national interests to pursue.

- Different governments have responded differently to the domination of the EC by the French and Germans, and the British have found some support at times for their sceptical stance towards Franco-German initiatives from the Italians and the Dutch in particular.

The 1973 entrants

- Both Denmark and Ireland entered the EC because, such was their trade dependence on Britain, they felt that they had no choice once Britain had decided to go in.

- Whereas Denmark regretted this necessity because it separated the Danes from their Scandinavian partners, Ireland welcomed it because it offered a route to reduce an almost total dependence on Britain.

- The two countries have adopted very different attitudes towards further integration, Ireland becoming a big supporter of all moves except those involving security and defence, while Denmark has become one of the more Eurosceptic member states.

The 1980s entrants

- The 1980s saw the accession of three mediterranean states to the EC, Greece in 1981 and Spain and Portugal in 1986. All three states had been ruled by dictators. EC membership therefore promised greater political stability as well as economic prosperity.

The 1995 entrants

- For Austria, membership of the EU was tied up with issues of national identity and neutrality. It was pursued ultimately for economic reasons. However, by the end of 1999, the EU was less popular in Austria than in any other member state except Sweden.

- The declining importance of political neutrality after the cold war and the narrowing of the gap between Sweden's welfare provision and that elsewhere in Europe paved the way for Sweden's accession. However, shortly after joining, public opinion became negative towards the EU again.

- The economic collapse of Russia, Finland's main trading partner, and Sweden's EC application provided the push for Finnish membership. Despite a narrow vote in favour of membership, Finland has since demonstrated above-average support for the EU.

QUESTIONS

1 How important have economic issues been for states seeking to join the EC/EU?

2 What explains the timing of each member states' accession to the EC/EU?

3 How easily have new member states adjusted to membership of the EC/EU?

FURTHER READING

The best source for information on public opinion in all the member states, including those three for which there are separate chapters, is the EU's *Eurobarometer*, which can be accessed via the Commission's web site (http://europa.eu.int/comm) using the link for the directorate-general for Education and Culture. Surveys are published every six months.

On the economic structure and orientation of individual states, two periodical publications are invaluable: *Economist Intelligence Unit: Country Profiles*, (published quarterly), and *OECD Economic Surveys* (published six-monthly).

An excellent regional survey (although it does not contain information on Greece) is: Europa Publications, *Western Europe 2000* (London: Europa Publications, 2000). There is a good general text on the Nordic countries: L. Miles (ed.) *The European Union and the Nordic Countries* (London: Routledge, 1996).

On specific member states, there are more recent books that can be used for follow-up reading. In the order that the states appear in this chapter:

J. Fitzmaurice, *The Politics of Belgium: A Unique Federalism* (London: Hurst, 1996).

G. Newton (ed.), *Essays on Politics, Language and Society in Luxembourg* (Lampeter: Edwin Mellon, 1999).

R. Andeweg and G. Irwin, *Dutch Government and Politics* (Basingstoke and London: Macmillan, 1993).

M. Bull, and M. Rhodes, (eds.) *Crisis and Transition in Italian Politics* (London: Frank Cass, 1997).

K. E. Miller, (ed.) *Denmark: A Troubled Welfare State* (Oxford: Westview Press, 1996).

B. Chubb, *The Government and Politics of Ireland* (London: Longman, 1992).

K. Featherstone and K. Ifantis (eds.) *Greece in a Changing Europe: Between European Integration and Balkan Disintegration?* (Manchester: Manchester University Press, 1996).

J. Gibbons, *Spanish Politics Today* (Manchester: Manchester University Press, 1999).

P. Lanca, *The Good Apprentice: Portugal and the European Union* (London: Institute for European Defence and Strategic Studies, 1996).

V. Lauber, (ed.) *Contemporary Austrian Politics* (Oxford: Westview Press, 1996).

Part Four

Institutions

Both theories deriving from international relations and those deriving from the analysis of domestic policy-making include positions that emphasize the importance of institutions. In the IR literature on international regimes, there is an emphasis on institutions as, 'persistent and connected sets of rules (formal and informal) that prescribe behavioral roles, constrain states, and shape expectations' (Keohane, 1989*b*: 3). In the 'new institutionalist' approaches to the study of domestic policy-making there is a similar emphasis on the importance of institutions, broadly defined. Essentially our argument is that *institutions matter*. Of course, it is not only institutions that matter. Nor is it the case that only formal institutions matter. However, to understand the outcomes of the EU polity it is necessary to know something about the nature of the formal institutions and the relationship between them.

There are six chapters in this section of the book. The opening chapter on **The institutional architecture** provides essential introductory information on the institutions, the treaties, and the legislative and budgetary processes. It contains little analysis, but presents the context within which the institutions operate, and provides the background to understanding the debates that are developed in the later chapters.

In the rest of this section, the choice of subjects for inclusion in individual chapters is perhaps the most straightforward in the book. There is a broad consensus that the EU has four 'main' institutions: the **Commission**; the **Council of Ministers**; the **European Parliament**; and the **European Court of Justice**. Each receives separate treatment. There is also growing acknowledgement of the importance that organized interests play in the decision-making process. This is the subject of the concluding chapter of this section.

18 The institutional architecture

SUMMARY

The EU has no formal constitution, but it is governed by a series of treaties that have been concluded since 1951. These have now largely been codified into two: the Treaty on European Union (TEU), and the Treaty establishing the European Community (TEC). The EU itself consists of three pillars: the EC pillar, which is governed by the TEC, and two intergovernmental pillars, the Common Foreign and Security Policy pillar, and the pillar on

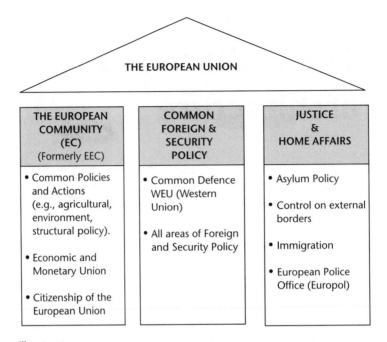

Fig. 18.1 The three-pillar structure
(*Source*: adapted from European Parliament slides)

Justice and Home Affairs. In the EC pillar, the Treaties make the European Commission the sole proposer of legislation, and the Council of Ministers and the European Parliament are the joint legislative decision-makers. A similar division of functions exists for budgetary decision-making. The Economic and Social Committee (ESC) and the Committee of the Regions and Local Authorities (CoR) also have a right to be consulted on legislative proposals.

Implementation of legislation once it has been passed is partly a responsibility of the Commission, but mostly it is the responsibility of the member states. The Commission and the European Court of Justice act as watchdogs to ensure that the member states fulfil their obligations. The Court of Auditors performs a similar role for the budget. These powers and procedures do not apply in the two intergovernmental pillars, where the Commission has to share the right of initiative with the member states, and the EP has only a right to be consulted and informed about developments.

Introduction

The institutions of the EU and the formal relationships between them are laid down in the Treaties (Box 18.1, p. 215). These formal relationships are only the start of the story, as subsequent chapters will explain. The institutions, once created, become political actors in their own right, and strive to achieve their objectives through a variety of informal means; but the formal relationships are

---

Box 18.1 **The European Union**

The Treaty on European Union (TEU), as its name implies, created a new organization known as the European Union (EU). This consisted of three 'pillars' (see Fig. 18.1, p. 214): the European Communities (pillar 1); provisions on a Common Foreign and Security Policy (CFSP) (pillar 2); provisions on co-operation in the fields of Justice and Home Affairs (pillar 3). Thus it is not correct to say that the European Union 'replaced' the European Communities. It superseded the EC in the sense that it incorporated the three communities into a wider structure; but the three communities continued to exist, and it is legally correct to speak of 'EC law', not 'EU law', because it is only in the EC pillar that law can be made. The other two pillars are 'intergovernmental' pillars. The powers of the institutions are different under these pillars.

The Treaty of Amsterdam modified the Maastricht architecture in various ways. In particular, it moved policy on visas, immigration, and asylum from the third pillar to the first, EC pillar, and it renamed the third pillar 'Police and Judicial Co-operation in Criminal Matters'.

(Duff, 1997: pp. xxiii–xv)

---

important. The institutional architecture both empowers institutions by giving them certain rights in the various decision-making processes of the EU, and acts as a constraint on the political influence that institutions can exercise (see Ch. 2, pp. 20–2).

This chapter examines the pattern of institutions and the formal rules that govern them. It also gives information on the composition of the less important institutions, although for the main institutions—the Commission, the Council, the European Parliament (EP), and the European Court of Justice (ECJ)—that information is provided in the separate chapters devoted to them.

The chapter starts with a review of the Treaties that form the founding 'constitutional' documents of the EU. The main institutions involved in the processes of decision-making are then introduced. Decision-making covers both the budgetary and legislative procedures, which are quite complex. They are explained. The chapter then looks at the implementation of decisions once they have been made. Finally, the rather different processes that operate in the intergovernmental pillars of the EU are outlined.

Fig. 18.2 Decision-making institutions of the European Union

The Treaties

The EU does not have a formal constitution. Instead various treaties govern its operation. There are three 'founding treaties', the Treaty of Paris and the two Treaties of Rome. They were supplemented in ways that affected the powers of the institutions by three further Treaties in the 1960s and early 1970s. One of these merged the Councils and the Commissions of the three Communities, while the other two were concerned with budgetary provisions. After the last of these, in 1975, there were no further major revisions of the Treaties for another decade, but then there were three new Treaties in the next fifteen years: the Single European Act, the Treaty on European Union, and the Amsterdam Treaty (Box 18.2, p. 216).

The staff of the EU institutions constantly refer to the Treaties. They are always careful to check the treaty-base of any action that they take. The Commission is formally obliged to state in the preamble of any proposal that it makes for legislation under which article of the Treaties it is making the proposal. This incessant engagement with the text of the Treaties has led the internal discourse of the institutions to be peppered with references to articles of the Treaties, usually just citing them by number.

However, as the founding treaties were amended and added to by the later treaties, the numbering grew more and more complex, with letters having to be used in addition to numbers. Finally, at Amsterdam in June 1997 the heads of government agreed to renumber the articles. This reasonable decision had the unfortunate consequence that familiar phrases in the discourse of the EU became obsolete. Everyone working in or studying the institutions knew what the Article 113 Committee was (see below, p. 392), or what an Article 177 referral to the ECJ meant (see below, p. 279). After Amsterdam they had to adjust to calling them respectively the Article 133 Committee and an Article 234 referral. Many other similar adjustments had to be made.

Authors of textbooks on the EU have also had to cope with the changed numbering system. In this book, the new number of a Treaty Article is given, followed by the old one in brackets, except where the reference is purely historical, when the numbering current at the time is given first followed by the new numbering in brackets. In all cases the reference is to what is now called the 'Treaty establishing European Community' (TEC), unless it is indicated that it is to the Treaty on European Union (TEU). The texts of both treaties can be found on the EU web site at: http://europa.eu.int/eur-lex/en/treaties/index.html.

Box 18.2 **The Treaties**

- The Treaty of Paris (signed 1951; took effect 1952) created the European Coal and Steel Community (ECSC).

- The two Treaties of Rome (signed 1957; took effect 1958). The first of these created European Atomic Energy Community (Euratom); the second created the European Economic Community (EEC).

- The Treaty Establishing a Single Council and a Single Commission of the European Communities, also known as the Merger Treaty (signed 1965; took effect 1967).

- The Treaty Amending Certain Budgetary Provisions of the Treaties (1970).

- The Treaty Amending Certain Financial Provisions of the Treaty (1975).

- The Single European Act (1985).

- The Treaty on European Union—also known as the Maastricht Treaty (signed 1992; took effect November 1993).

- The Treaty of Amsterdam (signed 1997; took effect 1999).

The decision-making institutions

The main decision-making institutions of the EU are those that were set up in the Treaty of Rome (EEC):

- the Commission
- the Council of Ministers
- the European Parliament.

There are also two consultative committees:

- the Economic and Social Committee, which was in the original Treaty of Rome (EEC)
- the Committee of the Regions and Local Authorities, which was set up by the TEU.

The Commission

The Commission submits proposals to the Council of Ministers for EC legislation; it also draws up the draft annual budget of the EC for discussion in the Council of Ministers and the EP. It is the sole institution with the right to propose legislation under the various EC Treaties, although this is not true of the intergovernmental pillars of the TEU (see below, pp. 228–9). Its proposals can only be amended by the Council of Ministers if the Council acts unanimously. Also, the Commission may withdraw or amend its own proposals at any stage as long as the Council has not acted on them.

To say that the Commission is the sole proposer of legislation does not imply that it works on legislative proposals in isolation. In practice it consults widely with interest groups, and with committees of technical experts and representatives of national bureaucracies. Nevertheless, it defends its right of initiative vigorously. Although the Commission and the EP have usually been allies in attempting to lever powers away from the national governments, the Commission has strongly resisted persistent demands from the EP that it also be allowed the right to initiate legislative proposals. In the view of the Commission it is only its monopoly of the right of initiative that allows a coherent agenda to emerge for the EC as a whole. For this reason the Commission was also opposed to the idea that co-operation on a Common Foreign and Security Policy (CFSP)

and on Justice and Home Affairs (JHA) should be developed outside of the decision-making framework of the EC, although it lost this argument (see below, pp. 228–9).

The Council of Ministers

The Council of Ministers consists of representatives of the member states, although most meetings under the Council heading are not of Ministers themselves, but of various committees of national government officials (see Ch. 20, pp. 252–4). Nearly all business for the meetings of Ministers is filtered through these committees, and then through the Committee of Permanent Representatives (COREPER), which consists of the ambassadors from the member states to the EU (see Ch. 20, pp. 252–4). The Council makes decisions on proposals from the Commission on the basis either of unanimity or Qualified Majority Voting (QMV) depending on the issue. As explained in chapter 8, de Gaulle blocked the formal transition to QMV in 1965, but the SEA introduced it for legislative acts related to the single market programme, and it was extended in the TEU to cover a range of other policies (Box 18.3, p. 218). The weighting of votes is indicated in Box 18.4, p. 218.

The European Parliament (EP)

In the original blueprint for the ECSC, Monnet did not include any parliamentary body, but in an attempt to make the new community more democratic a European Parliamentary Assembly was added to the Treaty of Paris (Diebold, 1959: 62). This body was carried over into the Treaties of Rome. The EP has consistently tried to insert itself more effectively into the decision-making process of the EC, especially since 1979 when it became a directly elected body. It has made some limited progress. In the original legislative process the Council of Ministers was obliged to consult the EP before disposing of legislative proposals made by the Commission, but it could

Box 18.3 Policy areas covered by qualified majority voting

QMV applied in the following policy areas following the TEU:

- the free movement of workers;
- freedom of establishment;
- mutual recognition of qualifications;
- the internal market;
- public health;
- consumer protection;
- co-ordination of national provisions on the treatment of foreign nationals;
- competition;
- transport;
- trans-European networks;

- environment;
- development co-operation.

In the Treaty of Amsterdam, QMV was extended to:

- equal pay and treatment of men and women;
- the framework programmes for research and development;
- access to official documents;
- combating fraud;
- customs co-operation.

QMV also applies to the implementation of the European Social Fund (ESF) and the European Regional Development Fund (ERDF).

Box 18.4 Weighting of national votes under qualified majority voting

Country	Votes	Country	Votes	Country	Votes
Austria	4	France	10	Luxembourg	2
Belgium	5	Germany	10	Netherlands	5
Britain	10	Greece	5	Portugal	5
Denmark	3	Ireland	3	Spain	8
Finland	3	Italy	10	Sweden	4

A blocking minority consists of 26 votes, but if there are 23 votes against a measure it is withdrawn for a period of reflection before being reintroduced.

ignore the EP's opinion if it wished. This remains the case in several policy areas, but in others the EP has further powers, and in several it has the right to block legislation altogether. These powers are outlined under the heading 'Decision-Making Procedures' below. The EP is also formally a co-decision maker with the Council on the annual budget, and its approval is necessary for the budget to be given effect. The formal budgetary process is also outlined below in the section on Decision-Making Procedures.

The Economic and Social Committee (ESC)

The ESC consists of representatives of various economic and social interests (Box 18.5, p. 219). The Commission, or the Council as appropriate, has to consult the ESC on a range of issues including agricultural matters, freedom of movement for workers, the right of establishment, social policy, internal market issues, measures of economic and social cohesion, and environmental policy. In addition, the Commission may consult it on any matter that it thinks appropriate; and the ESC has the right to issue

---

Box 18.5 The Economic and Social Committee

- The ESC consists of representatives of producers, farmers, workers, professionals, and of the general public. Members are proposed by national governments and formally appointed by the Council of Ministers. They sit on the ESC in a personal capacity and formally may not be bound by any mandatory instructions from their organizations.

- It is divided into three Groups representing employers, workers, and 'various interests'. The last Group includes farmers, the professions, the self-employed, consumers, and environmental groups. There are also some members who choose not to take any group affiliation (currently there is only one).

- It has six sections, which are the equivalent of the committees in the EP. They are:
  — Agriculture, Rural Development, and the Environment;
  — Economic and Monetary Union and Economic and Social Cohesion;
  — Employment, Social Affairs and Citizenship;
  — External Relations;
  — The Single Market, Production, and Consumption;
  — Transport, Energy, Infrastructure, and the Information Society.

- A secretariat-general is responsible for the Committee's administration.

Box 18.6 The Committee of the Regions and Local Authorities

- The CoR has 222 full members and an equal number of substitute members.

- They are chosen by the member states and officially appointed by the Council of Ministers for a four-year, renewable term.

  Germany, France, Italy and the United Kingdom each have 24 members; Spain has 21; Belgium, Greece, the Netherlands, Austria, Portugal, and Sweden each have 12; Denmark, Ireland, and Finland each have 9; Luxembourg has 6.

- They participate in the work of seven specialized

commissions, which are responsible for drafting the Committee's opinions.

- The Bureau, which organizes the work of the Committee and its commissions, has 36 members. These include the chairman, a first vice-chairman and one vice-chairman from each of the 15 member states, whom the members of the assembly elect for two-year terms. They also include the chairmen of the political groups.

- A secretariat-general is responsible for the Committee's administration.

(*Source*: Web Site of the CoR: http://www.cor.eu.int/)

---

opinions on any matter on its own initiative, except for subjects that fall under the remit of the ECSC, which still has its own Consultative Committee. In practice the ESC is not particularly influential. This is because it has chosen not to be selective in issuing opinions, which are of very variable quality. There is thus a lot of paper coming out of the secretariat of the ESC, much of it not very constructive, and as a result little of it is read with any great attention.

The Committee of the Regions and Local Authorities (CoR)

CoR was created by the TEU, and was given the right to be consulted on proposals that affected regional and local interests, and the right to issue opinions on its own initiative (Box 18.6, p. 219). At first sight the CoR appears to be another incarnation of the ESC, with which it originally shared a meeting chamber and support staff. However, there is an important difference: the CoR is strongly backed by political

---

Box 18.7 Representation of Member States in the Committee of the Regions

Austria	12	Netherlands	12	Luxembourg	6
Denmark	9	Belgium	12	Portugal	12
France	24	Finland	9	Spain	21
Greece	12	Germany	24	United Kingdom	24
Italy	24	Ireland	9	Sweden	12

Source: CoR website

---

actors of considerable influence. It was put into the TEU at the insistence of the German Federal Government under pressure from the Länder, the states that make up the German federation. They appear to see it as an embryonic European equivalent of the Bundesrat, the upper house of the Federal German Parliament in which the Länder are represented (Box 18.7, p. 220 for the representation of member states). This interpretation of the future of the CoR is shared by regional authorities from some other member states, particularly Belgium and Spain, although the Spanish central government is less keen. With the political weight and the resources of these significant

regional actors behind it, there is a possibility that the Committee will turn into a much more influential institution than the ESC. The Commission therefore has every incentive to work closely with the Committee, particularly because the Commission itself has long favoured the emergence of a 'Europe of regions' which would break down the domination of all decision-making by the central governments of the member states. So, as well as being another constraint on the freedom of action of the Commission, the CoR provides it with a potential ally against the governments.

Decision-making procedures

There are two types of decision-making procedure: that for adopting the annual budget of the EU—the budgetary procedure—and the various legislative procedures.

The budgetary procedure

The budgetary procedure is laid down in Article 272 (previously Article 203) of the Treaty, although it has been modified as a result of interinstitutional agreements. The budget is divided into 'compulsory' and 'non-compulsory' items of expenditure. Compulsory expenditure consists mainly of agricultural expenditure, which remains the largest single item in the budget. The EP can only propose modifications to the compulsory items by an absolute majority of its

members. However, it has the right to amend the draft budget for non-compulsory items with the effect that the EP has a final say on these items of expenditure within the constraints imposed by the multi-annual financial perspectives.

In 1988 the EP, the Council, and the Commission signed an Interinstitutional Agreement on Budgetary Discipline. This instituted multi-annual financial frameworks, and agreed ceilings for both compulsory and non-compulsory expenditure that would have the effect of shifting the balance to the non-compulsory items. The balance between compulsory and non-compulsory expenditure in the budget is obviously of considerable importance in determining the level of influence that the EP may exercise. The first financial perspective covered the years 1988–92 and the second 1993–9. In March 1999, agreement was reached on a third financial perspective to cover the period 2000–06. Although they did increase the influence of the EP by shifting the balance of the budget away from compulsory expenditure, in practice the financial frameworks are predominantly negotiated between the Commission and the member states, and allow for only very limited change within budget headings. They thus provide little opportunity for the EP to increase or decrease expenditure to any very significant extent in particular areas on a year-by-year basis.

The budget process begins with the Commission drawing up a Preliminary Draft Budget, which it has to do under the Treaty by 1 September of each year, but which it normally completes by June. The work is performed by the Budget Directorate-General (previously DG XIX) in consultation with the other services of the Commission and under the supervision of the Budget Commissioner. In preparing this document, the Commission is constrained by the multi-annual budgetary framework agreements. The Budget DG holds a meeting with representatives of the Council and the EP to discuss the precise interpretation of the framework in the specific conditions of the current financial year. The Commission also takes the opportunity to establish the financial priorities of the other two institutions.

Once the Preliminary Draft Budget is prepared, and agreed by the Commissioners as a whole, it is sent to the Council of Ministers, which formally has until 5 October to adopt a Draft Budget. Often, however, the Draft Budget has been adopted by the end of the Council presidency for the first half of the year, which means by the end of June. Most of the detailed work at this stage is done by the Budget Committee of the Council, which consists of the financial attachés to the offices of the Permanent Representatives, operating under QMV. Before the adoption of the Draft Budget an informal meeting is held with the Budget Committee of the EP to try to resolve any issues that could delay the process later.

The Draft Budget is then sent to the EP for a first reading, which has to be completed within forty-five days. At this stage the Budgetary Committee of the EP takes the lead, co-ordinating with the other specialized committees. The EP can simply approve the budget at this stage, but it invariably proposes a lot of amendments to the Preliminary Draft Budget, most of which increase expenditure to the maximum permissible level. The maximum rate of increase is determined by the increase over the previous year of the gross national product of the EU, the increase in national budgets, and the rate of inflation. It can only be exceeded by agreement between the Council and the EP.

Once adopted by the full EP, the Draft Budget goes back to the Council. The Council then has fifteen days to consider its response to the amendments proposed by the EP. At this stage there is a meeting between the Council and the EP, with the full participation of the Commission, to try to reach agreement on priorities within the budget. Despite this 'Conciliation' meeting, the Council usually rejects most of the amendments proposed by the EP.

The final stage is for the EP to complete a second reading within fifteen days of receipt of the Amended Draft Budget. The EP will restore whatever it has the power to restore of its original amendments. This is where the distinction between 'compulsory' and 'non-compulsory' expenditure is particularly important: the EP does not have the right to re-amend compulsory expenditure, only non-compulsory. To do this it has to muster the votes of a majority of all members, and three-fifths of those voting. It then has to adopt or reject the Budget as a whole. Rejection requires a majority of all members, and three-fifths of the votes cast. If the budget is rejected, as it was five times between 1979 and 1988, efforts to reach an agreement continue, but if no agreement can be reached by 1 January, when the new financial year begins, the EU has to operate on a system known as 'provisional twelfths'. This means that each month one-twelfth of the previous year's budget total is released to cover expenditure. This will obviously prove cumulatively more restrictive as the year progresses, and in particular it will mean that new programmes, which had no budget line the previous year, will not be able to begin operation. The introduction of the multi-annual financial perspectives, has, though, considerably reduced the prospects of rejection.

There is one other part to the budgetary process. Every year the Commission is required to submit to the Council and the EP the accounts of the previous financial year. These are considered by both institutions in the light of the annual report from the Court

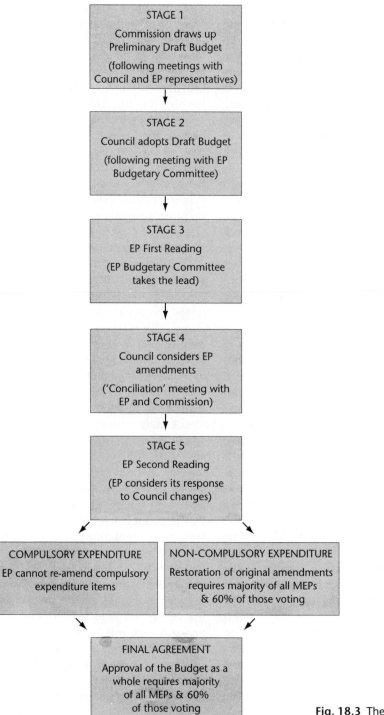

STAGE 1

Commission draws up
Preliminary Draft Budget

(following meetings with
Council and EP representatives)

STAGE 2

Council adopts Draft Budget

(following meeting with EP
Budgetary Committee)

STAGE 3

EP First Reading

(EP Budgetary Committee
takes the lead)

STAGE 4

Council considers EP
amendments

('Conciliation' meeting with
EP and Commission)

STAGE 5

EP Second Reading

(EP considers its response
to Council changes)

COMPULSORY EXPENDITURE

EP cannot re-amend compulsory
expenditure items

NON-COMPULSORY EXPENDITURE

Restoration of original amendments
requires majority of all MEPs
& 60% of those voting

FINAL AGREEMENT

Approval of the Budget as a
whole requires majority
of all MEPs & 60%
of those voting

Fig. 18.3 The budgetary procedure

of Auditors. The EP receives a recommendation from the Council, and in the light of this and its own deliberations, gives discharge to the Commission in respect to implementation of the budget. This means that the EP formally acknowledges that the Commission has implemented the budget properly and efficiently. It is not clear what happens if the EP does not feel that it can do so.

Legislative procedures

So far as legislative proposals are concerned, there are many different procedures that operate under the EC pillar of the EU. The four main procedures with which students of the EU need to be familiar are:

- consultation;
- co-operation;
- co-decision;
- assent.

The consultation procedure

The original 'consultation procedure' for deciding on EC legislation involved the Commission submitting a proposal to the Council of Ministers, which was then obliged to seek the opinion of the EP, and, where required by the Treaty, of the ESC. In the Isoglucose Case (1980), the ECJ ruled that the Council could not act legally in disposing of a proposal from the Commission without receiving the opinion of the EP. However, having received that opinion, the Council could if it so wished simply ignore it and agree to the proposal or reject it. Amendments could only be made by unanimity in the Council. This procedure still exists for certain categories of business, mainly agricultural policy issues and the policy sectors that were transferred under Amsterdam from the third to the first pillar (asylum, immigration, and visas).

The co-operation procedure

In the SEA the EP was given a right of second reading over legislation that was in future to be covered by QMV. This was most legislation relating to the single market programme, although some areas, such as veterinary regulations and the harmonization of taxation, were specifically excluded. In the areas subject to QMV, in addition to the right to be consulted, the EP was given a second chance to propose amendments. Under this procedure, often known as the 'co-operation procedure', the Council adopts a 'common position' by QMV after the first round of consultation. This position is then communicated to the EP, together with a statement of the Council's reasons for adopting it, and a statement of the Commission's view on the position. The EP has three months in which to approve or reject the common position, or to propose amendments. If the EP approves the common position, or if it does not act at all within the three months allowed, the Council may adopt the common position as the final version of the proposal. To propose amendments, or to reject the common position, the EP must be able to do so by an absolute majority of all its members. If the EP rejects the common position, the Council may only proceed to a second reading if it agrees to do so unanimously.

If the EP proposes amendments to the common position, the next stage is for the Commission to decide within one month whether it accepts these amendments. If it does, the amended proposal goes back to the Council of Ministers, which can only re-amend it if it acts unanimously. If the Commission does not accept the EP's proposed amendments, they are reported to the Council which can decide to adopt them, but only by unanimity. This gives the Commission considerable discretion in the process. Under this procedure, the Council has the final say on the legislation adopted, unless the EP rejects the common position and the Council cannot achieve unanimity, in which case the EP can block legislation.

The co-operation procedure is now almost only of historical interest, as in the Treaty of Amsterdam it

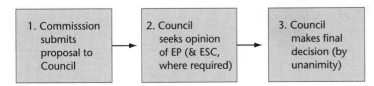

Fig. 18.4 The consultation procedure

1. Commisssion submits proposal to Council → 2. Council seeks opinion of EP (& ESC, where required) → 3. Council makes final decision (by unanimity)

was replaced by co-decision in nearly all areas to which it had applied. The exceptions were in the field of monetary union, which was not dealt with at Amsterdam. Other policy areas that became subject to QMV for the first time in the TEU, such as environmental policy, were covered by the older co-operation procedure, but these were changed to co-decision by the Treaty of Amsterdam. Under the TEU, two policy areas that were subject to the co-decision procedure—cultural policy, and the

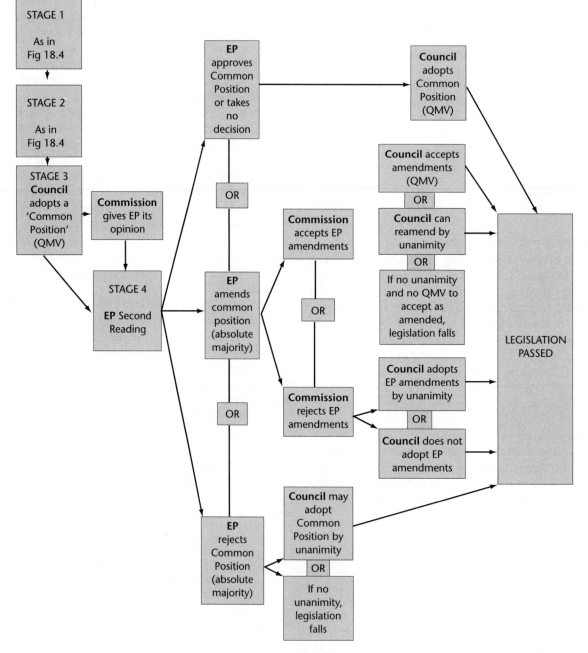

Fig.18.5 The co-operation procedure

multi-annual technological research and development framework programmes—differed from the other areas in that unanimity applied at the Council stages. At Amsterdam this was changed for the framework programmes, which now come under QMV, but the anomaly was retained for cultural matters, and social security for migrant workers, the rights of the self-employed, and citizens' rights were added to this category. It was also agreed at Amsterdam that visa procedures and uniformity rules would be governed by co-decision after five years.

The co-decision procedure

Co-decision gave the EP even stronger powers than co-operation. In its early stages it parallels the co-operation procedure; but if the EP rejects the common position, or the Council does not approve the EP's amendments, then a Conciliation Committee is set up. This consists of representatives of the members of the Council, and an equal number of representatives of the EP. With the help of the Commission, the Conciliation Committee tries to negotiate a mutually acceptable compromise text, which can

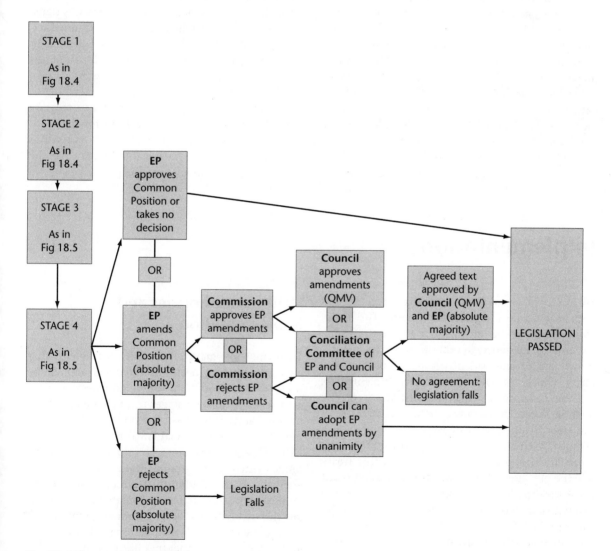

Fig. 18.6 The co-decision procedure

then be recommended to both institutions. The Committee has six weeks in which to do so, operating on the basis of QMV for the Council members and simple majority voting for the EP members.

If the Conciliation Committee agrees a joint text, the EP and the Council have six weeks in which to adopt it. The EP has to do so by an absolute majority, the Council by a qualified majority. If either institution fails to adopt the text, the proposal is effectively dead. Under the rules adopted in the TEU, the next stage was very complex, but it was simplified at Amsterdam. Under the original procedure, should the Conciliation Committee fail to agree a joint text, the Council could reaffirm its adoption of the original text within six weeks. If it did not do so, the measure fell; if it did do so, the EP had a further six weeks in which to reject the adopted text by an absolute majority. If it did not, the measure was adopted; but if it did, the measure fell. Under Amsterdam this extremely complex stage, which many felt advantaged the Council over the EP, was simplified so that now, if the Conciliation Committee fails, the measure falls. Amsterdam also simplified the co-decision procedure by allowing the Council to adopt a measure where it and the EP are in agreement, or where the EP is unable to muster the majority needed to pass amendments.

Assent

The EP can also block legislation under the assent procedure. This was originally introduced for agreements with non-member states, but was extended in the TEU to cover other areas. These included citizenship of the EU, amendments to the statute of the European System of Central Banks, elections to the EP in accordance with a uniform electoral procedure, and establishment and reform of the structural funds. Under Amsterdam, citizens' rights was transferred to co-decision (although with the Council acting by unanimity), while assent was extended to sanctions against a member state for serious and persistent breach of fundamental rights. Assent is a simple extension of the consultation procedure in which the assent of the EP is required for a measure to be adopted. There is no provision for the EP to amend proposals. However, the fact that its assent is required does give it considerable influence at the stage when proposals are being prepared.

Implementation

The policy process does not end once agreement has been reached on a legislative proposal. The agreement still has to be implemented before the policy has any real existence. In other words, implementation is an integral part of the policy process. For many types of legislation the primary implementers are the governments and administrations of the member states. The Commission has a central role in the case of other types of legislation, and is also charged by Article 211 (previously Article 155) of the Treaty to 'ensure that the provisions of this Treaty and the measures taken by the institutions pursuant thereto are applied'. In performing this latter task the Commission has recourse to judicial authority through the referral of cases to the ECJ. Finally, the implementation of all financial instruments is subject to scrutiny by the Court of Auditors.

National authorities and implementation

There are three main types of EC instruments that are legally binding: decisions, directives, and regulations (Box 18.8, p. 227). Where directives are concerned, there are two stages to implementation by national authorities. First, the directives have to be incorporated into national law through appropriate national legal instruments. Second, they have to be implemented on the ground; that is, they have to be applied by national administrative authorities. Regulations do not have to be incorporated into national law through national legal instruments, but it is still usually the responsibility of national administrative authorities to ensure that they are applied.

> ## Box 18.8 Legally binding EC instruments
>
> - Decisions are addressed to particular individual legal actors such as companies or individual states.
> - Directives are the most common form of general legislation agreed in the Council of Ministers; it is left to individual member states to decide how they are incorporated into national law.
> - Regulations are directly applicable in all member states.

In the case of both aspects of implementation the record of member states in actually doing what they have agreed to do varies considerably. This means that the outcomes of EU decisions are not always the same as the intention. Although Denmark and Britain have often been accused of being less than enthusiastic members of the EU, in most league tables of implementation Denmark comes out at or very near the top, and Britain is rarely far behind. Some of the member states that are most ready to sign up to integrative measures are the least willing to implement that to which they have agreed.

The Commission and implementation

Formally, the Commission has overall responsibility for the implementation of EC decisions. There are several processes of implementation in the EU, in each of which the Commission has a role.

- First, there is the implementation of common policies that are centrally administered by the Commission itself. These are few, but some of the powers of the Commission under the ECSC and Euratom Treaties fall under this heading, as does competition policy, including the control of large-scale mergers. A slightly different area is the administration of international policies such as the provision of food-aid, where again the Commission is the sole responsible EU body, although it has to work in conjunction with other organizations.

- Second, there is the implementation of common policies which takes place partly at the European level and partly at the national level: the administration of the CAP and the structural funds come under this heading.

- Third, there is the implementation of Council directives, where the Commission has a dual role as guardian of the Treaties: to ensure that directives are promptly and accurately incorporated into national law in the member states, and to ensure that they are actually implemented on the ground.

Under Article 226 (previously Article 169), if the Commission considers that a member state has failed to fulfil its obligations, it is required to deliver a reasoned opinion on the matter after giving the government of the member state concerned the opportunity to submit its own observations. If the state does not comply with the reasoned opinion, the matter may be brought before the Court of Justice. Another member state may also bring an alleged infringement of obligations to the attention of the Commission, which is required to act on the matter within three months, or the case automatically goes to the Court.

The European Court of Justice

Article 220 (formerly 164) of the Treaty charges the ECJ to ensure that the law of the EC is observed. It is the final arbiter on the interpretation of the Treaties and the application of EC law. As such it is a referee in disputes between institutions and member states.

Where the ECJ is asked to rule on whether a member state has fulfilled its obligations under EC law, the decision of the ECJ is final. Originally there was no penalty other than moral pressure if a member state still failed to fulfil its obligations after the ECJ had ruled against it. However, the TEU amended Article 171, EEC (now Article 228), to allow the Commission to return to the ECJ if it felt that a state was not complying with a ruling, and to request a financial penalty be levied against the state.

Box 18.9 **The Court of Auditors**

The Treaty confers upon the European Court of Auditors the main task of auditing the accounts and the implementation of the budget of the European Union with the dual aim of improving financial management and the reporting to the citizens of Europe on the use made of public funds by the authorities responsible for their management.

- It is based in Luxembourg

- It consists of one member from each member state appointed for a renewable six-year period.

- Members must have belonged to national audit offices, or be especially qualified for the office, and their independence must be beyond doubt.

- The members of the Court themselves elect a President from among their number for a period of three years.

- It has 550 staff, of whom 250 are auditors.

(Source: Court of Auditors website http://www.eca.eu.int/EN/coa.htm)

In the 1990s the profile of the Court of Auditors was raised considerably by the concern in member states over the level of fraud against the EC (Laffan, 1997a: 185; Peterson, 1997). Its annual report for 1994 indicated that fraud, payments made in error, and spending that did not achieve its objectives amounted to 500 m. ecus in 1994, and the Court called for substantial change in the financial management culture of the EU. Its report on the 1996 budget pointed to serious examples of maladministration in the Leonardo Youth Training Programme and the Humanitarian Aid Programme (ECHO). This led to a parliamentary motion of censure against the Commission, and to fundamental changes both in the administration of programmes and in the internal mechanisms for identifying fraud and maladministration. The Court's report on the 1997 budget alleged that errors affected 5 per cent of all payments from the budget.

The Court of Auditors

In 1975 the Treaty Amending Certain Financial Provisions of the EEC created a new institution, the Court of Auditors (Box 18.9, p. 228). This Court examines the accounts of all revenue and expenditure of the EC to determine whether the revenue has been received and the expenditure incurred in a law-ful and regular manner. It provides the EP and the Council with a statement on the reliability of the accounts, and publishes an annual report. It also prepares special reports on aspects of the audit, either on its own initiative or at the request of another institution; and it delivers opinions on request from the other institutions concerning the financial implications of proposed legislation.

The intergovernmental pillars of the EU

The TEU introduced two new areas of co-operation to the Treaties. The Common Foreign and Security Policy (CFSP) was a renaming of what had first appeared in the SEA as 'European Co-operation in the Sphere of Foreign Policy' (Box 18.10, p. 229). Justice and Home Affairs (JHA) was entirely new as a Treaty commitment (Box 18.11, p. 229). In both cases actual co-operation had begun before incorporation in the Treaties. Because the member states were not ready to risk any surrender of control over such sensitive areas of national policy, these areas were not brought under the decision-making rules of the EC. Instead they were put into two separate 'intergovernmental' pillars where the Commission did not have the sole right of initiative

In these two 'intergovernmental' pillars the Commission, the EP, and the ECJ do not have the same powers that they have under the EC pillar. In both pillars the Commission is to be 'fully associated' with actions taken, and it does have the right to

> ## Box 18.10 Common Foreign and Security Policy
>
> CFSP has the following objectives:
>
> - to safeguard the common values, fundamental interests and independence of the Union
>
> - to strengthen the security of the Union and its member states
>
> - to preserve peace and strengthen international security
>
> - to promote international co-operation
>
> - to develop and consolidate democracy and the rule of law, and respect for human rights and fundamental freedoms.
>
> (Treaties Article 11, previously Article J.1)
>
> These objectives are to be pursued:
>
> - by establishing systematic co-operation between member states in the conduct of policy;
>
> - by gradually implementing joint actions in the areas in which the member states have important interests in common.

> ## Box 18.11 Justice and Home Affairs
>
> Under the heading of JHA the TEU committed the member states to pursue co-operation in the following areas:
>
> - asylum policy
>
> - controls on people crossing the external frontiers of the Union
>
> - immigration policy
>
> - combating drug addiction
>
> - combating fraud on an international scale
>
> - judicial co-operation in civil matters
>
> - judicial co-operation in criminal matters
>
> - customs co-operation.
>
> (Treaties Article 29, previously Article K.1)

propose actions to the Council of Ministers, but it shares this right with the member states. The EP is to be consulted by the member state holding the presidency on the main aspects of both areas of co-operation, is to be regularly informed by the presidency and the Commission of developments, and be allowed to ask questions of the Council and make recommendations to it. It is also required to debate developments in each pillar annually.

The Amsterdam Treaty modified the commitment under JHA by transferring asylum and immigration to the first (EC) pillar. Although voting was to remain by unanimity, the transfer had the effect of bringing these areas within the jurisdiction of the ECJ. Amsterdam also formally changed the name of the JHA pillar to 'Police and Judicial Co-operation in Criminal Matters'.

Conclusion

The decision-making procedures of the EC are extremely complex. In particular, several different legislative procedures exist depending on the policy sector concerned. In many cases the procedure to be followed is by no means immediately apparent, and here the Commission can exercise some discretion in deciding under which articles of the treaties it will bring forward its proposals. Sometimes this has been challenged. For example, in 1990 the Commission brought forward proposals on maternity rights under what was then the new Article 118A of the EEC Treaty (now Article 138), which the SEA had introduced. This meant that the measure was subject to QMV in the Council, rather than unanimity. The British government objected to the Treaty base, and threatened to refer the matter to the ECJ, before eventually accepting a compromise solution.

Whatever treaty base is chosen, the main actors

remain the same; only the relative balance of influence is shifted. The Commission, the Council of Ministers, and the EP are the dominant institutional actors. Behind the scenes of the formal constitutional arrangements, interest groups always exercise a considerable influence on both the content of proposals and the outcome of the decision-making process. At the implementation stage, the Commission and the ECJ are particularly important among the EU institutions, but national governments are often the key to how policies are implemented.

The formal relationships outlined in this chapter are only one part, although an important part, of the analysis of the role of the EU institutions. The informal relationships between the institutions themselves, and between the institutions and the member states, are the part not covered here. In the chapters that follow, these informal relationships become central to the discussion, and attention focuses on the academic debates that have been generated about these relationships and their implications.

A key issue of debate concerning the Commission has been the extent to which it is an actor with independent influence over the process of European integration. One view is that it is merely an agent of the member states, and acts only in accordance with their wishes; the alternative view is that it has a good deal of autonomy, and can push the member states in directions that they do not wish to go. This is one of the debates considered in Chapter 19. The other relates to the role of the Commission in the implementation of policy, where it is widely perceived to be less efficient than it is in making policy proposals.

The main issue of academic debate about the Council of Ministers centres on how far it is really an intergovernmental organization through which the member states successfully control the EU. Some analysts have argued that the complex nature of the structure of committees that make up the Council, and the frequency with which the same individuals meet in these committees, has weakened the control by central government actors over the processes and outcomes. On this view, the Council committees have developed an identity of their own, and do not follow the will of the core executives of their states. This debate is reviewed in Chapter 20.

For the EP the key academic debates have concerned the extent of its power and influence in the legislative process. Rational choice institutionalists have contested the common observation that the EP has steadily increased its influence over legislative outcomes. This has sparked a considerable debate, which is reviewed in Chapter 21.

The ECJ is sometimes believed to have overstepped its proper judicial function as an interpreter of the treaties and an impartial referee in disputes between states. It is accused of having become a political actor, pushing forward European integration in a partisan manner. The evidence for this view is reviewed in chapter 22.

Finally, although not part of the formal structure of institutions, organized interests play a considerable role in the decision-making of the EU behind the scenes, as has been suggested from time to time in this chapter. Their influence is assessed in Chapter 23.

KEY POINTS

The Treaties

- There are three 'founding treaties', which have been amended and supplemented by later treaties.

- Together these treaties form the 'constitution' of the EU.

Decision-making institutions

- The Commission has the sole right to initiate legislation.

- The Council of Ministers has to agree to proposals for them to become law.

- The EP has long had significant budgetary powers, although only over 'non-compulsory' expenditure.

- Since it became directly elected in 1979, the powers of the EP have grown, particularly in relation to the legislation process, until today it is effectively the co-legislature with the Council of Ministers in many policy areas.

Decision-making procedures

- The EU budget passes through a complex process which involves the Commission, the Council, and the EP

- There are four main legislative procedures under the EC pillar: consultation; co-operation; co-decision; and the assent procedure

- Co-decision is now the most common procedure for EC legislation, although consultation and co-operation remain for some matters. The assent procedure covers measures for which the agreement of the EP is required.

- The ESC provides a formal input into EC decision making for organized economic and social interests

- The CoR provides a formal input into decision making for the representatives of member states' regional and local authorities

- The ESC has remained a rather 'toothless tiger' while the CoR has the potential to exercise greater political authority

Implementation

- Implementation is an integral part of the policy-making process.

- Three main types of EC instruments are legally binding: decisions, directives and regulations.

- While the Commission has formal responsibility for implementation, in practice national authorities play an important role.

- The ECJ has the power to interpret EC law, and its decisions are final.

- Created in 1975, the Court of Auditors checks the legality and regularity of EC expenditure.

The intergovernmental pillars

- The two intergovernmental pillars of the European Union cover Common Foreign and Security Policy (CFSP) and Justice and Home Affairs (JHA)/Police and Judicial Co-operation.

- Under these pillars, the Commission, the EP and the ECJ have less authority than under the EC pillar

QUESTIONS

1 How has the formal balance of powers between EU institutions changed since the founding treaties?

2 What are the different legislative procedures that exist for EU decision making?

3 Why is implementation an integral part of the EU policy-making process?

FURTHER READING

The standard work on the institutional structure of the EU is N. Nugent, *The Government and Politics of the European Union* (Basingstoke and London: Macmillan, 1999). Good commentaries on the later treaties are provided by C. H. Church and D. Phinnemore, *European Union and European Community: A Handbook and Commentary on the 1992 Maastricht Treaties* (London: Prentice Hall, 2nd edn. 1995) and A. Duff, *The Treaty of Amsterdam: Text and commentary* (London: Federal Trust/Sweet & Maxwell, 1997). On the budget the standard work now is B. Laffan, *The Finances of the European Union* (Basingstoke and London: Macmillan, 1997).

Reading on other institutions is given at the end of each of the chapters devoted specifically to them.

19 The European Commission

SUMMARY

There is considerable academic debate about whether the Commission is merely an agent of the member states, or whether it is an autonomous actor in its own right. Intergovernmentalists argue that the Commission is simply fulfilling the aims of the member states, which have various means of keeping a check on what it is doing and of reining it in if it starts to act in ways of which they do not approve. The supranationalists point to the resources in the possession of the Commission that allow it to achieve a degree of independence from the member states to pursue its own objectives.

There is also debate about the extent to which the Commission is able to fulfil efficiently its implementation tasks. It is argued that the Commission is geared up to be a proposer of legislation, but that as the amount of EC legislation in existence increases, its implementation and management roles become more important. While the Commission struggles to prove its worth in this regard, others have argued for implementation functions to be handed to independent agencies. The Commission's position on implementation has not been strengthened by widespread perceptions of fraud and financial mismanagement which reached crisis point in 1999 with the resignation of the whole Commission. As such, the EC's management deficit is indeed proving to be as important to its future as the widely debated democratic deficit.

Introduction

At the heart of the EC is the European Commission. It consists of a College of Commissioners and a permanent civil service of some 20,000 staff, of which only around 15,000 are administrators, the rest being employed either in scientific research or as translators and interpreters. This is the 'Brussels bureaucracy' which is frequently attacked or ridiculed by opponents of the EC. In fact it is a very small organization in comparison with not just national civil services, but even individual departments of state in national civil services.

The term 'the Commission' is used to refer both to the College of Commissioners and to the Services of the Commission. However, these should be clearly distinguished. The composition of the College of Commissioners is outlined in Box 19.1 (p. 234); the role of its President in Box 19.2 (p. 234); the current Commissioners are listed in Box 19.3 (p. 235). The Services are divided into twenty-four Directorates General (DGs), plus a number of special services. They are listed in Box 19.4 (p. 235). The DGs are the equivalent of national civil service departments of state. They used to be known by their number only

---

Box 19.1 **The College of Commissioners**

The commissioners themselves are nominated by national governments. Each state has one commissioner, and the larger member states (France, Germany, Italy, Britain, and Spain) have two each. There were therefore:

- 9 commissioners when the EC had six member states;

- 13 after the accession of Britain, Denmark, and Ireland in 1973;

- 14 following Greece's accession in 1981;

- 17 following the accession of Spain and Portugal in 1986;

- 20 following the 1995 enlargement to take in Austria, Finland, and Sweden.

The commissioners are appointed by their governments. Originally they were appointed for a four-year renewable term, but this was extended to five years in the TEU. Commissioners are sworn to abandon all national allegiances during their tenure of office.

Box 19.2 **The President of the Commission**

One commissioner acts as President for the five-year term. This person is chosen by agreement between the governments of the member states ahead of the rest of the Commission, and is consulted about the other nominations. The Treaty of Amsterdam strengthened this right to be consulted, saying that the other commissioners would be appointed by common accord of the member states with the President. The term of the President is also renewable: Jacques Delors held office for two full terms of four years each, plus an interim two-year period to bring the period of office of the Commission into line with that of the EP following the TEU.

There are no formal rules on the nationality of the president, but there are unwritten understandings that the presidency rotates between member states. There are also two vice-presidents, but their position is nowhere near as influential as that of the president has become. The commissioners are bound by the principle of collegiality: all actions are the responsibility of the Commission as a whole.

Box 19.3 Commissioners and their portfolios (as from 2000)

Romano Prodi
   (President)
Neil Kinnock — Administrative Reform
   (Vice President)
Loyola de Palacio — Relations with the European
   (Vice-president) — Parliament, Transport &
   Energy
Mario Monti — Competition
Franz Fischler — Agriculture, Rural Devel-
   opment & Fisheries
Erkki Liikanen — Enterprise & Information
   Society
Frits Bolkestein — Internal Market
Philippe Busquin — Research
Pedro Solbes Mira — Economic & Monetary
Poul Neilson — Affairs
   Development & Humanitarian
Günter Verheugen — Aid
Chris Patten — Enlargement
Pascal Lamy — External Relations
David Byrne — Trade
Michel Barnier — Health & Consumer Protection
Viviane Reding — Regional Policy
Michaele Schreyer — Education & Culture
Margot Wallström — Budget
Antonio Vitorino — Environment
Anna Diamantopoulou — Justice & Home Affairs
   Employment & Social Affairs

Box 19.4 The Services and Directorates General of the Commission

Secretariat General	Legal Service
Press and Communication	Economic and Financial Affairs
Enterprise	Competition
Employment and Social Affairs	Agriculture
Transport	Environment
Research	Joint Research Centre
Information Society	Fisheries
Internal Market	Regional Policy
Energy	Taxation and Customs Union
Education and Culture	Health and Consumer Protection
Justice and Home Affairs	External Relations
Trade	Development
Enlargement	Common Service for External relations
Humanitarian Aid Office– ECHO	Eurostat
Personnel and Administration	Inspectorate General
Budget	Financial Control
European Anti-Fraud Office	Joint Interpreting and Conference Service
Translation Service	Publications Office

(e.g. DGIV for the Competition Directorate-General), but Romano Prodi abolished the numbering, and also tried to bring the structure of the DGs more into line with the designation of portfolios within the College.

There is considerable debate around the role of the European Commission in the policy-making process. There is no doubt about its formal role. It has the sole right to initiate proposals for legislation. Without a proposal from the Commission, neither the Council of Ministers nor the EP can act. However, the debate centres on whether the Commission can actually determine the direction in which the EU moves.

The story of the decline and revival in the fortunes of the Commission has been told in Chapters 8 to 13 (pp. 87–139). Theorizations of the role of the Com-

mission moved from the neofunctionalist emphasis on it as the 'motor of integration' to the intergovernmental view of it as just the servant of the member states. This balance of opinion swung back after the launch of the single market programme in the mid-1980s. After this development, it rapidly became a widely-accepted view that:

The renewed drive for market unification can be explained only if theory takes into account the policy leadership of the Commission   (Sandholtz and Zysman, 1989: 96).

This view did not go unchallenged, though. The disagreements over the role of the Commission in the single market programme represented fundamental disagreements about the nature of the Commission in more general terms. Is it simply an agent of the member states, acting at their behest and under their control; or is it an autonomous actor in its own right, capable of playing a leadership role in the EU?

A second, separate question about the Commission concerns its role in the implementation of EC legislation. Much attention in the past has focused on the role that the Commission can play in promoting new legislation, and the Europeanization of new policy sectors. However, the Commission has always had an implementation role. This came to the fore with the rapid growth in EC legislation that was produced by the single market programme. Sub-sequently concern also grew about the effectiveness of the Commission's management of its finances, and the various spending programmes under its control. Both sets of concerns have led to proposals for reform of the implementation and management functions of the Commission.

The rest of this chapter will examine first the debate over the leadership role of the Commission, then the issues raised by concern over its ability to ensure the smooth and even implementation of EC legislation, and some of the proposals for reform.

The policy-making process

If the argument that the EU is an intergovernmental organization is to hold, then those who defend the position have to confront the assertion that the Commission is the prime mover of the process of European integration. This assertion was made from the early days of the EEC by Lindberg (1963) and other neofunctionalists. The counter-argument is that the Commission is simply an international secretariat like many others that help the member states of international organizations to achieve their collective aims. It is simply an agent of the member states, acting on their behalf and in accordance with their will.

The Commission as an agent of the member states

The first view of the Commission is that it is only an agent of the member states. On this view, the Commission is like the secretariat of any other international organization. Its function is to make it easier for governments to find agreement on the details of co-operation with each other. Where there is agreement on the broad agenda for co-operation, it is convenient for member states to delegate some control over the detailed agenda to the Commission. They see it as a reliable source of independent proposals because it has technical information, and is a neutral arbiter between conflicting national inter-ests. Delegating the making of proposals to the Commission in this way reduces the costs of co-operation by reducing the risk that 'decisions will be delayed by an inconclusive struggle among competing proposals, or that the final decision will be grossly unfair' (Moravcsik, 1993: 512). Where there are alternative proposals that might win majority support, the choice is often decided by which proposal is backed by the Commission.

Although this delegation of the right to make detailed proposals gives the Commission a certain formal power to set the agenda, on this view the Commission does not determine the direction in which the EU moves. It is only helping the member states to agree on the details of what they have decided that they want to do anyway. Nor is the Commission always effective. It is not the only potential source of proposals, nor of package deals to facilitate compromise between different national positions. Other actors are able to perform these functions, and often do so.

The Commission may use the margin of discretion that the member states allow it to try to manoeuvre the member states towards objectives that they had not anticipated. It is difficult for the states to keep a check on exactly what the Commission is doing because it is in possession of more information than they are. That is, after all, the point of delegating to it. Nevertheless, there are ways in which the member states can keep a check on the Commission (Pollack, 1997). First, they have set up a whole complex of committees of national experts to monitor the actions of the Commission: Management Committees, which operate mainly in the agricultural policy sector, can refer a Commission decision to the Council of Ministers for review by QMV; Regulatory Committees, which operate in a range of policy sectors, have to support the Commission by QMV or the proposed measure is referred to the Council of Ministers for review. Second, Article 230 (previously Article 173) of the Treaty allows challenges through the ECJ to the actions of the Commission should any individual member state or any directly affected individual or company believe that it has overstepped its mandate. Other EU institutions such as the EP and the Court of Auditors also monitor the activities of the Commission, providing member states with the information that they need to keep a check on it.

The Commission as an autonomous actor

The alternative to the view that the Commission is no more than an agent of the member states is that it can and does act autonomously to provide policy leadership to the EU. Defenders of this view point to key resources that allow it to do so: its sole right of initiative in the legislative process of the EC, its ability to locate allies among influential interest groups, and its powers under the competition clauses of the Treaties to act against monopolies. (See also Box 19.5, p. 238).

The Commission does not have to wait passively for the member states to ask it to bring forward proposals. It can identify a problem that has already started to concern governments, and propose a European solution, as it did with the single market programme. It can use its sole right of initiative to package issues in the form least likely to engender opposition in the Council of Ministers. Where there is opposition from member states to the full-blown development of a policy, the Commission may propose instead a limited small-scale programme; where there is resistance to a directive or regulation, the Commission may propose a less threatening rec-

ommendation or opinion. In each case, the limited step establishes a precedent for action in the policy sector and can be followed up later with further steps if and when the environment in the Council of Ministers is more conducive (Cram, 1997: 162–3).

The Commission can also act to put the Europeanization of a policy sector onto the agenda of governments. By involving domestic interests at the EU level through instruments such as advisory committees, the Commission seeks to win converts to the idea that an issue can best be handled at the European level. These allies may help to soften up the governments of the member states to allow the Europeanization of the policy sector (Cram, 1997: 164–5).

Similarly, the Commission can utilize, and if necessary create, transnational networks of producers who will be its allies in the private sector and bring pressure to bear on governments to Europeanize a sector. It did this in the case of technology policy (Sharp and Shearman, 1987; C. Sharp, 1989; Peterson, 1991), and in the cases both of telecommunications (Dang-Nguyen et al., 1993; Fuchs, 1994) and energy (Matlary, 1993). In each of these latter sectors it encouraged industrial users to press governments to move away from national monopolies to create a European market under European regulation.

Once governments have become aware of a problem, and faced up to the possibility of a European solution, the Commission can use technical experts to increase the pressure on governments, as it did with the Cecchini report of economists for the single market (see Box 25.4, p. 331), or for monetary union, the Delors Committee which consisted mainly of central bankers (see Ch. 26, p. 348).

Nevertheless, any move to Europeanize a policy sector will produce counter-pressures from groups that benefit from the status quo. The Commission can break down this opposition by threatening the use of existing powers under the competition clauses of the Treaties if actors in the sector will not co-operate to find a negotiated way forward. Again it did this to achieve the opening up of national monopolies in telecommunications and energy supply. In each case DGIV (the Directorate-General for Competition) threatened to use its powers under what was then Article 90 (now Article 86) of the Treaty. This Article specifically said that national

---

Box 19.5 **Nugent on the leadership resources of the Commission**

Nugent (1995: 605–13) identified a number of resources available to the Commission to exercise leadership in the EU.

Constitutional powers

The Commission has the sole right to propose legislation. It can also exploit lack of precision in the wording of the treaties to expand its competencies. (605–7)

The standing of Commissioners

Despite legitimacy problems that arise from the Commissioners being appointed rather than elected, almost all Commissioners are now former politicians of some standing in their domestic political systems. They thus arrive in Brussels in possession of political prestige, and a range of political skills. (607–8)

Knowledge and expertise

This is the classical resource of bureaucrats, and the Commission is well placed to exercise its unrivalled knowledge of the content and impact of EU policies. (608)

Impartiality and neutrality

Although Commissioners and officials are not immune from national preferences, 'generally speaking the Commission is seen to be seeking to act in the interests of the EU as a whole'. (609).

The 'duty' of the Commission to be the engine of integration

The continued presence of a sense of commitment to the ideal of European integration amongst Commission employees is an important mobilizing resource internally. (609–10)

The position of the President

Although officially no more than a *primus inter pares*, 'it is clear that a forceful and activist President can do much to enhance the Commission's general standing and leadership capacities' (611).

The (relative) cohesion of the Commission

Although the Commission 'is highly pluralistic, with a divergence of preferences, styles, working procedures and cultures', it is nevertheless a more cohesive institution than either the Council or the EP, and therefore in a stronger position to exercise leadership (611–12).

The strategic position of the Commission in the EU system

Although its position varies according the issue, 'looking at the EU's policy spectrum as a whole, none of the Commission's 'competitor institutions' is engaged in policy to anything like a comparable degree'. (613).

---

public monopolies were subject to the rules prohibiting the prevention of competition within the common market. The vested interests against change were therefore faced with the alternative of reaching an agreement with the relevant DG of the Commission to allow phased and regulated competition, or having DGIV make a full-frontal attack on its protected position. In both the cases cited, the alternative of having some say in how the transition from national monopoly to European market was carried out proved more attractive than the uncertainty of the alternative of legal proceedings, and the resistance to the Commission's proposals was seriously weakened as a result.

Implementation

The EC has a management deficit at least as significant for its future effectiveness as its more widely recognised democratic deficit. (Metcalfe, 1992: 118)

In 1991 the Secretary General of the Commission, David Williamson, in a lecture to the Royal Institute of Public Administration in London, admitted to the failings of the Commission when it came to implementing the growing body of EC legislation. He argued that the Commission had to enhance its capacity to manage the post-1992 EC without becoming a central monolith.

This analysis echoed that of Metcalfe and other academic observers, who had noted that the Commission was better adapted to proposing policies and legislation than to implementing them once they were agreed. It has long been argued that the two functions of initiation and implementation require different types of organizational structure, which Coombes (1970) identified as *organic* and *mechanistic* organizations. He described the Commission as an organic organization, well equipped to generate proposals, but lacking sufficient of the qualities of a classical mechanistic bureaucracy to implement them effectively. Others have seen this bias against implementation as embodied in the culture of the Commission.

There has always been a bias within the Commission in favour of policy formulation as opposed to policy execution. (Ludlow, 1991: 107)

Since Williamson's lecture in 1991, the implementation problems of the Commission have increased as a result of several factors.

- First, the success of the 1992 programme and other policy initiatives taken under the Delors presidency has left the Commission with a much larger body of legislation to implement.

- Second, EU competencies have moved into new policy sectors, such as social and environmental policy, which raise different problems of implementation from those that the Commission may already have encountered in policy sectors where it previously had competence. (Peters, 1997: 191).

- Third, the crisis over the ratification of the TEU, and the subsequent renewed stress on the principle of subsidiarity (Box 22.7, p. 284) has complicated the relationship between the Commission and the member states (Laffan, 1997*b*: 425).

In 1992, the year after Williamson spoke, the Commission published a report by a working party under the chairmanship of the former Commissioner Peter Sutherland which called for a deeper partnership between the Commission and the member states to make the single market effective. (Laffan, 1997*b*: 426).

The question of consistent implementation of single market rules became an issue because of the wide disparities between member states that were shown up by Commission monitoring reports. The states with the better records felt that they were being placed at a competitive disadvantage in comparison with states that were less meticulous about applying the rules. The call for more effective enforcement of the rules came to be seen as a specifically British demand, but Britain was only the most vocal member state to express concern.

The Commission as implementer

There are very few policy sectors where the Commission has direct implementation powers. The most notable is competition policy, which has been called 'the first supranational policy' (McGowan and Wilks, 1995). Others are fisheries and some of the programmes involved in the external relations of the EU, such as the Humanitarian Aid Programme, and the programmes for assisting the transition to capitalism and liberal democracy in the former Communist states of central and eastern Europe. For most internal policies, the Commission sits at the apex of a multilevel system of implementation that extends down to the central authorities of the member states, then below them to sub-national authorities and agencies. Whereas for both policy-making and direct implementation, the Commission acts as the agent of the member states, for the bulk of implementation national and sub-national actors are the agents of the Commission. The problem for the Commission is ensuring that these agents do not pursue their own agendas.

This problem is compounded by two circumstances. First, the Commission does not have the resources to ensure effective performance, lacking both adequate staffing levels and independent information (Metcalfe, 1992: 126). Second, the number of agents which it has to monitor has been increased by the decentralization of public administration that has taken place in many member states under the banner of the 'New Public Management' (Peters, 1997: 198). The shift from government to governance within member states presents the Commission with a proliferation of agents to monitor.

Under these circumstances, Metcalfe argued that it was necessary for the Commission to learn to function as the manager of European networks, rather than seek to manage European integration alone. In this role, it would seek to prompt the development of organizational capacities and inter-organizational co-ordination. Although he did not use the phrase, Metcalfe here was also talking about how the Commission could adapt to the process of governance; or, governing in a situation where there is a variety of actors with shared or contested responsibility for policy implementation rather than one identifiable unitary authority as had traditionally been the case (Rhodes, 1995).

The increasing challenge facing the Commission over implementation has led to demands for its implementation functions to be hived off to separate functional agencies. In other words, implementation in an age of governance requires greater decentralization than the Commission alone can provide. We return to this issue later in the chapter.

Financial management

Alongside the Commission's burgeoning implementation problems, concern has also grown about effective financial management of EC programmes. As Laffan (1997b: 427) noted, for many years the annual reports of the Court of Auditors highlighted weaknesses of the Commission's financial management. However, as the EC budget grew, the number of member states that were net contributors to EC funds also grew. The 1995 enlargement added three more net contributors (Laffan, 1997b: 427). Both increased payments and an increase in the number of net contributor states led to greater concern that EC money should be spent effectively. This concern was reflected in changes made in the TEU. The TEU raised the status of the Court of Auditors to that of a full EC institution and raised the status of budgetary discipline and sound financial management to EC principles (Laffan, 1997b: 429).

In the context of increasing concern from member states, the Santer Commission made improvements in financial management central to its programme. Santer appointed the Finn, Erkki Liikanen, as Budget Commissioner, and enhanced his status by requiring all proposals that had expenditure implications to be sent to Liikanen for approval before being circulated to the College of Commissioners. Santer also appointed Anita Gradin from Sweden to be in charge of an anti-fraud unit within the Commission. However, despite the efforts of the Santer Commission to put this aspect of implementation on a sound footing, in 1999 the Commission was almost voted out of office on a motion of censure from the EP because of alleged lax financial control. (Box 19.6, p. 241)

Despite the events leading up to the 1999 crisis, it is still uncertain exactly how much fraud there is within the EU (Peterson, 1997). There is no doubt that the issue of fraud has been blown up to inflated proportions by media attention. However, it is equally certain that the public perception of fraud and financial mismanagement contributes to undermining the legitimacy of the EU among citizens and changing this perception remains an outstanding challenge for the Commission.

Implementing through decentralization

Metcalfe (1992: 120) noted that the Commission had many of the characteristic weaknesses of national civil services: a hierarchical structure in which vertical lines of authority are more highly developed than horizontal links, leading to over-centralization and problems of co-ordination within as well as between DGs. These problems were identified much earlier in the Spierenburg Report, which was produced in 1979, but: 'The report had little impact and did not lead to action' (Metcalfe, 1992: 125).

Another effort was made in the mid-1980s, focusing on the modernization of the internal management of the Commission, and initiated by Commissioner Henning Christophersen. It did raise awareness about management deficiencies, but did not produce significant changes. The record of reform has not been good. The Commission has come late to the process of modernizing public management. This has taken off in western states since the early 1980s, and a key element has been decentralization of decision-making on implementation.

One proposal for improving implementation that was mentioned by David Williamson was to create

Box 19.6 The 1999 crisis

The report of the Court of Auditors on the 1996 budget led the EP's Budget Committee in March 1998 to refuse to recommend discharge of the budget by the whole EP. The Committee was particularly concerned about alleged mismanagement of the Humanitarian Aid budget, which at that time had been under the control of Commissioner Manuel Marin, who was by 1998 a Vice-President of the Commission.

In October 1998 Santer, together with Emma Bonino who was by then in charge of the European Community Humanitarian Aid Office (ECHO) appeared before the Budget Committee to admit that an investigation by the Commission's internal fraud unit had indeed revealed irregularities in the expenditure of funds allocated to ECHO. In fact, ECHO had apparently not audited any of its external contracts until 1995, and the Commission therefore had no guarantees of how money had been spent between 1993 and 1995. The internal fraud unit had discovered that at least two contracts, for personnel and equipment for operations in Bosnia and in Africa, had been completely fictitious, and that most of the money appeared to have been spent on extra administrative staff for the Brussels office. However, some 400,000 to 600,000 ecus of the money had proved untraceable.

Despite an offer from Santer to re-create the fraud office as a separate agency outside of the Commission, the EP in December 1998 refused discharge of the 1996 budget. It expressed concern about the ECHO affair, and also about what appeared to be nepotism in making appointments under the LEONARDO Youth Training Programme, which was the responsibility of the French Commissioner, Edith Cresson. In the meantime, the Court of Auditor's report on the 1997 budget had appeared, and indicated that some 5 per cent of total EC expenditure could not adequately be accounted for.

The EP laid down a motion of censure on the Commission, which did not achieve the two-thirds majority required to remove the Commission from office, but which did achieve the largest vote for a motion of censure since the EC began: 232, with 293 against and 27 abstentions. This result was despite the Socialist Group, the largest single party group in the EP, officially deciding to vote against the censure.

In an attempt to head off the censure, Santer produced a plan of action which he put to the EP on 11 January 1999. This involved:

- new codes of conduct for Commissioners, their cabinets, and all Commission staff

- the setting up of an independent fraud unit outside of the Commission itself

- an audit of all the Commission's activities and departments, leading to proposals for restructuring

- a promise of proposals to modernize the administration of the Commission

- a review of budgetary management and of appointments to senior positions

- the negotiation of an agreement with the EP on how MEPs would be kept informed on financial expenditure, and how to ensure effective EP scrutiny of spending.

This compromise at first seemed to have averted a crisis, but in March 1999 a committee of five independent experts that had been set up to look into the internal management of the Commission issued a damaging report, which suggested widespread malfunctioning of the system. Santer and his whole College of Commissioners then resigned just after midnight on 15/16 March. The European Parliament claimed this as a great victory for their persistence in scrutinizing the activities of the Commission.

special-purpose agencies along the lines of the Next Steps initiative in the UK. Williamson was cautious about going in this direction, lest such agencies conflict with the policy decisions or broad executive authority of the Commission (Hennessy, 1991). Nevertheless, the idea does have strong advocates, like F. Vibert (Box 19.7, p. 242)

The proposal along these lines that has received the strongest political support has been that for a European Cartel Office (ECO), which has come from the German Federal Cartel Office (Bundeskartellamt—BKartA) supported by the German Federal Economics Ministry. To reproduce the German model of competition policy at the European level 'has become something of a German obsession' (Wilks and McGowan, 1995: 260). Three main arguments are put forward for an independent cartel office:

Box 19.7 A proposal to break up the Commission

Vibert (1994) agreed with the view that the Commission is not well organized to manage implementation, 'because it has put its greatest effort into its political role as initiator . . . rather than into management' (Vibert, 1994: 2). He was quite clear that the European Council and the Council of Ministers should give political direction to the EU, while the Commission should concentrate on its managerial tasks. To facilitate this he advocated unbundling the tasks of the Commission into three main areas:

- a Single Market Commission,

- a Treasury Board,

- an External Trade Commission.

In addition, he would transfer the implementation powers of the Commission over competition policy and over the application of trade instruments such as anti-dumping measures to independent agencies. The Commission's role as implementer of aid policy would be transferred to the European Investment Bank and the EBRD.

Vibert's justification for breaking up the Commission was that: 'These are quite different functions that require different terms of reference and different professional skills' (Vibert, 1994: 13). As such, there was no justification for them being handled by a single authority. At the same time, the reorganization would allow functions that overlapped to be handled in a more co-ordinated way than they tended to be within a Commission that was divided into 'fiefdoms and functionally organised directorate-generals' (Vibert, 1994: 13).

For Vibert, the viability of the single market was the key to the future prosperity of the EU, and he therefore wished to see a Single Market Commission that would be under the supervision of the Single Market Council and would bring together those DGs that dealt with sectoral matters such as environmental, employment and social affairs. The membership of the Single Market Council might vary, involving Ministers for Industry, Economics Ministers, or Ministers for Enterprise, depending on the organization of individual member states. However, the important point was that oversight would be provided by ministers with a general responsibility for competitiveness in the single market, rather than sectoral ministers who might be tempted to pursue an agenda that would benefit vested interests in their particular sector.

Under Vibert's proposals, the Treasury Board would take over the work of the Financial DGs, XIX (Budget), XX (Financial Control), and XXI (Customs Union and Indirect Taxation) along with the main spending DGs. This Board would be overseen by the Council of Finance Ministers; one of the main advantages being that the hands of Finance Ministers would be strengthened against colleagues pressing for more spending. A Trade Commission would take over the functions of DG I relating to external trade, but the negotiation of new trade agreements would be handled by a special trade representative appointed by the member states, not by a Trade Commissioner.

Competition policy would be administered by a separate free-standing agency, a Competition Authority, which would investigate and adjudicate on all competition, monopoly, and merger cases currently handled by the Commission. This Authority, rather than the Trade Commission, would take over the work of the directorates of DG I dealing with 'trade instruments' and non-tariff barriers. It would not be accountable directly to any Council of Ministers, but Vibert would allow the Council a political override of decisions of the Authority by an 80 per cent majority (Vibert, 1994: 16).

1. The existing system is politicized because the final decision on whether to approve a merger is taken by the College of Commissioners.

2. The existing system lacks transparency; all discussions take place in secret between the companies concerned and the Commission's merger task force; this allows informal deals to be made, which may increase the efficiency of the process, but is also damaging to strict application of competition criteria.

3. Subsidiarity (Box 22.7, p. 284) is not allowed to apply; some mergers may have more serious competition implications for individual national markets than for the European market as a whole. Although there is the so-called 'German clause' (Article 9) in the Merger Regulation, which allows national cartel authorities to request that a merger which is eligible to be considered at European level should nevertheless be considered by the national authority, the Commission has been very reluctant to grant such requests.

Together these arguments constitute the German case for an independent European Cartel Office, which would have the same sort of political independence from both national governments and from the Commission that the BKartA has from political control in the German system. There are remarkable parallels here with the arguments about the independence of the European Central Bank, which are examined in chapter 26 below.

In other policy sectors independent agencies already exist, two since 1975. Agreement was reached on creating a further eight in 1993. These are listed in Box 19.8, below. These agencies vary tre-

mendously in both the nature of their activities and in their degree of independence from the Commission and from the member states. It has been suggested that they could form the instrument that the Commission lacks to monitor implementation of policies in the member states. Because they are independent of the Commission, they can help to improve co-ordination between the relevant agencies in the member states, while avoiding the problem that the member states do not wish to see further powers assigned to the Commission, nor to increase its staffing to levels that would be necessary to perform implementation functions effectively (Kreher, 1997).

Box 19.8 **Independent agencies**

AEE – European Environment Agency

AER – European Agency for Reconstruction

CDT – Translation Centre for the Bodies of the European Union

CEDEFOP – European Centre for the Development of Vocational Training

EMEA – European Monitoring Agency for the Evaluation of Medicinal Products

ETF – European Training Foundation

EUMC – European Monitoring Centre on Racism and Xenophobia

EUROFOUND – European Foundation for the Improvement of Living and Working Conditions

OCVV – Community Plant Variety Office

OEDT – European Monitoring Centre for Drugs and Drug Addiction

OHIM – Office for Harmonisation in the Internal Market (Trademarks and Designs)

OSHA – European Agency for Safety and Health at Work

Source: *http://europa.eu.int/agencies/carte_en.htm*

Conclusion

The debate over the role of the Commission remains central to explanations about the nature and pace of European integration. It is clearly central to one of the themes of this book: the debate about the nature of the EU itself. If the Commission can be shown to be an autonomous actor, the argument that the EU is an intergovernmental organization is severely weakened. Up to now the debate is inconclusive.

The Commission has been fiercely criticized in its role as manager of EC policies and finances. While policy implementation is never straightforward

within member states, it becomes even more difficult to achieve policy objectives in a union of fifteen member states, where the Commission is dependent on national governments and national administrations for effective compliance. Added to this, the proliferation of actors involved in the policy process, giving rise to the term governance, has made the Commission's task even more difficult. Yet the impact of these failings has fed into the debate about one of the other themes of the book: the issue of the legitimacy of the EU. While there is a lot of discussion about the democratic deficit, Beetham and Lord (1998) pointed to a wider legitimation deficit, of which the democratic deficit was only one aspect. Another aspect that they identified as feeding the legitimacy deficit was performance: 'the ability [of the EU] to deliver effective policy in the areas it undertakes, to meet some basic criteria of effective decision making, and to demonstrate a capacity for correction and renewal in the event of 'failure'' (Beetham and Lord, 1998: 23–4). The relevance of this to the above discussion of the Commission's 'management deficit' should be obvious.

KEY POINTS

The policy-making process

- There is considerable debate about the degree of independence of the Commission in determining the pace and direction of European integration.

- One view is that the Commission is merely the agent of the member states, which have several means of ensuring that it complies with their wishes.

- Another view is that the Commission has various means at its disposal to act independently of the member states.

Implementation

- The Commission appears better equipped to perform its role in policy formulation than in implementation.

- Its implementation problems have increased in the 1990s.

- Disparities in the implementation records of member states have led to calls for more effective enforcement of EC rules.

- The Commission has weaknesses typical of national civil services, notably a hierarchical structure that leads to over-centralization and problems of co-ordination across DGs.

- It has been slow to follow trends in member states that have decentralized key implementation functions.

- The 1990s witnessed growing concern over the financial management of EC programmes, particularly through the growth of the budget and the increase in net contributor member states.

- Despite prioritizing improvements in financial management, the Santer Commission was almost voted out of office by the EP for its lax financial control in January 1999, and eventually resigned in March 1999 after persistent criticism from the EP.

- Some have called for the Commission's implementation functions to be passed to separate agencies.

QUESTIONS

1 To what extent is the Commission an autonomous political actor?

2 How important to the future of the Commission is the challenge posed by widespread perceptions of fraud and financial mismanagement?

3 What can be done to secure more effective policy implementation?

FURTHER READING

M. Cini, *The European Commission: Leadership, Organisation and Culture in the EU Administration* (Manchester: Manchester University Press, 1996) is probably the best starting point for further reading on the subject. G. Edwards and D. Spence (eds.), *The European Commission* (Harlow: Longman, 1994) is a useful collection of articles, as in more analytical mode is N. Nugent (ed.), *At the Heart of the Union: Studies of the European Commission* (Basingstoke and London: Macmillan, 1997).

P. Ludlow, 'The European Commission' in R. O. Keohane and S. Hoffmann (eds.), *The New European Community: Decisionmaking and Institutional Change* (Boulder, San Francisco, and London: Westview Press, 1991), 85–132 remains impressively insightful, although now slightly dated. N. Nugent, 'The Leadership Capacity of the European Commission', *Journal of European Public Policy* 2/4 (1995) 603–23, is a very good discussion of the leadership capacity of the European Commission. T. Christiansen, 'A Maturing Bureaucracy? The Role of the Commission in the Policy Process', in J. Richardson (ed.), *European Union: Power and Policy-Making* (London: Routledge, 1996), 79–95 was written in the run-up to the 1996 IGC, but explores a number of interesting themes.

B. Laffan, *The Finances of the European Union* (Basingstoke and London: Macmillan, 1997) is an excellent discussion of the implementation deficit of the Commission.

20 The Council

SUMMARY

The Council is a hybrid institution that appears in several different manifestations: the European Council, the Council of Ministers, COREPER, and the technical committees. The European Council, the meetings of heads of government, was originally set up in part to reassert national government control over the EC, and it remains the most unambiguously intergovernmental of the manifestations of the Council. The Council of Ministers itself meets in several guises, with different ministers present depending on the subject under discussion. Those that meet more frequently may start to develop a collegiality which will erode the pure intergovernmental nature of their discussions. More significantly, a large majority of decisions are made before they reach the ministers, at the level of the Permanent Representatives or technical committees. There is some evidence that these groups do develop a collective identity that undermines the simple description of them as intergovernmental bargaining forums.

Introduction

The term 'the Council' is used here to cover a complex of institutions (Box 20.1, p. 247). It includes both the European Council, which is the correct name for the periodic summit meetings of heads of state and government, and the Council of Ministers, which itself is a multi-part institution that does not have a constant membership, but involves different ministers depending on the policy under consideration. Even that, though is not the full extent of the complexity of the Council. The work of the meetings of ministers is prepared by a myriad of committees consisting of national and European officials and experts. Estimates of the exact number of committees vary, but generally fall between 150 and 200 at any one time. The work of all these expert committees is brought together by the Committee of Permanent Representatives (COREPER), which itself meets as both COREPER I and COREPER II (Box 20.2, p. 248).

At first sight it seems obvious that the Council is an intergovernmental organization. However, this is a simplification of a complex situation. First, it is clear that the Council as a collective entity is a supranational institution, because it can and does agree to legislation which is then binding on all the member states. Second, it is not clear that the Council, in all its manifestations, operates simply as an intergovernmental bargaining forum. Wessels (1991: 136) insisted that 'the Council is not an 'interstate body' . . . but a body at the supranational level'. Hayes-Renshaw and Wallace (1997: 278) were less sure of that, but were clear that it was 'not a wholly 'intergovernmental' institution'. As they put it,

For the analyst the Council and its processes embody the recurrent tension in the construction of the EC between the supranationalists and the intergovernmentalists. (Hayes-Renshaw and Wallace, 1997: 2)

The question of the relationship between the intergovernmental and supranational features of the Council is a theme that runs through this chapter. The theme is closely related to the debate covered in Chapter 19 (pp. 236–8) about whether the Commission is an autonomous actor in the policy-making process. The discussion here is not about the relationship between the Council and other institutions: it is about the relationships within the Council; about whether the constituent parts of the Council

---

Box 20.1 The structure of the Council

The European Council

Summit meetings of the Heads of Government (and the French Head of State), held at least twice per year, with provision for additional meetings.

The Council of Ministers

Consists of a representative of each member state 'at ministerial level', authorized to commit the government of the member state. It meets in more than twenty different forms depending on the subject matter under consideration.

The Committee of Permanent Representatives (COREPER)

The Permanent Representatives are the ambassadors of the member states to the EU. Their deputies meet as COREPER I and the Representatives themselves as COREPER II. They filter business for the meetings of ministers (Box 20.2, p. 248).

The presidency

A representative of the member state currently holding the presidency chairs all meetings of the Council. The presidency rotates on a six-monthly basis.

The Secretariat

The state holding the presidency is assisted by a Council Secretariat of around 2,000 staff, about a tenth of whom are senior administrators.

> ### Box 20.2 The Committee of Permanent Representatives
>
> - The Permanent Representatives perform some formal functions in Brussels, but their main task is to co-ordinate the work of the various committees that meet under the banner of the Council of Ministers, and to sift through the reports of these committees before they go to the Council of Ministers.
>
> - COREPER meets at least weekly at ambassador level as COREPER II, and at deputy level as COREPER I. Both prepare the agendas of meetings of the Councils of Ministers, except that of the Agriculture Council, for which there is a Special Committee on Agriculture to perform the same task.
>
> - COREPER II is responsible for the agendas for meetings
>
> of the General Affairs Council (consisting of Foreign Ministers), the Development Council, the Economic and Finance Ministers Council (ECOFIN), and the Budget Council. It also prepares the agendas for meetings of the European Council. The Antici Group of officials, named after the Italian official who was the chair of the first such group, assists it in this task. COREPER I is responsible for the agendas of all other Councils except Agriculture.
>
> - COREPER divides the agendas of Council meetings into points A and points B. The A points are normally agreed at the Council meeting without discussion, although any Member State can request at the start of a meeting that an item be moved from the A to the B list.

act as agents of the core executives of national central governments. By 'the core executive' we mean the Prime Ministers, Foreign Ministers, and other members of what in Britain is called 'the cabinet', and in other member states is known as 'the council of ministers' (which is where the EU institution gets its name from).

Below, each of the manifestations of the Council is examined in turn: the European Council, the Council of Ministers, COREPER, and the technical committees. The co-ordination of this complex institutional conglomerate falls to the Presidency and the Council Secretariat, which are considered separately.

The European Council

The origins of the European Council were in the summit meetings that started with the 'relaunching of Europe' at The Hague in 1969 (see Ch. 9, pp. 98–102). Agreement was reached in Paris in 1974 to institutionalize the summit meetings and to call them meetings of the European Council. The first formal meeting of the European Council was in Dublin in 1975.

Originally meetings were scheduled to take place three times per year, but in the SEA that was reduced to twice per year, or once per presidency. However, such is the prestige of hosting a meeting of the European Council, and such are the opportunities for attracting a lot of business into hotels, bars, and restaurants in major cities, that presidencies often manage to find an excuse to have more than one

European Council in their country during their six months in charge.

Reasons for inventing the European Council

There are a number of reasons why the European Council was set up in the first place. In an era of events such as currency fluctuations, crises in energy supplies, and stagflation, summitry was a prominent feature of the international system in the 1970s as governments sought to maintain economic control. It was at this time of recurrent global crises that the international economic summits, now known as the G7/G8, began (Box 20.3, p. 249). Just like

Box 20.3 The G7/G8

Like the European Council itself, the origins of the present G8 meetings lie with an initiative by Giscard d'Estaing. He convened an economic summit at Rambouillet in November 1975, at which he and Chancellor Schmidt of West Germany proposed that such economic summit meetings should become regular events. Originally there were five members of the group: France, Germany, Britain, the United States, and Japan. In 1976–7 the group's membership was extended to seven with the addition of Italy and Canada. At the same time it was agreed that the President of the European Commission could attend summit meetings to represent the views of the other member states of the EC. The group came to be known as the G7.

Initially the summits were concerned purely with economic issues, but in the 1980s political and strategic defence issues began to appear on the agenda. At the same time meetings of Finance Ministers started to take place separately from the summits. Following the end of the cold war, Russia started to participate in the meetings, originally as an observer, but eventually as a full member of what is now the G8.

(*Source*: British Foreign Office web site for the 1998 Birmingham G8 meeting: http://www.g8summit.gov.uk/brief0398/what.is.g8.shtml).

these wider forums, the European Council was a response by states to the demands of complex interdependence.

However, the European Council was also an attempt by governments to reassert national control over the development of the EC. After de Gaulle's resignation in 1969 there was a wish by the national governments to start the development of the EC moving again, but in the direction that they, not the Commission, decided; hence the Hague summit. The 1965 crisis led to a crisis of confidence inside the Commission, which partly explains the lack of movement in the 1965–9 period. If the Commission was not going to drive the EC forward, another motor would be needed. The agreement to formalize summits in the form of the European Council was an indication that the governments were determined to keep control.

A further explanation for the establishment of the European Council was that as the EC increased the number of policy sectors in which it had competence, the risk emerged of policy segmentation through there being no single body that could take an overview of events. As explained above, the Council of Ministers meets with a different membership depending on the policy under discussion. The General Council, consisting of Foreign Ministers, is supposed to act as the co-ordinator, but the heads of government have more authority to play that role.

Finally, the European Council was also an attempt to present a united front to the outside world. It has always been in effect what it has been constitutionally since the TEU, i.e. the highest body of both the European Community (EC) and European Political Co-operation (EPC)/Common Foreign and Security Policy (CFSP). It was therefore an attempt to co-ordinate overall policy towards the rest of the world. This is another function that the heads of government have usurped from the Foreign Ministers meeting in the General Council and the EPC/CFSP Council of Foreign Ministers.

Functions

The European Council has a number of important functions (see Box 20.4 p. 250). In carrying out these functions, the European Council faces some serious problems. These can be summarized as problems of overload, over-optimism, over-cautiousness, and over-expectation.

Overload

During the late 1970s and into the 1980s there was a tendency for more and more problems to be referred up from the Council of Ministers to the European Council, so that it often found itself considering quite detailed and technical issues. Because it only met three times a year, and now only meets twice a year on a routine basis, there was a danger of it becoming overwhelmed with mundane business at the expense of its more strategic functions. However, since the introduction of QMV into the work of the Council of Ministers in the SEA and TEU, the tendency for matters not to be resolved at lower levels has receded.

Box 20.4 The functions of the European Council

- *As a court of appeal for the resolution of problems that cannot be resolved lower down the system.*

If agreement cannot be reached in the Council of Ministers, the issue is pushed further up the hierarchy to be resolved at the next meeting of the European Council.

- *As a 'Board of Directors' giving general guidance to the EU on its future direction.*

Although the details have to be filled out by interaction between the Commission and the Council of Ministers, if the European Council gives a lead, the presumption is that the Commission will make proposals and the Council will try to reach agreement on a policy.

- *As a means of attracting publicity to the EU.*

Much of the work of the EC in particular is technical and unexciting, except for the specialists, hence it is rarely reported. European summits are probably the only occasion when most members of the public hear about the EU other than when there is crisis. The European Council feeds the desire of the media to have pictures of pomp and ceremony, and to focus on individuals. Perhaps Kirchner (1992: 113) slightly overstated the case when he said, 'European Councils are a media stunt', but there is an element of truth in the accusation.

- *As a forum for personal contact between Heads of Government.*

The meetings have become more formal, but the original intention of Giscard and Schmidt was that they would be informal get-togethers by heads of government to help them to understand each other's problems, and just to get to know each other. European Councils do still fulfil this function to a certain extent, and it is the reason given for meals being scheduled to last for long periods, because during meals the heads of government are free of officials and able to relate to each other as individuals.

Box 20.5 Over-optimism in the European Council

At a press conference on 20 March 1996, Jacques Santer complained about the phenomenon of over-optimism, which had resulted in heads of government not putting up the money to fund the projects that they had launched at various European Council meetings. He gave a list of things that European Councils had said should be supported, but for which the money had not been forthcoming:

- Trans European Networks (i.e. infrastructure projects in transport and power supply)

- the Northern Ireland peace initiative

- financial aid to Armenia and Georgia

- extra Commission posts for the 1995 entrants.

Some of these commitments went back to 1994, but adequate funds had never been made available.

(*Financial Times*, 21 March 1996).

Over-optimism

Sometimes the atmosphere of mutual co-operation that can be generated, together with the expectation that something will come out of every European Council, can lead to commitments being made which subsequently prove difficult to honour. When they go home after the meeting, heads of government may not be able to get the agreement of their own political parties or their cabinets/councils of ministers to carry through the commitment (see Box 20.5, p. 250).

Over-cautiousness

The publicity can make it more difficult for heads of government to make concessions that might be made in a less exposed bargaining context.

Over-expectation

If the meetings do not produce dramatic results, this can cause disillusionment amongst the European public because the media has built up expectations.

The Council of Ministers

It has already been established that the Council of Ministers itself is not an institution with a constant membership. It meets in a variety of manifestations depending on the subject under discussion. Formally there is no hierarchy between different Councils, but there is a recognized unofficial hierarchy. The General Council, consisting of Foreign Ministers, normally meets monthly, and has a co-ordination function between the various technical councils. It is therefore perceived to be the highest level at which the Council of Ministers meets. It also has some direct responsibility for external relations, but the same participants meet under different rules of procedure as the Council of Foreign Ministers in the CFSP pillar of the EU.

The Council of Economic and Finance Ministers (ECOFIN) also normally meets every month. These meetings have a high position in the unofficial hierarchy because of the importance and centrality of the subject matter with which they deal. This position was enhanced in the late 1990s because the issue of monetary union dominated the agenda of the EU. The start of the single currency (the Euro) on 1 January 1999 complicated the institutional position because now the Finance Ministers from those member states that are also members of the Eurozone meet prior to the full meetings of ECOFIN to discuss single currency matters.

The Council of Agriculture Ministers also has a privileged status because of the importance of agriculture to the EU, although this position is threatened by attempts to reduce the extent to which agricultural expenditure dominates the budget. Like the other senior councils, the Agriculture Council meets monthly during most of the year, and sometimes more frequently when negotiations are taking place on the annual fixing of agricultural prices in the first half of each year.

Other Councils can be divided into those that cover subjects for which there is a recognized EC competence, and those such as education where the member states are attempting to co-ordinate their policies (Kirchner, 1992: 74). The frequency of meetings varies considerably, though most of the sectoral councils meet between twice and four or five times a year (Hayes-Renshaw and Wallace, 1997: 30).

Fritz Scharpf (1989) contrasted 'problem solving' and 'bargaining' as modes of negotiation within the EC. His distinction at least partly corresponds to the differences between theorists about how to understand the operation of the Council. For intergovernmentalists the Council is simply 'a forum for hard bargaining' (Lewis, 1998: 479). For those who adopt a more supranational theoretical perspective, bargaining takes place between actors whose positions are influenced, at least partially, by their social interaction with their ministerial colleagues from other member states; 'communicative rationality' is at least as important as 'instrumental rationality', which means that the discussion is about how to find a solution to common problems rather than just about playing a negotiating game to win; and there is an instinct to proceed consensually (Lewis, 1998: 480–81).

If it were possible to research these theories, the hypotheses that they generate are fairly clear. If the supranational theorists are correct, one would expect to find more collegiality, and a discourse more oriented to joint problem-solving, in Councils that meet more frequently than in those that meet less frequently, and also in the more technical councils rather than in the more political councils (although deciding what is technical and what is political is notoriously difficult).

The extent to which ministers meeting in the different Councils engage in hard-headed intergovernmental bargaining, or adopt a more supranational approach, is difficult to research because of the secrecy that surrounds such meetings. Minutes are not publicly available. Anecdotal evidence suggests that some manifestations of the Council are more collegial than others. For example, it was said that after John Major became British Prime Minister in late 1990, he became increasingly disillusioned with the political nature of interactions between the heads of government, having previously only experienced meetings of ECOFIN which were much more oriented towards common problem-solving than to political points-scoring.

One particularly interesting research finding in this respect is that very few issues are actually decided by the ministers themselves. Hayes-Renshaw and Wallace (1997: 78) estimated that approximately 85 per cent of all decisions are effectively made either at the level of COREPER, or at the level of the technical committees that operate below COREPER. The issues are either decided before they go to the Council, which just rubber-stamps them (the 'A-points' on the agenda) or they are decided in outline by the Council of Ministers but then referred back to the committees for the details to be negotiated.

Van Schendelen (1996: 542), who managed to obtain the Minutes of all meetings of the Agriculture Council for 1992 and 1993, calculated that only 13 per cent of decisions were actually finally made in the Council, while 65 per cent were left to be made by auxiliary bodies (the remainder were still under consideration when he wrote). The interest of this lies in the expectation that negotiations in COREPER and the technical committees are more likely to be oriented to problem-solving than to bargaining. This is because the national representatives meet more frequently than ministers, and they are both less political and more concerned with the minutiae of technical issues than are ministers.

COREPER and the technical committees

It is at the level of the Council committees, up to and including COREPER, that the argument is most convincing that the Council is not an intergovernmental organization at all, but a supranational institution. Although it formally only prepares the agenda and meetings of the Council, COREPER has a great deal of discretion about what it classifies as A-points or B-points on the agenda. A-points are simply accepted by the ministers without discussion. Although any minister may request that an A-point be turned into a B-point, this is usually only done as a gesture by a member state that has lost the argument at committee level but wishes to enter a further reservation (Van Schendelen, 1996: 40).

It is also the case that issues move up and down the hierarchy of committees. So although COREPER and the working groups formally prepare the meetings of the ministers, in one sense the ministers can be said to prepare the meetings of the committees. This is the case where an issue has been discussed at ministerial level, and broad consensus has been reached, but the issue is then referred back down the hierarchy for the detail to be filled in.

All studies of COREPER indicate that its members consider themselves to have a dual role. According to Hayes-Renshaw et al (1989: 136), while the Perman-

ent Representatives 'are the trustworthy executors of the instructions from their respective capitals', they also have strong ties of solidarity with their colleagues in COREPER. These ties are developed as a result of intensive social interaction in Brussels. Committee members eat, drink, and breathe EU issues seven days a week. Every six months they and their wives go on trips to tourist locations in different member states, which helps to cement the bonds between them (Barber, 1995: I). Lewis (1998: 487) argued that this constant interaction between the same individuals built up a considerable legacy of what he called 'social capital'. This means that the individuals concerned trust one another, and understand and have sympathy for each other's points of view.

The ties are also the result of all the Permanent Representatives being in the same position vis-à-vis their national governments. All of them will have sympathy with one of their number who is bound by a tight mandate on a particular issue, because they are sometimes placed in that position themselves. In such a situation they will try to help each other out, perhaps by persuading their own government to make concessions if they feel that the issue is not so important for them.

The attitude of the Permanent Representatives to a negotiation is ambivalent: they all want their government's position to prevail; but they also want to reach agreement even at the cost of not achieving all of their own government's objectives in the negotiation (Hayes-Renshaw *et al.*, 1989: 136). When Permanent Representatives make concessions, or urge their governments to make concessions, it is not just because they feel a sense of social solidarity with their counterparts from other member states. It is also indicative of the strong sense that they have of being involved in a continuous process of bargaining with the same partners. In the language of games theory, they are involved in *iterated* games (i.e. the same game is repeated several times with the same participants). This changes the calculation of what is rational as compared with isolated games. In a one-off game it is rational to take any step to damage your opponent's position and to further your own, even so far as cheating on the rules if you can get away with it. In iterated games the use of such tactics is likely to backfire during a subsequent round. If you have reneged on a deal in one round of negotiations, it will be difficult to get anyone to conclude a deal with you in subsequent rounds.

This logic of iterated games in EU bargaining is more apparent to Permanent Representatives than it sometimes is to ministers, who have many other concerns and are less intensively socialized into the Community method of bargaining. It means that Permanent Representatives are often involved in trying to educate their governments about the nature of the EU bargaining process. This can lead to them being seen as the representative of the EU in the national capital: one German Permanent Representative punned that he was known in Bonn not as the *ständiger Vertreter* (Permanent Representative) but as the *ständiger Vertrager* (the permanent traitor) (Barber, 1995: I; Lewis, 1998: 483).

Although this sort of suspicion may occasionally exist in national capitals, it would be a foolish government that did not listen seriously to the advice of the Permanent Representative when deciding on its national negotiating position. This could be taken as evidence that the intergovernmentalist view, that national preferences are formulated independently of influence from the EU level, is false.

Moving down the hierarchy from COREPER, the technical groups that prepare recommendations for the Permanent Representatives involve intensive interaction between national and Commission officials. The processes of socialization that Lewis and others argued apply to COREPER also apply here. Although the people who work on these committees are national representatives, research by Beyers and Dierickx (1998: 307–8) showed that members of working groups soon started to judge other members on the basis of the level of expertise that they showed in the committee rather than on nationality. Ludlow (1991:103) went further to argue that 'Commission officials act as thirteenth members of the Council machinery', implying that the distinction between national and Commission representatives was almost meaningless in the work of these groups.

The thrust of all these arguments is that the members of the technical groups develop a sense of collegiality and engagement in a joint enterprise that makes it more sensible to see them as individuals participating in a team effort than as representatives of individual states. Here we are operating very much at the 'problem-solving' end of Scharpf's spectrum of types of negotiation. Agreements are reached on the basis of convincing arguments, not political weight or bargaining skill.

The relationship between the ministers on the one hand and COREPER and the technical groups on the other can be seen as similar to the relationship between the member states and the Commission as outlined in Chapter 19 (pp. 236–8). In an argument similar to that used to define the degree of autonomy available to the Commission, Van Schendelen (1996: 543) said that members of these 'auxiliary bodies' had a discretionary freedom within broadly defined parameters because of:

- the technical nature of the dossiers, which the ministers struggle to understand;

- the fact that the ministers are too busy to monitor their agents' performance in detail;

- the fact that instructions from national governments are often loosely drawn, arrive late, or are weak;

- the discretion that the agents are allowed in

response to the argument that they need to be given room for manoeuvre in negotiations;

- the agents' ability themselves to influence the

national negotiating position, and to educate the national ministry on what is feasible.

The Council presidency

Every six months a different member state assumes the presidency of the Council. During its period of office, that member state has responsibility for organizing and chairing meetings of the Council of Ministers and its various committees. In the course of its six months in charge, the presidency can expect to arrange and chair some ninety separate meetings of ministers, and many more times that of committees. In addition, there will be at least one European Council meeting during the six months. In this considerable task, the civil service of the state holding the presidency is assisted by the Council Secretariat (Box 20.6, p. 254). However, much of the burden of administering the presidency inevitably falls on national officials.

Kirchner (1992: 72–3) pointed to the increase in the role of the presidency in the 1970s as a result of several developments. First, the 1970s saw national positions diverging because of the differential impact on the member states of the international economic crises. Reaching agreement between the member states thus became more difficult at the very time that the Commission was at its least effective. In this context the Council presidency's role as mediator became more salient. Second, the development of EPC in the 1970s emphasized the intergovernmental method, sidelined the Commission, and again increased the salience of the presidency. Third, the increased role of the European Council also enhanced the presidency, because it prepared the agenda, drafted compromises between heads of government, and drafted the final communiqué.

The current system has been subject to two main criticisms: that six months is too brief a period for the tenure of the presidency; and that the scale of demands on the country holding the presidency has grown to outstrip the capacity of all but the largest member states to cope.

Box 20.6 The Council Secretariat

The Secretariat is a relatively small body of 2,300 people, a tenth of whom are at the senior A-grade. It is based in Brussels in the Justus Lipsius building. It is internally divided into the private office of the Secretary-General, a Legal Service, and ten Directorates-General.

The Secretariat is another potential mediator in disputes between member states, a role that it came to play more prominently after Niels Ersbøll of Denmark became Secretary-General in 1980. Ersbøll gave the Council Secretariat a new role through the active support he gave to successive presidencies during the 1985 IGC (Dinan 1994: 236). He was actively involved in the discussions about institutional reform in 1990–1, and in the drafting of documents for the IGC on political union (Dinan, 1994: 18–81). Ersbøll was also widely credited with having brokered a deal at the Edinburgh European Council on the concessions that needed to be made to the Danish government to allow them to win a second referendum on the TEU.

As Wessels (1991: 140) put it, the Secretary-General 'intentionally maintains a low profile but is known to be highly influential in attaining consensus'. From the viewpoint of intergovernmentalist theorists, this further undermines the claim of the supranational theorists that the Commission is essential to the process of reaching agreement in the EU. However, the Secretariat-General itself is also a supranational body, so its role hardly disproves the contention that supranational actors are influential in the EU.

Brevity

Six months is not long to hold the presidency, 'scarcely longer than the learning curve' (de Bassompierre, 1988: 153), and the frequency of changes disrupts continuity. On the other hand, with fifteen members, the presidency comes around only once every 7½ years, and following enlargement it might come around only once every ten or twelve years. This is too long a gap for collective expertise to be retained because staff have moved on, so the learning has to begin anew with every turn at the presidency.

In an attempt to get round this problem, a system known as the Troika was introduced in 1983, whereby the current presidency works in close liaison with the immediate past and next presidency states. The Troika system also provides a partial solution to the problem that the frequent changes in the presidency can confuse the EU's partners in other parts of the world.

Domestic political instability can seriously disrupt a six-month presidency. Of the seven presidencies between January 1993 and June 1996, only that of Belgium (January to June 1994) was not disrupted by either elections or political crisis. Perhaps the worst crisis was during the Danish presidency (January to June 1993), when the government resigned weeks before it was due to take over, and everything had to be put on hold while new ministers came into office and mastered their briefs. But other presidencies in this period were severely disrupted by domestic politics (see Box 20.7, p. 255)

Scale of demands

Some of the smaller member states have difficulties in coping with the sheer range of topics on which they might be expected to produce papers during a presidency. There is a lot of room for concern about whether the political and administrative infra-

> ### Box 20.7 Disruption to Council presidencies, July 1994–June 1996
>
> - Germany (July to December 1994) had a federal election during the presidency.
> - France (January to June 1995) had a presidential election during its presidency.
> - Spain (July to December 1995) faced a crisis over the domestic budget, and was in a pre-election phase with a government seriously weakened by scandals.
> - Italy was without an elected government for most of its presidency (January to June 1996), and held elections during the presidency.

structure of the new members who are expected to join in the next few years will be up to the task. It is also the case that after enlargement there will be far more small and medium-sized states than large states, and the turn of a large state will not come around very often. Sometimes it takes the resources of a large state to break the backlog that has built up.

Proposals for reform

Various proposals have been made. These include:

- a longer term of office, lasting from one to two years;
- the creation of presidential teams of perhaps four or five countries;
- consolidation of the Troika system so that the presidency is shared between three states at a time on a rolling basis.

Conclusion

To try to analyse the role of the Council as a whole would be a mistake. It is important to disaggregate the Council's component institutions in order to understand at exactly which point in the machinery issues are dealt with. Only with this knowledge can an informed judgement be made concerning the key actors involved and their motivations. Even then,

the task is complicated by the secrecy that surrounds Council activity in virtually all of its manifestations. The usual justification for this is that the Council meetings are intergovernmental negotiations, and if they were subject to public scrutiny it would become more difficult to reach agreements. There is an echo here of one of the arguments about the problems faced by the European Council: that the publicity given to meetings encourages over-cautiousness. Ironically, it is very difficult to establish whether the premiss of this argument is correct because of the secrecy that is justified by reference to that premiss.

The most informed research suggests that a high proportion of Council decisions are taken relatively low down in the decisional hierarchy. It is here, within COREPER and the technical committees, that observers find the greatest evidence of supra-nationalism in Council activities. At the ministerial level, decisions tend to be more politicized and national positions less open to negotiation. However, to complicate matters further, anecdotal evidence suggests that even at the ministerial level, some Councils are more collegial than others. The conclusion must be, therefore, that the argument between intergovernmental and supranational theorists cannot be settled finally so far as the Council is concerned, but that there are some grounds for not assuming too readily that because the Council is the institution where the governments of member states are most directly represented, it is necessarily an intergovernmental body.

While the debate between academics continues, the Council faces major practical problems in the context of future enlargement. Some of these concern the viability of the presidency. Others concern related issues such as the weighting of votes under QMV (Box 20.8, p. 256). However, these practical concerns are not as far removed from the academic debate as might appear at first sight. Whether the

---

Box 20.8 The reweighting of votes under QMV following enlargement

Successive enlargements have increased the number of small states in the EU. Most of the applicants for the next round of enlargement are also small states. Because the number of votes allocated to a state under QMV is not directly proportional to its population, the increase in the number of small member states has produced a situation in which measures can be passed under QMV with the support of the representatives of a decreasing proportion of the total population of the EU. In the original six states votes representing 70 per cent of the population were needed to pass a measure; by 1995 this had been reduced to 58.3 per cent; and on the basis of reasonable assumptions about the identity of the members and therefore about the numbers of votes to which they will be entitled on the existing formula, with 26 member states the proportion required could be only 50.3 per cent.

Council can continue to operate with over twenty members may depend on how far it is only a forum for intergovernmental bargaining, or how far it is a genuinely collegial, problem-solving body. In the first case, the prospects for it functioning effectively after enlargement are not good; in the second, after a period of socialization of new members, they are much better.

KEY POINTS

The European Council

- A number of factors explain the establishment of the European Council in the 1970s. It provided a collective response to the challenges of economic interdependence; allowed national governments collectively to control the direction of the EC; and presented a united front to the outside world.

- The European Council has a number of important functions. These include providing general direction to the EC and acting as a 'Court of Appeal' for EC decisions that cannot be resolved lower down the decisional hierarchy.

- The European Council faces a number of problems. For example, there are often unrealistic expectations about what the summits can achieve.

The Council of Ministers

- The Council of Ministers meets in a variety of manifestations depending on the subject under consideration.

- Although there is no formal hierarchy of Council meetings, informally, those concerning foreign affairs, finance, and agriculture have the highest status.

COREPER and the technical committees

- While much attention is paid to Council decisions, research has indicated that a large proportion of 'Council' decisions are actually taken lower down the decisional hierarchy within COREPER and technical committees.

- Arguments that the Council is a supranational entity are strongest at the level of COREPER and the technical committees.

- The Permanent Representatives of national governments interact regularly and develop trust and solidarity which makes agreement between them easier than between politicians who are less regularly engaged and who have broader concerns.

- National representatives on technical groups also undergo a process of socialization which produces a problem-solving approach where decisions are taken more on the strength of evidence rather than political weight.

The presidency

- The Council presidency rotates between member states every six months. This system has been criticized on the grounds of brevity and for the scale of the demands it places on smaller member states.

QUESTIONS

1 What evidence is there for (a) supranationalism and (b) intergovernmentalism in the complex of institutions that comprises the Council?

2 Is the European Council essential or could its functions be undertaken by an alternative EC institution?

3 What are the implications of the secrecy that surrounds meetings of the Council??

4 What relevance has the debate about the intergovernmental or supranational nature of the Council to practical concerns about the impact of enlargement on the working of the Council?

FURTHER READING

The most comprehensive treatment of the functioning of the Council is by F. Hayes-Renshaw and H. Wallace, *The Council of Ministers* (Basingstoke and London: Macmillan, 1997).

An early assessment of the strengths and weaknesses of the institutionalized summit meetings, which remains relevant, is in S. Bulmer and W. Wessels, *The European Council:*

Decision-Making in European Politics (Basingstoke and London: Macmillan, 1987). A later assessment from one of the same authors is provided in: W. Wessels, 'The EC Council: The Community's Decision-Making center', in R. O. Keohane and S. Hoffmann (eds.), *The New European Community: Decisionmaking and Institutional Change* (Boulder, San Francisco, and London: Westview Press, 1991), 133–54.

E. J. Kirchner, *Decision-making in the European Community* (Manchester: Manchester University Press, 1992) is a rich source of ideas and insight, while M. Westlake, *The Council of the European Union* (London: Catermill, 1995) is even more up-to-date, and informed by something of an insider's perspective (Westlake works for the Commission).

J. Lewis, 'Is the "Hard Bargaining" Image of the Council Misleading? The Committee of Permanent Representatives and the Local Elections Directive', *Journal of Common Market Studies* 36 (1998), 479–504 is a constructivist contribution to the debate about whether the Council is intergovernmental or supranational in nature, and a similar insight is provided by: J. Beyers and G. Dierickx, 'The Working Groups of the Council of the European Union: Supranational or Intergovernmental Negotiations?', *Journal of Common Market Studies* 36 (1998), 289–317.

21 The European Parliament

SUMMARY

The European Parliament (EP) is unique among EU institutions as the only directly elected body. The introduction of direct elections increased the legitimacy of the EP. This legitimacy has provided the platform from which the EP has sought to increase its powers. To a degree, it has been successful in this through pursuing a two-pronged minimalist and maximalist strategy, at times assisted by the Commission and the ECJ. However, while the EP is directly elected, European elections remain a relatively low-key affair within member states, often having a similar domestic status to local government elections. Moreover, they tend to be fought on domestic rather than European issues.

Despite its limitations, the EP remains for many the most obvious and most effective way of closing the democratic deficit that exists in EU decision-making. As such, the EP and its supporters will continue to press for a further expansion of its competencies. For others, the development of a European identity is an important prerequisite to a powerful EP. This, it seems, remains a distant prospect.

Introduction

The European Parliament (EP) is the one directly elected institution in the EU. The Members of the EP (MEPs) are elected once every five years, and since the first direct elections in 1979 the EP has campaigned for its powers to be increased. Although it is still not satisfied with the situation, there has been some increase in its powers. This struggle for increased powers is discussed in more detail below, but the basic functions and powers of the EP are summarized in Boxes 21.1 and 21.2 (see pp. 260 and 261).

MEPs are divided between the member states on a basis that is approximately proportionate to size of population, although the small countries are somewhat over-represented. The distribution of the 626 seats following the 1995 enlargement is shown in Box 21.3 (see p. 261). The internal structure of the EP is summarized in Box 21.4 (see p. 262).

The central theme for discussion in this chapter is the extent to which the EP has become an effective

---

Box 21.1 The functions of the European Parliament

Legislative function: The EP has emerged as a co-legislature with the Council of Ministers in most areas of EC legislation. The various legislative procedures, and the powers of the EP in each of them, are discussed in Chapter 18, pp. 223–6.

Budgetary function: The EP and the Council of Ministers are the joint budgetary authorities on the EC. The budgetary procedure, and the role of the EP in it, is described in Chapter 18, pp. 220–3.

Supervisory function: the EP exercises democratic supervision over all Community activities.

- It was given the right under the TEU to be consulted by the governments of the member states when they were agreeing on a new president of the Commission. The Treaty of Amsterdam extended this power so that the nomination had to be formally approved by the EP. A new Commission is subject to a vote of approval by the EP, and the EP has the power to dismiss the whole of the Commission on a vote of censure; but in neither case can it target individual commissioners. A motion of censure requires a positive vote from an absolute majority

of MEPs and two-thirds of the votes cast. The EP also has the right to ask the Commission written and oral questions.

- It can table written and oral questions about the activities of the Council of Ministers, and the Foreign Minister of the state holding the presidency of the Council reports to the EP at the beginning and end of the presidency. For the European Council, there is no mechanism of parliamentary accountability, although the presidency does give the EP a report on European Council meetings.

- The Council Presidency consults the EP on the main aspects of the common foreign and security policy and ensures that Parliament's views are taken into consideration. The EP is regularly informed by the presidency and the Commission of developments in the Union's foreign and security policy.

- The EP can also set up its own committees of inquiry.

Source: EP web site: http://www.europarl.eu.int/presentation/en/powers.htm)

Box 21.2 The powers of the European Parliament

Political

- Approves appointment of Commission President
- Approves appointment of Commission after public hearings
- Questions the Council and Commission
- Can censure and dismiss whole Commission

Legislative

- Delivers opinions on Commission proposals

- Shares final decision on most proposals with Council (Co-decision procedure)
- Assent required for enlargement of European Union and agreements with third countries

Budgetary

- Can modify certain proposed expenditures
- Annual approval required for annual budget
- Budgetary Control Committee Checks expenditure (together with Court of Auditors)

Box 21.3 Distribution of seats in the European Parliament

Germany	99
France, Italy, United Kingdom	87
Spain	64
Netherlands	31
Belgium, Greece, Portugal	25
Austria	21
Denmark, Finland	16
Ireland	15
Luxembourg	6
Total	626

independent actor in the affairs of the EU, and how far it will continue to move in that direction in the future. This clearly parallels the discussion in the previous two chapters, on the Commission and the Council.

The chapter looks first at the record of the EP in increasing its power, and then turns to the closely related question of whether these gains have led to a real increase in the influence of the EP in the legislative process. It then considers the prospects for a further increase in the powers and influence of the EP. Two factors that will influence the ability of the EP to extend its powers and influence further are the quality of the MEPs, and the independence of the party groups from control by domestic political parties. The chapter considers these two issues, then turns to examine the two main arguments that the EP has used as a means of levering extra power from the member states: that direct elections confer especial legitimacy on it as an institution; and that there is a need to increase its powers to close the democratic deficit that is widely believed to have opened up in the EU.

The struggle for power

Over the years since it has been directly elected, the EP has struggled to get its powers increased. In this it has adopted a two-pronged strategy, what Lodge (1990*a*) called a minimalist and a maximalist strategy.

The minimalist strategy consists of making the most extensive use possible of its existing powers, and trying to stretch the definition of those powers. 'It rests on the supposition that anything not explicitly forbidden the EP by the EC treaties is

---

Box 21.4 **The structure of the European Parliament**

The EP meets in plenary session every month, except August, in Strasbourg. Committee meetings are held in Brussels.

The President is elected by the MEPs from among their number for a 2½ year renewable term. The President represents the EP on official occasions, and in relations with other institutions, presides over debates during plenary sessions, and chairs meetings of the Bureau and the Conference of Presidents.

The Bureau consists of the President, fourteen vice-presidents, and five 'quaestors' who deal with administrative and financial matters relating to MEPs. The members are elected by the MEPs for a term of two-and-a-half years.

The Conference of Presidents consists of the President and the Chairs of the Political Groups. It draws up the agenda for plenary sessions, fixes the timetable for the work of parliamentary bodies and establishes the terms of reference and size of parliamentary committees and delegations.

The Committees. Most of the work of the EP is channelled through seventeen standing committees (p 000). In addition, the EP can establish temporary committees and committees of enquiry.

The Secretariat consists of approximately 3,500 administrative and clerical staff, headed by the Secretary-General. Around one-third of the staff are in the language service, concerned with translation and interpretation. In addition to the secretariat, the political groups have their own administrative support.

Source: EP web site: http://www.europarl.eu.int/presentation/en/ how.htm)

Box 21.5 **The Isoglucose Case**

The most significant example of a judgement of the ECJ stretching the powers of the EP was the Isoglucose case in 1981. In 1980 the Council of Ministers agreed a Commission proposal for a Regulation before the EP had delivered its opinion under the consultation procedure. The failure was not a deliberate withholding of the opinion: the EP had just not got around to dealing with the issue. However, when the Council proceeded without its opinion, the EP took the issue to the ECJ claiming that the Council had acted beyond its powers. The ECJ agreed and in effect gave the EP a right to delay legislation, although it also made it clear that the EP was obliged to deliver an opinion, so the ruling did not hand it a veto power.

---

permitted.' (Lodge, 1990*a*: 11). In this the EP has found an ally in the ECJ. A number of judgements of the ECJ, on cases brought to it by the EP, have given a more far-reaching interpretation of the constitutional powers of the EP than the member states had foreseen (e.g. Box 21.5, p. 262).

The EP has also exploited its limited powers of control over the Commission. In 1998 its Budgetary Affairs Committee refused to discharge the 1996 budget because it was unhappy with the response of the Commission to certain charges of lax financial administration. Jacques Santer, the President of the Commission, made the issue one of confidence by challenging the EP either to give discharge to the budget or to lay down a motion of censure on the whole Commission. This the EP did, although when it was voted on in January 1999 it failed to get even a majority, let alone the two-thirds majority that was required. However, the vote of 232 for and 293 against was the biggest vote ever for a motion of censure, and prompted the Commission to agree to set up a committee of independent experts to report to the EP on fraud, mismanagement, and nepotism in the Commission. When the report appeared in March 1999 it was so damning of the level of mismanagement by some Commissioners, that the whole Commission resigned. Although the EP had not managed to summon the substantial majority needed to censure the Commission formally, it had managed to raise the public awareness of the issues identified by the Court of Auditors to the point where the position of the Commission became untenable. By adept use of its limited powers, the EP achieved a considerable victory (see Box 19.6, p. 241).

The *maximalist* strategy, which has been pursued by the EP alongside the minimalist strategy, is 'based on the overt goal of advancing European Union through not merely treaty amendment but the supplanting of the old treaties by a new one, a constitution for the European Union' (Lodge, 1990*a*: 12). The biggest step taken in this direction was the agreement to a Draft Treaty on European Union in February 1984 (Lodge, 1986). This initiative was pushed by the Italian federalist Altiero Spinelli and the Crocodile Club of MEPs, who took their name from the restaurant in Strasbourg where they met. The Draft Treaty formed a possible constitution for a federal Europe, and came at a time when change was in the air because of concern about 'Eurosclerosis' (see Ch. 10, pp. 110–11). In September 1983 the heads of government had agreed to a Solemn Declaration on European Union at the Stuttgart European Council. The Spinelli Draft Treaty went much further, though. Its significance is subject to some difference of opinion between scholars, but some of its ideas were incorporated into the SEA, and further ideas into the TEU, most notably the introduction of the co-operation procedure in the SEA and of the co-decision procedure in the TEU (see Ch. 18, pp. 223–6).

Effective influence

An increase in formal power does not necessarily mean an increase in effective influence. Indeed, some analysts argued that the EP had less effective influence on legislation under the co-decision procedure than it had under co-operation. (Garrett and Tsebelis 1996, and Tsebelis and Garrett 1996). Their argument was as follows.

Under the *consultation* procedure the Council had the strongest say on the final form of legislation, because although the Commission drafted the proposal, the Council had to accept it unanimously. The Commission therefore had to formulate each proposal in such a way that even the member state least favourably disposed towards integration would be able to accept it, which meant that the Commission had little room to exercise its own discretion. After the SEA introduced QMV in the Council, the Commission became more influential in those few areas that still came under consultation. This was because the Commission only had to draft a proposal that would be preferred to the *status quo* by a qualified majority of members of the Council. Here, the EP was restricted to a consultative role, and its opinion could be ignored whether the voting rule was unanimity or QMV.

Under the *co-operation* procedure the Commission and the EP shared the power to determine the final form of the legislation. This was because of the combination of QMV in the Council, and the introduction of a second reading with a conditional power of veto for the EP. At the second reading, if the EP was unhappy with the version of the draft legislation that had been adopted by the Council as its 'common position' (which in effect meant if the EP's proposed amendments had largely been ignored), the EP could reject the common position by an absolute majority of its members. This constituted a veto, but the Council could override it if it acted by unanimity. A key element in the balance of influence here was the attitude of the Commission to the EP's proposed amendments at second reading. If the Commission accepted the amendments, the Council had to act by unanimity to overturn them; but the Council could accept the amended proposal by QMV. This meant that if the EP and the Commission could agree on a proposal that was acceptable to a coalition in the Council that constituted a qualified majority, they together had the decisive influence on the form of the legislation.

Under the *co-decision* procedure, according to Tsebelis and Garrett, the formal power to determine the final wording of the legislation passed to the Council of Ministers. This was in complete contrast to the general view that co-decision was a significant increase in the power of the EP. The procedure gave the EP:

- three readings of legislation
- the right to negotiate directly with the Council via a conciliation committee on any amendments for which there was an absolute majority in the EP but with which the Council did not agree
- an absolute right of veto.

The reasoning of Tsebelis and Garrett was as follows:

1. The position of the Commission was fatally weakened because after the second reading the Council and the EP could convene a conciliation committee and negotiate a text bi-laterally which could overrule the Commission text.

2. On the assumption that the EP would normally prefer to see some legislation rather than no legislation, it was engaged in an uneven negotiation with the Council. If agreement could not be reached in the conciliation committee, the Council could either allow the proposal to drop by simply not acting on it, or could adopt the original common position. In the latter case the EP could reject the common position by an absolute majority, but the effect was to revert to the status quo.

These conclusions were strongly contested by Scully (1997a, 1997b). He accepted the general framework of the model put forward by Tsebelis and Garrett, but pointed to certain flaws in the argument.

1. The role of the Commission was underestimated. It still had the sole right of initiative for legislative proposals, and drafted the initial text. If it worked in conjunction with the EP at this stage, and if the two institutions acted strategically to agree proposals that could command a qualified majority in the Council, then they had the same joint influence as under the co-operation procedure.

2. Tsebelis and Garrett seriously underestimated the importance of the EP's power of veto under both the co-operation and conciliation procedures. If the issue was a matter of detail, then the willingness of the EP to threaten to veto a proposal might produce concessions from the Council, which would be reluctant to lose a measure on which it was agreed in principle because of a detail.

3. Tsebelis and Garrett were incorrect to argue that after the EP's second reading the Commission was marginalized. The Commission did consider the proposed amendments, and if it rejected them it effectively forced a conciliation committee to be convened. At this stage the Commission could still play an effective role as a negotiator, and try to find a position that was still based on its original text but which would avert conciliation, where both sides stood to lose everything that they hoped to gain from the legislation.

In practice much of Tsebelis and Garrett's analysis was based on ignoring the informal aspects of the inter-institutional bargaining process. This failing is perhaps related to the rational choice framework of analysis that they adopted, which does not place much emphasis on empirical research. Scholars whose approach involved intensive research 'in the field' were clear that, 'the informal dimensions of inter-institutional relations are of major significance in understanding policy-making in the EC' (Judge, Earnshaw, and Cowan, 1994: 45).

The importance of the informal aspect is related to the EP's vigorous pursuit of the minimalist strategy of making the greatest possible use of its formal powers. This first emerged with reference to the consultation procedure in the aftermath of the Isoglucose judgement (Box 21.5, p. 262). As a result of the judgement, the EP was able to force the Commission to interact more intensively with it to try to ensure that it would not delay legislation. Under the *renvoi* procedure the EP refused to deliver a formal opinion until it had received some indication from the Commission of how it proposed to react to the amendments that the EP was suggesting. The level of informal interaction in particular increased, and in 1990 the Commission offered a code of conduct which committed it to keeping the EP informed. This was accepted, and was extended in 1995 in the light of changes in the TEU.

On the same theme, Earnshaw and Judge (1997: 560) made the following assessment of the effect of the co-operation procedure:

the co-operation procedure served to 'hyphenate' the relationship between Parliament and the other two institutions and so to transform the Council–Commission dialogue into an asymmetrical Council–Commission–Parliament trialogue.

However, in strict constitutional terms, Parliament still remained the 'outsider' in this relationship. Nonetheless, the true importance of the formal procedure was that it facilitated the exertion of greater *informal* parliamentary influence over EU legislation. Thus, in interview, MEPs and officials alike pointed to the importance of informal negotiations between Parliament and the Commission in determining the eventual legislative impact of the EP.

On the co-decision procedure, the same researchers (Earnshaw and Judge, 1995: 645) agreed with Tsebelis and Garrett that the role of the Commission had been weakened. It was placed in 'a considerably more ambiguous, and weaker, position than in the co-operation or consultation procedures'. However, they disagreed that the procedure had left the EP with less influence than previously:

Under co-decision Parliament is certainly a more equal partner in the legislative process, and now has a rightful place alongside the Council in several important policy areas—despite the weighting of the procedure towards the Council (Earnshaw and Judge, 1995: 647).

As with the other developments treated above, though, the biggest impact of the change was on the informal contacts: 'informal inter-institutional linkages have expanded as a result of co-decision' (Earnshaw and Judge, 1995: 647–8).

Overall, then, it seems that the informal increase in the influence of the EP has actually exceeded the formal increase in its powers as a result of the Treaty changes. This is a finding that is directly relevant to the question of whether the EU still has a democratic deficit in its operation (see below, pp. 269–71).

The quality and independence of MEPS

In the early years of the EP, few MEPs were in their prime. They were predominantly either older or younger than most national MPs. Most of the older politicians had exhausted their career options in their home state and were serving out their years to retirement in the well-paid but relatively undemanding role of an MEP. The young politicians were mostly keen to pursue a national political career, but found that it was easier to get started with a European seat than with a national seat. Over the years this seems to have changed to some extent. Research by Martin Westlake (1994) indicated that there was increasing professionalization and careerism among MEPs. Although this still had far to go, the European Parliament might be becoming 'more, rather than less, attractive' to ambitious politicians (Westlake, 1994: 268).

There is still a problem about the lack of an obvious career route at the European level. National MPs can aspire to enter government, or at least to become an official spokesperson for their party if it is in opposition. At the European level the executive is not drawn from the EP, which means that there is no obvious progression. However, as Hix and Lord (1997: 117) pointed out, if the Commissioners from the new member states were excluded, eleven out of

seventeen members of the Santer Commission had been MEPs. This does not indicate, though, that the EP is influential in the appointment of Commissioners, but rather that being an MEP can provide useful relevant experience for individuals who hope to be nominated as Commissioners. The decision still lies with national party leaders.

Another point about career progression, is that in the United States the executive is not chosen from members of the legislature, but that has not prevented the emergence of professional members of Congress who aspire to occupy senior committee chairs. As the powers and influence of the EP grow, so a similar career route might come to be followed by MEPs.

The existence of a European career structure, independent of national party leaderships, is important to the prospects of attracting MEPs of sufficient calibre to allow the EP to maximize its influence, and giving those MEPs the opportunity and the incentive to act independently. At present those prospects are not good. The lack of an independent career structure means that most MEPs remain subordinate to their parties' national leaderships, and this tendency is reinforced by the way in which the political groups in the EP operate.

Party groups

MEPs do not sit in the EP in national delegations, but in transnational party groups (Box 21.6, p. 266). A full list of the groups, and their level of representation in the 1999–2002 Parliament is given in Box 21.7 (p. 266).

There are definite advantages to being a member of one of the party groups. The groups receive funding from the EP to cover their administrative costs. Memberships of committees, and their chairs and rapporteurs, are allocated to groups in proportion to their size. (For a list of EP committees see Box 21.8, p. 267.) It is not surprising, therefore, that national parties and individual MEPs who cannot find an ideological group to join will seek to band together to form a disparate group of their own. This was the nature of the Rainbow Group in the 1984–9 Parliament. It consisted of members of environmentalist parties, regionalist parties, and anti-EC Danish MEPs; the only thing that they had in common was a wish to draw down the funding and other advantages that would be denied them if they did not join a group.

However, even the groups that may appear to be more homogeneous can contain within them a wide variety of divergent ideological positions. The Liberal and Democrat Group contains economic liberals, who believe in free market economics and are conservative on social issues, and social liberals, who are nearer to social democrats on social issues and on the need to regulate the market than they are to some of their colleagues in their own Group. Even bigger divergence existed over many years between the French and Italian Communists in what used to be the Group of the Democratic Left: the Italian Communists were pro-European integration, whereas the French Party was hostile.

Even within the ideologically more cohesive groups, which includes the two largest groups of the Socialists and the conservative European People's Party, differences can emerge around national perspectives on issues. In early 1999, when the EP voted on a censure motion against the Santer Commission, the Socialist Group officially said it would vote

---

Box 21.6 The Structure and purpose of party groups in the European Parliament

- A party group may be established by 12 MEPs if they are drawn from three or more member states; by 18 MEPs if they are drawn from two member states; or by 23 MEPs if they are drawn from only one member state.

- Each party group has its own administrative and support staff, paid for out of the central budget of the EP.

- Groups are co-ordinated by a bureau, consisting of a chair, a vice-chair, and a treasurer as a minimum. The members of the bureau are elected by the members of the group as a whole.

- The groups play an important role in setting the agenda of the EP, choosing the *rapporteurs* for committees, and allocating speaking time in plenary sessions.

Box 21.7 Membership numbers of political groups in the European Parliament (as at 31.8.00)

Group	MEPs
The European People's Party and European Democrats	233
The Party of European Socialists	180
European, Liberal, Democratic and Reformist Group	51
Greens/European Free Alliance	48
European United Left/Nordic Green Left	42
Union for a Europe of Nations	30
Technical Group of Independent Members	18
Europe of Democracies and Diversities	16
Independents	8
Total	626

(*Source*: http://www.europarl.eu.int/)

Box 21.8 Committees of the EP (as from September 1999)

- Committee on Foreign Affairs, Human Rights, Common Security and Defence Policy

- Committee on Budgets

- Committee on Budgetary Control

- Committee on Citizens' Freedoms and Rights, Justice and Home Affairs

- Committee on Economic and Monetary Affairs

- Committee on Legal Affairs and the Internal Market

- Committee on Industry, External Trade, Research and Energy

- Committee on Employment and Social Affairs

- Committee on the Environment, Public Health and Consumer Protection

- Committee on Agriculture and Rural Development

- Committee on Fisheries

- Committee on Regional Policy, Transport and Tourism

- Committee on Culture, Youth, Education, the Media and Sport

- Committee on Development and Cooperation

- Committee on Constitutional Affairs

- Committee on Women's Rights and Equal Opportunities

- Committee on Petitions

Source: EP web site: http://www.europarl.eu.int/presentation/en/how.htm)

---

against the motion. However, almost all its German members voted for the censure. This reflected the fact that criticism of the Commission had become a popular cause in the press in Germany, to a greater extent than in other member states.

Not only can genuine differences of national perspective lead to divergence in voting behaviour: the MEPs in the party groups are subject to pressure from their national parties. In 1980, the first directly-elected EP blocked the passing of the budget for 1981 in a test of strength against the Council. For several months the EC had to survive on the system of 'provisional twelfths', whereby it is allowed to spend each month an amount equivalent to one-twelfth of the previous year's budget. Eventually the MEPs came under tremendous pressure from their national parties to lift their veto, which they did without winning any further concessions from the Council.

In many, although not all member states, the proportional representation (PR) electoral systems that operate make it easier for national party leaders to put pressure on their MEPs, because European elections are held on the basis of closed party lists. The chances for an individual of being elected depend on where he or she is placed on the list. As the lists are drawn up by the national party organizations, the MEPs face the prospect of being dropped down the list, and of their seats being jeopardized, if they offend the national party leadership too much.

This raises directly the issue of the independence of MEPs. The system is still dominated by national parties, and this has a number of adverse consequences for MEPs, not least in denying them the vital quality of electoral legitimacy. The observation is made below that European elections are treated as second-order national elections. The main reason that this situation persists is the domination of the process by national political parties that have their own concerns.

The central aim of domestic political parties in any electoral contest is gaining control of national government offices. European elections are thus fought on the performances of the parties holding national government offices. . . . As long as national parties decide who are the candidates in the elections and control the attention of the media during campaigns, there is little the EP groups or the party federations can do to break their hold over the process. (Hix and Lord, 1997: 211)

Direct elections

The forerunner of the present EP was the indirectly-elected European Parliamentary Assembly (EPA). Members of the EPA were members of national parliaments who were seconded to the EPA. They were full-time national MPs and part-time European MPs. Agreement to replace the EPA with a directly-elected body was reached at the Rome meeting of the European Council in December 1975. The date agreed for the first direct elections then was May/June 1978; but the first elections were not held until 1979, because of delay in passing the necessary enabling legislation in Britain.

The reason why the heads of government agreed to direct elections is concealed by the aura of secrecy that surrounds all the work of the European Council. However, given that Germany, Italy, and the Benelux countries had long favoured a directly-elected EP, the crucial shift was on the part of France. Giscard d'Estaing was the first President of the Fifth Republic not to belong to the Gaullist party. Although his own Independent Republicans did not support direct elections to the EP prior to Giscard becoming President, the small parties in the centre of the French political spectrum did, and Giscard needed their support to move away from dependence on the Gaullists for his parliamentary majority in France. So the agreement to direct elections to the EP may have been the result of domestic political calculations.

Britain, newly joined in 1973, was more reluctant to accept direct elections because it implied a degree of federalism in the constitution of the EC that was greater than British politicians from either of the main political parties wanted to see. Why the Labour government agreed is difficult to understand, but there may have been a deal behind the scenes on French support for the renegotiated terms of entry.

The British Labour government found it difficult to get acceptance of direct elections in the British Parliament. At this time Labour was not a pro-European party; but the government did not have a majority in the House of Commons and was dependent on the support of the Liberal Party, which was pro-European. The Liberals were also strong supporters of PR as a system of election, which most Labour MPs strongly opposed. In response to Liberal demands the government introduced a European elections bill that incorporated PR, but had to retreat to a system based on single-member constituencies in the face of the combined opposition of the Conservatives and a majority of its own backbenchers. This delayed the legislation, but it delayed implementation even further because the constituency system required extensive work to draw boundaries. As a result of domestic British politics, the first elections were put back a year, until June 1979.

Even then the elections did not take place under a uniform electoral system as envisaged in the Treaty, because the rest of Europe outside Britain used PR. They also all used different variations on PR, some adopting closed party lists, others allowing the elector to vote for an individual; some treating the whole country as one constituency, others dividing it into separate geographical constituencies. This variety was less significant, though, than British exceptionalism because of the distortion of party representation that first-past-the-post imposes on the overall results. Once elected, the MEPs sit in party groups in the EP, and the British system consistently deprived the Liberal and Democrat Group of any British members, while disproportionately enhancing the number of members of whichever British party got the largest number of votes. The timing of European elections meant that this was usually the party that was not in office at home.

Turn-out in European elections has been consistently low. It varies between member states, but in every state is much lower than for national elections. This reflects the fact that the European elections do not affect which party or coalition governs the EU. The outcome affects neither the composition of the Commission nor that of the Council of Ministers, the two most powerful institutions in the system.

European elections are treated by the electorate as 'second order national elections', which means that they are seen as being on a par with local government elections. The campaigns are fought predominantly on domestic issues rather than European issues. Although the main party groups issue European manifestos, these are framework documents from which the national parties draw when they prepare their national manifestos. Most of the actual campaigning centres on the record of the national government rather than on the differences between the parties on European issues. One consequence of this is that the results tend to reflect the protest nature of voting in second-order elections. The party that is in office nationally will tend to do badly if it is in the middle of its term because voters use the European election as a means of indicating their dissatisfaction. Of course, the national electoral cycles of member states map onto the schedule of European elections in different ways; and there may well be parties of different political complexions in office in the different member states. However, there is a tendency for European electorates to move to the right or left in a manner that may not be co-ordinated, but does produce clusters of conservative or Socialist governments at any one time. So, during most of the 1980s and 1990s there was a majority of conservative governments in the Europe, and the Socialist parties formed the largest group in the EP because protest votes in European elections were directed against the national conservative governments. Following a swing to the left in the large majority of member states in the late 1990s, it was predictable that the conservative parties would overtake the Socialists in the EP elections of 1999.

This effect of separating out the majorities in member states and the majority in the EP was perhaps less significant in a situation where the main concern of the EP was to press for further European integration. There is a tendency for individuals who stand for election to the EP to be pro-European whether they are from the right or left of the political spectrum. It can be argued, though, that in the aftermath of the completion of the single market the issues that face the EU are classic left-right issues of how much public control there should be over business, how much legal protection should be given to workers, etc. If this is true, and it is a plausible argument, the disjuncture between the ideological orientation of the national and European majorities could become a serious barrier to effective governance. National opposition parties will try to use the EP to continue their struggle against national governments. The result will most likely be to increase the reluctance of national governments to give more power to the EP.

The democratic deficit

One of the strongest arguments used by the EP to secure an increase in its powers is that the EU suffers from a democratic deficit which can only be filled by giving more say in decision making to the only directly democratically elected institution.

The origins of the democratic deficit can be traced back to the original blueprint for the ECSC (Featherstone, 1994). Jean Monnet, the architect of the system, was a technocrat who came from a political system, France of the Fourth Republic, in which politicians had short tenure in office, and the real motors of change were the technocrats. In his original plan, Monnet made no provision for a Parliamentary Assembly: this was added in during the negotiations at the insistence of the smaller states and under

pressure from the French National Assembly (see Ch. 5, pp. 62–3). Its inclusion was an anomaly: the main thrust of the institutional structure was elitist.

The EPA began campaigning for an increase in democratic control over the EC from an early stage. Initially the demand was for direct elections. This was resisted on the argument that the EPA had no real power, and therefore there was no point in electing it. The argument was circular: demands from the EPA for more power were inevitably met by the argument that it had no claim to increased powers because it was not directly elected. The main opponent of direct elections was always the French government; but eventually, as explained above, Giscard d'Estaing changed his position for domestic political reasons. Once direct elections were achieved, the EP used this fact to press for more power.

The argument gained extra force with the introduction of QMV into the Council of Ministers. So long as it was possible for any member state to veto any proposal, it could be argued that, in principle at least, national parliaments could exercise democratic control by mandating their ministers not to accept a measure except under specified conditions. Once it became possible for the minister to be outvoted, the national parliaments lost even this nominal, negative control over decisions. Under these circumstances, the democratic deficit grew wider and the arguments for filling it by increasing the powers of the EP grew stronger.

The extension of the range of policy issues with a European dimension also contributed to making the problem more serious. So long as it was only agriculture and a few other areas that were decided in Brussels, the extent to which democratic control was lost to national electorates was limited. Whether entirely accurate or not, Jacques Delors's prediction in July 1988 that 'In ten years 80 per cent of economic legislation—and perhaps tax and social legislation—will be directed from the Community' (Debates of the European Parliament, 1988–9, 2–367/140) indicated something of the scale of the change in the relevance of European legislation and decision-making to the peoples of Europe.

The consequence of the original technocratic blueprint and the success of the EC/EU in pursuit of its objective of ever closer union was:

a reduction in the degree of policy control by individuals within member states; and intrusion of the EU into functions that were previously performed by the nation state; a weakening of legislative control over the executives within nation states; and an overall lack of democratic accountability and transparency.   (Weale, 1997: 667)

There are arguments against the idea that simply increasing the powers of the EP can fill the democratic deficit. The nature of European elections as second-order national elections is an indication not only of the dominance of national parties over European parties, but also of the attachment of national electorates to domestic politics. This in turn reflects an unevenly developed sense of political identity (Lord, 1998: 126). People feel a much stronger sense

of national identity than they do of European identity.

While there are those who argue that the answer is to build a sense of European identity on the basis of a common cultural inheritance, others are sceptical, arguing that European history contains as many things that divide nations as potentially unite them. There is even a view that the nation state represents the 'final equilibrium' in identity formation. It is the product of a unique historical development that is not replicable. The circumstances in which national identity emerged have now passed. While nations continue to confer a sense of identity on individuals, national identity is a declining element of individual identity in the contemporary world. Nations have been in existence so long that they are capable of attracting loyalty long after the conditions that produced the original grant of loyalty have disappeared (Beetham and Lord, 1998: 37). New state-like organizations have little chance of attracting such loyalty; indeed, if European nation-states did not exist, it might be impossible to invent them.

The very fact that states do exist, and that they incorporate key institutions by which individual identities are reproduced such as education, language, and news media, means that,

When attempts have been made to create a European political arena, notably with direct elections to the European Parliament, it is the Euro-politicians who have had to adapt to compartmentalized national debates and identities, rather than the other way round. (Beetham and Lord, 1998: 37)

National parliaments are perceived as more legitimate than the EP, and they can help to close the deficit by being allowed to exercise a stronger scrutiny of European legislation. However, they cannot alone fill the democratic deficit. Besides the argument rehearsed earlier, that QMV in the Council of Ministers means that ultimately national parliaments cannot prevent measures being passed which they dislike, Lord (1998: 125–6) pointed out other barriers.

1. The workload of national parliaments tends to crowd out effective scrutiny of European developments.

2. There is a problem about the level of expertise

that national parliaments can muster on European matters, and indeed about the amount of information to which they can gain access without it being controlled and filtered by national governments.

3. There is a lack of congruence between action at the European level and control at the national level. No one national parliament could bring the whole of the EU leadership to account.

The solution that many observers see to this dilemma is for closer co-operation to take place between national parliaments and the EP. The EP can gain democratic legitimacy by operating as the partner of the national parliaments; and the national parliaments can gain access to expertise and information that will allow them to perform their scrutiny function more effectively. Some such solution is being pursued through the Conference of European Affairs Committees of the Parliaments of the European Union (COSAC). This body, which has been meeting since November 1989, brings together representatives of all the national parliaments' European Affairs Committees and representatives of the EP. In the Treaty of Amsterdam the role of the COSAC was recognized for the first time in the Treaty by the adoption of a Protocol on the role of the national parliaments.

Conclusion

The themes of the book that are brought out in this chapter are particularly those concerned with the supranational or intergovernmental nature of the EU, and with the democratic and legitimacy deficits of the EU.

The issue of the nature of the EU as an organization is clearly affected by the view that is taken of the effective influence of the EP. If it is accepted that the successive changes in its formal role have made it a co-legislator with the Council of Ministers, then the view that the EU is no more than an intergovernmental organization cannot be sustained. There is no other such organization where the member states have to share decision-making with a directly-elected institution. This is true whether or not the formal role translates into effective influence. It can be dismissed as no more than an appearance of supranationalism, though, if there is no real power attached to the role.

On legitimacy, the main reason why the powers of the EP have been extended has been in response to the argument that this would help to close the democratic deficit, and therefore the legitimacy deficit of the EU. The evidence does not indicate that much has been achieved in that direction. There are clear limits to the legitimacy of the EP's democratic mandate which may only be eased with the development of a stronger sense of European identity among EU citizens. For now, the best prospect of reducing the democratic deficit appears to lie in closer working relations between the EP and national parliaments.

In other respects, though, the EP may be helping to close the legitimacy deficit. Its strong line towards the management failings of the Commission, culminating in what was effectively the forced resignation of the Santer Commission, may be helping to convince European publics that the efficiency issue is being addressed. Also the role of the EP as an alternative point of access to the policy-making process for interests that feel excluded elsewhere by the domination of business interests could help to build a sense of European identity among such groups in the longer term.

KEY POINTS

The struggle for power

- Lodge (1990*a*) identified a two-pronged strategy by the EP to get its powers increased.

- The *minimalist* strategy involves making the greatest use of existing powers and seeking to stretch the definition of these powers. In this strategy, the EP has an ally in the ECJ.

- The *maximalist* strategy pursues treaty amendments and supplanting old treaties by a new one.

Effective influence

- The increase in the EP's formal powers does not necessarily mean an increase in its effective influence.

- Tsebelis and Garrett argued that, contrary to popular belief, co-decision actually weakened the influence of the EP over EC legislation.

- Critics of this argument suggested that it underestimated the importance of the informal powers of the EP in the inter-institutional bargaining process.

The quality and independence of MEPs

- Research has suggested that being an MEP is increasingly attractive to ambitious politicians and that this trend is likely to continue as the EP's influence grows.

- The lack of a European-level career structure acts as an obstacle to MEPs acting independently of their national parties.

Party groups

- MEPs sit in transnational party groups, which can contain within them a wide variety of ideological positions.

- Different national perspectives and pressures from national parties can lead to divergent voting behaviour within transnational party groups.

- The weakness of European-level party groups relative to national parties undermines the effectiveness and independence of the EP.

Direct elections

- The first direct elections to the EP took place in June 1979.

- Turn-out for elections to the EP is lower than for national elections and they are fought primarily on domestic issues.

- The electorate in all member states tends to vote as in European elections as it does in second-order national elections. The elections are seen as a chance to protest against an unpopular government.

- This makes it likely that the political complexion of the EP will tend to be different from that of the Council.

- This in turn makes it less likely that the governments of the member states will be willing to grant further increases in power to the EP.

The democratic deficit

- Supporters of the EP argue that increasing its powers is the most effective way of closing the democratic deficit in the EU.

- This argument is undermined by low turn-outs for EP elections and the fact that they are fought primarily on domestic issues.

- One solution to this problem may lie in greater co-operation between the EP and national parliaments.

QUESTIONS

1 How has the EP achieved increases in its formal powers?

2 What is the argument for the view that the EP has less influence on legislation under co-decision than under co-operation? How valid is it?

3 What are the challenges to the effectiveness of transnational party groups?

4 Why do elections to the EP have relatively low status within member states?

5 Does the EP have sufficient legitimacy to justify a further increase in its powers?

FURTHER READING

For general guides to the EP see R. Corbett, F. Jacobs, and M. Shackleton, *The European Parliament* (London: Catermill, 3rd edn. 1995), and M. Westlake, *The European Parliament: A Modern Guide* (London: Pinter, 1994). A more focused recent study is J. Smith, *Europe's Elected Parliament* (Sheffield: Sheffield University Press/University Association for Contemporary European Studies, 1999). Among the many shorter pieces that have been published on the EP, some of the most perceptive are by Juliet Lodge, 'Ten Years of an Elected Parliament', in Lodge (ed.), *The 1989 Election of the European Parliament* (Basingstoke and London, 1990), 1–36, and 'The European Parliament and the Authority-Democracy Crisis', in P.-H. Laurent (ed.), *To Maastricht and Beyond* (spec. edn. of *The Annals of the American Academy of Political and Social Science*, Jan. 1994), 69–83.

On the wider issues of the democratic deficit there are two excellent, short books that complement each other nicely: D. Beetham and C. Lord, *Democracy and the European Union* (London and New York: Longman, 1998) and C. Lord, *Democracy in the European Union* (Sheffield: Sheffield Academic Press/University Association for Contemporary European Studies, 1998).

On the political parties, the most impressive survey is S. Hix and C. Lord, *Political Parties in the European Union* (Basingstoke and London: Macmillan, 1997).

22 The European Court of Justice

SUMMARY

The European Court of Justice (ECJ) makes binding decisions on disputes over Treaty provisions or secondary legislation. It therefore plays an essential role in the developing EU. There is consensus on the need for the ECJ to exist as an authoritative interpreter of both the Treaties and the secondary legislation (directives, regulations) put in place by member states; but in carrying out this task, it has been criticized for stepping beyond its legal role into the realm of politics. Specifically, it has been accused of generally ruling in favour of integrationist solutions to disputes. This has provoked hostility from member states who see their national sovereignty being undermined by Court rulings. In the period after the Maastricht ratification crisis, the ECJ was subjected to increased criticism from member states for its radical jurisprudence. The British and German governments were at the forefront of this criticism. Yet while the 1990s may have seen some questions raised about the Court's influence, its centrality to the process of European integration remains intact.

Introduction

Everything written on this subject begins with a warning not to confuse the ECJ with the European Court of Human Rights (ECHR). The warning is very necessary, as even serious newspapers and media routinely confuse the two. The ECJ is an integral institution of the EU. It is the final arbiter in disputes about the interpretation of the EU Treaties, or secondary legislation based on the Treaties. The ECHR is not part of the EU. It is an institution under the auspices of the Council of Europe, and is concerned solely with cases brought under the European Convention on Human Rights. Our concern here is exclusively with the ECJ.

The structure of the ECJ is outlined in Box 22.1 (p. 275) and its functions in Box 22.2 (p. 276). In 1989 a Court of First Instance was created to help the ECJ with the sheer volume of business that it had to get through. It structure and functions are outlined in Box 22.3 (p. 277).

Judges are usually thought of as conservative. Not so these judges. It has been argued that the ECJ has done more than any other institution to advance European integration (Freestone, 1983: 43). Its approach has been heavily criticized by some commentators as stepping beyond the bounds of legal interpretation to become political (Ramussen, 1986; Smith, 1990). Perhaps this lack of conservatism is because many of the members of the ECJ are not judges by profession. The Treaties require the appointment of people 'whose independence is beyond doubt and who possess the qualifications required for appointment to the highest judicial offices in their respective countries or are juriconsults of recognised competence' (Article 223, formerly 167). Many of the appointees have been academics rather than professional lawyers. Whatever

> ## Box 22.1 **The structure of the ECJ**
>
> - The Court of Justice comprises 15 judges and 9 advocates general.
>
> - It meets in Luxembourg.
>
> - The judges and advocates general are appointed by common accord of the governments of the member states and hold office for a renewable term of six years. They are chosen from jurists whose independence is beyond doubt and who are of recognized competence.
>
> - The judges select one of their number to be President of the Court for a renewable term of three years. The President directs the work of the Court and presides at hearings and deliberations.
>
> - The advocates general assist the Court in its task. They deliver legal opinions on the cases brought before the Court.
>
> *Source*: ECJ web site: http://curia.eu.int/en/pres/co.htm)

the reasons, the ECJ has followed a radical jurisprudence which has involved it in consistently reaching decisions that have advanced the process of European integration. It has done this both in judgments on the proper powers of the institutions and in Article 234 (formerly 177) referrals from national courts seeking clarification of points of EC law.

This chapter looks at some of the main rulings of the ECJ and examines their significance. It first considers rulings on the powers of the institutions, then judgments on issues of EC law made in response to

Box 22.2 Functions of the ECJ

It is the responsibility of the Court to ensure that the law is observed in the interpretation and application of the Treaties establishing the European Communities and of the provisions laid down by the competent Community institutions.

To enable it to carry out that task, the Court has wide jurisdiction to hear various types of action and to give preliminary rulings. The types of action it may hear are:

Proceedings for failure to fulfil an obligation.
A member state may be taken to the Court by the Commission or by another member state for failing to act to meet its obligations under the Treaties or EC secondary legislation. If the Court finds against the state so charged, it must comply without delay. If it fails to do so, it may be taken back to the Court and a fine imposed on it.

Proceedings for annulment
A member state, the Council, the Commission and, in certain circumstances, the Parliament, may apply to the Court of Justice for the annulment of all or part of an item of Community legislation, and individuals may seek the annulment of a legal measure which is of direct and individual concern to them.

Proceedings for failure to act
The Court may review the legality of a failure to act by a Community institution, and penalize silence or inaction.

Actions for damages
In an action for damages, the Court rules on the liability of the Community for damage caused by its institutions or servants in the performance of their duties.

Appeals
The Court may hear appeals, on points of law only, against judgments given by the Court of First Instance in cases within its jurisdiction.

Preliminary rulings are discussed at length below (pp. 279–82).

Source: ECJ web site: http://curia.eu.int/en/pres/comp.htm)

---

questions referred to the ECJ by national courts. Its relationship with national courts has been crucial to the legitimacy of the ECJ's judgments, and the chapter examines this relationship before looking at the reaction of national politicians to the radical jurisprudence of the ECJ.

ECJ rulings on the powers of the institutions

The biggest beneficiary of the ECJ's distinctive approach to institutional relations has been the EP. In a series of judgments the ECJ has interpreted the powers of the EP in an expansive manner. The key cases, which are considered here, were:

- Roquette v. Council (1980) (the 'Isoglucose' case) Case 138/79.

- Parti Écologiste, 'Les Verts' v. Parliament (1986). Case 294/83.

- European Parliament v. Council (1988) (the Comitology case). Case 302/87.

- European Parliament v. Council (1990) (the Chernobyl case). Case C-70/88.

The Isoglucose Case (1980)

In March 1979 the Commission submitted to the EP a draft regulation on fixing quotas for the production of isoglucose, to take effect from the beginning of July. The draft regulation went to the EP's Committee on Agriculture, which reported to the May plenary session of the EP. However, the plenary rejected the report of the Committee that contained an opinion on the regulation. This effectively meant that the quotas could not be introduced at the beginning of July (1979 was an election year for the EP, so there was no June plenary). In the meantime, the Council had considered the draft regulation and agreed to adopt it. Faced with a possible delay of four months or more, the Commission acted on the approval of the Council and published the directive in the Official Journal.

Subsequently, an individual who was directly affected by the directive brought a case to the ECJ under Article 173 (now Article 230) (Box 22.4, p. 277), claiming that the Council and Commission had acted beyond their powers by adopting the directive without having received the opinion of the EP. The Court could have decided that the EP had been consulted, and the fact that it had been unable to deliver an opinion in time for the regulation to take effect at the date planned was its own fault. In other words, it could have decided that 'consultation' meant submitting the proposal a reasonable time before a decision was needed. Instead it upheld the complaint, choosing to interpret 'consult' to mean that the formal opinion of the EP had to be delivered before the Council could act.

In its judgement, the Court insisted that the EP had a duty to give an opinion within a reasonable length of time, without defining what would be considered reasonable. Thus, the judgment did not give the EP an effective power to veto legislation under the consultation procedure, but it did give it a significant power to delay legislation by holding back on formally delivering its opinion. (This case is also discussed in Ch. 18, p. 223; Ch. 21, Box 21.5, p. 262.)

Les Verts v. European Parliament

In 1984 the French Green Party (*Les Verts*) stood candidates for election to the EP for the first time. In doing so it discovered that those of its opponents that had been represented in the previous Parliament had been voted funds by the EP to defray their election expenses. Subsequently the Greens brought a case to the ECJ under Article 173 claiming that the EP had acted beyond its powers in effectively supporting the election of existing parties at the expense of new parties.

The immediate issue here was whether any such case could be brought to the Court. Article 173 explicitly said:

The Court of Justice shall review the legality of acts of the Council and the Commission.

There was no mention of the ECJ reviewing the legality of acts of the EP. The Court nevertheless accepted the case on the grounds that, although the Treaty did not explicitly make the actions of the EP subject to judicial review, this omission was not in keeping with the spirit of the Treaty.

The Court argued, without any real evidence to support the assertion, that the EP must have been omitted from Article 173 because when the Treaty was signed the EP had no real powers. Subsequently it had acquired powers that would normally be subject to judicial review. These included the powers that were contested in this case, and as these *should* be subject to judicial review, the Court would review them.

In this judgment the ECJ increased its own powers by a unilateral reinterpretation, some would even say rewriting, of the Treaty. Although apparently acting in a way that would restrict the powers of the EP, the judgment also took the first step towards giving the EP a legal personality that it had not been granted by the member states when they signed the Treaty. Once it had been decided that the EP could be a defendant in an Article 173 hearing, it seemed logical that it should also be accorded the right to be a plaintiff; that is, that it be allowed to bring cases to the Court under the same Article. The Court was given the opportunity to take this step in the next case reviewed below.

Parliament v. Council (The Comitology Case) (1990)

This case was brought by the EP under article 175 (now 232), which said:

Should the Council or the Commission, in infringement of this Treaty, fail to act, the Member States, and the other institutions of the Community may bring an action before the Court of Justice to have the infringement established.

The EP argued successfully that it was allowed to bring a case under this Article because it was one of the 'other institutions of the Community'. But it also argued that it should be allowed to bring a case under Article 173 if the issue was one of another institution acting beyond its powers, rather than of not acting at all. The EP argued that it was illogical for it to be allowed to bring a case under 175, but not under 173. It also quoted the Court's judgment in *Les Verts* that the EP could be a defendant under Article 173, and argued that if it could be a defendant it was illogical that it should not be allowed to be a plaintiff.

Surprisingly, the Court rejected the EP's arguments. It said that there was no logical link between the circumstances outlined; that the EP could normally rely on the Commission to take up a case under Article 173 on its behalf; and that the member states had recently had the opportunity to grant this right explicitly to the EP in the SEA and had declined to do so, despite a submission from the Commission to the IGC explicitly recommending this revision. However, within a short period of time the Court appeared to have a change of heart on the issue.

European Parliament v. Council (The Chernobyl Case) (1990)

In this case, the EP applied to the Court for a review of the procedure adopted for agreeing a regulation on public health. This regulation set limits for the permissible radioactive contamination of food that could be sold for public consumption following the Chernobyl disaster (Box 22.5, p. 279). The Commission proposed the regulation under Article 31 of the Euratom Treaty, which dealt with basic standards for

Box 22.5 Chernobyl

On 26 April 1986 a major accident occurred at the Chernobyl nuclear power station in Ukraine. Radioactive pollution extended over a vast geographical area. Contamination was detected in the food chain as far west as Ireland. The EC introduced standardized rules on the permissible levels of radioactive contamination, and provided financial support for the farmers worst affected.

the protection of the health of the general public arising from radiation. Proposed legislation under this Article was subject to the consultation procedure. The EP maintained that the matter was a single market issue, and therefore should have been introduced under Article 100A of the EEC Treaty, as revised by the SEA. This would have brought it under the co-operation procedure, and given the EP a second reading. The EP wished to challenge the treaty base under which the regulation was adopted, but first had to establish that its case was admissible because it was invoking Article 173.

Although the Court's decision in the *Comitology* case was surprising, its decision in this case, coming so soon after, was even more surprising. Here, the

Court decided that the EP could bring the case after all, despite what it had said in its *Comitology* judgment. Its reasoning was that the job of the Court was to preserve the institutional balance. In the *Comitology* judgment the Court had asserted that the Commission could normally be relied upon to protect the prerogatives of the EP where Parliament required an Article 173 case to be brought. However, in this instance the dispute over the treaty base pitted the Commission against the EP. Therefore in this, and similarly limited circumstances, the EP had to be granted the right to be a plaintiff in an Article 173 case. The other argument that had appeared in the *Comitology* judgment, that the member states had only recently declined to grant this power explicitly to the EP, now disappeared from view. A sceptic commenting on the *Chernobyl* judgment, soon after it appeared, said:

The fundamental flaw in this decision is of course the Court's failure to give effect to the wholly unambiguous provision of Article 173 . . . the judgement rests on the unsatisfactory concept of 'institutional balance', which is not to be found, still less defined, in the Treaties. Moreover, the Court's own failure to define the notion adequately means that, should it decide in future cases that the prerogatives of the Commission or the Parliament in other areas are not sufficiently safeguarded, the requirement of 'institutional balance' may be used to justify providing a remedy   (Smith, 1990: 20).

ECJ rulings on the nature of EC law

If the jurisprudence of the ECJ has pushed back the limits of the Treaty in judgments based on Article 173 cases, it has been even more radical in its judgments on Article 177 (now Article 234) referrals from national courts (Box 22.6, p. 280). In a number of controversial judgments the Court laid out principles of EC law that took it beyond the limits that the member states would like to put on it. The following cases were particularly important:

- Van Gend en Loos (1963). Case 26/62.

- Costa v. ENEL (1964). Case 6/64.

- Van Duyn v. Home Office (1974). Case 41/74.

- R. v. Secretary of State for Transport, ex parte Factortame (1991). Case C-221/89.

- Francovich v. Italy (1991). Cases C-6, 9/90.

Van Gend en Loos (1963)

In this early case, the Court first asserted the principle that EC law conferred rights on individuals as well as on member states. This was the principle of 'direct effect', which has no explicit authority in the Treaties, and is a dramatic departure from international law. Under international law, treaties are

> ### Box 22.6 Article 234 (formerly Article 177)
>
> The Court of Justice shall have jurisdiction to give preliminary rulings concerning:
>
> (a) the interpretation of this Treaty;
>
> (b) the validity and interpretation of acts of the institutions of the Community and of the ECB;
>
> (c) the interpretation of the statutes of bodies established by an act of the Council, where those statutes so provide.
>
> Where such a question is raised before any court or tribunal of a Member State, that court or tribunal may, if it considers that a decision on the question is necessary to enable it to give judgment, request the Court of Justice to give a ruling thereon.
>
> Where any such question is raised in a case pending before a court or tribunal of a Member State against whose decisions there is no judicial remedy under national law, that court or tribunal shall bring the matter before the Court of Justice.

held to impose obligations on the states that sign and ratify them, but neither to confer rights nor impose obligations directly on individual citizens.

A Dutch company claimed that its rights under the EC Treaty had been breached by the Dutch government, which had levied a higher rate of duty on formaldehyde after the date on which it was agreed in the EEC Treaty that there would be no increase in internal EEC tariffs. The Dutch government maintained that the company had no power to claim a right deriving from an international treaty. The Court disagreed. It maintained that a new legal order had come into existence with the signing of the Treaty, in which citizens could claim rights against their governments. The ruling of the Court contained the following famous phrase:

the Community constitutes a new legal order of international law for the benefit of which the states have limited their sovereign rights, albeit within limited fields, and the subjects of which comprise not only member states but also their nationals. Community law therefore not only imposes obligations on individuals but is also intended to confer upon them rights that become part of their legal heritage. (Quoted in Kuper, 1998: 5)

The full significance of this doctrine only became apparent years later.

Costa v. ENEL (1964)

In this case, the year after *Van Gend en Loos*, the Court first asserted the supremacy of EC law over national law. Again there was no explicit authority for this in the Treaty. An Italian court referred the case to the ECJ, but the point of law at issue was very pertinent to the United Kingdom, because the Italian constitution, while it is a written constitution, was originally modelled on British practice and principles. This is mentioned to clarify that the principle was established well before Britain became a member of the EC, and should have been known to the British government when it made its second and third applications.

Under both Italian and British law, Parliament is sovereign (strictly speaking in Britain it is the Queen in Parliament). This means that statute law (that is, a written law that has been passed by Parliament) takes precedence over all other forms of law. Where statutes come into conflict, the principle that prevails is '*lex posterior priori derogat*': the later law overrides the earlier. This is necessary if the democratic principle that no Parliament can bind its successor is to be observed.

In the Italian case, the issue was whether an Act of the Italian Parliament, passed later in time than the Act that embodied an EC directive into Italian law, took precedence over the earlier EC law. The Court said it did not, because if there was to be a single body of EC law throughout the Community, it could not be subject to interpretation in each member state in the light of the individual laws of that state. This was a perfectly logical position, but it did directly conflict with both Italian and British constitutional principles.

Van Duyn v. Home Office (1974)

A Dutch national who had been debarred from entering Britain because she was a member of the Church of Scientology, which the British Home Office considered to be a socially undesirable organization, brought a case in the English courts challenging the ruling. This case was brought on the grounds that Article 48 of the EEC Treaty committed the member states to allow free movement of workers, and that the British government had accepted Directive 64/221 which implemented this Treaty provision as part of the *acquis communautaire* when it joined the EC. The Court was asked to decide whether rights could be acquired directly in this way from a directive that had not yet been incorporated into national law.

The extension of the principle of direct effect to directives seemed unlikely because Article 189 (now Article 249) made a very clear distinction between a regulation, which 'shall be binding in its entirety and directly applicable in all Member States', and a directive, which 'shall be binding, as to the result to be achieved, upon each Member State . . . but shall leave to the national authorities the choice of form and methods'.

Despite this apparently clear distinction between an instrument that was directly applicable and one that was not, the Court still decided that the directive did have direct effect. Although the relevant directive had not yet been explicitly incorporated into English law, the Court maintained that the defendant could still quote it as grounds for her opposition to the British government's position.

Factortame (1990)

This was the highly-publicized case in which Spanish fishermen had been purchasing British fishing vessels, and with them the quotas that the boats had been allocated to catch fish under the Common Fisheries Policy of the EC. In effect the Spanish fishermen had been catching fish on the British quota and landing it in Spain. The British government had responded by passing the 1988 Merchant Shipping Act, which required 75 per cent of the shareholders and directors of a company to be British in order for the company to be able to register as British. The Spanish fishermen claimed that this was a breach of their rights as EC citizens to be given equal treatment with other EC citizens.

The Court first granted an injunction to the Spanish fishermen, which the government agreed that the Law Lords could instruct British courts to recognize. This was the first time that British courts had been allowed to set aside an Act of Parliament. The ECJ subsequently agreed with the Spanish fishermen that the Merchant Shipping Act was in breach of EC law on the equal treatment of citizens, thus overturning the British Merchant Shipping Act. Each of these steps caused a furore in the British Parliament, both because of what was seen as the manifest unfairness of allowing Spanish fishermen to take fish on the British quota, but also because of the constitutional implications. Here was a stark example of the ECJ overruling an Act of Parliament. Although no new principles were enunciated by the Court, the full impact of its radical jurisprudence only really came home to many British parliamentarians with this case.

Francovich v. Italy (1991)

Before this case arose, the Italian government had already been taken to the ECJ by the Commission and charged with not incorporating into Italian law a directive that gave redundant workers the right to compensation, and made such compensation the first claim against the assets of a bankrupt employer. It had still not been incorporated when workers for a bankrupt Italian company took a case to court in Italy because they had received no compensation for redundancy. On an Article 177 referral, the advocate-general argued that the Italian government should be liable for damages because it had already been found in breach of its obligations. The full Court went further. It said that the fact that the Italian government had been taken to the Court previously was irrelevant. Any government that did not properly implement EC law was liable to damages claims by its own citizens.

Subsequently the Court used the same principle, that a government that did not properly implement EC law was liable to damages claims, to decide that the Spanish fishermen in the *Factortame* case were eligible for compensation from the British government for loss of earnings during the period when they were prevented from catching fish on the British quota. It also decided, in another case (*Brasserie du Pêcheur*), that a French brewery could claim damages from the German government for the period when the German government enforced its beer purity laws, which the Court had subsequently ruled to be an illegal barrier to trade. So in these two cases, the liability of a government that had not properly applied a directive to be sued for damages was extended beyond its own citizens to cover other citizens of the EU.

The European Court and national courts

The evidence that the ECJ has been instrumental in considerably advancing the cause of European integration is convincing. However, the question then arises of how the Court is able to get away with its radical jurisprudence. For its legal doctrines to be effective they have to be accepted by national courts. This seems to have happened. By making Article 177/234 references, national courts have been the main accomplices of the ECJ in its 'constitutionalization' of the Treaties. Why has this collaboration taken place?

Burley and Mattli (1993) suggested that a sort of legal neofunctionalism was at work. Spillover was implicit in the concept of EC law itself, but it was cultivated by the ECJ to give the most integrationist interpretation possible to the existing laws. Other actors—national courts, private individuals—fed the process simply by pursuing their own self-interest in a rational manner within the changed context: e.g. individuals did so by bringing cases against their own governments under European law when they felt that their rights had been breached.

Alter (1996) went further, arguing that the Article 177 procedure actually empowered lower national courts. They were used to having their judgments overturned on appeal by higher national courts, but by making Article 177 references they could directly influence the evolution of national legal principles. Higher courts might be able to overturn the substance of their judgments, but they were unable to challenge the points of European law on which they were based.

The ECJ has also been careful always to get the national courts on its side by proceeding in what Mancini (1991: 185) described as a 'courteously didactic' manner. The judges:

developed a style that may be drab and repetitive but explains as well as declares the law, and they showed unlimited patience vis-à-vis the national judges, reformulating questions couched in imprecise terms or extracting from the documents concerning the main proceedings the elements of Community law that needed to be interpreted with regard to the subject matter of the dispute. (Mancini, 1991: 185)

In this way the European judges won the confidence of their national colleagues. Those who presided over even the lowest courts knew that they would receive sympathetic treatment if they made an Article 177 referral, and were therefore more inclined to do so.

Although this may seem surprising given the earlier comments about the radicalism of their judgments, another technique used by the European judges was to proceed cautiously.

A common tactic is to introduce a new doctrine gradually: in the first case that comes before it, the Court will establish the doctrine as a general principle, but suggest that it is subject to various qualifications; the Court may even find some reason why it should not be applied to the particular facts of the case. The principle, however, is now established. If there are not too many protests, it will be re-affirmed in later cases; the qualifications can then be whittled away and the full extent of the doctrine revealed (Hartley, 1994:88)

The alliance forged between the ECJ and lower national courts is not the whole of the story, though. The reception of the jurisprudence of the ECJ by national supreme courts has been less enthusiastic. Problems have arisen with the reception of the judgments of the ECJ by the Italian, French, British, and German supreme courts (Kuper, 1998: 19–27). In no case has a national supreme court attempted to negate a decision of the ECJ. Were one to do so it would cause a constitutional crisis. In several cases, though, the national supreme court has disagreed with the reasoning of the ECJ, while finding alternative lines of legal reasoning to arrive at the same substantive decision. In particular, the doctrine of the supremacy of EC law over national law has not been universally accepted by member states.

The British Law Lords have always preferred to give primacy to EC law on the basis that the British Parliament must be presumed to want its legislation to be compatible with EC law, unless it says otherwise, so that any incompatibility must be accidental and unintended. This allows the constitutional principle of the sovereignty of Parliament to be preserved in principle. It also means that should a future British Parliament explicitly express its view that a statute should override EC law, the British courts could be expected to apply the statute and not the EC law. This is the exact opposite of the outcome that would be expected under the constitutional principle that the ECJ favours, of the supremacy of EC law.

The strongest challenge to the doctrines of the ECJ in this respect has come from the German Constitutional Court. The first disagreement between the two courts was over the *Internationale Handelsgesellschaft* case of 1970 (Case 11/70). In this case a German import–export firm appealed against having to forfeit a deposit that it had made to the Commission in order to obtain an export licence for maize groats. It had been unable to complete the contract, but claimed that the loss of the deposit was a breach of its constitutional right to engage in trade under the German Basic Law. The ECJ applied its doctrine of supremacy of EC law, and insisted that it made no difference that this issue affected one of the fundamental individual rights that the German constitution guaranteed. The German Constitutional Court dissented from this view on the grounds that the EC itself had no provision for the protection of individual rights, and therefore the application of EC law potentially undermined the fundamental rights of citizens. The ECJ accepted that there was a problem here, but proposed to solve it by ensuring that respect for those individual rights that were the common principles of national constitutions would be applied in its judgments. In effect the ECJ set about writing a bill of rights into the constitution of the EC, with no support at all from the Treaties.

While this radical solution helped to put the dispute into abeyance, the principle at issue was not resolved. It came to a head again in 1993 when Manfred Brunner, a German citizen and a former Commission official, brought a case to the German Constitutional Court challenging the legality of the TEU, and specifically the commitment made therein to the single currency. The German Court decided that the TEU was not unconstitutional, but clearly stated the principle that every EC law had to be either implicitly or explicitly authorized by national parliaments. If there were any doubt about whether a specific law had been so authorized, it was the prerogative of the national constitutional court to adjudicate. Paul Kirchoff, a member of the German Constitutional Court who was also a professor of law, spelled out the reasoning behind the judgment more fully. He argued that in a sovereign state the people (*Volk*) recognized themselves as a single community, bound together by historic ties. To give expression to this sense of community, and to protect the community, the people were prepared to delegate the power to make decisions which affected their lives to the state. However, there was no such entity as a European people. The EU was not and could not be a sovereign entity in the same way as a state. Any authority it had flowed from the membership of states, not directly from the people. It followed that the states must remain the masters of the Treaties, and that all transfers of authority from the state to the EU must be approved by the representatives of the people, which meant the national parliaments.

Political reactions to the radical jurisprudence of the ECJ

The judgment of the German Constitutional Court in the Brunner case typifies what was something of a backlash against the process of European integration generally, and against the ECJ more particularly in the 1990s. The difficulties that were encountered in several member states in getting ratification of the TEU reinforced a tendency that had already been apparent in the inclusion in that Treaty of clauses on subsidiarity (Box 22.7, p. 284). The desire to limit the transfer of competencies from member states to the EU institutions was not confined to Britain, although John Major's government pressed the case for subsidiarity to be written into the Treaty. The French government actually pressed for the whole *acquis communautaire* to be reviewed in the light of subsidiarity. The importance of this step should not be underestimated.

The formal introduction by the Maastricht Treaty (TEU) of subsidiarity as a general principle into EC . . . law both symbolized and contributed to a gradual change in the political and legal culture of the European Community. If much of the Community's legal activity before the 1990s reflected a self-conscious teleology of integration, the teleology of subsidiarity suggests a rather different future. (de Búrca, 1998: 218)

As well as the general change of mood away from pro-integration sentiments, the implications of the Court's judgments in the *Francovich*, *Factortame*, and *Brasserie du Pêcheur* cases led the British and German governments to sponsor a proposal to the 1996 IGC that the right to damages should only apply where there was 'grave and manifest disregard of their obligations' by governments; that is, not where governments believed in good faith that they were abiding by EC law and applying the relevant directives. The Court, not surprisingly, did not want to get into having to make these decisions, which are far from clear-cut.

It should be noted at this point that even the attitude of the British Conservative government to the Court was not uniformly hostile. The 1996 White Paper (HMSO, 1996) said:

The Government is committed to a strong, independent Court without which it would be impossible to ensure even

---

Box 22.7 Subsidiarity

Subsidiarity is an ambiguous concept. It is interpreted by the British government to mean that action should not be taken at the EU level unless it can be shown that the objectives of the action can be better achieved at that level than at the national level. This interpretation appears to be supported by the wording of Article 5 (formerly 3b) of the TEC.

The German government interprets it more generally to mean that decisions should be taken at the lowest level of government at which they can be made effective. This implies a commitment to internal devolution of power within states. This interpretation appears to be supported by the wording of Article 1 (formerly A) of the TEU.

Article 5 (formerly Article 3b) of the TEC

In areas which do not fall within its exclusive competence, the Community shall take action, in accordance with the principle of subsidiarity, only if and insofar as the objectives of the proposed action cannot be sufficiently achieved by the Member States and can therefore, by reason of the scale or effects of the proposed action, be better achieved by the Community.

Article 1 (formerly Article A) of the TEU

This Treaty marks a new stage in the process of creating an ever closer union among the peoples of Europe, in which decisions are taken as closely as possible to the citizen.

application of Community law, and to prevent the abuse of power by the Community institutions. . . . The ECJ safeguards all Member States by ensuring that partners meet their Community obligations.

This moderate approach was disliked, though, by Eurosceptic backbench Conservative MPs, sixty-six of whom had voted in April 1995 for the United Kingdom to be exempt from ECJ rulings.

A sign that not only the British government was finding it difficult to live with the rulings of the Court came in April 1998 when the German government announced that it would ignore a ruling by the ECJ that citizens could 'shop around' in all member states for health care, and then charge the cost to national health insurance schemes. The cost implications of such an arrangement were clearly unacceptable. However, more such issues are likely to be raised in the future, as member states have to come to terms with the full implications of the single market rules to which they signed up in the SEA.

Conclusion

This review of the role of the ECJ particularly raises two of the themes that run through the book. The first, is the theme that has been most prominent in the chapters on the institutions: the intergovernmental-supranational debate about the nature of the EU. A second theme is that of legitimacy.

If the role of the ECJ is approached in the same way as the discussion in Chapter 19 (see pp. 236–8) about role of the Commission, that is, whether it is an agent of the member states or an autonomous actor in its own right, there is little doubt that the judgments of the Court have gone beyond what the governments of the member states were expecting. The radical jurisprudence of the Court may represent the logical consequences of the actions of the member states, but it is not a logic that was thought through by their governments, nor is it always welcome to them. In this sense the ECJ has proved itself to be an autonomous actor in the process of European integration.

As intergovernmentalists would point out, the member states can rescind those powers that they have given to the Court; but this is not easy, because without an independent and authoritative interpreter of the law, all the rules put in place by the Treaties and by EC secondary legislation would be subject to different interpretation by different parties. There has to be an authoritative source of interpretation, and it has to be unquestionably independent. Some parties to any dispute will not like some of the decisions of the independent arbitrator, but they will abide by them rather than see the collapse of the system from which they benefit generally. The 'ratchet effect' also makes it difficult to recall powers once delegated. Treaty changes require unanimity, and if even one member state is happy with the thrust of the ECJ's decisions, it will not be possible to reduce its powers because its one supporter has a veto on any attempt to do so.

There is no question that the ECJ has the formal right to reach the decisions that it does. Whether those decisions are accepted as legitimate is another matter. Most decisions of the Court have not impinged on the consciousness of national politicians or members of the public. They have received legitimacy through being accepted by national courts, especially those lower down the legal hierarchy. When ECJ judgments have come to the attention of national politicians, there has sometimes been a strong negative reaction, suggesting that the legitimacy of the Court's doctrines does not extend beyond the national courts and professional judges. The strength of reaction in Britain to the *Factortame* judgment is indicative of this.

The highest courts in the member states have been less comfortable than have lower courts with the judgments of the ECJ, which have often raised difficult constitutional issues. Essentially the ECJ has been in the business of forging a new constitution for the EU from the raw material of the Treaties. It has had plenty of scope to impose its own interpretation of what that constitution should look like, because treaties are not carefully-crafted legal documents: they are the outcome of diplomatic negotiations and compromises. These far-from-watertight documents leave judges plenty of space to fill in the gaps. In doing so, the ECJ has enunciated principles that conflict with some fundamental national constitutional principles. The legal conflict shows the impossibility of taking fifteen national constitutions and reconciling them with one overarching constitution. The political reaction raises again the issue of identity, which appears in the discussion of the legitimacy of the EP in Chapter 21 (pp. 269–71). National politicians and publics find it difficult to accept that decisions made by their democratically-elected national institutions can be overruled by an organization which has far less legitimacy in their eyes.

The existence of national identity, and the nonexistence of any equivalent European identity, was also the basis for the reasoning of the German Constitutional Court in the Brunner case. The implications of this for the future of the EU are far reaching. If Kirchoff's gloss on the judgment is accepted, then the EU can never move from its present ambiguous situation to become a federal entity. His argument that the states must remain the masters of the Treaties points up the relevance for practical concerns of the academic debate about the extent to which the EU has already run out of the control of the governments of the member states.

KEY POINTS

ECJ rulings on the powers of the institutions

- The EP has been the major beneficiary of the Court's radical jurisprudence.

- Although on occasions, the Court has found against an extension of the EP's legal position, it has also reversed this in subsequent judgments.

- In particular, the Court has used the principle of 'institutional balance' to extend Parliament's prerogatives.

ECJ rulings on the nature of EC law

- The ECJ has been most radical in cases referred by national courts under Article 177 (now 234).

- In early rulings, the Court stated the principles of 'direct effect'—that EC law confers rights on individuals—and the supremacy of EC over national law. Subsequent rulings confirmed these principles.

- A series of later cases also produced rulings that surprised the governments of the member states, because they imposed on them obligations to which they did not think that they had agreed.

The European Court and national courts

- A number of explanations are offered for why national courts have accepted the radical jurisprudence of the ECJ. Most point to shrewd tactics on the part of the Court. These include introducing new doctrines gradually for them to be confirmed in later judgments; explaining as well as declaring decisions; and forging alliances with lower national courts.

- Despite the advances of the ECJ, the principle of the supremacy of EC law over national law has yet to be fully accepted by national supreme courts.

Political reactions to the radical jurisprudence of the ECJ

- Unlike many courts, the ECJ has a reputation for radical jurisprudence.

- It has been criticized for stepping beyond its legal role and behaving politically in favouring judgments that advance European integration.

- Partly because of a general anti-integrationist mood in the 1990s, the ECJ was subjected to increased criticism by member states for its perceived political activism.

- The importance of the Court is not questioned, but there is division on how it should interpret its role.

QUESTIONS

1 In what ways has the ECJ acted to strengthen the position of the European Parliament?

2 What evidence is there that the ECJ acts in a political manner?

3 In what ways might EC law, as interpreted by the ECJ, come into conflict with national constitutional principles?

4 What explains the success of the ECJ in advancing the cause of European integration?

FURTHER READING

An excellent, non-technical introduction to the role of the ECJ is provided by R. Kuper, *The Politics of the European Court of Justice* (London: Kogan Page, 1998). Readers of this book who turn to that one, as they should, will recognize the debt that the present authors owe to it. Another clear non-technical introduction to the ECJ is R. Dehousse, *The European Court of Justice: The Politics of Judicial Integration* (Basingstoke and London: Macmillan, 1998).

More technical accounts of the impact of EC law, including the controversial rulings of the Court are T. C. Hartley, *The Foundations of European Community Law* (Oxford: Clarendon Press, 3rd edn. 1994), and, J. Steiner and L. Woods, *Textbook of EC Law* (London: Blackstone, 5th edn. 1996).

Well-argued cases on the political power of the ECJ are put in: K. Alter, 'The European Court's Political Power', *West European Politics* 19 (1996), 458–87; G. De Búrca, 'The Principle of Subsidiarity and the Court of Justice as a Political Actor', *Journal of Common Market Studies* 36 (1998), 217–315; J. H. H. Weiler, 'Journey to an Unknown Destination: A Retrospective and Prospective of the ECJ in the Arena of Political Integration', *Journal of Common Market Studies* 31 (1993), 133–54.

An intellectually exciting theoretical explanation for the way in which the Court has been able to get its judgments accepted is provided by A.-M. Burley and W. Mattli, 'Europe before the Court: A Political Theory of Legal Integration'. *Political Organization* 47 (1993), 41–76.

23 Organized interests

SUMMARY

Interest group activity in Brussels has increased considerably since the start of the single market programme, involving several different types of groups. Moves to institutionalize interest representation in a form that would echo the arrangements made at national level in most EU member states have not been very successful, and the system that has emerged resembles the 'pluralist' system of interest representation that is typical in the United States.

In this form of representation, there is competition for influence between groups, which take part in 'lobbying' the institutions. In this process, the better-resourced groups tend to be at an advantage, although the skilful use of strategy and tactics is also important. Attempts have been made to regulate the lobbying activity of groups, and the Commission in particular has tried to correct the imbalance in favour of well-resourced interests. The system nevertheless favours business interests over others because their resources are considerably superior.

Introduction

The term 'interest group' is used to describe a range of organizations, outside of the formal institutions, that seek to influence decision-making. They provide a link between state actors and the rest of society. For some, interest groups play an essential role in giving voice to concerns otherwise neglected by formal institutions, and are an important source of information and advice for policy-makers. For others, interest groups distort democratic decision making by giving undue weight to those social actors and organizations that have the necessary contacts, time, finance, and skill to promote their objectives.

Within the political systems of member states, interest group activity is long-established. This chapter examines the development of interest group activity at the EU level. It looks first at the general growth of interest group activity at the European level, before analysing the forms of representation open to interests, the types of groups that try to influence EU policy-making, and the strategies and resources that they bring to the task. The chapter then looks at how groups lobby the different institutions, and at attempts to regulate their activity.

The growth of interest group activity

Interest group activity aimed at EU decision makers has grown spectacularly, particularly from the launch of the single market programme in the mid-1980s. By the end of the 1990s Mazey and Richardson (1999: 105) could speak of 'a dense European lobbying system . . . which now exhibits many of the features of interest group intermediation systems long familiar in Western Europe'. Finding precise statistics on this growth is more difficult, but Commission figures suggest there are around 3,000 interest groups active in Brussels, with around 10,000 individuals involved in the lobbying industry (Greenwood, 1997: 3).

For many organized interests, the development of direct representation at the EU level is accompanied by continuing attempts to influence national governments as part of their overall strategy to shape EU policy. However, the Brussels end of the strategy is increasingly important. Factors that contribute to this include:

- the growing policy competence of the EU
- the perception of a shifting balance of institutional power in Brussels, most notably in favour of the EP
- the receptiveness of EU officials to interest group representations
- the 'snowballing' effect of groups following the lead of others so as not to risk being disadvantaged.

In line with the maxim that 'where power goes, interest groups follow', the increasing competence of EU institutions is an important reason for the rapid growth in interest group activity at the European level. Whereas in the early years the coal and steel industries and agriculture were the most affected by the setting up of the European communities, there is now scarcely any policy sector that does not have an EU dimension. The switch to QMV within the Council of Ministers for most policy sectors makes it less sensible to lobby only at the national level, because a single state no longer has a veto over legislative proposals. There has also been a perceived shift of power within the policy-making process away from the Council of Ministers to other institutions, particularly the EP. Although this is a contested interpretation (see above, Ch. 21, pp. 263–5), the perception itself is enough to encourage interest groups to feel that it is worth lobbying the other institutions.

The EU provides relatively easy access for those seeking to influence decision making, which provides, 'part of the explanation for the intensity of participation in the process by so wide a range of political and economic actors' (Wallace and Young 1997: 250). There are several advantages for policy-makers of good relations with interest groups:

Put simply, it is very difficult to make effective public policy without the *specialized expertise* which interest groups possess. Moreover, their cooperation in the *implementation* of public policy is a prime condition for implementation success. Finally, from the bureaucratic perspective, the mobilization of a constituency of *support* is vital to the long-term survival of bureaucracies.   (Mazey and Richardson, 1999: 106)

The importance of organized interests to policy-makers, particularly in the complex emerging system of the EU, means that many groups find themselves greeted by an open door when they seek discussions in Brussels.

Once groups have started to shift their activity to Brussels, a momentum builds up that carries other groups along with it. Mazey and Richardson suggested that: 'rather like bees around a honey pot, interest groups are attached to regulatory institutions in swarms. Once one set of groups begins to exploit incentives and opportunity structures at the European-level, others are bound to follow; they cannot afford to be left out, whatever the cost' (1999: 107). This last point is important. No one can be sure of the benefits of lobbying activities, so the fear of missing-out has become another motivating factor for EU-level activity. Aspinwall and Greenwood (1998: 18–19) referred to the potential costs of 'non-membership': 'it is the fear of losing out that drives membership decisions in the face of vague and ill-defined incentives, rather than the wish to take advantage of specific benefits'.

Types of interest group and forms of interest representation

A broad range of organized interests seek to influence EU policy-making through a variety of means, but the form of interest representation that has emerged at the European level has to some extent determined the types of interest groups that have emerged, rather than the other way around.

Types of interest group

Interest groups that operate in Brussels can be classified under seven headings (Mazey and Richardson, 1999: 108):

1. *European associations*, (e.g. Association of Petrochemicals Producers of Europe, Greenpeace International–European Unit);

2. *National associations*, (e.g. Confederation of British Industry, Federation of Swedish Industry);

3. *Individual firms*, (e.g. Imperial Chemical Industries, Ford Motor Company);

4. *Lobbying consultancy firms* (e.g. European Public Policy Advisers);

5. *Public bodies* (e.g. regional governments and local authorities);

6. *Ad hoc coalitions for single issues*, (e.g. European Campaign on Biotechnology Patents; Software Action Group for Europe);

7. *Organizations of experts and epistemic communities*, (e.g. European Heart Network; Federation of Veterinarians of Europe).

Each of these seven types of organization has grown in the past two decades.

Different types of organizations can represent any given set of interests at the same time. Business interests provide a good example. Business representation in Brussels takes the form of individual companies, collective national organizations (such as the Confederation of British Industry), and collective European organizations. The last category includes the Union of Industrial and Employers' Confederations (UNICE), which brings together national business associations, and the European Round Table of Industrialists (ERT), which is made up of Chief Executives of major firms. The ERT was particularly active in moves to launch the single market programme in the mid-1980s (see Ch. 25, pp. 330–1). In addition, firms individually or collectively might employ lobbying consultancy firms to advance their case, and may also become involved in single-issue campaigns.

Business interests were represented in Brussels from a very early stage in the existence of the EC. Hix (1999: 192) noted that individual firms were the most numerous type of interest represented there. Nevertheless, following the logic that activity by one set of interests stimulates competing interests into activity, there is now a wide range of groups that act as countervailing forces to business lobbying in Brussels. Trade unions, consumer groups and environmentalists are examples of this in relation to business interests, although these groups were late to the game and only really become prominent in the 1990s.

The other type of group that has exploded in numbers in Brussels is the lobbying consultancy firm. This more than any other development indicates the extent to which the form of representation has become predominantly pluralist—other forms having failed to take a firm hold within the EU system.

Forms of interest representation

Three forms of interest representation coexist in the EU:

- the full institutionalization of representation through the Economic and Social Committee (ESC);

- the semi-institutionalized 'social dialogue';

- the pluralist system based on competitive lobbying.

The ESC has its origins in the 'corporatist' institutions that were set up between the wars in Germany and France to bring together labour, management, the self-employed, and the government: the German Economic Council and the French *Conseil Economique et Social* (Box 23.1, p. 291). Similar institutions were recreated in five of the six member states after the war, Germany being the exception.

The ESC did not prove to be a particularly effective institution (Ch. 18, pp. 218–19), and when new forms of institutionalized relations between government, business, and trade unions were tried in several member states of the EC during the 1970s, attempts to replicate them at the EC level did not involve the ESC. Instead, the ministers of social affairs and economic and financial affairs organized a series of Tripartite Conferences bringing together European business and trade union organizations. These met six times in 1978 to discuss issues such as employment, inflation, wage restraint, fiscal policy, vocational training, and measures to increase productivity (Schmitter and Streeck, 1994: 177). The business groups were reluctant participants in the process, though, and by the end of 1978 the European Trade Union Confederation (ETUC) had withdrawn from the process because of lack of progress.

The idea was revived by Jacques Delors when he became President of the Commission. In 1984 he proposed the creation of a 'social space', a term that had first been used in 1981 by the French Socialist

Box 23.1 Corporatism

The term 'corporatism' comes from the Latin verb *corporare*, meaning to form into a body. The process of forming individuals into collective bodies produces corporations, which are artificial persons created by individuals, who authorize the corporation to act on their behalf.

Between the wars in Europe the idea of the 'corporate state' emerged, in which representation of the people would not be by geographical constituencies but through vocational corporations of the employers and employees in each trade and industry. It was seen as an alternative 'third way' between capitalism and Communism. In practice corporatism came to be most closely associated with the Fascist regime in Italy after 1928, and was widely imitated by other authoritarian regimes. This association discredited the term in the eyes of the Anglo-Saxon states, but the idea still held some resonance in Catholic social thought, hence its revival without the formal title of corporatism in the post-war constitutions of some west European states.

In the 1970s academics coined the term 'neo-corporatist' to describe the less formal but nevertheless institutionalized patterns of consultation on policy between governments, business, and trade unions in several leading west European states.

government of which Delors was a member. Subsequently Delors linked this phrase to the 1992 project to free the internal market. In 1985 an approach was made to both ETUC and UNICE to open a 'social dialogue'. Delors suggested that if the idea were accepted, the Commission would refrain from introducing further items of social legislation, and would instead let them emerge out of the dialogue. Initially two working parties were set up, on employment policies and on new technology and work. They met at the chateau of Val Duchesse outside Brussels and the dialogue therefore became known as the 'Val Duchesse process'.

From the outset, though, there were difficulties about the status of the discussions. UNICE insisted that they should lead to the publication of 'joint opinions', not 'agreements', and that the opinions should not lead to legislation; ETUC clearly saw the process as one that would result in legislation. The

social dialogue was incorporated into the social protocol of the Maastricht Treaty. It was agreed that where the social partners could negotiate agreement on any aspect of social legislation, that agreement would automatically be accepted by the Commission and formulated as a proposal to the Council of Ministers, with the expectation that it would become part of the social legislation of the EC, although not applying to Britain, which at that time had an opt-out from the social protocol of the TEU. The first piece of legislation to be agreed in this way, in 1995, concerned paid parental leave. However, there has been little progress in this direction since, because UNICE has been reluctant to make the system work. The fact that the British government signed the social protocol at Amsterdam, thereby allowing it to be incorporated into the Treaty as the social chapter, obviously owed something to the change from a Conservative to a Labour government, but it is also indicative of how little the system is seen as a threat even to the state that has always been least keen on it. The changed mood of the EU towards a stress on subsidiarity (Box 22.7, p. 284) does not augur well for the future of this system of decision-making.

The continuous lack of enthusiasm of UNICE and its member organizations for EU-level neo-corporatism reflects the fact that business interests are in a stronger position to get their views heard under the alternative, pluralist system of interest representation. This involves interest groups lobbying the formal institutions to try to get their preferred legislative options. It is a competitive system of seeking influence, but although early pluralist theories suggested that there was a level playing-field of competition, it is now generally accepted that some groups have greater resources than others, and so benefit more from this form of interest representation (see below, pp. 293–5). Schmitter and Streeck (1994: 187) argued that Brussels is more like Washington in the dominance of this form of interest representation than it is like national EU capitals.

Finally, although it constitutes a very different activity from lobbying, for certain categories of interest groups, targeting the ECJ has been a particularly fruitful activity. Mazey and Richardson (1999: 115) noted that: 'Women's and environmental groups (and also trade unions) have been adept in

ORGANIZED INTERESTS **293**

securing favourable ECJ decisions which have been just as, if not more, effective than bringing about change in EU policy via other means.' Here, 'whistle-blowing' activity of groups in highlighting non-compliance with EU decisions by member states has been prominent.

Resources, strategies, and tactics

For individual or collective interests that can afford it, a Brussels base is considered highly advantageous. Brussels has acquired the status on 'an insider's town' (Greenwood, 1997: 55), and those who do not have a presence there are operating at a disadvantage. Even in the age of rapid electronic communication, personal contact and 'networking' are extremely important in keeping abreast of the latest information and gossip, and building relationships of trust. However, the simple fact of having representation in Brussels is not everything. Just because the business lobby now co-exists in Brussels with a broad range of other competing groups does not necessarily mean that the competition is equal.

The aim of most interests is to achieve 'insider status'. Insider groups have the ear of policy makers. They build up a relationship of trust with the policy makers, forming what was referred to in Chapter 2 (pp. 23–4) as a 'policy network' with them. There are two factors that determine the effectiveness of groups in achieving this insider status: the resources at their disposal; and the skill with which they deploy those resources, that is the strategy and tactics that they adopt.

Resources

The extent to which groups command resources of varying types is crucial to understanding their relative influence. The control of key resources determines whether a group will secure 'insider status' with policy-makers or remain outside the core process. In the final analysis, the resources available to organized interests are generally decisive.

Greenwood (1997: 18–20) identified eight types of resources of importance to interests (Box 23.2, p. 293). As a general rule, the more of these resources

> **Box 23.2 Resources available to interest groups**
>
> - Information and expertise
> - Economic muscle
> - Status
> - Power in implementation
> - The organization of the interest into a non-competitive format
> - Coherent organization with representative outlets able to make decisions with ease and alacrity
> - The ability to help the overloaded Commission with carrying out policies
> - The ability of a group to influence its members

an interest group has, the more likely it is to secure 'insider' status and have an ongoing influence over policy-making. It is here that the unequal nature of the pluralist competition for influence becomes apparent. As Greenwood (1997: 187) himself pointed out, 'business groups possess more resources of the type required for insider status than do non-business groups'. Other commentators have argued that big business interests possess far more of the resources than any other groups, including small business interests:

The diffuse character of the Brussels process within and between institutions means that to be a participant often requires covering several access points in order to find the most useful one. Small groups, and small firms, thus find it much harder to engage than the better resourced organizations or firms. (Wallace and Young, 1997: 244).

One way for smaller organizations to become more effective is to pool resources. Kohler-Koch (1997: 58) provided the example of business: 'Large firms find it easy to become privileged interlocutors of the political-administrative system, thanks to their economic importance, while small and medium-sized firms rely more heavily on their collective force.' However, while there are resource advantages in separate interests coming together, such combinations of interests increase the risk of 'problems of collective action' (Olson, 1971). The interests aggregated within a combined group may find it difficult to agree among themselves about priorities and tactics.

The disadvantages of small business interests when compared with big business interests are even greater when it comes to non-business groups. As Kohler-Koch (1997: 60) noted, 'Organizing at the European level cannot redress the balance of power between interests that stems from differences in economic strength . . . The relative power of capital and labour is not altered by the fact that trade-union bodies are subsidized by the Commission, or granted the opportunity to take part in working groups and committees, or offered a "social dialogue".'

Despite the advantages for resource-rich groups in the EU's multilevel, multi-arena system, even these groups 'have to make rational calculations as to how to target those resources to the best effect' (Mazey and Richardson 1999: 111). In other words, the most effective organized interests are those that combine the control of key resources with the use of the most effective tactics at a given moment.

Strategies and tactics

The strategies and tactics of interest groups will vary depending on the target decision-maker and/or the issue concerned. There is no magic formula for success in lobbying. There are, however, tried and tested practices that suggest some approaches are better than others. Greenwood (1997: 8) offered some advice for lobbying Brussels (Box 23.3, p. 294). Much of this advice amounts to good common sense. Policy-makers are often under great pressure and even those who respond to interest group approaches need to feel this is a good investment of

---

> **Box 23.3 How to lobby in Brussels**
>
> - Have a clear strategy.
>
> - Develop long-term, even permanent, relations with authorities. Establish a track record as a provider of useful, accurate, well-researched information.
>
> - Find out who is drafting an item and make your representations early.
>
> - Prepare well for meetings. Beware of using hired hands to present cases where their knowledge of your issue will inevitably be limited.
>
> - Present with brevity and clarity.
>
> - Be aware of all sides of the argument. Keep it low-key; do not over-lobby. Appreciate the limits of what can be achieved.
>
> - Keep all viable channels of communication open.
>
> - Know the system, and get to know the points of entry to the decision-making process.
>
> - Remain vigilant.
>
> *Source*: Greenwood, 1997: 8

---

their time. Those interests that are professional in their approach, who keep to the point and do not waste time, and who have realistic expectations of the policy process, are likely to develop the best relationships with decision-makers.

This advice also indicates clearly the importance of timing in the lobbying process. For many groups, making representations early is vital, particularly in relation to policy formation. As Greenwood noted (1997: 8), 'If you have not been able to influence the Commission draft proposal you have probably lost the case.' Related to this is the need to maintain ongoing relationships with Brussels policy-makers to ensure that there is a good flow of information so that issues can be identified quickly. Ongoing relations are also important in responding to issues, in that 'If you need to start forming a relationship when there is a problem it is probably too late' (Greenwood 1997: 8).

Moreover, the impact of lobbying is affected by the extent to which the views of an interest group 'chime with the emerging prevailing wisdoms of policy and with the quest of European policy makers (including those from national governments) for a form of legitimation for their proposed actions' (Wallace and Young 1997: 245–6). Even interests that are effective in every way advocated by Greenwood may well find that their efforts are without success if they advocate views that are out of line with the views of key decision makers.

As any card-player knows, skill in playing the hand that you have been dealt can allow you to win even when your opponents have better cards. There are limits, though, to how far effective strategy and tactics can equalize the disparity of resources. As argued above, attempts by other interests to combine resources may reduce the effectiveness with which they can be deployed because of tensions within the coalition about priorities. Also, big business has the financial resource to buy the expertise that it needs

to take the maximum advantage of its already strong hand.

There is one other strategic approach open to interests that fail to achieve insider status. They can in effect turn over the gaming table by politicizing the issue. Policy communities are cosy relationships between organized interests and officials. Politicians are sometimes included in these relationships, but are usually peripheral to them. The policy community can get on with the business of making public policy without interference so long as the issues do not attract the notice of the politicians or the public. If the profile of the issue is raised above the political threshold, then the nature of the process changes. The strategy of excluded groups with interests in the field is therefore to seek access by politicizing issues. As issues become politicized, they disrupt the exclusive relationships between public agencies and insider interests (Greenwood 1997: 23).

Organized interests and the institutional actors

The complexity of EU institutional arrangements provides a variety of both formal and informal channels through which interest groups can seek to influence decision-makers. It is quite probable that on a particular issue, an effective interest group may seek to influence actors involved in the Council, the Commission and the EP. Such simultaneous lobbying has increased in recent years, as a result of the new policy-making procedures.

Changes to the institutional balance of power under the SEA, and the TEU, mean that it is essential for an interest to engage all the institutions of the EU. The complexity which these changes have brought means that often the same proposal will be under consideration at the same point in time by the different institutions.   (Greenwood 1997: 55)

Although the fragmented nature of the EU institutional structure provides multiple channels through which organized interests may seek to influence policy-making, 'the exact combination of channels that is used, and the relative emphasis that is placed on them, will depend on the particular

issue being addressed' (Grant 1993: 29). The nature of the institution will also influence whether it is targeted by different organized interests, in that the different institutions 'encompass institutional biases which privilege certain interests against others' (Mazey and Richardson 1999: 111). In other words, effective interest groups recognize where they are most likely to gain a sympathetic hearing.

The Commission

For a number of reasons, the Commission is an important target for interest groups:

- it has a role in setting the agenda;
- all proposals have to pass through it;
- it is there that the detail of proposals is decided;
- it is receptive to approaches from interest groups.

The Commission's agenda-setting role is of particular importance to interest groups. If they want to get particular issues placed on the agenda of the EU, the Commission is a good place to start lobbying. Alternatively, if they want to block measures coming onto or rising up the agenda, influence in the Commission is vital. All policy proposals 'have to pass through the Commission gateway and are subject to detailed *processing* at that institutional site' (Mazey and Richardson, 1999: 112). This means that the Commission is an important channel to monitor. It also means that it is the primary place for influencing the detail of proposals, which is often what concerns interest groups.

The Commission is widely recognized as being receptive to interest group representations. This is not least because the Commission's limited human resources make it more dependent than other institutions on the information and expertise that interest groups can offer. Moreover, the Commission 'has actively promoted the organization of the less represented social interests in order to achieve more balanced participation' (Kohler-Koch, 1997: 53). It has also sought alliances with influential groups to strengthen its position vis-à-vis the Council in the EU system. Authoritative and representative interest groups can provide the unelected Commission with legitimacy in its arguments with the Council. The Commission has thus encouraged the formation of Euro-groups. These are able to provide a cross-national consensus on an issue, which may be absent within the Council. Greenwood (1997: 4) argued that the Commission preferred interaction with Euro-groups where possible:

Places on its advisory committees are handed out to Euro groups first. Drafts of directives and other policy initiatives are often given to European business sector associations to comment on. Although single-firm representations to the Commission are heard, the firm concerned is usually told that the Commission would wish to explore the issue further by talking to the interest group concerned in order to ensure that it gets a more representative opinion.

Contacts between interest groups and the Commission take place in a number of ways. These include:

- face-to-face meetings between Commission officials and interest group representatives;
- conferences and workshops;

- permanent and ad hoc advisory committees;
- telephone conversations and correspondence.

The relative openness of Commission officials to approaches by organized interests results in regular contact for many groups. Groups may target specific officials in the Commission who are important on a particular matter or may focus their efforts on a relevant advisory committee or working party. When interest groups are unable to present their arguments face-to-face, they maintain their profile with the Commission by providing research reports, policy documents, and briefings on matters of interest. The methods used will vary according to a number of factors. For example, interests without a permanent base in Brussels are less likely to develop close face-to-face relationships with officials and are more likely to employ the 'long-range' methods of communication, such as telephone calls and correspondence.

The Commission has increasingly sought to formalize contacts with organized interests. As a contribution to this, it has produced a guide for its own staff which lists interest groups by policy sector, 'as part of a 'procedural ambition' to maximize Commission consultation with European civil society', and, 'where the Commission identifies that a European-level group is missing, it attempts to create and sustain one' (Hix 1999: 206).

The Council

The authority of the Council makes it an important target for interest groups. Yet in reality there is little opportunity for them to lobby either the European Council or the Council of Ministers directly. These institutions meet behind closed doors and, generally, groups do not have direct access. Because its members are supported by national administrations and permanent officials in Brussels, the Council has less need for the information resources of interest groups than does the Commission, and is thus less receptive to approaches. The consequence is that most lobbying of the Council is indirect rather than direct.

To influence the Council indirectly, groups seek contact with individual national governments.

Initially, of course, they will try to influence their own national government; but as understanding of the EU policy process has grown, interest groups' lobbying techniques have become more sophisticated, and interest groups in one member state will now seek to influence governments in other member states. Which governments matter will vary with the issue. For obvious reasons, the government holding the Council presidency will be a particular target.

Although lobbying national governments is only an indirect way of influencing EU affairs, it is a process that is familiar to most interest groups. It is, as Greenwood (1997: 32) argued, an arena 'where established policy networks operate which can equally well be used for the purposes of EU representation as they can for the governance of domestic affairs'. Moreover, for those groups that do not have the necessary resources to lobby EU institutions, the national route may remain the only real option. However, the value of lobbying individual governments has declined with the extension of QMV in the Council. Even where a group has successfully persuaded a government of its case, under QMV it is far from certain that the government will be able to assist. As such, 'it is one thing to argue that the majority of groups still rely on the national opportunity structures, but quite another to conclude that this is an efficacious form of behaviour. It is no accident that large firms appear to show a growing preference for Euro-level lobbying' (Mazey and Richardson, 1999: 119).

The European Parliament

Despite the fact that the EP has traditionally had less influence over decision-making than either the Council or the Commission, it has still attracted considerable attention from interest groups. This is largely because of its long-standing advisory role, which has been viewed as an indirect route to influencing the other institutions. Moreover, MEPs are relatively accessible. In particular, those with a constituency interest in an issue will be the focus of attention. More generally, the EP is seen as a 'natural ally' for groups lobbying on behalf of consumers, human rights, and the environment. This is 'not because MEPs necessarily favour their demands, but because their interests match. MEPs are eager to take up those issues which attract a broad public interest and are grateful for any external support which mobilizes public attention, because this will increase their political weight in the decision-making process' (Kohler-Koch 1997: 55–56). In addition to representations to individual MEPs, they can also be targeted collectively through the numerous intergroups that bring together MEPs with similar interests in a relatively formal arena. As the logic of interest group activity suggests, activity around EP plenary sessions and committee meetings has increased with the enhancement of Parliament's powers under first the SEA, and subsequently the TEU and Amsterdam (Ch. 18, pp. 223–6).

Like the Commission, the EP lacks the national administrative support that is available to the members of the Council, and so it also leans heavily on interest group information and expertise. The consequence is that 'in the process of writing reports and proposals for EP resolutions, *rapporteurs* seek out key interest groups to canvass their views. Indeed, some EP reports have even been written by representatives from European interest associations' (Hix 1999: 206).

Many of the methods used to lobby the EP are similar to those used in dealings with the Commission. Again, meetings take place between group representatives and individual MEPs, presentations are made to committees and ad hoc or permanent parliamentary groupings. Reports and briefings are sent to targeted MEPs and contact will be maintained through correspondence, telephone calls, and e-mails. Some MEPs will have strong links with particular interest groups and may unofficially speak on their behalf.

Regulating lobbying

It is a sign of the development of EU lobbying that the issue of regulating the activities of interest groups emerged as an important issue in the 1990s. The first moves were taken by the EP, in response particularly to concerns expressed by the Socialist Group. A report produced by the Belgian MEP, Marc Galle in October 1992 ran into problems over the definition of what constituted a lobbyist. However, the Galle Report raised an important issue that the Commission soon sought to address. In 1993, Commission attempts to persuade interests to introduce a self-regulatory code failed, despite warnings that the absence of a voluntary code would probably prompt regulatory instruments drawn up by other institutional actors, who might be less sympathetic. The code that was ultimately produced by lobbying firms in 1994 provided minimum standards in line with the Commission's wishes (Greenwood 1997: 86). This, however, did not satisfy the EP, which returned to the issue following the elections of 1994. The result was a report produced by Glynn Ford MEP, a British member of the Socialist Group.

Ford rejected the self-regulatory approach to lobbying. He was also able to get around the problem of defining lobbying activities by developing an approach based on incentives. The proposal was to issue passes to those who sought to access the EP on a regular basis because they wished to provide information to MEPs. These passes would ensure easy regular access, rather than requiring individuals to apply for a one-day pass on each occasion. In exchange for passes, the recipients would agree to register their interests and activities with the EP.

The attractive simplicity of the Ford Report got lost when its fate became linked to the more complex and more controversial Nordmann Report on members' interests. In effect, 'what started life as a debate about the regulation of lobbying in the Parliament ended as a highly politicised contest between party groupings over the declaration of members' assets and receipts of gifts' (Greenwood 1997: 97). The effect was to delay acceptance of Ford's proposals, along with those of Nordmann, until they were eventually passed together by the EP in July 1996.

This decision required that passes would be issued to interested parties in exchange for their agreement to the establishment of a code of conduct and the creation of a register of interests. While action on the regulation of lobbyists was generally welcomed, there was concern that this format might formalize the role of insider groups at the expense of those interests in less frequent contact with EU actors. In other words, these proposals, even if fully implemented, would not achieve the level playing field sought by many.

Despite these reservations, the acceptance of the Ford and Nordmann schemes did at least mark a starting point in regulating lobbying activity, which might be built upon in future. It is clear that key institutional actors in the EU have a vested interest in ensuring the effective participation of organized interests. The Commission in particular has developed a consultative approach that encourages broad participation, which is part of its wider strategy for mobilizing support for European integration. In this context, the Commission is likely to be an important force in the future of interest group intermediation. Mazey and Richardson (1999: 125) suggested that: 'the Commission seems intent on a process of *institutionalization* as a means of creating stability and predictability in the policy process . . . it means a growing number of permanent consultative structures.' The outcome of this is likely to be 'the emergence of more and better organized groups, and the further proliferation of EU opportunity structures accompanied by institutionalization, which will further bind interest organizations into the European project' (Mazey and Richardson 1999: 126).

Conclusion

This chapter raises issues connected with two of the themes of the book. The first is the theme of supranational versus intergovernmental interpretations of the nature of the EU. The second is the theme of national models of capitalism, and the model that will emerge at the EU level.

Interest group activity may provide a litmus test for the degree to which the supranational institutions of the EU exercise independent influence over the policy process. If interest groups transfer their lobbying activities away from national governments to Brussels, this might be taken as an indication that the EU is a supranational organization. However, such a conclusion has to be modified in the light of arguments and evidence presented in this chapter. First, the increased level of interest group activity in Brussels has not replaced activity at the national level, but has generally supplemented it. Second, although groups must have some reason to expend financial resources on establishing a presence in Brussels, this does not mean that the reasons are well founded. They may simply be afraid of missing out on something. There is a point at which the sight of other groups swarming to Brussels will lead groups to follow on the assumption that there must be something going on, even if there is not.

Once located in Brussels, groups will not all be equally effective in influencing the institutions. Observations to this effect run throughout the chapter. Most studies suggest that business interests are more influential than other interests, such as organized labour, consumers, or environmental groups. Whether this relative influence matters, of course, depends on the answer to the question of how much independent influence the supranational institutions have over policy outcomes. If they do have some influence, and if it is true that business interests have the most influence over the supranational institutions, then this could provide one explanation for the observation that the policies that emanate from Brussels tend to be in line with an Anglo-American model of capitalism.

Schmitter and Streeck (1994) argued that the shift of policy-making competencies from the national to the EU level would be accompanied by a shift in the pattern of interest-mediation from that typical of the 'organized capitalism' that prevailed in most European states to a pattern much more akin to the pluralism of the United States. Under 'organized capitalism', especially after the economic crises of the 1970s, business and trade unions were given an institutionalized role in national policy-making alongside government. This was thought to be necessary to get the compliance of organized labour with the changes in economic policy that were needed to respond to the turbulent international economic environment. Business interests were never happy with the influence that these 'corporatist' arrangements gave to organized labour, and were keen to dismantle them as soon as they no longer seemed necessary. However, this did not prove easy, and only in Britain under the Thatcher governments was it carried through.

From this perspective, European business interests welcomed the opportunity to circumvent the influence of labour by supporting a shift of policy competence to the EU. Moves under Delors to reconstitute neo-corporatist arrangements at the European level, under the banner of 'the social dimension of 1992', were successfully resisted, and the system that is described above emerged instead. In describing this system as 'pluralist', Schmitter and Streeck did not fall into the trap of assuming that there was a fair competition between different types of interests. They accepted many of the arguments put in this chapter about the reasons why the competition is tilted towards business interests. If they are correct, it is less surprising that EU policy resembles the business-friendly policies of the Anglo-American model of capitalism rather than some average of the different national policies of the member states. It is precisely to achieve this outcome that business, and perhaps the governments of member states also, have collaborated in the shift of policy competence to the EU. That, though, assumes that there has been a genuine shift of competence.

KEY POINTS

The growth of interest group activity

- Interest group activity in Brussels has increased greatly since 1985.

- Factors in this growth are: the growing policy competence of the EU; the perception of a shifting balance of institutional power in Brussels, most notably in favour of the EP; the receptiveness of EU officials to interest group representations; and the 'snowballing' effect of groups following the lead of others so as not to risk being disadvantaged.

Types of interest group and forms of interest representation

- There are at least seven types of interest organization active in Brussels.

- Business interests were the first to locate in Brussels, and still account for the largest number of groups.

- Interest groups representing workers, consumers and the environment have become increasingly active.

- Three forms of interest representation exist in the EU: 'corporatist', 'neo-corporatist', and pluralist.

- Of these three, pluralism is the strongest form.

- Some groups have also had success in making their voices heard through bringing cases to the ECJ.

Interest group resources

- The most effective interest groups in a pluralist system are generally those that control key resources such as information and expertise, economic muscle and status.

- Small organizations can pool resources, but they may then find problems in agreeing on priorities and tactics.

Interest group strategies

- It is possible to identify good practice in lobbying.

- Developing good ongoing relationships with policy-makers, through providing relevant and focused information, is particularly important.

- The timing of interventions is important.

- To be influential groups need to be in tune with the prevailing thinking of policy-makers.

Organized interests and EU policy-making

- Interest groups can use a variety of formal and informal channels in seeking to influence EU policy-making and are active at different stages of the policy process.

- For some EU actors, interest groups are an important source of information and legitimation and as such are enthusiastically consulted

- The Commission is a prime example of an institution that is receptive to interest groups. The advantages of wide consultation brought to the Commission have led it to seek formalization of relations with many interests.

- The Council is less reliant on organized interests than other institutions and as such is less open to approaches. Most lobbying of the Council is indirect, through individual national governments.

- The EP is a key target for organized interests, particularly following the growth of its powers since the mid-1990s. MEPs are thought to be particularly sympathetic to representations on issues of broad public interest that will strengthen the position of the EP within the decision-making process.

- Attempts to regulate lobbying have been made in recent years, indicating its increased importance in the system.

QUESTIONS

1 Why are some interests more influential than others at EU-level?

2 How important are strategies and tactics to the success of organized interests?

3 Why is the Commission particularly receptive to interest group approaches?

4 What are the difficulties involved in regulating the activity of lobbyists?

FURTHER READING

For a thorough and comprehensive review of organized interests in the EU, see J. Greenwood, *Representing Interests In the European Union* (Basingstoke and London: Macmillan, 1997). In addition to considering interest group strategies, resources, and channels of influence, this book includes separate chapters on some of the major interests, including business, labour, and territorial interests.

The edited collection by J. Greenwood and M. Aspinwall (eds.), *Collective Action in the European Union: Interests and the new Politics of Associability* (London and New York: Routledge, 1998) looks at the motivation for and problems of collective action in the EU, drawing on a number of case studies including business, the professions and consumer groups. The edited collection by H. Wallace and A. R. Young (eds.), *Participation and Policy-Making in the European Union* (Oxford: Clarendon Press, 1997) focuses on participation in the fields of market regulation and policies for industry, while S. Mazey and J. Richardson (eds.), *Lobbying in the European Union* (Oxford: Oxford University Press, 1993) bring together contributions on the European lobbying process in general and in specific sectors.

P. Schmitter and W. Streeck, 'Organised Interests and the Europe of 1992' in B. Nelsen and A. C-G. Stubb (eds.), *The European Union: Readings on the Theory and Practice of European Integration* (Boulder and London: Lynne Rienner, 1st edn., 1994), pp. 169–87, offers a stimulating discussion of the wider issues raised by the form of interest representation that is emerging at the EU level. A. Butt Philip, 'Pressure Groups and Policy-Making in the European Community', in J. Lodge (ed.) *Institutions and Policies of the European Community* (London: Pinter, 1983), 21–6 provides a rare early overview of interest group activity in the EC, while the recent contribution by S. Mazey and J. Richardson, 'Interests', in L. Cram, D. Dinan, and N. Nugent, *Developments in the European Union* (Basingstoke and London: Macmillan, 1999), 105–29 provides an excellent summary of developments.

Part Five

Policies

The scope of policies now within the EU remit makes it difficult to provide comprehensive coverage. Beyond those policies for which the EU has formal competence, it has an emerging role in others. In terms of this book the essential choice here was between coverage in breadth or in depth. We settled for depth. Each of the six chapters in this part provides a detailed account of the development of one EU policy area.

CHOICE OF POLICIES

There are probably equally convincing cases for many alternative combinations to the policy areas we have covered here. Still, we offer a few comments to justify our selection.

Agriculture and **Regional and Structural Policies** account for over three-quarters of EU spending. This alone makes them significant. In addition, agriculture was the first EC common policy and has a central place in the history of the early development of what is now the European Union. Regional and Structural Policies have taken an increasing share of the EU budget, now around one-third of all spending. This policy sector has been at the forefront of EU experiments with innovative programmes and modes of governance: it was here that the partnership principle was first developed for EU policies. The importance of this policy sector has been consolidated in recent years with the proposed enlargement of the EU to include the countries of central and eastern Europe, who will become the principal recipients of aid following membership and for whom some of the innovative principles of structural policy will present interesting challenges.

The creation of a common market has been a central objective of the European Union since the signing of the Treaty of Rome in 1957. Moreover, the **Single Market** project of the mid-1980s provided the impetus which relaunched the stumbling process of European integration. There is a clear link between this policy area and that of **Economic and Monetary Union**. Of the two, however, it is the latter which has proved more controversial and for most of the EU's history, more elusive. The control of national currencies has been viewed by some member states as the greatest threat to sovereignty posed by EU member-ship. That this view still prevails in some states goes some way to explaining why some member states did not join the single currency when it was eventually launched in 1999.

External Relations has two aspects: trade and foreign policy. Both are of major importance to the EU, but have developed at a different pace. The prospect for greater economic prosperity through European integration has been a major motivation for member states and this prosperity is linked to trade relations beyond the EU's borders. As an emerging regional bloc, the EU appears to many as an obvious territorial level at which some foreign policies should be developed. There has not been full agreement on this issue, but the pressures remain.

Enlargement is a particular aspect of the EU's relations with the rest of the world which requires special treatment because of its profound implications for the operation of the EU as a whole.

Although we can make justifications for our selections, we are aware of important omissions. Above all, the policy areas chosen should be seen as illustrative case studies. We are keen to emphasize the importance of disaggregating the EU by policy area to understand the full complexity of decision-making. In different policy sectors, there are different policy networks. Within these networks, actors that are influential in one policy sector may be less influential than in others. The resources available to actors in different policy networks vary considerably. Even across issues within the same policy area there are fluctuations in the power of various actors. In other words, seeking to develop a general theory about the nature of the European Union is highly problematic if not futile. Once research is conducted down 'amongst the weeds' of day-to-day processes in different sectors, the variations revealed are considerable.

24 Agriculture

In the case of agriculture an attempt has been made to devise a common policy to cope with economies having different levels of involvement in agriculture and food processing, a variety of historical agricultural traditions, and which display divergences in the structure of agriculture in terms of such variables as farm size, ownership patterns and commodities produced. It is not surprising that attempts to devise such a policy have encountered considerable difficulties and it has been necessary to evolve expensive and often incoherent policy compromises

(Grant 1997: 2–3).

....

SUMMARY

The common agricultural policy (CAP) has been at the centre of controversy throughout its history. Developed to ensure security of food supplies in the Community, the CAP has proved highly expensive, with overproduction by farmers keen to maximize subsidies. Despite widespread criticism, the CAP has proved notoriously difficult to reform. Farmers' groups have fiercely resisted change and their importance in the domestic politics of key member states has ensured that reform has been slow and piecemeal. Only in the context of external pressures in the 1990s was significant change secured. Yet the CAP still claims a major proportion of the EU budget and pressures for further reform continue.

Introduction

The common agricultural policy (CAP) was the first redistributive policy of the EC, and for many years the only one. The success of agriculture sustained the hopes of the advocates of integration during the 1960s, when it was seen as the start of a process that would lead to other common policies, but the other common policies did not appear. As a result, agriculture dominated payments from the common budget. This became one of the bases for the protracted dispute over British net contributions to the budget in the 1970s and early 1980s.

The main features of the CAP, as it operated before reform in the 1980s, are summarized in Box 24.1 (p. 307). Every year the national Ministers of Agriculture decided the level of prices for agricultural products that were covered by the CAP. These prices were ensured by the intervention of the Commission in the market to buy up enough of each product to maintain the agreed price. If prices subsequently rose above the agreed level, the produce that the Commission had purchased and placed into storage would be released onto the market to bring the price back down; but in practice this did not occur.

Prices tended to be set at the level that would ensure the least efficient farmers in the EC an adequate income. However, this was also a level that encouraged the more efficient, large-scale farmers to maximize their output, because the price was more than adequate to guarantee them a return on their investment. Thus surpluses in most products became permanent. The Commission's interventions in the market were all in one direction: to keep up prices by intervention buying. The amounts of produce in storage constantly grew and became an embarrassment, prompting press reports of 'food mountains' and 'wine lakes'. The cost of storage in itself became a significant burden on the Community budget, so attempts were made to reduce stocks by subsidizing exports. This, though, incurred the anger of the United States, which saw the subsidies as a threat to its own agricultural exports.

These problems stemmed from the failure of agricultural policy itself to develop. What is commonly known as the CAP is in effect only one part of a common agricultural policy: it is a policy on agricultural price support. Sicco Mansholt, the commissioner in charge of agriculture during Hallstein's presidency, saw a clear line of spillover from price support to the restructuring of European agriculture to create fewer, larger, more efficient farms. This would have allowed guaranteed prices to be reduced. At the request of the Council of Ministers, Mansholt

---

Box 24.1 The price-support system of the CAP

The system of price support for different commodities uses slightly different terminology, but the basic principles are the same.

- The *target price* is the wholesale price that Ministers of Agriculture agree on every year, commodity by commodity. This is the price that the EU is aiming to see prevail in the market. It is supported by import levies, export subsidies, and intervention buying.

- The *market price* is the price level that prevails within the EU without intervention by the authorities. If the market price falls too far below the target price, the authorities will intervene to buy up produce so as to

raise the price; if it rises too far above the target, the authorities will intervene to release stored produce onto the market to depress the price.

- The *intervention price* is the level at which the EU will start to buy up produce on the open market in order to prevent the market price from falling below the target price. It is set at a level a little below the target price. All produce that is offered for sale at this price will be purchased.

- The *threshold price* is the price of imports from outside of the EU below which levies will charged. It is set below the target price by an amount that takes account of transport and handling costs.

---

introduced proposals for such a restructuring in the late 1960s. However, in the end there was no agreement on a Community approach which would have placed responsibility in the hands of the Commission, nor was there progress on restructuring by national governments. Despite repeated attempts, no effective reform was achieved until the 1990s.

This chapter, then, tries to answer the following questions:

- What was peculiar about agriculture that it was possible to agree a common policy in this sector?
- Why was the price-support system chosen as the basis of the CAP?
- Why did restructuring of the farming sector not follow agreement on price support?
- Why did reform of the CAP prove so difficult?
- Why did reform eventually succeed in the 1990s?

The peculiarities of agriculture

The most obvious difference between agriculture and other sectors where integration could occur is the extent of the commitment to a common policy actually written into the Treaty of Rome. Agriculture was one of only four common policies that had its own Title in the Treaty. (The others were the free movement of goods; the free movement of persons, services, and capital; and transport.)

The privileged position afforded to the sector reflects other peculiarities of agriculture, particularly the importance that French governments of the Fourth Republic attached to it. For them, agriculture was both politically and economically important. Politically, there was constant electoral pressure on

all the parties of the centre-right from small farmers who were inefficient producers but were determined to retain their independence. This, in effect, meant that the farmers had to be subsidized by the state through the national price-support system. Economically, France also had an efficient agricultural sector, and produced a considerable food surplus.

Part of the price that the French insisted on for their participation in the common market in industrial goods was the subsidization of the cost of maintaining their small farmers, and the guarantee of a protected market for French agricultural exports. France was assisted in placing agriculture at the head of the list of possible common policies by the agreement of all the other participants that agriculture was different from other economic sectors. All the member states, including West Germany, had national support policies for agriculture, and it was generally accepted that the social and environmental implications of allowing a completely free market in agricultural products would be unacceptable.

Had the EC simply abolished restrictions on free trade in foodstuffs, the effect would have been to produce a competition between member states to see which government would be prepared to give the highest level of support to its farmers. So free trade was not viable. Yet it was also recognized that the equalization of food prices was an important factor in ensuring fair competition in industrial products, because of the effect of food prices on wages. Higher food prices meant that workers demanded higher wages, thus raising industrial production costs. The argument was that to have a level playing field of competition between different national industrial producers, cost differences arising from the effect of food prices needed to be limited. The same reasoning could be applied to other elements in industrial production costs, such as tax levels or energy costs. The difference in the case of food was that West Germany, which had low tax rates because of low social security benefits and low energy costs because of efficient production plant, had high food costs because of the political influence of its farmers. Thus the equalization of costs was more acceptable to West Germany where food was concerned than where other costs were concerned. This created something near to unanimity within the Community.

The existence of high food prices in West Germany was indicative of the problems that the CDU/CSU governments had in reconciling their commitment to economic modernization with their conservative political image. The same difficulty faced the Gaullist governments of the Fifth Republic in France. On the one hand, their commitment to modernization meant that they wished to keep down labour costs and to see the movement of workers from agriculture to industrial employment. This was essential if industrial expansion was to be maintained during the long post-war boom. On the other hand, these parties depended on votes from the agricultural population to keep them ahead of the parties of the left in electoral terms. As such, they were under pressure to maintain farm incomes, although the cost would be a burden on industry, and they were reluctant to see too rapid a reduction in the rural population lest their electoral position be undermined. Hence there was the basis for a Franco-German agreement on agriculture: the French would get their subsidy to maintain a significant rural population and the Germans would get the equalization of food prices throughout the common market.

West Germany was less happy on the issue of agricultural protection against the rest of the world. West German industry felt that its exports to countries such as Argentina would be adversely affected if West Germany stopped importing foodstuffs from them in order to give preference to EC produce. There was also the influence on the West German government of the United States, which was very unhappy about the idea of any restriction on trade in this sector.

However, another peculiarity of agriculture in the policies of the EC was relevant here: it was the only issue on which the French government was on the same side as the Dutch government. As a major agricultural producer itself, The Netherlands also wished to gain guaranteed access to the West German market. This unity of ambition meant that France and The Netherlands were in alliance against West Germany, whereas on almost every other question that arose during de Gaulle's presidency, the Dutch government opposed what it saw as France's attempt to dominate the smaller states. This was an important factor in overcoming West German resistance, because The Netherlands was normally closely allied to the German position. In addition, Adenauer did not wish West Germany to appear to be throwing its weight around where small states were concerned: there was a reputation to be lived down.

The price-support system

The detail of the agricultural policy was not included in the Treaty of Rome. It was agreed in negotiations that took place in Stresa, Italy in July 1958 that the CAP would be based on a system of common prices (see Box 24.1, p. 307). It was this system that eventually became the cause of the high cost of the CAP, and of the high price of food. As such, the system came in for sustained criticism, especially in Britain, where the high cost of food under the CAP was an important issue in the debate on entry.

For many British consumers it was impossible to understand why the original six Community member states ever set up such a patently irrational system of farm support, and why they were so reluctant to see it changed. For most people in Britain it was obvious that the old British system of deficiency payments to farmers, to compensate them for loss of income due to low prices, was much more sensible. It meant lower food prices for the consumer, and it allowed the government to bring pressure on individual farmers to improve their efficiency.

The first point that British critics of the CAP price-support system overlooked was that French peasant farmers rejected any suggestion of a system that would allow the government to put pressure on them to do anything other than they wished. In fact, any system involving a direct and obvious subsidy from the government would have upset the peasant spirit of independence. There were, then, good political reasons for choosing a price-support system and these were strengthened by administrative considerations. It is much more difficult to operate a system of direct deficiency payments where there are large numbers of small farmers concerned.

It was not so much the price-support system in itself that was irrational, but the level at which prices were set in a context of mixed farming sizes. The original price level that was set for cereals, in 1964, was not particularly high. This was because the French cereal producers were mostly large-scale and efficient, so there was no reason for the French government to hold out for a price that would raise the cost of living and put pressure on industrial wages. But the reaction in West Germany to a cereals price

level that was below the prevailing national price was instructive as a guide to why later price agreements were consistently high.

The West German farmers were uniformly small-scale, high-cost producers. They opposed the whole idea of the CAP, fearing that it would reduce their incomes, and they vehemently opposed the low level of cereal prices as a vindication of their worst fears. But on this occasion a combination of industrial pressure in favour of lower food prices and the personal commitment of Adenauer to the process of integration overruled them. In fact, in the early 1960s de Gaulle exerted considerable influence over Adenauer and made German agreement to the cereal-price settlement a test of their friendship. The corollary of Adenauer's support on cereal prices was de Gaulle's continued support for Adenauer's hard line towards Eastern Europe. The consequence of Adenauer's adherence to this deal was a further undermining of his position within the CDU, and the political enmity of the FDP, which was determined to pose as the protector of the farmers. Adenauer's removal from the Chancellorship in October 1963 was thus made more certain, and it in turn put Ludwig Erhard in the hot seat (Ch. 14, p. 154). His defence of the agreement helped to strain his relations with the FDP. At the same time the neo-Nazi National Democratic Party (NPD) was formed, and was to enjoy some success among disillusioned rural CDU supporters.

Under the pressure of these political developments, the West German government held out for a higher level of prices for the beef and dairy sectors. These they obtained because in those sectors the French, who had small producers of their own, were more interested in a generous support level than in reducing food costs. But at this stage in the story it was the West Germans who were most concerned about setting higher price levels because of the need of the CDU/CSU to retain the farm vote in the face of the threat from the NPD and the challenge from the FDP. The influence of the FDP continued to be exerted on the side of high price settlements after the arrival of the SPD/FDP coalition in office in 1969.

Although the French are frequently blamed for high support prices, successive German governments have often been supporters of high prices for domestic political reasons. This is not to argue that the French had no responsibility for the high prices. In the early years of the CAP they were perhaps less responsible than were the Germans, partly because in the 1960s the rapid growth of the French economy meant that policies fostering a movement off the land were favoured rather than those aimed at maintaining a rural population. But after 1973 the slow growth of the economy shifted this emphasis in French policy quite markedly. There was more need to maintain a rural population for social reasons, because there were not enough jobs available for the existing non-agricultural work force. High support prices therefore became more important to the French government.

The change in economic circumstances is a factor often overlooked by critics of the price-support system. At the time that it was set up it was predictable that political pressures would tend to push price levels upwards, but that situation was not expected to persist. It was a period of rapid change in agriculture, with a fast rate of depletion of the rural population. In the 1960s, the problem seemed to be how quickly the last remaining areas of agricultural inefficiency could be eliminated in order to free more labour for industry, which was beginning to suffer from labour shortages in all parts of the EC. It seemed that the elimination of the smallest farms would soon reduce the pressure for high support prices, which would allow the system to function without placing too great a burden on the Community budget.

In the meantime Commissioner Mansholt saw the burden that high prices would place on the budget as an incentive for the member states to press forward to the next stage of the agricultural policy, the restructuring of European agriculture. This had been an agreed priority of the Stresa Conference of July 1958. It was reasonable to assume that it would be handled as a Community policy rather than through national policies, because in that way governments could maintain a certain distance from measures that might be electorally dangerous. By the late 1960s the cost of the price-support system was already causing concern, and the Council asked the Commission to examine the problem in October 1967.

Restructuring agriculture: the Mansholt Plan

The Council's request that the Commission examine the price support system came in the year that West German GDP actually fell by 2 per cent. It was pressed by the CDU/SPD coalition at a time when budget problems and the problems of industry were understandably dominant concerns. It came also at a time when the French government was itself thinking along the same lines. In 1968 the Vedel Plan for the reform of French agriculture appeared, which showed that labour-supply for industrial expansion was taking precedence over the maintenance of a rural population in the thinking of the government. Rising inflation increased for all member states the incentive for a reduction in farm prices. The signs for agricultural restructuring were favourable.

In December 1968 the Commission produced a memorandum entitled 'Agriculture 1980', which came to be known as 'the Mansholt Plan' (European Commission, 1969). It proposed a restructuring of agriculture, based upon encouraging small farmers to leave the land and giving financial support to the amalgamation of holdings. The 'carrot' of incentives would include grants, pensions to farmers over 55, and assistance to younger farmers in finding new jobs. The other side of the scheme was the 'stick': a proposal that price levels be cut so that inefficient farmers would be forced off the land. This last proposal was considered by the Community's farming pressure group, COPA, to be a 'psychological blunder' (Rosenthal, 1975: 88). It certainly guaranteed the hostility of the French and West German farmers.

In France the larger farmers took the lead in organizing opposition to the plan, arguing that it would mean the death of the family farm. Their concern with the family farm may have been sentimental, but it is also clear that they did not like the prospect of the removal of their high profits once the small farmer disappeared. 'Save the family farm' was a better campaign slogan than 'Save our excess profits'.

Yet despite the outcry, the reaction of the French government was not too hostile to the plan. As was explained above, the Vedel Plan for French agriculture appeared in the same year as the Mansholt Plan. The Gaullists gained a large majority in the 1968 elections to the National Assembly, which were held in the aftermath of the strikes and riots of May, and were in a strong position to go ahead with their rationalization proposals. So the French government's reaction to the Mansholt Plan was moderate, but emphasized the need for the implementation of the plan to be in the hands of national governments and not of the Commission. This was in line with de Gaulle's general approach to Community policies. Had the position of the government been less secure, the French might not have insisted on national control: they might have preferred to hide from political unpopularity behind the Commission. Circumstances, though, made it more important for de Gaulle that the nationalist principles of Gaullism be observed.

The main opposition to the Mansholt Plan came from West Germany. This was for a combination of reasons. First, the reaction of the German farmers was very much the same as that of the French farmers, but their influence was enhanced because there was a Federal election due in 1969. Neither of the parties in the Grand Coalition wished to argue too strongly for Community proposals that upset the farmers: the CDU/CSU feared that their position might be damaged by a loss of votes to the NPD; the SPD was hoping to conclude a coalition agreement with the FDP. Second, the government parties collectively were worried about the potential cost of the proposals. They foresaw a considerable short-term burden on the Federal budget, since West Germany would be bound to provide the largest share of the funding. The government therefore announced that it was unhappy with the plan and would prefer to see the problem of surpluses tackled by a system of quotas on the amounts that would be bought into intervention.

When Mansholt produced his revised plan ('mini-Mansholt') in 1969 (European Commission, 1970) he rejected the West German suggestion, arguing that it would be a cumbersome bureaucratic system which would have to be permanent, whereas his restructuring scheme was a long-term solution to the problem. But the political doubts slowed down progress on the plan, and it was overtaken during 1969 by changes of government in France and West Germany, and by the Hague summit at the EC level. The exchange-rate crises of 1969 put economic and monetary union higher on the agenda than agricultural reform, and once enlargement was accepted in principle it constituted another reason for delay on the CAP. This was because the applicant states, particularly Ireland and Denmark, would find it difficult to negotiate terms of entry if there was uncertainty about agriculture, which was of central importance to them.

The one applicant likely to favour the Mansholt Plan was Britain, and Mansholt attempted to gain advantage from this by visiting the country in late June 1969. He met agricultural interest groups, gave a press conference, and recorded a BBC interview. His message was that unless his proposals were implemented, the Community market for some products, particularly butter, would simply collapse. He also warned the British people that without reform of the CAP they would find themselves paying high food prices and making high contributions to the Community budget to finance the intervention buying. He was right, of course, but his message did not prompt the British government to make reform of the CAP a condition of entry. Heath was too eager to conclude negotiations to want to introduce new difficulties. All that Mansholt succeeded in doing was to infuriate the French government, which saw his intervention as an attempt to interfere with the decision-making process within the Council of Ministers.

When the Council of Agricultural Ministers eventually met to discuss the plan, in March 1971, they were accompanied to Brussels by 80,000 demonstrating farmers. The farmers hung Mansholt in effigy, burned cars, tore up street signs, broke windows, killed one policeman, and injured 140 more of the

3,000 deployed to restrain them (Rosenthal, 1975: 92). Their anger had been increased by low price rises in 1970, which had resulted in a drop in their incomes, yet had not solved the problem of the surpluses. But the presence of the farmers in the streets probably did not have a great influence on the outcome of the meeting. The French were angry with Mansholt for his attempt to ally Britain to his cause, and were determined to get the issue settled before Britain became a member, in case the Mansholt intervention had worked. They were also determined to get it settled in a way that would leave responsibility for the implementation of restructuring in the hands of national governments. The West Germans were equally determined to keep the cost of the restructuring exercise as low as possible, and under the SPD/FDP coalition government were not prepared to commit themselves to measures that would anger their farmers too much.

The modified version of the plan which the Council of Ministers finally accepted did not significantly increase the amount to be spent on restructuring over what was already available through the Guidance section of the CAP. It also left the member states full discretion for the implementation of the restructuring. Although Mansholt welcomed the agreement as 'the beginning of a vast process of reform' (*The Times*, 26 Mar. 1971), he was putting a brave face on what was obviously a personal defeat. He retired the following year.

The vast programme of reform never even got started. In 1972–3 a combination of bad weather, poor harvests, and an increase in world demand led to big price rises on international markets, so that world prices actually exceeded EC prices. This took off the immediate pressure for reform. Then in 1973 the OPEC oil-price rises sparked off the world recession which led to high unemployment, and meant that all governments had an incentive not to force labour off the land. A combination of national political and economic considerations and international economic developments therefore led to the complete failure of the attempt to extend the CAP beyond the level of guaranteed prices.

Agriculture in the 1970s

The economic recession of the 1970s led to resistance by those governments that had considerable agricultural populations to the introduction of restructuring measures. There was also a tendency for price settlements to remain high because of the political influence of farmers, which was everywhere considerable. Even Britain, despite loud protestations about the cost of the CAP, connived in allowing high price settlements through the Council of Agricultural Ministers. At the same time, the high prices acted as a burden on the Community budget, and put a particular burden on the national budgets of West Germany and Britain, the two largest net contributors to the Community budget.

West Germany here, as in other areas, faced a dilemma. On the one hand its belief in balanced budgets and sound finance meant that the West German government wished to reduce its budgetary commitments to the minimum. This was especially so at a time when the recession meant that the Federal government was receiving less in tax revenue, and was having to disburse more in social security payments. On the other hand, the electoral salience of the farm-vote remained high, especially for the FDP. When Helmut Schmidt took over as Chancellor in 1974 it looked for a time as though he was determined to resolve the dilemma in favour of budgetary restraint. In September 1974 he vetoed the farm price settlement that had been accepted by Josef Ertl, the FDP Minister of Agriculture. It was a move that shocked the rest of the EC, though not nearly so much as it shocked Ertl and the FDP. The consequent strain on coalition relationships led to the veto being revoked, and though Schmidt continued to speak out in favour of reform of the CAP, West Germany did not seek to take the lead in forcing the issue.

Britain eventually provided that lead. The British problem with the CAP was that as a net importer of food, and an efficient producer with a small farming sector, it ended up contributing more to the EC budget than it should have on the basis of its relative prosperity within the Community. The domination of the budget by the CAP distorted the pattern of disbursements, giving Britain the greatest incentive to press for change. Yet the 1974–9 Labour governments made no real effort to bring about change. John Silkin, the Secretary of State for Agriculture for much of this period, adopted a tough image in his dealings with the EC, presumably for domestic political purposes. But he repeatedly acquiesced in high price settlements, claiming victory if he could offset the effect on British prices by obtaining special subsidies on butter or by manipulating the artificial 'green' rate of exchange which was used for calculating agricultural prices in national currencies. The government as a whole seemed to prefer to engage in bruising public fights for annual rebates on Britain's budgetary contributions rather than going for fundamental reform.

The difficulty for the Labour government may have been that it could see little prospect of gaining agreement to the modification of the CAP from the other members of the EC. France was opposed to any fundamental changes: and the fact that it was Britain, a latecomer to the club and an uncooperative member on almost every other issue, which was leading the challenge led to a closing of ranks by the original members. This was where an unambiguous West German commitment to reform would have been useful, but it was not forthcoming.

Of the other new members, neither Ireland nor Denmark wished to see the CAP dismantled because they too were big beneficiaries. The only other alternative solution to the problem was a considerable expansion of the budget to accommodate other common policy funds from which Britain would benefit, so that British payments would increase but so would British receipts, leaving it a net beneficiary. But this line of approach was ruled out for the Labour government because of the hostility of so much of the Labour Party to any increase in integration, which was seen as a further loss of sovereignty.

The Conservative government that succeeded Labour in 1979 followed a very similar line. For it, the blockage to a permanent settlement that would involve a larger Community budget was formed more by economic doctrine than by nationalism. Thatcher's approach was opposed to increased governmental expenditure either at the national or the Community level, and she adhered to that position even where its relaxation would have benefited the British Treasury.

The tensions set up by a single common policy standing alone provided vindication of the neofunctionalist idea of functional spillover pressures (Ch. 1, pp. 9–12). But there was no spillover into other policy areas, only an uneasy and unstable condition of immobility. Political spillover pressure was not succeeding, though the interest groups in the agricultural sector were acting as effective gatekeepers, barring the way to a retreat from the level of integration already achieved. Governments were trying to avoid the implications of their position, but the strains were threatening to break something, possibly even the EC itself. In only one direction had the governments been able successfully to fudge the issue of spillover, and that was in the direction of monetary union, one of the ways in which it had been expected by the Commission that spillover from agriculture would occur.

The Commission believed that the CAP would act as an incentive for the EC to move rapidly towards economic and monetary union as stable exchange rates between national currencies were essential to the system of common agricultural prices. In fact, when exchange-rate instability hit the EC in 1969 it was not allowed to destroy the CAP, but the defence was not to move to monetary union either. Instead a complex arrangement of green currencies and monetary compensatory amounts (MCAs) was introduced (Box 24.2, p. 314).

In the international monetary chaos that followed the ending of the convertibility of the dollar in 1971, frequent changes in the relative values of Community currencies were prevented from destroying the CAP only by allowing six green currencies to grow. In this way, the linkage between the CAP and monetary policy, which the Barre Report on economic and monetary union had made the centrepiece of its argument in 1969, was avoided. However, this was only at the expense of destroying one of the main justifications for the CAP, the argument that food prices should be the same in all member states so as to equalize the pressure on wage rates.

Box 24.2 Green currencies and monetary compensatory amounts

A *green currency* was an artificial rate of exchange between a national currency and the European unit of account (EUA) used to calculate agricultural prices, which were set in EUA but had to be applied in national currencies. They originated at the end of the 1960s, and disappeared in January 1999 with the start of the single currency.

When, in August 1969, the French franc was devalued, the French government declared that it would like to phase in the effect of the devaluation on agricultural prices so as to alleviate the inflationary effects. Had the full devaluation been applied to agricultural prices they would have increased sharply because the Community support-price levels were calculated in EUA. This was a fictional currency based on the average value of the member states' national currencies, so the devaluation would have meant that the same price expressed in EUA would have translated into a higher price expressed in francs. To accommodate the French government, the Council of Ministers agreed that for a limited period the agricultural prices would be calculated as though the franc had not been devalued. The CAP would operate on the basis of a fictional 'green' franc for the purpose of calculating national agricultural price levels. The intention was that the green franc would be devalued in stages until it eventually came into line with the real franc's international value.

Almost immediately a problem arose. The green-currency arrangement meant that it became more profitable for French agricultural produce to be sold in Community markets outside France than in France itself. This was because the EUA price could be obtained in another national currency, which could then be converted into francs at the normal rate of exchange, so yielding more

francs than if the produce had been sold in France at the artificially low translation of the EUA price. As speculators began to buy up agricultural produce throughout France, the Community moved more swiftly than usual to correct the price imbalance by inventing Monetary Compensatory Amounts (MCAs).

An MCA is either a levy or a refund which is paid to an exporter or importer at the border between two states. In the French case, a levy or tax was charged on all agricultural produce leaving France to bring its price up to the difference between the rates of exchange of the green franc and the real franc. All importers were paid a subsidy of the same amount to compensate them for the lower price that they would receive in France.

There is little doubt that the French government did see these measures as purely temporary and exceptional. As a net exporter of food to the rest of the EC, France had no interest in seeing such obstacles to free trade become a permanent feature. But in October the green-rate system was extended to the Deutschmark. The upwards revaluation of the Deutschmark should have led to a drop in farm incomes in West Germany. The effect of a revaluation was to lower food prices in the revaluing state, for precisely the opposite reasons to those that increased prices in devaluing states: the rate of exchange against the EUA was changed, so that the same price translated into Deutschmarks came out at a lower price on the West German market. Lower prices would mean lower farm incomes. This was politically unacceptable to the FDP, which had just re-entered government in coalition with the SPD. So, for far less worthy reasons than the French, the West German government requested that the currency revaluation should not be reflected in agricultural prices, and a green mark was created.

The CAP in the 1980s

In the course of the early 1980s the pressures built up for reform of the CAP. The main sources of pressure were its escalating cost, increasing concern about its environmental effects, spillover from the single market programme, and external pressures. Together these did produce some reforms in 1984 and 1988 (Box 24.3, p. 315).

The cost of the CAP

Between 1974 and 1979 the cost of the CAP rose by 23 per cent, twice the rate of increase of incomes. It then stabilized between 1980 and 1982 because the exceptionally high value of the dollar in 1981–2 brought higher world food prices and reduced the cost of export subsidies and the need for intervention buying. In 1983, as the value of the dollar declined, the cost of the CAP soared by 30 per cent. Even with the true cost of the CAP obscured by the high dollar, the EC reached the ceiling of expenditure that could be covered from its own resources. Agreement to lift the limit had to be unanimous, and the British government would not agree to any increase without firm measures to curb the cost of the CAP. This led to the 1984 agreement on dairy quotas, and on a system of budgetary discipline whereby a maximum limit would be set to the size of the budget each year before the annual round of negotiations on agricultural prices. Ministers of Agriculture would therefore be negotiating within fixed parameters. Any budgetary overshoot would be clawed back in the following years.

In the event this system did not work because there was no automatic mechanism for making the necessary adjustments to costs in the years following an overrun. Between 1985 and 1987 the cost of the CAP increased by 18 per cent per annum. Dairy products remained largely under control thanks to the system of quotas set in 1984; but cereals were the new cause of difficulty, due to increased yields which resulted from technological advances and a consequent decline in world prices which increased export subsidies.

Although the EC did not appear to face the immediate exhaustion of its financial resources as it had in 1984, there was an estimated budgetary shortfall of 4–5 million European currency units (ecus) in 1987. This was covered by creative accountancy that simply pushed the problem forward in time. By this time, also, Spain and Portugal had joined the EC, bringing new demands on the budget that could only be met by either diverting money away from existing beneficiaries or expanding the size of the budget. This situation was compounded by the insistence of the Spanish, Portuguese, and Greek governments that they would not be able to participate in the freeing of the internal market of the EC by the end of 1992 unless the structural funds were substantially increased. At the London meeting of the European Council in December 1986 agreement was reached in principle on the doubling of the structural funds by 1993 (see Ch. 27, pp. 369–71), thus requiring an increase in the resources of the EC.

Environmental pressures

Environmental pressures bore less on member states than financial ones, but in the 1980s there was growing concern about the environment in general, and about the effect of the CAP in particular. The main beneficiaries of the CAP were large farmers who responded to the high prices by maximizing output. To do this they pumped more and more fertilizer into the land, and hormones into animals, to improve yields. The rise of environmentalism provided a counterweight to the general sympathy of European public opinion for farmers, and made it politically easier for governments to respond to the financial pressures with reform measures.

Spillover from the single market programme

The 1992 programme to free the internal market did not directly involve agriculture, but the fact that the CAP had not achieved one of its original objectives, that of equalizing food prices, did act as a barrier to a genuine level playing-field of competition. Also, the existence of 'green' exchange rates and MCAs did offer a barrier to the removal of internal frontiers, which was one of the ultimate objectives of the single market for most member states (Warley, 1992: 121).

External pressures

External pressures proved the most formidable incentive for change in the CAP. The United States made the phasing out of agricultural subsidies a central part of its negotiating position for the Uruguay Round of GATT talks which began in 1986. It was joined by the Cairns Group of fourteen agricultural-producing states, including Australia, Canada, New Zealand, and several Latin American states. All felt that they suffered from the dumping of the EC's agricultural exports onto world markets, which drove down prices and prevented them selling some of their own production.

These pressures led to the reforms described at the start of this section. But those reforms were ineffective in restraining the growing cost of the CAP. They were both too modest in their aims, and lacked effective enforcement mechanisms. This reflected two aspects of the reforms. First, they were drawn up by an EC agricultural policy community that consisted of DG VI of the Commission, the European Agriculture Commissioner, and the representatives of farmers in COPA. These groups had developed close working relationships, and were unlikely to produce proposals that would seriously damage the interests of farmers, or reduce the importance of agriculture as an EC policy sector. Second, the proposals had to be agreed by the Council of Agriculture Ministers, most of whom were strongly influenced by national farmers' representatives.

These circumstances operated most strongly for the 1984 reforms. By the time of the 1988 reforms, according to Moyer and Josling (1990: 86–7), the coalition against change had been weakened by the formation within the Commission of an inner circle. This inner circle consisted of the president, Jacques Delors, the agriculture commissioner between 1985 and 1989, Frans Andriessen, and the budget commissioner, Hening Christophersen. Delors's reason for supporting reform was the damage that failure to achieve it might do to the single market programme. 'Delors had made the single European market something of a personal crusade and could not easily see this goal frustrated by agricultural stalemate' (Moyer and Josling, 1990: 86). Under pressure from the Commission, which was prepared to take the Council of Ministers to the Court of Justice if it did not agree a budget for 1988, a system of price-stabilizers for agricultural produce was accepted in February 1988. That did not resolve the problems, though, and further reform was planned within the Commission during 1990.

The CAP in the 1990s

In the 1990s the external pressures for reform of the CAP finally forced effective action to be taken. Initially this was in the context of the Uruguay Round of GATT negotiations. Subsequently the pressure for reform was maintained by the need to prepare for the eastward enlargement of the EU.

The MacSharry reforms

In May 1992 the EC member states reached an agreement to cut guaranteed prices for cereals by 29 per cent over three years, together with smaller but still significant reductions for other surplus products. The price reductions were accompanied by a rural development dimension that encouraged set-aside, early retirement, reforestation, and the adoption of more organic forms of farming (Ross 1995: 200).

These reforms were the result of the same combination of internal and external pressures that had produced the 1988 reforms, but the real change had come from an intensification of the external pressures (Box 24.4, p. 317). Delors and the new commissioner for agriculture, Ray MacSharry, saw

Box 24.4 External pressures for CAP reform in the 1990s

- Budget pressures again became significant as the USA allowed the value of the dollar to decline and reintroduced agricultural export subsidies of its own. This forced down world prices, and so increased the cost of export subsidies.

- The reunification of Germany brought into immediate membership of the EC considerable grain-producing areas, as well as extra dairy and beef livestock, adding to the problems of overproduction.

- The need to stabilize democracy and capitalism in the states of Central and Eastern Europe demanded that the West buy exports from them to allow them to obtain the hard currency necessary to buy from the West to re-equip their industries. These countries had

few products in which they had any comparative advantage. Agricultural products were among the few. If the CAP had not prevented it, several of the states could have exported their agricultural goods to the EC.

- By 1992 the Uruguay Round of the GATT had reached a critical stage. In previous rounds of the GATT, agriculture had been raised as an issue, but had always been eventually left on one side because the participants did not want the overall package to collapse. This time the fate of farmers was so serious that both the USA and the Cairns Group appeared to be prepared to collapse the deal unless it were included. Eventually in 1992, with the original deadlines for agreement already well past, the Cairns Group agreed to allow the United States to negotiate directly with the EC on agriculture.

particularly the linkage between reform of the CAP and the GATT negotiations as a useful way of pressing the necessity for reform on the member states. 'The threat of trade war inherent in the GATT negotiations could lessen internal opposition to CAP reform while the gestation of CAP reform might give the United States pause before pushing too hard on trade' (Ross, 1995: 141). However, as Grant (1997: 77) explains, there was also frequent denial of the linkage because any suggestion that the reforms were being forced on the EU from the outside would have stiffened the resistance of the Ministers of Agriculture.

Commissioner MacSharry introduced his reform proposals in July 1991, and they were agreed with some modifications, and side-payments to sweeten the pill, in a very rapid ten months, by May 1992. Although known as the 'MacSharry reforms', they nevertheless bore the imprint also of President Delors and his *cabinet*. The package involved a sharp decrease in the prices for cereals and beef, to bring them more into line with world prices, linked to a move from supporting farmers through subsidies on production to direct support for rural incomes. More land was to be taken out of production altogether, with the farmers being compensated by direct payments; an early retirement scheme was introduced to encourage older farmers to cease production; and

more environmentally-friendly farming was encouraged, with the implication that this would lower yields.

Sceptics claimed that the reforms would not solve the problem, and in the short term would even increase the cost of the CAP. However, at the end of November 1993 MacSharry's successor, René Steichen, claimed that cereal production for 1993 was 16 million tons lower than it would have been without the reforms (*The Week in Europe*, 2 Dec. 1993). More significantly, the reforms accepted for the first time that support for farmers could be separated from production. Surprisingly, in his farewell speech to the European Parliament in January 1995, Delors said that getting this agreement on reform of the CAP was in his own view his greatest achievement.

The Uruguay Round: the Blair House Agreements

Acceptance of his reform package allowed MacSharry to turn his attention to negotiating with the United States in the context of the GATT talks. Agreement was reached in December 1992, but the implications caused widespread protests from French farmers, and the Socialist government, faced with elections before the end of the year, chose not to reinforce its unpopularity by implementing the agreement. However, the conservative government of Edouard Balladur, which was elected in March 1993, had little choice but to accept the agreement because of the implications for the French economy if the GATT round were not successful. France was the world's fourth largest exporter after the United States, Germany, and Japan; and it was the second largest exporter of services, with ten per cent of total world trade (*Independent*, 7 Nov. 1993).

Even this proved not enough to satisfy the United States within the GATT negotiations, though. In November 1992 Delors reached the limit of his willingness to compromise. MacSharry had almost reached a deal in direct talks with the United States at the Blair House hotel in Chicago, when he received a telephone call from Delors telling him that the concessions he was proposing to make were not acceptable. They went beyond the limits of the CAP reform that had been agreed, and would not be acceptable to the member states. If MacSharry persisted with the deal, Delors would oppose it in the College of Commissioners.

MacSharry flew back to Brussels and took up the challenge from Delors by resigning as one of the Commission's negotiators for the GATT. Delors was outvoted in the College of Commissioners, MacSharry resumed his mandate and reached an agreement with the United States. Delors suffered a severe blow to his prestige, which contributed to undermining his future effectiveness.

Agenda 2000

The external pressure on the EU to continue the process of reform of the CAP became greater as the former Communist states outside what had been the Soviet Union began to press ever more strongly for full membership of the EU. After some initial reluctance, most member states came round to the realization that this would be necessary. Germany in particular became a strong advocate of eastern enlargement. However, reports prepared by the Commission indicated that the existing CAP could not simply be applied to the applicant states without dramatic consequences for the budget of the EU.

Extension of the Common Agricultural Policy in its present form to the acceding countries would create difficulties. Given existing price gaps between candidate countries and generally substantially higher CAP prices, and despite prospects for some narrowing of these gaps by the dates of accession, even gradual introduction of CAP prices would tend to stimulate surplus production, in particular in the live-stock sector, thus adding to projected surpluses. World Trade Organization (WTO) constraints on subsidized exports would prevent the enlarged Union to sell its surpluses on third markets.   (quoted in Avery & Cameron, 1998: 153)

However, the difficulties of negotiating the political obstacles to further reform of the CAP were clearly demonstrated in November 1995. At this stage, Germany joined France and the Mediterranean states in rejecting a proposal from the Commission that the permitted exports of agricultural produce from six central European states (the Czech Republic, Poland, Hungary, Slovakia, Bulgaria, and Romania) be increased by 10 per cent per annum. Five per cent annual increase was all that these states were prepared to accept (*Financial Times*, 17 Nov. 1995). Despite paying lip-service to the need to allow the eastern states into the EU, they were not prepared to risk the wrath of their own farmers to facilitate this.

Pressure also increased on the world trade front. At the conclusion of the Uruguay Round of GATT it had been agreed to open a further round of trade talks at the end of 1999. It was clear that the compromises reached at Blair House were provisional, and that agriculture would be a central element of the new round. In June 1996 the British National Farmers' Union (NFU) produced a paper explaining why the EU would come under great pressure in these trade talks to reform the CAP further. At the end of the Uruguay Round, agreement had been reached to allow both the EU and the USA to continue to subsidize cereal and livestock farmers. These measures had, in the terminology of the agreement, been placed in a 'blue box'. This meant that the subsidies did distort production, but could be continued without legal challenge until 2003 provided that they were not increased. Another 'green box' was created of support for farmers which did not distort production. These included measures such as those that had already been introduced into the CAP by the MacSharry reforms: measures to take land out of production, or to encourage environmental protection. Since the agreement the USA had unilaterally moved almost all of its support measures out of the blue box into the green box, leaving the EU alone in the blue box. Although the blue box measures could be sustained until 2003, the EU would now be under tremendous pressure to reciprocate the unilateral US gesture (NFU, 1996).

It was in this context that Frans Fischler, Agriculture Commissioner in the Santer Commission, produced a package of proposals for further reform in November 1995. These continued the pattern of the 1992 reforms, decoupling support for farmers from production and linking it to social and environmental objectives (European Commission, 1995b). They were subsequently incorporated into the Commission document *Agenda 2000: For a Stronger and Wider Union* (European Commission, 1997). This document 'consisted essentially of the Commission's recommendations for the Union's financial framework for the period 2000–2006; the future development of the Union's policies, and in particular its two most important spending policies—the cohesion and structural funds, and the Common Agricultural Policy; and the strategy for enlargement of the Union.' (Avery and Cameron, 1998: 101). On CAP it proposed large reductions in support prices and giving compensation to farmers in the form of direct payments, with a ceiling on the level of aid that any one individual could receive. Although explicitly linked to the eastern enlargement in *Agenda 2000*, these reforms were in line with shifting support from the GATT 'blue box' to the 'green box'.

When negotiations began on the CAP proposals of *Agenda 2000* in February 1999, the French government predictably pressed for more limited reform. This position was supported by 30,000 farmers—mainly from France, Germany, and Belgium—protesting on the streets of Brussels, the biggest demonstration since those against the Mansholt reforms in 1971. After a temporary suspension of the negotiations, the Agriculture Ministers agreed on 11 March to cut cereal prices by 20 per cent, as proposed by the Commission, but to do so in two stages—a half in 2000–1 and the other half in 2001–2. They agreed to lower milk prices by 15 per cent in line with the Commission's proposals, but only over three years starting in 2003, and dairy production quotas were actually raised slightly. They also agreed that beef prices should be cut by 20 per cent, but this was only two-thirds of the cut proposed by the Commission.

Fischler hailed the agreement as the most far-reaching reform of the CAP for forty years; but the states that had most strongly supported reform—Britain, Italy, Sweden, and Denmark—expressed their disappointment. They did not like the delays in implementing the cuts that had been forced through by France and Germany (which held the Presidency of the Council). They were to be even more disappointed following the Berlin European Council that was intended to approve the reform.

In Berlin, President Chirac of France simply refused to accept what the French Minister of Agriculture had negotiated. This reflected the fact that Chirac was a conservative President who was forced to work with a Socialist government. He was blatantly playing domestic politics. However, so important was it to the German government to get an agreement during its presidency, and not to break publicly with France, that Chancellor Schröder eventually agreed to support a significant further dilution of the reform package. The dairy reforms were further delayed, and the cuts in cereal prices were scaled back from the compromise level reached by the Ministers of Agriculture. The other member states went along in return for side-payments: Spain and Greece got agreement to continuation of the cohesion fund (see Ch. 27, pp. 376–9); Britain got agreement to the continuation of the British budgetary rebate with only minor concessions. However, the emasculated package of farm reforms by the end fell far short of anything that would either prevent problems after enlargement or, more significantly, would satisfy the USA in the forthcoming trade talks.

Conclusion

For many years agriculture seemed like a sector that could not be reformed. Farmers' groups effectively played the role of gatekeepers, preventing the rolling back of the level of integration already achieved. They also managed to achieve consistently high increases in guaranteed prices by working together with officials in national ministries of agriculture and in DG VI of the Commission in the nearest thing that the EC had to a closed policy community.

Spillover pressures did exist as a result of the CAP. The distorting effect of the domination of the budget by agricultural expenditure provided an argument for the development of other common spending policies that would balance its effect. However, the spillover pressures were not strong enough to force the EC forward into other common policies. Governments, aided and abetted by the Commission, showed a remarkable ability to evade the problems caused by functional spillover through the adoption of *ad hoc* solutions. During the whole period from the collapse of the Mansholt Plan to the mid-1980s the Commission did not take the lead in pushing agricultural reform. Nor did the member states, with the partial exception of the British government, although Britain did not push wholeheartedly for reform until after the election of the Thatcher government in 1979 and was generally isolated and without allies anyway.

In the end reform was forced by the escalating cost of price-support operations, a function of long-term increases in productivity resulting from technological advances that increased yields, together with a number of short-term circumstances that boosted

the cost of the CAP, and especially the cost of export rebates. Reform moved to the top of the agenda in 1984, when the cost of the CAP threatened to exhaust the funds available to the EC, and again in 1987 under similar circumstances. In both cases the external environment had a profound effect on reform of an internal Community policy, because changes in the world price of food and changes in the value of the dollar both contributed to the rapid escalation of the cost of the CAP. Enlargement also increased the need for reform by adding to the overall cost of the budget.

The external environment was the most important incentive for further reform in the 1990s. The centrality of agriculture to the GATT negotiations and the importance of agriculture to the economies of the states of central and eastern Europe both provided strong incentives to change. The Commission manipulated all of these pressures. Although Delors got cold feet over the MacSharry agreement with the United States because it went beyond what he thought France could accept, he was fully involved with the drawing up of the package of reforms that carried the name of MacSharry. He also worked as hard as anybody to get them accepted by the member states, using all the influence that he had over the French government. The fate of the Agenda 2000 proposals, though, indicated that the limits of CAP reform might have been reached while still falling well short of what was necessary in order to accommodate the external pressures. At the end of the 1990s the CAP remained a problem for the EU.

KEY POINTS

Peculiarities of agriculture

- Agriculture was politically and economically important to France. The French government made it a condition of agreeing to the common market in industrial goods that agriculture be included in the Treaty.

- There was general agreement between the governments of the Six that agriculture was special and could not be subject to market rules.

- It was necessary to equalise food prices between the member states to ensure a level playing field of competition in the common market because food prices were an important determinant of industrial wage costs.

- France and The Netherlands were allies on this issue, forming a powerful lobby in favour of an agricultural policy.

The price-support system

- The price support system was introduced for both political and administrative reasons, with the concerns of French peasant farmers paramount.

- Political resistance to the CAP in Germany was exacerbated when Adenauer, as part of a political deal with de Gaulle, forced acceptance of lower prices for cereals than had previously been guaranteed to German farmers. Because of the reaction to the cereals price level, the German government held out for high guaranteed prices for beef and dairy products.

- After the collapse of the post-war economic boom there ceased to be any advantage in forcing farmers off the land because they would only be adding to the level of unemployment. The CAP then became a system of welfare support for farmers.

The Mansholt Plan

- The Mansholt Plan proposed a restructuring of agriculture, based upon encouraging small farmers to leave the land and giving financial support to the amalgamation of holdings. This provoked hostility from farmers' groups.

- The French government objected to allowing the restructuring to be in the hands of the European Commission.

- The main opposition came from West Germany. The elections in 1969 enhanced the already considerable political influence of German farmers on the government.

- The Mansholt plan faced further difficulties as the 1969 exchange-rate crisis put economic and monetary union higher up the agenda than agricultural reform. Reform was further delayed by the need to negotiate enlargement.

- The modified version of the plan which the Council of Ministers finally accepted did not significantly increase the amount to be spent on restructuring. It also left the member states full discretion for the implementation of the restructuring.

Agriculture in the 1970s

- In the 1970s, economic recession and the political influence of farmers blocked reform, despite the high cost of the CAP distorting the overall Community budget.

- The move from holding intervention stocks in storage to paying export subsidies caused tensions in trade relations with the United States.

- Spillover pressures from agriculture to monetary union were circumvented by inventing the system of 'green currencies' and monetary compensatory amounts.

The CAP in the 1980s

- Some progress on CAP reform came in the 1980s. This was driven by:

- — escalating costs;

- — growing environmental concerns;

- — the single market programme;

- — other agricultural producing countries, particularly the United States.

- Reform was resisted by farmers and, when it did come, was rendered ineffective by the policy community of the Commission DGVI and COPA, and the reluctance of Ministers of Agriculture to upset farmers.

- Towards the end of the 1980s the forces for reform began to be manipulated by key figures in the Commission who feared that an unreformed CAP would damage the single market programme.

The CAP in the 1990s

- External pressures were crucial in forcing CAP reform in the 1990s: the collapse of Communism increased pressure to allow the East European states to export their agricultural produce to the EU; and, agricultural reform became linked to the success of the Uruguay Round of GATT talks.

- In the face of these pressures the MacSharry reforms were agreed in 1992, establishing the principle of separating support for farmers from production subsidies.

- The agreements on agriculture made at the end of the Uruguay Round left unfinished business for a further round of trade talks at the end of the 1990s when the EU would face strong pressure to reform the CAP further.

- Applications for membership of the EU from the states of central and eastern Europe meant that the CAP had to be revised to accommodate their agricultural sectors once they became members, otherwise the EU budget would be bankrupted.

- The Agenda 2000 reforms of the CAP continued the process begun by the MacSharry reforms, but were so watered down on French insistence in particular that they were still an unsatisfactory basis for the future.

QUESTIONS

1 Why did the CAP develop in the particular form that it did?

2 Why has agricultural policy proved so difficult to reform?

3 Why did the MacSharry reforms succeed where earlier efforts had failed?

4 What is the importance of external events to CAP reform?

FURTHER READING

The best general introduction to the CAP is W. Grant, *The Common Agricultural Policy* (Basingstoke and London: Macmillan, 1997). The same academic has established a web site that is an invaluable reference tool for up-to-the-minute comment on developments in the CAP: http://members.tripod.com/~WynGrant/WynGrantCAPpage.html

An interestingly different perspective, linking the CAP to the post-war European welfare state, is: E. Rieger, 'The Common Agricultural Policy', in H. and W. Wallace (eds.), *Policy-Making in the European Union* (Oxford: Oxford University Press, 3rd edn. 1996), 97–123.

On the difficulties and prospects of reform of the CAP, in chronological order see: H. W. Moyer and T. E. Josling, *Agricultural Policy Reform: Politics and Process in the EC and the USA* (Ames: Iowa State University Press, 1990); A. Swinbank, 'CAP Reform 1992', *Journal of Common Market Studies* 31 (1993), 359–72; W. Grant, 'The Limits of Common Agricultural Policy Reform and the Option of Denationalization', *Journal of European Public Policy* 2 (1995), 1–18; W. D. Coleman, 'From Protected Development to Market Liberalism: Paradigm Change in Agriculture', *Journal of European Public Policy* 5 (1998), 632–51.

CHRONOLOGY

1958
July   CAP system of common prices agreed at Stresa Conference

1968
December   Commission produces 'Mansholt Plan' for restructuring EC agriculture

1971
March   Farmers demonstrate in Brussels against Mansholt Plan; Council of Agricultural Ministers agree a modified version of the Plan

1984
March   System of quotas for dairy products agreed

1988
February   Legal limit placed on increases in spending on agricultural support

1991
July   Agriculture Commissioner MacSharry introduces reform proposals

1992
May   MacSharry proposals agreed by Agriculture Ministers

1995
November   Commission proposal to increase imports from central European states rejected; Agriculture Commissioner Fischler introduces reform proposals, subsequently incorporated into *Agenda 2000*

1999
February   Negotiations over *Agenda 2000* proposals for agriculture begin
March   Modified Agreement on Agenda 2000 proposals reached at Berlin European Council

25 The single market

SUMMARY

The development of a single European market from the creation of the EEC through the 1990s was uneven. Following the Treaty of Rome, there was initial progress on the completion of a single market in the 1960s, before global economic recession in the 1970s led to a growth of member state protectionism and a retreat from European solutions. Revival came in the changing political and economic circumstances of the 1980s and was led by the entrepreneurial Delors Commission. This led to the 1985 White Paper, agreed by member states, which set 1992 as the target date for completion of the single market. By 1992, 95 per cent of the measures had been agreed. This success was qualified, however, by problems in transposing and enforcing these measures within member states. Nonetheless, the relative success of the single market programme brought in its wake implications for integration in other areas, not least for the completion of monetary union.

Introduction

Article 9 of the Treaty of Rome (EEC) states, 'The Community shall be based upon a customs union'; also, a substantial section of the Treaty (Title III, Articles 39–69, previously 48–73) is devoted to the free movement of persons, services, and capital. Together these objectives constitute the construction of a single European market. Progress in achieving the objectives varied in line with fluctuations in the world economic cycle. After rapid initial progress in the 1960s there was a period of stagnation and even retreat from the unified market in the 1970s and early 1980s, before the adoption in 1985 of a new programme to free the internal market by the end of 1992 sparked off a second period of rapid progress.

This chapter looks first at the original decision to create a common market, then at the moves to complete the internal market, what became known as the single market programme, in the 1980s. Throughout, the following questions are raised:

- Why were the decisions taken to create a common market, and to complete the single market?
- What role was played by supranational actors?
- What role was played by domestic economic interest groups?
- What role was played by the autonomous calculation of national interests by national governments?

The common market: the original decision

The decision to create a common market reflects two of the main motivations for setting up the EEC: to avoid any return to the national protectionism that had been economically disastrous for Europe between the wars, and to promote economic expansion by creating a large internal market for European producers that would rival the large US market. The

history of the decision is recounted in Chapter 6 (pp. 72–5).

There is little evidence of supranational actors playing a key role in this original decision. Whereas the scheme for Euratom emerged from the lobbying activities of Jean Monnet's Action Committee for the United States of Europe, the proposal for the EEC, although adopted by the Action Committee, originated with the Dutch government supported by the Belgian government, and was a revival of a scheme that they had long favoured and had implemented on a more limited scale between themselves in the form of the Benelux economic union. The initiative was taken therefore by the political and administrative elites in small states in pursuit of what they perceived as their national interest in being part of a larger economic grouping.

Neofunctionalism (Ch. 1, pp. 9–12) does not provide an adequate framework for understanding the original commitment in the Treaty of Rome to the common market; but it was, after all, a theory about what would happen once the first steps had been taken in the integrative process. In one sense the first steps were taken with the Treaty of Paris, but in another sense the ECSC was something of a false start, based upon a view of integration as a process that would proceed sector by sector. It was only with the EEC Treaty that the framework was laid for a form of integration based on a general common market.

Initial reaction from producer-groups in the member states of the ECSC to the proposal for a general common market were much more mixed than neofunctionalist theory might have predicted. According to neofunctionalism, the success of the ECSC ought to have led other groups of producers to put pressure on their governments to extend the common market to their products so that they too could benefit. Yet there is no evidence that any national group of producers lobbied for the extension of the ECSC.

Although the experience of the coal and steel industries with the ECSC had been generally beneficial, it was also clear, especially in the case of coal, that as well as winners from a common market there would be losers. The reactions of different national interest groups reflected the extent to which they expected to be winners or losers from a general common market (Box 25.1, p. 326). So the experience of the creation of the EEC does not lend support to the neofunctionalist concept of political spillover. Nor does it support the view that important steps in the process of European integration have been taken as a result of the lobbying of national governments by economic interests. Rather it illustrates the

---

Box 25.1 Reactions of national groups to the proposal for a common market

- German industrialists were mostly supportive of the idea; they were in buoyant mood because of their experience of remarkably high rates of economic growth in the early 1950s, and they saw the common market as an opportunity to sustain that expansion (Haas, 1968: 172).

- French industry, on the other hand, had not by the mid-1950s shaken off the generally negative, safety-first culture that had dominated between the wars, and the CNPF campaigned against French participation in the EEC (Haas, 1968: 191–3). They were, however, overruled by the French state-elites.

---

inadequacies of a simple pluralist view of the nature of politics and the way in which public policy is made in capitalist democracies. The state is not just a cipher, a black box into which demands are fed, and which processes those demands to produce outputs that reflect the balance of the forces making those demands. It is an independent actor, consisting of politicians and administrators who may sometimes take a short-term view of policy (especially perhaps the elected politicians, who wish to be re-elected) but who also have to take a view of what will be in the longer-term interests of the country. If they do not take that longer-term view, they will find that they are running into more and more intractable problems. Short-termism has its limits, and they are soon reached.

Thus it was clear that the creation of a customs union would result in an uneven distribution of benefits and losses between the member states; and although the precise distribution of those benefits and losses could not be predicted in advance, there were reasonable grounds for believing that West German industry might gain more than French industry. That is why French negotiators were anxious to ensure that other commitments were made in the Treaty of Rome, to develop policies in areas where their country could be expected to benefit more than West Germany, particularly agriculture. But the reason why the plunge was taken to create the EEC was that all six states expected their economies to be better off as a result of creating the internal market, even if some benefited more than others.

Towards completion of the internal market

After the original decision had been taken to create a common market, there was rapid progress in that direction; but the progress faltered in the mid-1960s, and there was no further advance in the 1970s. It was not until the 1980s that the programme was revived, in a form that was updated to take account of the changed global circumstances in the meantime.

Progress in the 1960s

If the original decision to create a common market did not lend support to the neofunctionalist idea of political spillover, the surprisingly rapid progress that was made in the 1960s towards that objective did seem to do so. In particular, a decision taken by the Council of Ministers in 1960 to accelerate the original timetable for removing internal tariffs and quotas, and erecting a common external tariff was celebrated by Leon Lindberg (1963: 167–205) as a graphic illustration of political spillover at work.

The EEC Treaty specified (Article 14) a precise timetable for the progressive reduction of internal tariffs. On the original schedule it would have taken at least eight years to get rid of all internal tariffs. This rather leisurely timetable reflected the concerns of some industrial groups about the problems of adjustment involved in ending national protection. However, once the treaty was signed and it became obvious that the common market would become a reality, those same industrial interests responded to the changed situation facing them. Even before the treaty came into operation on 1 January 1958, companies had begun to conclude cross-border agreements on co-operation, or to acquire franchised retail outlets for their products in other member states. Just as the neofunctionalists had predicted, changing circumstances led to changed behaviour.

Corporate behaviour adjusted so rapidly to the prospect of the common market that companies became impatient to see the benefits of the deals concluded and of the new investments made. This led to pressure on national governments to accelerate the timetable. Remarkably, the strongest pressure came from French industrial interests, which had opposed the original scheme for a common market.

On 12 May 1960, the Council of Ministers agreed to a proposal from the Commission to accelerate progress on the removal of internal barriers to trade and the erection of a common external tariff, and on the creation of the CAP. Interest groups had only pressed for the first of these to be accelerated. Progress was slow on agriculture; the negotiations had been dogged by disagreements over the level of support that ought to be given to farmers for different commodities. But the issues were clearly linked: progress on the CAP to accompany progress on the industrial common market had been part of the original deal embodied in the EEC treaty.

In keeping the linkage between the two issues in the forefront of all their proposals to the Council of Ministers, the Commission played a manipulative role that coincided with the view of neofunctionalism about the importance of central leadership. As described by Lindberg (1963: 167–205), the progress of the EC between 1958 and 1965 involved the Commission utilizing a favourable situation to promote integration. Governments found themselves trapped between the growing demand from national interest groups that they carry through as rapidly as possible their commitment to create a common market, and the insistence of the Commission that this could only happen if the same governments were prepared to overrule the conflicting pressures on them from other groups and reach agreement on the setting of common minimum prices for agricultural products. (But see also Box 8.2, p. 90.)

The Dark Ages: the 1970s

De Gaulle's actions in 1965 were to blame for taking much of the momentum out of the EC (see Ch. 8, pp. 92–3). However, de Gaulle did not stop the completion of the customs union, which was complete by July 1968. He did cause a delay, though, in the implementation of the rest of the Treaty. The wait turned out to be much longer than just for the retirement of de Gaulle. By the time that Pompidou became President of France, and adopted a more accommodative attitude to the EC, world economic circumstances had begun to shift away from the high growth of the 1950s and 1960s. By the time that the negotiation of the entry of Britain, Ireland, and Denmark had been completed, clearing the way for a further deepening of the level of economic integration, the capitalist world was teetering on the brink of recession, and was soon to be pushed over the edge by OPEC (Ch. 9, pp. 97–8).

Throughout the 'stagflation' years (Box 9.1, p. 97) of the 1970s further progress on the creation of a genuinely free internal market became almost impossible (Hodges and Wallace, 1981; Hu, 1981). Given the economic problems that they were experiencing, and the political problems that resulted, governments became particularly prone to short-termism, and sensitive to the protectionist impulses of interest groups and wider public opinion. This was not a favourable environment for strengthening the internal market. Indeed, throughout the 1970s there was a marked retreat from the common market by the member states. Unable to raise tariffs or quotas against imports from other members of the EC, governments became adept at finding different ways of reserving domestic markets for domestic producers. Non-tariff barriers (NTBs) proliferated (see Box 25.2, p. 328).

Project 1992: freeing the internal market

In the mid-1980s the situation in the EC began to change rapidly, again in response to the changing international economic environment. In June 1984, at the Fontainebleau meeting of the European Council, two major steps were taken in breaking

Box 25.2 Non-tariff barriers (NTBs)

These NTBs took a wide variety of different forms. Some, such as state aids to industry, were against the competition clauses of the EEC Treaty, and the Commission frequently took member states to the European Court of Justice. However, the compliance of guilty states with the rulings of the Court was often tardy and only effected once an alternative system for supplying the aid had been devised. The long process of investigation by the Commission, issuing of warnings, reporting to the Court, and waiting for the case to make its way to the top of the Court's increasingly long agenda then had to begin all over again.

Other NTBs were more subtle. Particularly prevalent were national specifications on the safety of products, some of which were so restrictive that only nationally produced goods could meet them without modification to their basic design. Differing regulations could prevent a single manufacturer from producing on the same production line for the whole EC market; in effect the market was fragmented into a series of national markets again. Governments also used border customs formalities to make importing difficult, and only placed public contracts with national companies (Pelkmans and Winters, 1988: 16–53).

out of the *immobilisme* that had been afflicting the EC. First, agreement was reached on the long-running dispute over British contributions to the Community's budget; second, a committee was set up to look into the need for reform of the institutional structure and decision-making system of the EC.

At the beginning of 1985 a new Commission took office under the presidency of Jacques Delors, and in June 1985 Lord Cockfield, the British Commissioner for Trade and Industry, produced a White Paper on the freeing of the internal market from non-tariff barriers to trade in goods, services, people, and capital (European Commission, 1985). This listed some 300 separate measures, later reduced to 279, covering the harmonization of technical standards, opening up public procurement to intra-EC competition, freeing capital movements, removing barriers to free trade in services, harmonizing rates of indirect taxation and excise duties, and removing physical

Box 25.3 The Commission white paper on freeing the internal market

The White Paper provided no simple definition of what 'freeing the internal market' constituted, but it dealt with four 'freedoms':

- free movement of goods
- free movement of services
- free movement of labour
- free movement of capital.

The aim of the White Paper was to remove physical barriers, fiscal barriers, and technical barriers to these four freedoms of movement.

Physical barriers were dealt with by a series of proposed directives to end elaborate border checks on goods crossing from one EC member state to another, which were costly in themselves and caused long delays.

Fiscal barriers were dealt with in a series of proposals to harmonize rates of value added tax (VAT) and excise duties.

Technical barriers was a portmanteau term covering a range of different things, including national standards for products, barriers to the free movement of capital, the free movement of labour, and public procurement rules.

- National standards were dealt with by the adoption of the so-called 'new approach'. This was based on the principle enunciated by the ECJ in its judgement in the *Cassis de Dijon* case (case 120/78, 1979). Ruling that the German government had acted illegally in preventing the sale of a French liqueur in Germany because its alcohol content was lower than specified in German law, the ECJ stated that any product that could legally be offered for sale in one member state should also be allowed to be offered for sale in every other member

state. The only exceptions allowed to this were on health and safety grounds. In order to overcome this potential barrier, the Commission proposed that minimum health and safety standards for all products should be laid down by two European standards authorities, each of which is known by the initial letters of its name in French: CEN (the European Committee for Standardization), CENELEC (the European Committee for Standardization of Electrical Products). If products met these minimum standards, they would be awarded a 'CE' mark, and could not legally be prevented from being put on sale in any member state.

- Barriers to the free movement of capital had already started to disappear within the EC, and the White Paper simply proposed to complete this process through three directives covering cross-border securities transactions, commercial loans, and access to stock exchanges in other countries.

- Barriers to the free movement of labour were to be tackled by directives covering the extension of rights of residence that already existed for workers to citizens who were not active members of the labour force (students, retired people, the unemployed), and guaranteeing non-discrimination in access to social and welfare benefits. The Commission also undertook to prepare guidance and draft directives on the mutual recognition of professional and educational qualifications.

- Public procurement referred to the purchasing policies of public authorities, which in most member states discriminated in favour of national suppliers and contractors. The aim was to open the largest contracts to competitive bidding by firms from across the EC.

---

frontier controls between member states (Box 25.3, p. 329). The list was accompanied by a timetable for completion.

At the Milan European Council in June 1985 the heads of government accepted the objectives of the White Paper and the timetable for its completion by the end of 1992. It was also agreed, against the protests of the British Prime Minister, to set up an IGC to consider what reforms of the decision-making process should accompany the initiative to free the market. The outcome of this IGC was the Single

European Act, which was agreed by the heads of government at the Luxembourg European Council in December 1985, and eventually came into force, after ratification by national parliaments, in July 1987. It introduced qualified majority-voting into the Council of Ministers, but only in respect of measures related to the freeing of the internal market, and even here certain areas—including the harmonization of indirect taxes and the removal of physical controls at borders—were excluded at British insistence.

Explaining the 1992 programme

The decision to adopt the 1992 programme provoked a fierce academic debate about the explanation. All voices in this debate agreed that structural factors favoured the single market. The differences concerned the role of supranational versus national actors.

Structural factors

The structural context was the sluggish recovery of the European economies from the post-1979 recession in comparison with the vigorous growth of the US and Japanese economies. In particular, the tide of direct foreign investment turned, so that by the mid-1980s there was a net flow of investment funds from western Europe to the United States. This augured badly both for the employment situation in Europe in the future, and for the ability of European industry to keep abreast of the technological developments that were revolutionizing production processes.

It was in response to the worry that Europe would become permanently technologically dependent on the United States and Japan that President Mitterrand proposed his EUREKA initiative for promoting pan-European research and development in the advanced technology industries. It also lay behind the promotion by the new Commission of framework programmes for research and development in such fields as information technology, biotechnology, and telecommunications (Sharp and Shearman, 1987). But when European industrialists were asked what would be most likely to encourage them to invest in Europe they replied that the most important factor for them would be the creation of a genuine continental market such as they experienced in the United States. It was therefore in an attempt to revive investment and economic growth that governments embraced the free-market programme. The pressure to break out of the short-termism that had prevented the EC from making progress in the 1970s and early 1980s came from the objective situation that faced governments. The EC,

as only one part of a global capitalist economy, was seeing investment flow away from it to other parts of that global economy, and was already being left behind in rates of economic growth and in technological advance by rival core-areas within the system. It was a calculation of the common national interests of the member states that led them to agree a new contract, in the form of the White Paper and the Single European Act.

The role of supranational actors

Among scholars and commentators . . . a conventional wisdom has emerged about the origins of the SEA . . . The decisive impulse stemmed from far-sighted Commission officials like Etienne Davignon, Jacques Delors, and Arthur Cockfield . . . backed by a coalition of visionary multinational businessmen who, strongly supportive of market liberalization, convinced or circumvented reluctant national leaders. (Moravcsik, 1998: 316–7)

Although in the above quotation he is setting up a position in order to knock it down, Moravcsik is not erecting a straw man. According to Sandholtz and Zysman (1989: 96): 'The renewed drive for market unification can be explained only if theory takes into account the policy leadership of the Commission.' It manipulated a conjunction of international events and domestic circumstances to push forward the process of European integration in much the way that neofunctionalists had expected it would back in the 1960s. In their explanation the Commission was seen as providing the essential leadership to exploit the prevailing international and domestic circumstances. In one of the earliest assessments of the single market programme (Hoffmann, 1989), even Stanley Hoffmann, who had been the main advocate of intergovernmentalism in the 1960s, emphasized the importance of Jacques Delors (Box 25.4, p. 331). Sandholtz and Zysman also emphasized the role of supranational business interests in pushing the single market, mentioning particularly the role of the ERT. This too became almost accepted wisdom, with Cowles (1995) making the strongest

Box 25.4 Jacques Delors and the single market programme

Before assuming office in January 1985, Delors spent much of the autumn of 1984 casting around for a 'big idea' that would provide a focus and an impetus for the incoming Commission (Grant, 1994: 70). Institutional reform, monetary union, and defence co-operation were all considered, but eventually the completion of the single market was chosen. There were two main reasons for this decision:

- First, extensive consultations indicated that each of the other possibilities would be strongly resisted by the governments of some member states, but the opening up of the European market would command general support. Indeed, there was already a momentum underway to dismantle the barriers that were fracturing the market and hindering economic development.

- Second, Delors believed that market integration would inevitably bring other important issues onto the agenda. For example, it would only be possible to pass all the laws necessary to complete the single market if there was a reform of the decision-making process; and

movement towards a more integrated market would raise the question of monetary integration.

So, Delors was instrumental in giving the single market objective a high priority. He promoted it in the early months of his presidency through speeches, interviews, and in his dealings with national governments. He encouraged the members of the European Round Table of Industrialists (ERT) to bring pressure to bear on governments to support the single market programme, thus utilizing a transnational network to push forward the issue. He commissioned the Cecchini Report (Cecchini *et al.*, 1988) of leading European economists to put the weight of technical experts behind the project.

The issue was already on the agenda, but Delors singled it out and pushed it to the top of that agenda. He acted as a policy entrepreneur, recognizing an opportunity to promote a policy that went with the grain of existing thinking, that would increase the level of integration between the member states, and that would put other integrative measures onto the agenda in its wake.

statement of the importance of the role of the ERT. Against this 'accepted wisdom' Moravcsik (1991) contested explanations that stressed the role of supranational forces (Box 25.5, p. 332). Instead he put the emphasis on the positions of national governments.

National actors and the single market programme

Britain

The adherence of the British government to the single market programme is not difficult to explain. The Thatcher government had a strong ideological commitment to liberalization. It had carried through a programme of domestic economic liberalization within Britain, and had been advocating international liberalization in a variety of fora for some time. Indeed, it was because of the predictable support that the Thatcher government was prepared to give to the programme that it was chosen as the centrepiece of Delors's strategy to relaunch the EC. As Helen Wallace (1986: 590) explained:

The internal market is important not only for its own sake, but because it is the first core Community issue for over a decade . . . which has caught the imagination of British policy-makers and which is echoed by their counterparts elsewhere. . . . The pursuit of a thoroughly liberalized domestic European market has several great advantages: it fits Community philosophy, it suits the doctrinal preferences of the current British Conservative government, and it would draw in its train a mass of interconnections with other fields of action.

It was with the 'mass of interconnections with other fields of action' that the British government was to have most difficulty (see below). Initially its problems were with just one aspect: the link that was made between the single market and institutional reform.

Box 25.5 **Moravcsik on supranational actors and the Single European Act**

Moravcsik (1991) considered two broad explanations for developments that furthered European integration: supranational institutionalism and intergovernmental institutionalism.

Supranational institutionalism covered explanatory factors such as pressure from the EC institutions (primarily the European Parliament and the European Court of Justice), lobbying by transnational business interests, and political entrepreneurship by the Commission; it was therefore a model consistent with neofunctionalist theory. Moravcsik tested it against the empirical evidence relating to the SEA and found it wanting. He argued that the European Parliament was largely ignored in the negotiation of the SEA; the transnational business groups came late to the single market, when the process was already well under way as a result of a consensus between governments on the need for reform; the Commission's White Paper on the single market was 'a response to a mandate from the member states' rather than an independent initiative from a policy-entrepreneur (1991: 45–8).

Intergovernmental institutionalism stressed bargains between states, marked by lowest-common-denominator bargaining and the protection of sovereignty. It was an example of what Keohane (1984) had described as the 'modified structural realist' explanation of the formation and maintenance of international regimes, but it took more account of domestic politics. Indeed, in his application of the model to the SEA, Moravcsik put a good deal of emphasis on domestic politics, and he ended his article in 1991 with a plea for more work on this aspect of EC bargaining. He subsequently (Moravcsik, 1998) answered his own plea.

The codification of the commitment to majority voting as a formal amendment of the founding treaties, and as part of a potentially wider reform of the institutional procedures for making decisions, was resisted strongly by Mrs Thatcher. The whole issue of institutional reform was one of several where the British government differed from most of its continental European partners. Thatcher insisted at Milan that no institutional reform, and so no IGC, was necessary. However, it seems that she was persuaded by her Foreign Secretary, Sir Geoffrey Howe, and her adviser on European affairs, David Williamson, that unless a legally binding commitment were made to an element of majority-voting in the Council of Ministers the measures necessary to implement the Cockfield White Paper would never be agreed.

Germany

The 1992 proposal met with the favour of the CDU/CSU/FDP coalition, which took office in 1982 and was returned in the 1983 Federal election, for four reasons:

1. West Germany was an export-oriented economy, and over half of its exports went to the rest of the EC. Moves to open up the market further would therefore appeal to any German government.

2. Although business support for market liberalization varied according to sector, the German federation of industrialists (*Bundesverband der Deutschen Industrie*—BDI) came out in favour of the proposals in the White Paper (Moravcsik, 1998: 328).

3. Public support in Germany for European integration in general was high. Unlike the situation in Britain, it was a vote-winning platform. The FDP was particularly associated with pro-EC policies through its leader and Foreign Minister, Hans Dietrich Genscher. It was therefore both a matter of internal coalition management and public popularity for the new Chancellor, Helmut Kohl, also to embrace a relaunching of the EC.

4. The new coalition was concerned to reform the German economy to make it more competitive. This meant introducing domestic liberalization measures that would run into opposition from economic vested interests, and particularly from the trade unions. Signing up to the 1992 programme allowed the government to pursue unpopular policies that it believed necessary under the cover of pursuing European integration, which was popular (Moravcsik, 1998: 330).

France

The position of the French government was pivotal in ensuring the acceptance of the 1992 proposal. The turning point was the decision of Mitterrand to keep the French franc in the ERM in 1983. This was followed by the reversal of policy which was outlined in Chapters 11 (p. 116) and 15 (pp. 173–4). From this point on the reasons for French support closely parallel those of Germany.

1. The French economy had become more export-oriented, and there was concern about the effect of NTBs elsewhere, and particularly in Germany, on the export industries.

2. The CNPF leadership supported both domestic and external policies of liberalization (Moravcsik, 1998: 337).

3. Mitterrand's reversal of policy required justification to his electorate, which thought it had voted for the Socialist policies of the first three years. Mitterrand chose to justify the new direction by declaring a European mission for himself and for the Socialists.

4. The abandonment of the 1981–3 Socialist experiment implied that the French economy must be opened up to international competition, which meant that it was necessary to pursue modernization of the less competitive sectors. As in Germany, this was bound to stir up opposition. It was therefore convenient for the Socialists to be able to hide behind Brussels to force through the reforms.

Beyond 1992

The deadline of the end of 1992 was the target date for the Council of Ministers to agree all the 279 measures in the White Paper. To facilitate meeting the deadline, the Commission drew up a timetable for proposals to be made and to be agreed. As a result of this, over 95 per cent of the measures mentioned in the White Paper had been agreed by the end of 1992 (Calingaert, 1999: 157). This remarkable record of success, however, needs to be set against three further considerations:

1. Agreement in the Council does not in itself mean that the single market is working. Before that stage is reached there are two further requirements: transposition and enforcement.

2. The 5 per cent of the measures that had not been agreed included some of the most intractable and controversial in the White Paper.

3. The White Paper did not cover some areas where businesses wanted to see liberalization because they were considered too controversial.

Transposition

Once a directive has been agreed by the Council of Ministers, it has to be transposed into the national laws of the member states. This process was slower in some states than in others. The Commission kept a running tally of the record of member states on transposition, and published the results annually as a league table. These showed that Germany did particularly badly until 1997, when criticism from other member states led to a concerted effort to catch up. The other poor performers were Austria and Belgium. At the other end, Denmark and Britain, allegedly poor Europeans, were consistently near the top of the league tables.

During 1998, Mario Monti, the Commissioner for the Internal Market, made a determined effort to persuade member states to transpose the remaining outstanding legislation before the Euro came into operation. He argued that once exchange rates were eliminated as an economic instrument, and once prices became transparent across the Euro-zone, the political pressures on governments to adopt protectionist measures might become irresistible if they did not already have the legislation in place (*Financial Times*, 16 Feb. 1998).

Enforcement

Even when the member states have transposed internal market legislation, it still has to be enforced, and the record of national governments on this is very variable. A survey was conducted by Mori for the British Chambers of Commerce and the CBI in October 1995 showed that of 5,000 British companies, two-thirds claimed to have experienced some form of unfair restriction of competition in other EU markets. At the same time, 40 per cent complained about over-zealous enforcement of regulations by British authorities in comparison with their counterparts elsewhere (*Financial Times*, 7 Nov. 1995). Again, the German government scored very badly. In May 1996, Germany and Belgium had the most proceedings against them for not conforming with the requirements of single market legislation. Two areas where the record on enforcement is particularly bad are those products for which there are no harmonized EU standards, and public procurement.

Where there is no uniform EU standard for a product, the national authorities should accept the standards of other member states. However, this rarely happens. Companies found their products being subjected to a battery of national test and certification requirements, especially in France and Germany. The British Department of Trade and Industry even set up its own Single Market Compliance Unit to pursue cases where British manufacturers had been discriminated against in this way, and if necessary to report the offending state authorities to the Commission.

The situation on public procurement is that eight directives were agreed by the end of 1993 obliging all public authorities to advertise for tenders for public contracts over 5 million ecus in the *Official Journal* of the EC. However, very few contracts are ever actually awarded to non-national firms, and there are a number of celebrated cases of governments blatantly flouting the rules.

Problem Areas

Some issues that were included in the White Paper have proved particularly difficult. Two that stand out are tax harmonization and company law. Arguably both are necessary if there is to be a genuine single market in which companies can operate without regard to national boundaries. Without harmonization of taxes and a common company statute, companies that operate in several different states face a complex of regulations and paper work.

Pressures for tax harmonization have also come from spillover. The removal of restrictions on the purchase of goods such as alcohol has led to cross-border shopping by consumers taking advantage of different levels of excise duty and VAT. This has particularly hit countries such as Denmark, which has high duties but is close to Germany which has low duties. Danes travel to Germany to buy alcohol more cheaply.

Ironically, cross-border shopping has also hit Britain. In 1988 the British government argued that rates of excise duty and VAT should be allowed to sort themselves out. States with higher rates of excise duty and VAT would have to lower their rates to match those of their neighbours. The British government believed that this would benefit consumers by reducing taxes across the EU. At the same time, it clearly believed that Britain would suffer little from cross-border shopping (George, 1998: 196–7). Yet by mid-1995 the British Brewers' and Licensed Retailers' Association was arguing that unless the level of excise duty on beer was reduced, many pubs and off-licences would be driven out of business by the influx of cheap beer bought by British day-trippers to France. Predictably, though, the states with low excise duties refused to consider raising their levels.

A second spillover from the single market to tax harmonization came from the freeing of capital movements. This led to competition between states to attract savings from other countries by reducing taxes on the interest paid on them. Germany has suffered most from low levels of taxes on savings, in Luxembourg in particular. In all cases the reduction of taxes on savings has led to the lost revenue being replaced by higher taxes on less mobile factors such as labour. The Commission has identified this as one

Box 25.6 **The liberalization of telecommunications**

Telecommunications in Europe is traditionally dominated by national monopoly suppliers—the Post, Telephone and Telegraph (PTT) public utilities. Attempts by the Commission to involve itself in the sector prior to 1982 proved fruitless. It was a sector dominated by national policy communities, which collaborated at the international level to preserve the status quo.

An opportunity was opened for the Commission by the implications of deregulation of the telecommunications market in the United States in the early 1980s. This led to pressure from the government of the United States for the EC to open its markets for telecommunications equipment. AT&T, which had been forced to open up its domestic operations, was anxious to recoup lost revenue by moving into Europe, and IBM was looking to diversify into what promised to be an increasingly profitable market (Dang-Nguyen *et al.*, 1993: 103).

The Commission (DG XIII) responded by commissioning a number of reports on how Europe was losing out to the United States following US deregulation. It used these to build a momentum in the same way that Delors and Cockfield used the Cecchini Report on the 'Costs of Non-Europe' (Cecchini *et al.*, 1988) to build up momentum for the internal market. It also mobilized producer groups that had an interest in seeing an increase in the efficiency and a decrease in the cost of telecommunication services: UNICE, and the Information Technology User Group (INTUG). Another element in the strategy was that the Commission tried to ride its project on the back of the single market programme. Its discourse on telecommunications drew heavily on the 1992 programme. Its approach assumed that a single market required a common infrastructure, of which telecommunications would be a part. Thus the creation of a European policy for telecommunications gathered momentum by association with the 1992 programme (Fuchs, 1994: 181).

Having established the legitimacy of a European policy for the sector, the Commission produced a *Green Paper on the Development of the Common Market for Telecommunications, Services and Equipment* in 1987. This discussion document became the basis for the development of a policy in the sector much as the White Paper on the internal market had been the basis for the 1992 programme. It advocated deregulation and increased competition, proposals that were consistent with developments in those member states that had begun to respond to the problem at national level. The Green Paper advocated the separation of regulation of the sector from operation of the system, a reform that had already been introduced in Britain, France, and Germany; and the introduction of Open Network Provision (ONP), so that rival operators could compete using a common infrastructure. A concession to the PTTs was that they would remain in control of the provision of network services.

In 1988, the year after the publication of the Green Paper, DG IV (Competition) issued an administrative directive on the liberalization of the terminal equipment market. The Commission argued that it had the right to act without specific approval by the Council of Ministers because it was acting in pursuance of Article 90 paragraph 3 of the Treaty of Rome (EEC), under which the Commission is charged to ensure that special rights conferred on national companies by their governments do not prevent the completion of the common market. Although the Council of Ministers had approved the Green Paper, which listed liberalisation of the market amongst its objectives, France, Belgium, Germany, and Italy took the Commission to the European Court of Justice, alleging that it had exceeded its powers by not seeking the approval of the Council for the directive. In March 1991 the Court found in favour of the Commission.

Dang-Nguyen *et al.*, (1993: 108) interpreted this incident as evidence of a conflict between the interventionist philosophy of DG XIII and the free-market philosophy of DG IV, and stated that: 'The Directive was issued by DG IV without consulting DG XIII.' However, given the internal procedures of the Commission on consultation of all DGs with an interest in a sector, it is difficult to see how this could have been the case. An alternative explanation is that the directive was another element in the strategy of the Commission as policy entrepreneur. In effect DG IV was playing the 'hard-cop' to DG XIII's 'soft-cop'. Faced with the prospect of an enforced opening of telecommunications monopolies by DG IV's exploitation of Article 90 of the Treaty, the PTTs were more likely to co-operate with a negotiated process under the auspices of the Task Force.

Box 25.7 **The liberalization of energy supply**

According to Matlary (1997), a similar approach was used to push forward a common energy policy to that used in the case of telecommunications. Like telecommunications, the energy sectors were dominated by national monopolies, which were most commonly publicly-owned. An open market in energy was originally part of the White Paper on the single market, but the opposition of national monopoly suppliers led to it being excluded. However, the Commission returned to the issue in 1989, making proposals for a phased dismantling of national monopolies over the electricity grids and gas supply networks. The linking of energy policy to the single market programme was explicit. In April 1991 Sir Leon Brittan, the Commissioner for Competition Policy, said that there were two sectors that were vital to the internal market, telecommunications and energy.

It was unlikely that the national monopolists themselves would support liberalization moves, but the Commission was able to mobilize the support of large industrial users of energy, working through the existing institutionalized networks of UNICE and the ERT.

At the same time as the proposals for a phased dismantling of national monopolies were being negotiated, DG IV was stepping up its attacks on monopolistic practices using its powers under Article 90 of the EEC Treaty. As in

the case of telecommunications, although the threat never became as explicit, the vested interests resisting integration were faced with a choice between a hardline free-market approach from DG IV or a negotiated softer approach from another DG, in this case from DG XVII.

Negotiations in the Council of Ministers were protracted. The French government in particular was reluctant to end the monopoly of Electricité de France (EdF) over the distribution of electricity in France. It claimed that its primary concern was to protect the access of rural French domestic consumers to electricity at the same price as was available everywhere else in France. This was the public service argument. However, it was also bowing to intense pressure from the Confédération Générale du Travail (CGT) trade union, which feared that liberalization would mean job losses.

Eventually, in June 1996, agreement was reached on a phased liberalization of electricity supply over six years, but it would only apply to large industrial users. The whole process of negotiation then had to be repeated to secure an agreement on liberalization of the market in gas supply, with the French government fighting as hard to protect the position of Gaz de France as it had to protect EdF. Eventually another compromise deal was reached in December 1997.

of the reasons why the single market has not produced the numbers of extra jobs predicted in the Cecchini report. Yet no progress has been made on the issue. Britain in particular has opposed agreement on a harmonized level of withholding tax on savings, reflecting the benefits that accrue to the City of London.

Agreement on a European company statute has been blocked by the insistence of the German government that it must contain a requirement for workers' representatives to sit on supervisory boards and to be consulted on all management decisions that affect the workforce. This is the position in Germany. The German trade unions fear that if it is not a requirement at EU level, German firms will operate under the European rules, reducing the influence of workers. Other member states are opposed to this German system being imposed at the EU level, resulting in stalemate.

Areas omitted from the White Paper

Cockfield's White Paper made no mention of extending the single market to telecommunications. Although it did mention energy, this was subsequently dropped. Yet these have been identified by businesses in the EU as two of the areas that most raise their costs of production in comparison with the United States. They were omitted from the White Paper because they were both sectors that had traditionally been in public ownership in the member states, and they both had a public service aspect to them. However, the Corfu European Council in June 1994 recognized that the extension of the internal market to the two sectors was a priority action to raise European competitiveness. The Commission then tried, and to a certain extent succeeded, in liberalizing these market sectors (Boxes 25.6, p. 335, and 25.7, p. 336).

Conclusion

The story of the various moves to create a single internal market in the EC illustrates several of the themes that run through this book. In particular it has been a key intellectual battleground for the supranational–intergovernmental debate. This has also involved debate about the role of interests, and ideas. The influence of the external environment, on the other hand, has been accepted by all sides in the debate.

The supranational–intergovernmental debate remains unresolved, and individuals will have to weigh the evidence for themselves and decide whether they believe that the role of supranational actors has been significant. The original decision to create a common market was taken by national governments against a background of enthusiasm for federalist ideas, but in response to urgent practical problems, particularly the need to sustain the post-1950 economic expansion. There were no significant supranational actors to cloud the analysis of the original decision; but disagreement continues over the role that the Commission played in pushing forward the process. Even less is there consensus on the relative role of the Commission in the 1985 decision to adopt the single market programme.

As for the role of organized interests, there is agreement that larger businesses have supported the single market, while smaller businesses have been more hesitant about its impact on them. This did not apply across the board to the original decision on the common market: business interests were divided on essentially national lines; but it did apply to the 1985 decision. However, there is disagreement about whether the channel used for exerting influence was through national governments, or through supranational institutions, with the European Round Table being identified by some analysts as a key ally of the European Commission. Once the first steps had been taken, the pressure from the larger industrial interests helped to prevent any backsliding from governments, and helped to sustain, even to accelerate the momentum; just as in the 1960s industrial pressures led to the acceleration of progress to the original common market. Once industrial interests

began to gear themselves up to the existence of a genuine internal market they were anxious that it should come about, otherwise their efforts and investments would prove in vain. As one of their number put it: 'it is the entrepreneurs and corporations who are keeping the pressure on politicians to transcend considerations of local and national interest' (Agnelli, 1989: 62). The support of large users of telecommunications and energy was important to counteract the pressure of vested interests within the states against extension of the single market to these sectors.

Ideas played a role in the form of the manipulation of the Cecchini report by the Commission. This group of economists comprised an epistemic community in the sense that they did not have a vested interest in the outcome, as did sectors of business; but they did have a commitment to the ideas that underpinned the programme. Also, once the single market was accepted, the ideas that informed the project became part of the common outlook of the Commission and the member states, making much easier the extension of the competitive principles to sectors such a telecommunications and energy supply.

The role played by the global economic environment in fostering both the original common market decision and the 1985 decision is clear. The background of the cold war and the threat of Communism in the 1950s was combined both with pressure from the United States, and with the hope on the part of European, especially French, leaders that they could make Europe as strong an economic actor as the United States. The background of the relative failure of the EC to recover from the recession of the end of the 1970s and the sight of both the United States and Japan establishing what might prove to be a permanent lead was crucial in prompting the 1985 decision.

The form taken by the single market programme gave an extra twist to globalization. It led to the dismantling of a whole array of protectionist devices that individual states had used to try to shelter their populations from the full impact of global competition. It did not replace these with EC-level protection against the encroachment of US and other non-European companies into the European market. At the same time, the failure to provide the accompanying social measures that Delors had envisaged helped to structure EC capitalism on a pattern that looked more like the Anglo-Saxon or American model than it did the various continental European models.

By making it more difficult for national governments to protect jobs, the single market contributed to undermining the legitimacy of the EC.

KEY POINTS

The common market: the original decision

- The original decision to create a common market was based on avoiding national protectionism and providing a large market to rival that of the USA.

- This decision was not promoted by supranational actors, but by the Dutch and Belgian governments.

- Support for the common market from national interest groups was ambiguous and varied by country and by sector. The acceptance of the common market reflected the commitment of key national political elites.

Towards completion of the internal market

- Industrial interests responded to the creation of the common market by adjusting their commercial behaviour. They became advocates of faster completion of the common market, and pressured governments to accelerate progress.

- The Commission responded by linking acceleration on the common market with acceleration of the CAP in a classic package-deal to 'upgrade the common interest'.

- The 1965 crisis slowed momentum on completing the common market.

- A focus on enlargement in the early 1970s and developing economic problems for member states throughout the decade held back further market integration.

- Changing economic circumstances in the early 1980s prompted new attempts to revive the EC.

- In 1985 a new Commission under the presidency of Jacques Delors published a White Paper on freeing the internal market. This was approved the European Council, which agreed 1992 as the target date for completion of the necessary measures.

Explaining the 1992 programme

- All commentators agree on the importance of the global economic context to the decision to take the 1992 initiative.

- There is a commonly accepted view that the solution to the problem of 'Eurosclerosis' through freeing the internal market was driven by a combination of supranational actors: the Commission and supranational business interests organized in the ERT.

- The Commission (and specifically President Delors):

  — raised the issue to the top of the agenda

— mobilized experts to produce reports arguing the advantages of the single market

— mobilized business interests (the ERT) to press the case on governments.

- The alternative view, put by Andrew Moravcsik, is that the initiative came from national governments, and reflected the coincidence of the policy and political priorities of the governments in Britain, Germany, and France.

National actors and the single market programme

- The British government embraced the single market programme enthusiastically because of its ideological commitment to free markets, but it had difficulty with some of the associated policies, including the introduction of QMV into the Council of Ministers.

- The German coalition government was intent on modernizing the German economy, and the single market programme allowed it to do this while linking unpopular restructuring measures to the project for European integration, which had popular support.

- The French Socialist government had just turned away from the policies on which it was elected, and hoped to use the single market as a substitute popular platform. Like the German government, it too was looking to modernize the national economy behind the cover of a commitment to European integration.

Beyond 1992

- The Council had agreed 95 per cent of the White Paper measures by the end of 1992.

- Transposition of Council agreements into national law has been much slower.

- Enforcement of legislation varies both by member state and by sector.

- No progress has been made on tax harmonization or a European company statute.

- The Commission has extended the single market to telecommunications and energy.

QUESTIONS

1 What explains the uneven progress towards the completion of the single European market?

2 What were the main pressures for the creation of a single European market?

3 To what extent did the Commission act as a 'policy entrepreneur' in the development of the single market programme in the 1980s?

4 What were the implications of the completion of the single market for integration in other policy areas?

5 What have been the unintended consequences for governments who signed up to the single market programme?

6 Was monetary union a necessary corollary to the single European market?

FURTHER READING

The great debate between theorists about the single market begins with W. Sandholtz and J. Zysman, 'Recasting the European Bargain', *World Politics* 42 (1989), 95–128, and continues with A. Moravcsik, 'Negotiating the Single European Act', in R. O. Keohane and S. Hoffmann (eds.), *The New European Community: Decisionmaking and Institutional Change* (Boulder, San Francisco, and Oxford: Westview Press), 41–84—a view now slightly revised by the author in A. Moravcsik, *The Choice for Europe: Social Purpose and State Power from Messina to Maastricht* (London: UCL Press, 1998), 314–78. An interesting contribution is made by M. Green Cowles, 'Setting the Agenda for a New Europe', *Journal of Common Market Studies* 33 (1995), 501–26. On telecommunications the texts to look at are G. Dang-Nguyen, V. Schneider, and R. Werle, 'Networks in European Policy-Making: Europeification of Telecommunications Policy', in S. S. Andersen and K. A. Eliassen (eds.), *Making Policy in Europe: Europeification of National Policy-Making* (London: Sage, 1993), 93–114, and G. Fuchs, 'Policy-Making in a System of Multi-Level Governance: The Commission of the European Community and the Restructuring of the Tele-communications Sector', *Journal of European Public Policy* 1 (1994), 177–94. On energy, the key text is J. H. Matlary, *Energy Policy in the European Union* (Basingstoke and London: Macmillan, 1997).

CHRONOLOGY

1958
January   EEC Treaty sets objective of a customs union and the free movement of persons, services and capital

1960
May   Council of Ministers agrees to Commission proposal to accelerate progress towards single market

1968
July   Customs Union completed and common external tariff established

1984
June   Fontainebleau European Council resolves issues blocking further market integration

1985
June   Trade and Industry Commissioner Cockfield produces White Paper on the freeing of the internal market

June   Milan European Council accepts Commission White Paper and its timetable for completion by the end of 1992

December   Single European Act agreed in principle by heads of government at Luxembourg European Council

1986
February   Single European Act signed by Foreign Ministers in Luxembourg (nine states) and subsequently the Hague (the remaining three states).

1987
July   Single European Act comes into force following ratification by national parliaments

1994
June   Corfu European Council agrees to extend internal market to energy and telecommunications

26 Economic and Monetary Union

Among economists, there is no consensus on the desirability of monetary integration, much less on its functional necessity.

(Sandholtz, 1993: 21)

SUMMARY

Plans for Economic and Monetary Union (EMU) go back to the 1960s. The first serious attempt to tie together the value of national currencies came in the early 1970s, but collapsed in the face of turbulence in the global monetary system. In the late 1970s the European Monetary System (EMS) was set up. This was initially an attempt to produce more monetary stability in the EC, and was generally successful. Building on the experience of the EMS, and the success of the single market programme, proposals for another attempt to move to monetary union were pursued at the end of the 1980s, leading eventually to the commitment in the TEU to a single currency. In deciding on the detail of how the single currency would be managed, the French and German governments put forward very different proposals, with the German position prevailing on every significant issue. In January 1999 eleven member states of the EU joined the single currency. A range of factors have been identified as significant in explaining these developments: cultivated spillover, the role of an epistemic community, concerns about the credibility of anti-inflationary commitments, the domination of the EMS by German policy priorities, the strength of political leadership from Kohl and Mitterrand, the impact of German reunification, and concern about the use that the United States made of the international dominance of the dollar to benefit the US economy.

Introduction

Economic and monetary union (EMU) first came to the fore as a primary objective of the EC in 1969. Each element in the term has a maximalist and a minimalist meaning. Economic union implies that the member states will, at most, cease to follow independent economic policies, and at least will follow co-ordinated policies. Monetary union means, at most, the adoption of a single EC/EU currency, at least the maintenance of fixed exchange rates between the currencies of the member states.

Over the years the economic aspect of EMU has been emphasized less, and the monetary aspect more. This is partly because co-ordination of economic policy has occurred, quietly and away from intense public scrutiny, while an early attempt at monetary union at the start of the 1970s collapsed in the face of turbulence in the global monetary system following President Nixon's decision in August 1971 to end convertability of the dollar into gold, and the member states were thereafter cautious about trying

the experiment again. The European Monetary System (EMS), which began operation in March 1979, had a much less ambitious aim: to create a zone of monetary stability in Europe. Although it went through several crises, it did eventually prove to be successful. However, the project for monetary union was revived in the wake of the success of the single market programme, and despite opposition from the British government, and scepticism in several quarters, a single European currency, the 'Euro', formally came into existence in January 1999.

This chapter examines the various attempts to achieve EMU between 1969 and 1999, and analyses the reasons for the relative successes and failures up to and including the launch of the Euro. It then looks at the interpretations and explanations that have been given by various academic commentators. It does not go on to examine the record of the Euro since it was set up because the story was still unfolding at the time of writing, and hasty judgements did not seem appropriate.

The first attempts

Prior to 1969 some progress was made in institutionalizing the co-ordination of national economic and financial policies. In 1960 arrangements for the co-ordination of short-term economic policy were made, with the setting up of a Short Term Economic Policy Committee, consisting of representatives of the member governments and of the Commission. In 1964, on a proposal from the Commission, a Committee of Governors of Central Banks and a Budgetary Policy Committee were set up along the same lines. At the same time a Medium Term Economic Policy Committee was set up, which attempted to co-ordinate the medium-term programmes of the member states. Its work was hampered, though, by the very different degrees to which the member governments were prepared to engage in planning, and it never managed to move beyond forecasting to real indicative planning.

In February 1969 the Commission produced the Barre Report, arguing the case for a full economic and monetary union, and in December of the same year the Hague summit meeting of the EC heads of government made a commitment to the achievement of EMU. What followed is detailed in Chapter 9 (pp. 100–1). Analysing the reasons for these first attempts to move to EMU, and the reasons for their relative success and failure, provides a basis for understanding the later efforts that resulted in the Euro.

The Barre Report was the last time that discussion of EMU centred on spillover from the customs union and the CAP. By 1969, international considerations were already coming to the fore. In the background to the Hague summit were the devaluation of the French franc and the revaluation of the Deutschmark, symptoms of the disintegration of the international monetary systems agreed at Bretton Woods in 1944. They gave added weight to the argument in the Barre Report that the common market and the CAP would be threatened by fluctuating exchange rates.

To make the commitment to EMU was one thing: to agree how to do it was another. International considerations prompted the commitment: different national economic strategies caused problems in implementation. The French, looking for a subsidy from the EC for their national development plans, wanted a system for mutual support of fixed exchange rates. They argued that this would produce economic convergence, the essential requisite of a common economic policy. The Germans rejected that approach because they believed that it would involve them using their considerable foreign currency reserves to support the currencies of states that were following irresponsibly lax and inflationary economic policies. For the Germans, common economic policies had to come first; and they wanted their preference for monetary stability, rather than the growth-orientated policies of France, to be the basis of the common policies.

This fundamental disagreement produced the compromise proposals of the Werner Committee in November 1970 that the co-ordination of economic policy and the narrowing of exchange-rate fluctuations should proceed in parallel. This arrangement for approximating the exchange rates of member currencies one to another became known as the 'snake-in-the-tunnel'. In its first stage the snake was to contain no institutionalized mechanism for mutual support of currencies. Each state had to maintain its own currency within the parameters of the system. Even in the second stage, the aid from one member to another would be in the form of loans, not grants, the bulk of which would be short-term and repayable within three months. Where longer-term credits were granted they would be accompanied by conditions on the economic policies to be adopted by the recipient.

Even this limited arrangement was entered into reluctantly by West Germany. However, the world monetary crisis and the Smithsonian agreements (Ch. 9, p. 101) were not used as an excuse to end the experiment. On the contrary, concern about the way in which the United States had handled the situation increased the German wish to establish some degree of autonomy from US domination of the world monetary system. Also, there was a threat to West German exports to the rest of the EC implicit in the Smithsonian agreements. The Deutschmark was permitted to fluctuate by 2¼ per cent against the dollar in either direction, a maximum divergence from the established rate of 4½ per cent. But since all other currencies were fixed in terms of the dollar, and could each fluctuate by a maximum 4½ per cent, there was a possibility that the Deutschmark might appreciate against the other EC currencies by as much as 9 per cent, while the dollar could not appreciate by more than 4½ per cent. There was thus a risk that US products might become more competitive in EC markets than West German products. For this reason there was an incentive for the Germans to pursue a reconstitution of the snake even after the collapse of the first experiment following the ending of dollar convertibility in August 1971.

After the snake was reconstituted in April 1972 it ran into the same problems as its predecessor when it came to West Germany supporting weaker currencies. In 1972 the Federal Bank (Bundesbank) in Germany refused to intervene in the foreign exchanges to support the pound because the British were only prepared to repay any debts that were incurred in this way in dollars, and the Federal Bank refused to accept, in effect, dollars in exchange for Deutschmarks. The consequence was that speculation forced sterling out of the snake. In an attempt to prevent a repetition of this, the Council of Economic and Finance Ministers agreed in April 1973 to move at the start of 1974 to the second stage of the original Werner plan. It would also set up a European Monetary Co-operation Fund which would co-ordinate mutual support measures and the payment and repayment of loans in an acceptable currency. The West Germans agreed to this only reluctantly: they were very unhappy with the progress that was being made, or rather that was not being made, in the co-ordination of economic policies.

In fact co-ordination of economic policy was always going to prove difficult simply because the French, and other member states, could not accept that they should follow the German policy-priority of restraining inflation. This difference of viewpoint was exacerbated by the international economic developments of the early 1970s.

The slowing of growth affected different national economies very differently; and so did the oil-price rises of December 1973. By 1974 economic divergence was glaringly apparent in the EC, indicating that there were definite structural weaknesses in the economies of the peripheral states, including Britain. France sat delicately balanced on the edge between centre and periphery. It was these strains that caused the complete collapse of the original EMU experiment after 1973. But they were made worse by a US policy of allowing the dollar to depreciate on the foreign exchanges, at a time when the snake was being pulled upwards by the strength of the Deutschmark. Hence the departure of Italy in February 1973, finding itself unable to compete with US products even on its domestic market, but unable to boost its exports to its biggest customer, West Germany, because it could not devalue the lira against the Deutschmark. The French struggled against the same competitive disadvantage for longer, in the interests of encouraging West German independence from the United States, but finally capitulated after the oil-price rises, in order to ease the consequent deficit on the balance of trade. With the departure of the franc, the snake ceased to be even a possible route to EMU.

The EMS: origins

Despite the failure of the snake to move the EC towards EMU, it still served a purpose in 1977. It held together, within tight margins of fluctuation, seven currencies covering an area of high economic interdependence based on strong mutual trading links. In effect the snake constituted a Deutschmark zone within which West Germany conducted 25 per cent of its export trade. The proportion was even higher for the other participants. Given the failure to hold all the EC currencies together, this was a reasonable alternative, and few people thought that West Germany would be interested in any attempt to revitalize the original conception of the snake. Roy Jenkins's initiative in October 1977 to revive EMU was therefore greeted with some scepticism (Tsoukalis, 1977b).

Jenkins's initiative was taken up by Helmut Schmidt, largely because of the effect on the West German currency of the US policy of benign neglect of the dollar. Since the start of the 1970s the dollar had been depreciating, and there had been a corresponding upward pressure on the Deutschmark. The Deutschmark and the Yen were the safest currencies to hold. There was no chance of a devaluation, or depreciation of the Deutschmark, and every prospect of an upward movement which would represent a profit. The extent of the movement of funds into the Deutschmark ensured that it would appreciate in value. This was what made it so difficult for the other EC currencies to remain in the original snake.

The influx of funds into the Deutschmark increased long-term inflationary pressures, and the appreciation of the currency adversely affected the price competitiveness of German exports. After France and Italy left the snake their currencies depreciated, making their goods more competitive than German goods. Even the exclusion of a million migrant workers could not prevent the growth of unemployment in West Germany, and consequent political strains, including a widening rift on economic policy between the SPD and the trade unions.

Even worse, despite the best efforts of the Bundesbank to prevent it, there were signs that the Deutschmark was about to become an international reserve currency. Trade and investment deals were being concluded in Deutschmarks, and there began to emerge a Euromark market which rivalled the Eurodollar market as an uncontrolled source of credit. This was the last thing that the West Germans wanted: they had seen the effect on Britain and the United States of having to conduct economic affairs through the medium of a national currency that was also an international reserve currency. It was with this prospect in mind that Schmidt proposed the creation of the ecu, which could form the basis of an alternative reserve currency to the dollar without having the same damaging effect on West German economic freedom.

At the same time as these considerations were encouraging the German leadership to reconsider an EC monetary arrangement, one of the main factors that had been a barrier to German enthusiasm about the original snake was now removed. Gradually the governments of the other member states were coming round to accepting the German economic priority of controlling inflation.

Mainly this reassessment of policy was because of the acceleration of inflation following the 1973 oil-price rises. It was obvious that the economies that were having the least success in controlling inflation were also those with the highest rates of unemployment, and the poorest record on growth. The trade-off between inflation and growth did not appear to be working, and accelerating inflation threatened economic collapse. In these circumstances the economic doctrine known as 'monetarism' came increasingly to be accepted in western Europe. This doctrine returned to the traditional view that governments could only control inflation by balancing their budgets. They must either cut spending or raise taxes. The difficulty was in implementing it. The refusal of both organized and non-union workers to accept willingly a decline in their living standards meant that anti-inflationary policies were politically dangerous. It is in this light that the acceptance of the EMS idea by Giscard can be understood.

The victory of the anti-inflation priority in French economic policy was marked by the appointment of Raymond Barre as Prime Minister in succession to Chirac in 1976. But Giscard and Barre had difficulty in convincing the centre parties of the necessity of such policies. The EMS was an ideal opportunity for Giscard to remove internal dispute within his government on the issue. Acceptance of the EMS could be presented as a pro-EC and integrationist move. As such it was pleasing to the centrists. But it could also be used as an argument for following deflationary policies, since only by reducing France's rate of inflation to the West German level could the franc be kept in alignment with the Deutschmark. The EMS therefore served the French President as a useful external constraint on domestic economic policy, allowing him to plead that he could do no other than he was doing, and avoiding the admission that he would have chosen to do it anyway.

In December 1978 the Bremen European Council created the European Monetary System (EMS). The central element was the exchange rate mechanism (ERM) for holding fluctuations in exchange rates within narrow bands. Britain joined the EMS, but did not enter the ERM.

The EMS in the 1980s

Despite predictions of its early demise, the new monetary system, which began operations in March 1979, did survive. The main reason for its survival in the early stages was the surprising weakness of the Deutschmark. Partly this was due to the end of the weakness of the dollar. The new strength of the US currency meant that there was no speculative pressure on the German currency to revalue. Partly also it was a reflection of the very real problems for the West German balance of payments caused by the second oil shock of 1979. For a time the balance of payments was in deficit, and there was even speculation at one stage that the Deutschmark might have to be devalued within the EMS. Under these circumstances it was relatively easy for the other member states to remain within the system.

The ease with which the other currencies were able to live with the Deutschmark had a negative aspect: the EMS did not have the anticipated disciplinary effects on national economic policies. Member states were not obliged to adopt stringent measures against inflation in order to keep up with the Germans. The result was greater economic divergence, and inflation rates in particular moved wider apart. Under these circumstances the Germans were not prepared to accept the automatic movement to the second stage of the scheme, the setting up of the EMF, and in December 1980 this was postponed indefinitely.

The postponement of the second stage was partly a reflection of the domestic political difficulties of the scheme's two main architects. Although Helmut Schmidt had won the October 1980 Federal election, his health was not good, and growing dissension within the government coalition weakened his position. The financial elite in the Economics Ministry and at the Bundesbank, who had always opposed the EMS, were therefore able to become the dominant voice in the West German camp (Ludlow, 1982: 136–8). In France, Giscard faced a difficult presidential election campaign in which he would have to defend himself against Gaullist charges that he was intent on compromising France's monetary sovereignty, so he could hardly fight too openly on behalf of the EMF.

The result of the French election, the victory of Mitterrand and the subsequent election of a Socialist government, led to a rapid flow of funds out of the franc, putting it under tremendous pressure to devalue. This combined in the autumn of 1981 with a revival in the fortunes of the Deutschmark. The West German balance of payments began to move back into surplus, while the dollar weakened temporarily. Funds flowed back into the Deutschmark from the dollar, and funds leaving the French franc were also converted into Deutschmarks. The combination of downward pressure on one and upward pressure on another of the main currencies within the system inevitably produced a major realignment. In October 1981 the Deutschmark and the Dutch guilder were revalued, while the French franc and the lira were devalued. Within five months the Belgians and the Danes were also obliged to devalue.

Stability did not last long. The French franc remained under pressure, as the Socialist government increased its budgetary deficit in an attempt to reduce unemployment. Ironically, the French budgetary deficit in 1981 was less than the West German budgetary deficit. The difference was that the French government was deliberately increasing the size of its deficit at a time when inflation was already, at 14 per cent, double the West German level. The effect was to produce another realignment of EMS currencies in June 1982. This time, though, there was a significant new development. The French franc was devalued, but the Deutschmark was also revalued, although it had not experienced great upward pressure. The reason for the revaluation was to improve France's relative trade position without France having to devalue by as much as it really needed to in order to take account of the weakness of the franc. The advantage for France was that every percentage point that it devalued increased the cost of imported oil proportionately. The cost to West Germany was a reduction in the price competitiveness of its exports.

But the German gesture came with conditions. It was accompanied by commitments from the French Finance Minister to reverse the expansionary economic policies of the government, to attempt to cut the budgetary deficit, and to introduce a prices freeze. The Italians, who also devalued, made the same commitments.

The EMS now seemed to be working as originally intended by Schmidt. The importance of the West German economy as a market for other EC states' exports allowed the Germans to offer them help in maintaining the value of their currencies, while extracting the price of economic policies that followed the German priority of restraining inflation. The EMS looked like creating a zone of monetary stability.

Nevertheless, the change of course by the French did not take the pressure off the franc, and in March 1983 there had to be yet another realignment. This time there were recriminations. The new West German government was not happy at the idea of revaluing the Deutschmark yet again in order to help the French, particularly since the new course for the French economy had already been marked out, so that there were few concessions that could be extracted in return. But the French threatened to withdraw from the system if the Germans did not agree to bear the bulk of the burden of readjustment. Chancellor Kohl was hesitant about causing the collapse of his predecessor's achievement: it might rebound against him in the forthcoming Federal elections. So the Germans agreed to a 5½ per cent revaluation of the Deutschmark, against only a 2½ per cent devaluation of the franc. The West German press reaction was uniformly hostile, though to France and not to Kohl.

This wrangle did spoil somewhat the image of the EMS as a symbol of unity; but more serious was the continued non-participation of Britain. When the Conservatives took over from Labour in 1979 there were hopes that Britain would enter the ERM; but the Thatcher government at first maintained that it was against its economic principles to intervene in any way to control the value of the pound. The market should decide the value of currencies, according to this view, and the correct exchange policy was to float the national currency. This dogmatic phase of British external monetary policy lasted only until mid-1981, after which the Bank of England did begin to intervene to prevent large fluctuations in the value of sterling; but Britain still refused to enter the ERM. This was seen within the EC as one example among many of the lack of pro-EC spirit in Britain.

The single market programme and monetary union

Moves to strengthen and extend the EMS were part of the programme of the Delors Commission from the outset. However, the issue really came into the forefront of debate in the aftermath of the decision to free the internal market by the end of 1992, and it became the most serious issue of dissension between the British government and the rest of the EC. In the revival of the project for monetary union in the later 1980s, evidence can be seen of functional spillover pressures being skilfully manipulated by the Commission to move integration forward; in the resistance of the British Prime Minister to such moves many observers detected a personal influence reminiscent of that of de Gaulle in the middle 1960s; domestic political pressures played their part in the story; and so did international pressures.

Delors, in presenting the programme of his new Commission to the EP in January 1985, said that he wanted to develop the EMS by bringing sterling into membership and making the ecu a reserve currency (*Debates of the European Parliament*, 12 Mar. 1985, 2–324/3–6). At the end of that year the Luxembourg European Council agreed on the terms of the SEA, including a commitment to monetary union despite the objections of the British.

Further progress had to wait until the June 1988 Hanover European Council, but in the meantime there was growing support for the idea of a single currency controlled by a European central bank, a concept that Margaret Thatcher totally rejected. The Hanover European Council agreed to set up a committee of central bankers and technical experts, under the chairmanship of the president of the Commission, to prepare a report on the steps that needed to be taken to strengthen monetary co-operation. The report of this committee (Box 26.1, p. 348) was accepted by the June 1989 European Council meeting in Madrid.

Thatcher made it clear that she was unhappy about both the route and the destination mapped out by Delors. However, at Madrid she did lay down concrete conditions for putting sterling into the exchange-rate mechanism, going beyond her previous formulation that Britain would join 'when the time was ripe'. The conditions were that the British rate of inflation must be on a falling trend towards convergence with the rates in other member states, that there must have been tangible progress towards the achievement of the internal market, and that other member states must have dismantled their controls on the movement of capital. The momentum was sustained when the December 1989 European Council in Strasbourg agreed to set up an IGC to consider the institutional changes that would be necessary in order to move towards monetary union. The British Prime Minister voted against the IGC on monetary union, but she made it clear that Britain would continue to play a full role in the EC despite its differences with the other members.

Events in eastern Europe gave a new urgency to the timetable for unity within the EC in the latter part of 1989. François Mitterrand told the European Parliament in December that the EC needed to accelerate its integrative moves in response to developments in

---

Box 26.1 The Delors Report

The 'Delors Report' proposed a three-stage progress to monetary union.

1. The EC currencies that remained outside the exchange-rate mechanism of the EMS (those of Britain, Greece, Portugal, and Spain) would join, and the wider band of fluctuation would disappear.

2. Economic policy would be closely co-ordinated, the band of fluctuation of currencies within the EMS would be narrowed, and the governors of central banks would meet as a committee to prepare the ground for the institution of a European Monetary Co-operation Fund (EMCF).

3. National currencies would be irrevocably locked together, and the ecu would become a real currency in its own right, administered by the EMCF.

---

the East (*Debates of the European Parliament*, 25 Oct. 1989, 3–382/150). Although these comments were a prelude to a Franco-German proposal for an IGC on political union to run alongside that on monetary union, the argument was intended to apply also to monetary union. Although the British government rejected the logic of treating the collapse of Communist regimes in eastern Europe as a reason for changing the internal plans of the EC, most other member states seemed prepared to accept the argument. This put additional pressure on the British Prime Minister not to allow Britain to be left behind; pressure that was eventually central to her political downfall in 1990.

Monetary union in the 1990s

Before the two IGCs began to meet in 1991, Margaret Thatcher was replaced as British Prime Minister by John Major. Britain entered the negotiations adopting a new and more co-operative tone of voice. Nevertheless, the IGC on monetary union took as its negotiating text the report of the Delors Committee, which recommended that movement to monetary union should be to a timetable, rather than adopting the British idea for an evolutionary approach.

Early in the negotiations there was a consensus

that a monetary union would only be sustainable if it were underpinned by a considerable degree of economic convergence. The TEU provided four convergence criteria that would have to be met by any state before it could take part in the monetary union (Box 26.2, p. 342). These criteria reflected the policy priorities of the German government in that they were all concerned with monetary stability. Although these criteria were stringent, the Treaty did appear to leave room for some relaxation if states were moving in the right direction on all the relevant indicators. At the same time, it was written into the Treaty that any state that did qualify would join the monetary union when it was set up, which would be in 1997 if possible, and not later than 1999. Only Britain was initially allowed to opt-out of signing up for the monetary union in advance.

For John Major it would have been extremely difficult to persuade his party, and the British Parliament, to ratify the Maastricht Treaty if it had tied Britain into a commitment to joining the monetary union. The influence of his predecessor on the thinking of the Conservative Party was too strong. The governments of the other member states understood this, and were prepared to let him off the hook by granting Britain the right to decide whether it would participate when the union was about to come into

effect. The British government would have preferred the right to decide later to be a general right, thus avoiding Britain appearing to be isolated yet again. However, the other member states were not prepared to accept this because of fears that the German parliament, the Bundestag, might decide against taking Germany into the monetary union. That would have defeated the object of the exercise. Following the rejection of Maastricht in the Danish referendum in June 1992, Denmark was granted a similar opt-out clause in a protocol to the Treaty.

On 16 September 1992 Britain was forced out of the exchange rate mechanism by intensive speculation against the pound (Box 26.3, p. 350). The incident damaged Anglo-German relations because the Chancellor of the Exchequer, Norman Lamont, accused the Bundesbank of making little effort to support the British currency, whereas full support was given to the French franc when it came under pressure. The next day the Italian lira also had to leave the mechanism. Then in August 1993 the system came under so much pressure that the 'narrow bands' had to be widened to 15 per cent either side of parity to allow it to survive.

One interpretation of these developments was that the member states were not ready for a single currency if they could not hold their exchange rates. Another interpretation was that the episode showed how important it was to move to a single currency so that speculators could not push the economies of the members apart. Certainly the problems did not deflect either the French President or the German Chancellor from their commitment to monetary union.

It was not entirely clear, though, how much support the President and Chancellor had in their own countries. In France high unemployment made the policy of tying the franc closely to the Deutschmark increasingly unpopular, and the country was paralysed by strikes in the later months of 1995 as the government tried to introduce policies that would allow it to meet the convergence criteria. In Germany, public opinion polls showed growing opposition to abandoning the Deutschmark, despite a conspiracy amongst the political élite to insist that the monetary union was the only course for the country: in November 1995 a poll published in *Die Woche* indicated that 61 per cent of the German

Box 26.2 The Maastricht Convergence Criteria

Prospective members would have to have:

- a budget deficit of not more than 3 per cent of GDP
- a public debt of not more than 60 per cent of GDP
- a level of inflation no more than 1.5 percentage points above the average level achieved by the three states with the lowest levels of inflation
- interest rates that were no more than 2 per cent above the average level of the three states with the lowest levels
- a record of respecting the normal fluctuation margins of the exchange rate mechanism for two years.

Box 26.3 'Black Wednesday': Britain's exit from the ERM

1. The Background

In October 1990 the British government finally took the pound sterling into the ERM. The Prime Minister, Margaret Thatcher, had resisted taking the step despite pressure from her senior cabinet colleagues. When she did agree to go in it was at a parity of 2.95 Deutschmarks. This was a parity of her choosing, and reflected her wish that the pound should be seen as a strong currency. Many observers in both Britain and the rest of Europe thought it too high. The rate at which sterling entered should have been a matter for negotiation with the other members, but they were presented with a take-it-or-leave-it offer, which caused some resentment, particularly on the part of the German central bank, the Bundesbank, which would be expected to defend the parity in case of a crisis.

2. The Run-up

In mid-1992 German interest rates were high following the monetary unification between the Deutschmark and the Ostmark at a politically-determined one-for-one rate of exchange (Box 14.4, p. 158). ERM membership meant that the interest rates of other members of the system had to be set in line with German rates, even if this was not an appropriate rate for their economies.

In mid-1992 the British economy was in recession. The British government had been urging the Bundesbank for some time to lower rates, and had been supported by the other governments, including the French.

On 1 July 1992 Britain assumed the presidency of the EC. The Chancellor of the Exchequer, Norman Lamont, convened a meeting of Economics and Finance Ministers (ECOFIN) in Bath over the weekend of 5 September to discuss the forthcoming annual meeting of the IMF. Lamont used the occasion to attack the policy of the Bundesbank, and angered its president, Helmut Schlesinger, who was present at the meeting, by repeatedly demanding that the Bundesbank lower interest rates.

3. The Crisis

Over the next week both the pound and the Italian lira came under intense speculative pressure to devalue from their internal parities within the ERM.

On the following weekend, 12 September, the lira was devalued. The British government refused to apply to devalue the pound.

On 15 and 16 September the pound came under irresistible pressure to devalue. The Bank of England spent over $30 billion of its foreign currency reserves defending the value of the currency, an unprecedented amount. The Bundesbank refused to intervene in the markets to assist by buying sterling. Eventually the British government had to admit defeat, withdraw sterling from the ERM altogether and let it 'float' (i.e. allow it to find its own level against other currencies through free market transactions).

Source: Dyson and Featherstone, 1999: 682–6.

---

people were opposed to the single currency (*Financial Times*, 11–12 Nov. 1995).

Because of public scepticism about the single currency, the German government was in a strong position in the bargaining about the detail of the arrangements. It could always argue that unless the German public was confident in the arrangements made, there would be no German participation, and therefore no single currency. In this way, Germany won all the main arguments. First it was agreed that the European Central Bank (ECB) (Box 26.4, p. 351) would be located in Frankfurt; then, that the name of the new currency would not be the 'ecu', which the French preferred because it was the name of an old French coin, but the 'Euro', because the German people did not have confidence in the existing ecu (the acronym for the European currency unit).

France put up a stronger fight on three other issues:

(1) the level of political control that would be exerted over the ECB;

(2) the rules that would govern budgetary policy after the start of the single currency;

(3) the identity of the first President of the ECB.

On the level of political control, the Kohl government insisted that the ECB should be as independent as it was possible to make it. This was the only way that the German people would have confidence that the single currency would be run on a sound basis. The French conservative government prior to June 1997 never accepted this. It wanted the ECB to be answerable to national governments.

This fundamental philosophical clash also under-

Box 26.4 The European Central Bank

The TEU set up a European Central Bank (ECB) charged with conducting the monetary policy of the Euro zone. Its governing council consists of an Executive Board plus the governors of the national central banks. The Executive Board consists of a President, a Vice-President plus four other members. They are appointed by common accord of the member states for a non-renewable term of eight years, and must be 'of recognized standing and professional experience in monetary and banking matters' (Treaty A. 109a).

In May 1998 there was an unseemly dispute at the special European Council meeting in Brussels which had been called to launch the single currency, when the French President, Jacques Chirac, refused to accept the nomination of the Dutchman Wim Duisenberg as the first President of the ECB. Duisenberg had been the President of the forerunner of the ECB, the European Monetary Institute, and was the first choice of the clear majority of member states, including Germany. Eventually, in order to satisfy the intransigent French President, Duisenberg apparently agreed to step down half-way through his term of office to allow the Governor of the Banque de France, Jean-Claude Trichet, to take his place (Financial Times, 4 May 1998). However, Duisenberg subsequently told the EP that he had not made such a precise commitment on when he would retire, and that he would decide when was the time for him to go (Financial Times, 8 May 1998).

---

lay the differences between the two governments on the issue of the terms of the budgetary rules that would apply after the start of the single currency. The Germans wanted in effect a continuation of the Maastricht convergence criterion for budget deficits on a permanent basis: that budget deficits should not exceed 3 per cent of GDP. They also wanted a system to penalize states that overshot this target, and proposed a fine that would be automatic. The French government argued that the fine should be discretionary, and that the Finance Ministers should decide the issue in the light of prevailing economic circumstances.

At the Dublin European Council in December 1996 it was agreed that states which ran a deficit in excess of 3 per cent of GDP would be fined, but the fine would be automatically waived if the GDP had fallen by more than 2 per cent in the previous year. If GDP had fallen by less than 2 per cent, but by more than 0.75 per cent, the Finance Ministers would have discretion to decide whether a fine should be imposed. This compromise allowed everyone to claim that they had won, but the fundamental principle was that of the Germans.

When the Socialist government was elected in France in June 1997, it made clear that it was unhappy with the stability pact that had been agreed at Dublin. Although the Finance Minster, Dominique Strauss-Kahn, said that he did not want to renegotiate it, he also said that he was not sure that it could be accepted in its existing form. Once again a compromise had to be found to keep the Germans and French on board. At the Amsterdam European Council in June 1997 it was agreed that the stability pact would be supplemented by a growth and employment pact, and this was written into the Treaty as a new Title 6a. However, the terms of the employment pact did not involve any commitments to new EU expenditure, nor were they particularly interventionist in nature. The member states committed themselves: to review their tax and benefits systems to see whether there were measures that were disincentives to job creation that could be removed; to pursue measures to make their labour markets more flexible; to institute programmes of education and training to improve the employability of the workforce.

Over the five months following Amsterdam, national plans of action were drawn up. These were debated at a special 'jobs summit' in Luxembourg in November 1997, and adjustments were made to co-ordinate the measures. Nevertheless, the outcome at Amsterdam on monetary union has to be seen as another German victory. The French government accepted the stability pact in return for much less than the employment chapter that they had originally wanted to be written into the Treaty; and the principles of the pact were based on the ideas of the modernizing social democrat parties, particularly the British Labour government, rather than the old-style socialist interventionist principles that the Jospin government claimed to represent.

The French position received a temporary boost following the election victory of the SPD/Green coalition in the October 1998 German federal election. The new German Finance Minister, Oskar Lafontaine, declared himself to be in favour of the same sort of interventionist principles as his French counterparts. He formed a strong bond with his French opposite-number, Dominique Strauss-Kahn, and together they put pressure on the national central banks to lower interest rates to boost employment. After 1 January 1999, when the third stage of EMU became operative, they put the same pressure on the ECB. However, the independent bank resisted the pressure, and in March 1999 Lafontaine resigned following heated exchanges with the German Chancellor, Gerhard Schröder. Thereafter German policy reverted to something similar to its priorities under the CDU/CSU/FDP governments, and France was once again isolated in its demands for political interference in the setting of monetary policy.

Having lost almost every argument to the Germans, the French made an issue of the identity of the first president of the ECB. In 1996 Alexandre Lamfalussy of Belgium, the first head of the European Monetary Institute (EMI), the predecessor of the ECB, retired. This was unexpected. Most governments had assumed that he would retire when the EMI came to the end of its term, leaving them to choose a new president for the ECB. Lamfalussy was replaced by the president of the Dutch central bank, Wim Duisenberg. This was resented in France and elsewhere as a move by the central bankers to influence the decision on the first ECB president; but the German government favoured Duisenberg for the post anyway. Given that it would clearly be unacceptable to the rest of the EMU members to have a German head the bank, Duisenberg was the German government's preferred choice.

In November 1997, the French President Jacques Chirac and the Prime Minister Lionel Jospin jointly proposed the president of the French central bank, Jean-Claude Trichet, as a candidate to be the first president of the ECB. This was a surprise initiative, coming so late in the process and more than a year after Duisenberg had succeeded Lamfalussy at the EMI. There followed several months of open lobbying by the Dutch and French governments for their respective nominees, with increasing talk of a compromise whereby Duisenberg would be nominated as the first president, but would agree to step down

half-way through the eight-year term in favour of Trichet. Although Duisenberg publicly rejected this solution at the end of January 1998, in May 1998 agreement on just such a deal was announced following the special Brussels European Council that was called during the British presidency of the EU to launch the single currency.

The deal was widely criticized in both Germany and France. It was also condemned by the EP, which approved the nomination of Duisenberg, but also voted an amendment which called on him to avoid a situation in which there would be 'early or simultaneous succession of both the president and vice-president'. The first vice-president, a Frenchman, was appointed for four years. The clear implication was that the EP would cause trouble if asked to approve the nomination of Trichet to replace Duisenberg after four years. Duisenberg himself subsequently indicated that he had no intention of being forced to retire after four years: he would decide for himself when it was appropriate for him to retire.

The launch of the single currency was only slightly marred by this political controversy, and the financial markets reacted calmly to the shenanigans. The Euro formally came into existence on 1 January 1999 with eleven members. Only Greece in the end was excluded by the convergence criteria. Britain, Denmark, and Sweden met the criteria but excluded themselves. Britain and Denmark were allowed to do this under the terms of their 'opt-outs'. Sweden was able to claim on a technicality that it had not fulfilled the conditions because it had not been a member of the ERM for two years prior to the launch of the Euro. The inclusion of Italy caused some misgivings because the budget-deficit criterion had been met partly by what seemed to be a purely temporary expedient: the government levied a one-off 'Euro tax' to offset the deficit in the year for which the criteria were applied. The inflation criterion did not prove to be a problem in the context of a slowing in European economic activity. The criterion relating to the debt:GDP ratio was effectively ignored on the grounds that it only required the ratio to be moving in the right direction. As Belgium and Italy both had ratios that were double the 60 per cent target, and were not showing clear evidence of coming down, this seemed to be a fudge.

Nevertheless, monetary union happened. Almost thirty years after the Hague summit declared EMU to be a priority objective, half of the union was achieved. The existence of a single currency made at least the minimalist definition of economic union

inevitable. Close co-ordination of economic policy was required by the stability pact, and by the necessity of living together in the same currency area. The question is why eleven states chose to abandon their monetary sovereignty in this way.

Explanations of EMU

The collapse of the Bretton Woods international monetary system provided the context for European moves towards EMU. The first decisive steps were taken in the late 1960s, culminating in a commitment to complete EMU taken at the Hague Summit of 1969. The road from this declaration to the introduction of the single currency in 1999 was a difficult one. Along that road, a number of important steps were taken and explanations for these are contested.

It could be argued, as it was argued by the Commission, that pressure for monetary union came as spillover from the decision to free the internal market. Making a reality of the single market implied eliminating the fluctuations in exchange rates that were a source of interference with trade across national boundaries. However, Sandholtz (1993: 20–22) rejected the argument that there was a clear functional spillover from the single market to a single currency. The reasoning behind it was contentious:

Among economists, there is no consensus on the desirability of monetary integration, much less on its functional necessity. (Sandholtz, 1993: 21)

However, he argued that there was clearly what others have called 'cultivated spillover'. The Commission used 1992 as an argument to press for a single currency, and it met with a receptive audience among the public, business, and political elites because the success of the 1992 programme had provided a favourable environment. Tsoukalis (1996: 293) reinforced this argument about cultivated spillover. He suggested a strategic approach by the Commission which resembled that identified in Chapter 25 (p. 335) as the approach of the policy entrepreneur.

In terms of decision making, the negotiation on

EMU during the Maastricht IGC bore considerable resemblance to earlier European initiatives and especially the one which had led previously to the adoption of the internal-market programme. The gradual build-up of momentum, the steady expansion of the political base of support through coalition-building, and the isolation of opponents were combined with an effective marketing campaign orchestrated by the Commission and addressed primarily towards opinion leaders and the business community. Central bankers were closely involved early on, notably through their participation in the Delors Committee which produced the report on EMU. Later, they played an active role in the drafting of the relevant articles of the Treaty. Functional spillover was also successfully mixed with high politics and the appeal to 'Eurosentiment'—a recipe which had proved quite successful in the past.

Verdun (1999: 317) identified the central bankers as an 'epistemic community'. They all agreed that the aim of monetary policy was to achieve price stability. They all agreed that to achieve this, monetary policies had to be freed from political influence. They all supported a supranational regulatory agent in the form of the ESCB. She also argued (Verdun, 1999: 320) that the Delors Committee itself fulfilled the four main requirements laid down by Haas (1992) for an epistemic community:

(1) a shared set of normative beliefs: that monetary union would benefit the EC;

(2) a shared set of causal beliefs: on the causes of inflation, on the importance of stable exchange rates, that the dominance of European monetary policy by the Bundesbank was unsatisfactory; that it was undesirable to have economic policy centrally directed;

(3) shared notions of validity;

(4) a common policy enterprise.

Verdun appeared to accept the intergovernmentalist view of the dynamics of monetary union, arguing that the member states invoked the assistance of this epistemic community in order to legitimate policy decisions that they wished to take. An alternative interpretation is to see Delors's use of the epistemic communities as entirely in line with the way in which he had used the epistemic community of economists in the form of the Cecchini Report to push forward the single market programme.

Acceptance of Verdun's explanation would involve stressing the wish of national governments to transfer decision making to central institutions to allow them to disclaim responsibility for some of the unpopular economic measures that might be necessitated by the requirements of maintaining competitiveness in the single market. Votes are closely correlated to the sense of economic well-being of the population of a state, and this has been a powerful factor encouraging parties in office to bow to protectionist demands which they may know not to be in the long-term national interest. If governments are increasingly losing their room to influence the short-term performance of the national economy, it would clearly be in their interest to make this as obvious as possible to the electorate. The EU could then be blamed for adverse economic fortunes.

Linked to this argument are concerns about the credibility of anti-inflationary commitments. Sandholtz (1993: 34–6) argued that for the governments of some states their commitment to combating inflation was in doubt because of their previous record, and because of political obstacles to carrying through the necessary policies. In this context, a government might welcome having its hands tied by commitments to the EC/EU:

monetary union would provide price stability for governments that would be unable, for domestic political reasons, to achieve it on their own.   (Sandholtz, 1993: 35)

This hypothesis might explain why the German preferences prevailed on the issues of the independence of the ECB and the constitutional commitment for the ECB to produce price stability above other goals. Whatever the public protestations of other governments that they found the German preferences too

restrictive, in private they welcomed the opportunity to be tied into policies that they believed to be right, but did not believe that they could persuade their electorates to support. In states where the general value of the EU was never in doubt this technique could be used without undermining the legitimacy of EU membership itself. In other states the outcome of the monetary union negotiations contributed to undermining the legitimacy of the EU.

Another explanation for EMU starts from the experience that member states had of the EMS. Sandholtz (1993: 27–30) noted that the EMS was working well, but that there was growing discontent in France and elsewhere with the way that interest rate decisions were made by the Bundesbank in the light of conditions only in Germany, and these were then transmitted throughout the EMS member states because of the need to keep all currencies aligned in a context of open capital markets. This was the main motivation for the French government proposing to move beyond the EMS to a single currency in a paper circulated in January 1988. Sandholtz (1993: 30) felt, though, that this explanation ignored the possibility of a greater say for the other members of the EMS being achieved by reforms of the EMS system. In short, the goal of a greater voice for France and for other countries in EC monetary policy could have been achieved by other means and did not require movement toward EMU (Sandholtz, 1993: 30).

This objection was met in part by the argument of Cameron (1997), who identified three asymmetries in the EMS which were unwelcome to France and other participants. First there was the asymmetry of influence in making decisions on interest rates which has already been noted above. Second, there was an asymmetry in adjustment costs, which fell particularly heavily on the weak-currency states. If the exchange rate of a weak-currency country threatened to fall below the range of its parity, it was expected to take the necessary action to support its currency. Failure to maintain the parity could lead to a devaluation, which would again place adjustment costs on the weak-currency state by feeding inflationary tendencies. Third, there was an asymmetry in the impact on the prosperity of strong-currency and weak-currency states. If realignments could be avoided (and they became less frequent the longer the system lasted) states that had higher levels of inflation would find that their exports were becoming relatively less competitive. States with lower rates of inflation would find their exports becoming steadily more competitive. This is how Germany came to run large surpluses with all its main EC trading partners. To these, Loedel (1998) added a fourth asymmetry: in international monetary influence. It was with Germany that the USA conducted such dialogue as it held on international monetary matters. Other members of the EMS had no say in such monetary diplomacy.

On this argument, then, spillover pressures from the experience of the EMS led member states other than Germany to want to transfer control of monetary policy from the national to the European level; as things stood under the EMS, the German central bank had effective control over the monetary policy of other member states. While reform of the exchange rate mechanism might have tackled this problem, there were other disadvantages to the system which made movement to full monetary union preferable.

It is clear, though, that the asymmetries in the EMS do not explain why Germany supported the single currency. After all, it was a system that favoured German interests. Here Sandholtz (1993: 31–4) invoked German foreign policy aims. Genscher, who initially welcomed the French proposal, had a long record of wanting to balance German policy to the east with strengthening its links within the EC. In the context of the accelerating collapse of Communism in eastern and central Europe, this aim came to be shared by Kohl. The issue also became linked to German reunification. In late 1989 Kohl produced a ten-point plan for German unification. Shortly afterwards, the EC states agreed to convene the IGC on EMU in 1990. Sandholtz suggested that this decision was precipitated by the concern of France and other neighbours of Germany that the reunified German state would lose interest in the EC, and might even become nationalist again. This danger became a theme of speeches given by Helmut Kohl in defence of the single currency. He repeatedly associated the single currency with European integration, and European integration with the avoidance of war in Europe. The single currency was an essential step on the way to political union, which in turn was essential to peace and stability.

Moravcsik (1998: 381) was dismissive of the explanation based on German reunification because, he maintained, the timing was not right. Firm commitments by France and Germany to move decisively forward with EMU—and opposition by Britain to that goal—predated the fall of the Berlin Wall and remained unchanged after unification was completed in August 1990. On the other hand, he did allow that in this decision the influence of the commitment of both Kohl and Genscher to European integration could not be dismissed:

Genscher and Kohl appear to have been strongly predisposed toward integration, even in advance of a clear economic justification for it. (Moravcsik, 1998: 403)

At the same time he argued that there was a German economic interest in monetary integration. The steady appreciation of the Deutschmark against other currencies was reducing the competitiveness of German exports, and merging it into a wider European currency offered the opportunity to dampen down this trend. Concerns about currency appreciation intensified in the 1990s in the face of the large costs of reunification and the collapse of the ERM in 1992 (Moravcsik, 1998: 392).

On domestic politics, Sandholtz (1993: 23–7) argued that key domestic interest groups came to support the single currency. The 1992 programme led to a big increase in cross-border mergers, which increased the constituency of firms that would benefit from the disappearance of currency-exchange costs. However, he acknowledged that the business support came after the single currency had become the leading project of the member states, so that it could not be used as the explanation for the commitment, although it could help to explain why the commitment was carried through against all obstacles. Public opinion was generally pro-EC in the aftermath of the successful agreement on the 1992 programme, but it also could not be seen as a cause of the commitment to the single currency. Rather it was a permissive factor in most member states. Later, when it came to ratification of the Maastricht Treaty, less enthusiastic public opinion became an obstacle to carrying through the commitment.

Finally, international pressures were present at two stages in the story. From at least the early 1980s on, there was continuing and growing concern about the extent to which the United States was prepared to use the still dominant position of the dollar in the international monetary system to benefit the US domestic economy. Large fluctuations in the value of the dollar threw off course the economic and budgetary plans of the EC, and gave it a strong incentive to develop a single European currency that could displace the dollar from its position of pre-eminence in the international system, which it continued to hold more by default than because of the strength of the currency.

Conclusion

Economic and monetary union raises many of the issues that are consistent themes of this book. The debate between supranational and intergovernmental interpretations of the nature of European integration rages as fiercely here as it does for the single market programme, and the creation of another independent supranational institution, the ECB, feeds the argument between the same positions about the nature of the EU and its institutions. The form of monetary union that has been adopted gives another twist to the erosion of different national models of capitalism, and in doing so further helps to undermine the legitimacy of the EU, which the symbolic aspects of the move had already damaged.

In terms of the supranational–intergovernmental debate, while there is some evidence of spillover from the single market programme, it is largely of what the neofunctionalists called 'cultivated spillover'. The Commission, and Jacques Delors in particular while he was president of the Commission, repeatedly asserted that the single market needed to be completed by a single currency, but there was no consensus on this among economists. Nor is there strong evidence that the project was driven forward by interest groups. It seems to have been an intergovernmental project, specifically a project taken forward by two national leaders, Mitterrand and Kohl.

The previous history of attempts to achieve EMU clearly indicated that the attempt at the end of the 1980s would have to face up to the difficult issue of the form that the monetary union would take. French and German views on the matter had long differed. France favoured institutional arrangements that would put the ECB directly under the guidance and ultimate control of the governments of the member states. Germany favoured an independent central bank, not because the German government wanted to increase the degree of supranationalism inherent in the EC's institutional architecture, but because the German post-war tradition was that the value of the currency should not be subject to political interference, but should be determined by an independent bank. The Bundesbank had always been fiercely independent of the Federal government in Germany, and the confidence of the German people in the new currency would be vitally dependent on similar arrangements applying to the ECB. The German view prevailed, with the result that the degree of supranationalism of the EU may have been increased, even if that was not the intention.

German priority to preserving the value of the currency was a fundamental and indigenous aspect of the German model of capitalism. However, an emphasis on keeping control of inflation through a rigorous monetary policy was also part of the Anglo-Saxon model. The British government, although operating with an opt-out from the single currency, supported the German position in the negotiations on the institutional form of monetary union, as did the epistemic community of central bankers who formed the core of the Delors Committee. Institutionalizing this anti-inflation priority undermined the ability of other member states to protect employment at the risk of higher inflation. This was a fundamental part of the models of capitalism that operated in France, Italy, and elsewhere in the EU. The removal of another policy instrument from the tool-kit of national governments took the EU nearer to adopting the Anglo-Saxon model, and risked undermining the legitimacy of the EU when recession cost jobs and the government could not respond effectively.

Even before the form of monetary union had been negotiated, the decision to abandon national currencies caused an undermining of the legitimacy of the EU. National currencies are a symbol of national identity. In Britain in particular the debate about entry to the single currency became a debate about national identity more than about the economic merits of the move. Similar considerations applied in Germany. The result of the agreement of the German government at Maastricht to agree to monetary union was a rapid drop in the level of public support for the EU in Germany. The government did not suffer directly, because the main political parties took common cause in defence of the move; but the German people, who were not consulted in a referendum on the abandonment of the Deutschmark, made clear their distaste for being forced into a monetary union with countries that had very different traditions when it came to preserving the value of the currency.

The international context was not so clearly important in the decision to move to a monetary union as it had been in the case of the single market, but throughout the history of EMU there was a persistent tendency to see a single currency as means of establishing greater European independence of the United States. US hegemony meant that the dollar became the main international reserve currency, and commodities such as oil were traded in dollars. If the EU is to challenge the dominant position of the United States, escaping from the dominance of the dollar is an important part of any such project.

KEY POINTS

The first attempts

- Moves to EMU took place in the context of the collapse of the Bretton Woods international monetary system.

- There was tension over EMU between Germany and France. Germany made anti-inflationary policies the priority; France made economic growth the priority even at the risk of higher inflation. This disagreement led to the compromise proposals of the Werner Committee for closer co-ordination of economic policy accompanied by tying together the exchange rates of member states within narrow margins of fluctuations (the 'snake in the tunnel').

- First established in 1971, the snake collapsed following the ending of dollar convertibility in August 1971; it was reconstituted in April 1972.

- The snake was ultimately broken by a combination of divergence in the economic performance of the members and the US policy of allowing the dollar to devalue.

The EMS: origins

- In October 1977 the Commission President, Roy Jenkins, called for a new attempt at EMU.

- This initiative was supported by German Chancellor Helmut Schmidt, who feared the Deutschmark was about to become an international reserve currency, which would have a detrimental effect on West German economic freedom.

- In the period following the oil crisis, other member states began to follow Germany's lead in supporting a low-inflation policy. This removed a major barrier to greater currency co-operation. Also important, the deflationary effects of the EMS would provide President Giscard with a politically helpful external constraint to facilitate domestic policies of budget restraint in France.

The EMS in the 1980s

- The EMS survived initially because the Deutschmark was weak.

- In 1981, a change of government in France coinciding with an upturn in the fortunes of the Deutschmark led to currency realignments. Further alignments were necessary in 1982 and 1983.

- In return for taking some of the burden of the adjustment in rates, Germany forced policy changes onto the French government.

- Britain remained outside of the ERM.

The single market programme and monetary union

- Moves to strengthen the EMS after the single market programme became a major point of contention between the British government and the Commission

- The rapid collapse of Communist regimes in Eastern Europe persuaded most member states of the need for greater cohesion within the EC: Britain rejected this logic.

Monetary union in the 1990s

- The 1991 IGC set a timetable for completion of monetary union which would be not later than January 1999.

- The Maastricht Treaty (1991) set stringent criteria to ensure the convergence of member state economies prior to participation in monetary union

- Only Britain was initially allowed to opt-out of signing up for the monetary union in advance. Following the rejection of the Maastricht Treaty in the Danish referendum in June 1992, Denmark was granted a similar opt-out.

- In September 1992 Britain was forced out of the ERM by intensive speculation against the pound. The following day the Italian lira also had to leave the mechanism.

- In August 1993 the 'narrow bands' of the ERM had to be widened to 15 per cent either side of parity to allow it to survive.

- German public scepticism about monetary union placed the German government in a strong position to negotiate the detail of monetary union. One consequence was that the ECB was located in Frankfurt.

- Franco-German tensions over the conditions for sustaining monetary union after 1999 culminated in a dispute over who should head the new ECB. This controversy only slightly marred the launch of the Euro in January 1999. Only Britain, Denmark, and Sweden refused to take part, while Greece failed to meet the qualifying criteria.

QUESTIONS

1 How important were the experiments of the 1970s and 1980s to the ultimate creation of a single currency?

2 To what extent can monetary union be explained as a form of spillover from internal market pressures?

3 What explains why eleven rather than fifteen member states joined the single currency in January 1999?

4 'The chief motivating factor for national governments in creating a single currency was the desire to rival the international monetary supremacy of the US dollar'. Discuss.

FURTHER READING

The essential starting point for further reading is D. R. Cameron, 'Economic and Monetary Union: Underlying Imperatives and Third-Stage Dilemmas', *Journal of European Public Policy* 4 (1997), 455–85, which examines why the member states perceived EMU to be in their national interest, and considers some of the practical problems involved in operating a single currency. W. Sandholtz, 'Choosing Union: Monetary Politics and Maastricht', *International Organization* 47 (1993), 1–39, reviews the history of the decision on monetary union, and analyses it in the light of theoretical perspectives, including neofunctionalism and intergovernmentalism. Unsurprisingly, the intergovernmental viewpoint is best represented by A. Moravcsik, *The Choice for Europe: Social Purpose and State Power from Messina to Maastricht* (London: UCL Press, 1998), 379–471. An excellent, detailed history is provided by K. Dyson and K. Featherstone, *The Road to Maastricht: Negotiating Economic and Monetary Union* (Oxford: Oxford University Press, 1999); while the perspectives of a political scientist and an economist are combined in M. Levitt and C. Lord, *The Political Economy of Monetary Union* (Basingstoke and London: Macmillan, 2000).

CHRONOLOGY

1969
December   Hague Summit makes commitment to achieving EMU by 1980

1970
November   Werner Committee proposes system for linking exchange rates

1971
March   Start of joint float of European currencies
August   Collapse of first EMU experiment

1972
April   Joint float reconstituted as the 'snake in the tunnel'

1972
June   British Pound withdrawn from the 'snake'

1973
February   Italian Lira withdrawn from the 'snake'
April   Council agrees to move the second state of the original Werner plan at the start of 1974

1977
October   Commission President Jenkins attempts to revive EMU

1978
December   Bremen European Council creates the European Monetary System (EMS), with the Exchange Rate Mechanism (ERM) as the central element

1979

March   Start of EMS

1980

December   Second stage of the EMS scheme postponed indefinitely

1982

June   EMS currencies realigned

1983

March   EMS currencies realigned again

1985

January   New Commission President Delors declares aim of developing EMS by bringing Britain into membership and making the ecu a reserve currency

1988

June   Hanover European Council sets up committee of central bankers and technical experts under Delors to report on measures for strengthening monetary co-operation

1989

June   Madrid European Council accepts the 'Delors Report', which proposes a three-stage progress to monetary union

December   Strasbourg European Council sets up an IGC to consider institutional changes necessary for completing monetary union

1991

December   Maastricht Treaty sets out convergence criteria for participation of states in monetary union

1992

September   Britain forced out of ERM by intensive speculation against the pound/Italian Lira leaves the ERM the following day

1993

August   The ERM's 'narrow bands' have to be widened to 15 per cent to allow it to survive

1996

December   Dublin European Council agrees a 'stability pact' to support monetary union

1997

June   Amsterdam European Council agrees to supplement the stability pact with a growth and employment pact

1998

May   Special European Council meeting in Brussels to launch the single currency/Wim Duisenberg agreed as the first president of the European Central Bank (ECB)

1999

January   Third stage of EMU becomes operative with the launch of the single currency, the 'Euro'/Greece excluded by the convergence criteria/Britain, Denmark and Sweden exclude themselves

27 Regional and structural policies

[S]tructural policy has provided subnational governments and the Commission with new political resources and opportunities in an emerging multilevel policy arena.

(Gary Marks, 1993: 403)

SUMMARY

The EC had a problem of regional disparities in economic performance from its inception, but serious efforts to tackle them at EC level only date from the agreement at the Paris summit meeting of heads of government in October 1972 to set up a European Regional Development Fund (ERDF). The intergovernmental bargaining on the detail of the policy that followed the framework decision resulted in a fund of very modest size, which did nothing to counteract growing regional differences over the next decade. The Mediterranean enlargements of the 1980s, combined with the impact of the adoption of the single market programme, led to a fundamental reform in 1988, which increased the size of the ERDF and other 'structural' funds considerably. This round of reform also gave the Commission more discretion in the management of the funds, although some of its autonomy was removed by a further round of reform in 1993. The imminence of enlargement of membership of the EU to take in central and east European states necessitated another reform in 1999 as part of the Agenda 2000 proposals from the Commission. Bargaining over these reforms also demonstrated the intergovernmental nature of the EU; but the degree of autonomy that the Commission retains in this policy sector also provides some support for supranational theories of the nature of the EU.

Introduction

Disparities between Europe's regions have been long reported by both the Commission and independent experts. As early as 1958 it was noted that noted that the regional GDP in Hamburg was five times greater than in Calabria (Halstead, 1982: 55). Yet the Treaty of Rome made no specific commitment to the creation of a Community regional policy. It did though provide a more general objective of promoting throughout the Community 'a harmonious development of economic activities, a continuous and balanced expansion' (Article 2). The preamble to the Treaty also made reference to 'reducing the differences between the various regions and the backwardness of the less favoured regions' (Swift 1978: 10). At this stage, it was not clear whether these disparities would be addressed through member state or Community regional policies, or a combination of both.

For almost two decades, the responsibility for regional policy remained with the member states, but wide disparities between EC regions persisted. In 1970 the gap in GDP per head between the ten richest and the ten poorest regions in the EC was approximately 3 : 1. This represented a narrowing of the gap that had existed in the mid-1960s, when the ratio was nearer to 4 : 1; but this narrowing was based

Box 27.1 The European structural funds

Several terms which have quite specific meanings are often used interchangeably in this policy field. EU *regional* policy is concerned with correcting economic and social disparities between European regions that are caused by the creation of a single European market. The main financial instrument of EC regional policy is the European Regional Development Fund (ERDF). Other EU policies have regional dimensions, but are primarily aimed at assisting specific social groups. Of particular importance among other EC financial instruments in this respect are the European Social Fund (ESF) and the 'Guidance' section of the European Agricultural Guarantee and Guidance Fund (EAGGF).

Since 1988, the ERDF, ESF, and EAGGF collectively have been known as the *structural funds*, informed by *structural policy*. Thus structural policy has both regional and non-regional dimensions. In 1993, the Financial Instrument of Fisheries Guidance (FIFG) was added to the structural funds. To complicate the picture further, the term *cohesion policy* came into use after the Single European Act of 1986. This term describes a range of EU measures, including the structural funds, that are aimed at reducing economic and social disparities in Europe. The main non-structural fund financial instrument is the Cohesion Fund.

on a high level of labour migration from the poor to the rich regions. (Eurostat 1980). Eventually agreement was reached at the Paris summit in October 1972 to create a European Regional Development Fund (ERDF). This move reflected the increased salience of the issue following the first enlargement of the EC, and subsequent enlargements have also been significant in producing reform of the ERDF and other structural funds that were subsequently added to the budget **(Box 27.1, p. 363)**.

This chapter looks first at the early moves to try to co-ordinate regional policies between the member states, before turning to the formation of the ERDF. The negotiations around the ERDF are considered in some detail as an illustration of how the process of intergovernmental bargaining has from the outset been critical to the development of regional and structural policy. The subsequent rounds of reform in 1988, 1993, and 1999 are also considered in some detail. The central question of the chapter is whether the experience of regional and structural policy lends more support to intergovernmental theories of the nature of the EU or to supranational theories.

Early moves

The Commission showed recognition of regional problems in 1961 when it convened a conference in Brussels to consider what a European regional policy would constitute. This set in train a process of deliberations which led to the establishment in 1967 of a Commission Directorate General (DG XVI) for regional policy. This brought together those parts of the Commission of the EEC and the High Authority of the ECSC with responsibility for existing regional measures. The merger provided additional impetus to the development of Community regional policy.

In 1969, the Commission made proposals to the Council for the co-ordination of member states' regional policies and of Community policies with a regional impact, and the creation of a European Regional Development Fund (ERDF). The ERDF would be targeted through regional programmes and overseen by a standing committee on regional development made up of representatives from member states' governments and the Commission.

The Commission's proposals were not well received by the Council. Only Italy, which contained the poorest regions in the EC, was really keen to see progress in that direction. West Germany was already feeling concern at the financial implications of the CAP, and was not keen on making any further open-ended commitments of a similar nature. France had both political and economic reasons for opposing a common regional policy. Politically, President Pompidou had to avoid antagonizing his Gaullist supporters by appearing to cede further member state sovereignty to the EC; economically, France's exceptional growth rates in the 1960s, which were continuing with a 7.9 per cent increase in GNP in 1969 (OECD 1970: 1), meant that despite her own problem regions, she might well become a net contributor to any ERDF.

After 1969, a combination of factors elevated the status of regional policy: the issue of economic and monetary union (EMU); the proposed enlargement of the Community to include Britain and Ireland; and the issue of member state aids to industry. The Werner Report of 1970 gave impetus to the Treaty of Rome's objective of completing economic and monetary union (Ch. 26, pp. 343–4). This Report planned to achieve economic and monetary union in the Community within ten years, requiring further institutional reform and closer political integration. The Report argued that continued regional disparities within the Community would work against this objective. From the subsequent agreement to work towards EMU, taken at the Hague Summit of 1969, came recognition from the Council that action was necessary to address the problem of regional imbalances.

The proposed enlargement of the Community to include Britain, Denmark, and Ireland would bring a new set of disadvantaged regions to deal with in two of these countries. While the problems of Ireland, largely related to agriculture, might have been dealt with by reforming the European Agricultural Guarantee and Guidance Fund (EAGGF), Britain had a number of regions suffering industrial decline. Moreover, Britain was also likely to be a net contributor to Community funds and was keen to explore potential forms of reimbursement.

The third factor providing the context for the introduction of EC regional policy was the Commission's plans for controlling member states' aid to industry. In June 1971, the Commission recommended to the Council that state aids should be clearly measurable (transparent) and that a distinction should be made between the 'central' or wealthy areas of the Community and the 'peripheral' regions. It proposed that the level of state aid to central areas should be no more than 20 per cent of total investment. In line with the commitment to fair competition in the Treaty of Rome, the Council endorsed this proposal in October 1971. The effect was to encourage a higher proportion of member states' aid to be targeted at poorer regions. This decision placed constraints on member states' regional policies and consequently intensified interest in developments at Community level.

The creation of European regional policy

In the changing circumstances of the early 1970s, a new coalition in favour of European regional policy emerged, but the British position was crucial (Box 27.2, p. 365). As a result, the Commission's regional policy proposals were accepted unanimously by the European Parliament in March 1972 and the Council agreed to decide on the issue by October. At the Paris Summit of October 1972, the new member states were involved in discussing future priorities for the first time and it became clear that senior political

leaders had accepted the case for a regional policy. The final communication of the summit outlined the agreement that a 'high priority' should be given to correcting the Community's structural and regional imbalances that might affect the realization of economic and monetary union. Further, the heads of government instructed the Commission to prepare a report on the Community's regional problems and suggest appropriate solutions. It was also agreed that member states would undertake to co-ordinate their regional policies and that a regional development fund would be established.

The Thomson Report

The problems posed for the EC by the existence of wide and growing divergences in economic performance were summarized in the Commission's first major report on the subject, published in May 1973. The 'Thomson Report', as it became known after the British EC Regional Policy Commissioner, argued that regional problems prevented balanced expansion of the Community. Moreover, the poverty of the weaker regions limited the size of the potential market for the products of the stronger regions, thus limiting the potential for continuous expansion of the economy as a whole.

Thomson also emphasized that the commitment to EMU was jeopardized by regional disparities. While regional weaknesses did not coincide exactly with member states' boundaries, there was a ten-

dency for the weakest member states' economies to be comprised predominantly of regions that had the most serious problems, and for the stronger member states' economies to contain few problem regions. This placed pressure on the governments of countries with serious regional problems to follow national economic policies to alleviate them. In the context of a common market, manipulation of the rate of exchange of the national currency was one of the few policy instruments still available to governments for this purpose: EMU implied the loss of that instrument. If they were expected to abandon the last means of assisting their economies, the governments of the weaker states would expect Community aid for those regions that subsequently found themselves in difficulty.

Finally, the Thomson Report pointed out the threat of ongoing regional disparities to the common market, and so to the basis of the Community itself. The Report put this point bluntly: 'No community could maintain itself nor have meaning for the peoples which belong to it so long as some have very different standards of living and have cause to doubt the common will of all to help each Member to better the conditions of its people' (European Commission, 1973: 550). This warning took on a new immediacy in the context of the recession of the 1970s, as pressure began to grow for governments to take protectionist measures as a means of alleviating the unemployment problem.

The oil crisis

While the EC took a major step towards a regional fund at Paris in 1972, it was a difficult journey from this declaration to the establishment of the ERDF in 1975. The insistence of Britain, Ireland, and Italy that they could not take the first steps towards EMU if there were no regional fund was an important factor in securing West German acceptance. But the size of the proposed fund remained a serious point of contention between the potential recipients and the potential contributors.

Before this issue could be tackled, the 1973 oil crisis intervened to place discussion of energy at the top of the Community agenda. And on this issue the British reluctance to consider any Community interference with the distribution of North Sea oil drove a wedge between Britain and West Germany. The Germans, keen to get an agreement on energy-sharing, attempted to link the issue to that of a regional fund. It was a time-honoured Community method of working, but the British government, not used to such methods, rejected the linkage, annoying the Germans even further. West Germany then decided to take a hard line on the ERDF, and refused to continue negotiations. As the OPEC price-rises had thrown the international economic systems into such disarray that 'EMU by 1980' was no longer feasible, the Germans felt that they could afford to retract the commitment to set up the fund: there was little for them now to lose.

Domestic politics

Changes of government in 1974 in Britain, West Germany, and France also had their effect on the dispute. The election of a minority Labour government in Britain in February 1974 introduced a new dimension into negotiations. The new government was committed to renegotiating the British terms of entry into the Community and to holding a referendum on continued membership. With the British government's interest in the proposed regional fund marginalized, the prospects for agreement on regional policy became even more distant. The change of Chancellor in West Germany brought Helmut Schmidt into office, a man unlikely to compromise West German national interests and more concerned than his predecessor about the cost to the Federal German budget of membership of the EC. This made him less likely to agree to any further common funds to which his country would be a net contributor. The arrival in office in France of Giscard d'Estaing, and the rapport that rapidly developed between him and the new German Chancellor, meant that the two leaders were able to work together on the issue of Britain's renegotiation. This marked the beginning of the Franco-German alliance that was to dominate the EC for the next seven years; an alliance that was not inclined to look favourably on any revival of the ERDF proposal. Yet agreement *was* reached on the setting up of an ERDF at the summit in Paris in December 1974.

This unexpected development was a direct result of desperate action by the Irish and Italian governments, which still had a major interest in seeing such a fund come into existence. They threatened to boycott the summit unless they were promised progress on the creation of the fund. Such a move would have been unwelcome to Giscard. He had called the summit to establish his position as a leading European statesperson, and to launch his scheme for the institutionalization of summits in the form of the European Council. To save his summit, Giscard was prepared to accept the demand for an ERDF, and to persuade Schmidt to do so. In fact, the removal of the British from the coalition of states pressing for the ERDF made it easier for West Germany to agree to the Italian and Irish demands. Relations between Britain and West Germany were so cool at this time that Schmidt would have been reluctant to back down on his refusal to create a regional fund if it had been the British asking for it. Since it was not, the summit was able to reach agreement on the size and distribution of the ERDF. Concerns remained primarily about the Fund's distribution and the eligibility criteria. However, largely in response to Irish and Italian threats, member states agreed at the Paris Summit to establish a regional fund for a three-year period to begin on 1 January 1975. Initially the French government interpreted this as a trial period, but following the angry reaction of the Irish and Italian governments, all parties accepted that the Fund would be permanent but should be reviewed triennially.

The 1975 agreement

While the agreement to create a regional fund was politically significant, the imbalance of influence between the member states pressing for the fund and those resisting it limited the initial allocations significantly. Commissioner Thomson had initially proposed a fund of 3 billion European Units of Account (EUA) (approximately £1,260 million), which was reduced to 2.4 billion EUA before the proposal even left the Commission. Already this was a 'political' figure, designed to gain Council approval, rather than a realistic figure in view of the size of the problem. The supplicant states had considered it inadequate. Eventually the Paris summit reached agreement on a fund of 1,300 million EUA (approximately £540 million), only just over 50 per cent of what the poorer member states had originally considered an inadequate sum.

The Fund would provide up to 50 per cent of the cost of regional development projects in targeted regions. It was a requirement under the funding rules that the remainder had to be provided domestically. This 'match funding' requirement was designed to ensure that EC and member states' initiatives would be co-ordinated and complementary. In addition to this requirement, the Fund regulations called for close co-operation between Community and member states' authorities in implementing regional policy.

ERDF-funded projects were concerned either directly or indirectly with job creation. Applications for funding were to be submitted by member states to DG XVI of the Commission, which was authorized to select projects for approval by the Fund Management Committee (composed of representatives of the member states and chaired by the Commission). A Regional Policy Committee was also created, consisting of two representatives of each member state and one from the Commission, with the Commission also providing the secretariat. The chief tasks of this Committee were to co-ordinate domestic regional policies and to set the overall framework for regional policy in the Community. The Regional Policy Committee also considered funding applications for large-scale infrastructure projects (over 10 million EUA).

Member states' governments refused to accept the Commission's proposals for 'objective' Community criteria, insisting instead that the regional fund should be allocated according to national quotas. Moreover, each government demanded a quota, even though this meant regions in richer member states were eligible despite having a greater per capita GDP than some ineligible regions in poorer member states. This intergovernmental carve-up meant funding was dispersed rather than concentrated on areas of greatest need. In its first phase, the ERDF was to cover some 60 per cent of the geographical area of the Community and 40 per cent of the total popula-

Table 27.1 ERDF National Quotas (1975)

	Percentage (%)
Belgium	1.5
Denmark	1.3
France	15.0
Germany	6.4
Italy	40.0
Ireland	6.0
Luxembourg	0.1
Netherlands	1.7
United Kingdom	28.0
Total	100

Note: Ireland was also to receive a further 6 MUA taken proportionally from the other countries, with the exception of Italy

Source: Preston 1984: 75

tion (Mawson, Martins, and Gibney, 1985: 30). Three member states would be net beneficiaries of the fund—Britain, Ireland, and Italy—with the other six being net contributors. The quotas agreed are set out in Table 27.1, p. 367.

Guiding principles

The German government was an important ally for the Commission in seeking precise rules for the implementation of regional policy. This was particularly the case with the principle of *additionality*. The intergovernmental disputes following the outbreak of the Yom Kippur War led the German government to adopt a more 'hard headed' approach to the ERDF, particularly in seeking to ensure rules that would prevent governments spending grants as they saw fit. Consequently, the wording on additionality in the original ERDF regulations stated that,

the Fund's assistance should not lead Member States to reduce their own regional development efforts but should complement these efforts.   (European Commission, 1975)

Securing the additionality of regional funds would have been a major step towards a genuine supranational element in EC regional policy. However, effective implementation of this key principle could not be assumed.

The 1988 reform of the structural funds

EC regional policy underwent reforms in 1979 and 1984, the history of which was 'largely one of a struggle to throw off the many restrictions imposed by the Council of Ministers in the original 1975 Fund Regulation' (Armstrong 1989: 172). The package introduced in 1975 was subject to much criticism. The ERDF was considered too small and too dispersed. It had also become clear that the principle of additionality was largely ignored by member states. In short, progress towards the development of a Community regional policy had 'been marred by national control over all the major aspects of the policy' (Keating and Jones, 1985: 54).

Where the Commission did make progress before 1988, it did so through its agenda-setting powers. Thus, while member states' governments rejected and diluted many of the Commission's proposals for regional policy from the 1960s through to the early 1980s, some were adopted. The introduction of a non-quota section of funding and the development of programme contracts were both illustrations of this. Both allowed the Commission greater controls over the allocation of funding and were moves towards a genuinely supranational policy (Bache 1998: 53–66). Yet advances for the Commission depended on securing sufficient support within the Council, which often did not materialize. Additionality was an important example of this and the Commission's failure to make progress on this key principle was an illustration of the member states' governments' resilience on matters of public expenditure.

The reform of the structural funds in 1988 provided another opportunity for the Commission to strengthen the redistributive impact of regional policy. While the reforms of 1979 and 1984 failed to convert ERDF from a system of reimbursement to an effective instrument of regional policy, they contained the seeds for future policy development as seen in the 1988 reform.

The 1988 reform

Two important developments provided the political and economic context of the major reform of the structural funds that came into effect on 1 January 1989: the enlargement of the Community to include Portugal and Spain in 1985; and the push towards greater economic and social cohesion given expression in the Single European Act (SEA) of 1986.

The accession of Spain and Portugal meant a considerable widening of regional disparities in the EU, leading to a doubling of the population of regions with a per capita GDP of less than 50 per cent of the Community average (European Commission 1989: 9). This in itself required an increase in regional allocations. The accession of Spain and Portugal was also important in prompting the introduction of a new type of regional development programme in 1985, the Integrated Mediterranean Programmes (IMPs). These programmes involved the Commission in all aspects of programming and also, for the first time, involved subnational actors with detailed knowledge of local problems. This was the Commission-inspired concept of 'partnership'. Through the development of this principle in particular, the IMPs proved to be important forerunners for the reform package of 1988.

Moves to complete the internal market in the mid-1980s led to talk of a 'Golden Triangle' connecting the prosperous parts of the Community which would benefit most from the single market. This 'served to alert the poorer regions of the Community that the completion of the internal market could lead to a concentration of wealth in the EC's core economies' (McAleavey, 1993: 92). In response to the concerns of the poorer regions, Article 130A of the SEA (now Article 158, TEC) set out the need to strengthen 'economic and social cohesion' within the EC, in particular through aiming at 'reducing disparities between the various regions and the backwardness of the least-favoured regions' (European Commission, 1989: 11). The term *cohesion* subsequently came into use to describe a range of Community policies, including structural policy, aimed at reducing regional and social disparities. The concept was developed within the Commission as the counterpart of the moves to completing the internal market. Cohesion had a dual meaning:

It summarized a novel policy rationale to deal more effectively with the old problem of regional economic disparities, but it also held a political promise to involve subnational actors more openly in European decision-making . . . subnational mobilization was crucial to its success. (Hooghe, 1996b: 89)

Article 130D of the SEA (now Article 161 of the TEC) called for a reform of the three structural funds (ERDF, ESF, and EAGGF), through a framework regulation on their tasks, their effectiveness 'and on co-ordination of their activities between themselves and with the operations of the EIB and other financial instruments' (European Commission 1989: 11). The Brussels European Council of February 1988 agreed the draft regulations in principle and also agreed to a doubling of structural fund allocations by 1993. The final details were agreed in three main Regulations that came into effect on 1 January 1989.

Provisions of the 1988 reform

The Council agreed that allocations to the three structural funds would double in real terms between 1987 and 1993, with allocations in the final year of this period up to ECU14 bn.; approximately 25 per cent of the EU budget. This contrasted sharply with the initial allocation of ECU257.6 m. in 1975 which had represented 4.8 per cent of total EC spending and the 1987 allocation of ECU3,311 m. (9.1 per cent) (Marks, 1992: 194). Approximately 9 per cent of the structural fund budget would be allocated through Community Initiative (CI) programmes, for which the Commission had greatest influence over both design and implementation. CIs superseded the existing non-quota section allocations.

The operation of the structural funds would be guided by four complementary principles (Box 27.3, p. 369), which were essentially those the Commission had advocated throughout the development of regional policy. Several 'Objectives' were defined on the basis of which eligibility for funds would be determined (Box 27.4, p. 370). Together with alloca-

---

> **Box 27.3 Principles guiding the operation of the structural funds**
>
> **concentration** of the funds on the areas of greatest need as defined by the accompanying objectives (see Box 27.4, p. 370).
>
> **programming**: multi-annual programmes would be the norm for all funding, to ease the Commission's administrative burden and promote a more coherent approach.
>
> **partnership**: partnerships would be established to oversee the administration of the funds and would require the formal involvement of local and regional actors for the first time.
>
> **additionality**: the additionality requirement would be strengthened by a new regulation and by the greater involvement of the Commission and local and regional actors in the new partnership arrangements.

---

tions from the non-regional Objectives 3, 4 and 5a the share of structural funding received by each member state is detailed in Table 27.3, p. 373.

Despite the creation of new Objectives with detailed criteria for eligibility, the decisions on which regions (and thus member states) received assistance under both Objectives 1 and 2 were either taken or heavily influenced by member states' governments. Yet, as McAleavey (1995a: 159) put it: 'Even if an element of the 'carve-up' approach did remain, the advances made by the European Commission on the other key principles were more radical.'

Programming

After more than a decade of trying, the Commission finally secured Council support for multi-annual programmes for all structural funding. This switch promised more coherence in formulating strategies for regional development and brought greater certainty to the spending process. Objective 1 regions received programme funding for five years and Objective 2 regions for a shorter period of three years to allow flexibility for structural funding to respond to problems caused by unforeseen industrial decline.

Programming would follow a three-stage process.

Box 27.4 Priority objectives of the 1988 reform

Following the principle of concentration, structural fund expenditure was focused on five objectives, three with an explicit regional dimension (Objectives 1, 2, and 5a). The bulk of spending was focused on the most disadvantaged regions eligible under Objective 1 (approximately 65 per cent of total structural fund allocations).

Objective 1: promoting the development of 'less developed regions', i.e. those with per capita GDP of less than, or close to, 75 per cent of the Community average under 'special circumstances' (ERDF, ESF, and EAGGF—Guidance Section)

Objective 2: converting the regions seriously affected by industrial decline (ERDF, ESF)

Objective 3: combating long-term unemployment: assisting people aged over 25, unemployed for over a year (ESF)

Objective 4: assisting the occupational integration of young people, i.e. people below the age of 25 (ESF)

Objective 5: (a) accelerating the adjustment of agricultural structures (EAGGF—Guidance Section); (b) promoting the development of rural areas (EAGGF—Guidance Section, ESF, ERDF)

In addition to the 'mainstream' structural funds allocated according to the five objectives, approximately 9 per cent of the ERDF budget was retained for 'Community Initiatives'. These were programmes devised by the Commission to meet outstanding regional needs. As with the non-quota and Community programmes, such as RESIDER (steel areas) and RENAVAL (shipping and ship-building areas), Community Initiative programmes would primarily address the needs of particular categories of regions, such as those suffering from the decline of a dominant industry.

First, after full consultation with the sub-national implementers, governments were to submit regional development plans to the Commission. Each of these would detail regional problems, set out a strategy which indicated priorities and provide an estimate of required funding. Second, the Commission would incorporate member states' views in Community Support Frameworks (CSFs) that would prioritize spending, outline the forms of assistance, and provide a financial plan. Third, detailed operational programmes would be agreed by the partners to allow partners to implement the objectives of the CSFs. These would identify appropriate measures, beneficiaries and costings. Beyond this, each programme would be monitored and assessed to ascertain whether money had been spent appropriately (European Commission, 1989).

Partnership

The principle of partnership formed part of the Commission's view of regional policy from the 1970s (McAleavey, 1995a: 167). However, early Commission attempts to involve sub-national authorities in regional policy-making had received a mixed response. In Britain for example, the 1984 reform agreement on this had little impact on a

government, 'reluctant to allow local authorities much say in the preparation of the non-quota programmes . . .' (Mawson, Martins, and Gibney, 1985: 49). The partnership principle of the 1988 reform made the consultation of appropriate local and regional authorities a formal requirement for the first time. The framework regulation adopted by the Council in 1988 formally defined partnership as:

close consultation between the Commission, the member states concerned and the competent authorities designated by the latter at national, regional, local or other level, with each party acting as a partner in pursuit of a common goal. (Regulation (EEC) 2052/88)

The partnership principle was an attempt to make regional policy more effective by engaging in policy-making those actors closest to the problems and priorities of targeted regions. Partnerships were to be active in the management, presentation, financing, monitoring, and assessment of structural fund operations, including: preparation of regional development plans for submission to the Commission; negotiation of the CSFs; implementation of the Operational Programmes; and monitoring and assessment of measures taken.

Additionality

The 1988 reform provided the Commission with a major opportunity to strengthen its position for securing additionality. The final wording on additionality agreed by the Council stated:

In establishing and implementing the Community Support Frameworks the Commission and the member states shall ensure that the increase in the appropriations for the (structural) funds ... has a genuine additional impact in the regions concerned and results in at least an equivalent increase in the total volume of official or similar (Community and national) structural aid in the member states concerned, taking into account the macro-economic circumstances ... (Article 9 of Regulation 253/88 EEC)

The Commission also believed that more widespread use of programming would enhance additionality. While the 1988 reform appeared to improve the Commission's prospects of ensuring effective implementation, the issue provided one of the major obstacles in the negotiations, with the British government being the key objector to the re-wording of this part of the regulation (Bache 1999).

Environmental protection

The 1988 ERDF framework regulation reflected increased awareness of the potential environmental threat posed by economic development operations. The regulation stated that:

Measures financed by the Structural Funds receiving assistance from the EIB or from another existing financial instrument shall be in keeping with the provisions of the Treaties with the instruments adopted pursuant thereto and with Community policies, including those concerning ... environmental protection.   (Official Journal of the European Communities, 1988, L185/9, Art. 7)

The CSF for Objective 1 regions also included a requirement that measures should satisfy Community legislation on the environment and that member states should supply appropriate information to allow the Commission to evaluate the environmental impact of measures funded (Scott, 1995: 81).

The 1993 reform of the structural funds

The general thrust of the 1993 reform was one of continuity rather than radical change, with the principles and structures of the 1988 reform remaining largely intact. Yet the political and economic context in which the 1993 reform took place was very different from that of 1988, and so, consequently, was the scope for advancing Commission preferences.

While enlargement again formed part of the context, negotiations to include Austria, Finland, and Sweden were relatively straightforward. The new members were relatively prosperous and posed no major sectoral problems for other member states. In terms of regional policy, this enlargement involved three concessions: part of Austria gained Objective 1 status; Objective 6 status was created for sparsely populated areas; and EC competition rules were adapted to accommodate the subsidy practices of the Nordic states (Wishlade, 1996: 57). However, the crucial factor in shaping the context of the 1993 reform was the signing of the TEU at Maastricht in December 1991.

The TEU upgraded the importance of EC regional policy in the context of further moves towards closer economic and political union. Yet the period between the Maastricht European Council and the 1993 reform of the structural funds was marked by a change in the political and economic climate. In particular, 'growing unemployment and other economic difficulties within some northern member states heightened concerns about the costs and the cost-effectiveness of Community policies' (Wishlade, 1996: 48). Subsequent problems involved in ratifying the Treaty prompted concern over the progress and timetable for economic and monetary union (Ch. 13, pp. 130–1).

By the Edinburgh European Council of December 1992 'agreement on the future Community budget (providing funding for the commitments entered into at Maastricht) was the most critical item requiring decision' (Bachtler and Michie, 1994: 790). The compromise that was reached included an increase in the structural funds' budget to ECU27.4 bn. by 1999, virtually doubling the amount previously allocated. The context of monetary union was crucial in securing this increase.

Following the budgetary envelope agreed at Edinburgh, the Commission's proposals for the 1993 reform were framed within the principles of concentration, partnership, programming, and additionality set out in the 1988 reform. The main proposals related to eligibility criteria, programming periods, and administrative arrangements. When agreement was reached by the European Council in July 1993, following the intervention of Commission president Delors, 'secrecy surrounded the final compromise figures . . . and uncertainty remained as to whether the promised allocations matched or exceeded the sums agreed at Edinburgh' (Bachtler and Michie, 1994: 790).

Provisions of the 1993 reform

Official Commission documentation suggested that in the 1993 reform 'the major principles adopted in

1988: concentration of effort, partnership, programming and additionality, are maintained or strengthened' (European Commission, 1993b: 7). Yet the evidence suggested the relatively minor changes made to the four guiding principles were in some cases driven by the preferences of member states' governments (below). The principle of concentration continued attempts to focus aid on the areas of greatest need. To do this, some amendments were made to the existing priority objectives (see Box 27.5, p. 372).

The Commission's initial proposals for the 1993 reform were intended to address member states' concerns over the operation of the funds after 1988. Despite this, member states' governments 'proceeded to change the substance of the Commission's proposals in several nontrivial ways to respond to concerns about the distribution of funds, efficiency, and member state control of the funds' operation' (Pollack, 1995: 381). Again, the designation of eligible areas proved controversial as a number of governments pressed for, and secured, the inclusion of regions that did not meet the objective Community criteria.

More generally, governments again pressed their claims for a share of the total fund allocations. In

Box 27.5 Priority objectives of the 1993 reform

Objectives 1 and 2 were not changed from 1988. Objectives 3 and 4 were merged to create a new Objective 3. This aimed at 'facilitating the integration . . . of those threatened with exclusion from the labour market' (European Commission 1993b: 11). The new Objective 4, was designed to give effect to new tasks laid down in the Maastricht Treaty to, 'facilitate workers' adaption to industrial changes and to changes in production systems' (European Commission 1993b: 11). Objective 5a maintained its initial goal of accelerating the adjustment of agricultural structures as part of the CAP reform, but a new fund was added to assist the fisheries: the Financial Instrument of Fisheries Guidance (FIFG). Problems arising from the decline in fishing and fish-processing activities would also be addressed through Objectives 1, 2, and 5b. Objective 5b changed slightly from the 'development of rural areas' to the 'development and structural adjustment of rural areas' (European Commission 1993b: 11). Objective 6 status (above) was added to the list.

Objective 1: promoting the development of 'less developed regions' (ERDF, ESF, and EAGGF—Guidance Section)

Objective 2: converting the regions seriously affected by industrial decline (ERDF, ESF)

Objective 3: combating long-term unemployment and promoting entry into the labour market (ESF)

Objective 4: facilitating the adaptation of workers to industrial change (ESF)

Objective 5: (a) accelerating the adjustment of agricultural and fisheries structures (EAGGF—Guidance Section, FIFG); (b) promoting rural development and structural adjustment (EAGGF—Guidance Section, ESF, ERDF)

Objective 6: developing sparsely populated Nordic areas (ERDF, ESF, EAGGF—Guidance Section)

particular, the Irish government claimed to have been promised a 13.5 per cent share of allocations at the Edinburgh European Council of December 1992 in return for concessions on allocations to the new Cohesion Fund (below). The Irish government threatened to veto the 1993 reform agreement if this promise was not honoured, which ultimately it was (Pollack, 1995: 381–2).

In addition to conflicts over redistributive matters, the Council also amended the Commission's proposed administrative arrangements. Four issues were important:

1. Provisions for the monitoring and assessment of structural fund operations were strengthened, largely at the insistence of the British government.

2. Member states were given a more important role in the designation of Objective 2 and 5b regions. Here the governments of France, Germany and Britain were most influential.

3. The Council made amendments to the Commission's proposed wording on additionality, adding that it should take account of 'a number of specific economic circumstances, namely privatizations, an unusual level of public structural expenditure undertaken in the previous programming period and business cycles in the national economy'. This allowed member states to reduce spending on domestic structural measures without contravening the additionality requirement.

4. The Council insisted on the creation of a management committee to facilitate greater national government control over Community Initiative programmes (Pollack, 1995: 382–3)

The Cohesion Fund

During the negotiations over the Maastricht Treaty, the Spanish government argued for a new compensatory mechanism additional to the structural funds. Spain was worried it would be a net contributor to Community funds by 1993. While the Spanish government did not convince other governments to introduce a compensatory financial instrument, it did secure the support of the governments of other relatively poor member states—Portugal, Greece, and Ireland in arguing for additional resources to compensate ongoing regional disparities. Ultimately, faced with the threat of veto from the Spanish government, the Council agreed to establish a new Cohesion Fund (Morata and Munoz, 1996: 215). This had allocations of approximately ECU 16 bn. for the period 1993–9 (European Commission, 1996a: 147).

The Cohesion Fund provided broadly equal amounts for environmental improvements and transport infrastructure projects. The Fund was targeted at member states with a GDP of less than 90 per cent of the Community average, not at specific

Table 27.2 Cohesion Fund Allocations 1994–9 (estimated)

	%	ECU m. (1994 prices)
Spain	55	7950
Portugal	18	2601
Greece	18	2602
Ireland	9	1301
	100	14454

Source: Commission 1996a: 147

Table 27.3 Scale of Structural Intervention (including Cohesion Fund and Community Initiatives) 1994–9 (allocations for 1989–93 in brackets)

	% Share of EU aid	Eu aid as % of national GDP
Austria	1.13 (0)	0.19 (0)
Belgium	1.25 (1.18)	0.18 (0.11)
Denmark	0.50 (0.59)	0.11 (0.08)
Germany	12.97 (11.46)	0.21 (0.13)
Greece	10.58 (12.51)	3.67 (2.65)
Spain	25.30 (20.57)	1.74 (0.75)
Finland	1.19 (0)	0.40 (0)
France	8.92 (9.46)	0.22 (0.14)
Ireland	4.42 (6.68)	2.82 (2.66)
Italy	12.92 (16.0)	0.42 (0.27)
Luxembourg	0.06 (0.10)	0.15 (0.17)
Netherlands	1.56 (1.11)	0.15 (0.07)
Portugal	10.53 (12.9)	3.98 (3.07)
Sweden	0.93 (0)	0.37 (0)
United Kingdom	7.75 (7.27)	0.25 (0.13)

Source: Calculated from figures in Commission 1996a: 144

regions. It would support up to 85 per cent of the costs of projects, a higher intervention rate than with any of the structural funds. As with the structural funds, the Cohesion Fund—and the interim instrument established before the Fund came into operation—was subject to indicative allocations: (Greece 16–20 per cent; Spain 52–58 per cent; Portugal 16–20 per cent; and Ireland 7–10 per cent) (Scott, 1995: 38) (Tables 27.2, p. 373, and 27.3, p. 373).

Some key principles guiding the structural funds did not apply to the operation of the Cohesion Fund. As Scott (1995: 39) noted: 'In the first instance, nowhere in the interim instrument or in the European Council guidelines regarding the main elements of the forthcoming Cohesion Fund Regulation is there any reference to the concept of partnership.' Instead, decisions on projects (*not* programmes) to be funded would be made by the Commission in agreement with the 'member state' concerned. In

terms of additionality, the preamble to the interim regulation stipulated that member states should not 'decrease their investment efforts in the field of environmental protection and transport infrastructure', but the more tightly defined principle of additionality included in the structural fund regulations did not apply.

While the relaxed requirements on additionality and partnership left the implementation of these principles to the discretion of member states, this had to be understood in the context of moves towards monetary union that required severe constraints on public expenditure. In this context, governments were left with considerable discretion over how Cohesion Fund allocations would be spent. In particular, insistence on additionality would have created serious tension with the objective of reducing public expenditure in the 'Cohesion Four' countries.

Implementing the structural funds 1988–1998

As noted above, the framework of implementation provided by the regulations for the period after 1988 was relatively consistent. This section focuses on the implementation of the principles of partnership, additionality, and environmental protection.

Partnership

Hooghe (1996a) co-ordinated the most comprehensive study to date of the impact of the partnership arrangements across member states. This study considered the impact of the partnership arrangements on 'territorial restructuring' within eight member states. It sought to answer two related questions: 'Have diverse territorial relations converged under pressure of this uniform EU policy, hence moving towards a systematic involvement of subnational authorities in all member states? Or are uniform European regulations being bent and stretched so as to uphold existing differences in member states?' (Hooghe, 1996a: 2). The study found that the

implementation of the partnership principle varied considerably across member states. Actors at different levels—national, sub-national, and supranational—controlled different resources in different member states, influencing their ability to shape policy implementation within the framework set by EU-level agreements. The study of Britain (Bache, George, and Rhodes, 1996) also illustrated variations in implementation across regions within a member state.

In centralized member states, where central government actively sought to play a gatekeeper role over the political impact of the new arrangements, such as in Britain, it met with considerable success. There was sufficient scope within the requirements for governments to dominate partnerships, where they had the will to do so. Here, sub-national actors were mobilized, but not necessarily empowered. In more decentralized member states, sub-national authorities—normally regional governments—were better placed to take advantage of the opportunities provided by the partnership requirement. In 1998, the Commission (1998b: 11) stated that: 'While significant progress has been made in involving regional authorities, in particular where regionalization is least developed, the involvement of local authorities most directly concerned . . . is still very patchy.'

Additionality

After 1988, the European Commission singled out Britain as the only member state to continue breaching the principle of additionality (Bache 1996: 274). The additionality problem in Britain culminated in a dispute over the Rechar programme for declining coal-mining areas. The way in which the British government tried to implement the expenditure of Rechar funds led directly to a confrontation with the Commission. The dispute began in December 1990 and lasted for over a year.

The details of the dispute are complex. The British government had long been suspected of not providing genuine additionality, but the Treasury had always maintained that it built into each year's regional expenditure plans an element to cover expected ERDF funds. Without the ERDF, spending in the regions would be less. However, this excuse did not hold for Rechar because the programme had not even existed when the British budgetary plans for the Rechar funding period (1990– 3) were made. After a prolonged struggle between the government and the Commission, during which Commissioner Bruce Millan withheld the British share of the Rechar money, the government backed down and in February 1992 announced its intention to introduce new arrangements for implementing additionality.

This dispute, and the generally enhanced autonomy of the Commission in the regional policy sector, was central to the development by Gary Marks (1993) of the theory of multilevel governance (Ch. 2, pp. 25–6). However, the Commission's success on additionality in Britain proved to be short-lived. An assessment of additionality following the implementation of the government's new arrangements showed little evidence of extra spending in targeted regions as a result (Bache, 1999).

Environmental provisions

Despite provisions in the 1988 reform seeking to address the environmental problems caused by structural developments, in practice environmental concerns took a low priority. The Commission was inadequately resourced to monitor environmental impacts, with only six Commission officials dedicated to overseeing this aspect of operations across all member states. Moreover, member states were reluctant to supply full information on environmental implications and the Commission had no clear powers under the regulations to insist that governments comply with the request in the regulations (Scott, 1995: 82). Non-governmental environmental organizations were equally powerless to ensure adequate implementation of environmental requirements. Scott (1995: 83) noted that these groups were 'entirely excluded from national or regional monitoring committees in theory as well as practice—committees which at any rate do not have an explicit environmental remit'.

The 1993 structural fund regulations sought to strengthen the Commission's powers for regulating the behaviour of member states in ensuring respect for the environment, but these provisions fell short on a number of counts:

1. The 1993 reform provisions were so vague as to leave member states with considerable discretion.

2. There remained a need for environmental assessment to be strategic, rather than project-based.

3. The amendments failed to take account of the limited effectiveness of the Environmental Impact Assessment Directive of 1985 in relation to structural fund operations.

4. The new regulations failed to open up the structural fund planning process to non-governmental organizations (Scott, 1995: 94–97).

Assessing implementation

The 1988 reform of the structural funds provided a classical illustration of how EU-level agreements could be frustrated at the policy-implementation stage. The principles of partnership and additionality were implemented very differently by member states in practice. Yet the partnership principle remained key to the Commission's pursuit of an effective regional policy. In its proposals for the 1999 reform, the Commission argued for a deepening of partnerships, so that partners would be more involved throughout the process of financing from the structural funds (below). Perhaps more significantly, the Commission noted the 'very patchy' involvement of local authorities, environmental authorities and other bodies (the social partners, local voluntary organizations, non-governmental bodies etc.) who were 'dealing with matters of major concern to the Community, such as employment, sustainable development and equal opportunities for men and women' (European Commission, 1998b: 11).

In terms of theoretical developments, perhaps the main lesson from the implementation of the 1988 reform was that:

Analysts who want to predict developments in EU cohesion policy from the great bargains risk overlooking the ambivalence in the regulations; the active role of the European Commission, national administrations, and subnational actors in exploiting these ambiguities; and the effects of policy learning. (Hooghe, 1996b: 119)

In particular, where governments were determined to resist unwanted outcomes from developments at EU level, they would carry their 'gatekeeper' role over into the policy-implementation stage.

In a study of the implementation of the principles of the 1988 reform in Britain, it was argued that existing explanations of the EU policy process would be strengthened by analysing the impact of implementation on policy outcomes. For those in the pluralist tradition, there was much evidence of multilevel *involvement* in the implementation of EU regional policy in Britain, but the extent to which this constituted multi-level governance was unclear. Certainly, in relation to the principles of additionality and partnership, analysis of policy outcomes suggested that the gatekeeper role of the British government was played with some success at the implementation stage. For intergovernmentalists, this research suggested that where the gatekeeper notion was useful in describing the behaviour of governments in EU policy-making, it made sense to refer to an *extended gatekeeper* that could operate at all stages of the policy process, including implementation (Bache, 1999).

The 1999 reform of the structural funds

Negotiations over policy reforms for the post-2000 period took place in the context of a majority of member states joining the single currency (Ch. 26, pp. 352–3) and ongoing negotiations to enlarge the EU to include countries of central and eastern Europe. As one commentator put it:

The political climate in which the latest round of regional policy reforms is being negotiated is very different from that surrounding previous exercises over the past decade. After the successive expansion of regional and social funding in 1988 and 1993, the emphasis now is very much on budgetary consolidation. (Watson, 1998: 16)

Enlargement to include countries from central and eastern Europe, with an average GDP per capita typically at around one third of the existing EU average, had obvious implications for structural policy. Clearly, it would not be possible to apply the existing structural fund criteria to the new member states. Under the structural fund regulations for 1994–9, the entire territories of the countries of eastern and central Europe would qualify for Objective 1 and Cohesion Fund assistance. Extending the existing funds to Poland, Hungary, the Czech Republic, and Slovakia would increase the total cost of the funds to approximately ECU48 bn., and would double the funds if all 10 countries of central and eastern Europe, Cyprus, and Malta became members after 2001 (CURDS, 1997: 55). Somehow, the Commission's proposals for reform had to strike a balance between the demands of existing member states and the need to facilitate enlargement. The context was not favourable towards major Commission advances on regional policy. In addition to the challenges of proposed enlargement, EMU was crucial in framing a mood of uncertainty within member states, creating a political atmosphere against further integration.

Commission proposals

In March 1998, the Commission presented its proposed regulations for governing the structural funds for the period 2000–6. The proposed reform was centred on three priorities: greater concentration, decentralized and simplified implementation, and a strengthening of efficiency and control set against a background of budgetary discipline (European Commission, 1998*a*: 2).

Box 27.6 **Priority objectives of the 1999 reform**

Objective 1: would continue to assist the least-developed regions, defined as those with a GDP per capita at 75 per cent or less of the EU average over the previous three years. Henceforth, this criterion would be strictly enforced. In addition, the new Objective 1 included the regions that previously qualified under Objective 6, which were the sparsely populated regions of Finland and Sweden.

Objective 2: The changes to designation here were more significant. The existing Objectives 2 and 5b were merged into the new Objective 2, which thus covered 'areas undergoing socioeconomic change in the industrial and service sectors, declining rural areas, urban areas in difficulty and depressed areas dependent on fisheries' (Wishlade 1999: 39). Also significant was that Objective 2 would be concentrated on no more than 18 per cent of the EU population, with the safety-net mechanism ensuring that no member state's Objective 2 population would be less than two-thirds of its coverage under the 1994–9 programme period.

Objective 3: would apply across the EU, except for Objective 1 regions, and would assist in modernizing systems of education, training, and employment.

The Commission proposed to maintain the four governing principles of the structural funds—partnership, concentration, additionality, and programming (Box 27.6, p. 377). However, the partnership principle would be reformed so that the responsibilities of each of the partners would be defined 'so as to implement better the principle of subsidiarity and permit improved application of Article 205, under which the Commission is responsible for implementation of the Community budget' (European Commission, 1998*b*: 10). The Commission proposed introducing a fifth principle—efficiency—to reassure people that public money allocated to the structural funds was well used. While the four principles of 1988 remained intact, and a fifth principle of 'efficiency' would be added, the Commission's proposals were relatively modest and in some areas hinted at a further renationalization of the funds.

The Commission signalled its intention to take a lesser role in the day-to-day management of the funds. This meant withdrawing its officials from involvement in partnership activities below programme monitoring committees, where this had been the practice. In defence of this withdrawal, Commission officials emphasized that they would still be involved in programme monitoring committees, and these would take on a more strategic role than previously. In addition, the Commission proposed retaining 10 per cent of the structural funds as a performance reserve for it to allocate during the programme period to those regions performing well.

The proposed enlargement of the EU focused the Commission's efforts on concentrating the funds on a smaller proportion of the existing EU's population. While existing member states accepted the need for concentration in principle, agreeing which areas would be affected by greater concentration in 1999 would be fiercely contested. Moreover, the proposed regulations suggested that in addition to determining Objective 1 areas, the Council would also have more control over the designation of Objective 2 areas.

The convergence criteria for monetary union established at Maastricht had provided a loose interpretation of the additionality requirement after the 1993 reform. While the Commission's proposal for negotiated additionality, if accepted, appeared to be

Table 27.4 Structural Funds: Breakdown by Member State for the period 2000–6 (in EUR million at 1999 prices)

Member State	Obj. 1	Transitional support for former Obj. 1 areas	Obj. 2	Transitional for former Obj. 2 and 5(b) areas	Obj. 3	Fisheries Instrument (outside Obj. 1 areas)	Total
Belgium	0	625	368	65	737	34	1 829
Denmark	0	0	156	27	365	197	745
Germany	19 229	729	2 984	526	4 581	107	28 156
Greece	20 961	0	0	0	0	0	0
Spain	37 744	352	2 553	98	2 140	200	43 087
France	3 254	551	5 437	613	4 540	225	14 620
Ireland[a]	1 315	1 773	0	0	0	0	3 088
Italy	21 935	187	2 145	377	3 744	96	28 484
Luxembourg	0	0	34	6	38	0	78
Netherlands	0	123	676	119	1 686	31	2 635
Austria	261	0	587	102	528	4	1 473
Portugal	16 124	2 905	0	0	0	0	19 029
Finland	913	0	459	30	403	31	1 836
Sweden[b]	722	0	354	52	720	60	1 908
UK[a]	5 805	1 166	3 989	706	4 568	121	15 635
EU15[c]	127 543	8 411	19 733	2 721	24 050	1 106	183 564

Notes:
[a] Including Peace (2000–2004).   [b] Including the special programme for Swedish coastal zones.   [c] EU totals for all fifteen member states

Source: Inforegio Newsletter No. 65, June 1999, pp. 3–4.

an improvement on this, its success would depend in large part on what the Commission would be able to negotiate with member states, most of whom were about to experience the first challenges of monetary union. The Commission proposed taking a specific indicator of additionality for each objective to facilitate more effective monitoring.

Programming remained a relatively uncontroversial principle of structural funding in 1998. Its value had been widely accepted. One proposal for improvement was to reduce the three-stage programming process to two stages, except for very large allocations. Partnership remained at the core of Commission thinking and the principle would be strengthened if the proposals for 1999 were accepted. The Commission sought to build on the existing provisions by increasing the emphasis placed on involving the social partners, environmental agencies, and other non-governmental organizations involved in social and economic development. The need to reduce the number of Community Initiatives to simplify procedures and reduce duplicative structures was accepted by the Commission. While CIs were reduced to three in number, this meant more resources for each remaining CI.

Provisions of the 1999 reform

The General Affairs Council formally adopted the new structural fund regulations in June 1999, following political agreement at the Berlin European Council in March and approval by the European Parliament in May. The same meeting also adopted the regulations for the Cohesion Fund and the pre-accession structural instrument (ISPA), which would be used to help the applicant states adjust their economies in preparation for membership.

Financial allocations to the structural funds were EUR195 bn. over the period 2000–6, with a further EUR18 bn. provided for the Cohesion Fund. In addition, EUR7.28 bn. was set aside for pre-accession structural assistance to applicant states. Total funding under these measures remained at 0.46 of the EU's GNP over the period. Allocations by member state and by Objective are outlined in Table 27.4 (p. 378).

The guiding principles proposed by the Commission were accepted. On *concentration*, this meant that the number of structural fund Objectives would be reduced from six to three (see Box 27.6, p. 377). Also, as proposed by the Commission, the number of Community Initiatives would be substantially reduced from the existing thirteen. The Commission had proposed three Initiatives:

- Interreg (cross border, transnational and inter-regional cooperation)
- Leader (rural development)
- Equal (tackling discrimination in the labour market).

However, at the insistence of the European Parliament, a fourth programme was retained:

- Urban (to regenerate inner cities).

The *programming* process was retained, with the Commission adopting a more strategic role and delegating greater responsibility to domestic actors for the day-to-day implementation and monitoring of programmes. The reworded *partnership* principle required the involvement of organizations that reflected the 'need to promote equality between men and women and sustainable development through the integration of environmental protection and improvement requirements' (OJ L161, 26/6/99: 12). The principle of *additionality* was maintained, although its verification would depend on baseline figures of domestic spending which member states' governments would play a key role in determining. Finally, in line with the principle of *efficiency*, a performance reserve was agreed by member states. However, this was limited to 4 per cent of each member state's share of funding, rather than the 10 per cent the Commission had proposed.

Conclusion

Since 1975, the regional policy sector has been subject to significant fluctuations in the influence of key actors. While the Commission has long pushed for a genuinely redistributive policy, the Council has intervened at key moments in ways to protect member states' allocations and governments' control over the distribution of funds.

All the major decisions on the creation of regional policy were taken by the heads of government; in particular at the summits in Paris 1972 and 1974 and Copenhagen 1973. The Commission's influence over initial allocations and policy guidelines was at first limited, although the Commission was important in keeping the issue of the regional policy alive in the difficult circumstances of the 1960s and early 1970s. Yet while the eventual establishment of the ERDF in 1975 owed a great deal to Commission persistence, intergovernmental politics ensured that it fell some way short of the redistributive policy instrument the Commission sought.

While a number of member states sought to limit the increase in the fund allocations in the 1988

reform, the doubling of allocations owed much to the commitment of larger member states to the single market programme. Although the funds continued to benefit regions in the more prosperous member states, the main impact of the doubling of the funds was to transfer resources from Belgium, Denmark, Germany, France, and the Netherlands to Greece, Spain, Ireland, Italy, and Portugal, with the impact on Britain largely neutral (Marks, 1992: 194).

Pollack (1995) argued that agreement to major reform in 1988 could be explained by changes in the preferences of the various member states—in particular net contributors such as Britain, France, and Germany—and as a result of the accession of Greece, Spain, and Portugal. The preferences of the net contributors changed in three ways. First, with the Iberian enlargement, the proportion of structural funds received by the 'big three' member states decreased significantly. This meant that for these governments, 'the idea of greater Commission oversight seemed less like an intrusion into the internal affairs of one's own state, where EC spending was minimal, and more like a necessary oversight of the poor member states where the bulk of EC money was being spent' (Pollack, 1995: 372). Second, the Iberian enlargement made France, like Britain and Germany, a net contributor to the EC budget, thus giving the 'big three' governments a common interest in the efficient use of the structural funds. Third, the spiralling costs of both the CAP and the structural funds made the level and efficiency of EC spending a 'political issue' of increasing concern to the governments of France, Germany and Britain in the 1980s (Pollack, 1995: 372).

In terms of the budgetary envelope agreed in 1988, an intergovernmentalist interpretation found favour amongst most commentators. The more prosperous member states strongly supported the completion of the single market and wanted this market extending to include Spain and Portugal. In this context, the doubling of the structural funds was accepted by the likely paymaster governments as a 'side-payment to Ireland and the Southern nations' in exchange for their political support on other issues (Moravscik, 1991: 62). Marks (1992: 198) conceptualized the side-payment argument as an illustration of *forced spillover*, 'in which the prospect of a breakthrough in one arena created intense pressure for innovation in others'.

Consensus between scholars over other aspects of the 1988 reform is harder to find. For example, Hooghe (1996*b*: 100) argued that the Commission emerged 'as the pivotal actor in designing the regulations' through its 'monopoly of initiative on the institutional design'. A good example was the inclusion of the partnership principle in the regulations, which was the major innovation of the 1988 reform. In contrast, Pollack (1995) suggested that this shift was a response to national government pressure to secure 'value for money' in the funds' administration. While there is some truth in Pollack's argument, in the context of the single market programme and enlargement, negotiations over the reform of the structural funds in 1988 allowed the Commission to advance its objective of an effective supranational regional policy. Yet securing changes in the regulations was one thing; effective implementation could not be taken for granted, as later evidence proved.

While the context of the 1988 reform gave the Commission considerable scope for advancing its policy preferences, the 1993 reform represented a reassertion of member states' government control in key areas. A good example was additionality. The tenacity with which the Commission had sought the implementation of additionality after 1988 was met by member states' governments effectively diluting the requirement in 1993. Indeed in the context of the convergence criteria for monetary union agreed at Maastricht, for the Commission to pursue genuine additionality at this time would have been difficult: while additionality required member states to demonstrate additional public expenditure, the convergence criteria put a squeeze on domestic public spending.

Other changes in 1993 reflected the reassertion of government preferences. For example, while the partnership principle was confirmed, governments remained in control of the designation of 'appropriate partners'. Finally, the creation of the Management Committee to oversee CIs created a degree of national government involvement that would curtail Commission discretion. In the conflict over the implementation of additionality after 1988, the Commission had used its control over the content, coverage and timing of CIs to undermine the British government's arguments. The 1993 changes meant this would be less possible in future.

In summary, the 1993 reform provided a measure of how the relative influence of actors fluctuated over a short period of time. The context of regional policy reform changed dramatically in the five years after the 1988 reform. This led to a shift in the balance of political resources away from the Commission to the Council at the EU level, which was reflected in the 1993 outcome.

As with previous reforms, the budgetary envelope for the 1999 reform of the structural funds was decided at Council level. In addition to limiting total allocations, member states' governments were also instrumental in securing safety-net mechanisms and transitional arrangements to protect their assisted regions from a sudden and dramatic reduction of funding. Moreover, the reduction of the proposed performance reserve from 10 to 4 per cent was accompanied by provisions for member states' involvement with the Commission in determining the allocation of this reserve to regions that were performing well.

While the partnership principle was maintained, and its requirements made more precise, the selection of partners remained with governments. The additionality principle was also retained, but the new regulations did not suggest that member states' compliance would be any easier for the Commission to ensure. The reduction in the number of and financial allocations to Community Initiatives would limit the Commission's scope for autonomy and innovation somewhat, although in its proposals the Commission had acknowledged the need for such a reduction. Institutional politics aside, CIs had been subject to much criticism from a broad range of actors who deemed some programmes as unneces-

sarily bureaucratizing the structural fund process further.

In summary, while the 1999 reform was not simply a renationalization of the structural funds, a number of changes from the Commission's initial proposals reflected the preferences of governments. Perhaps more significantly, in the context of proposed enlargement, the Commission's initial proposals were themselves relatively modest. Yet the Commission retained a key role in the process, for example over issues of eligibility, programming, allocating the performance reserve, and in the design and implementation of Community Initiatives. Moreover, the key principles guiding the operation of the funds essentially remained those developed by the Commission.

KEY POINTS

Early moves

- The Treaty of Rome made no specific commitment to regional policy.

- Until the 1970s, regional policy remained a domestic matter for member states.

- In the early 1970s, three factors combined to make European regional policy more likely: the issue of economic and monetary union (EMU); the proposed enlargement of the Community to include Britain and Ireland; and the issue of member states' aids to industry.

The creation of European regional policy

- The Paris Summit of 1972 agreed to set up the ERDF.

- Commissioner Thomson's (1973) report emphasized the importance of regional policy to the project of European integration as a whole.

- The 1973 oil crisis and political changes within member states threatened to jeopardize agreement on regional policy.

- A deal was eventually reached only when the Italian and Irish governments threatened to boycott the Paris Summit of 1974.

- Initial ERDF allocations were disappointing. Moreover, there were no guarantees that the funds would be spent by member states as the Commission intended.

The 1988 reform of the structural funds

- After 1975, ERDF was criticized for being inadequate to meet the needs of disadvantaged regions.

- Member states' governments dominated the policy process and there was no major movement towards the creation of a supranational policy. However, developments before 1988 provided the seeds for policy change.

- Enlargement and the single market programme provided the context for a major reform of the structural funds in 1988.

- The 1988 reform doubled financial allocations, strengthened the additionality principle and introduced the principle of partnership.

The 1993 reform of the structural funds

- The 1993 reform of the structural funds maintained the guiding principles established in 1988, although aspects of the reform reflected a reassertion of member states' government control.

- In 1993, the Cohesion Fund was established as an additional compensatory instrument for the poorer member states.

Implementing the structural funds 1988–1998

- The implementation of the principles of additionality, partnership and environmental protection left much to be desired from a Commission perspective.

- Evidence suggested that member state governments have considerable scope for frustrating EU-level agreements at the implementation stage.

The 1999 reform of the structural funds

- Proposed enlargement and completion of monetary union provided the context for the 1999 reform. In this context, the Commission's proposals were relatively modest.

- The final agreement maintained allocations at 0.46 per cent of EU GNP and retained the principles of additionality, concentration, partnership and programming while adding the principle of efficiency.

QUESTIONS

1 What explains the growth in size of the structural funds?

2 To what extent have member states' governments acted as gatekeepers in relation to EU regional policy?

3 How successful has the Commission been in advancing its regional policy agenda?

4 What problems has the Commission faced in securing effective regional policy implementation?

5 What are the implications for EU regional policy of enlargement to include states from eastern and central Europe?

FURTHER READING

While most introductory texts and collected editions on the EU provide a chapter on regional and structural policies, four books with a specific focus on the subject are particularly relevant for the discussion here.

I. Bache, *The Politics of European Union Regional Policy: Multi-Level Governance or Flexible Gatekeeping?* (Sheffield: Sheffield Academic Press/University Association for Contemporary European Studies, 1998) provides an overview of the key developments in the politics of EU regional policy from the 1950s to 1998, focusing on the struggle for control over the policy sector.

A. Evans, *The EU Structural Funds* (Oxford: Oxford University Press, 1999) provides a comprehensive review of the structural funds and other EU financial instruments, focusing on the contribution of these to the objective of cohesion.

L. Hooghe (ed.), *Cohesion Policy and European Integration* (Oxford: Oxford University Press, 1996) is an edited collection that brings together detailed coverage of the political impact of the partnership principle in eight member states, assessing the degree of multi-level governance evident.

Finally, J. Scott, *Development Dilemmas in the European Community: Rethinking Regional Development Policy* (Buckingham and Philadelphia: Open University Press, 1995) argues for a reconsideration of the purposes of regional policy and provides particularly good coverage on the environmental dimension.

In recent years there has been a proliferation of shorter pieces on structural policy. From his analysis of the 1988 reform of the structural funds and subsequent disputes over implementation, G. Marks, 'Structural Policy and Multilevel Governance in the EC', in A. Cafruny and G. Rosenthal (eds.), *The State of the European Community*, ii. *The Maastricht Debates and Beyond* (Boulder, Colo., and Harlow: Lynne Rienner and Longman, 1993), 391–410, developed his arguments about multi-level governance. M. Pollack, 'Regional Actors in an Intergovernmental Play: The Making and Implementation of EC Structural Policy', in C. Rhodes and S. Mazey (eds.), *The State of the European Union*, iii. *Building a European Polity?* (Boulder, and Harlow: Lynne Rienner and Longman, 1995), 361–90, reflects on both the 1988 and 1993 reform and provides an essentially, though 'not mindlessly', intergovernmental response to the arguments of Marks.

I. Bache, 'The Extended Gatekeeper: Central Government and the Implementation of EC Regional Policy in the UK', *Journal of European Public Policy* 6 (1999), 28–45, argues that in these accounts, either inadequate or insufficient attention is given to the process of implementation in shaping regional policy outcomes.

CHRONOLOGY

1961
December Commission convenes first conference on European regional policy

1967
July   Commission Directorate General for regional policy (DG XVI) established

1972
March   European Parliament unanimously accepts Commission proposals for creation of EC regional policy
October   Paris Summit accepts the case for EC regional policy and requests the Commission to prepare a report on the issue

1973
May   'Thomson Report' on regional problems presented to the Council

1974
December   Heads of government meeting in Paris agree principles of regional policy, including creation of ERDF

1975
January   ERDF comes into operation

1979   First reform of EC regional policy

1984   Second reform of EC regional policy

1988   Reform of the 'structural funds'—ERDF, European Social Fund (ESF) and the 'Guidance' section of the European Agricultural Guarantee and Guidance Fund (EAGGF)/ Allocations to the structural funds doubled/new policy principles agreed

1989
January   1988 reform provisions come into operation

1991
December   Council agrees to create a Cohesion Fund to assist Greece, Spain, Ireland, and Portugal

1993   Reform of the structural funds/Financial Instrument for Fisheries Guidance (FIFG) added

1994
January   1993 reform provisions come into operation

1999   Reform of the structural funds/financial assistance for applicant states introduced

28 External relations

International events have helped to concentrate the minds of EC governments on what unites them in their foreign policies in a way that perhaps few would have anticipated in the early 1970s.

(Lodge, 1989: 235)

SUMMARY

The external relations of the EU can be divided into economic and political, although the boundary is not so clear in practice.

The economic relations include a long-standing special relationship with a large group of African, Caribbean, and Pacific (ACP) states, and a common commercial policy. The relationship with the ACP states was until recently governed by the Lomé Conventions. The first Lomé Convention was widely seen as a model of relations between developed and underdeveloped countries, but relations deteriorated over time into a more traditional donor–recipient relationship.

The common commercial policy covers the economic relations of the EU with the rest of the world. It is subject to complicated decision-making procedures because, although the Treaty of Rome gave competence in commercial policy to the EC, the Commission has to negotiate trade deals on a mandate laid down and closely monitored by the member states. There is some room for independent initiative on the part of the Commission, but it is strictly limited.

The most important trade partner of the EU is the United States. Despite attempts by both sides to make the relationship work harmoniously, several serious trade disputes have arisen between the two partners, and the frequency of such disputes has increased since the start of the World Trade Organization.

External political relations have been handled outside of the EC framework, and initially outside of the treaty framework altogether. They are now governed by the second pillar of the EU, on Common Foreign and Security Policy (CFSP). Although this is officially an intergovernmental pillar, the Commission still has an important role to play. The record of achievement on CFSP has been patchy.

Introduction

The EU is the world's largest trading bloc. As such it is obliged to have an external economic policy. Economic relations with the rest of the world take several forms (Box 28.1, p. 387). The earliest external economic relationship was with the former colonies of member states. These are governed by special conventions. External trade relations with the rest of the world appear from the Treaty to be the responsibility of the Commission. There are also strong pressures on the EU to develop coherent political relations with the outside world. These are covered by the Common Foreign and Security Policy (CFSP), which forms the second pillar of the TEU and is predominantly intergovernmental. However, this division of competencies does not work out so neatly in practice. The member states share responsibility for external economic relations with the Commission; and the Commission is a central actor in the intergovernmental CFSP pillar of the TEU.

This chapter considers three aspects of relations between the EU and non-member states:

- relations with the African, Caribbean, and Pacific (ACP) states

- external trade relations

- external political relations.

In each case the focus is on how the interaction of internal and external factors has contributed to the development of policy.

Relations with the African, Caribbean, and Pacific states

Since 1975, trade and aid relations between the EC/EU and a growing number of ACP states have been governed by the Lomé Convention (see Table 28.1, p. 387). The ACP states were originally all former colonies of one or other of the member states, although as the Convention was regularly updated, other ACP states that had never been colonies of EU members joined. The Lomé Convention was eventually superseded by the Contonou Agreement in June 2000.

EC–ACP relations prior to Lomé

When the Treaty of Rome was signed in 1957, the vast majority of independent countries that are now in the ACP group remained the responsibility of colonial powers. In 1956 France, which had the largest number of colonies, requested associated status with the proposed EEC for its overseas territories. It wanted to protect itself from the economic costs of applying external tariffs to these territories. The French request was turned into a condition for

Table 28.1 The Lomé Conventions

	Period	ECU (bn.)	Innovations	ACP States
Lomé 1	1975–80	3.07	STABEX system	46
Lomé 2	1980–85	4.54	SYSMIN system	58
Lomé 3	1985–90	7.44	Emphasis on rural development for food security	65
Lomé 4	1990–00	24.63	Emphasis on human rights, democracy and good governance	68

Source: Figures from European Commission 2000: 1–2

signing the Treaty of Rome, following opposition from West Germany and the Netherlands. The Implementing Convention that was subsequently included in the Treaty therefore extended predominantly to Francophone Africa. The Convention had two main elements: the progressive establishment of a free trade area between the EC and the associated countries, with the reciprocal reduction of tariffs and quantitative restrictions; and the establishment of a European Development Fund (EDF) for the purpose of granting EC financial aid to the associated countries and territories to promote their social and economic development (Frey-Wouters, 1980: 14).

The Implementing Convention ran for five years before being succeeded in July 1963 by the first Yaoundé Convention, named after the capital of Cameroon, where it was signed. This Convention extended EC relations to the eighteen associated African States and Madagascar (AASM). The provisions of Yaoundé 1 were not significantly different from those of the Implementing Convention. The reciprocal granting of tariff preferences for industrial and some tropical products remained; EC preferences on a number of tropical products were unilaterally reduced or abolished; agricultural products exported by the AASM to the EC were regulated by special trade arrangements; and joint institutions at ministerial and parliamentary level were set up to administer the Convention (Frey-Wouters, 1980: 14).

Despite concessions to the Dutch and German governments, which had the effect of widening the coverage of EC policy, the first Yaoundé Convention again predominantly reflected French interests. A. H. Jamal, the former Tanzanian Minister of Communications, described the Convention as providing 'an institutional dependence on the part of some African countries on one particular metropolitan power—France' (Jamal, 1979: 134). Although modifications were made to the agreement at the signing of Yaoundé 2 in January 1971, these did not change the essential character of the arrangement.

The EDFs under the Implementing Convention and Yaoundé were described by one commentator as 'basically a device to offload the costs of French colonial mercantilism on the EEC in return for other EEC states receiving access to their markets and sources of supply' (Green, 1976: 50). Certainly, neither the Implementing Convention nor the Yaoundé Agreements marked a serious attempt to break with the traditional pattern of relations between Europe and the developing world. Many hoped that the first Lomé agreement would mark a turning point in these relations.

The Lomé Convention

Two factors shaped the particular nature of the first Lomé agreement:

1. The 1973 enlargement brought Britain into the EC. Britain retained close links with the Commonwealth countries, and this had a major bearing on the successor agreement to Yaoundé 2 being extended to forty-six ACP states.

2. The negotiations over the Lomé Convention took place in the context of the 1973 oil crisis, during which the OPEC states insisted on linking talks about energy supplies with a review of the whole system of relations between developed and developing countries.

Not only did this crisis alert Europe to the power of solidarity between developing countries, it also underlined the extent of international interdependence; in particular, the dependence of the North on the raw materials of the South. The call at this time for a move towards a new international economic order was strong; one that would allow less developed nations greater control over both their own development and international economic developments.

The first Lomé Convention came into operation in February 1975 and gave formal recognition for the first time to the interlinkages between trade and aid. The agreement was received by the ACP states more enthusiastically than its predecessors had been. As one observer put it: 'When Lomé 1 was signed, both sides claimed that it was qualitatively different from anything that had gone before; a contract between equal partners and a step towards a New International Economic Order' (Stevens 1984: 1).

A key innovation of the new agreement was the System for the Stablization of Export Earnings (Stabex). Stabex provided financial support for countries experiencing fluctuations in their revenues from the export of many primary commodities, mainly agricultural produce. In addition to Stabex, Lomé removed reciprocity in trade preferences. Products covered in the EC by the CAP were subject to negotiation, but generally the ACP states were given preferable treatment over third parties. A total of ECU3 bn. of EC aid was provided for the industrialization of ACP economies, and the institutions of permanent dialogue were reinforced with a Council of Ministers, a Council of Ambassadors, and a Consultative Assembly (now called the Joint Assembly) all being involved in overseeing the agreements.

The consensus among commentators was that while Lomé was an improvement on what had gone before, it was inadequate in relation to the nature and scale of development problems, and certainly fell short of what the ACP states had hoped for (see Cosgrove Twitchett, 1981; Stevens, 1984). Others were more scathing in their criticism. Galtung (1976: 37) argued that: 'the Convention is economistic, even classical, not only in its formulation but also in its consequences, by emphasising production, processing and marketing/trading without always keeping in mind the purpose of all that, the development of human beings rather than things, systems, structures.' Yet Galtung accepted that not much more could be expected from the EC, itself essentially a trading bloc.

Thus the main impact of Lomé 1 was to reinforce the established flow of raw materials in one direction (to Europe) and processed goods in the other (to the ACP). Lomé did require developed states to pay more for the supply of raw materials, but the cost of this to the ACP states was stabilization of the existing international division of labour.

The Second and Third Lomé Agreements

Lomé 2 came into effect in March 1980, ran until 1985, and was worth ECU4.5 bn. Despite criticisms of Lomé 1, the prospect of EDF grants meant the number of ACP signatory states increased. In terms of innovation, Lomé 2 was notable for the introduction of the Sysmin facility. This guaranteed a certain level of income from mineral exports, and thus

---

Box 28.2 **The Europe agreements**

At the end of the cold war, the EC signed technical co-operation agreements with the central and east European countries (CEECs). These were subsequently replaced with enhanced association agreements, called 'Europe Agreements', in recognition of the aspiration of the CEECs to become members of the EU. Agreements were signed as follows:

1991 with Poland, Hungary, and Czechoslovakia (the last was replaced by separate agreements with the Czech Republic and with Slovakia in 1993 after their separation).
1993 with Romania and Bulgaria.
1995 with Estonia, Latvia, and Lithuania.
1996 with Slovenia.

The agreements cover economic co-operation, but also foreign policy co-ordination and cultural exchanges.

---

protected the productive capacity of many ACP states, who were major suppliers of minerals to the EC. For the first time, human rights issues became a controversial feature of the negotiations, with the British and Dutch governments in particular pushing for provisions as part of the overall deal. This move was not well received by ACP states, especially as many European countries continued to trade with and invest in South Africa, where human rights abuses were endemic under the apartheid regime. Thus, in spite of Sysmin and other minor innovations, Lomé 2 was viewed as a disappointing successor to Lomé 1.

Lomé 3 was signed in December 1984 to cover the period from 1985 to 1990, providing ECU7.4 bn. of aid. The trading arrangements remained essentially the same as before, but there was an increased emphasis on private investment in ACP states, and also a shift away from loans and towards grants, for Stabex in particular. Lomé 3 marked a move towards rural development projects to promote food security and was notable for the inclusion of an agreement by all signatories to work for the eradication of apartheid in South Africa. The amount of aid increased in monetary terms, but it was not clear whether this would mean an increase in real terms. When inflation and population growth are taken into account the period up to Lomé 3 (1976–85) saw a fall in EC real capita transfers to ACP states by 40 per cent (Hewitt 1989: 291).

Lomé 4

In the period 1980–7, Africa's per capita GDP fell by an average of 2.6 per cent and its returns on investment were substantially down (Glaser 1990: 26). This meant that on top of the unfulfilled hopes of various aid schemes, many ACP countries were

under intense pressure to repay loans. By 1983, the IMF and the World Bank were implementing stabilization and structural adjustment programmes in response. This meant that the EC response to ACP problems had to be implemented in close co-ordination with these institutions. This situation placed the IMF in the driving seat 'with its own short-run conditions overwhelming those of all the other partners' (Hewitt, 1989: 296).

Thus, by the late 1980s, ACP states believed that Lomé seriously neglected their main concerns: the impossibility of servicing debt; the increasing demands of the World Bank and the IMF for changes in economic and social policies; and the ongoing problem of apartheid in South Africa. By the early 1990s, these concerns were added to by concerns over the effect of the completion of the single European market and concern over the aid demands of the former Communist countries of Eastern Europe.

Lomé 4 was signed in December 1989 by the EC and sixty-nine ACP states (Box 28.4, p. 391). It ran for a ten-year period to 2000 and ECU12 bn. was committed for the first five years with a further ECU14.6 bn. for the remainder of the period. The new Lomé was governed by the principle of *partnership* between the EC and the ACP states. Article 2 of the Convention stated that Co-operation should be based on:

- equality between partners, respect for their sovereignty, mutual interest, and interdependence
- the right of each state to determine its own political, social, cultural, and economic policy options
- security of relations based on the *acquis* of the system of co-operation (Laffan, 1997a: 162).

Partnership aside, the approach of Lomé 4 was essentially similar to its predecessors, albeit with greater emphasis on conditions for recipient states. It continued to address debt problems through the Stabex and Sysmin compensatory schemes, though some changes were made to enhance the effectiveness of these. To reflect the increased demands on the Stabex scheme in the context of deteriorating prices for agricultural commodities on the world market, Lomé 4 increased allocations to this programme by 62 per cent between 1990 and 1995 (Laffan 1997a: 167).

Box 28.4 The ACP states

African states

Angola, Benin, Botswana, Burkina Faso, Burundi, Cameroon, Cape Verde, Central African Republic, Chad, Comoros, Congo, Djibouti, Equatorial Guinea, Ethiopia, Gabon, Ghana, Guinea, Guinea Bissau, Ivory Coast, Kenya, Lesotho, Liberia, Madagascar, Malawi, Mali, Mauritania, Mauritius, Mozambique, Namibia, Niger, Nigeria, Rwanda, Sao Tome and Principe, Senegal, Seychelles, Sierra Leone, Somalia, South Africa, Sudan, Swaziland, Tanzania, Togo, Uganda, Zaire, Zambia, Zimbabwe.

Caribbean states

Antigua, Barbados, Barbuda, Bahamas, Belize, Dominica, Dominican Republic, Grenada, Guyana, Haiti, Jamaica, St Christopher and Nevis, St Lucia, St Vincent and Grenadines, Suriname, Trinidad and Tobago.

Pacific states

Fiji, Kiribati, Papua New Guinea, Solomon Islands, Tonga, Tuvalu, Western Samoa, Vanuatu.

New environmental protection measures were introduced in Lomé 4, including for example a ban on moving toxic and radioactive waste; more emphasis was placed on the role of the private sector in stimulating development; and the human rights provisions were strengthened by a joint declaration on the elimination of apartheid in South Africa and on the rights of ACP migrant workers and students. However, while human rights provisions were long a feature of Lomé, the EU began to place an increasing emphasis on democracy, the rule of law, and 'good governance' (below). In 1994, the EU brought a halt to aid negotiations with ten ACP states because of the 'deteriorating political situation in those countries' (Laffan 1997a: 168).

However, the conditions attached to Lomé 4's structural adjustment programme and other forms of assistance led the EC–ACP relationship to look increasingly like the traditional donor-recipient pattern of relations. Although partnership was an innovative feature of Lomé 4, the decline of ACP bargaining power resulting from the fall in commodity prices since the high point of the mid-1970s meant that EU-ACP partnership relations were highly asymmetrical. This was illustrated by the EU's unilateral decisions to suspend aid to states where it deemed political or human rights conditions to be unacceptable.

The Contonou Agreement

In September 1998 negotiations began over a successor agreement to Lomé 4, which was due to expire in February 2000. These negotiations followed a Commission 'green paper' highlighting the ongoing problems of ACP countries. The green paper noted (Commission, 2000: 6) that:

- ACP countries' share of the EU market had declined from 6.7 per cent in 1976 to 3 per cent in 1998 with 60 per cent of total exports concentrated in only 10 products;

- only a handful of nations registered economic growth as a result of the trade protocols and preferences (notably Ivory Coast, Mauritius, Zimbabwe, and Jamaica);

- per capita GDP in sub-Saharan Africa grew by an average of only 0.4 per cent per annum 1960–92, compared with 2.3 per cent for all developing countries;

- only 6 per cent of African trade was with other countries of the continent.

The green paper also noted that economic developments in many ACP countries had been accompanied by political conflict and major social and humanitarian problems. In other words, EU aid policy had taken insufficient account of the importance of the domestic context in which aid was spent. In negotiating Lomé 5, the EU was clear that ACP states would be expected to meet more stringent social, economic, and political conditions than previously. The EU negotiators demanded stronger commitments on democracy, human rights, and 'good governance'.

A successor agreement to Lomé was signed in June 2000, in Contonou, Benin. This agreement would cover a twenty-year period, allowing for a revision every five years. Financial allocations would also be made on a five-yearly basis. Amendments to the agreement would be decided by the ACP–EC Council of Ministers, which would normally meet on an annual basis. The agreement placed a greater emphasis on dialogue between the EU and recipient states. Clarity was given to the partnership principle, so that it would 'encourage greater participation by civil society, the private sector and trade unions' (European Commission, 2000*b*: 1). In the first five-year period, the Agreement provided ECU13.5 bn. for development projects. Other objectives included: the encouragement of equality between men and women at every level—political, social, and economic; the promotion of sustainable management of the environment and of natural resources; and the gradual replacement of the system of trade preferences by a series of new economic partnerships based on the progressive and reciprocal removal of trade barriers (European Commission, 2000*b*: 2).

The common commercial policy

Article 133 of the Treaty (Article 113 of the original Treaty of Rome) gives the EC exclusive competence in commercial policy, including external trade negotiations. However, the trade negotiations are to be conducted by the Commission, 'in conjunction with a special committee appointed by the Council'. This committee, known as the Article 133 committee (previously the Article 113 committee), consists of senior civil servants of the member states who monitor the position taken by the Commission at every stage of trade negotiations to ensure that it is in line with a negotiating mandate laid down by the Council of Ministers. Once an agreement has been reached in the negotiations, it has to be ratified by the member states meeting in full Council.

Not only is the Commission closely monitored in trade negotiations: it also does not have full competence, except for trade in goods. Trade in services and intellectual products, which were not subject to trade negotiations when the Treaty of Rome was drawn up, are not included. In 1994 the ECJ ruled that the Commission did not have sole competence in negotiations on such matters, but shared the competence with the member states. In September 1996 the Commission asked the Council of Ministers to extend its remit to these sectors, but met with a cool response. In the Treaty of Amsterdam the member states inserted a clause that allowed them to give the Commission full competence in these sectors in future negotiations, without further change to the Treaties, but only if they were unanimous in agreeing to do so.

Shared responsibility for trade negotiations produces a complex pattern of bargaining. Putnam described the making of foreign policy for a state as a 'two-level game'. This insight was incorporated by Moravcsik (1991, 1993, 1998) into his theorizations of the nature of the relationship between the EC/EU and its member states. At one level the government of each member state has to find a position that will satisfy the balance of pressures in the domestic political arena. It then has to play a game at the level of the international negotiations to try to achieve an agreement that falls within the parameters of what is acceptable domestically. This produces a complicated bargaining situation. However, the position in EC trade negotiations is even more complex (Collinson, 1999). The nature of the relationship between the member states, the Commission, and the trade partners means that it is a three-level rather than a two-level game (Box 28.5, p. 393).

Matters are made even more difficult by the multi-issue nature of trade talks. It has already been suggested that when the Treaty of Rome was drawn up, certain issues that are central to contemporary world trade were not considered to be part of the trade agenda. Trade in the 1950s was predominantly in goods. Today there is growing trade in services and intellectual property. In addition, agriculture, which was effectively excluded from the earliest rounds of GATT negotiations by a tacit agreement between participants, has become a crucial issue area. Each of these sectors has its own policy networks within it

> ## Box 28.5 The three-level game of EC trade negotiations
>
> 1. The government of each of the member states has to find a negotiating position that reflects the domestic constraints.
>
> 2. All the governments then have to negotiate around these positions in determining together the negotiating mandate for the Commission in the wider trade talks.
>
> 3. The Commission then has to negotiate in the wider talks within the tight parameters of this mandate.
>
> If it is necessary to go beyond these parameters to reach a deal, the Commission has to refer back to its constituency in the Council, and the members of that constituency (the governments of the member states) have to refer back to their domestic arenas.

(Collinson, 1999), and some, especially agriculture and the cultural industries (part of intellectual property issues) are politically extremely sensitive. For example, the French government had great difficulty in accepting the November 1992 Blair House agreements between the European Commission and the USA on agricultural trade, and almost collapsed the whole GATT package-deal because of the difficulty of selling the agreement to its domestic political constituency. France also objected to the inclusion of cultural industries in the GATT package because of fears that the dominance of US films and television programmes would undermine its distinctive national culture.

Indicative of the clash of interests in making EC trade policy was the 1997 dispute over the imposition of anti-dumping measures against imports of unbleached cotton cloth. The measures against China, Egypt, India, Indonesia, and Pakistan were demanded by Eurocoton, the association of European producers of cotton fabrics; but they were opposed by European producers of finished cotton goods who benefited from the cheaper semi-finished products imported from the non-EU countries. The member states were evenly divided, with Germany abstaining when the first vote was taken in March

1997. This indicated the balance of industrial interests between producers of raw cotton cloth and producers of finished cotton goods in the different member states. Eventually, in May 1997, the German government decided to oppose the anti-dumping measures, to the fury of the French. Underlying the specific issue, which was a straight division on the basis of national economic interest, there was also a more general issue about free trade versus managed trade.

This difference was nicely illustrated at a meeting in Otranto in Italy in April 1996, when during a discussion of the twenty-six free-trade agreements that the Commission had negotiated, the French representative said that the Commission appeared to want to have free trade with the whole world. This might well have been the ultimate aim of the British Commissioner for trade, Sir Leon Brittan. The extent of the philosophical difference is indicated by the fact that the French representative apparently considered it to be a bad thing.

The thrust of EC trade policy has been in the direction of free trade. Given the qualms of France and other southern member states, some of the explanation must lie in the role of the Commission, and particularly of Commissioner Brittan. The divisions within the EU between member states, combined with the need for the Council to approve trade agreements by a qualified majority rather than unanimity, opened up an opportunity for active and committed Commission leadership to influence the direction of policy. Brittan provided such leadership, a task made easier by the 1995 enlargement, because all three of the new member states were favourable to free trade. He became a vigorous defender of the view that the single market gave the EU the opportunity to set the future trade agenda, rather than responding to the lead of the United States. This may also have helped his cause in building support within the Council of Ministers, because French governments have generally been favourably disposed toward any policy of European leadership in defiance of the United States.

Trade relations with the United States

Relations with the United States are central to the external relations of the EU in both economics and politics. There is a high degree of commercial interdependence between the EU and the United States. In 1996, two-way trade in goods and services amounted to more than ECU355 bn., of which trade in goods amounted to more than ECU227 bn., and the fast-growing trade in services ECU128 bn. (Smith, 1998: 561–2).

The public authorities on the two sides of the Atlantic would seem to have a strong incentive to work together to maintain open trading relations. However, EU–US trade has been dogged by a series of intractable disputes (Box 28.6, p. 394). Yet at the same time as these disputes were causing tensions,

---

Box 28.6　Trade disputes between the EU and the United States

- Since the WTO began operation in January 1995, the United States and the EU have struggled to dominate the procedures and the agenda, or at least to ensure that the other does not dominate.

- In 1995 the United States demanded compensation for the trade diversion effects of the northern enlargement, as it had after every previous enlargement, and threatened to make a formal complaint to the WTO before agreement was reached in December.

- The United States objected to the proliferation of free trade agreements between the EU and other states in the 1990s. The EU justified them as stepping stones to global free trade, but the United States saw them as bilateral measures that damaged US access to the third markets.

- In October 1996 the EU made a formal complaint to the WTO against the United States' policy of operating sanctions against companies that invested in Cuba. Under the 1996 Helms-Burton Act, the US reserved the right to impose financial penalties against non-US companies trading with Cuba, and even to deny access to the United States to individuals who were shareholders, directors, or executives of the companies concerned. The US Congress also passed legislation (the D'Amato Act) in May 1996 allowing similar action to be taken against companies dealing with Libya or Iran. As well as making a complaint to the WTO, the EU in 1996 gave itself the power to retaliate against US companies and individuals if the United States implemented the terms of Helms-Burton or D'Amato against EU companies or citizens.

- In 1998 a fierce dispute blew up over the EU's banana regime. This was part of the Lomé agreements with former French and British colonies, and gave preferential access to the EU market for bananas grown in those Caribbean and Pacific states. The United States objected to the discrimination against bananas produced in Latin America, mainly by US-owned companies. The WTO had already ruled against the EU's regime in September 1997, and given it until January 1999 to produce a revised scheme that complied with WTO rules. The EU produced a revised scheme, but the United States insisted that it still did not comply with WTO rules, and in October 1998 threatened unilaterally to impose sanctions. The EU maintained that this would be a breach of WTO procedures, and that if the United States was not satisfied with the new banana regime it would have to start complaints procedures all over again. The United States said that this was a recipe for endless delay. The EU then asked the WTO to rule on the legitimacy of Section 301 of US trade law under which the unilateral sanctions were threatened. Eventually, in April 1999, the WTO did authorize the imposition of sanctions by the United States, although at a much reduced level from those originally proposed. The whole issue generated a surprising amount of bitterness and heat considering that it concerned a product which was grown in neither the EU nor the United States.

- In 1999 the United States won a complaint to the WTO against a ban by the EU on the import of hormone-treated beef. The ban reflected the strong prejudice of EU consumers against meat that contained hormones, and was first imposed in 1987. The United States maintained that this action was against WTO rules because there was no scientific evidence that there was any risk to human health from eating such meat. The EU insisted that it wanted to complete its own scientific tests before agreeing to lift the ban. Early in 1999 the WTO ruled against the EU, and the United States said that it would impose retaliatory sanctions unless the ban was lifted.

Box 28.7 Attempts to improve EU–US commercial relations

- During 1995 a Transatlantic Business Dialogue (TABD) was instituted with the aim of developing co-operation on issues such as mutual recognition of standards.

- In December 1995 a New Transatlantic Agenda was signed in Madrid by US President Bill Clinton, EU Council President Felipe Gonzalez, and Commission President Jacques Santer. The EU and United States produced a transatlantic action plan to develop four areas of collaboration:

  (1) promotion of peace, stability, democracy, and development;

  (2) responding to global challenges such as environmental threats and drugs trafficking;

  (3) contributing to the expansion of world trade;

  (4) building 'Atlantic bridges' through collaboration in areas such as education.

- In November 1996 the TABD produced a declaration on Mutual Recognition Agreements, advocating the recognition by public authorities on each side of the Atlantic of the testing procedures for health and safety that were in force on the other side. In June 1997 a pact on mutual recognition of testing and certification procedures was signed between the EU and USA covering trade worth £29 bn. ($47 bn) a year. It involved each side agreeing to accept the other's procedures as adequate to ensure safety, thereby reducing the barriers to imports and exports.

---

steps were being taken to improve commercial relations (Box 28.7, p. 395).

The tensions in the trade relations between the EU and the United States are indicative of the differences of interest between two large trading blocs which are inevitable. Politics also comes into it. The strength of the US reaction to the EU's defence of its banana regime (Box 28.6, p. 394, bullet point 5) was widely believed to reflect the influence in Congress of Carl Lindner, the Chairman of Chiquita Bananas, and a large contributor to the funds of both the major US political parties. On the EU side, the sensitivity of the relationship with the former colonies of the two large ex-imperial member states (France and Britain) clearly counted for a lot, especially when it is borne in mind that the German public was hostile to the banana regime because of its passionate attachment to the larger 'dollar bananas'. Another factor that weighed heavily was the refusal of the EU to be pushed around in world trade matters by the United States.

External political relations

While the trade relations of the EC with the rest of the world are covered by the TEC and come under the auspices of the Commission, the member states have also developed machinery for formulating common positions on matters of foreign policy. This initially developed outside of the framework of the treaties under the name of European Political Co-operation (EPC). It entered the treaties as Title III of the SEA, although still on an intergovernmental basis. Title V of the TEU set up a Common Foreign and Security Policy (CFSP) as the second pillar of the EU. Some additions were made to the machinery of the CFSP in the Amsterdam Treaty.

European political co-operation

EPC was suggested by President Pompidou at the Hague summit in 1969, but was seen at the time as little more than a sop to his Gaullist supporters. Few participants or observers thought that it would amount to anything, because it closely resembled the Fouchet Plan, which had already been rejected (Box 8.3, p. 91), and because it proposed co-operation in the field of 'high politics' as defined by Hoffmann (1964, 1966), an area where national interests would be expected to get in the way of common action.

The machinery of EPC consisted mainly of regular meetings to co-ordinate national stances to particular areas of the world, or to particular issues. Foreign Ministers met at least twice a year, but in practice much more often. Immediately below the ministerial level, Foreign Office political directors met, on the original plan every three months, but in practice monthly. Until 1987 these meetings had no secretariat to give administrative back-up. This was provided by whichever member state held the presidency of the Council at the time. However, the additional strain that it placed on the state holding the presidency, and the need for proper continuity across changes of presidency, led to the creation in the SEA of a small secretariat, situated in Brussels. EPC was originally set up as a parallel process to that of economic integration within the EC, but the two became closely linked. The distinction between matters proper to EPC and EC matters was rigidly maintained in the early years of the operation of EPC at the insistence of the French. This reached the heights of absurdity in November 1973, when the Foreign Ministers of the then nine member states met in Copenhagen one morning under the heading of EPC, and then flew to Brussels to meet in the afternoon of the same day as the EC Council of Ministers. This rigid separation finally broke down with the opening of the Euro-Arab dialogue in 1974. The Arab participants in these talks insisted on maintaining a clear linkage between trade and political questions, which forced the EC to fudge the lines of demarcation on its side. Once the artificial distinction had broken down here, it soon became less evident elsewhere in the external relations of the EC.

The Commission, originally excluded from meetings under the machinery of EPC, was soon admitted to them at all levels, and came to play a vital co-ordinating role between EPC and the Council of Ministers. This arose for two reasons: the lack of an EPC secretariat until 1987; and the fact that Foreign Offices tended to send different people to the two different categories of meeting, while the Commission, with a considerably smaller staff upon which to draw, usually sent the same people. Where questions arose that overlapped the two forums, the Commission representatives were the most likely to spot the overlap and to be able to guide a meeting away from making decisions that were incompatible with those already made elsewhere.

EPC also started to be reported upon to the EP. The reports were originally made only to the Parliament's Political Affairs Committee, but subsequently they came to be made in a full plenary session, usually as part of the same statement on progress in Community affairs that is made by the Foreign Minister of the state holding the Council presidency. Members of the EP were allowed to question the Minister about EPC matters as well as about more strictly Community matters.

So procedurally EPC made big strides in the course of the 1970s, and became intertwined with the institutions and procedures of the EC in a way that furthered European integration more than any steps taken in the 'low politics' areas, where the neofunctionalists expected there to be progress. These advances were formalized in the Single European Act.

Although EPC was described as an example of 'procedure substituting for policy' (Wallace and Allen, 1977), it had several substantive successes (Box 28.8, p. 397). Admittedly, there were also failures (Box 28.9, p. 397); on balance, though, there were more successes than there were failures, and it could at least be argued that these successes dragged the procedure along in their wake rather than vice versa. As one observer put it:

International events have helped to concentrate the minds of EC governments on what unites them in their foreign policies in a way that perhaps few would have anticipated in the early 1970s. (Lodge, 1989: 235)

The SEA gave EPC a written basis for the first time, but the articles relating to it were not subject to judicial interpretation by the ECJ. This represented a compromise between the original position of the German and Italian governments in particular, that the Act should become a basis for a genuine political union, and the reservations of some other member states, particularly Ireland. In Ireland the possible

Box 28.8 Successes for EPC

- EPC formulated a common position on the Middle East, which allowed the EC, through the Euro-Arab dialogue, to pursue its clear interest in improving trade with the Arab OPEC states in the 1970s. In June 1980 this common policy culminated in the Venice Declaration, which went further than the United States was prepared to go in recognizing the right of the Palestinians to a homeland.

- The then nine member states were extremely successful in formulating a common position at the Conference on Security and Co-operation in Europe (CSCE) in Helsinki in 1975, and at the follow-up conferences in Belgrade in 1977, and Madrid in 1982–3. Again the common position adopted by the EC ran somewhat contrary to the position of the United States. The Americans regarded the Helsinki process with some suspicion because they thought it risked legitimating Communist rule in eastern Europe. In January 1995 the CSCE took on more permanent form as the Organization for Security and Co-operation in Europe (OSCE).

- The member states achieved a high degree of unity in the United Nations, voting together on a majority of resolutions in the General Assembly, and developing a reputation for being the most cohesive group there at a time when group-diplomacy was becoming much more common.

Box 28.9 Failures of EPC

- It proved difficult to find a joint position on the invasion of Afghanistan by the Soviet Union in December 1979. The British government argued strongly for following the lead of the United States in boycotting the Olympic games in Moscow, while the French in particular were not prepared to do so, and the Federal German government was unhappy at the way that the United States used the issue to heighten East–West tension.

- In the early 1980s it proved extremely difficult for the member states to find agreed positions on the issue of sanctions against South Africa (Holland, 1988).

compromising of the state's constitutional neutrality was a tremendously controversial issue.

At the end of the 1980s the issue of extending EPC arose once again in the context of the dramatic political changes in eastern and central Europe. The collapse of Communist rule left a potentially unstable situation in that part of the world. The western states had to prepare contingency plans for responding to any outbreak of violence. In particular, the resurgence of nationalist sentiment held the threat that intercommunal conflict might break out. In this situation there needed to be some sort of regional military force available that could act quickly if the need arose. The Bush administration in the United States made it clear that it could not be expected to provide this force. Although the administration did not wish to withdraw US troops completely from western Europe, it needed to cash in the so-called 'peace dividend' from the ending of the cold war to help it tackle the large budgetary deficit that it had inherited from the Reagan administration. Also, even if the west Europeans could have been persuaded to provide financial support for the US troops, there was no possibility of a US President being able to risk the lives of US troops by intervening in European nationalist conflicts. Yet just how poor were the prospects of a rapid response to regional problems by the member states of the EC was shown clearly by the Gulf crisis that broke out in the autumn of 1990 (Box 28.10, p. 398). A second crisis that severely tested the limits of EPC soon followed in Yugoslavia (Box 28.11, p. 399).

The EC's response to these crises lent some support to the view that the differences between the perceptions and national interests of the member states remained too diverse to accommodate within a single foreign policy. However, it also supported the view that some of the problems at least lay in the existence of inadequate machinery for dealing with crises. Two observers of the Gulf crisis defended the latter view in these terms:

The structural problems which arose were of significance in that it was necessary for various institutions to be involved where only one would have sufficed. This created a greater problem with decision-making than existed before, and led to independent national responses and the absence of consensus. A structural vacuum exists in the EC, in the absence of one institution endowed with binding power to create and

Box 28.10 The Gulf Crisis

When Iraq invaded Kuwait in August 1990, the initial response of the EC was decisive. The invasion was immediately condemned, and economic sanctions were imposed against Iraq. On 21 August the Foreign Ministers meeting under EPC discussed the aggressive actions being taken by the invading Iraqi troops against EC embassies in Kuwait, which included cutting off water and electricity supplies. It was agreed that the embassies would be kept open, but that if any embassy was forced to close, the other EC embassies would act for the citizens of those states (prefiguring a later agreement in the TEU on European citizenship). When Iraqi troops entered the French embassy on 14 September, the EC issued a joint condemnation, and demand for the release of the hostages.

However, the first cracks started to appear in the united front on precisely this issue. The subsequent release of the French hostages by Iraq raised suspicions that the French government had engaged in some sort of unilateral negotiation, perhaps making commitments to Saddam Hussein. This was vigorously denied by the French, but it may have reduced the likelihood that the British and the Dutch, the most Atlanticist of the member states, would agree to subsequent French initiatives designed to avoid the military solution that the United States increasingly favoured. This split came to the fore in January 1991 when the French government submitted to the Foreign Ministers a conciliatory seven-point plan to secure a peaceful Iraqi withdrawal from Kuwait. The British, Dutch, and Germans all found it difficult to accept parts of the plan, which involved organizing an EC–Iraq meeting without the participation of the United States.

The EC had always experienced difficulties in agreeing on military action. Sanctions were a relatively easy matter: although they overlapped EPC and EC competencies, they had been used before, for example against South Africa. However, as a civilian power, the EC was not equipped to exercise force, and the issue had to be discussed in the forum of the Western European Union (WEU) (Box 28.12, p. 400). The United States in the meantime was able to act decisively in support of the United Nations in threatening to utilize force. When a UN military force was dispatched to the Gulf, it was under US leadership.

Although the EC states formally backed action through the UN, on 14 January 1991 France broke ranks, and just before the scheduled start of the UN military operation launched an independent peace initiative that had not been discussed with the other member states of the EC. This was clearly in breach of the agreement under EPC to discuss all major foreign policy initiatives with the other states, which had been set out in the London Report of October 1981. The French blamed the British and Dutch for showing such a dedicated and inflexible loyalty to the United States that they were unable to make a joint EC approach.

---

implement foreign policy. Therefore, as a civilian power asked to go to war, the EC was unable to take a leading role. The only institution in a position to fulfil this role was European Political Cooperation, which ultimately is only a discussion forum and has no powers of application. (Poulon and Bourantonis, 1992: 28)

Maastricht: from EPC to CFSP

While it was struggling to deal with crises in the Gulf and former Yugoslavia, the EC was also transforming itself into the EU. The IGC on political union, which began in January 1991, had the future evolution of EPC as a central item on its agenda. The more radical agenda, supported by Delors and by the German government, was to bring EPC into the framework of the EC, with the Commission perhaps not having the sole right of initiative but being centrally involved, and majority-voting applying to decisions in the Council of Ministers. Security and defence would be added to the remit of this new mechanism for a common foreign policy. The opposite pole was marked out by the British, who argued against majority voting on issues that were central to the sovereignty of the member states, and were particularly concerned that any moves to establish a common policy for security and defence should not undermine the NATO alliance.

The two voices in this debate drew opposite conclusions from events in the Gulf. Both sides agreed that the failure of the EC to respond effectively to the crisis indicated how far there still was to travel to a common policy. However, whereas Delors told the European Parliament that the ineffective response

Box 28.11 The Yugoslav Crisis

As in the Gulf, the immediate reaction was positive. When fighting broke out in June 1991 between the federal Yugoslav army and Croat and Slovenian separatist forces, representatives of the EC Troika, consisting of the previous, present, and immediate future presidencies of the Council, flew into the area three times in the first week of hostilities to try to broker a cease-fire, which they did successfully. Peace monitors were then sent to the area to help maintain the cease-fire. Economic sanctions were imposed by the EC on Yugoslavia in November 1991.

The European Council meeting in Luxembourg in June 1991 issued a declaration that implied support for the continued existence of Yugoslavia in some form. However, by the end of the year the pressure of public opinion in Germany had pushed the German government to a position where it insisted on recognition of the independence of Croatia and Slovenia or it would act unilaterally. Both France and Britain, the two countries most likely to have to commit troops if the fighting escalated and required a military response, were opposed, but had to give way in the face of German insistence on recognition.

The recognition went ahead in spite of the fact that the Badinter commission on the future of Yugoslavia, which the EC had itself set up, in its report in January 1992 gave only qualified support to the claims of Croatia to become independent. The commission did, however, support the claim of Macedonia to be recognized; but Greece objected to the recognition of its neighbour under the name of Macedonia, which Greece claimed was tantamount to a territorial claim against its northern region of the same name. It was not until 1993 that Macedonia achieved independence in the eyes of the UN, under the name of the Former Yugoslav Republic of Macedonia (FYROM).

Even this did not satisfy the Greeks, and in February 1994 the EU was faced with the serious embarrassment of the country that then held its presidency unilaterally refusing the Macedonians the right of access to the port of Salonika. When exhortation failed to move the Greeks, the Commission took the Greek government to the European Court under the previously unused Article 225 of the Treaty of Rome (EEC). This Article allowed the Commission or any member state to take to Court a member state which was believed to be misusing the claim that its national security interests were threatened to act in breach of its obligations under the Treaty. No decision was reached by the ECJ before the issue was resolved, but the Commission's move underlined the seriousness of the divisions within the EC.

Faced with such embarrassing disunity, the EC was probably sensible to try to widen the basis for action at an early stage. The UN was called in to help within four months of the start of the war, and in April 1993 the EC declared that it would in future only take action in support of UN initiatives. When military force was eventually used in Bosnia it was initially under UN auspices, but when air power was needed it was supplied by NATO. The main WEU military contribution was to send warships to the Adriatic in July 1992 to help enforce the UN sanctions. Even then, the use of NATO communications infrastructure proved to be necessary (Nuttall, 1994).

When a peace agreement was eventually signed, it was brokered by the United States (the Dayton Agreements). The EU undertook responsibility for the tasks of reconstruction and rehabilitation of refugees. This proved to be a job of formidable complexity, and the EU faced what some felt was unfair criticism from the United States for its slow progress. This all added to a sense of the inadequacy of EPC to provide a response to crises.

indicated the urgency of pushing forward to political union (*Debates of the European Parliament*, 23 Jan. 1991, 3–398/139), John Major told the House of Commons that this failure clearly indicated that Europe was not ready for a common policy (*Hansard*, 22. Jan 1991, col. 162).

The British position had moved, though. Whereas Margaret Thatcher had been opposed to any common European position on security and defence, despite the fact that the Bush administration was pressing for it, Douglas Hurd indicated in the

Winston Churchill Memorial Lecture in February 1991 that the government was now prepared to back the idea that the WEU should be used as a bridge between the EC and NATO (Hurd, 1991) (see Box 28.12, p. 400).

France and Germany continued throughout the IGC to promote the idea of defence coming under EC rules, to which the British government responded by formally tabling a joint proposal with the Italian government at a meeting of Foreign Ministers in October 1991 stressing the primacy of NATO. France

Box 28.12 The Western European Union (WEU)

WEU was the organization that had been set up in 1954 following the collapse of the Pleven Plan for a European Defence Community. It had apparently become moribund, but proposals to revive it as a vehicle for co-ordinating European positions had been made by the French government. Margaret Thatcher had rejected these calls, and made it quite clear that she thought too strong a WEU would undermine the role of NATO. In 1999 the British Foreign Secretary indicated that such a revival would be acceptable to the British government, and he supported the idea that had already been floated by France, Germany, and Italy for it to come under the political guidance of the European Council; although he rejected the Italian suggestion that once the WEU treaty formally expired, the organization should be absorbed into the EC. To facilitate closer co-ordination, in 1992 the WEU secretariat was moved from London to Brussels, where both the European Commission and NATO headquarters were located. In June 1992 the WEU Petersberg Declaration said that member states would allocate armed forces to peace-keeping and humanitarian tasks in Europe.

and Germany responded by announcing the expansion of the Franco–German brigade, which had been formed three years earlier, to lay the basis for a European rapid-response force. This upset the British government, because NATO had the previous May established its own rapid-response force under British command, to which the Germans were the second biggest contributors.

Despite this apparent determination to adopt a united front, the French and Germans did not succeed at Maastricht in getting the EPC brought into the EC. Instead a three-pillar structure was adopted, with the CFSP and Justice and Home Affairs forming intergovernmental pillars of the new EU alongside the EC pillar. Majority-voting in the second pillar was restricted to the implementation measures needed to carry through decisions of principle that would have to be taken by consensus, and even then the majority-voting would only apply if all states agreed to accept it in a particular case. Although

there was provision for a review of the structure in 1996, the Treaty on European Union represented a victory for the minimalist position on the CFSP.

Common Foreign and Security Policy

How did the CFSP differ from the EPC that it succeeded? Title V of the Treaty:

> provided the legal basis upon which to upgrade EPC operations; bring the old EPC secretariat inside the Council of Ministers and give it a larger and more permanent staff and budget; better relate the Rome Treaty-based foreign economic powers of the European Community . . . with the foreign political activities of EPC . . . to form more rounded and consistent EU policies; open up the possibility that some decisions may be reached by qualified majorities . . . It seemed as if the EU would be poised to adopt new kinds of higher profile foreign policy actions previously not thought possible. (Ginsberg, 1994: 13)

However, the first actions undertaken under the new heading were all in areas that built on EPC. Monitors were sent to observe the elections in Russia in December 1993; humanitarian aid for Bosnia was co-ordinated; a new political framework was developed for aid to the West Bank and Gaza. Subsequently observers were sent to monitor the first non-racial elections in South Africa; and the EU played an active role in the preparations for elections in the Palestinian homeland.

A more ambitious proposal that originated with French Prime Minister Edouard Balladur came to fruition in March 1995, when 52 states from Western and Eastern Europe signed a Stability Pact binding themselves to be good neighbours, and to respect the rights of minorities. Although there were several flaws in the Pact, especially the exclusion for one reason or another of all the Yugoslav successor states, the pattern was adopted later in the year by the Spanish presidency to develop a regional pact for the Mediterranean, in the face of growing concern in Southern Europe about Islamic fundamentalism in the Arab world and about illegal immigration from there.

On security and defence, the tragedy in former Yugoslavia did have a beneficial effect in bringing

France and Britain closer together. The common experience of operating under UN auspices in Bosnia led to increased co-operation on the ground, which spread into the creation of a joint air-force command unit. Nevertheless, when in 1998 a further crisis occurred in the Kosovo province of Serbia, the EU again proved unequal to the task of making a rapid response. It was NATO that undertook a bombing campaign against Serbia to force it to retreat from the persecution of the ethnic Albanian minority in Kosovo. The United States spearheaded the NATO effort.

The Amsterdam Treaty made some modifications to the CFSP, particularly in agreeing to the appointment of a High Representative who would be the first point of contact for CFSP matters. In November 1999 it was agreed to appoint the NATO secretary-general, Javier Solana to this post. The Commission had argued that the post should go to one of the Commissioners, but the heads of government decided to make it a position within the Council framework, thus storing up potential for problems in the co-ordination of the work of the two institutions.

Amendments to the TEU at Amsterdam drew a distinction between, on the one hand, deciding the principles and general guidelines of the CFSP, and common strategies in pursuit of these, and on the other the adoption of joint actions, common positions, and implementing decisions. The first category of decision had to be unanimous; qualified majority could decide the second. Also, a member state could abstain in a vote and make a formal declaration that it would not be bound by the vote. This would allow the EU as a whole to be committed to the decision, but not the individual abstaining state, which would only be obliged not to act in any way that would conflict with the pursuit of the action by the EU. The complicated procedure led one critic to say of the CFSP provisions of Amsterdam:

The engaged citizen . . . may wonder whether any of this is much of an advance on the old system of 'European Political Cooperation' that preceded Maastricht.   (Duff, 1997: 125)

Political relations with the United States

As in economic relations, the political and military relationship with the United States is central to the external relations of the EU. It is one of the key lines of division within the CFSP. France has consistently taken the line that Europe must act independently of the United States, whereas Britain, Germany, the Netherlands, and usually Italy have all held to the position that security and defence issues need to be handled on a transatlantic basis. However, after the end of the cold war positions shifted. France moved to collaborate more with NATO, which showed realism about the importance of NATO infrastructure to any attempt to act effectively in the military and security fields. Britain and Germany responded to prompting from the United States to try to make a success of the CFSP, so that the EU could be a more equal partner for the United States in dealing with international crises.

Verbal encouragement from the United States for a stronger partner in Europe was nothing new. Equally, when it came to the reality of a crisis, the United States was usually unwilling to stand back and leave it to its European allies to sort out. So long as there was no effective EU force to act decisively, there was every excuse for the United States to intervene. For example, when Greece and Turkey came into confrontation over the disputed Imia islands in the Adriatic in February 1996, the EU was unable to act decisively, and the United States stepped in to head off the crisis. Richard Holbrooke, the US Deputy Secretary of State, in an interview with the *Washington Post*, said that while President Clinton had been on the telephone to Ankara and Athens, the EU had been sleeping. This caused intense irritation in the EU, but the US intervention, if not strictly necessary, was facilitated by the lack of an immediate EU response. The question arises of what the situation would have been had the EU also responded quickly, especially as Greece is an EU member state, whereas the United States tends to be more favourable to Turkey.

Conclusion

It is hardly surprising that the external environment has had an impact on the external relations of the EU. This still leaves the question of what form that impact has taken. It also leaves the questions of what other influences have affected the development of external relations, and whether the evidence indicates anything about the nature of the EU.

The deterioration of the Lomé relationship can be directly related to a changing global environment. When the Yaoundé Convention was agreed in the 1960s, the former colonies were hardly consulted, and the terms reflected the neo-colonial relationship that still existed. By the time that the original Lomé Convention was negotiated, the actions of OPEC had indicated the potential power of producers of primary commodities to disrupt the industrial economies of the capitalist world, and so the ACP states had some real bargaining power. Subsequent Conventions were negotiated against a changing background, in which the ability of OPEC to sustain high prices for oil was shown not to be as great as believed in the early 1970s, and other commodity-producer cartels failed to materialize. The Contonou Agreement should be understood as a response to the challenges of ACP states in the context of globalization. Spreading global free trade had gradually eroded the benefits of the special arrangements that Lomé had made for the access of ACP goods to the EU's market. The new arrangements reflected this. They also reflected the increasing diversity among the ACP economies; and the increased emphasis that the EU put on social objectives, particularly in the face of pressure from organized labour which feared that global free trade would erode the rights that they had fought so hard for in the past unless those rights were extended to other parts of the world.

The common commercial policy has followed the world trend to extending free trade. This has not prevented conflict with the United States in particular. Neither side in the transatlantic trade disputes has yet broken ranks with the rulings of the WTO, although every time a decision goes against the United States there are threats from Congress to withdraw support and act unilaterally. The EU has a different internal political structure from the United States, and so the direct impact of domestic politics on trade issues is not so obvious. Sometimes the issues show up divisions within the EU itself; but probably the trade disputes with the United States have done more to foster a sense of European identity among economic actors and governments than they have to drive a wedge between them. The interests of the EU and the United States do inevitably come into conflict; yet each has an interest in trying to maintain a stable framework for global trade and commerce. The end of the era of US hegemony in the international economic system has both opened up an opportunity for the EU to assert itself—an opportunity which the Commission has been keen to exploit—and presented problems of co-ordination to both the world's trading giants.

The demand for a common external political approach has come mainly from outside of the EU itself. The fact that the EC was the largest trading bloc in the world inevitably meant that other states and groups of states expected to be able to deal with it as a unified political entity. As Delors (*Debates of the European Parliament*, 23 Jan. 1991, 3–398/139) put it:

The EC is now perceived as a major power. Much is expected of it. We must remember this and . . . take the necessary steps to give ourselves the political, legal and financial resources to shoulder our responsibilities.

The decline of US hegemony has been a factor reinforcing this general expectation. Since the end of the cold war the United States itself has frequently complained that the EU has not done enough to help stabilize the world, especially in its own region. This demand has helped moves towards CFSP, because it has helped to overcome the hesitancy of traditionally pro-NATO member states of the EU about developing an independent EU capability in the area of security and defence.

It is more difficult to argue that spillover from internal policy developments has been responsible for the development of external policy, although in an increasingly interdependent world, few internal policies do not have external effects. Competition policy is, 'an area in which the growth of transnational alliances and communications has made the internal/external distinction almost meaningless at times' (Allen and Smith, 1998: 75). Transport policy, so far as it affects air transport, has also become an aspect of external policy because of the number of issues that involve agreements between European and US carriers. Environmental issues have also become increasingly an international concern, overlapping the internal/external division. This overlapping of internal and external issues is likely to increase in the future. Issues of human rights, for example, are involved in trade relations with countries as diverse as Turkey and China, and the EP has become increasingly vocal in demanding that European standards of human rights should inform trade relations.

On the question of what external policy says about the supranational or intergovernmental nature of the EU, the evidence is mixed. The common commercial policy looks from the TEC as though it is supranational, but in practice it is formulated in a continuous dialogue between the Commission and the member states. On the other hand, the CFSP looks from the TEU as though it is clearly intergovernmental, but the practice is again much more mixed. In the TEU, the Commission was given the right to participate in all CFSP meetings, and a right to take initiatives, albeit not an exclusive right. As Ginsberg (1994: 15) pointed out, 'CFSP is not a wholly intergovernmental undertaking.' Against this, the decision taken at Amsterdam to appoint a High Representative and locate the post outside of the Commission indicates the reluctance of member states to allow a supranational organization too much influence in this area.

Caution on the part of governments about allowing CFSP to run out of their own control reflects Hoffmann's argument about high and low politics (Hoffmann, 1964, 1966). Foreign policy, defence, and security are definitely high politics. The decisions made affect matters of life and death if troops are to be committed to back up a policy. This is why the elaborate arrangements have been devised by the EU to allow member states to opt out of specific actions without preventing the others from pursuing them in the name of the EU as a whole. The legitimacy of the whole process would be severely tested if national soldiers of a state where the population did not approve of a particular action were killed in pursuit of that action. On the other hand, *Eurobarometer* polls show that a clear majority of over two-thirds of EU citizens favour a European approach to foreign policy (Leonard, 1998: 46). This is an area where the potential for progress is considerable, and the indications are that effective progress will increase the legitimacy of the EU.

KEY POINTS

Relations with African, Caribbean, and Pacific states

- Relations between the EC and the former French and Belgian colonies were governed by the terms of the Yaoundé Conventions, signed in the capital of Cameroon in 1963 and 1969.

- When Britain joined the EC it became necessary to negotiate a new set of agreements to cover the former British colonies (although the states of the Indian subcontinent were excluded).

- The first Lomé Convention was signed in the capital of Togo between the EC and eighteen African, Caribbean, and Pacific (ACP) states in 1975 and ran until 1980. It was succeeded by Lomé II (1980–85), III (1985–90) and IV (1990–2000, with a mid-term review in 1995).

- At each stage more states joined. These included, but were not restricted to, the former colonies of Spain and Portugal when they became member states of the EC. By the time of the fourth convention, seventy ACP states were covered.

- Under Lomé, virtually all ACP exports enter the EU free of tariffs, while their export earnings on commodities and minerals are partially protected by stabilization programmes.

- In 2000, the Lomé Convention was set to be superseded by a new agreement signed in Contonou, Benin.

The common commercial policy

- The Treaty of Rome allocated responsibility for commercial policy to the EC.

- In practice the competence is shared between the EC and the member states. The Commission represents the EC in external trade negotiations, but it negotiates to a mandate given it by the member states, and it is monitored by representatives of the member states in the Article 133 Committee.

- The EC does not even have formal competence over trade in services and intellectual products, which were not subject to international trade negotiations when the Treaty of Rome was signed. The member states have so far not agreed to extend the relevant Treaty Article to cover these increasingly important areas.

- Trade negotiations are the subject of a complex 'three-level' game. At level one the member states each try to establish a position that will be acceptable to their domestic constituencies. At level two the member states collectively bargain over a mandate for the Commission. At level three the Commission negotiates with other states on this mandate.

- Trade relations with the United States are particularly important to the EU. Despite attempts by both sides to help relations run smoothly, they have been subject to increasing tensions and disputes.

External political relations

- External political relations are handled outside of the EC framework under the intergovernmental 'third pillar' of the EU, under the title 'Common Foreign and Security Policy' (CFSP).

- The predecessor arrangement to the CFSP was European Political Co-operation (EPC). It had a number of substantive successes to its name. Initially the Commission was excluded from meetings of Foreign Ministers under EPC, but it became increasingly apparent that the linkage between external commercial policy and external political relations was too close for this to work, and gradually the role of the Commission increased.

- The end of the cold war, demands from the United States that the EC play a larger role in ensuring the security of the post-cold war world, and the ineffectiveness of the EC in the Gulf and Yugoslav crises all gave momentum to attempts to strengthen co-operation on external political relations. The TEU introduced the CFSP.

- A decision was made at Amsterdam in 1997 to appoint a High Representative to be the public face of the CFSP. The decision to put the post into the Council machinery rather than to appoint a member of the Commission raised the prospect of co-ordination problems.

- As US hegemony has declined the United States has encouraged the EU to play a larger role in security matters, and this has helped progress in CFSP.

QUESTIONS

1 What explains the nature and extent of co-operation on external relations?

2 How important is the Commission in external economic relations?

3 What are the problems involved in EU foreign policy-making?

4 Why is CFSP predominantly intergovernmental?

FURTHER READING

On Lomé there is an informative official document available on the web: European Commission (2000), *The Lomé Convention* (*http://www.europa.eu.int/comm/development/contonou/Lomé_history_en.htm*). The new Contonou agreement is also available through the same medium: European Commission, 'The European Commission and its member States Sign a New Partnership Agreement with the African, Caribbean and Pacific States in Contonou, Benin', *Press Release* (11 July 2000). Commentary and analysis are available in B. Laffan *The Finances of the European Union* (Basingstoke and London: Macmillan, 1997); M. Lister, *The European Union and the South: Relations with Developing Countries* (London: Routledge, 1997), and M. Lister (ed.), *European Union Development Policy* (Basingstoke and London: Macmillan, 1998).

The common commercial policy of the EU is analysed as a multilevel game in S. Collinson, '"Issue Systems", "Multilevel Games" and the Analysis of the EU's External Commercial and Associated Policies: A Research Agenda', *Journal of European Public Policy* 6 (1999), 206–24. B. Y. Hanson, 'What Happened to fortress Europe? External Trade and Liberalization in the European Union', *International Organization* 52 (1998), 55–85, examines the reasons why the 'threat' of a fortress Europe did not materialize, and the factors behind the liberalization of EU trade policy. S. Meunier and K. Nicolaïdes, 'Who Speaks for Europe? The delegation of Trade Authority in the EU', *Journal of Common Market Studies* 37 (1999), 477–501, analyses the political factors behind the refusal of the member states to extend full negotiating authority to the Commission in the areas of trade in services and intellectual property, and speculates about the implications of this for the future conduct of the EU's external trade policy.

An excellent recent introduction to the CFSP is provided by F. Cameron, *The Foreign and Security Policy of the European Union: Past, Present and Future* (Sheffield: Sheffield Academic Press, 1999). An important contribution to the debate about the external political relations of the EU which is frequently quoted and well worth reading is C. Hill, 'The Capability–Expectations Gap, or Conceptualising Europe's International Role', *Journal of Common Market Studies* 31 (1993), 305–28. The analysis is followed up in Hill, *The Actors in Europe's Foreign Policy* (London: Routledge, 1996), while the overall record is assessed in M. Holland (ed.), *Common Foreign and Security Policy: The Record and Reforms* (London: Cassell, 1997).

CHRONOLOGY

1954
October   Treaty creating Western European Union (WEU) signed
1958
January   EEC Treaty gives Commission competence for external trade negotiations
January   Implementing Convention of the EEC Treaty comes into effect

1963
July   First Yaoundé Convention succeeds the Implementing Convention

1971
January   Second Yaoundé Convention signed

1975
February   First Lomé Convention comes into operation
August   Signing of the 'Final Act' at the Conference on Security and Co-operation in Europe
              (CSCE) in Helsinki

1979
December   USSR invades Afghanistan

1980
March   Start of Lomé 2
June   EC makes Venice Declaration recognizing right of Palestinians to a homeland

1981
October   'London Report' on European Political Co-operation published

1984
December   Lomé 3 signed

1989
December   Lomé 4 signed

1990
August   Iraq invades Kuwait

1991
January   France breaks ranks with EC position on Iraq conflict and launches independent peace
              initiative/start of IGC on political union
June   Start of conflict between federal Yugoslav army and Slovenian separatist forces
November   EC imposes economic sanctions on Yugoslavia

1992
January   Badinter Committee gives support for recognition of Macedonia and qualified support
              for Croatian independence
June   WEU Petersberg Declaration
November   Blair House agreements between EU and USA

1993
April   EC declares that it would in future only take action in support of UN initiatives
December   EU monitors observe Russian elections

1994
February   Greek government refuses Macedonia access to the port of Salonika

1995
January   WTO begins operation/CSCE becomes Organization for Security and Co-operation in
              Europe (OSCE)
March   Stability Pact signed by 52 states from western and eastern Europe

1996
October   EU makes formal complaint to WTO against US sanctions against Cuba

1997
May   German government opposes EU anti-dumping measures
June   EU and US agree mutual recognition pact on testing and certification procedures for
              health and safety

1999
April   WTO agrees to US sanctions over banana dispute
December   Successor to Lomé 4 agreed

29 Enlargement

SUMMARY

This chapter provides an overview of the series of enlargements to the EC/EU. It begins with the accession of Britain, Denmark, and Ireland in 1973 and concludes with a discussion of the issues facing the EU as it considers further enlargement at the end of 2000. In doing so, the chapter highlights the recurring themes of enlargement: the key issues for the applicant states; the key issues for the EC/EU; and the precedents set during each enlargement process.

Introduction

The EC/EU has expanded its membership four times, and at the end of the twentieth century was contemplating a fifth enlargement that would take membership to as many as 27 member states. Enlargement is not simply about incorporating additional states into existing practices. Each enlargement has had important implications for the EC/EU in relation to both policies and institutions. While each of the previous enlargements has brought challenges, the nature and potential scale of enlargement in the early years of the twenty-first century poses the biggest set of challenges to date.

The first enlargement

In 1970, the EC was in accession negotiations with four applicant states: Britain, Denmark, Ireland, and Norway. On 1 January 1973 the first three of these states became members of the EC, while Norway did not. The reasons behind the first enlargement were primarily economic, with the British application pivotal.

There was a strong constituency of support for British entry within the EC, especially among the smaller member states, but France had blocked such a move previously. The change of French president, particularly the departure of General de Gaulle in 1969, cleared the way. More important, though, were changed economic circumstances. The post-war economic boom faltered in the late 1960s. British entry in particular offered the prospect of giving a boost to the EC economies.

France's President Pompidou had to ensure that British entry did not compromise French interests. That is why he agreed to a compromise that allowed the EC to move to an 'own resources' system of funding the budget. De Gaulle had blocked such a move in 1965 because he objected to the idea, which became linked to the proposal as part of a package deal, that the budgetary powers of the EP should be increased. Pompidou was prepared to make concessions on this, difficult though it was for him to do so in terms of domestic politics, because the new system would benefit France once Britain was a member. Britain, with a small and relatively efficient agricultural sector, would become a net contributor to a common budget that was dominated by the CAP. France, which had a large agricultural sector and a lot of small farmers who were eligible for financial support, would become a net beneficiary.

The procedure that was established at the time of the first enlargement was that the existing member states would sort out arrangements that suited them before the new members were admitted. The corollary of this was French insistence that accession for the new members could only be on the basis of acceptance of the complete *acquis communautaire* (Preston, 1995: 452: see Box 8.4, p. 91). This was to ensure that Britain did not try to slip out of the uncomfortable budgetary position into which the French believed that they had manoeuvred it. The implicit understanding that there was a deal in operation here explains the strength of French (and German) resistance to subsequent British demands for a correction of the budgetary imbalance.

The position of Ireland and Denmark in relation to EC membership followed closely that of Britain. The extent of trade dependence between these countries and Britain made this so. If Britain was to accede to membership, these countries had a strong economic incentive to follow suit. Moreover, while joining the EC along with Britain would protect their existing trade relationships, it would also open up other opportunities that would allow their dependence on Britain to be reduced over time.

In Ireland, early concerns were expressed over the

implications for the country's neutrality of EC membership. As entry became a more realistic prospect in the early 1970s, more specific concerns surfaced. These included the threat to the Irish fishing industry and concerns over the relative lack of economic development in parts of Ireland. On the first of these, the EC allowed Ireland a temporary concession on its fishing rights and recognized Irish concerns on structural development by adding a protocol to the Accession Treaty committing the Community to addressing these problems. Despite these issues, the Irish accession was relatively smooth. As Preston (1997: 41) noted: 'Irish negotiating priorities threatened neither the overall acquis nor any powerful domestic interest groups in the EC. At that stage in the development of the EC's foreign policy identity, Ireland's neutrality did not prove problematic either.'

Like Britain, Denmark had a reputation for scepticism about European integration. Instinctively, Danish politicians preferred deeper co-operation with their Nordic counterparts. However, as a major exporter of food to Britain, Denmark had a strong incentive to follow the first British application to protect its exports. When this application broke down, Denmark pursued the prospect of a Nordic customs union. However, the revival of the British application in the late 1960s coincided with problems in the Nordic negotiations and persuaded politicians and public alike that EC membership provided the better option. While Denmark was keen to secure confirmation of the status of the national veto in EC decision-making, economic factors ultimately overrode political concerns in the Danish decision to join the Community.

Norway shared with Denmark both close trade links with Britain and concern over the political implications of European integration. Like Denmark, the Norwegian application followed that of Britain in the early 1960s and, when this failed, Norway participated in the Nordic customs union negotiations. However, unlike Denmark, Norway did not ultimately join the Community following the reactivation of its membership application in the late 1960s. While the EC moved some way to meeting Norwegian concerns, particularly over agriculture and fisheries, membership was ultimately rejected in a referendum held in September 1972. While the majority against membership was slim (53.5 per cent), the public concerns expressed during this period over the threat of membership to national political and economic identity have ensured that Norway has remained outside the European Union ever since.

The Mediterranean enlargement

The second and third enlargements of the EC are often treated as a single 'Mediterranean' enlargement. Greece became a member state in January 1981, and Spain and Portugal in January 1986. In all three cases political considerations overrode economic factors in the decision to enlarge. Each of the states concerned had just emerged from a period of dictatorship, and the desire to consolidate democracy and guard against a resurgence of authoritarianism featured strongly in the reasons for the applications and the reasons for their acceptance. It was assumed that EC membership, conditional on democratic government, would help to achieve that. Ensuring stability on the southern periphery of western Europe was a particular concern of France and West Germany.

Greece first signed an Association Agreement with the EEC in July 1961, with the intention of applying for full membership later. However, this agreement was suspended by the EC following the military coup in Greece in April 1967. The subsequent military dictatorship collapsed in July 1974 following the Turkish invasion of Cyprus, which led to a division of the island between Greek and Turkish communities. This invasion, along with the collapse of the right-wing dictatorship in Portugal (below), threatened the stability of the region. In both cases the end of undemocratic governments was followed by a period of uncertainty about the direction the country would take, with a growing concern that the southern flank of NATO would be weakened.

The failure of the United States to restrain Turkey over Cyprus produced a wave of anti-American sentiment in Greece. Greek forces were withdrawn from the NATO command structure, signalling a danger that the alliance might be damaged in a strategically important geographical location. The EC responded by accepting an application for membership from the Greek government in June 1975.

The Commission gave a very hesitant official Opinion on the Greek application, expressing concerns over Greco-Turkish relations, the economic implications of accession and the potential impact of Greek membership on EC decision-making and policy development (Preston, 1997: 50–1). However, the Council overrode the Commission's opinion and the application was accepted, largely at the insistence of the German government. Ultimately, strategic considerations overcame the economic and diplomatic problems that the Commission had correctly identified. This set a precedent for later acceptance of applications from a range of former communist states in central and eastern Europe with weak economies following the collapse of communism in 1989. More immediately, the Greek accession provided a rehearsal for further Mediterranean enlargement.

Portugal was a founder member of EFTA in 1960 and as such was part of the free trade area between EFTA and the EC, created by the Special Relations Agreement, which came into effect in January 1973. While the end of dictatorship was a pre-requisite of full membership, the April 1974 revolution against the right-wing government threatened to run out of the control of the pro-capitalist democratic forces. For nearly two years there was political turmoil, with strong support emerging for the Communist Party and for a variety of left-wing socialist movements.

To avert the possibility of Portugal being removed from the NATO alliance, funds were channelled to the democratic parties through international political party organizations. The largest support was channelled from the ruling Social Democratic Party in West Germany via the Socialist International to the Portuguese Socialist Party (PSP) of Mario Soares. In 1976, a PSP government was elected under Soares, which submitted a formal application for membership of the EC in March 1977. Despite serious doubts about structural weaknesses in the Portuguese economy, this application was also accepted, again for essentially political reasons.

Eight years after its first request, Spain eventually signed an Association Agreement with the EEC in 1970. As with Greece, this agreement signalled a longer-term ambition for full membership. Spain's formal application for membership was submitted by the Suarez government in July 1977, merely twenty months after the country emerged from dictatorship following the death of Franco.

Although with slightly less urgency than in the Portuguese case, strategic considerations applied for EC states with the application of Spain. Spain had not been a member of NATO, but its absence had left a gap in the Mediterranean coverage of the alliance, which had been partially plugged by close collaboration between the United States and the right-wing dictator. As in Greece, the United States had damaged its image in the eyes of the indigenous democratic forces, so again it fell to the EC to stabilize the position. Spain's membership of NATO was achieved against considerable domestic opposition as part of an implicit bargain that membership of the EC would follow. This was desirable for Spain because its emerging engineering-based industries needed access to the wider market. However, it was clear that other sectors of the Spanish economy would require support from the EC if they were not to be decimated by membership. Again, the EC took on an immediate economic burden in order to achieve a geostrategic objective.

The EFTA enlargement

In the course of the 1980s, the states of the European Free Trade Association (EFTA) (Box 29.1, p. 411) became concerned about the impact on investment in their economies of the EC's decision to create the single internal market. Businesses wanted to be inside the single market, and investment began to flow in that direction. Even large national companies of the EFTA states, such as Volvo of Sweden, were locating their investments inside the EC and not in the EFTA countries. This led the EFTA states to enquire about closer links with the EC, despite the unpopularity of the idea of membership inside some of the states concerned. At the time the EC was trying to process the legislation that was needed to make a reality of the internal market. It was also looking to the next stage in the process, which in the view of the President of the Commission (Jacques Delors), the Chancellor of Germany (Helmut Kohl), and the President of France (François Mitterrand) was movement to a monetary union.

To prevent another round of enlargement dominating the attention of the organization, and possibly deflecting the course of the spillover from the single market to the single currency, in January 1989 Delors proposed the idea of the European Economic Space (EES), which was later renamed the European Economic Area (EEA). This would give the EFTA states membership of the single market without them becoming full members of the EC. For the governments of the EFTA states this had the advantage that the compromise might be easier than full membership to sell to their electorates, because they had to get domestic ratification of any deal. The disadvantage was that they would have no voice in the ongoing negotiation of the regulation of the single market. They would be obliged to accept agreements reached in their absence.

The EEA negotiations were successfully concluded in 1991, and a treaty was signed in 1992; but it became increasingly apparent that businesses were simply not prepared to believe that members of the EEA would be full members of the single market. Investment flows did not revert to previous patterns. The EEA suffered a further blow to its credibility when the Swiss people rejected membership of it in a referendum in December 1992. The government of Austria had already applied for full membership of the EC in July 1989, and Finland, Norway, and Sweden did likewise between July 1991 and November 1992. Not only had the EEA proved to be an unsatisfactory compromise solution: the events of 1989 in Eastern Europe had also removed one of the main objections of opponents of membership within the EFTA states. Austria, Finland, and Sweden were all neutral states during the cold war, and there had been doubts about whether membership of an organization that was developing a common foreign and security policy was compatible with neutrality. The end of the cold war called into question the meaning of neutrality, and effectively dissipated the doubts on that score.

Box 29.1 EFTA at the end of the 1980s

By the late 1980s, EFTA consisted of seven states of varying size.

Country	Population (000s)
Sweden	8,640
Austria	7,820
Switzerland	6,790
Finland	5,030
Norway	4,260
Iceland	256
Liechtenstein	30

- The economies of the EFTA states had been linked with those of the EC since the 1970s by a series of bilateral free-trade agreements.

- By the end of the 1980s, EFTA was economically closely integrated with the EC.

- The EC did 25 per cent of its trade with EFTA, a higher proportion than with the United States, while the EFTA states sent 56 per cent of their exports to the EC, and bought 60 per cent of their imports from the EC.

By this time the prospect had emerged of an eventual eastern enlargement to embrace states that were economically considerably less developed than the existing member states. The EFTA applicants were wealthy, and potential net contributors to a common budget that would come under much greater pressure if the central and east European states were eventually accepted. So, while there were sensitive negotiations over agriculture in particular, the EFTA applications were accepted, and Austria, Finland, and Sweden became EU members at the start of 1995. Norway, as in 1972, narrowly rejected membership in a referendum after terms of entry had been agreed.

The main significance of the EFTA enlargement was that it raised for the first time some of the issues concerning the institutional architecture of the EC/EU that were to emerge with more urgency when the eastern enlargement came to the top of the agenda. The weighting of votes in the Council of Ministers was particularly problematical. Britain and Spain raised it as an issue during the negotiations on the accession of Austria, Finland, and Sweden, pointing out that if the existing rules on what constituted a qualified majority (or a blocking minority) were simply extrapolated upwards on enlargement, it would become possible for states representing 41 per cent of the population to be outvoted. This would be compounded with further enlargement because of the number of small states applying,

and it would soon be possible for a majority of the population of the EU to be outvoted. Eventually a compromise was reached at a meeting of Foreign Ministers in Ioannina in Greece in March 1995. They agreed that the blocking minority would be increased to 26 in line with the increased total number of votes, but if there were 23 votes against there would be a delay in proceeding with the measure during which time the Commission would try to find an acceptable compromise amendment to its proposal.

The other institutional issues raised by the EFTA enlargement were the extension of the practice of QMV, and the size of the Commission. It soon became obvious that the increase from 12 to 15 member states increased the complexity of bargaining and coalition formation more than proportionately to the expansion of the number of actors. The prospect emerged of the organization becoming paralysed if it expanded its membership further without agreeing to remove the national veto. At the same time, the formation of a coherent Commission also became more difficult. Because the larger member states had two Commissioners, a membership of 15 states meant a Commission of 20 members, and there were simply not sufficient significant portfolios to go round, as Jacques Santer discovered in 1995 when he tried to accommodate all the national nominees without upsetting anyone by giving them inadequate responsibilities.

Future enlargement

In the later months of 1989 the process of the collapse of communism in central and east Europe gathered pace. The fall of the Berlin Wall in November marked a further acceleration of the process, and the Soviet Union began to disintegrate as states such as Lithuania and Estonia (both March 1990) declared their independence. In the summer of 1990 NATO declared that it no longer considered the Warsaw Pact to be an enemy. The cold war had ended.

The first moves to provide support for the transition of former communist states to democracy and

capitalism came from the Paris summit of the G7 states in July 1989, which agreed that the European Commission should co-ordinate aid to Poland and Hungary from the broader G24 (the 24 most industrialized countries). The EC's own contribution to this wider effort was the programme of assistance known as Poland, Hungary: Actions for Economic Reconstruction (PHARE). This acronym stuck even after 1990, when following the total collapse of communism the programme was extended to other central and eastern European states. The G24 also

Box 29.2 The European Bank for Reconstruction and Development

The European Bank for Reconstruction and Development (EBRD) was established in 1991. It exists to foster the transition towards open market-oriented economies and to promote private and entrepreneurial initiative in the countries of central and east Europe and the Commonwealth of Independent States (CIS) which are committed to and applying the principles of multiparty democracy, pluralism, and market economics. Through its investments it promotes private sector activity, the strengthening of financial institutions and legal systems, and the development of the infrastructure needed to support the private sector.

The 26 states that are eligible for support from the EBRD are:

Albania, Armenia, Azerbaijan, Belarus, Bosnia and Herzegovina, Bulgaria, Croatia, Czech Republic, Estonia, the Former Yugoslav Republic of Macedonia, Georgia, Hungary, Kazakhstan, Kyrgyzstan, Latvia, Lithuania, Moldova, Poland, Romania, the Russian Federation, the Slovak Republic, Slovenia, Tajikistan, Turkmenistan, Ukraine, and Uzbekistan.

Source: EBRD Web Site http://www.ebrd.com/english/index.htm

accepted the legitimacy of this aspiration, and took the first step towards further enlargement by laying down the criteria that potential applicants would have to meet in order to be considered (Box 29.3, p. 413). It was not long after Copenhagen that the first applications for membership were submitted. Hungary and Poland applied within a week of each other, in April 1994, to be followed in the course of 1995 and 1996 by eight other central and eastern European states (Table 29.1, p. 414). Encouragement was given to this aspiration for membership by at least some of the applicants when Helmut Kohl used the prerogative of the German Presidency of the EC to invite the heads of state of Poland, Hungary, and the Czech and Slovak Republics to make an appearance at the Essen European Council in December 1994.

That the German gesture was targeted at specific applicants became clearer in the following year. Germany gave strong support to the idea that the applications of Poland, Hungary, and the Czech Republic should be prioritized; but at the Madrid European Council in December 1995 agreement was reached to open negotiations with all the applicants simultaneously, within six months of the IGC, which the same European Council decided would open officially in Turin on 29 March 1996.

acted to establish the European Bank for Reconstruction and Development (EBRD) (Box 29.2, p. 413).

In 1991 the first of a series of 'Europe Agreements' were signed by the EC with the former communist states. These were association agreements such as the EC had concluded with a variety of other states. They committed the EC to co-operate with the associated states in political and economic matters, and offered freer access to the EC market for the exports of the associated states. They stopped short, however, of envisaging membership of the EC. This disappointed the associated states, although as Gower (1999: 5) pointed out, 'the first three Europe Agreements were signed in December 1991, barely two years after the fall of the Berlin Wall, and when the stability of the new democracies was still far from certain'.

Membership of the EC was the explicit aim of the former communist states. Less than two years later, in June 1993, the Copenhagen European Council

Box 29.3 The Copenhagen Criteria

The Copenhagen European Council in June 1993 approved the principle of the enlargement of the EC/EU to take in the associated states of central and east Europe, and laid down three broad criteria that were preconditions of membership:

- A political criterion:
  An applicant must have stable institutions, guaranteeing democracy, the rule of law, human rights, and the protection of minorities.

- An economic criterion:
  An applicant must have a functioning market economy and the capacity to cope with competitive pressures within the single market of the EU.

- A criterion relating to the *acquis communautaire*:
  An applicant must be able to take on the obligations of membership, including adherence to the aims of political, economic, and monetary union.

Table 29.1 Association agreements and accession applications

State	Date of association agreement	Date of accession application
Bulgaria	March 1993	December 1995
Cyprus	December 1972	July 1990
Czech Republic	October 1993	January 1996
Estonia	June 1995	November 1995
Hungary	December 1991	March 1994
Latvia	June 1995	October 1995
Lithuania	June 1995	October 1995
Malta	December 1970	July 1990
Poland	December 1991	April 1994
Romania	February 1993	June 1995
Slovakia	October 1993	June 1995
Slovenia	June 1996	June 1996
Turkey	September 1973	April 1987

Source: Europa web site: http://europa.eu.int/scadplus/leg/en/lvb/e40001.htm

The commitment to open negotiations with all applicants included, in addition to the ten central and eastern European states, two small Mediterranean island states, Cyprus and Malta, which had long had association agreements that did envisage eventual membership. Both applied formally for membership in July 1990. Turkey, which had an association agreement dating back to 1964, and which applied for membership in April 1987, was not included in the list of prospective members. The Turkish government was insulted by this omission, and in March 1997 threatened to block the enlargement of NATO, of which Turkey was a member, if it were not offered the prospect of eventual EC membership. Meanwhile Greece, in February 1997, threatened to veto the whole enlargement if negotiations with Cyprus embraced the northern Cypriot Turkish community, which had formed a separate state (unrecognized by the international community) since the 1975 Turkish invasion.

In late April 1996 the Commission sent the governments of all the central and eastern European applicant states a lengthy questionnaire, consisting of over 1,000 questions, to be returned by the end of July. The tight time-scale and the onerous nature of the questionnaire caused some resentment in the applicant states, although as Avery and Cameron explained (1999: 36–7) the approach was necessary because of the paucity of reliable official information

and statistics. Despite the difficulty of the exercise and the tight schedule, all the questionnaires were completed and returned by the end of July.

In July 1997 the Commission produced a report entitled *Agenda 2000* (European Commission, 1997), which comprised several documents. It contained a proposed Financial Perspective for the period 2000–2006, and proposals for the reform of the structural funds and the CAP which were held to be necessary before enlargement could be completed (see Chapter 24, pp. 318–19 and Chapter 27, pp. 376–9). Attached to the report were the Commission's Opinions on the applicant states' preparedness for membership, and a proposal to begin negotiations first with the applicants that were identified to be the best prepared—the Czech Republic, Poland, Hungary, Estonia, Slovenia, and Cyprus (Malta had withdrawn its application following a change of government in October 1996).

The Luxembourg European Council in December 1997 accepted the Commission's proposal to prioritize the applications of Cyprus and five of the central and eastern European states, but the other five (Bulgaria, Latvia, Lithuania, Romania, and Slovakia) were to remain involved. To help them feel a sense of involvement, it was subsequently agreed (by Foreign Ministers in October 1997) to hold an annual Europe Conference to allow an exchange of views between member states and all the applicant states. Turkey wanted parity with this second group, but Greece and Germany opposed such a move. Tensions remained between Greece and Turkey over Cyprus, while German concerns revolved around the prospect of large-scale Turkish immigration. The outcome was widely seen as a victory for Germany, which had long advocated prioritizing the applications of Poland, Hungary, and the Czech Republic, and had consistently opposed offering Turkey the prospect of membership. The agreement was angrily condemned by the Turkish Prime Minister, Mesut Yilmaz, who refused the invitation to the inaugural Europe Conference in London in March 1998.

Although the decision to prioritize their applications was welcomed by the five central and eastern European states who were selected, tension soon crept into their relationship with the EU. They complained that the new accession partnerships now proposed by the EU made aid that had been free of conditions under PHARE conditional on compliance with the programme of policies to adapt them for membership. They complained less when in November 1998 agreement was reached within the EU on two new funds to supplement PHARE. A pre-accession instrument to assist with structural adjustment, ISPA, was allocated 7 billion ecus for the period 2000–2006; and a pre-accession instrument to assist with agricultural adjustment, SAPARD, was allocated 500 million ecus per year, commencing in January 2000. The Berlin European Council confirmed these in March 1999, and also agreed to double existing pre-accession aid from 2000.

The Helsinki European Council in December 1999 acted to remove the sense of grievance felt by the applicants who had not been prioritized at Luxembourg by agreeing that accession negotiations should open with all the remaining applicants in January or February, with entry being determined by progress in meeting the conditions set. This meant that one or more of the second group could possibly overtake one or more of the first group. Malta, which had reapplied in September 1998, was included in this second group, and given the preparation that had already taken place prior to withdrawal of the original application, there was an expectation that it might reach the finishing line before some of those who had already begun negotiations. Latvia and Slovakia were also seen as possible rapid movers (Smith,

2000: 122–3). Slovakia in particular started from a sound economic base, and had only been refused inclusion in the first group in 1997 because of the authoritarian tendencies of the then government.

The same meeting decided to offer Turkey official applicant status in return for a guarantee that it would not act in such a way as effectively to block the accession of Cyprus. Such was the concern about Turkish susceptibilities, that Günter Verheugen, the Commissioner for Enlargement, and Javier Solana, the High Representative for CFSP, flew directly from Helsinki to Ankara to explain the offer to the Turkish government, which eventually did accept the deal.

There remained a great deal to agree before the enlargement could go ahead. The precise terms and conditions of entry still had to be settled for each individual applicant. In order to make concrete progress in the early stages, the more technical and less controversial 'chapters' of the *acquis* were dealt with at the start of the process. This left the more difficult issues such as agriculture and the free movement of workers to be tackled later, which meant that the process slowed down during 1999 and 2000. Also, as the conclusions of the Copenhagen European Council of June 1993 had emphasized, there was not only a need for the applicants to be prepared: the EC/EU itself had to be ready. This proved a difficult condition to fulfil.

Preparing the EU for enlargement

In order to be ready to take as many as 12 new members, the EU had to deal with some difficult issues requiring reforms of both policies and institutions. Two policy issues were particularly crucial to the prospects for enlargement: agriculture and the structural funds. The institutional questions were those that were already apparent at the time of the EFTA enlargement: the weighting of votes under QMV, and the size of the blocking minority; the abandonment of the national veto in more policy sectors; and the size of the Commission.

Agriculture accounted for 25 per cent of the GDP

of the applicant states, with production concentrated in the products that were already the most problematic for the EU: meat, dairy products, and cereals. Productivity within the applicant states varied considerably, but was generally lower than in the EU. Application of the CAP directly to the new entrants would be likely to encourage higher output. It would have an unsustainable impact on the cost of the CAP, and would generate increased surpluses in the products that were already most of a problem. At the same time, the higher cost of food to the consumer would have an inflationary effect in the new entrants, where expenditure on food accounted for a higher proportion of total household expenditure than it did in the west. The struggle to get the existing member states to accept the sort of far-reaching reform of the CAP that was necessary to pave the way for enlargement is told in Chapter 24.

The reform of the structural funds was similarly dogged by the refusal of existing beneficiaries from the policies to accept that they would have to give up much of their funding in order to allow enlargement to take place within existing budgetary ceilings. The Commission proposals unveiled in March 1998 would result in no state losing more than one-third of its eligibility for funding in terms of the percentage of its population covered by Objective 2. Long and generous transitional arrangements were made for regions that would lose Objective 1 status. Even

so, it proved difficult to get agreement, leading the Commissioner, Monika Wulf-Mathies, to warn a Council of Ministers meeting in Glasgow in June 1998 that governments had to stop pretending that enlargement would be possible without making sacrifices on structural funding.

Difficulties in getting agreement on policy issues were paralleled by problems in getting agreement on the institutional reforms that would also be necessary to facilitate enlargement. The Amsterdam European Council of June 1997 ended one IGC that was supposed to resolve these issues, but without agreement on them. A new IGC was convened in February 2000, and met throughout the year, but it also had produced no concrete agreed proposals on the most controversial issues by the time of the Nice European Council in December.

The Nice European Council

Nice turned out to be the longest European Council in the history of the EC/EU. For four days the heads of government haggled over the areas that would become subject to QMV, and over the weighting of votes. Membership of the Commission proved less difficult, although really tough decisions were deferred by allowing the size of the College of Commissioners to grow to 27 before there would be less than one Commissioner per member states; but in return for giving up their second Commissioner the large member states fought even harder on the weighting of votes in the Council. In the end an agreement was reached that just about opened up the prospect of the EU being ready for enlargement.

The veto was removed from 29 of the 70 Treaty articles where it still applied; but in important areas national interests prevented movement. Britain would not agree to the removal of the veto on tax or social security harmonization. Although QMV for trade negotiations was extended to services, at French insistence exceptions were made for audio-visual services, education, and health. Maritime transport was exempted from QMV at the insistence

of Denmark and Greece. Many aspects of immigration and asylum policy were not transferred to QMV at German and French insistence. Perhaps most significantly, though, Spain, with the support of Portugal and Greece, retained the right to veto changes to the cohesion funds until after the conclusion of the negotiations on the 2007–2012 Financial Perspective. This cast further doubt on the possibility of keeping the cost of enlargement to the common budget within limits acceptable to the net contributors.

On the way in which those areas subject to QMV would be decided, that is on the weighting of votes under QMV, the large member states seemed to gain an advantage over the small. The re-weighting, which would apply from 1 January 2005, left the small and medium-sized states with a smaller percentage of the total vote relative to the larger states than under the previous system. There was also the insertion of a clause requiring any measure agreed by QMV to comprise the votes of governments representing at least 62 per cent of the population of the EU. The effect was to put Germany, France, and Britain, or any two of these three plus Italy, in a position where they could effectively block progress on any measure on which they agreed to co-operate. In compensation the small states were allowed a clause that a measure agreed under QMV would also have to have the support of a majority of the member states. The cumulative effect of these two concessions to different coalitions of 'bigs' and 'smalls' was to make the decision-making system much more complex, and also to make it more difficult than previously to achieve a qualified majority.

Despite the weaknesses of Nice, the applicant states welcomed the agreement, especially because the member states also indicated that they would expect to accept new members from the end of 2002, in the hope that they would be able to take part in the next elections to the EP in 2004.

Analysing recent enlargement decisions

Given the difficulties that the enlargement decision caused, why was it taken? Why was the immediate reaction of the EC to the collapse of communism to offer the Europe Agreements, which did not make a commitment to eventual membership, and why was this approach subsequently abandoned and the applications of the central and eastern European states accepted? Why was it decided in Madrid in 1995 to open negotiations with all of the applicants, then in Luxembourg in 1997 to prioritize six of the applications, and then again in Helsinki in 1999 to open negotiations with all the remaining applicants? Why, if the EU was committed to making enlargement happen, were the member states not prepared to make sacrifices on trimming back their own entitlements under the structural funds and the CAP?

First, it has to be remembered that the collapse of communism came quickly and was not anticipated. The immediate response of the EC to developments focused on the implications of the rapid moves to reunify Germany (Friis, 1998: 323). It was clear that Chancellor Kohl was determined to seize this historic opportunity, and even his closest ally, François Mitterrand, was left trailing in his wake. The European Commission had to deal with the prospect of a sudden increase in the territory of the EC, and the adaptation of common policies to the addition of another 17 million people with a GDP per head well below the EC average. Attention inevitably focused on these issues until they were resolved.

Second, the negotiation of the EFTA enlargement was still at an early stage in 1989. Indeed, the EC was still following a policy of trying to persuade the EFTA applicants to become part of the single market without becoming members of the EC, the so-called European Economic Area negotiations. As with German reunification, this issue had to be settled before serious attention could be given to the position of the central and eastern European states. In addition, it would have been surprising had the central and eastern European states been given a perspective of membership before negotiations had opened on the applications of the prior EFTA applicants. The deal offered in the original Europe Agreements was similar to that on offer to the EFTA states at that stage: membership of the single market without membership of the EC.

Third, the EC was in 1989 about to embark on the process of agreeing to a monetary union. The Delors Report was published April 1989, before Hungary cut the first hole in the iron curtain by throwing open its borders to the west in May. The Madrid European Council in June 1989 agreed to set up an IGC to consider the Treaty changes needed to allow monetary union, and set a date for the start of stage 1 of the process outlined in the Delors Report. This process may have been accelerated by the events in central and eastern Europe, but essentially it was a separate process that had already begun, and another issue that occupied the attention of the member states and the Commission.

The change of policy, marked by the decision at Copenhagen in June 1993, can be explained by reference to the completion of other business, by the persistence of the central and east European states in requesting membership, and by geostrategic considerations.

Between 1990 and 1995 the three pressing issues identified above were all cleared out of the way. Formal reunification of Germany took place on 3 October 1990. The TEU, setting out the timetable and conditions for monetary union, was agreed at the Maastricht European Council in December 1991, and formally signed by Foreign Ministers in February 1992. Terms of entry for Austria, Finland, and Sweden were agreed in the early hours of 1 March 1994. Once these issues were resolved, removing what Friis (1998: 333) described as 'the negative spillover from internal negotiating tables', there was the possibility of contemplating further enlargement.

The persistence of the central and east European states in pressing for entry to the EC/EU was strengthened by the acceptance of the EC that the European Economic Area scheme was not going to work for the EFTA applicants. Membership of the single market without membership of the EC was not perceived by large capitalist enterprises to be the same as secure full membership of the single market. Investment continued to flow from the applicants to the EC. At the same time, the implications of having to accept the whole panoply of single market regulations—not just the *acquis*, but also what had not yet been agreed—without having any say in the negotiation of the rules, was unacceptable to the governments of the states concerned. It would have been difficult to convince the central and east European states that membership of the single market without membership of the EU would be any more successful or acceptable for them once the argument had been conceded for the EFTA applicants. It would have looked simply as though the EC/EU was prepared to accept prosperous member states and not those most in need of support.

Security considerations became more urgent in the context of growing instability in Russia (Friis and Murphy, 1999: 220). The USSR broke apart rapidly between August and December 1991. It formally ceased to exist on 31 December 1991. The Russian state that emerged after many of the former Soviet Republics had proclaimed independence was an insecure place in which nationalist voices received a hearing from the population, and in turn the governments under President Boris Yeltsin came under pressure to talk tough with 'the near abroad'. In these circumstances the concern of the central and east European states for security from an aggressive Russia led to increased demands for membership of both the EC and NATO. These two issues became intertwined. The United States was concerned not to expand NATO membership too precipitately for fear of alarming Russia, so it put pressure on the EC to offer membership as a sort of second-order guarantee of independence to the states most affected. There was particular pressure on the EC to offer membership to the three Baltic states—Estonia, Latvia, and Lithuania—because they were too close to Russia to make NATO membership feasible, but they were also too close to Russia for comfort given the rising nationalist sentiment there. Although it was never likely that the EC would accede to this demand, it had to show that it was prepared to move some way to contributing to the stabilization of the east. In addition, as Yugoslavia began to disintegrate on the very doorstep of the EC, concerns about security grew in the member states themselves.

The prevarication on whether to proceed with all 12 applications together or whether to prioritize some of the applicants reflected the different stakes that different member states had in the enlargement. Germany was particularly keen to see early enlargement to take in at least its closest neighbours: Poland, Hungary, and the Czech Republic. This was for both security and economic reasons. The security reasons are obvious: reunification rendered Germany once more a central European state itself, and instability in neighbouring states was highly undesirable. The economic motivations reflected the traditional economic links between Germany and its central European neighbours. France, on the other hand, had less of a stake in either consideration, as it has no contiguous land frontier with the central European states, and has fewer economic links.

For France and the other Mediterranean member states there was a real risk that eastern enlargement would reduce their influence in the EU, shifting the centre of gravity away from them towards Germany. The French government was therefore more prepared to take a leisurely approach, whereas the German government wanted as few obstacles as possible placed in the way of early accession for its favoured candidates. The European Commission's motivation in proposing to proceed with only some of the applications reflected particularly its concerns about its limited resources. The process of accession is long and complex, and can tie up a lot of the available resources of the Commission. Member states have never been prepared to provide all the extra resources necessary to allow the Commission to perform efficiently the task set for it, and there was no indication that they would do so on this occasion.

Acceptance of the Commission's proposal to limit the number of applicants with which accession negotiations would begin reflects a temporary meeting of minds between Germany and France. The link to NATO enlargement, and the pressure that the EU had come under from the United States to proceed rapidly on a broad front, made it very attractive for France to agree to a more limited start, to show that the EU was not going to be pushed around by the United States.

The change of tactic at Helsinki, to open negotiations with the remaining applicants, reflected a number of changed circumstances. First, the central and east European states that had not been placed in the first group had become increasingly restive about their treatment. Second, the pressure from the United States had receded as the threat posed by Russia appeared also to recede. Third, the change of heart in Malta opened the prospect to France, Spain, Portugal, Italy, and Greece of having another Mediterranean small state in the first group of members to off-set the influx of small and medium-sized central and eastern European states. Of the second six, Malta was the most equipped to catch up with some of the first six applicants and get membership early. Fourth, and very significantly, the reaction of Turkey to its exclusion from the list of potential applicants

had put in jeopardy the whole process. Without the co-operation of Turkey the problem of the division of Cyprus could not be solved, and Greece had repeatedly threatened to veto any enlargement unless Cyprus were part of the first wave.

The difficulties in agreeing to reform of the policies and institutional arrangements necessary to facilitate enlargement was partly an example of the familiar general phenomenon of willing the end without also being prepared to will the means. There were also more complex processes at work, though. The negotiations over Agenda 2000, and particularly over the IGC issues of institutional reform, indicate the extent to which the EU is a complex series of deals and bargains, involving concessions on one issue in return for concessions on others. An external shock such as the eastern enlargement threatened to unpick the thread of these deals (Preston, 1995: 460). Looking to the future, the changes needed to the institutional arrangements threatened more than just the pride of those states that were expected to make sacrifices on their voting strengths. The whole calculation of whether they would be able in future to bargain effectively for their interests was called into question. The ability of a state to be pivotal to any voting situation affects its influence in gaining concessions on matters of substance. This in turn is affected not just by the relative votes that it carries, but also by those that the other states carry. The drive of the larger member states at Nice was to try to ensure that even in an EU enlarged to 27 members, the big three of France plus Germany plus Britain could together constitute a blocking minority. This they practically achieved, but the move threatened to marginalize the small and medium-sized states as effective players in future policy negotiations.

Conclusion

While enlargement is not an inevitable consequence of developments in the EC/EU, there is evidence of a process of geographical spillover producing pressures on nearby states to co-operate more closely. In particular, as Preston (1997: 137) notes, 'changes in

internal trade regimes create demands from external interests for active involvement in policy development'. While these pressures may have been significant in each enlargement, this was illustrated most clearly with the EFTA enlargement which gained much of its impetus from the single market programme.

Each enlargement has brought challenges to existing EC/EU practices. In particular, the process of widening has been generally preceded by moves towards deepening. The institutional machinery established for an EC of six required reforms for an EC of nine, and so on. Without reform to decision-making processes, enlargement threatens institutional sclerosis. For example, in pure arithmetic terms, the more states that hold a potential veto over decisions, the greater the possibility for stalemate.

The proposed enlargement to include a large number of former communist states from central and eastern Europe would create an unprecedented diversity within the Union. The nature and scale of potential enlargement presented challenges in terms of policy and institutional reform that existing member states were still coming to terms with as the EU entered the twenty-first century. As such, this enlargement increased the prospect of flexible integration to allow those states wishing to integrate furthest to do so, while others opted-out (see Chapter 13, p. 132).

In theoretical terms, the most recent enlargement debate illustrates the inter-connectedness between developments in the EU and those outside. Before the end of the cold war, the current applicant states from central and eastern Europe were dealt with as part of EU external relations policy. After 1989, the prospect of an enlarged EU to include these states presented major implications for the full range of internal issues. At the time of writing, existing states remained embroiled in the process of dealing with these implications.

KEY POINTS

The first enlargement

- In January 1973, Britain, Denmark, and Ireland became members of the European Community. Norway rejected membership in a referendum in 1972.

- The replacement of de Gaulle by Pompidou as French president in 1969 combined with changing economic circumstances to boost British prospects of membership.

- Because of their trade dependence, the position of Ireland and Denmark in relation to EC membership followed closely that of Britain.

- It was made clear to applicant states that accession to membership was conditional on acceptance of the complete *acquis communautaire*.

The Mediterranean enlargement

- Greece became a member state in January 1981, and Spain and Portugal in January 1986. In all three cases political considerations overrode economic factors in the decision to enlarge.

- The primacy given to political considerations in the Mediterranean enlargement set a precedent for later acceptance of applications from former communist states in central and eastern Europe.

The EFTA enlargement

- The creation of the single market prompted EFTA states to explore closer relations with the EC in the 1980s.

- The creation of a European Economic Area, making EFTA states members of the single market but not the EC, proved to be an unsatisfactory compromise.

- The end of the cold war dissipated applicant states' concerns over political neutrality and EU membership. Austria, Finland, and Sweden became members in January 1995, while Norway again rejected membership through a referendum.

- The main significance of the EFTA enlargement was that it raised for the first time some of the issues concerning the institutional architecture of the EU that emerged later with more urgency over the proposed eastern enlargement.

Future enlargement

- The effective end of the cold war in 1989 opened up the prospect of enlargement for former communist states of central and east Europe.

- In 1991 the first of a series of 'Europe Agreements' were signed by the EC with the former communist states, which committed the EC to co-operate with the associated states in political and economic matters, and offered them freer access to the EC market.

- Between 1994 and 1996, ten former communist states applied for membership. Negotiations were opened with these states, plus Cyprus and Malta, but not Turkey, which had applied for membership in April 1987.

Preparing the EU for enlargement

- In order to be ready to take as many as 12 new members, the EU had to deal with some difficult issues requiring reforms of both policies and institutions.

- Two policy issues were particularly crucial to the prospects for enlargement: agriculture and the structural funds.

- The key institutional questions related to the weighting of votes under QMV, and the size of the blocking minority; the abandonment of the national veto in more policy sectors; and the size of the Commission.

- The IGC that concluded in the Amsterdam European Council of June 1997 failed to resolve the institutional issues.

- At the Nice European Council of December 2000, limited progress was made on some areas of institutional reform, enough to keep open the prospect of enlargement.

Analysing recent enlargement decisions

- Following the collapse of communism, the EC's focus was on the integration of East Germany into the Community. Alongside this, agreement on monetary union remained a priority. As these issues progressed, the persistence of the central and eastern European states in requesting membership, and geostrategic considerations combined to place enlargement at the top of the EU agenda.

- While existing states endorsed further enlargement, agreement on the necessary institutional reforms proved difficult. The deal struck at Nice sought to ensure that the big three states of France, Germany, and Britain could together constitute a blocking minority, with the prospect of smaller states being marginalized in future decision-making.

QUESTIONS

1 Why is 'deepening' viewed as an important prerequisite for the 'widening' of the European Union?

2 What problems have been encountered in securing agreement on institutional reforms in preparation for future enlargement?

3 What are the policy implications of the proposed expansion of the EU to include countries of central and eastern Europe?

FURTHER READING

C. Preston, *Enlargement and Integration in the European Union* (London: Routledge, 1997) provides comprehensive coverage of the first four enlargements. It contains sections on the accession process for each new member state and information on other applications. It considers the effects of enlargement on each member state, on the EU's policies and on the structure and processes of the EU. The concluding section reflects on the implications of, and prospects for, future enlargement.

Much of the writing on the prospective eastern enlargement of the EU is not very sophisticated, and simply recycles official information without offering much original analysis. An early exception was C. Preston, 'Obstacles to EU Enlargement: The Classical Community Method and the Prospects for a Wider Europe', *Journal of Common Market Studies* 33 (1995): 451–63. More theoretical analysis of the process of negotiation between the EU and the states of central and eastern Europe is in Lykke Friis, 'Approaching the "third half" of EU grand bargaining—the post-negotiation phase of the "Europe Agreement game"' *Journal of European Public Policy* 5 (1998): 322–38; and in Lykke Friis and Anna Murphy, 'The European Union and Central and Eastern Europe: Governance and Boundaries' *Journal of Common Market Studies* 37 (1999): 211–32.

Among the many edited collections on the eastern enlargement one that is worth looking at derived from a workshop sponsored by the University Association for Contemporary European Studies (UACES): K. Henderson, *Back to Europe: Central and Eastern Europe and the European Union* (London: UCL Press, 1999). This contains a useful overview by J. Gower on 'The Development of EU Policy towards Central and Eastern Europe' (pp. 3–19), but the definitive narrative of the unfolding relationship, complete with copious quotations from official documentation, is G. Avery and F. Cameron, *The Enlargement of the European Union* (Sheffield: Sheffield Academic Press/University Association for Contemporary European Studies, 1998).

To keep up to date with a rapidly changing picture on the eastern enlargement negotiations, students should consult the *Journal of Common Market Studies: Annual Review of Activities*. The last edition of this at the time of writing was for 1999/2000 and contained a piece by J. Smith on 'Enlarging Europe' (pp. 121–4).

CHRONOLOGY

1961
July–August Britain, Ireland, and Denmark apply for membership of EC.

1963
January   De Gaulle vetoes British membership.

1967

January	Britain, Ireland, and Denmark make second applications.
July	Norway makes second application.
December	France blocks re-opening of negotiations with applicants.

1969

April	Pompidou succeeds de Gaulle as French President.
July	Pompidou makes it clear that he has no objection in principle to British membership.
December	Hague summit agrees to widening to accompany completion and deepening.

1970

June	Accession negotiations begin with the four applicant states.

1972

January	Accession Treaties signed with the four applicant states.
September	Norwegian referendum rejects membership.

1973

January	Britain, Ireland, and Denmark become members of EC.

1975

June	Greece applies for membership of EC.
July	Accession negotiations begin with Greece.

1977

March	Portugal applies for membership of EC.
July	Spain applies for membership of EC.

1978

October	Accession negotiations open with Portugal.

1979

February	Accession negotiations open with Spain.
May	Accession Treaty with Greece signed.

1981

January	Greece becomes a member of EC.

1985

June	Accession Treaties with Portugal and Spain signed.

1986

January	Portugal and Spain become members of EC.

1987

June	Turkey applies for membership of EC.

1989

July	Austria applies for membership of EC.
	G7 agree to ask European Commission to co-ordinate G24 aid to Poland and Hungary, subsequently extended to other central and east European states.
November	Fall of Berlin Wall.

1990

July	Cyprus, and Malta apply for membership of EC.

1991

July	Sweden applies for membership of EC.
December	Association Agreements ('Europe Agreements') signed with Czechoslovakia, Hungary, and Poland (for dates of other Europe Agreements see Table 29.1, p. 414)

1992

March	Finland applies for membership of EC.

May	European Economic Area Agreement signed.
	Switzerland applies for membership of EC.
November	Norway applies for membership of EC.
December	Swiss referendum rejects EEA. Membership application to EC withdrawn.

1993

January	Czechoslovakia splits into two states: the Czech Republic and Slovakia.
February	Accession negotiations begin with Austria, Finland, and Sweden.
April	Accession negotiations begin with Norway.

1994

January	EEA begins.
March	Accession Treaties signed with Austria, Finland, Sweden, and Norway.
April	Hungary and Poland apply for membership of EU (for dates of other applications see Table 29.1, p. 414).
November	Norwegian referendum rejects membership.

1995

| January | Austria, Finland, and Sweden become members of the EU. |

1997

| December | Luxembourg European Council agrees to open accession negotiations with the Czech Republic, Poland, Hungary, Estonia, Slovenia, and Cyprus. |

1998

| March | Accession negotiations begin with Hungary, Poland, the Czech Republic, Slovenia, Estonia, and Cyprus. |

1999

| March | Berlin European Council agrees a Financial Perspective for 2000–6, and reform of the CAP and the structural funds. |
| December | Helsinki European Council agrees to open accession negotiations with remaining applicant states. |

2000

| December | Nice European Council agrees to institutional reforms to open the way to enlargement, and agrees to aim to accept new members from the end of 2002. |

Bibliography

Agnelli, G. (1989), 'The Europe of 1992' *Foreign Affairs* 68: 61–70.

Aldcroft, D. H. (1978), *The European Economy, 1914–1970* (London: Croom Helm).

Allen and Smith (1998), 'External Policy Developments' *Journal of Common Market Studies: The European Union, 1997, Annual Review of Activities* : 69–91.

Alter, K. (1996), 'The European Court's Political Power' *West European Politics* 19: 458–87.

Amoore, L., Dodgson, R., Gills, B. K., Langley, P., Marshall, D., and Watson, I. (1997), 'Overturning 'Globalisation': Resisting the Teleological, Reclaiming the "Political"' *New Political Economy* 2: 179–95.

Andersen, S. S., and Eliassen, K. A. (eds.) *Making Policy in Europe: Europeification of National Policy-Making* (London: Sage).

Andeweg, R., and Irwin, G. (1993), *Dutch Government and Politics* (Basingstoke and London: Macmillan).

Armstrong, K., and Bulmer, S. (1998), *The Governance of the Single European Market* (Manchester: Manchester University Press).

Arter, D. (1995), 'The EU Referendum in Finland on 16 October 1994: A Vote for the West, not for Maastricht' *Journal of Common Market Studies* 33: 361–87.

Aspinwall, M. (1998), 'Collective Attraction—The New Political Game in Brussels' in Greenwood and Aspinwall (1998): 196–213.

—— and Greenwood, J. (1998), 'Conceptualising Collective Action in the European Union: An Introduction', in Greenwood and Aspinwall (1998): 1–30.

Avery, G., and Cameron, F. (1998), *The Enlargement of the European Union* (Sheffield: Sheffield Academic Press/University Association for Contemporary European Studies).

Bache, I. (1995), 'Additionality and the Politics of EU Regional Policy Making' *Political Economy Research Centre Working Papers* no. 2 (Sheffield: Political Economy Research Centre, University of Sheffield).

—— (1996), *EU Regional Policy: Has the UK Government Succeeded in Playing the Gatekeeper Role over the Domestic Impact of the European Regional Development Fund?* (Sheffield: University of Sheffield, Ph.D. thesis).

—— (1998), *The Politics of European Union Regional Policy: Multi-Level Governance or Flexible Gatekeeping?* (Sheffield: Sheffield Academic Press/University Association for Contemporary European Studies).

—— (1999), 'The Extended Gatekeeper: Central Government and the Implementation of EC Regional Policy in the UK' *Journal of European Public Policy* 6: 28–45.

—— George, S., and Rhodes, R. A. W. (1996), 'Cohesion Policy and Subnational Authorities in the UK' in Hooghe (1996): 294–319.

—— and Jones. R. (forthcoming), 'Has EU Regional Policy Empowered the Regions? A Study of Spain and the United Kingdom', *Regional and Federal Studies*, 10/3.

Bachtler, J., and Michie, R. (1994), 'Strengthening Economic and Social Cohesion? The Revision of the Structural Funds' *Regional Studies* 28: 789–96.

Baker, D., Gamble, A., and Ludlam, S. (1993), '1846 . . . 1906 . . . 1996? Conservative Splits and European Integration' *Political Quarterly* 64: 420–34.

—— —— —— (1994), 'The Parliamentary Siege of Maastricht 1993: Conservative Divisions and British Ratification of the Treaty on European Union' *Parliamentary Affairs* 47: 37–60.

Barber, L. (1995), 'The Men Who Run Europe' *Financial Times: Weekend FT*, 11/12 March: I–II.

Baun, M. J. (1996), 'The Maastricht Treaty as High Politics: Germany, France and European Integration' *Political Science Quarterly* 110: 605–24.

Beetham, D., and Lord, C. (1998), *Democracy and the European Union* (London and New York: Longman).

Beyers, J., and Dierickx, G. (1998), 'The Working Groups of the Council of the European Union: Supranational or Intergovernmental Negotiations?' *Journal of Common Market Studies* 36: 289–317.

Boltho, A. (1982), *The European Economy: Growth and Crisis* (Oxford: Oxford University Press).

Branch, A. P. and Øhrgaard, J.C. (1999), 'Trapped in the Supranational-Intergovernmental Dichotomy: A Response to Stone Sweet and Sandholtz' *Journal of European Public Policy* 6: 123–43.

Brinkley, D., and Hackett, C. (eds.) (1991), *Jean Monnet; The Path to European Unity* (Basingstoke and London: Macmillan).

Bull, M., and Rhodes, M. (eds.) (1997), *Crisis and Transition in Italian Politics* (London: Frank Cass).

Buller, J. (1995), 'Britain as an Awkward Partner: Reassessing Britain's Relations with the EU' *Politics* 15: 33–42.

Bulmer, S. (1983), 'Domestic Politics and European Policy-Making' *Journal of Common Market Studies* 21: 349–63.

—— (1998), 'New Institutionalism and the Governance of the Single European Market' *Journal of European Public Policy* 5: 365–86.

—— and Paterson, W. (1987), *The Federal Republic of Germany and the European Community* (London: Allen & Unwin).

Bulmer, S., and Paterson, W. (1996), 'Germany in the European Union: Gentle Giant or Emergent Leader?' *International Affairs* 72: 9–32.

—— and Wessels, W. (1987), *The European Council: Decision-Making in Politics* (Basingstoke and London: Macmillan)

Burgess, M. (ed.) (1986), *Federalism and Federation in Western Europe* (London: Croom Helm).

—— (1989), *Federalism and European Union: Political Ideas, Influences and Strategies* (London and New York: Routledge)

Burley, A.-M., and Mattli, W. (1993), 'Europe before the Court: A Political Theory of Legal Integration' *International Organization* 47: 41–76.

Butler, F. (1993), 'The EC's Common Agricultural Policy' in Lodge (1993): 112–30.

Butt Philip, A. (1983), 'Pressure Groups and Policy-Making in the European Community' in Lodge (1983): 21–6.

—— (1992), 'British Pressure Groups and the European Community' in George (1990): 149–71.

Cafruny, A., and Rosenthal, G. (eds.) (1993), *The State of the European Community*, vol. ii.: The Maastricht Debates and Beyond (Boulder: Lynne Rienner; Harlow: Longman).

Calingaert, M. (1999), 'Creating a European Market' in Cram, Dinan, and Nugent (1999): 153–73.

Cameron, D. R. (1992), 'The 1992 Initiative: Causes and Consequences' in Sbragia (1992): 23–74.

—— (1997), 'Economic and Monetary Union: Underlying Imperatives and Third-Stage Dilemmas' *Journal of European Public Policy* 4: 455–85.

Cameron, F. (1999), *The Foreign and Security Policy of the European Union: Past, Present and Future* (Sheffield: Sheffield Academic Press/University Association for Contemporary European Studies).

Camps, M. (1967), *European Unification in the Sixties: From the Veto to the Crisis* (London: Oxford University Press).

Caporaso, J. (1998), 'Regional Integration Theory: Understanding our Past and Anticipating our Future' *Journal of European Public Policy* 5: 1–16.

—— (1999), 'Toward a Normal Science of Regional Integration' *Journal of European Public Policy* 6: 160–64.

—— and Keeler, J. T. S. (1995), 'The European Union and Regional Integration Theory' in Rhodes and Mazey (1995): 29–62.

Catterall, P. (ed.) (1990), *Contemporary Britain: An Annual Review* (Oxford: Blackwell).

Cecchini P. *et al.* (1988), *The European Challenge 1992: The Benefits of a Single Market* (Aldershot: Gower).

CEPS (1990) *1989 Annual Conference Proceedings*, vol. 1: *The Single Market and Economic and Monetary Union* (Brussels: Centre for European Policy Studies).

Christiansen, T. (1996), 'A Maturing Bureaucracy? The Role of the Commission in the Policy Process' in Richardson (1996*b*): 79–95.

Chubb, B. (1992), *The Government and Politics of Ireland* (London: Longman).

Church, C. H., and Phinnemore, D. (1995), *European Union and European Community: A Handbook and Commentary on the 1992 Maastricht Treaties* (London: Prentice Hall, 2nd edn.).

Cini, M. (1996), *The European Commission: Leadership, Organisation and Culture in the EU Administration* (Manchester: Manchester University Press).

—— and McGowan, L.(1998), *Competition Policy in the European Union* (Basingstoke and London: Macmillan).

Cipolla, C. M. (1976), *The Fontana Economic History of Europe*, vol. vi. *Contemporary Economies* (London: Fontana).

Cole, A. (1998), *French Politics and Society* (Hemel Hempstead: Prentice Hall).

—— and Drake, H. (2000), 'The Europeanization of the French Polity: Continuity, Change and Adaptation' *Journal of European Public Policy* 7: 26–43.

Coleman, W. D. (1998), 'From Protected Development to Market Liberalism: Paradigm Change in Agriculture' *Journal of European Public Policy* 5: 632–51.

Collinson, S. (1999), ' "Issue Systems", "Multi-Level Games", and the Analysis of the EU's External Commercial and Associated Policies: A Research Agenda', *Journal of European Public Policy* 6: 206–24.

Coombes, D. (1970), *Politics and Bureaucracy in the European Community* (London: Allen &Unwin).

Corbett, R. (1993), *The Treaty of Maastricht* (London: Longman).

—— Jacobs, F., and Shackleton, M. (1995), *The European Parliament* (London: Catermill, 3rd edn.).

Cosgrove Twitchett, C. (1981), *A Framework for Development: The EEC and the ACP* (London: Allen and Unwin).

Cox, A. (1982), *Politics, Policy and the European Recession* (Basingstoke and London: Macmillan).

Cox, R., with Sinclair, T. (1996), *Approaches to World Order* (Cambridge: Cambridge University Press).

Cram, L. (1996), 'Integration Theory and the Study of the European Policy Process' in Richardson (1996*b*): 40–58.

—— (1997), *Policy Making in the EU: Conceptual Lenses and the Integration Process* (London and New York: Routledge).

—— Dinan, D., and Nugent, N. (1999), *Developments in the European Union* (Basingstoke and London: Macmillan).

Criddle, B. (1993), 'The French Referendum on the Maastricht Treaty, September 1992' *Parliamentary Affairs* 46: 228–38.

CURDS (Centre for Urban and Regional Development Studies) (1997), *Written Evidence* in House of Lords (1997): 52–62.

Currid, J. N. (1998), *Explaining the Nature of Opposition in Britain to the European Community since 1973* (Sheffield: University of Sheffield, Ph.D. thesis).

Dang-Nguyen, G., Schneider, V., and Werle, R. (1993), 'Networks in European Policy-Making: Europeification of Telecommunications Policy' in Andersen and Elaissen (1993): 93–114.

De Bassompierre, G. (1988), *Changing the Guard in Brussels: An Insider's View of the EC Presidency* (New York: Praeger).

De Búrca, G. (1998), 'The Principle of Subsidiarity and the Court of Justice as a Political Actor' *Journal of Common Market Studies* 36: 217–315.

Dell, E. (1995), *The Schuman Plan and the British Abdication of Leadership in Europe* (Oxford: Clarendon Press).

Dehousse, R. (1998), *The European Court of Justice: The Politics of Judicial Integration* (Basingstoke and London: Macmillan).

Deubner, C. (1979), 'The Expansion of West German Capital and the Founding of Euratom' *International Organization*, 33: 203–28.

Deutsch, K. (1953), *Nationalism and Social Communication: An Inquiry into the Foundations of Nationality* (Cambridge, Mass.: MIT Press).

—— et al. (1957), *Political Community and the North Atlantic Area: International Organization in the Light of Historical Experience* (Princeton: Princeton University Press).

Devuyst, Y. (1999), 'The Community-Method after Amsterdam' *Journal of Common Market Studies* 37: 109–20.

Diebold, W., Jr. (1959), *The Schuman Plan: A Study in Economic Cooperation, 1950–1959* (New York: Praeger).

Dinan, D. (1994), *Ever Closer Union? An Introduction to the European Community* (Basingstoke and London: Macmillan).

Drake, H., and Milner, S. (1999), 'Change and Resistance to Change: Management of Europeanisation in France' *Modern & Contemporary France*, 7: 165–78.

Duchêne, F. (1994), *Jean Monnet: The First Statesman of Interdependence* (New York and London: W. W. Norton & Company).

Duff, A. (1997), *The Treaty of Amsterdam: Text and Commentary* (London: Federal Trust/Sweet & Maxwell).

Dyson, K., and Featherstone, K. (1999), *The Road to Maastricht: Negotiating Economic and Monetary Union* (Oxford: Oxford University Press).

Earnshaw, D., and Judge, D. (1995), 'Early Days: The European Parliament, Co-decision and the European Union Legislative Process post-Maastricht' *Journal of European Public Policy* 2: 624–49.

Edwards, G. (1992), 'Central Government' in George (1992): 64–90.

—— and Pijpers, A. (1997), *The Politics of European Treaty Reform: The 1996 Intergovernmental Conference and Beyond* (London and Washington: Pinter).

—— and Spence, D. (eds.) (1994), *The European Commission* (Harlow: Longman).

Europa Publications (2000), *Western Europe 2000* (London: Europa Publications).

European Commission (1969), 'Memorandum on the Reform of Agriculture in the European Economic Community' *Bulletin of the European Communities: Supplement 3/69* (Brussels: European Communities).

—— (1970), *Reform of Agriculture (Proposals of the Commission to the Council)*, COM (70)500 (Brussels: European Communities).

—— (1975), Preamble to Regulation (EEC) No. 724/75 of 18 March 1975 establishing a European Regional Development Fund, OJ L73, 21/3/75 (Brussels: European Commission).

—— (1985), *Completing the Internal Market* COM(85)310 (Brussels: European Community).

—— (1989), *Guide to the Reform of the Community's Structural Funds* (Brussels and Luxembourg: European Communities).

—— (1993a), *The Council's Common Position on the Revision of the Structural Fund Regulations*, Communication from the Commission to the European Parliament, SEC (93), final (Brussels: European Communities).

—— (1993b), *Community Structural Funds 1994–99, Revised Regulations and Comments* (Brussels and Luxembourg: European Communities).

—— (1995), *The Agricultural Situation in the European Union* (Luxembourg and Brussels: European Communities).

—— (1996a), *First Report on Economic and Social Cohesion* (Brussels and Luxembourg: European Commission).

—— (1996b), *Social and Economic Inclusion Through Regional Development: The Community Economic Development Priority in European Structural Funds in Great Britain* (Brussels: European Commission).

—— (1997), *Agenda 2000: For a Stronger and Wider Union* (Brussels: European Commission).

—— (1998a), *Proposed Regulations Governing the Reform of the Structural Funds 2000–2006*, preliminary version, 18 March, Inforegio (http://www.inforegion.org/wbpro/agenda 2000/compare/default_en.htm).

—— (1998b), *Reform of the Structural Funds, Explanatory Memorandum* (http://europa.eu.int/pol/reg/en/info.htm).

—— (1999), *The Amsterdam Treaty: A Comprehensive Guide* (Brussels and Luxembourg: European Communities).

—— (2000a), *The Lomé Convention* <http:www.europa.eu.int/comm/development/contonou/Lomé_history_en.htm>.

—— (2000b), 'The European Community and its Member States Sign a New Partnership Agreement with the African, Caribbean and Pacific States in Contonou, Benin' *Press Release*, 11/07/00 (http://www.europa.eu.int/rapid/start/cgi/guesten.ksh?p_action.gett?/640lg=).

Evans, A. (1999), *The EU Structural Funds* (Oxford: Oxford University Press).

Featherstone, K. (1994), 'Jean Monnet and the "Democratic

Deficit", in the European Union' *Journal of Common Market Studies* 32: 149–70.

Featherstone, K., and Ifantis, K. (eds.) (1996), *Greece in a Changing Europe: Between European Integration and Balkan Disintegration?* (Manchester: Manchester University Press).

Fitzmaurice, J. (1996), *The Politics of Belgium: A Unique Federalism* (London: Hurst).

Fohlen, C. (1976), 'France, 1920–1970' in Cipolla (1976): 72–127.

Forster, A. (1998), 'Britain and the Negotiation of the Maastricht Treaty: A Critique of Liberal Intergovernmentalism' *Journal of Common Market Studies* 36: 347–67.

Forsyth, M. G., Keens-Soper, H. M. A., and Savigear, P. (eds.) (1970), *The Theory of International Relations: Selected Texts from Gentili to Treitschke* (London: George Allen & Unwin).

Fraser, M. (ed.) (1998), *Britain in Europe* (London: Strategems Publishing Ltd).

Freestone, D. (1983), 'The European Court of Justice', in Lodge (1983): 43–53.

Frey-Wouters, E. (1980), *The EC and the Third World: The Lomé Convention and its Impact* (New York: Praeger).

Friis, L. (1998) 'Approaching the "third half" of EU grand bargaining – the post-negotiation phase of the "Europe Agreement game" ' *Journal of European Public Policy* 5: 322–38.

—— and Murphy, A. (1999) 'The European Union and Central and Eastern Europe: Governance and Boundaries' *Journal of Common Market Studies* 37: 211–32.

Fuchs, G. (1994), 'Policy-Making in a System of Multi-Level Governance—The Commission of the European Community and the Restructuring of the Telecommunications Sector' *Journal of European Public Policy* 1: 177–94.

Fursdon, E. (1980), *The European Defence Community: A History* (London: Macmillan).

Galtung, J. (1976), 'The Lomé Convention and Neo-Capitalism', *African Review* 6/1: 000–000.

Gamble, A., and Payne, A. (eds.) (1996), *Regionalism and World Order* (Basingstoke and London: Macmillan).

Garrett, G., and Tsebelis, G. (1996), 'An Institutional Critique of Intergovernmentalism' *International Organization* 50: 269–99.

George, S. (1989), 'Nationalism, Liberalism and the National Interest: Britain, France, and the European Community' *Strathclyde Papers on Government and Politics* no. 67 (Glasgow: University of Strathclyde).

—— (1990), 'Britain and the European Community in 1989' in Catterall (1990): 63–71.

—— (ed.) (1992), *Britain and the European Community: The Politics of Semi-Detachment* (Oxford: Clarendon Press).

—— (1994), 'Supranational Actors and Domestic Politics:

Integration Theory Reconsidered in the Light of the Single European Act and Maastricht' *Sheffield Papers in International Studies* no. 22 (Sheffield: University of Sheffield).

—— (1996a), *Politics and Policy in the European Union* (Oxford: Oxford University Press, 3rd edn.).

—— (1996b), 'The European Union: approaches from international relations' in Kassim and Menon (1996): 11–25.

—— (1998), *An Awkward Partner: Britain in the European Community* (Oxford: Oxford University Press, 3rd edn.).

—— (1999), 'Britain: Anatomy of a Eurosceptic State' *Journal of European Integration* 21: 1–19.

Gibbons, J. (1999), *Spanish Politics Today* (Manchester: Manchester University Press).

Gillingham, J. (1991a), *Coal, Steel, and the Rebirth of Europe, 1945–1955* (Cambridge: Cambridge University Press).

—— (1991b), 'Jean Monnet and the European Coal and Steel Community: A Preliminary Appraisal' in Brinkley and Hackett (1991): 129–62.

Ginsberg, R. H. (1994), 'The European Union's Common Foreign and Security Policy: An Outsider's Retrospective on the First Year' *ECSA Newsletter* (Pittsburgh: European Community Studies Association).

Glaser, T. (1990), 'EEC/ACP Cooperation: The Historical Perspective' *The Courier*, no. 120, March/April.

Gower, J. (1999) 'The Development of EU Policy towards Central and Eastern Europe' in Henderson (1999): 3–19.

Grant, C. (1994), *Delors: Inside the House that Jacques Built* (London: Nicholas Brealey Publishing).

—— (1998), 'Reconnecting Europe with its Citizens' in Fraser (1998): 148–51.

Grant, W. (1993), 'Pressure Groups and the European Community: An Overview' in Mazey and Richardson (1993): 27–46.

—— (1995), 'The Limits of Common Agricultural Policy Reform and the Option of Denationalization' *Journal of European Public Policy* 2: 1–18.

—— (1997), *The Common Agricultural Policy* (Basingstoke and London: Macmillan).

Green, R. H. (1976): 'The Lomé Convention: Updated Dependence or Departure towards Collective Self-Reliance', *African Review* 6: 43–54.

Green Cowles, M. (1995), 'Setting the Agenda for a New Europe: The ERT and EC 1992' *Journal of Common Market Studies* No. 33 vol 4: 501–26.

Greenleaf, W. H. (1983), *The British Political Tradition*, vol.1: *The Rise of Collectivism* (London: Methuen).

Greenwood, J. (1997), *Representing Interests in the European Union* (Basingstoke and London: Macmillan).

—— and Aspinwall, M. (eds.) (1998), *Collective Action in the European Union: Interests and the New Politics of Associability* (London and New York: Routledge).

—— Greenwood, J., Levy, R., and Stewart, R. (1995), 'The European Union Structural Fund Allocations: 'Lobbying to Win' or Recycling the Budget?' *European Urban and Regional Studies* 2: 317–38.

Guyomarch, A., Machin, H., and Ritchie, E. (1998), *France in the European Union* (Basingstoke and London: Macmillan).

Haas, E. B. (1958), *The Uniting of Europe: Political, Social and Economic Forces 1950–57* (London: Library of World Affairs).

—— (1968), *The Uniting of Europe: Political, Social and Economic Forces, 1950–1957* (Stanford, Calif.: Stanford University Press, 2nd edn.).

—— (1970), 'The Study of Regional Integration: Reflections on the Joy and Anguish of Pretheorizing' *International Organization* 24: 607–46.

Haas, P. (1992), 'Introduction: Epistemic Communities and International Policy Coordination' *International Organization* 49: 1–35.

Hall, P. (1990), 'The State and the Market' in Hall, Hayward, and Machin (1990): 171–87.

—— Hayward, J., and Machin, H. (eds.) (1990), *Developments in French Politics* (Basingstoke and London: Macmillan).

Halstead, J. (1982), *The Development of the European Regional Fund since 1972* (Bath: University of Bath, Ph.D. thesis).

Hanson, B. Y. (1998), 'What Happened to Fortress Europe? External Trade Policy Liberalization in the European Union', *International Organization* 52: 55–85.

Hardach, K. (1976), 'Germany, 1914–1970' in Cipolla (1976): 180–265.

Harrison, R. (1974), *Europe in Question* (London: George Allen & Unwin).

Hartley, T. C. (1994), *The Foundations of European Community Law* (Oxford: Clarendon Press, 3rd edn.).

Hayes-Renshaw, F., and Wallace, H. (1997), *The Council of Ministers* (Basingstoke and London: Macmillan).

—— Lequesne, C., and Mayor Lopez, P. (1989), 'The Permanent Representations of the Member States to the European Communities' *Journal of Common Market Studies* 28: 121–37.

Henderson, K. (ed.) (1999) *Back to Europe: Central and Eastern Europe and the European Union* (London: UCL Press).

Hennessy, P. (1991), 'Public Servant of a New World Order' *Independent*, 14 October.

Heurlin, B. (ed.) (1996), *Germany in Europe in the Nineties* (Basingstoke and London: Macmillan).

Hewitt, A. (1989), 'ACP and the Developing World' in Lodge (1989): 285–300.

Heyen, E. V. (ed.) (1992), *Yearbook of European Administrative History 4: Early European Community Administration* (Baden-Baden: Nomos).

Hill, C. (1993), 'The Capability-Expectations Gap, or Conceptualising Europe's International Role', *Journal of Common Market Studies* 31: 305–28.

—— (1996), *The Actors in Europe's Foreign Policy* (London: Routledge).

—— (1998), 'Closing the Capability-Expectations Gap', in Peterson and Sjursen (1998), 18–38.

Hirst, P., and Thompson, G. (1996), *Globalization in Question: The International Economy and the Possibilities of Governance* (Cambridge: Polity Press).

Hix, S. (1994), 'The Study of the European Community: The Challenge to Comparative Politics' *West European Politics* 17: 1–30.

—— (1999), *The Political System of the European Union* (Basingstoke and London: Macmillan).

—— and Lord, C. (1997), *Political Parties in the European Union* (Basingstoke and London: Macmillan).

Hodges, M., and Wallace, W. (eds.) (1981), *Economic Divergence in the European Community* (London: Butterworth).

Hoffmann, S. (1964), 'The European Process at Atlantic Crosspurposes' *Journal of Common Market Studies* 3: 85–101.

—— (1966), 'Obstinate or Obsolete? The Fate of the Nation State and the Case of Western Europe' *Daedalus* 95: 862–915.

—— (1982), 'Reflections on the Nation-State in Western Europe Today' *Journal of Common Market Studies* 21: 21–37.

—— (1989), 'The European Community and 1992' *Foreign Affairs* 68: 27–47.

Hogg, S. (1989), 'Trying to Market a New Species of EMU' *Independent* 4 September.

Holland, M. (1988), *The European Community and South Africa: European Political Co-operation under Strain* (London: Pinter).

—— (ed.) (1997), *Common Foreign and Security Policy: The Record and Reforms* (London: Cassell).

Holland, S. (1980), *Uncommon Market* (Basingstoke and London: Macmillan).

Hooghe, L. (1996a), 'Introduction: Reconciling EU-Wide Policy and National Diversity' in Hooghe (1996c): 1–26.

—— (1996b), 'Building a Europe with the Regions: The Changing Role of the European Commission' in Hooghe (1996c): 89–128.

—— (ed.) (1996c), *Cohesion Policy and European Integration* (Oxford: Oxford University Press).

House of Lords (1997), *Reducing Disparities within the European Union: The Effectiveness of the Structural and Cohesion Funds*, vol. ii. *Evidence*, Select Committee on the European Communities, Session 1996–97, 11th Report (London: HMSO).

Hu, Y. (1981), *Europe under Stress* (London: Butterworth).

Hurd, D. (1991), *The Churchill Memorial Lecture*. Transcript of speech given by the Foreign Secretary in Luxembourg on Tuesday 19 Feb. (London: Foreign and Commonwealth Office, News Department).

Jacobs, F., and Corbett, R. (1990), *The European Parliament* (Harlow: Longman).

Jamal, A. H. (1979), 'Preparing for Lomé Two' *Third World Quarterly* 1(4): 134–40.

Jenkins, R. (1977), 'Europe's Present Challenge and Future Opportunity: The First Jean Monnet Lecture delivered at the European University Institute, Florence, 27 October 1977' *Bulletin of the European Communities Supplement* 10/77 : 6–14.

—— (1989), *European Diary, 1977–1981* (London: Collins).

Jerneck, M. (1993), 'Sweden—the Reluctant European?' in Tiilikainen and Petersen (1993): 23–42.

John, P. (1994), 'UK Sub-National Offices in Brussels: Diversification or Regionalization?' *Regional Studies* 28: 739–59.

Jones, B. (ed.) (1998), *Politics UK* (London: Prentice Hall, 3rd edn.).

Jowell, R. *et al.* (1998), *British and European Social Attitudes: The 15th Report—How Britain Differs* (Aldershot: Ashgate).

Judge, D., Earnshaw, D., and Cowan, N. (1994), 'Ripples or Waves: The European Parliament in the European Community Policy Process' *Journal of European Public Policy* 1: 27–52.

Kaiser, W. (1995), 'Austria in the European Union' *Journal of Common Market Studies* 33: 411–25.

Kassim, H. (1994), 'Policy Networks, Networks and European Union Policy Making: A Sceptical View' *West European Politics* 17: 15–27.

—— and Menon, A. (eds.) (1996), *The European Union and National Industrial Policy* (London and New York: Routledge).

Katzenstein, P. J. (1997), *Tamed Power: Germany in Europe* (Ithaca, NY, and London: Cornell University Press).

Keating, M., and Jones, B. (eds.) (1985), *Regions in the European Community* (Oxford: Clarendon Press).

Keohane, R. (1984), *After Hegemony: Co-operation and Discord in the World Political Economy* (Princeton: Princeton University Press).

—— (1989a), 'Neoliberal Institutionalism: A Perspective on World Politics' in Keohane (1989b):

—— (ed.) (1989b), *International Institutions and State Power* (Boulder, San Francisco, and Oxford: Westview Press).

—— and Nye, J. S., Jr. (1977), *Power and Interdependence: World Politics in Transition* (Boston: Little, Brown).

—— and Hoffmann, S. (eds.) (1991), *The New European Community: Decisionmaking and Institutional Change* (Boulder, San Francisco, and Oxford: Westview Press).

Kirchner, E. J. (1992), *Decision-making in the European Community* (Manchester: Manchester University Press).

Kohler-Koch, B. (1997), 'Organized Interests in European Integration: The Evolution of a New Type of Governance?' in Wallace and Young (1997): 42–68.

Kreher, A. (1997), 'Agencies in The European Community: A Step towards Administrative Integration in Europe', *Journal of European Public Policy* 4: 225–45.

Kreile, M. (1977), 'West Germany: The Dynamics of Expansion' *International Organization* 31: 775–808.

Kuper, R. (1998), *The Politics of the European Court of Justice* (London: Kogan Page).

Laffan, B. (1983), 'Policy Implementation in the European Community: The European Social Fund as a Case Study' *Journal of Common Market Studies* 21: 389–408.

—— (1992), *Integration and Co-operation in Europe* (London and New York: UACES/Routledge).

—— (1997a), *The Finances of the European Union* (Basingstoke and London: Macmillan).

—— (1997b), 'From Policy Entrepreneur to Policy Manager: The Challenge Facing the European Commission' *Journal of European Public Policy* 4: 422–38.

Lanca, P. (1996), *The Good Apprentice: Portugal and the European Union* (London: Institute for European Defence and Strategic Studies).

Laqueur, W. (1972), *Europe Since Hitler* (Harmondsworth: Penguin).

Lauber, V. (ed.) (1996), *Contemporary Austrian Politics* (Oxford: Westview Press).

Laurent, P.-H. (ed.) (1994), *The European Community: To Maastricht and Beyond. Special Edition of The Annals of the American Academy of Political and Social Science*, January.

—— and Maresceau, M. (eds.), (1998), *The State of the European Union*, iv. *Deepening and Widening* (Boulder and London: Lynne Rienner).

Laursen, F., and Vanhoonacker, S. (eds.) (1992), *The Intergovernmental Conference on Political Union* (Maastricht: European Institute of Public Administration/Nijhoff).

—— and —— (eds.) (1995), *The Ratification of the Maastricht Treaty: Issues, Debates and Future Implications* (Maastricht: European Institute of Public Administration/Nijhoff).

Leonard, M. (1998), *Rediscovering Europe* (London: Demos).

Levitt, M., and Lord, C. (2000), *The Political Economy of Monetary Union* (Basingstoke and London: Macmillan).

Lewis, J. (1998), 'Is the "Hard Bargaining", Image of the Council Misleading? The Committee of Permanent Representatives and the Local Elections Directive' *Journal of Common Market Studies* 36: 479–504.

Lindberg, L. (1963), *The Political Dynamics of European Economic Integration* (Stanford: Stanford University Press; London: Oxford University Press).

—— (1966), 'Integration as a Source of Stress on the European Community System' *International Organization*, 20: 233–65.

Lister, M. (1997), *The European Union and the South: Relations with Developing Countries* (London: Routledge).

—— (ed.) (1998), *European Union Development Policy* (Basingstoke and London: Macmillan).

Lodge, J. (ed.) (1983), *Institutions and Policies of the European Community* (London: Pinter).

—— (ed.) (1986), *European Union: The European Community in Search of a Future* (Basingstoke and London: Macmillan).

—— (ed.) (1989), *The European Community and the Challenge of the Future* (London: Pinter, 1st edn.).

—— (1990*a*), 'Ten Years of an Elected Parliament' in Lodge (1990*b*): 1–36.

—— (ed.) (1990*b*), *The 1989 Election of the European Parliament*, (Basingstoke and London: Macmillan).

—— (ed.) (1993), *The European Community and the Challenge of the Future* (London: Pinter, 2nd edn.).

—— (1994), 'The European Parliament and the Authority–Democracy Crisis' in Laurent (1994): 69–83.

Loedel, P. H. (1998), 'Enhancing Europe's International Monetary Power: The Drive Toward a Single Currency' in Laurent and Maresceau (1998): 243–61.

Lord, C. (1993), *British Entry to the European Community under the Heath Government of 1970–4* (Aldershot: Dartmouth).

—— (1998), *Democracy in the European Union* (Sheffield: Sheffield Academic Press/University Association for Contemporary European Studies).

Ludlow, P. (1982), *The Making of the European Monetary System: A Case Study of the Politics of the European Community* (London: Butterworth).

—— (1991), 'The European Commission' in Keohane and Hoffmann (1991): 85–132.

—— (1997), *Dealing with Britain: The Six and the First UK Application to the EEC* (Cambridge: Cambridge University Press).

Mancini, G. F. (1991), 'The Making of a Constitution for Europe' in Keohane and Hoffmann (1991): 177–94.

McAleavey, P. (1992), 'The Politics of European Regional Development Policy: The European Commission's RECHAR Initiative and the Concept of Additionality' *Strathclyde Papers on Government and Politics* no. 88 (Glasgow: University of Strathclyde).

—— (1993), 'The Politics of the European Regional Development Policy: Additionality in the Scottish Coalfields', *Regional Politics and Policy* 3/2: 88–107.

—— (1995*a*), *Policy Implementation as Incomplete Contracting: The European Regional Development Fund* (Florence: European University Institute, Ph.D. thesis).

—— (1995*b*), 'European Regional Development Fund Expenditure in the UK: From Additionality to Subtractionality' *European Urban and Regional Studies* 2/3: 249–53.

McGowan, L., and Wilks, S. (1995), 'The First Supranational Policy in the European Union: Competition Policy', *European Journal of Political Research* 28: 141–69.

McLaughlin, A. M., and Greenwood, J. (1995), 'The Management of Interest Representation in the European Union' *Journal of Common Market Studies* 33: 149–65.

March, J., and Olsen, J. (1984), 'The New Institutionalism: Organizational Factors in Political Life' *American Political Science Review* 78: 734–49.

—— and —— (1989), *Rediscovering Institutions: The Organizational Basis of Politics* (New York and London: Free Press).

—— and —— (1996), 'Institutional Perspectives on Political Institutions' *Governance* 9: 247–64.

Marks, G. (1992), 'Structural Policy in the European Community' in Sbragia (1992): 191–224.

—— (1993), 'Structural Policy and Multilevel Governance in the EC' in Cafruny and Rosenthal (1993): 391–410.

—— (1996*a*), 'Exploring and Explaining Variation in EU Cohesion Policy' in Hooghe (1996*c*): 388–422.

—— (1996*b*), *An Actor Centred Approach to Multilevel Governance.* Paper presented at the American Political Science Association meeting, San Francisco, 29 Aug.–1 Sept.

—— Hooghe, L., and Blank, K. (1996), 'European Integration from the 1980s: State-Centric v Multi-Level Governance' *Journal of Common Market Studies* 34: 341–78.

Marsh, D. (1995), *Germany and Europe: The Crisis of Unity* (London: Mandarin).

Marsh, D., and Rhodes, R. A. W. (1992*a*), 'Policy Communities and Issue Networks: Beyond Typology' in Marsh and Rhodes (1992*b*): 249–68.

—— and —— (1992*b*), *Policy Networks in British Government* (Oxford: Oxford University Press).

Matlary, J. H. (1993), *Towards Understanding Integration: An Analysis of the Role of the State in EC Energy Policy, 1985–1992* (Oslo: University of Oslo, Ph.D. thesis).

—— (1997), *Energy Policy in the European Union* (Basingstoke and London: Macmillan).

Mawson, J., Martins, M., and Gibney, J. (1985), 'The Development of the European Community Regional Policy' in Keating and Jones (1985): 20–59.

Mayne, R. (1991), 'Gray Eminence' in Brinkley and Hackett (1991): 114–28.

Mazey, S. (1992), 'Conception and Evolution of the High Authority's Administrative Services (1952–1956): From Supranational Principles to Multinational Practices' in Heyen (1992): 31–47.

—— and Richardson, J. (eds.) (1993), *Lobbying in the European Union* (Oxford: Oxford University Press).

—— and —— (1999), 'Interests' in Cram, Dinan, and Nugent (1999): 105– 29.

Metcalfe, L. (1992), 'Can the Commission Manage Europe?' *Australian Journal of Public Administration* 51: 117–30.

Meunier, S., and Nicolaïdes, K. (1999) 'Who Speaks for Europe? The Delegation of Trade Authority in the EU' *Journal of Common Market Studies* 37: 477–501.

Michelmann, H. J., and Soldatos, P. (eds.) (1994), *European Integration: Theories and Approaches* (London and Lanham, Md.: University Press of America).

Middlemas, K. (1995), *Orchestrating Europe: The Informal Politics of European Union, 1973–1995* (London: Fontana).

Miles, L. (ed.) (1996), *The European Union and the Nordic Countries* (London: Routledge).

Miller, K. E. (ed.) (1996), *Denmark: A Troubled Welfare State* (Boulder, San Francisco, and Oxford: Westview Press).

Milward, A. S. (1984), *The Reconstruction of Western Europe, 1945–51* (London: Routledge).

Milward, A. (1992), *The European Rescue of the Nation State* (London: Routledge).

Mitrany, D. (1966), 'The Prospect of Integration: Federal or Functional' *Journal of Common Market Studies* 4: 119–49.

Monnet, J. (1962), 'A Ferment of Change' *Journal of Common Market Studies* 1: 203–11.

Morata, F., and Munoz, X. (1996), 'Vying for European Funds: Territorial Restructuring in Spain' in Hooghe (1996c): 195–214.

Moravcsik, A. (1991), 'Negotiating the Single European Act' in Keohane and Hoffmann (1991): 41–84.

—— (1993), 'Preferences and Power in the European Community: A Liberal Intergovernmentalist Approach' *Journal of Common Market Studies* 31: 473–524.

—— (1995), 'Liberal Intergovernmentalism and Integration: A Rejoinder' *Journal of Common Market Studies* 33: 611–28.

—— (1999), *The Choice for Europe: Social Purpose and State Power from Messina to Maastricht* (London: UCL Press).

—— and Nicolaïdes, K. (1999), 'Explaining the Treaty of Amsterdam: Interests, Influences, Institutions' *Journal of Common Market Studies* 37: 59–85.

Moxon-Browne, E. (1993), 'Social Europe' in Lodge (1993): 152–62.

Moyer, H. W., and Josling, T. E. (1990), *Agricultural Policy Reform: Politics and Process in the EC and the USA* (Ames: Iowa State University Press).

Murphy, B. (1973), *A History of the British Economy* (London: Longman).

Mutimer, D. (1994), 'Theories of Political Integration', in Michelmann and Soldatos (1994): 13–42.

Nanetti, R. (1996), 'EU Cohesion and Territorial Restructuring in the Member States' in Hooghe (1996c): 59–88.

Nelsen, B. F., and Stubb, A. C.-G. (eds.) (1994), *The European Union: Readings on the Theory and Practice of European Integration* (Boulder and London: Lynne Rienner, 1st edn.).

Newton, G. (1999), *Essays on Politics, Language and Society in Luxembourg* (Lampeter: Edwin Mellon).

NFU(1996), *NFU Briefing: 1996 US Farm Bill* (London: National Farmers' Union).

Nugent, N. (1992), 'British Public Opinion and the European Community' in George (1992): 172–201.

—— (ed.) (1994) *The European Union 1993: Annual Review of Activities* (Oxford: Blackwell).

—— (1995), 'The Leadership Capacity of the European Commission' *Journal of European Public Policy* 2: 603–23.

—— (ed.) (1997), *At the Heart of the Union: Studies of the European Commission* (Basingstoke and London: Macmillan).

—— (1999), *The Government and Politics of the European Union* (Basingstoke and London: Macmillan, 4th edn.).

Nuttall, S. (1994), 'Keynote Article: The EC and Yugoslavia—*Deus ex Machina* or *Machina Sine Deo?*' in Nugent (1994): 11–24.

Official Journal of the European Communities (1988), Council Regulation (EEC) No. 2052/88 on the tasks of the Structural Funds and their effectiveness and on coordination of their activities between themselves and with the operations of the European Investment Bank and the other existing financial instruments, 24 June.

Olson, M. (1971), *The Logic of Collective Action: Public Goods and the Theory of Groups* (Cambridge, Mass.: Harvard University Press).

Payne, A. (2000), 'Globalization and Modes of Regionalist Governance' in Pierre (2000): 201–18.

Peel, Q. (1986), 'Mrs Thatcher Finds the Middle Ground' *Financial Times* 4 Dec.

Pelkmans, J. (1994), 'The Significance of EC-1992' in Laurent (1994): 94–111.

—— and Winters, L. A. (1988), *Europe's Domestic Market* (London: Routledge).

Peters, B. G. (1992), 'Bureaucratic Politics and the Institutions of the European Community' in Sbragia (1992): 75–122.

—— (1997), 'The Commission and Implementation in the European Union: Is There an Implementation Deficit and Why?' in Nugent (1997): 187–202.

Petersen, N. (1993), ' "Game, Set and Match": Denmark and the European Union from Maastricht to Edinburgh', in Tiilkainen and Petersen (1993): 79–106.

Peterson, J. (1991), 'Technology Policy in Europe: Explaining the Framework Programme in Theory and Practice' *Journal of Common Market Studies* 31: 473–524.

—— (1992), 'The European Technology Community: Policy Networks in a Supranational Setting' in Marsh and Rhodes (1992): 226–48.

—— (1995a), 'Policy Networks and European Union Policy Making: A Reply to Kassim' *West European Politics* 18: 389–407.

—— (1995b), 'Decision-making in the European Union: Towards a Framework for Analysis' *Journal of European Public Policy* 2: 69–93.

—— (1995c), 'European Union Research Policy: The Politics of Expertise' in Rhodes and Mazey (1995): 391–412.

—— (1997), 'The European Union: Pooled Sovereignty, Divided Accountability' *Political Studies* 45: 559–78.

Philippart, E. and Edwards, G. (1999), 'The Provisions on Closer Co-operation in the Treaty of Amsterdam' *Journal of Common Market Studies* 37: 87–108.

Pierre, J. (ed.) (2000), *Debating Governance* (Oxford: Oxford University Press).

Pierson, P. (1996), 'The Path to European Integration: A Historical Institutionalist Analysis' *Comparative Political Studies* 29: 123–63.

—— (1998), 'The Path to European Integration: A Historical Institutionalist Analysis' in Sandholtz and Stone Sweet (1998): 27–58.

Pollack, M. (1995), 'Regional Actors in an Intergovernmental Play: The Making and Implementation of EC Structural Policy' in Rhodes and Mazey (1995): 361–90.

—— (1996), 'The New Institutionalism and EC Governance: The Promise and Limits of Institutional Analysis' *Governance* 9: 429–58.

—— (1997), 'The Commission as an Agent' in Nugent (1997): 109–28.

Porter, B. (1987), *Britain, Europe and the World 1850–1986: Delusions of Grandeur* (London: Allen & Unwin, 2nd edn.).

Poulon, C., and Bourantonis, D. (1992), 'Western Europe and the Gulf Crisis: Towards a European Foreign Policy?' *Politics* 12: 28–34.

Preston, C. (1983), 'Additional to What? Does the U.K. Government Cheat on the European Regional Development Fund?' *Politics* 3: 20–6.

—— (1984), *The Politics of Implementation: The European Community Regional Development Fund and European Community Regional Aid to the UK 1975–81* (Colchester: University of Essex, Ph.D. thesis).

—— (1995) 'Obstacles to EU Enlargement: The Classical Community Method and the Prospects for a Wider Europe', *Journal of Common Market Studies* 33: 451–63.

—— (1997) *Enlargement and Integration in the European Union* (London: Routledge)

Putnam, R. (1988), 'Diplomacy and Domestic Politics: The Logic of Two Level games' *International Organization* 42: 427–60.

—— (1993), *Making Democracy Work: Civic Traditions in Modern Italy* (Princeton: Princeton University Press).

Ramussen, H. (1986), *On Law and Policy in the European Court of Justice: A Comparative Study in Judicial Politics* (Dordrecht: Martinus Nijhoff).

Rattinger, H. (1994), 'Public Attitudes towards European Integration in Germany after Maastricht: Inventory and Typology' *Journal of Common Market Studies* 32: 525–40.

Rhodes, C., and Mazey, S. (eds.), (1995), *The State of the European Union*, vol. iii. *Building a European Polity?* (Boulder and London: Lynne Rienner and Longman).

Rhodes, R. A. W. (1988), *Beyond Westminster and Whitehall: The Sub-Central Governments of Britain* (London: Unwin Hyman).

—— (1995), *The New Governance: Governing without Government* (London: ESRC/RSA).

—— Bache, I., and George, S. (1996), 'Policy Networks and Policy-Making in the European Union: A Critical Appraisal' in Hooghe (1996c): 367–87.

Rhodes, M., and van Apeldoorn, B. (1997), 'Capitalism versus Capitalism in Western Europe' in Rhodes, Heywood, and Wright (1997): 171–89.

—— Heywood, P., and Wright, V. (eds.) (1997), *Developments in West European Politics* (Basingstoke and London: Macmillan).

Richardson, J. (1996a), 'Actor-based Models of National and EU Policy Making' in Kassim and Menon (1996): 26–51.

—— (ed.) (1996b), *European Union: Power and Policy-Making* (London: Routledge).

Richardson, K. (1997), 'Introductory Foreword' in Wallace and Young (1997): pp. xvii–xxiv.

Rieger, E. (1996), 'The Common Agricultural Policy' in Wallace and Wallace (1996), 97–123.

Risse-Kappen, T. (1996), 'Exploring the Nature of the Beast: International Relations Theory and Comparative Policy Analysis Meet the European Union' *Journal of Common Market Studies* 34: 53–80.

Rosamond, B. (1999), 'Discourses of Globalization and the Social Construction of European Identities' *Journal of European Public Policy* 6: 652–68.

—— (2000), *Theories of European Integration* (Basingstoke and London: Macmillan).

Rosenthal, G. G. (1975), *The Men Behind the Decisions: Cases in European Policy-Making* (Lexington, Mass.: D. C. Heath).

Ross, G. (1995), *Jacques Delors and European Integration* (Cambridge: Polity Press).

Royal Institute of International Affairs (1997), *An Equal Partner: Britain's Role in a Changing Europe: Final Report of the Commission on Britain and Europe* (London: RIIA).

Sabatier, P. (1988), 'An Advocacy Coalition Framework of Policy Change and the Role of Policy-Oriented Learning Therein' *Policy Sciences* 21: 129–68.

Sandholtz, W. (1993), 'Choosing Union: Monetary Politics and Maastricht' *International Organization* 47: 1–39.

—— (1998), 'The Emergence of a Supranational Telecommunications Regime' in Sandholtz and Stone Sweet (1998): 134–63.

—— and Zysman, J. (1989), '1992: Recasting the European Bargain' *World Politics* 42: 95–128.

—— and Stone Sweet, A. (eds.) (1998), *European Integration and Supranational Governance* (Oxford: Oxford University Press).

Sautter, C. (1982), 'France' in Boltho (1982): 449–71.

Sbragia, A. (ed.) (1992), *Euro-Politics: Institutions and Policymaking in the 'New' European Community* (Washington, DC: Brookings Institution).

Scharpf, F. (1989), 'The Joint-Decision Trap: Lessons from German Federalism and European Integration' *Public Administration* 66: 239–78.

—— (1999), 'Review Section Symposium—The Choice for Europe: Social Purpose and State Power from Messina to Maastricht. Selecting Cases and Testing Hypotheses', *Journal of European Public Policy* 6: 164–8.

Scheinman, L. (1967), 'Euratom: Nuclear Integration in Europe' *International Conciliation* no. 563.

Schlupp, F. (1980), 'Federal Republic of Germany' in Seers and Vaitsos (1980), 176–98.

Schmitter, P. (1970), 'A Revised Theory of Regional Integration' *International Organization* 24: 836–68.

—— (1996): 'Examining the Present Euro-Polity with the Help of Past Theories', in Marks, G., Scharpf, F., Schmitter, P., and Streeck, W., *Governance in the European Union* (London: Sage), 1–14.

—— and Streeck, W. (1994), 'Organised Interests and the Europe of 1992' in Nelsen and Stubb (1994): 169–87.

Scott, J. (1995), *Development Dilemmas in the European Community: Rethinking Regional Development Policy* (Buckingham and Philadelphia: Open University Press).

—— (1998), 'Law, Legitimacy and EC Governance: Prospects for "Partnership"' *Journal of Common Market Studies* 36: 175–94.

Scully, R. M. (1997a), 'The European Parliament and the Co-decision Procedure: A Reassessment' *Journal of Leglisative Studies* 3: 58–73.

—— (1975b), 'The European Parliament and Co-decision: A Rejoinder to Tsebelis and Garrett' *Journal of Leglisative Studies* 3: 93–103.

Seers, D., and Vaitsos, C. (1980), *Integration and Unequal Development: The Experience of the EEC* (Basingstoke and London: Macmillan).

Sharp, C. (1989), 'The Community and the New Technologies' in Lodge (1989): 223–40.

Sharp, J. M. O. (1997), 'Will Britain lead Europe?' *World Today* 53: 316–19.

Sharp, M., and Shearman, C. (1987), *European Technological Collaboration* (London: Royal Institute of International Affairs/Routledge and Kegan Paul).

Shonfield, A. (1969), *Modern Capitalism: The Changing Balance of Public and Private Power* (Oxford: Oxford University Press).

Smith, G. (1990), *European Court of Justice: Judges or Policy Makers?* (London: Bruges Group).

Smith, G., Paterson W. E., and Padgett, S. (eds.) (1996), *Developments in German Politics 2* (Basingstoke and London: Macmillan).

Smith, J. (1999), *Europe's Elected Parliament* (Sheffield: Sheffield Academic Press/University Association for Contemporary European Studies).

—— (2000) 'Enlarging Europe', *Journal of Common Market Studies: Annual Review of Activities, 1999/2000* (Oxford: Blackwell): 121–4.

Smith, M. (1998), 'Competitive co-operation and EU–US relations: can the EU be a strategic partner for the US in the world economy?' *Journal of European Public Policy* 5: 561–77.

Smith, M. P. (1997), 'The Commission Made Me Do It: The European Commission as a Strategic Asset in Domestic Politics' in Nugent (1997): 167–86.

Sowemimo, M. (1999), 'Evaluating the Success of the Labour Government's European Policy' *Journal of European Integration* 21: 343–68.

Spierenburg, D., and Poidevin, R. (1994), *The History of the High Authority of the European Coal and Steel Community: Supranationality in Action* (London:Weidenfeld).

Steiner, J., and Woods, L. (1996), *Textbook of EC Law* (London: Blackstone, 5th edn.).

Stevens, A. (1996), *The Government and Politics of France* (Basingstoke and London: Macmillan).

Stevens, C. (ed.) (1984), *The EEC and the Third World: A Survey. 4: Renegotiating Lomé* (London: Hodder and Stoughton).

—— (2000), 'Trade with Developing Countries: Banana Skins and Turf Wars' in Wallace and Wallace (2000): 401–26

Stone Sweet, A., and Sandholtz, W. (1997), 'European Integration and Supranational Governance' *Journal of European Public Policy* 4: 297–317.

Swann, D. (1995), *The Economics of the Common Market: Integration in the European Union* (Harmondsworth: Penguin, 8th edn.).

Swift, M. (1978), 'A Regional Policy for Europe' *Young Fabian Pamphlet 48* (London: Fabian Society).

Swinbank, A. (1993), 'CAP Reform 1992' *Journal of Common Market Studies* 31: 359–72.

Tiilkainen, T., and Petersen, I. B. (eds.) (1993), *The Nordic Countries and the EC* (Copenhagen: Copenhagen Political Studies Press).

Tranholm-Mikkelsen, J. (1991), 'Neofunctionalism: Obstinate or Obsolete? A Reppraisal in the Light of the New Dynamism of the European Community', *Millennium* 20: 1–22.

Tsakaloyannis, P. (1981), 'The Greco-Turkish Dispute in the Light of Enlargement' in *Sussex European Papers*, no. 11: *The Mediterranean Challenge VI* (Brighton: University of Sussex).

Tsebelis, G., and Garrett, G. (1996), 'Agenda Setting Power, Power Indices, and Decision Making in the European Union' *International Review of Law and Economics* 16: 345–61.

Tsoukalis, L. (1977a), *The Politics and Economics of European Monetary Integration* (London: Allen &Unwin).

—— (1977b), 'Is the Relaunching of Economic and Monetary Union a Feasible Proposal?', *Journal of Common Market Studies* 15: 231–47.

—— (1996), 'Economic and Monetary Union: The Primacy of High Politics' in Wallace and Wallace (1996): 279–99.

Urwin, D. W. (1985), *Western Europe since 1945: A Short Political History* (4th edn., London and New York: Longman).

—— (1995), *The Community of Europe: A History of European Integration since 1945* (London and New York: Longman, 2nd edn.)

Van Schendelen, M. P. C. M. (1996), ' "The Council Decides": Does the Council Decide?' *Journal of Common Market Studies*, 34: 531–48.

Verdun, A. (1999), 'The Role of the Delors Committee in the Creation of EMU: An Epistemic Community?', *Journal of European Public Policy* 6: 308–28.

Vibert, F. (1994), *The Future Role of the European Commission* (London: European Policy Forum).

Wallace, H. (1973), *National Governments and the European Communities* (London: Chatham House/PEP).

Wallace, H. (1977*a*), 'National Bulls in the Community China Shop: The Role of National Governments in Community Policy-Making' in Wallace, Wallace, and Webb (1977): 33–68.

—— (1977*b*), 'The Establishment of the Regional Development Fund: Common Policy or Pork Barrel?' in Wallace, Wallace, and Webb (1977): 137–63.

—— (1983*a*), 'Negotiation, Conflict and Compromise: The Elusive Pursuit of Common Policies' in Wallace, Wallace, and Webb (1983): 43–80.

—— (1983*b*), 'Distributional Politics: Dividing up the Community Cake' in Wallace, Wallace, and Webb (1983): 81–113.

—— (1986), 'The British Presidency of the European Community's Council of Ministers' *International Affairs* 62: 583–99.

—— (1997), 'Introduction' in Wallace and Young (1997), 1–16.

—— (1999), 'Piecing the Integration Jigsaw Together' *Journal of European Public Policy* 6: 155–79.

—— (2000), 'Flexibility: A Tool of Integration or a Restraint on Disintegration?' in Neunreither, K. and Wiener, A. (eds.) *European Integration After Amsterdam: Institutional Dynamics and Prospects for Democracy*, (Oxford: Oxford University Press), 175–91.

—— and Wallace, W. (eds.) (1996), *Policy-Making in the European Union* (Oxford: Oxford University Press, 3rd edn.).

—— and —— (eds.) (2000), *Policy-Making in the European Union* (Oxford: Oxford University Press, 4th edn.).

—— and —— and Webb, C. (eds.) (1977), *Policy-Making in the European Communities* (London: John Wiley and Sons, 1st edn.).

—— —— and —— (eds.) (1983), *Policy-Making in the European Communities* (London: John Wiley and Sons Ltd., 2nd edn.).

—— and Young, A. R. (eds.), (1997), *Participation and Policy-Making in the European Union* (Oxford: Clarendon Press).

Wallace, W., and Allen, D. (1977), 'Political Co-operation: Procedure as Substitute for Policy' in Wallace, Wallace, and Webb (1977): 227–48.

Warley, T. K. (1992), 'Europe's Agricultural Policy in Transition' *International Journal* 47: 112–35.

Watson, R. (1998), 'Sweetening the Bitter Pill of Budget Consolidation', *European Voice*, 26, March–April: 16.

Weale, A. (1997), 'Democratic Theory and the Constitutional Politics of the European Union' *Journal of European Public Policy* 4: 665–9.

Weiler, J. H. H. (1993), 'Journey to an Unknown Destination: A Retrospective and Prospective of the European Court of Justice in the Arena of Political Integration' *Journal of Common Market Studies* 31: 417–46.

Wessels, W. (1991), 'The EC Council: The Community's Decision-Making Center' in Keohane and Hoffmann (1991): 133–54

Westlake, M. (1994), *The European Parliament: A Modern Guide* (London: Pinter).

—— (1995), *The Council of the European Union* (London: Catermill).

Wilks, S., and McGowan, L. (1995), 'Disarming the Commission: The Debate over a European Cartel Office' *Journal of Common Market Studies* 33: 259–73.

Wincott, D. (1995), 'Institutional Interaction and European Integration: Towards an Everyday Critique of Liberal Intergovernmentalism' *Journal of Common Market Studies* 33: 597–609.

Wise, M., and Croxford, G. (1988), 'The European Regional Development Fund: Community Ideals and National Realities' *Political Geography Quarterly* 7: 161–82.

Wishlade, F. (1996), 'EU Cohesion Policy: Facts, Figures, and Issues' in Hooghe (1996*c*): 27–58.

Worre, T. (1995), 'First No, Then Yes: The Danish Referendums on the Maastricht Treaty 1992 and 1993' *Journal of Common Market Studies* 33: 235–57.

Wright, V. (1990), 'The Administrative Machine: Old Problems and New Dilemmas' in Hall, Hayward, and Machin (1990): 114–32.

Young, H. (1998), *This Blessed Plot: Britain and Europe from Churchill to Blair* (Basingstoke and London: Macmillan).

Young, J. W. (1993), *Britain and European Unity, 1945–1992* (Basingstoke and London: Macmillan).

General Index

Author Index